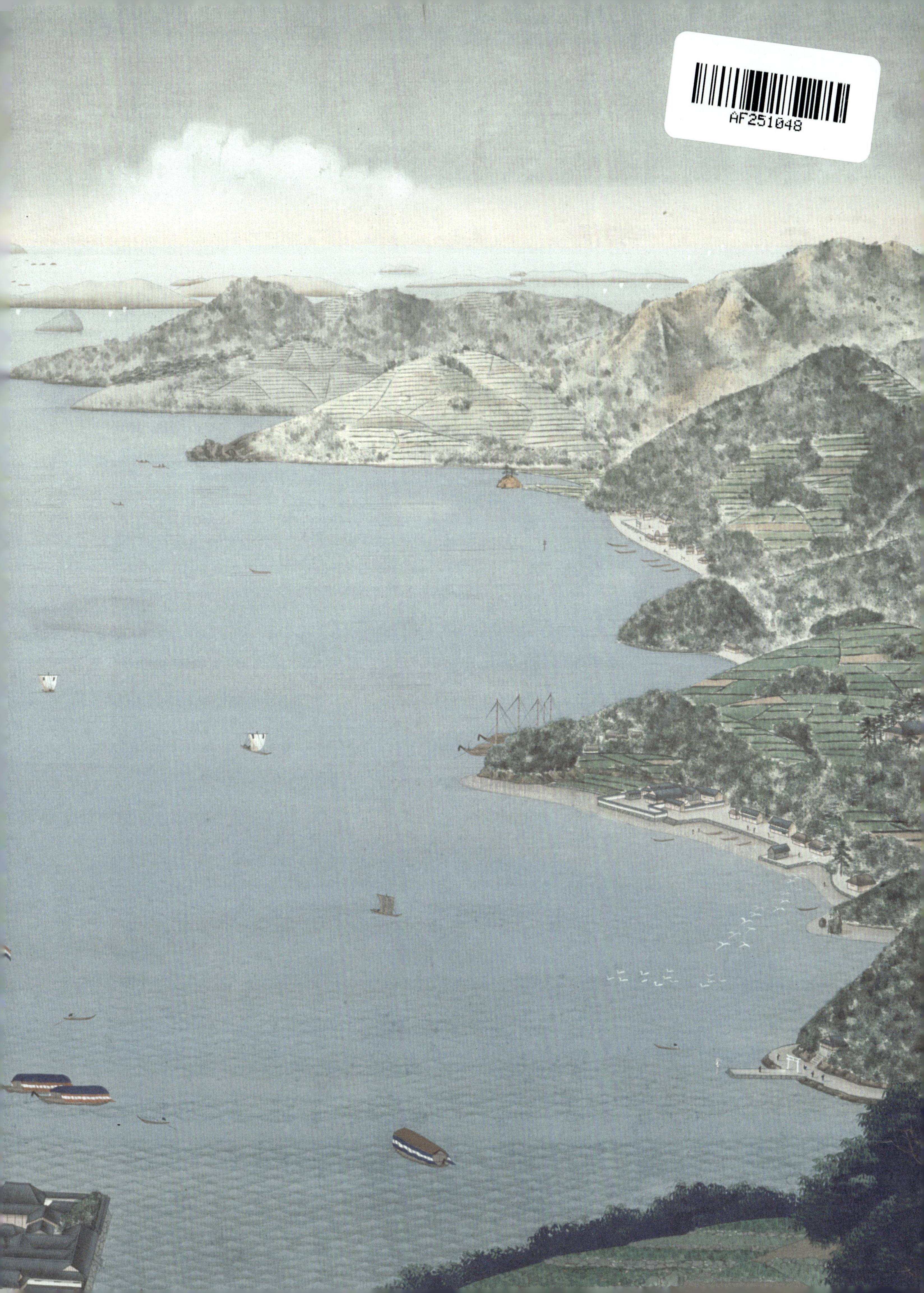

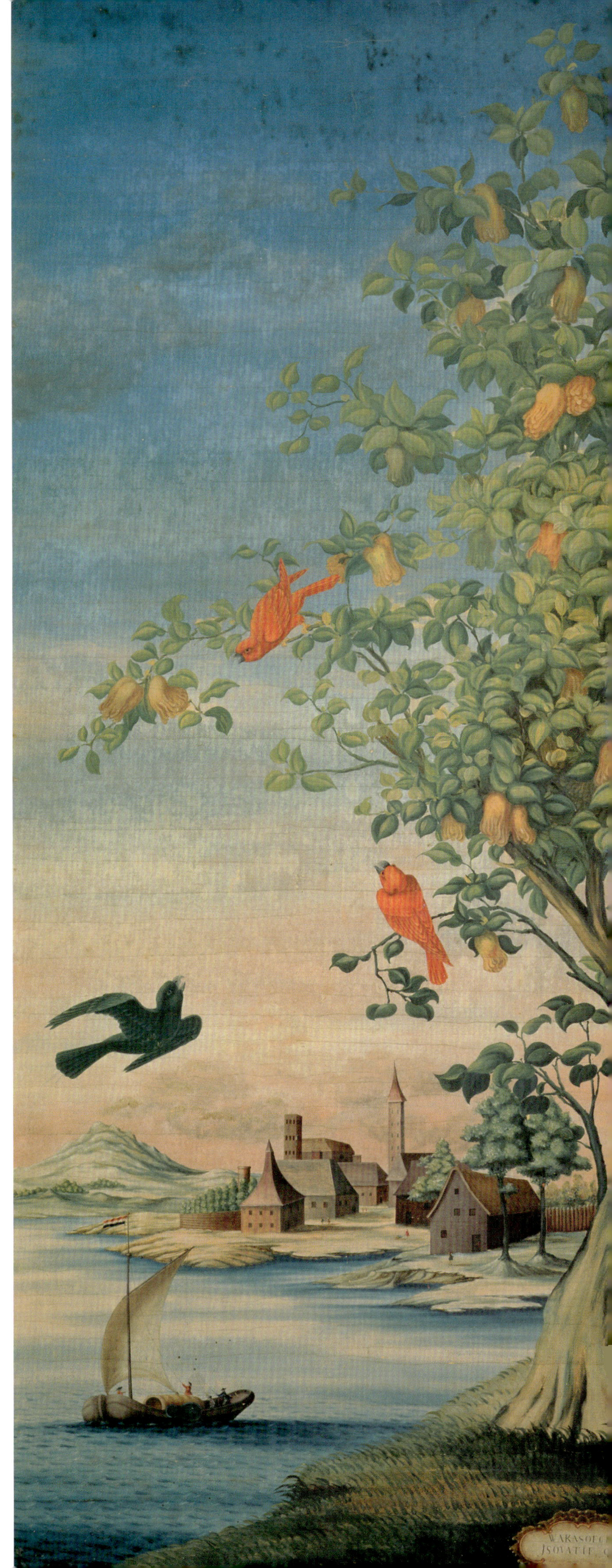

Japan

Envisions

the

West

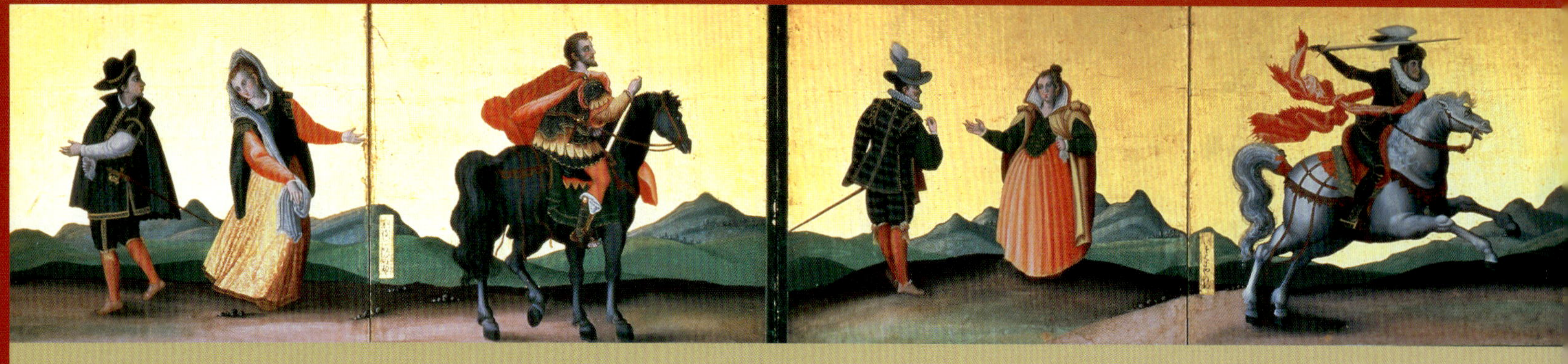

Seattle Art Museum   Edited by Yukiko Shirahara

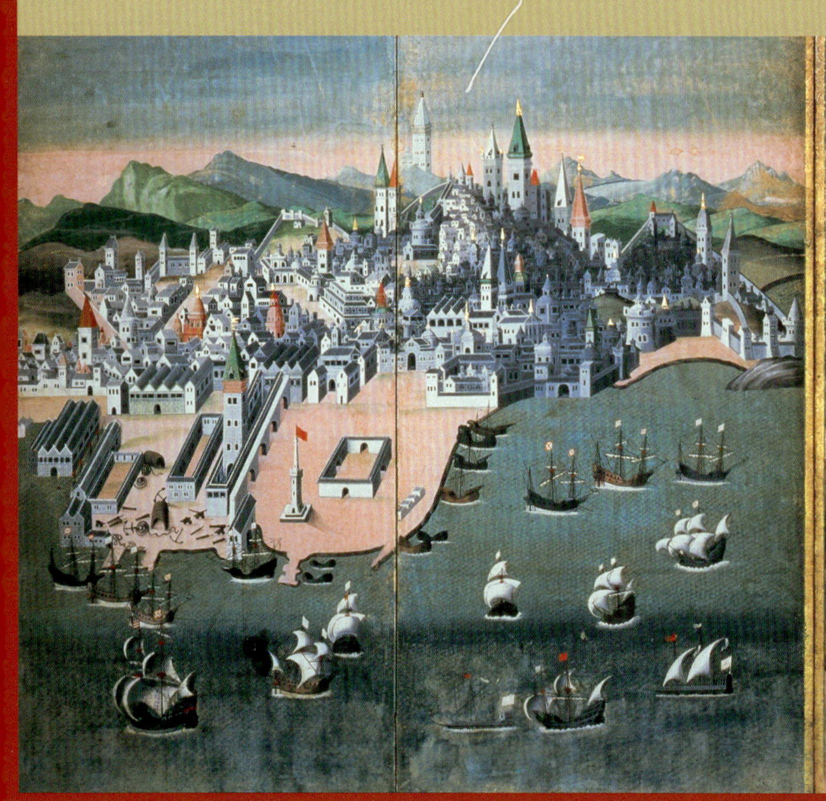

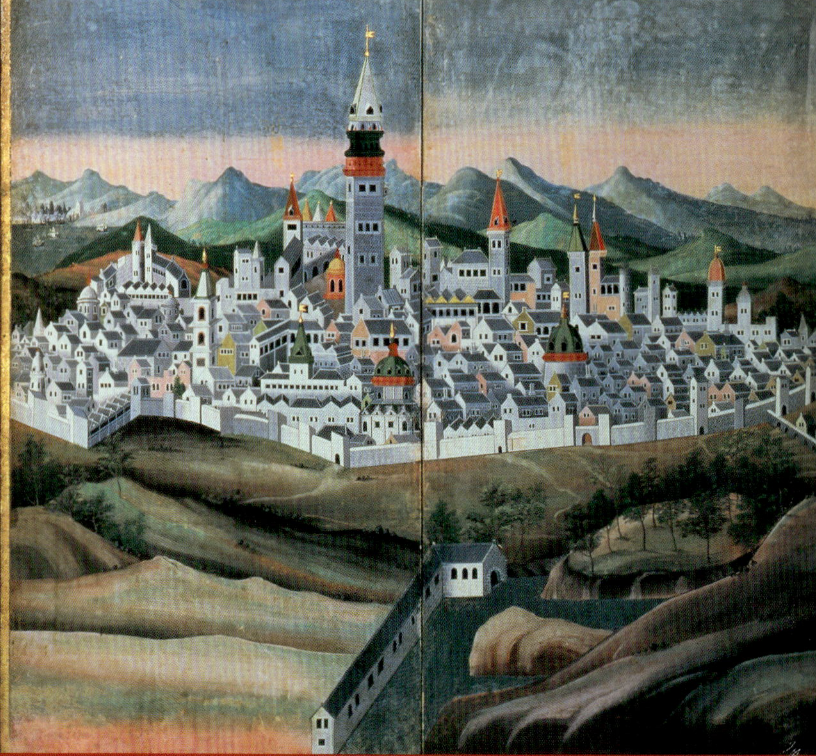

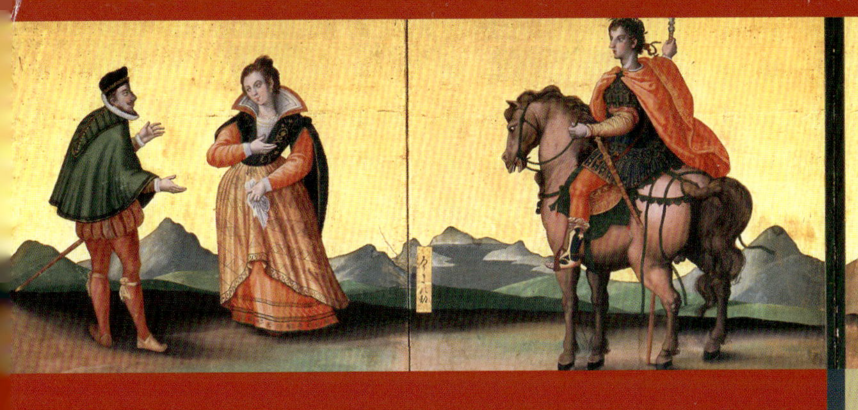
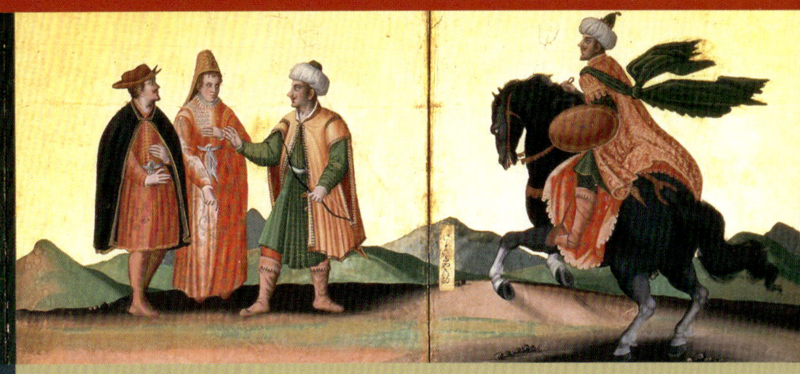

Japan Envisions the West

16th–19th Century

Japanese Art

from

Kobe City Museum

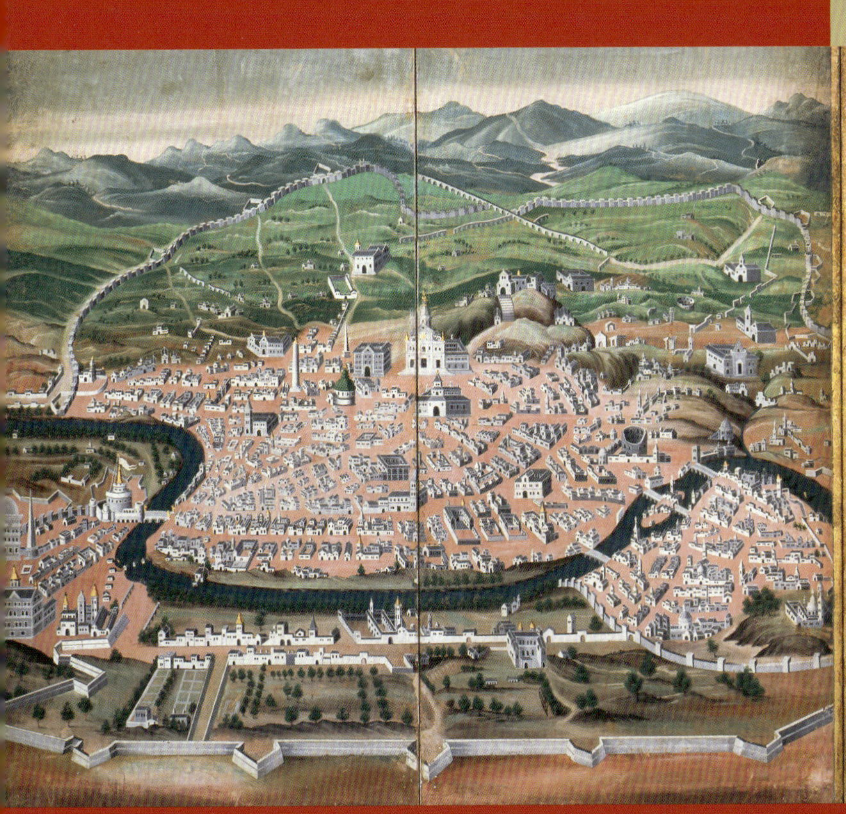
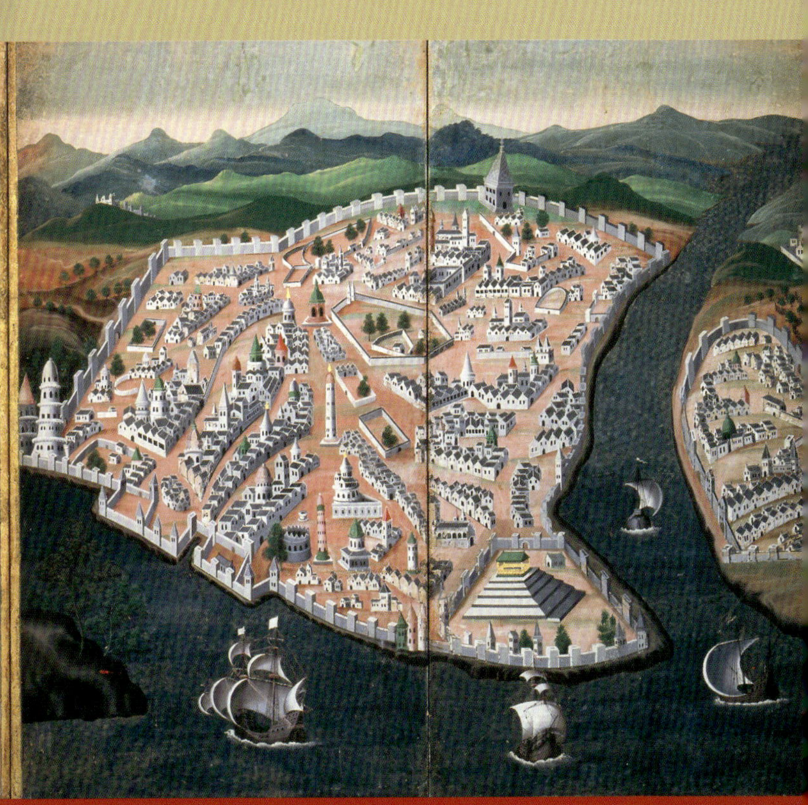

Seattle takes pride in its long history of trade and involvement with Japan. Over two hundred years ago the first trading ship left our shores for Japan; a hundred years later we were the first American port city to establish trade with Japan and the first to reestablish it again after World War II. Along with this history, our position on the Pacific Rim and proximity to Japan underscore the importance of international exchange to our region and the increasingly pivotal role we play in the socioeconomic stability of the Asia Pacific region.

Our sister city relationship with Kobe was the first one established, created soon after President Eisenhower initiated the program in 1956 to encourage people-to-people diplomacy between Americans and citizens of other countries. Back then a young attorney, Griffith Way, was instrumental in establishing the sister city connection, personally visiting Kobe as the first ambassador appointed by former Mayor Gordon Clinton. The success of this affiliation—ongoing for fifty years now—has produced invaluable results: we continue to gain insight, respect, and mutual understanding of our history and cultures, strengthening our shared friendship and prosperity. The exhibition *Japan Envisions the West: 16th–19th Century Japanese Art from Kobe City Museum* is a beautiful reminder of this reciprocal cultural and educational exchange. On behalf of the City of Seattle, I offer our congratulations and deep appreciation to the Kobe City Museum and the Seattle Art Museum for their spirit of cooperation that made this extraordinary presentation possible.

Greg Nickels

The City of Kobe is honored to lend these treasured works for this important exhibition in celebration of the fiftieth anniversary of our sister city relationship with Seattle. A history of more than thirteen centuries as an international port has endowed Kobe's citizens with an openness and desire to make cultural contributions to others, and to learn from them in return. The Kobe City Museum's collection of *namban* and *kōmō* art exemplifies the museum's key theme: international cultural exchange between East and West. This historic exhibition illustrates the unique qualities of Japanese art created when Japan encountered the cultures of the West in the premodern age.

The Asia Pacific region has become the center of gravity for our global economy. As partners in prosperity, Kobe and Seattle are representative of the major port cities on the Pacific Rim, and our sister city alliance is an important and valued one that contributes to regional stability. The continuity of sharing art and culture will ensure that our good relations are carried forward by generations to come. On behalf of the citizens of Kobe, I extend a hand of friendship and goodwill to Seattle and express our appreciation to the Seattle Art Museum for providing a forum for this vital international exchange.

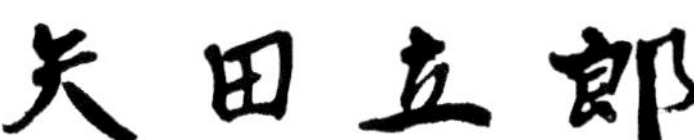

Yada Tatsuo

This book has been published in conjunction with the exhibition *Japan Envisions the West: 16th–19th Century Japanese Art from Kobe City Museum,* organized by the Seattle Art Museum in collaboration with the Kobe City Museum and on view at the Seattle Art Museum Downtown from October 11, 2007, through January 6, 2008. The exhibition, its programs, and the publication have been generously supported by

The Atsuhiko and Ina Goodwin Tateuchi Foundation
Office of Arts and Cultural Affairs, City of Seattle
The E. Rhodes and Leona B. Carpenter Foundation
National Endowment for the Arts

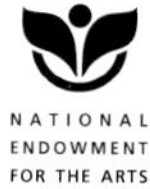

PONCHO (Patrons of Northwest Civic, Cultural, and Charitable Organizations)
U.S. Bank

Yoko and Minoru Arakawa
Obayashi Group
ORIX USA Corporation
Catherine and Taisuke Sasanuma
Starbucks Coffee Company

Richard and Peggy Danziger
Japan Foundation
Nintendo of America
Nippon Express Foundation
Worldbridge

Contributors to the Annual Fund

Contents

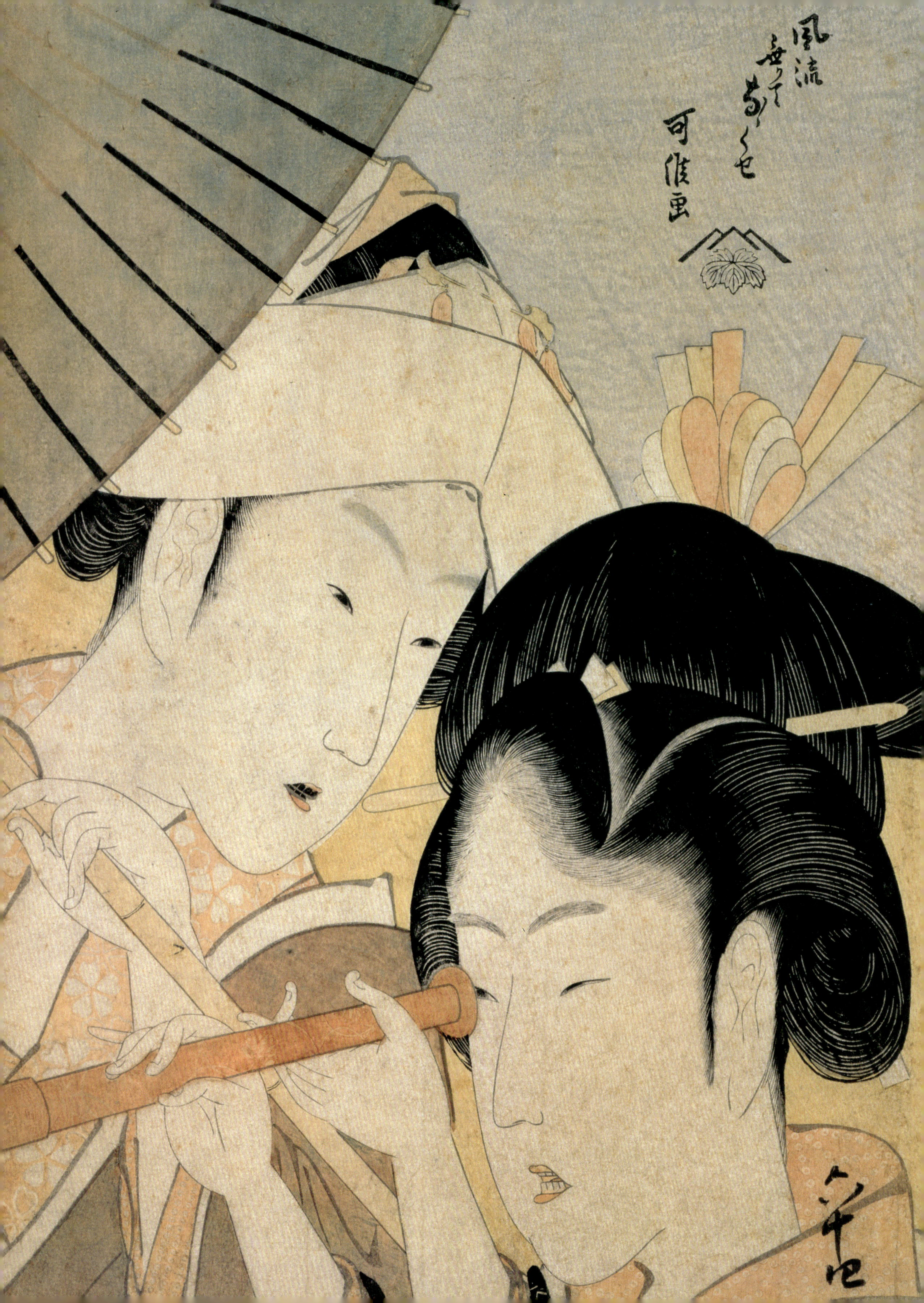

風流
無くて
七くせ
可侯画

Living in a fast-paced global age, it is easy to forget the complex histories created by the long-ago intersections of cultures and nations. While maps explicitly document how each culture's views of the world evolved over time, works of art, when scrutinized, provide a compelling reflection of how one culture saw another. Being in close proximity in East Asia, Japan, Korea, and China had constantly been in touch, but what took place when the Japanese came face to face with Westerners who ventured into their island nation? How did the Japanese view the West and Westerners? What elements of our artistic traditions influenced Japanese works of art and why? From what sources did the Japanese gain their knowledge of the West, its art and culture? How were Japanese works of art, especially ceramics and lacquerware, received in European markets? These important questions and many others are explored in the essays of this book and in the exhibition *Japan Envisions the West: 16th–19th Century Japanese Art from Kobe City Museum.*

Featuring a splendid variety of exquisite Japanese works of art, the exhibition provides a rare and intriguing window on the early interaction between Japan and the West, from 1543, when Westerners first set foot in Japan, through the period of seclusion from 1639, when only the Dutch and Chinese were permitted to live and trade at Nagasaki, until 1854, when Japan signed its first treaty with the United States. The Japanese responded to the foreign elements sifting in through Nagasaki—the only open port during this long era—with an artistic virtuosity and inventiveness that is truly breathtaking. The media they embraced range from large-format folding screens (such as two impressive examples included here, both designated Important Cultural Properties) to simple advertising circulars. From an initial reaction of pure curiosity developed an awareness of the sharp differences in Western and Japanese ways of seeing. Over time, in a fascinating process of acceptance, synthesis, and transformation, we see the ways in which Japanese artists assimilated Western conventions into their traditional aesthetics.

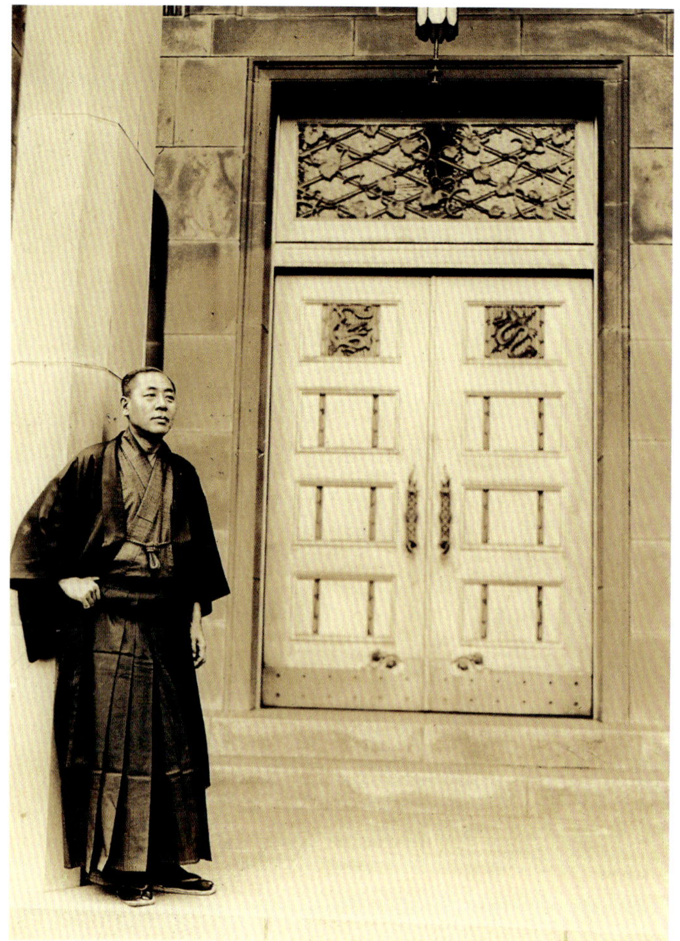

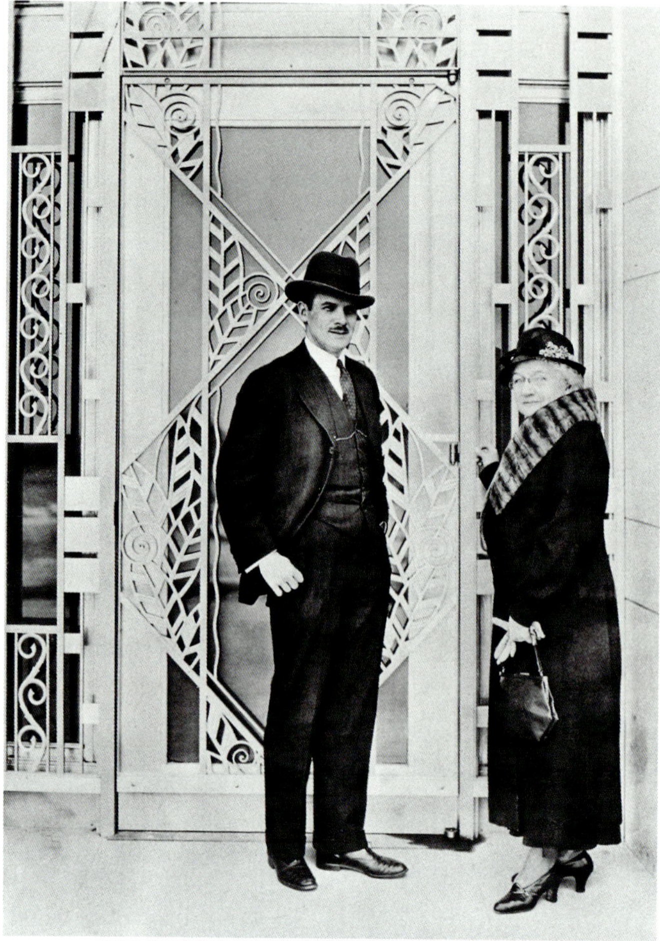

The international focus of Japan and its engagement with the West over three centuries are most fitting as this project celebrates the fiftieth anniversary of the Seattle-Kobe sister city relationship, formally established in 1957. Facing each other across the Pacific Ocean, the ports of Seattle and Kobe have had an especially intimate relationship. In addition to extensive trade which involves, among other things, heavy industry, information technology, and natural resources, Kobe and Seattle have long engaged in vibrant intellectual, educational, and cultural exchanges. The City of Seattle and the Seattle Art Museum are honored to be the only site to host this significant exhibition of treasures from the City of Kobe and the Kobe City Museum.

Our museums themselves share similar histories. The core holdings of each were shaped by individuals with a passion for collecting. Ikenaga Hajime (1891–1955) built his collection of Japanese art to include more than seven thousand pieces, and in 1940 he opened an art deco–style museum to the public. He made a gift of his collection to the City of Kobe in 1951, and these objects, together with the later donation of eight thousand historical maps from Manba Matsutarō and Akioka Takejirō, now form the heart of the Kobe City Museum. In Seattle, Richard E. Fuller (1897–1976) opened an art deco building in 1933 with his mother, Margaret E. MacTavish Fuller, to house their collection of Asian art, the early nucleus of the Seattle Art Museum.

Both museums have grown to become respected institutions with world-class art collections, and we are honored to partner with the Kobe City Museum as we celebrate its singular strengths in the arts of *namban* and *kōmō*—Japanese genres created on the basis of contact with foreigners. I extend gratitude to the museum's current director, Sasayama Kazutoshi, and its chief curator, Oka Yasumasa, for their leadership, generosity, and cooperative spirit, without which we could not have succeeded. In Seattle, the exhibition has been driven by the tireless energy and dedication of Yukiko Shirahara, John A. McCone Foundation Curator of Asian Art, who conceived the exhibition, established its key themes, and managed every aspect of its realization. To her, and to the distinguished scholars who contributed the essays in this volume, we extend our sincere thanks and appreciation.

An international project of this scope is an ambitious undertaking. Our planning and execution were guided by unwavering support from the prominent figures in the United States and Japan who formed our Honorary Committee. Cochaired by Kazuo Tanaka, Consul-General of Japan in Seattle, and trustee of the Seattle Art Museum Griffith Way, who has long fostered U.S.-Japan relations, the committee has enlisted many business and cultural leaders, including Mayor Greg Nickels, City of Seattle; Mayor Yada Tatsuo, City of Kobe; Michael H. Armacost and Thomas S. Foley, both former U.S. ambassadors to Japan; Governor Christine Gregoire of Washington State; and Governor Ido Toshizo of Hyōgo prefecture. It has been a great honor to welcome Gordon Clinton—mayor of Seattle at the time the Sister City relationship was established fifty years ago—to the committee.

A project of this magnitude is possible only with significant financial sponsorship. We gratefully acknowledge the generous support of the Atsuhiko and Ina Goodwin Tateuchi Foundation, the E. Rhodes and Leona B. Carpenter Foundation, PONCHO, the National Endowment for the Arts, U.S. Bank, Starbucks Coffee Company, Yoko and Minoru Arakawa, the Office of Arts and Cultural Affairs, City of Seattle; ORIX USA Corporation, the Obayashi Group, Catherine and Taisuke Sasanuma, and Nintendo of America. A grant from the Japan Foundation was instrumental in the publication of this book, and Worldbridge and Richard and Peggy Danziger made it possible for us to organize an international symposium in conjunction with the exhibition. Additional support was provided by the Nippon Express Foundation and contributors to the Seattle Art Museum's Annual Fund.

It is our sincere hope that this exhibition will advance knowledge of the rich art and culture of Japan, and offer keen insight into the history of cross-cultural exchange.

Mimi Gardner Gates
Ilsley Ball Nordstrom Director
Seattle Art Museum

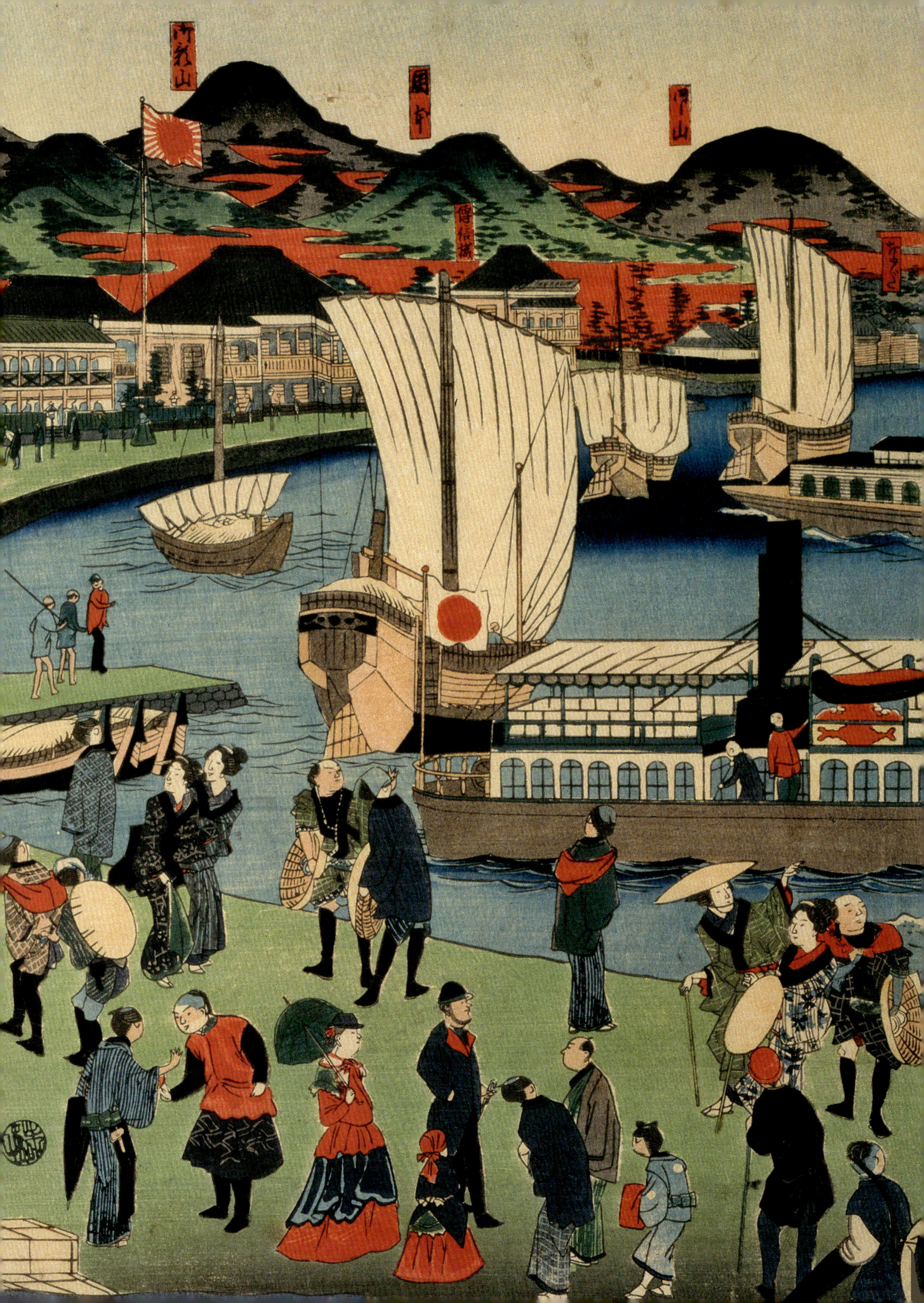

A few months after I moved from Japan to Seattle in 2002, Johsel Namkung showed me a picture taken in the 1960s at Shi Shi Beach in Olympic National Park at the far northwestern corner of Washington State. The Seattle-based photographer and his artist-friend George Tsutakawa sit in a simple arbor on the sand. They had spent the entire day occupied with things found on the beach—buoys from fishing nets, wooden barrels, and various odds and ends—all of which had floated to the shores of the Northwest from Japan.

Later, as I began to contemplate the origin and history of the cultural relationship between Seattle and Japan, I was reminded of this unintentional transmission of objects from one place to the other. As I studied and learned from historians and researchers in both places, I became fascinated by the many ways in which these "neighbors" have exchanged ideas and things. In particular, I was drawn to the story of a Japanese man called Otokichi (1819–1867), whose life, like that of so many others, was shaped by the powerful political, social, and cultural tides between the East and West.

In early 1834, nineteen years before Commodore Matthew C. Perry arrived in Japan, three Japanese boatmen drifted ashore near Cape Flattery, at the tip of the Olympic Peninsula. Native Makah people saved the men, who were the sole survivors of a fourteen-man crew that had been at sea for fourteen months. Their tiny ship, the *Hōjun-maru,* loaded with rice, had set sail for Edo from Toba (Mie prefecture) in the eleventh month of 1832. When a storm came up, they lost their mast and rudder, leaving them to drift helplessly eastward in the North Pacific Current, the same current that brings flotsam to Shi Shi Beach and the Northwest Coast. These men—Otokichi, Kyūkichi, and Iwakichi—were the first recorded Japanese to land in North America.

Even more than nature, global politics now trifled with their fate. The British governing the Oregon territory thought these Japanese would make a convenient excuse for a British ship to approach and possibly trade with Japan. Leaving from Fort Vancouver, the ship headed to London, where the British intended to show off the prosperity and advanced technology of their country, which, they reasoned, the Japanese would favorably report to their government. Accordingly, the men became the first Japanese to visit Great Britain, although just for a single day. Traveling on to Macao, they were in service for a year to Karl Gutzlaff, a German at the British Missionary Society, for whom they translated portions of the New Testament which appeared in the first Japanese Bible, published in 1837.

In the meanwhile, the British had turned their attention to China and lost interest in the Japanese drifters. The men ended up on an American merchant ship, the *Morrison,* which sailed to Edo from Macao in 1837 with trade and missionary intentions. But the Japanese shogunate invoked the Foreign Ships Expulsion Act (1825–42) and fired on the *Morrison,* driving it away without knowing it carried Japanese citizens seeking repatriation. The unlucky men had to pursue life outside Japan. Kyūkichi and Iwakichi remained in Macao, and Otokichi settled in Shanghai, working at a trading company and raising three children. Even after Japan withdrew its severe expulsion policy in 1842, Otokichi remained in China, where he assisted other Japanese trying to repatriate. He visited Japan twice, in 1849 and 1854, as an interpreter for the British Navy. In an interesting encounter, in 1862 Otokichi met members of Japan's official diplomatic delegation on their way to Europe. One of the delegates, Fukuzawa Yukichi (1834–1901), would later become famous for his championing of Western political, economic, and cultural institutions. Otokichi spent his later life in Singapore, his wife's country.

In 1879 one of Otokichi's children applied to Kanagawa prefecture for naturalization. In his application he stated that returning to Japan was his father's long-cherished wish, which he now wanted to realize. Among the numbers of nameless Japanese whose unique experiences were formed by events far from their control, Otokichi and his adventures bring a human perspective to the dynamic relationships among Japan, America, Great Britain, and China in those days.

In a fitting coincidence, Otokichi's son settled in Kobe, sister city to Seattle and home of the Kobe City Museum. The exhibition *Japan Envisions the West: 16th–19th Century Japanese Art from Kobe City Museum* features 142 works of art from its collections—maps, *namban, kōmō,* Yokohama *ukiyo-e,* and exported Japanese goods in ceramic and lacquerware. Twenty objects from the Seattle Art Museum supplement this selection. The exhibition focuses on the era from the late sixteenth century, when the first Europeans arrived in Japan, through the mid-nineteenth century. This period encompasses the long years of *sakoku,* which lasted from the 1630s, when Catholic missionaries and foreign traders (except the Dutch) were expelled from Japan, until the 1850s, when Japan signed trade pacts with America and other Western countries.

Sakoku—literally, "closed country"—is often misunderstood as a time of total isolation for Japan. In fact, art and knowledge flowed into Japan through four ports—Nagasaki, Matsumae, Satsuma, and Tsushima. In Nagasaki, the Dutch and Chinese conducted commercial trading under the direct control of the Tokugawa government. With the material objects transported from overseas came elements of art and culture that the Japanese absorbed and transformed in ways uniquely their own. Notably in the late sixteenth and early seventeenth centuries, before the country was closed off, the Japanese made so-called *namban* art under the influence of Roman Catholic Portugal and Spain. From the late seventeenth to early nineteenth century, during the heart of the *sakoku* period, Western artistic influence came via the Dutch, and art of this type is called *kōmō.* Meanwhile, ceramics and lacquerware exported from Japan to Europe had a profound impact on Western art. This reciprocal transmission and exchange of knowledge and culture is the essential concept behind *Japan Envisions the West.*

For this book, the contributions of six respected scholars of Japanese art establish a context and narrative by which to understand and appreciate these marvelous objects and the era in which they were made. The essayists are Oka Yasumasa, Chief Curator, Kobe City Museum; Katsumori Noriko, Onoda Kazuyuki, and Tsukahara Akira, Curators, Kobe City Museum; Narusawa Katsushi, Senior Curator, Kobe City Koiso Memorial Museum of Art; and Christiaan J. A. Jörg, Professor, History of the Cultural Interactions between Asia and Europe, Department of Art History, Leiden University. In an important overview, Oka discusses the various approaches taken by Japanese artists as they absorbed and adopted Western painting techniques, fusing them with traditional Japanese concepts and themes. From this basis, the following eight essays follow a nearly chronological path. Onoda discusses the role of maps in the exchange of ideas between Japan and the West. Narusawa considers the early impact of Western art on *namban* paintings, and he discusses the art scene that developed in and around Nagasaki, where the influences of the West and Qing Dynasty China were notable.

While the early impact and study of Western art occurred in Nagasaki, a second wave of interest in Western art and science bloomed in Edo from the middle of eighteenth century, and Katsumori reports on important direct relationships between published Dutch sources and the imagery of Japanese artworks during this time. Choosing among the Edo artists studying Western techniques, Tsukahara juxtaposes the approaches toward etching and perspective of two pioneers of Japanese copperplate printing, Shiba Kōkan and Aōdō Denzen. Oka proposes a new terminology—*hollandisme*—for the exotic items sought by Japanese townspeople throughout the Edo period and relates Western motifs to Japanese auspicious iconography. Jörg discusses the Japanese porcelain and lacquerware that exploded onto Western markets through the ambitious efforts of the Dutch East India Company and demonstrates their great impact on European wares. Finally, Tsukahara considers the fantastic images of America envisioned by the Japanese in Yokohama *ukiyo-e* and paintings at the dawn of their modern age.

Some might judge as quaint or ignorant the inaccuracies found in maps and prints of this era, or the perspective of some paintings as immature. But viewers should remember the ease with which we still misread other peoples and cultures, even in our Information Age. It is a conceit to think we can appreciate or understand a phenomenon based on one aspect of what is likely to be multifaceted. In the arts, an encounter with unknown aesthetic mores is a catalyzing event, stimulating the appearance of new styles and concepts. Through a process of fusion and adaptation, motifs and designs often take on new meanings, as witnessed in *namban* paintings and Western-inspired Japanese decorative arts. These objects are the beautiful fruits of the curiosity and progressive attitudes of those Japanese artists who sought to envision the strange, exotic world outside their borders.

My wish for this book is that it will introduce the excellent Kobe City Museum collection to a much wider audience while promoting scholarship in this unique field of Japanese art. It is a beautiful milestone in the relationship between the great cities of Seattle and Kobe.

Yukiko Shirahara
John A. McCone Foundation Curator of Asian Art

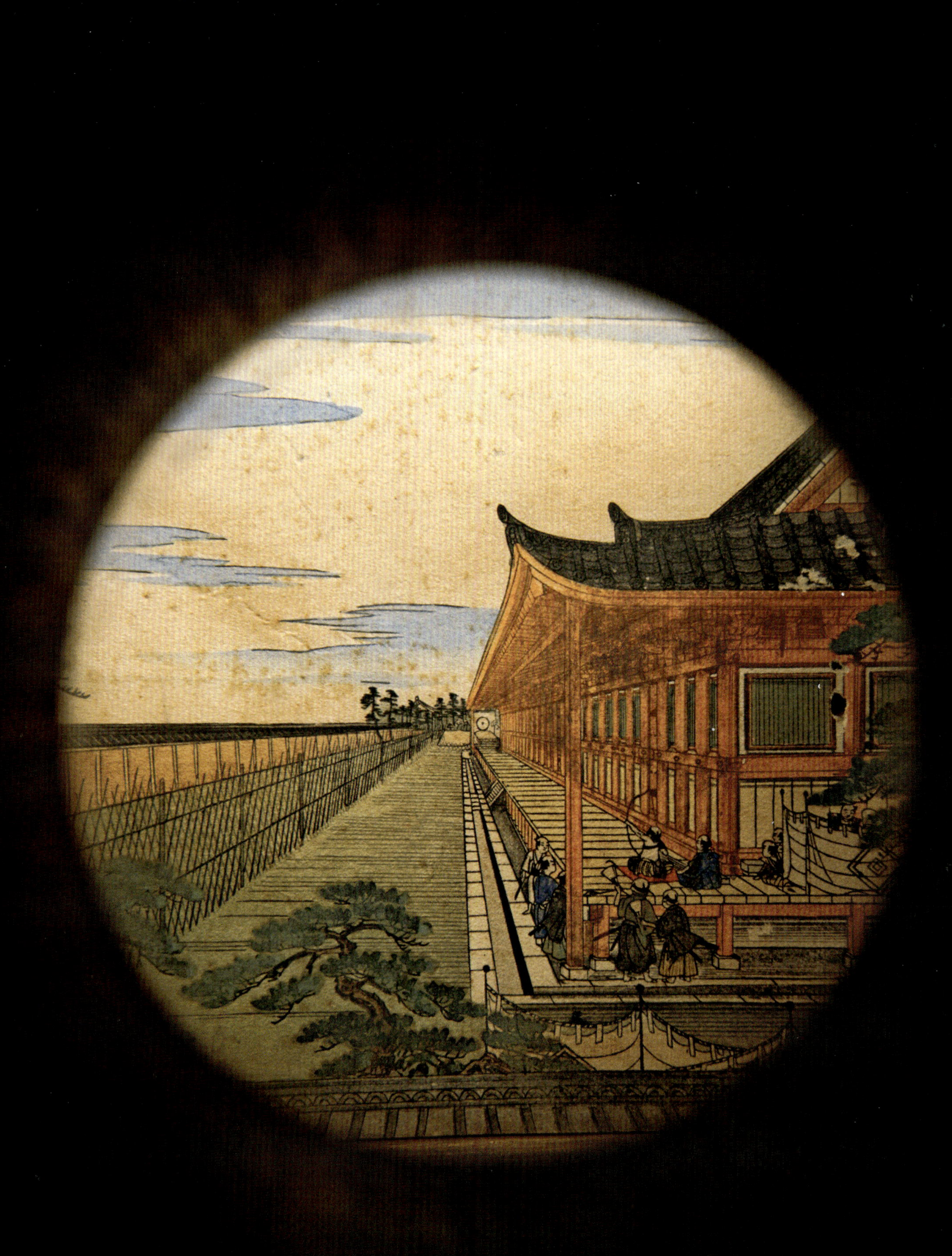

Oka Yasumasa

Introduction
The Painters of Japan and the West

The first Westerners appeared on Japan's shores in 1543, when a Chinese junk carrying two Portuguese men washed ashore on Tanegashima, an island off the southernmost tip of Japan (present-day Kagoshima prefecture).[1] From these Portuguese, the lord of Tanegashima acquired a matchlock gun, the first such weapon the Japanese had seen. The lord immediately ordered a swordsmith to replicate the weapon, but the smith had trouble with the unfamiliar screws at its breech, a problem solved only with the help of a Portuguese master blacksmith who came to Japan in 1544. From this beginning, the manufacture of matchlock guns came to be disseminated throughout Japan. The island of Tanegashima had produced iron since ancient times, and its craftsmen made swords, exporting them to China and the Ryūkyū Islands in the fifteenth century. Because Japan's blacksmithing technology was already highly developed for the production of swords and agricultural tools, it was readily adapted for gun manufacture.

A hundred years later, in 1639, when the Tokugawa shogunate had established its authority over Japan's feudal domains and succeeded in putting *sakoku* policies of national isolation into place, the necessity for firearms diminished. As a result, gun technology ceased to develop further in Japan. Similarly, because of sanctions on travel to foreign lands, Japanese ship design and maritime technology faltered.

This progression—the arrival of a new item or process, followed by its reproduction and further refinement in Japan, and finally its stagnation during the *sakoku* period—was paralleled in the development of Western-style oil paintings, engravings, and wooden or ivory carvings in Japan (plates 1, 2). European missionaries brought these items to be used as devotional aids as they sought Christian converts.

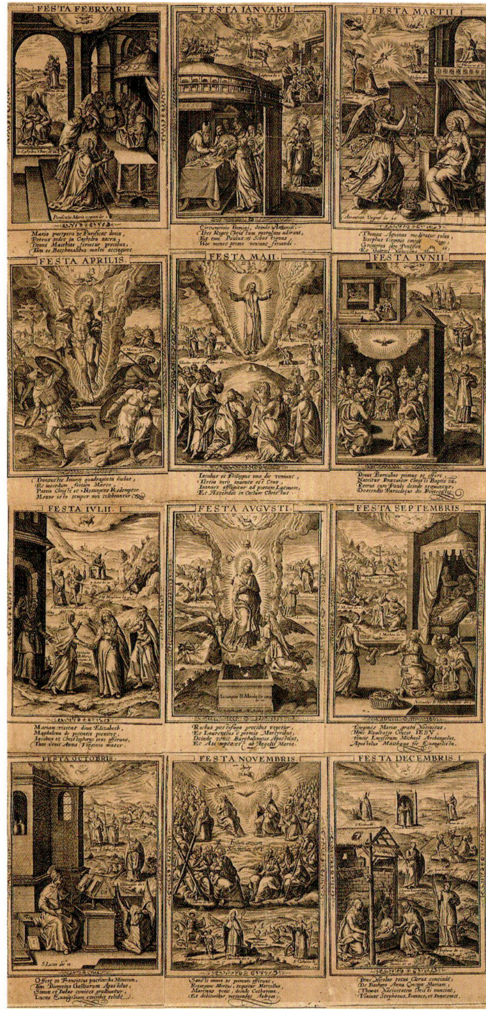

It is believed that in 1563 Takayama Hidano-kami (1527–1596), lord of Takatsuki Castle in Osaka and an early Christian daimyo, ordered a Japanese painter to copy a Western depiction of the Resurrection of Christ for his private chapel.[2] This is likely one of the earliest instances of a Japanese painter copying a Western work. Many metalwork replicas based on Western religious art and craftworks can be found among the items confiscated by authorities after the Christian prohibition of 1612.[3] Similar to the copying of the matchlock gun, it was the high skill level of Japanese painters and craftsmen that made such reproductions possible.

Copying Western paintings naturally introduced Western ways of seeing: artists incorporated perspective in their compositions, used *chiaroscuro* to create a sense of three dimensionality and mass on a flat surface, and projected shadows from light sources to replicate three-dimensional space (see detail, opposite). Japanese artists also acquired a method for rendering perspective through gradations of color. These Early Western-style Paintings (*shoki yōfūga*), as they are known, were created from the late sixteenth to early seventeenth century.

A world map in the collection of the Kobe City Museum (see plate 34b) is a beautiful example of this category and shows how its artist balanced Western painting technique with traditional Japanese modes of expression. In the depiction of North America, the upper edge of the continent has a grand mountainous view whose perspective is achieved through color: brown distinguishes the foreground from the green middle, and pale blue defines the far range. This coloristic technique must have been the result of the artist's study of Western models. Elsewhere the artist relied on a longstanding Japanese perspectival practice. By piling motifs in increasingly smaller scale from the bottom upward, as seen in the treatment of the ships and waves on the Atlantic Ocean, the artist conveys a sense of a more distant horizon at the top. The map is the artist's unconscious confession of his mixed acceptance of and adherence to differing artistic concepts.

Because Western ways of seeing were completely alien to the Japanese, painters and craftsmen worked to understand and engage with the culture that brought them these new ideas. It was in this process of reception, assimilation, and

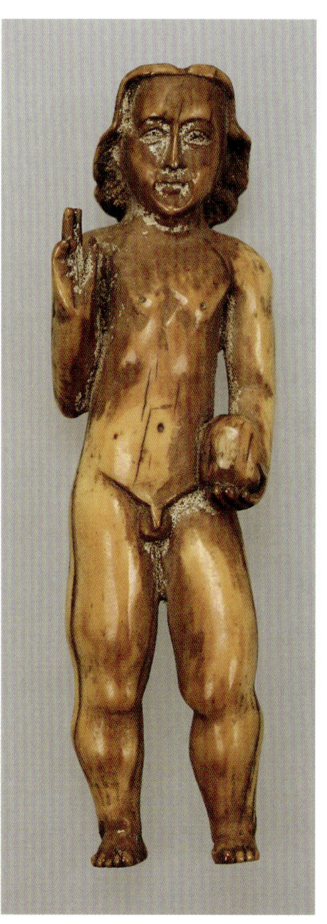

permeation that Japan truly discovered the West. The reception of a foreign culture can yield unexpected results in a short time when the receiving party responds actively and positively.

The Tokugawa shogunate prohibited Christian proselytizing in 1612, and the production of sacred pictures went directly into decline and soon disappeared. In the same studios in which the religious images had been produced, artists made purely decorative and domestic Early Western-style Paintings. For this they relied on imported sources such as world and city maps or military and genre scenes. Even though the naturalistic modes of expression that had been introduced to Japan with Christianity went into decline as the country's isolationism solidified, these techniques—creating a sense of spatial depth on a flat surface and replicating a three-dimensional space filled with air and light—would appear again in Japanese art in the mid-eighteenth century, when the study of Western science and culture (via the Dutch) resumed under the encouragement of Tokugawa Yoshimune (r. 1716–45).

Westernized Chinese pictures imported from Qing Dynasty China (plate 3) were the source from which Japanese artists first began to incorporate linear perspective into their work. The use of one-point perspective to emphasize the three-dimensionality of a scene appeared initially in the 1740s in the paintings and woodblock prints known as *uki-e* (plate 4). One such painting depicts the procession of a Korean mission to Japan (thought to be the tenth in 1748) and was created to order for a high-ranking warrior (plate 5). A composition of this type, with a line of figures receding into the background, had not

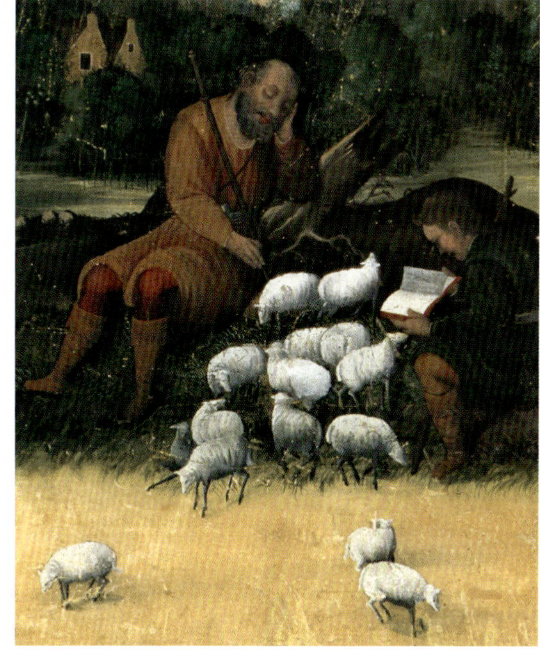

been seen in Japanese painting before this time. Another *uki-e*, from 1749, portrays the interior of a Kabuki theater (plate 6). Here, in a captivating use of trompe l'oeil, the artist seated a man on the very edge of the painting, while another figure seems to climb out and over the bottom of the scene. One can feel the artist's excitement and pleasure at using this novel technique.

By the 1750s, linear perspective can be found in the optical paintings known as *megane-e* (plates 7, 8). Meant to be viewed through a device with a convex lens, optical paintings gave the viewer a more realistic sense of depth in the landscape. With improving skill, the Japanese artist applied perspective to render more complicated and visually accurate compositions. Optical paintings would have a considerable influence on later Japanese landscape representations.

PLATE 3
Chinese, unknown artist
Chūgoku rōkaku zu (Interior of a Chinese Palace)
Mid-18th century
Ink and color on paper
11 × 16⅜ in.
(27.8 × 41.6 cm)

PLATE 4
Okumura Masanobu
(Japanese, 1686–1764)
Tōjinkan no zu (Interior of a Chinese Residence)
1741–48
(Kanpō-Enkyō era)
Woodblock print:
ink with hand color on paper
12⅜ × 16⅝ in.
(31.3 × 42 cm)

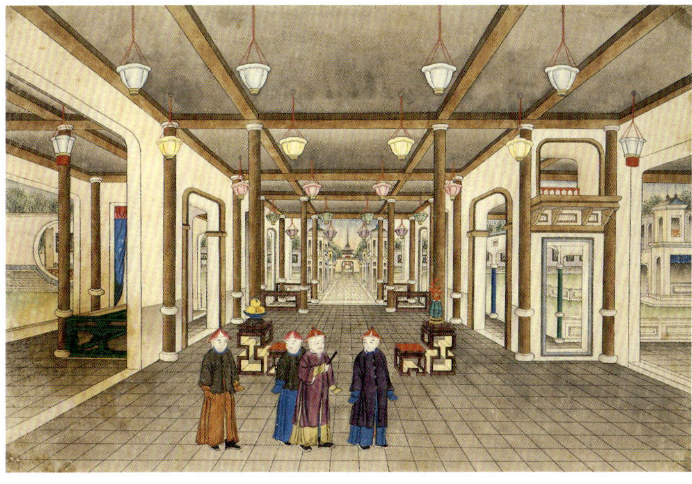

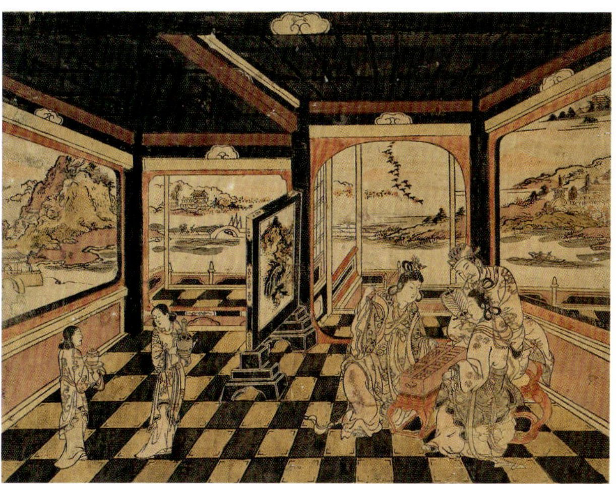

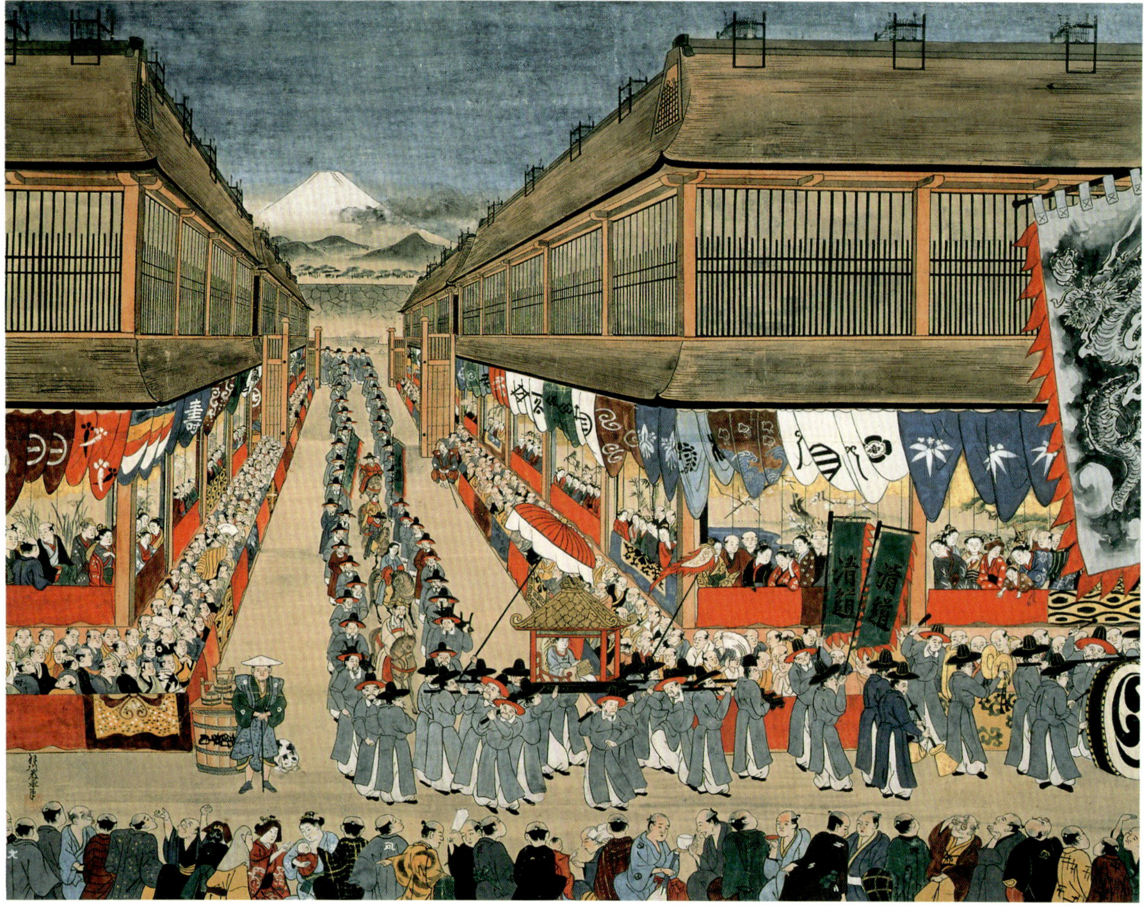

By the end of the eighteenth century, the second wave of Western-style paintings—by artists such as Shiba Kōkan (1738–1818) and those of the *Akita ranga* school—emerged in Japan. Combining Western illusionistic methods and naturalistic detail, their works resulted from the study of Western books, paintings, and prints brought to Japan via the Dutch trade as well as the influence of Chinese bird-and-flower pictures. It is too simplistic to say that Japanese artists learned to paint in Western style from the Dutch at Nagasaki; rather, they fused visual elements drawn from Japan, China, and the West. Shiba Kōkan, whose artworks disseminated the knowledge he was gaining from the Western natural sciences books of his scholar-friends, was but one of the growing number of Japanese artists to question established notions and to see the world from a positivistic, rational point of view. It was this attitude that most informed the late-eighteenth-century works of the Second Period of Western-style Paintings (*dainiki yōfūga*).

Even while enforcing the *sakoku* policy, the Japanese ruling elite continued to obtain information about the outside world, primarily through the trade center of Nagasaki and the domains of Tsushima, Satsuma, and Matsumae, which had been charged with maintaining foreign relations with particular countries. Nagasaki was the only port under the direct jurisdiction of the shogunate and would become the central point for the diffusion of European-style art in Japan. The *ukiyo-e* prints whose decorative effects would so profoundly affect European arts of the late nineteenth century were themselves produced under the influence of Europe. For instance, the beautiful women portrayed by the *ukiyo-e* masters Torii Kiyonaga or Kitagawa Utamaro stand in landscapes rendered with the Western method of linear perspective.

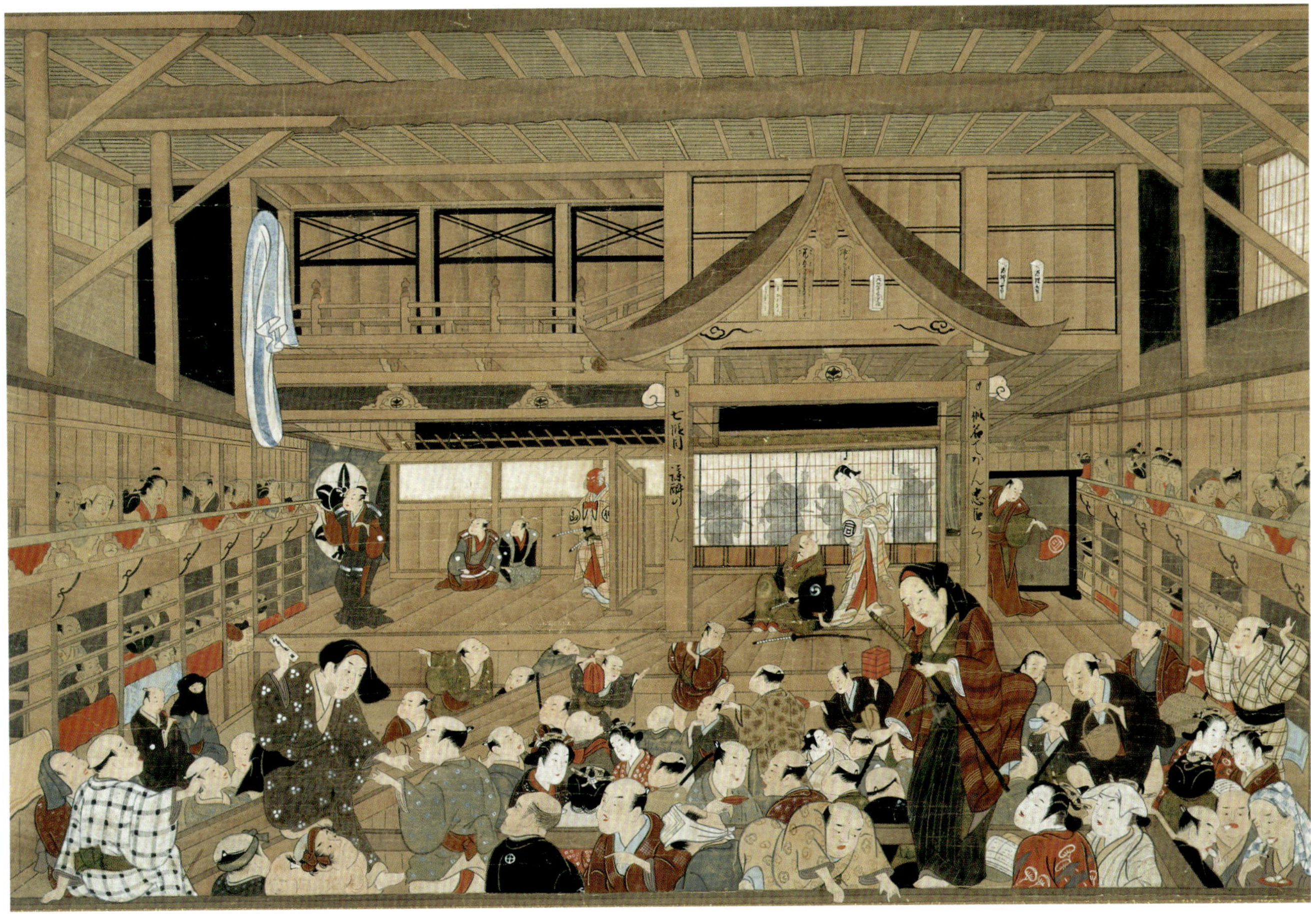

Masters and Pupils of Early Western-style Painting

In 1549 the Jesuit missionary Francis Xavier (1506–1552) sailed into the Japanese harbor at Kagoshima, just six years after the Portuguese had landed at Tanegashima. The number of early Christian converts in Kyūshū and its surrounding regions was surprisingly large. In 1579 Allessandro Valignano, supervisor of the Jesuit missions in Asia, arrived at Kuchinotsu harbor at Shimabara, Kyūshū. Concerned that missionary policies had generated conflicts with the Japanese, he changed the Jesuit focus to one of inculturation. Hoping to foster Japanese priests, Valignano founded secondary (*seminario*)– and college (*collegio*)–level schools to provide a European-style education. Western music and Latin were taught at the secondary level.

As the number of Christians increased, so did the demand for devotional pictures of Christ, the Virgin Mary, and the Virgin and Child. It was no longer practical to import devotional images and medals made in Europe or elsewhere in Asia, and the Jesuits looked for a way to produce these items in Japan. In 1583 Giovanni Niccolò, a Jesuit missionary who came from Naples, arrived in Japan to be an art instructor. The Italian Mannerism found in Early Western-style Painting was introduced to Japan through Flemish copperplate engravings or Italian oil paintings brought by Western ships and used by Japanese painters as models. But above all, these modes of expression found their way to Japan through Niccolò's instruction at the painting school called *gagakusha* (thought to be part of the *seminario*).[4]

Christian proselytizing in Japan reached a turning point in 1587, when Toyotomi Hideyoshi issued a deportation order for missionaries (*bateren tsuihō rei*). After Hideyoshi's death in 1598, Christianity came under the protection of Tokugawa Ieyasu for a short while, but in 1612 Ieyasu prohibited propagation of the faith, and in 1614 he expelled the missionaries as well as any of their followers with political influence in Japan. For the next thirty years, a storm of oppression and persecution against Christians, similar to that of Roman times, descended upon Japan.

During this time, the preparatory and painting schools survived by moving to various sites at Shimabara, Amakusa, and Nagasaki until finally forced to close by the 1614 deportation order. A registry of a Jesuit *collegio* at Nagasaki for 1613 lists Niccolò as a fifty-three-year-old painter and art teacher. Some of his Japanese pupils undoubtedly lived and remained in Nagasaki. The same registry includes, for example, an entry for the Japanese student "Louis Shiozuka—thirty-seven years old, painter, organist, conductor of church choir."[5]

With the ban on Christianity and the enforcement of *sakoku*, the evolving influence of early Western-style art from Roman Catholic countries was cut short, and such paintings were sealed away. After the prohibition, only art furnishings with little apparent Christian association survived; most religious images were lost during the persecution of Christians that now took place. Among the representative examples of Early Western-style Painting still extant are the medium-sized screens of Western genre or pastoral scenes called *seiyō fūzoku zu* (see plate 38a,b), which were

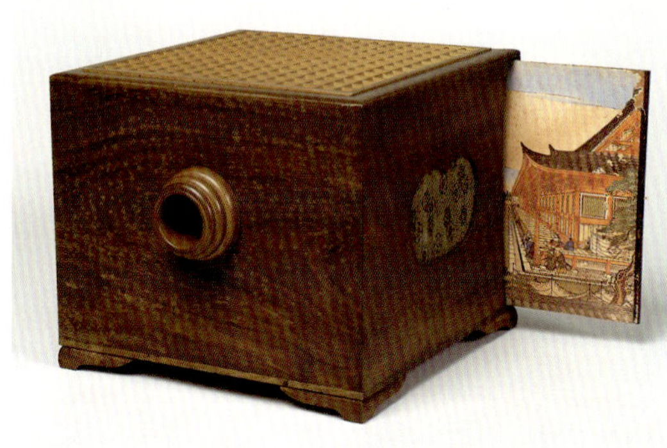

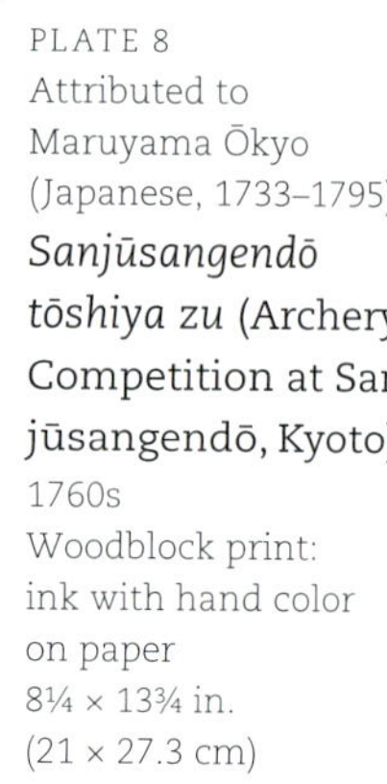

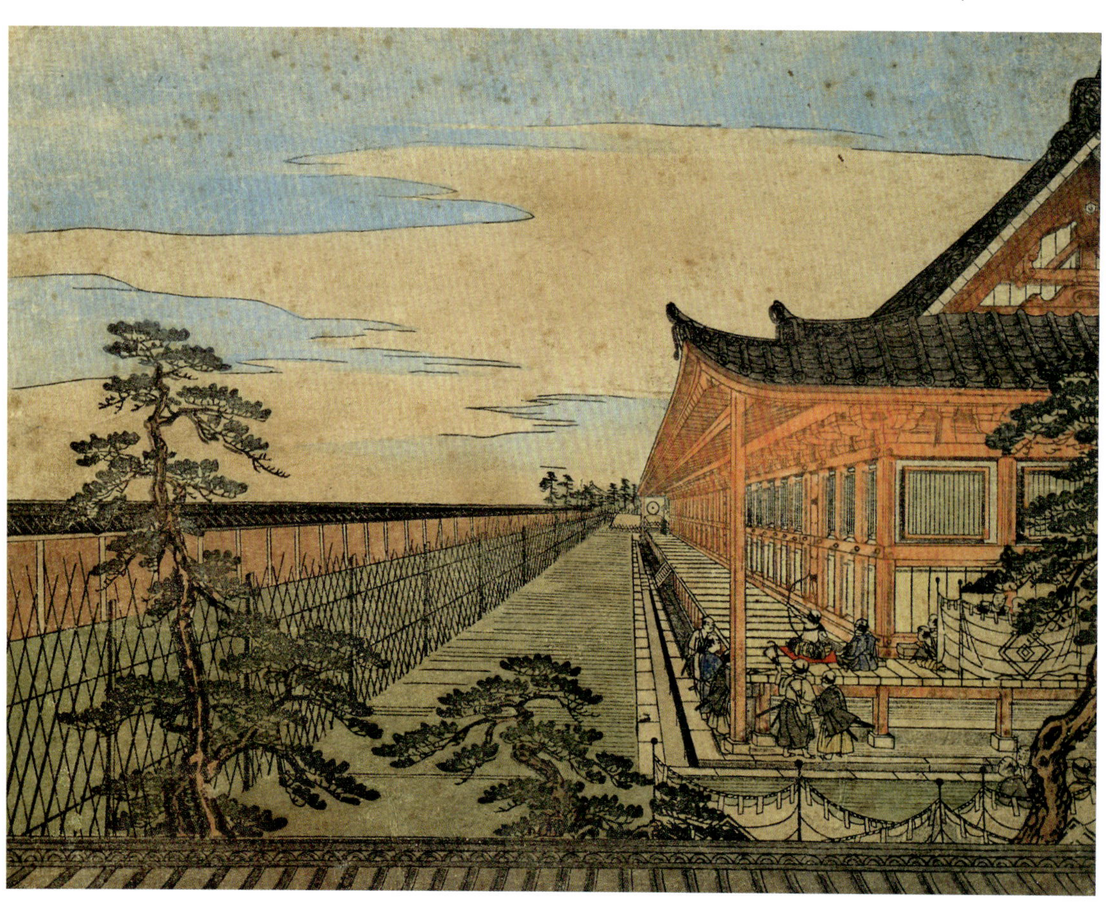

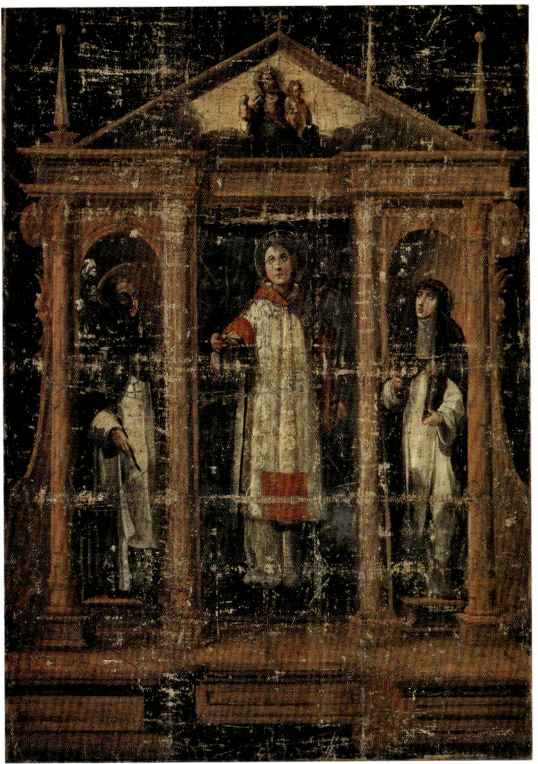

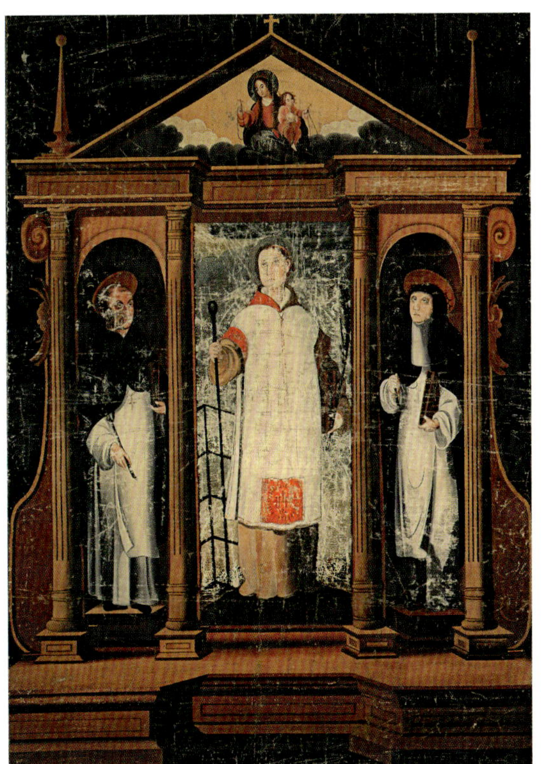

placed in domestic contexts, and the large screens meant for formal settings such as *Taisei ōkō kiba zu* (Foreign Emperors and Kings on Horseback, see plate 33) and *Yonto zu* / *Sekai zu* (Four Large Cities of the World / Map of the World, see plate 34a,b). The artists of these secular pictures were likely trained at the Jesuit painting school.

Two religious pictures confiscated by the Nagasaki magistrate during this time provide a telling example of the reception of Western technique in Japanese art. One is likely by a Western artist (fig. 1), and the other a Japanese copy (fig. 2). X-ray analysis of the first picture shows a build-up of white lead in Western impasto technique to render lights and darks. In the copy, however, the artist laid down a smooth, skin-colored surface for the figures' faces and used line and shading to render eyes and noses in a method reminiscent of *ukiyo-e*.[6] The Italian Niccolò and the painting school had not successfully passed on the basics of Western painting to all the Japanese students. Traditional modes of expression persisted despite the direct instruction of Western teachers, and one can surmise that after their departure, it was even more difficult to maintain or further develop an understanding of Western painting methods.

Tokugawa Ieyasu and the Map of the World Screens

Three monumental screens from the period of Early Western-style Painting offer a fascinating case study of the transmission, study, and adoption of Western sources as well as the purposes such screens may have served. The screens are *Bankoku ezu: Sekai zu* / *Nijūhachi toshi zu* (Picture of the Universe: Map of the World / Plans of Twenty-eight Cities, fig. 3), now in the collection of the Imperial Household Agency, and, from the Kobe City Museum, *Yonto zu* / *Sekai zu* (Four Large Cities of the World / Map of the World, see plate 34a,b) and *Taisei ōkō kiba zu* (Foreign Emperors and Kings on Horseback, see plate 33).[7] The shading, perspective, cast shadows, and the like employed on all three screens suggest that the unknown Japanese creators had been trained at the Jesuit painting school.

The map screens and the monarchs on horseback depicted on the screens have a common source: a revised version of a large wall map of the world produced in 1607 by the Dutch cartographer Willem Janszoon Blaeu (lost during World War II and known today only through a photograph, see fig. 9, p. 59). The revision itself, made in 1609 by the Dutch engraver Pieter van den Keere, does not survive. But at the Maritiem Museum in Rotterdam, one can find a world map made in 1646 by

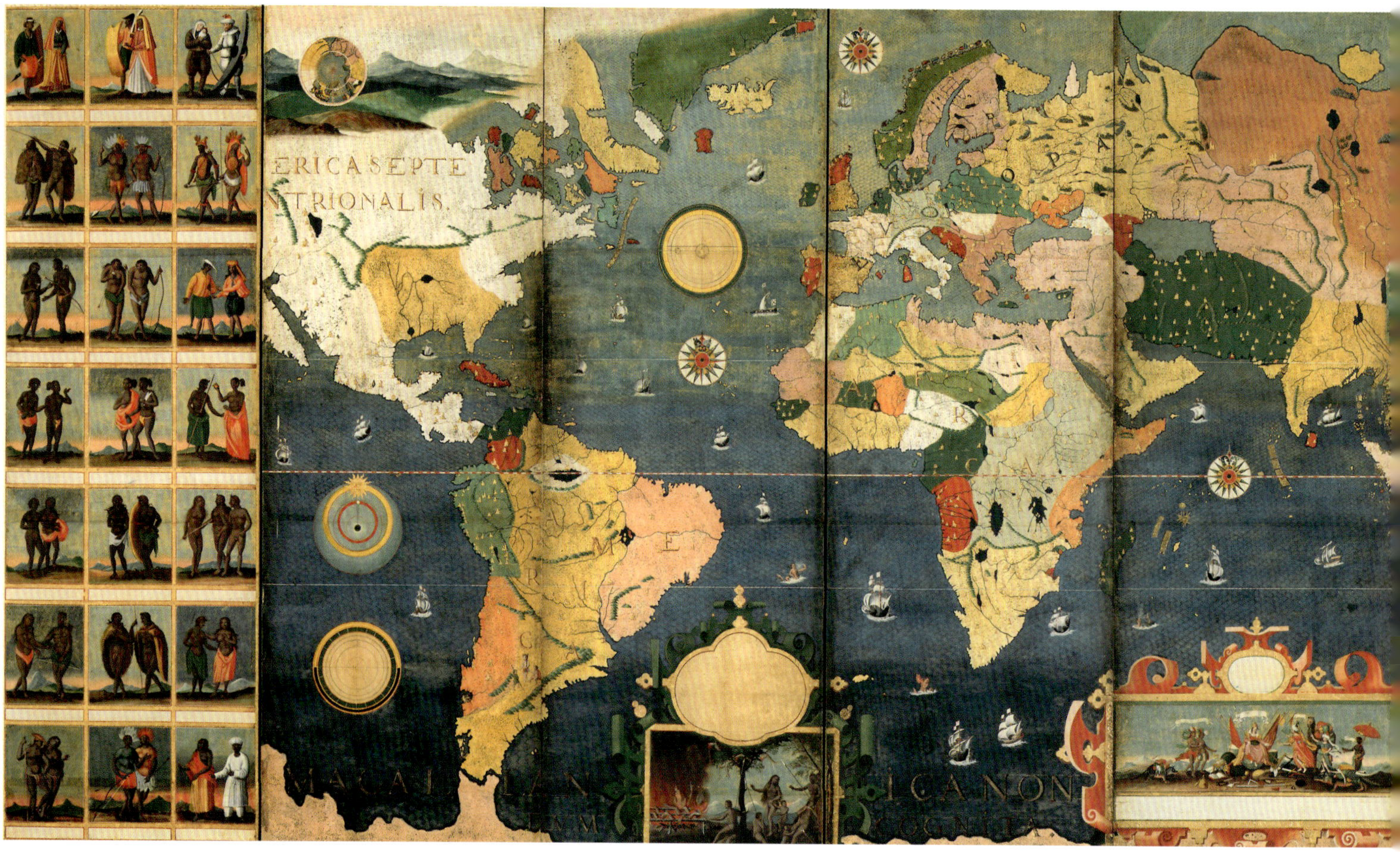

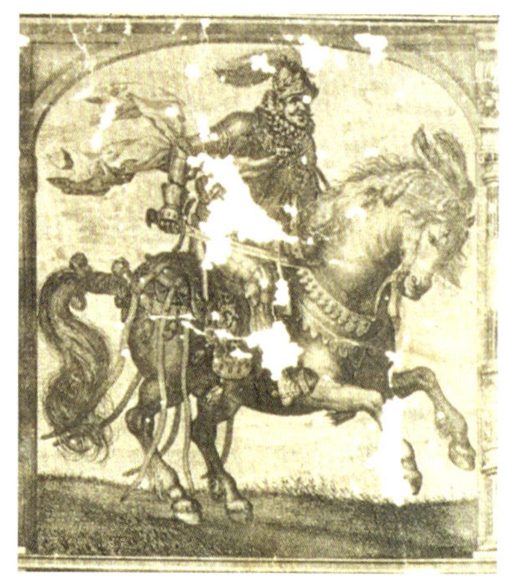

DETAIL
Horse and rider from
Blaeu source map (fig. 4)

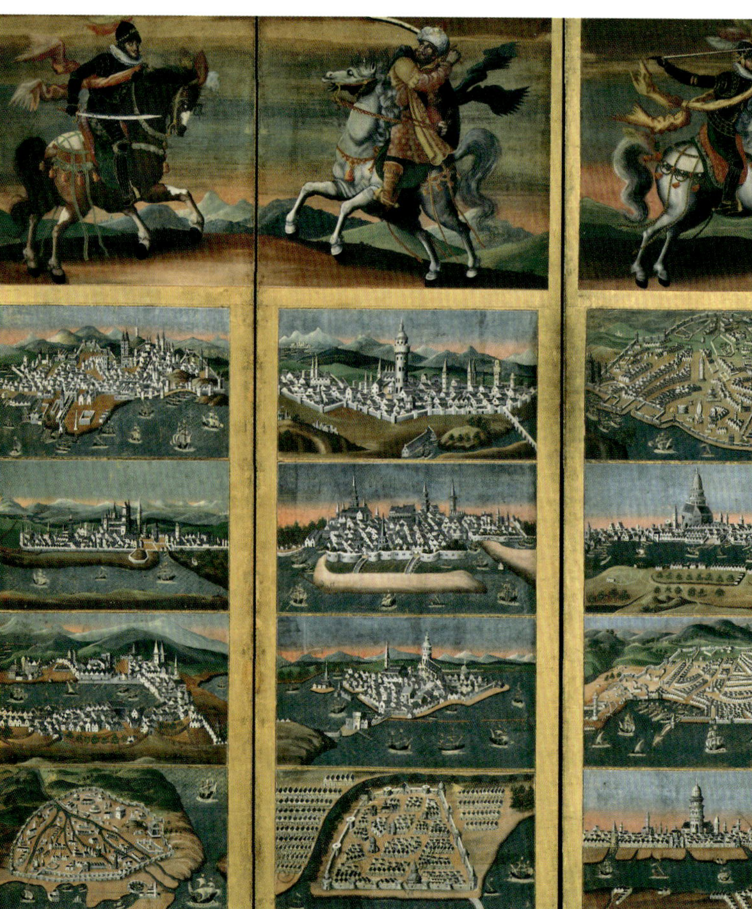

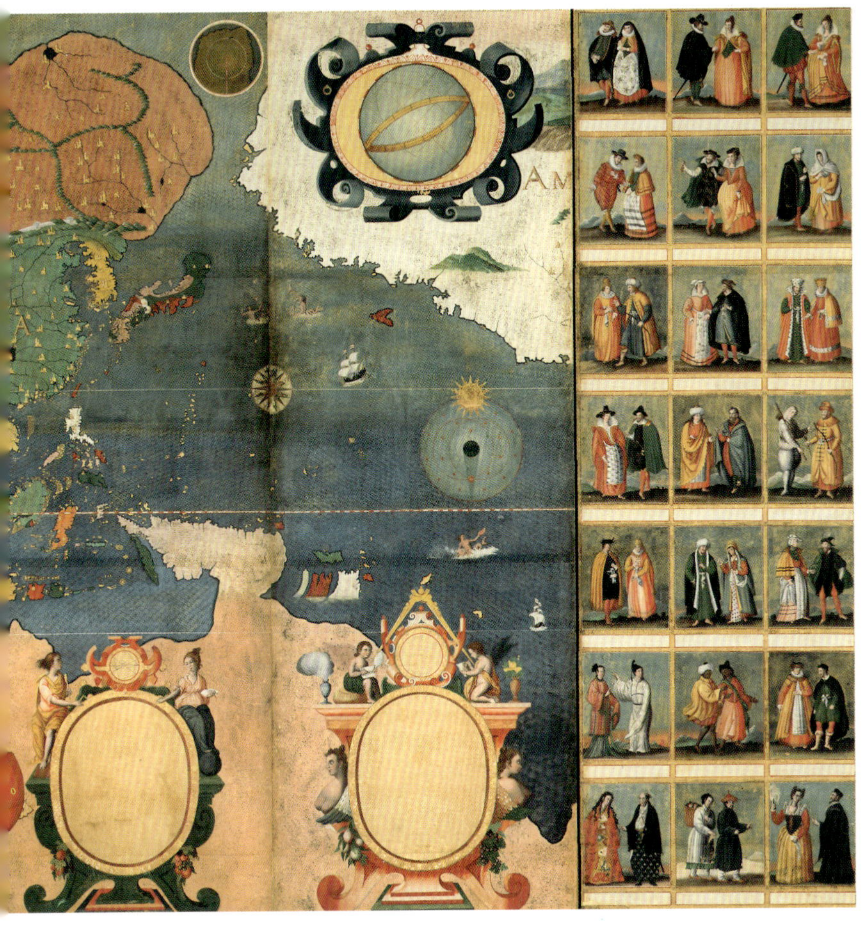

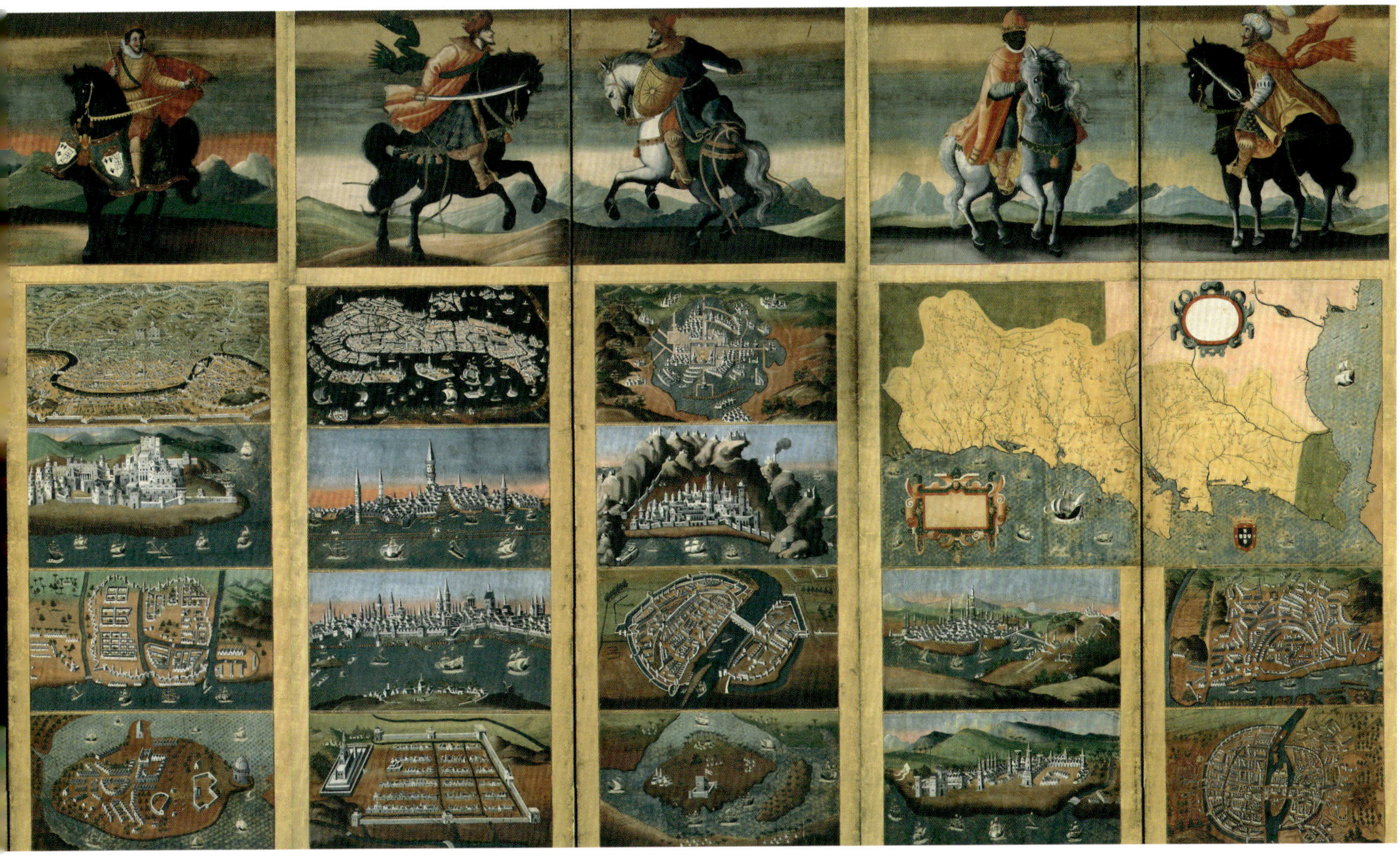

FIG. 3a,b
Japanese, unknown
artist
*Bankoku ezu: Sekai
zu/Nijūhachi toshi
zu* (Picture of the
Universe: Map of the
World/Plans of
Twenty-eight Cities)
Pair of eight-panel
screens: ink and
color on paper
70½ × 177 in.
(179 × 490 cm) each
Kunaichō Sannomaru
Shōzōkan, Tokyo

25

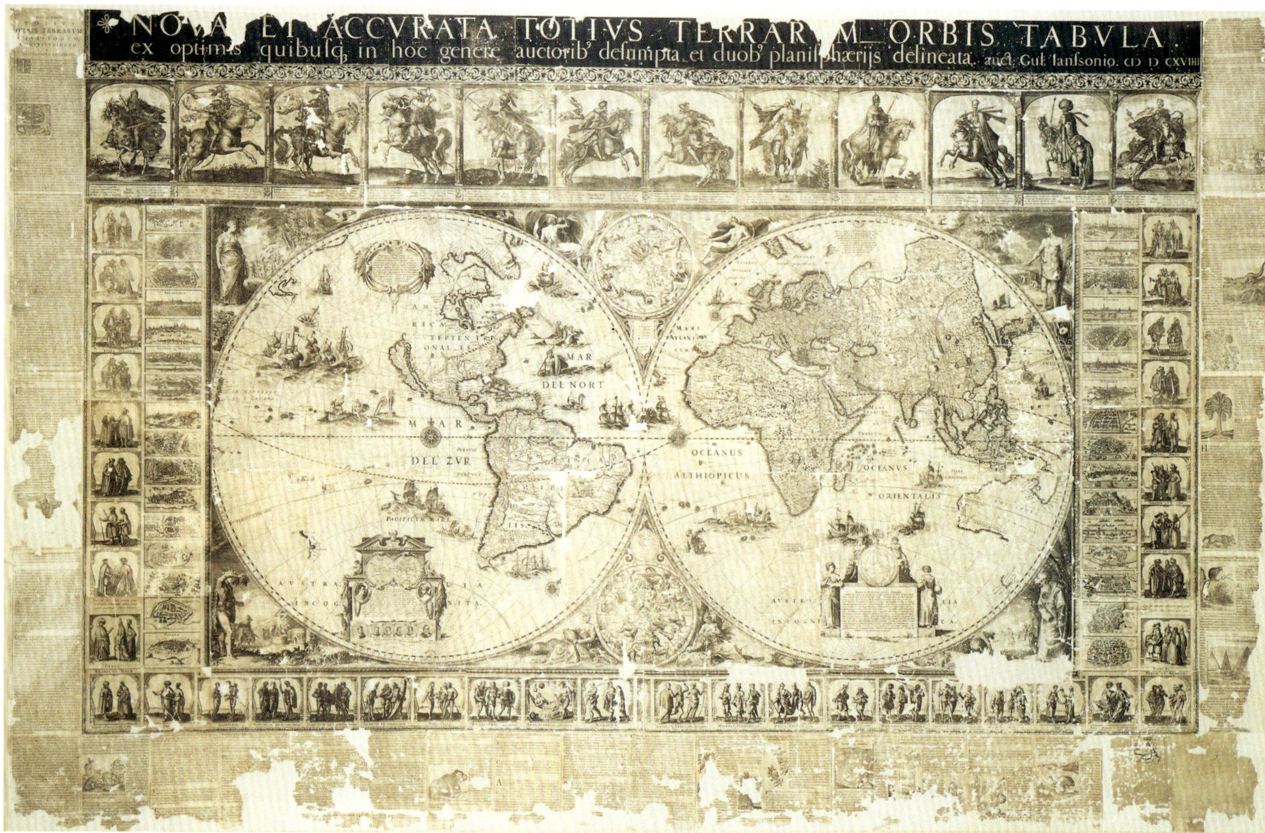

Willem's son, Joan Blaeu, who himself revised his father's 1619 version of the map (fig. 4). This is the oldest extent iteration of Willem Blaeu's 1607 world map. Based on documentary evidence (see below), the screens of *Bankoku ezu* are thought be the earliest reinterpretation of Blaeu's map in Japan, created shortly after the map came into the possession of the Jesuits at Nagasaki.

Standing before the world map in Rotterdam, one feels its overwhelming size (approximately 6 × 9 feet) and the density of its geographic information, its detail facilitated by the effects possible with copperplate engraving. When we compare the pictures of kings and cities on the Rotterdam map (see detail, p. 24) with those depicted in the Japanese screens, we see that the artists not only enlarged the original but also made changes that add dramatic impact. For example, the dynamism of the horses' poses was increased by the fore-shortening of their bodies, an alteration that contributes to the overall power of the compositions.

The *Bankoku ezu* screens were given by the Tokugawa family in Sunpu (Shizuoka) to the imperial family some time during the Meiji Restoration (1867–68). It appears that Tokugawa Ieyasu (1542–1616) had received them from the Jesuits as a gift, perhaps with the intention that such a gesture would enable the survival of the religious order in Japan. A record in the *Sunpu seiji roku* (Diary of Tokugawa Ieyasu at Sunpu) dated the twentieth day of the ninth month, 1611, reads: "[The retired Shogun, Ieyasu,] looked at the map screen. [And] spoke of the foreign countries."[8] Another reference is found in the *Sunpuki* (History of Tokugawa Ieyasu at Sunpu): "In the ninth month of 1611, a world map screen is brought from the West. [Ieyasu] has looked at it at Sunpu, where it was presented . . . and [he] has enquired about and discussed the state of world affairs."[9]

Large-scale screens were elaborate gifts made for men in power. The artist of Tokugawa Ieyasu's screens had probably studied at the Jesuit painting school, most likely with Niccolò. The Jesuits undoubtedly attempted to show off the prosperity and magnificence of Western cities by presenting the vastness of the world—which is to say, the smallness of Japan. In addition, they attempted to strongly impress the Japanese ruler with the glories of Portugal and places associated with the Society of Jesus, as well as the honor and reward of accepting Catholicism. Even so, in the end they were unable to stop the oppression of the Church that prevailed until the first half of the seventeenth century.

FIG. 4
Joan Blaeu
(Dutch, 1596–1673)
Nova et Accurata Torius Terrarium Orbis Tabula
[Map of the World]
1646
Copperplate print: ink on paper
69½ × 110⅞ in. (176.5 × 281.5 cm)
Marietiem Museum, Rotterdam

In 1639 the Tokugawa shogunate issued an order prohibiting Portuguese ships from entering Japan, and in 1641 the Dutch traders at Hirado were ordered to move to the artificial island of Dejima in Nagasaki harbor. The Dutch persevered despite humiliation and hardship, and theirs remained the single European country to trade with Japan. England had withdrawn from Japan in 1623, when they closed their trading post in Hirado. From this time until the opening of Yokohama harbor in 1859, Japan obtained limited information about Europe and its culture through the Dutch at Nagasaki.

Most of the pictures and books that arrived in Japan in these years were of Dutch origin, and many of the paintings and prints were of genre or landscape subjects (*petite genre*). The Japanese had little inclination toward large oil paintings, having no established custom of hanging framed pictures on a wall inside a room. Illustrations in expensive natural history books were brought to Japan, but high-quality paintings and prints were not in demand. Because so few samples were introduced, Western-style paintings did not reach the standard of a work of art in Japanese eyes, and artistic expression incorporating Western elements did not carry a higher aesthetic value than traditional art forms.

The Western influence recognized in Japanese artworks of the Edo period can be divided roughly into two categories. The first includes the pictures and craftworks produced in response to Japanese interest in Western subjects such as the natural sciences. The second encompasses Western-style craftwork manufactured for export to the specifications of Western buyers. Many of these were commercial goods or commemorative items. During the *sakoku* period, without direction from Western instructors, Japanese artists employed Western modes of expression in varying degrees in a process that says more about their traditional ways of seeing and, more generally, their approaches toward producing visual imagery. Whereas Western art focuses on depth perception and the totality of objects in space, the Japanese tradition emphasizes texture, interrelated flat shapes, and closely observed detail. Fixed Western stereotypes that ruled Japan at the time appear in the European landscapes and subjects produced by Japanese artists, such as the prominent noses and curly red hair invariably used to depict Dutch people. The few examples below illustrate how some Japanese artists responded to Western art models during *sakoku*.

The artist Tani Bunchō (1763–1841) famously copied a picture of flowers and birds by a minor Dutch painter that had been brought to Nagasaki in 1726 by the order of Tokugawa Yoshimune (see plate 61). Bunchō himself may have worked from a copy of the original made by Ishikawa Tairō and Mōkō (see fig. 12, p. 101). Depicted in Bunchō's picture are colorful flowers in a Classical krater-shaped vase, which is set in an arch and surrounded by realistically rendered birds in a manner that suggests the influence of the well-known Dutch painter Melchior d'Hondecoeter (1604–1653). Bunchō's vase sits well within the space of the arch, a placement emphasized by the tips of flowers that push forward to touch the top of the arch. The light source enters from the left rear of the depicted space, creating a shadow on the base of the vase. Bunchō's intention to create a sense of space and to replicate a light source is clear. Another artist, the little-known Zaiga, attempted to draw this same motif in 1729 in a monochrome print (plate 9). In Zaiga's picture, the vase sits in front of the arch, and the slanting lines he added to indicate shadow show little technical understanding of the concept of shading. Zaiga replicated the exotic picture of flowers, but unlike Bunchō, he did not master the artistic methods by which its spatial depth was rendered.

The next example is an illustration from *Ransetsu benwaku* (Clarification of Misunderstandings in Theories of the Dutch), written in 1799 by Ōtsuki Gentaku, a scholar of Dutch studies. With this book, Ōtsuki intended to correct Japanese misconceptions about the Dutch, and to this end he included a picture of a nude Dutch woman to show that she was no different from the Japanese. The original source was Govard Bidloo's *Anatomia Humani Corporis* (1685), most probably as interpreted by William Cowper in his *Anatomy of Human Bodies* (1698).[10] The artist of the source illustration was Gérard de Lairesse, whose *Het groot schilderboek* (Great Book of Painting) influenced a number of Western-style painters in Japan.

The differences in approach are apparent when we compare Lairesse's image with the Japanese copy. The Japanese artist struggled with his treatment of light source, shading, and three-dimensionality as well as the weight shift, or

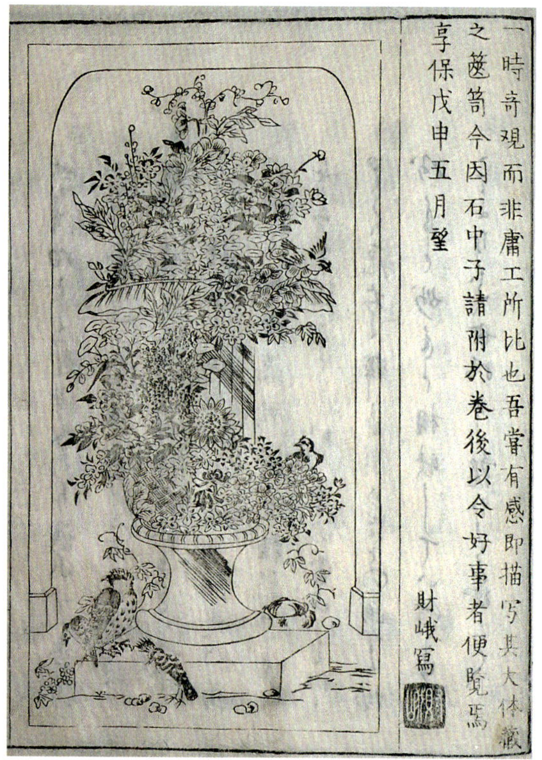

PLATE 9
Zaiga (Japanese, dates unknown)
Copy of Flowers-and-Birds by Willem Frederick van Royen
from *Gazu hyakkachō*, 1729 (Kyōho 14)
Book bound in Japanese style
Woodblock print: ink on paper
10¾ × 6⅜ in. (27.2 × 16.2 cm) page

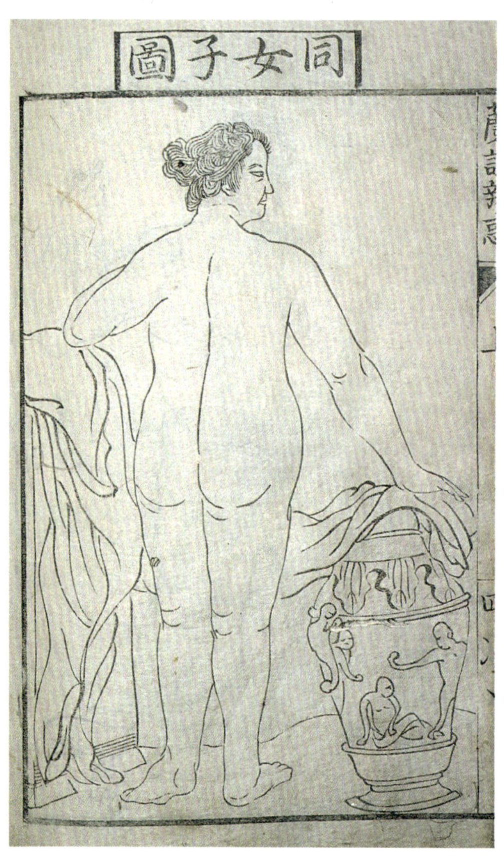

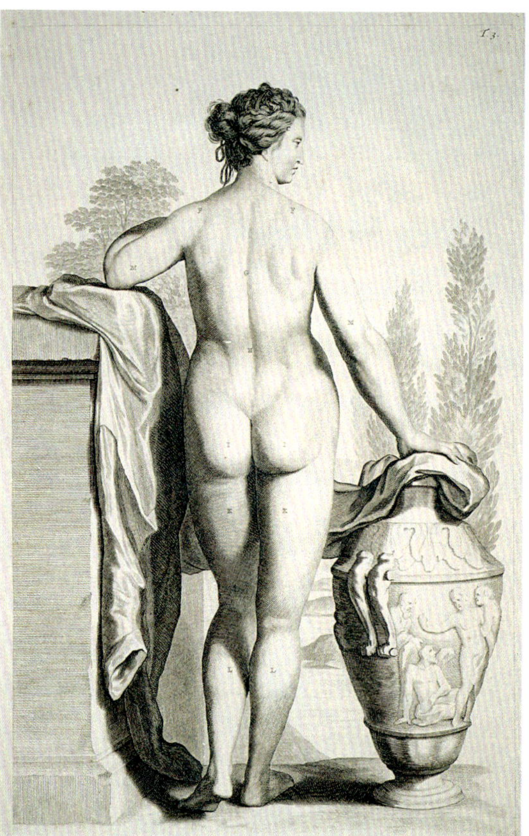

PLATE 10
Japanese, unknown artist
Nude
from Ōtsuki Gentaku, *Ransetsu benwaku*, 1799 (Kansei 11)
Two books bound in Japanese style
Woodblock print: ink on paper
7⅜ × 4⅜ in. (18.6 × 11 cm) page

PLATE 11
Gérard de Lairesse (Dutch, 1640–1711)
Nude
from Govard Bidloo, *Ontleding dea menschelyken lichaams*, Utrecht, 1728
Copperplate engraving and etching: ink on paper
20¾ × 14⅜ in. (52.5 × 36.5 cm) page

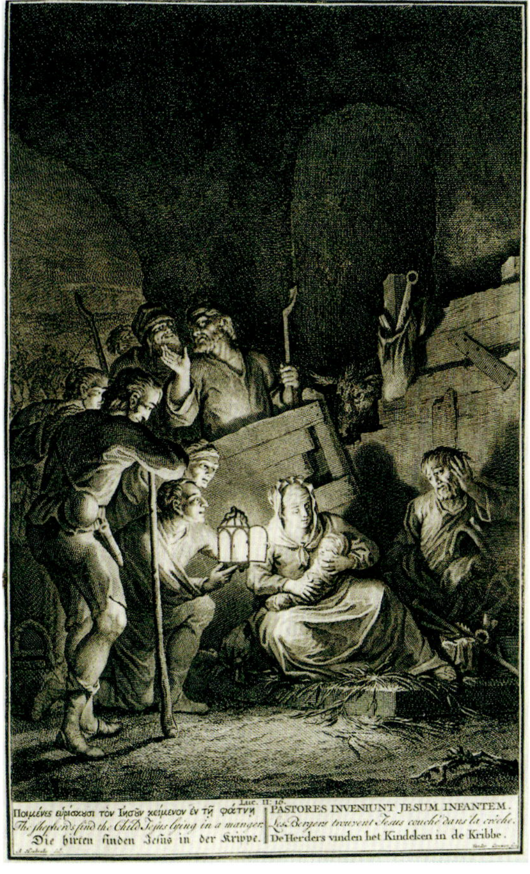

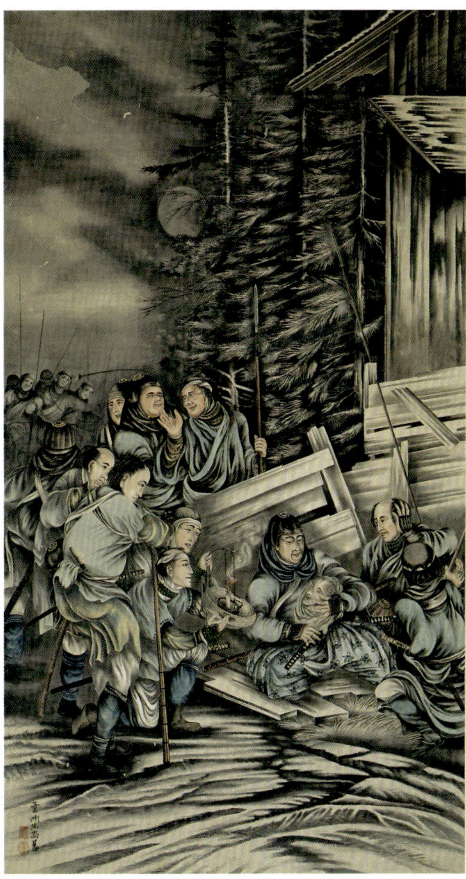

contrapposto, of the figure (plate 10). The artist did not grasp the idealization of the human form in the original, which was intended to express the beauty of a perfectly balanced human body. Even though intended for an anatomy book, Lairesse idealized the nude, setting her in an outdoor, light-filled space with a Roman amphora—elements that are reminiscent of an academic painting (plate 11). The Japanese artist, on the other hand, rendered the nude woman as a kind of specimen and ignored the ambient space. He did not possess the means to express three-dimensionality through modeling, and so the woman's body is flat, without texture or depth. The height of the woman's nose is emphasized, revealing a stereotype firmly held in the mind of the Japanese artist.

A final example comes from *Akōgishi hōshū zu* (Akō Retainers after Their Revenge), a hanging scroll produced in the Tenpō era by Yasuda Raishū, a Western-style painter from Edo. It depicts the famous Japanese story in which a group of Akō retainers achieve revenge by killing the murderer of their master. Its visual source, an engraved Adoration of the Shepherds by the Dutch artist Arnold Houbraken (1660–1719), was published in an illustrated bible in Amsterdam in 1720.[11] At first glance, it might seem that pictures of such disparate subjects could not be related, but the influences are surprisingly clear.

In rendering the biblical scene, Houbraken followed the Dutch tradition and did not idealize the Virgin Mary (fig. 5). He portrayed a benevolent woman with a measure of resolve. Joseph appears next to her, and a group of shepherds gathers around, the sincere wonderment of their expressions emphasized by the brightness of the sole light source, a lantern. In his illustration (fig. 6), Raishū omitted the ominously large shadow that looms over Houbraken's scene and suggests the darkness of the holy night. As if to provide an excuse for the even brightness illuminating the Akō retainers, Raishū placed a full moon in the sky. He added snow in the foreground, its whiteness imparting a supernatural quality to the lighting and, in turn, suppressing any effect of darkness and candlelight. In Houbraken's version, the light of the lantern hits the side of Mary's face and shines upon the shepherds as a radiance seemingly emitted by the infant Jesus, but Raishū did not incorporate this crucial *chiarascuro* effect in his work. It could have been the limitation of his artistic vision, but I prefer to think that Raishū's aesthetics led him to modify the strong contrast of the lantern light and surrounding dark of the original print to conform with the more traditional Japanese context of moonlight and snow.

The crucial factor is not how successfully Japanese artists learned Western painting concepts; it is how they adopted, fused, and transformed such completely different types of expression to create their own art. During the *sakoku* period, there were no instructors of Western painting in Japan, and artists had access to only a limited number of imported paintings and prints. Curiosity and the spontaneous or opportunistic study of Western painting led Japanese artists, from the seventeenth century on, to incorporate naturalistic three-dimensionality, one-point perspective, and shading techniques into their works. Throughout this period of artistic discovery, Japanese painters fully maintained and valued their traditional concepts and modes of expression. The combination of Western and Japanese perspectives, as well as the deeply felt attachment to Japanese aesthetics and motifs, instills Western-style painting of the premodern period with a marvelous and at times mysterious atmosphere. Because of this, these artworks still maintain the great appeal they held at the time of their creation.

NOTES

1. The arrival of the Portuguese in 1542 with a matchlock gun is recorded in *Teppōki* (History of the Gun), which was edited by Nanpo Bunshi in 1606 in response to a request from Tanegashima Hisatoki, a retainer of the Satsuma domain. This material is in the collection of the National Archives of Japan, Tokyo. The names of the Portuguese are given there as "Murashukusha" and "Kirishitadamōta." See "Rekishi no naka no teppō denrai," exh. cat. (Chiba: Kokuritsu Rekishi Minzoku Hakubutsukan, 2006), 168.

2. Matsuda Kiichi and Kawasaki Momota, "Kan'yaku Furoisu, Nihonshi 1, Oda Nobunaga hen I," (translation of Luis Frois's "Historica de Iapan") (Tokyo: Chūōbunko, Chūōkōronsha, 2000), 283.

3. Religious objects that had been confiscated by magistrates throughout Japan, including Christian icons, medals, and the so-called Maria Kannon (Virgin Mary in the Buddhist Avalokitesvara form), were added to the collection of Tokyo National Museum in 1879. Designated as Important Cultural Properties in 1977, they numbered 541 items as of 2001.

4. Niccolò himself also painted, which he must have done until he was deported from Japan to Macao in 1614.

5. *Nagasaki no korejio* (Nagasaki: Junshin Joshi Tanki Daigaku, 1985), 20–21.

6. Utada Shinsuke, *Abura-e o kaibō suru* (Tokyo: Nihon Hōsō Shuppankyōkai, 2002), 199.

7. Considering the degree of accuracy in the world maps and cities depicted in the extant examples, the most precise version, probably directly copied from the Dutch world map, is *Bankoku ezu*. A version in the collection of the Kōsetsu Art Museum (*Repanto sentō zu/Sekai chizu* [The Battle of Lepanto/Map of the World]) and *Yonto zu/Sekai zu* are thought to follow next. *Taisei ōkō kiba zu* is a slightly later work than *Bankoku ezu*.

8. A copy of *Sunpu seiji roku* (1611–16), attributed to Gotō Shōzaburō Mitsutsugu, can be found at the National Diet Library, Tokyo, among other locations.

9. *Sunpuki* (1611–15), attributed to Gotō Shōzaburō Mitsutsugu, is in the collection of the Cabinet Library in the National Archives of Japan, Tokyo. See also *Shiseki zassan,* vol. 6 (Tokyo: Gunsho Ruijū Kanseikai, 1995). There is a strong possibility but no direct confirmation that the screen now owned by the Imperial Household Agency is the same "world map screen" that came into Ieyasu's hands from "the West." It is odd that a screen, a Japanese-made work, would be described as arriving from abroad. The viewers at that time may have mistakenly believed that the world map screen had been produced in the West. Still it is undeniable that Ieyasu saw the screen in 1611 and asked about foreign countries.

10. I would like to thank Katsumori Noriko, curator at the Kobe City Museum, for providing this information.

11. Gilliam van der Gouwen etched Houbraken's design. I once proposed that Raishū's picture was based on the Christian iconography of the Adoration of Magi; see Oka Yasumasa, "Yasuda Raishū hitsu *Akōgishi hōshūzu* to jakkan no dōhanga sakuhin wo megutte," in *Kōbe shiritsu hakubutsukan kenkyū kiyō,* no. 2 (Kobe: Kobe City Museum, 1985). Subsequently, in 2005, Ad Stijnman, a printmaker and print historian in Oudewater, The Netherlands, and Anne Jaap van den Berg, librarian of the Nederlands Bijbelgenootschap, identified Houbraken's image as Raishū's source; see Oka Yasumasa, "Yasuda Raishū hitsu *Akōgishi hōshūzu* no genzu wo megutte," *Kokka,* no. 1342 (2007).

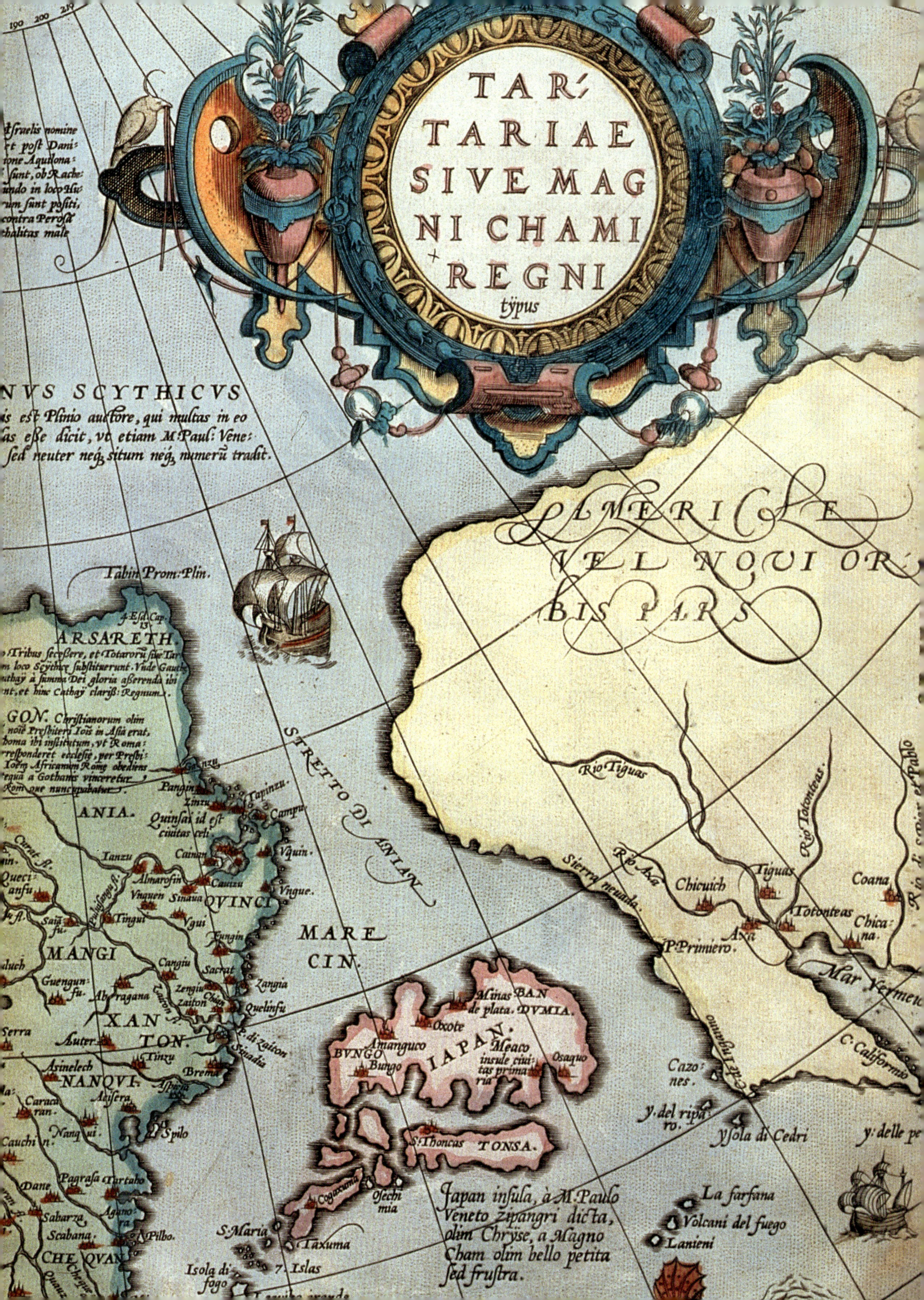

Japan insula, à M.Paulo Veneto zipangri dicta, olim Chryse, a Magno Cham olim bello petita sed frustra.

1

Onoda Kazuyuki

The Reception of Maps between Japan and the West

Westerners and the Japanese imagined and understood one another in the premodern period at two important historical junctures: the initial Japanese contact with Western Europeans, which lasted roughly from the later sixteenth century to the beginning of the seventeenth, and the era of renewed interest in things Western, especially European science, technology, and cultural forms, which occurred during the eighteenth and nineteenth centuries. Today, diaries, accounts, letters, and reports give us a wonderful glimpse into impressions of these times. These contemporaneous documents were produced by people of all backgrounds, including Jesuit missionaries, travelers, doctors, and the traders who were stationed on the artificial island of Dejima in Nagasaki harbor, the only place after the mid-seventeenth century where a closed and isolated Japan maintained contact with the West until the opening of the country by Commodore Matthew C. Perry in 1854.

In this essay I will explore how Japan was rendered visually in maps and the manner in which its representation changed over time. I will emphasize period world and regional maps, as well as maps that focus specifically on the Japanese archipelago. Of special interest is the manner in which different cultures accepted and absorbed cartographic techniques and geographic information, and made it their own. Issues of perception as well as the role maps played in the history of cultural exchange between Japan and the West will also be considered.

The Western perception of Japan prior to contact was driven by a fantastical vision of lands of great riches and wealth. One important figure who fuelled this idea was Marco Polo (1254–1324). In the famous record of his travels, he wrote:

> *Zipangu* [Japan] *is an island towards the east, in the high seas, 1500 miles from the continent. It is a very large island. The people are white, courteous, and handsome. They are idolaters. They are independent, and know no lordship but their own.*
>
> *You must know that they have immense quantities of gold, because it is found on the spot in great abundance. Moreover, no one ever brings the gold away from the country, for no one goes thither from the continent, not even merchants. This is why they have as much gold as I have said.*[1]

Polo goes on to describe a palace filled, incredibly, with gold, in a country itself brimming with treasures such as pearls and precious stones. Polo himself never visited Japan, but gained his impressions—and ideas of its location—from hearsay accounts, including those about Kublai Khan's attempted invasion of the island in 1281.

Once the fanciful idea of "Zipangu" as a legendary island of gold was born, it was reinforced visually in Western maps and book illustrations. In the succeeding centuries, as Western cartography developed and geographic knowledge about the Far East expanded, a more realistic view of Japan and the north regions of Asia took hold, finally dispelling invented notions of Japan from Western minds.

During the Renaissance, the rediscovery of a Classical text and maps by Ptolemy (c. 100–170 CE) moved Western map production away from the Christian-oriented worldview that had dominated medieval culture to one formulated on science, discovery, and exploration. Ptolemy's *Geographia* would lead to the discovery of new continents—it was Columbus's inspiration—and the broadening of geographic knowledge. First translated from Greek into Latin in 1406, *Geographia* soon was disseminated throughout western Europe.

In his edition of *Geographia* (1511), Bernardus Sylvanus (act. 1490–1511) included maps that still expressed classical ideas of the world rather than the most recent world geography. Of all the maps in this atlas, one is of particular interest (plate 12).

This heart-shaped world map places the Near and Middle East at its center, with the newly discovered American continent on the western edge, while Asia, its coastline vague, is at the eastern extreme. Even farther east, a triangular-shaped form labeled "Zampagu. Ins." (Japan Island), is located 140 to 150 degrees eastward from the Canary Islands (the location of the prime meridian in those days). This is an important variation from the world map found in Ptolemy's atlas. Sylvanus's *Geographia* was the first Western atlas to give a correct location for Japan.

The worldview held prior to the discovery of the New World is presented in the oldest known globe (fig. 7). Made by Martin Behaim (1459–1507) in 1492, the year Columbus made his voyage across the Atlantic, the globe is based on a world map by Henricus Martellus Germanus (act. 1480–96), a German cartographer who expanded and updated the Ptolemaic world map. Not surprisingly, the North and South American continents are absent from Behaim's globe. And although Japan's position relative to the West is extremely ambiguous on the globe, it seems that information regarding the island was actively being collected in western Europe at this time.

Japan, labeled "Cipangu jnsula," appears on the globe as a large island stretching in latitude between 85 and 95 degrees westward of the Canary Islands. Behaim drew a canopied royal tent on the island, and added labels reading "moscat nurwalt" (nutmeg forest) and "pfeffer walt" (pepper forest), an indication of the importance of the spice-producing areas that western Europe was so eager to dominate. Additional text off the island's east coast reads:

> *This island Zipangu lies in the east of the world. The inhabitants worship idols. The King is subject to no one. In the island is found exceeding much gold and likewise precious stones and pearls. This is stated by Marco Polo of Venice in his third book.*[2]

Descriptions of the form and position of "Zipangu" are apparent in both *Tabula Superioris Indiae et Tartariae Maioris,* published in 1522 by Martin Waldseemüller (1470–1521), and in a map of North and South America, *Die neüwen Inseln so hinder Hispanien gegen Orient bey dem land Indie ligen,* by Sebastian Münster (1489–1552). In the latter map (plate 13), published in the mid-sixteenth century, a ship, the *Victoria,* appears in the Pacific Ocean in recognition of Ferdinand Magellan's circumnavigation of the globe.[3] For both maps, the European cartographers relied on Marco Polo's conception of Japan's position and described the island as large and imposing, stretching from north to south.

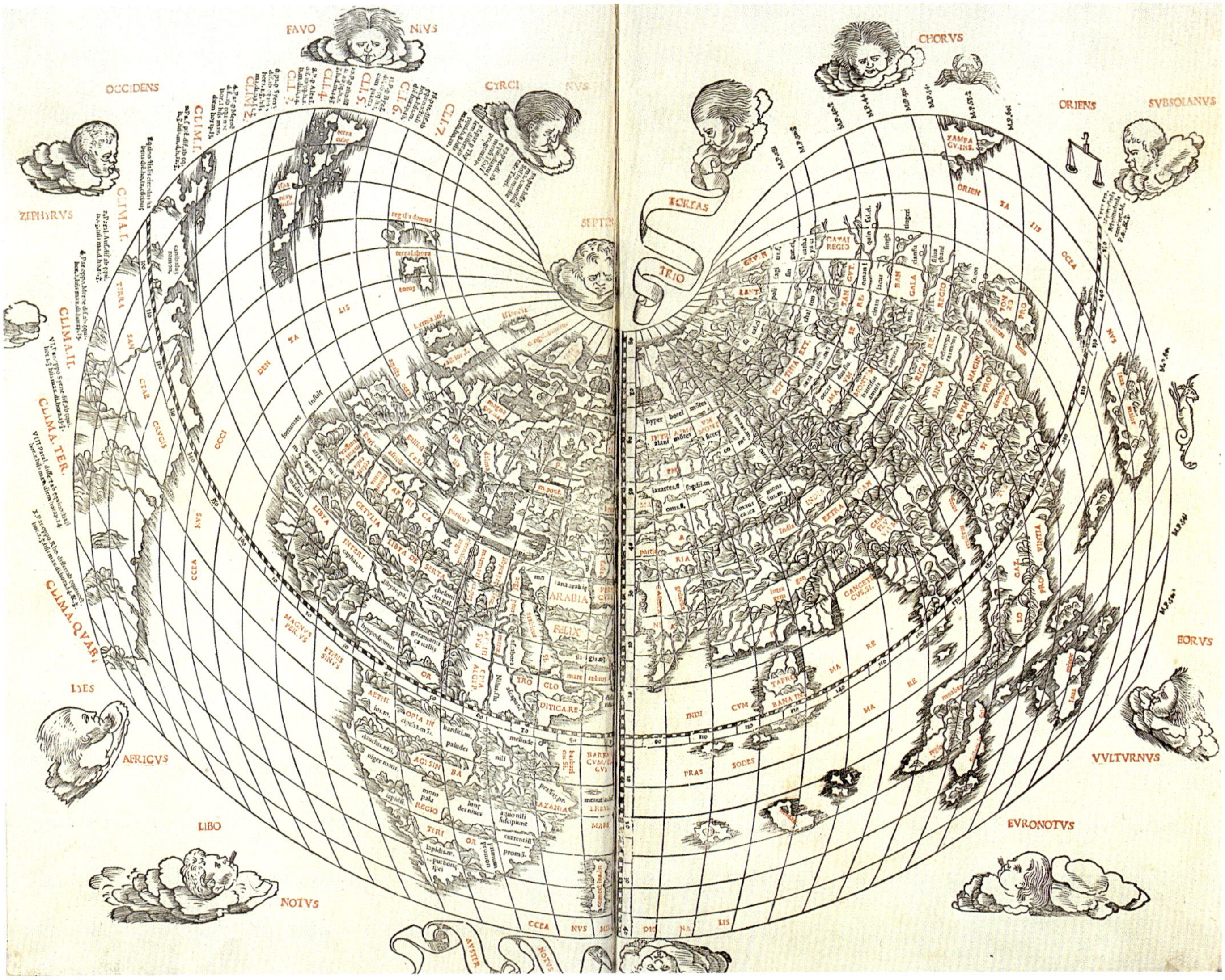

In *Universale della parte del mondo nuovamente ritrovata*, Giacomo di Gastaldi (c. 1500–1566) depicted Japan as one body of land stretching from east to west (plate 14). Gastaldi located "Giapam" at 30 degrees north and 155 to 165 degrees west.

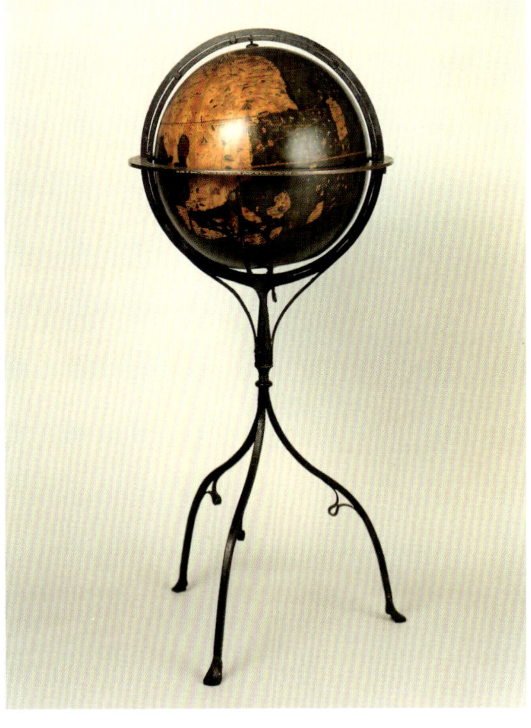

FIG. 7

World Globe

Modern reproduction, after Martin Behaim, Nürnberg, 1492 (original: Germanischesnational Museum, Nürnberg) diam. 20 in. (50.7 cm)

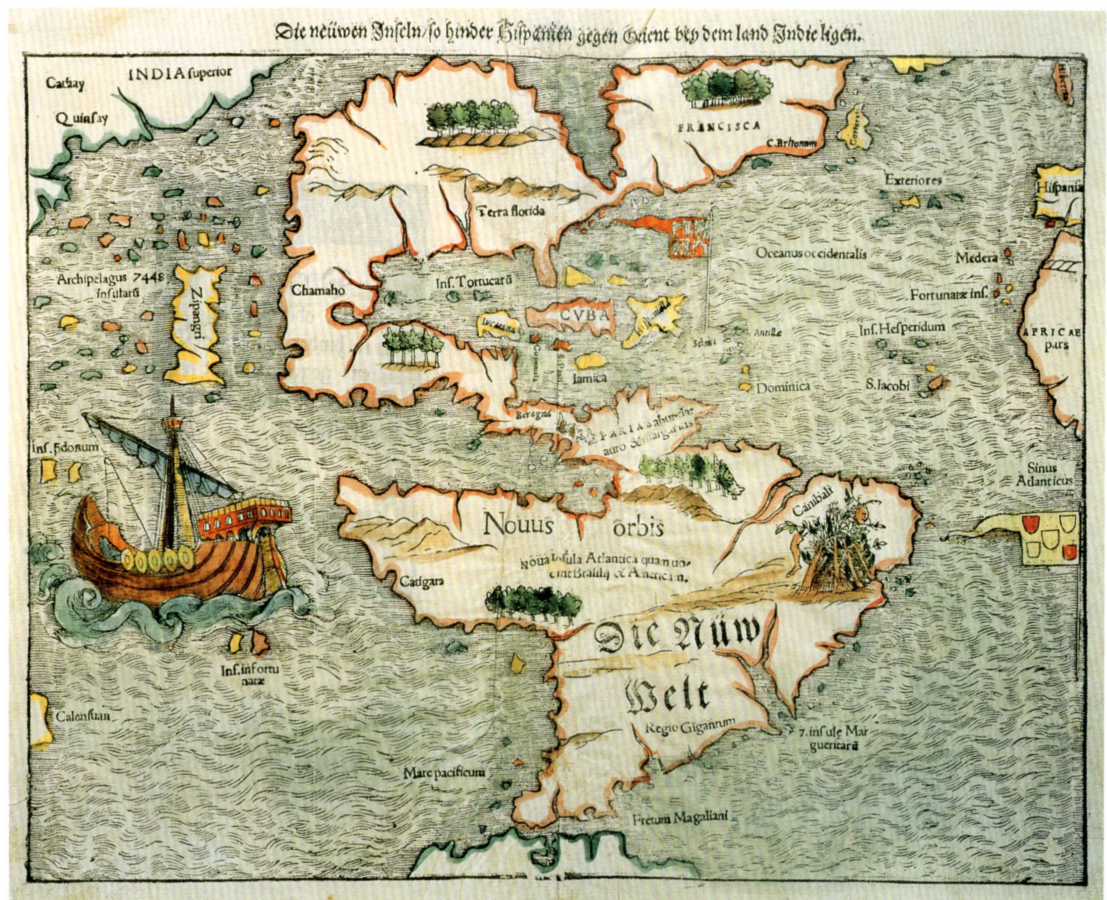

PLATE 13

Die neüwen Inseln so hinder Hispanien gegen Orient bey dem land Indie ligen (The New Islands Discovered in Our Times by the King of Spain in the Great Ocean)
from Sebastian Münster, *Cosmographia*, Basel, mid-16th century
Woodblock print: ink with hand color on paper
11⅛ × 15⅜ in. (29.3 × 38.8 cm)

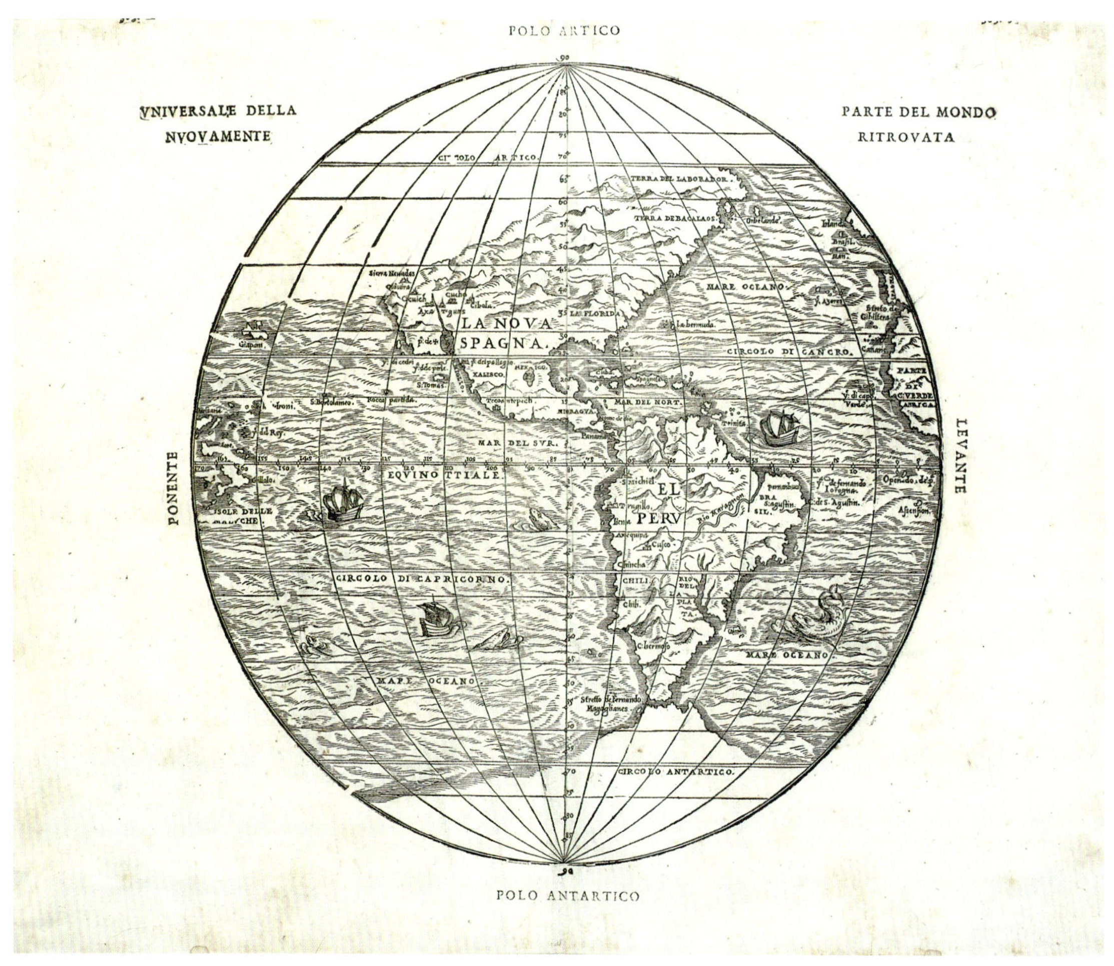

PLATE 14

Giacomo di Gastaldi (Italian, c. 1500–1566)
Universale della parte del mondo nuovamente ritrovata [Map of the Western Hemisphere]
from Giovanni Ramusio, *Delle navigatione viaggi*, Venice, c. 1550
Woodblock print: ink on paper
12½ × 15⅝ in. (31.5 × 39.6 cm)

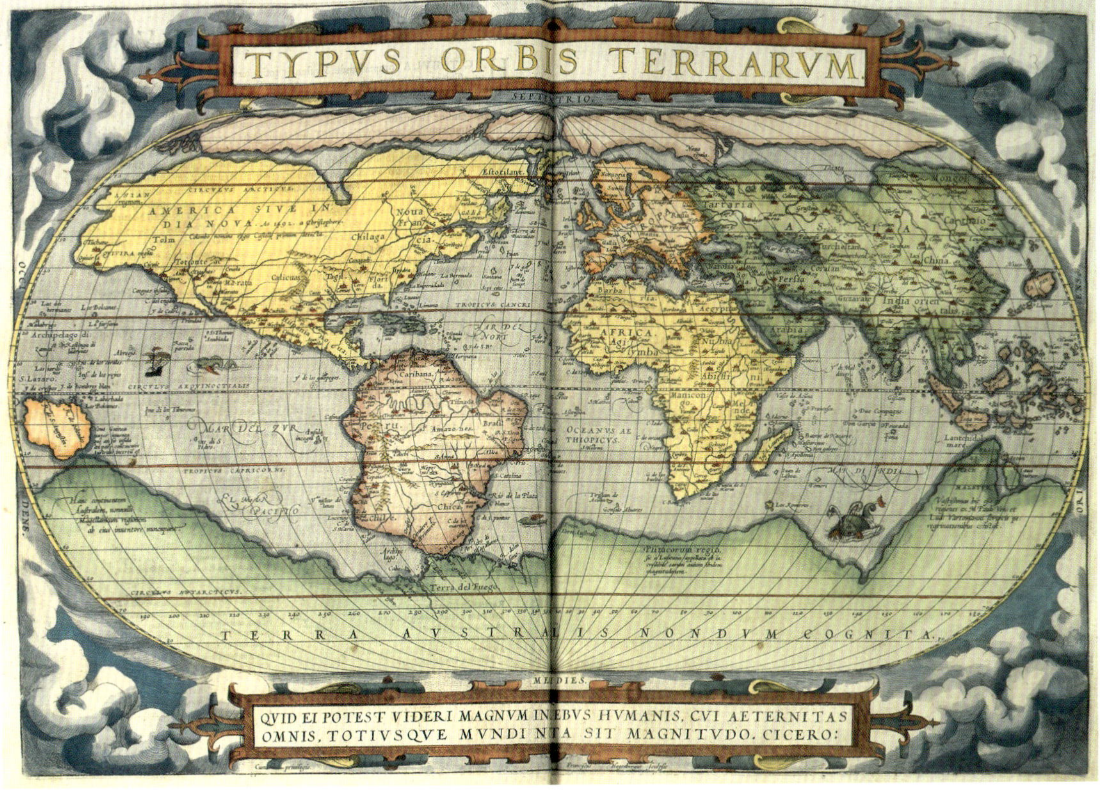

PLATE 15
Abraham Ortelius
(Dutch, 1527–1598)
Typus Orbis Terrarum
(Map of the World)
from *Theatrum Orbis Terrarum*, Antwerp, 1570
Copperplate engraving: ink with hand color on paper
16⅛ × 11¼ in.
(41 × 28.5 cm) at cover

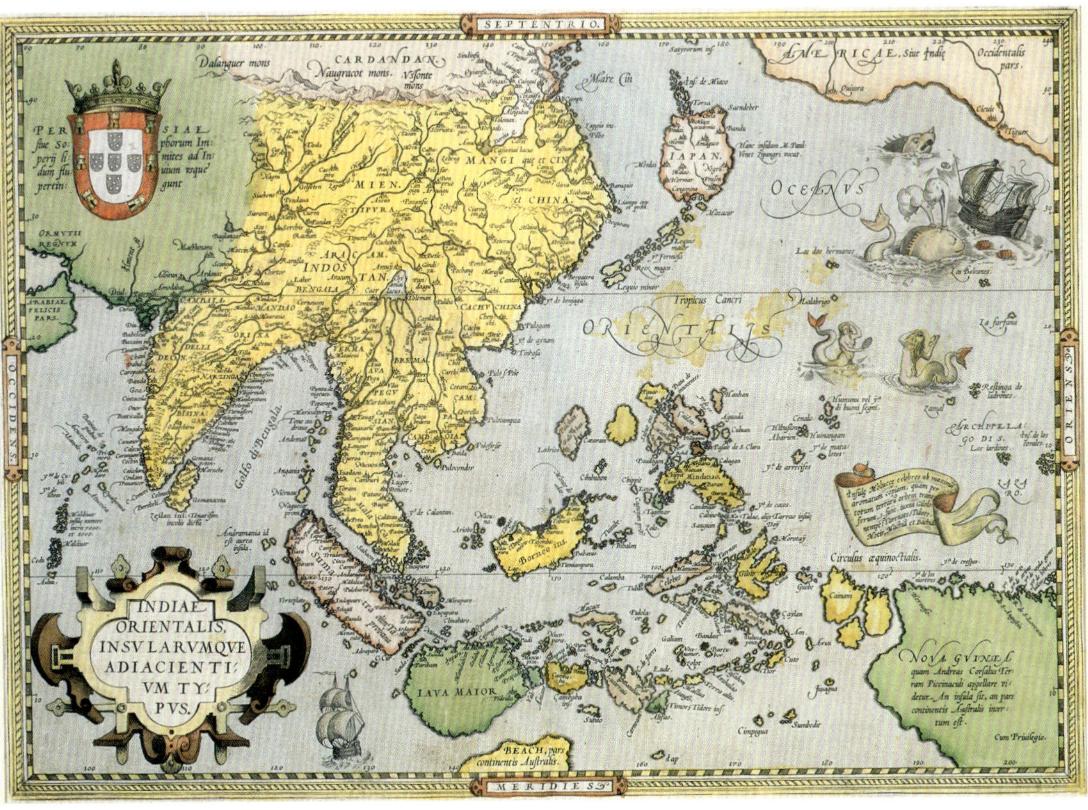

PLATE 16
Abraham Ortelius
(Dutch, 1527–1598)
Indiae Orientalis, Insula Rumque Adiacientium Typus
(Map of the East Indies and Surrounding Islands)
from *Theatrum Orbis Terrarum*, Antwerp, 1570
Copperplate engraving: ink with hand color on paper
16⅛ × 21 in.
(41 × 53.3 cm)

The year 1543 is significant in the history of exchange between Japan and the West. In this year some Portuguese were shipwrecked on the small Japanese island of Tanegashima, leading to what is thought to be the first European encounter with the Japanese on their home ground. As economic and cultural relationships developed throughout the remainder of the sixteenth and into the early seventeenth century, the sharing of geographic and other forms of knowledge would have a profound impact on how the Japanese and Europeans viewed one another.

From 1570, when it was first published, through much of the early seventeenth century, the important atlas *Theatrum Orbis Terrarum* by the geographer and cartographer Abraham Ortelius (1527–1598) was instrumental in disseminating an image of Japan to Europe. Many historians consider Ortelius's volume to be the precursor to the modern world atlas. In the decades after it was first released, *Theatrum* was translated into numerous languages, including French, Italian, and German, and was revised and reprinted forty-one times.[4] Ortelius lived in Antwerp, a city where the cultures and arts of the world intersected through its lively port and mercantile base. When *Theatrum* was first published, the center of map production in Europe was shifting from Italy and Germany, through Portugal and Spain, to Holland. Many historians have characterized *Theatrum* as a document that brought together different cultures, traditions, and approaches to mapmaking.

Given that geographic information about the Far East was still fairly scare and contradictory, representations of Japan vary greatly in the various editions of *Theatrum*. Subsequently, it is a wonderful source that reveals how Europeans imagined and visually documented Japan at the early stage of contact. In the first edition, Japan can be seen four times: in the first map, of the world (*Typus Orbis Terrarum*); the third map, of Asia (*Asia Nova Descriptio*); the forty-seventh map, of Tartary, Kublai Khan's lands (*Tartariae sive Magni Chami Regni Typus*); and the forty-eighth map, of East Asia (*Indiae Orientalis, Insula Rumque Adiacientium Typus*).

Typus Orbis Terrarum, employing an oval (Apian) projection (plate 15), shows the extent of Western knowledge of world geography. At the eastern edge, Japan can be seen at a latitude just above 30 degrees north. There is no other detail except for the labels "Iapan" and "Miaco."

A similar depiction of Japan is found in *Indiae Orientalis* (plate 16). Larger in scale and more detailed, this map allows us to better understand European perceptions of Japan. The presentation was adapted from the Dutch cartographer Gerardus Mercator's 1569 world map, which characteristically portrayed Japan as a single island ("Iapan"); multiple northern islands are labeled "Insula de Miaco." The map has many imaginary features and confuses various locations. Thirteen sets of towers symbolize cities, and labels include "Amaguco" (Yamaguchi) and "Miaco academia" (Miyako Academy). To the left of the island, a notation reads: "Hanc insulam M. Paul Venet Zipangri vocat" (Marco Polo of Venice calls this island Zipangri).

In the map of Tartary (plate 17), the depiction of Japan, labeled "Iapan," takes the so-called Ortelius pattern, which displays the islands of Honshū, Shikoku, and Kyūshū as themselves composed of multiple islands, stretching from east to west. Visible place names include "Meaco" and "Osaquo" (Osaka) as well as "Minas de plata" (the Iwami silver mine). A label beneath Japan provides more information: "Iapan Insula, à M. Paulo Veneto Zipangri dicta, olim Chryse, a Magno Cham olim bello petita sed frustra" (The isle of Japan, which Marco Polo of Venice called Zipangri, formerly called Chryse [Island of Gold],

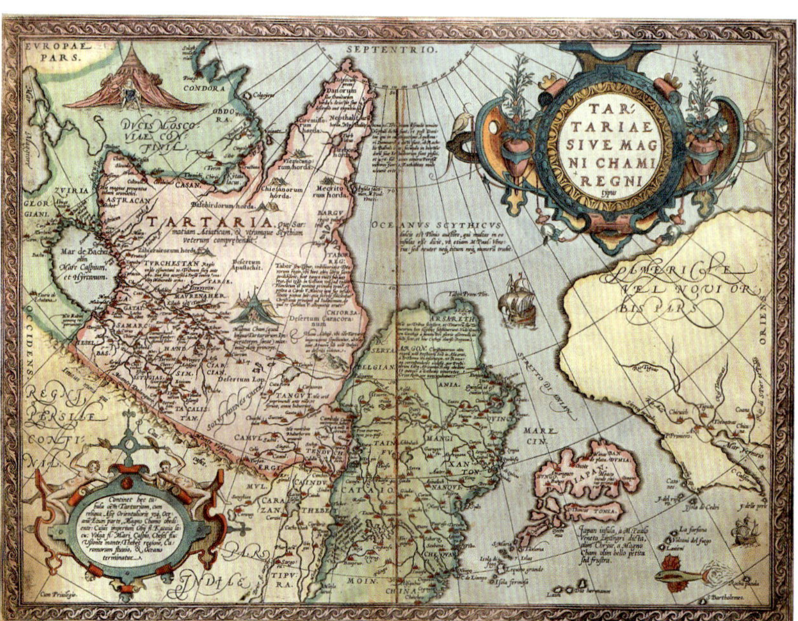

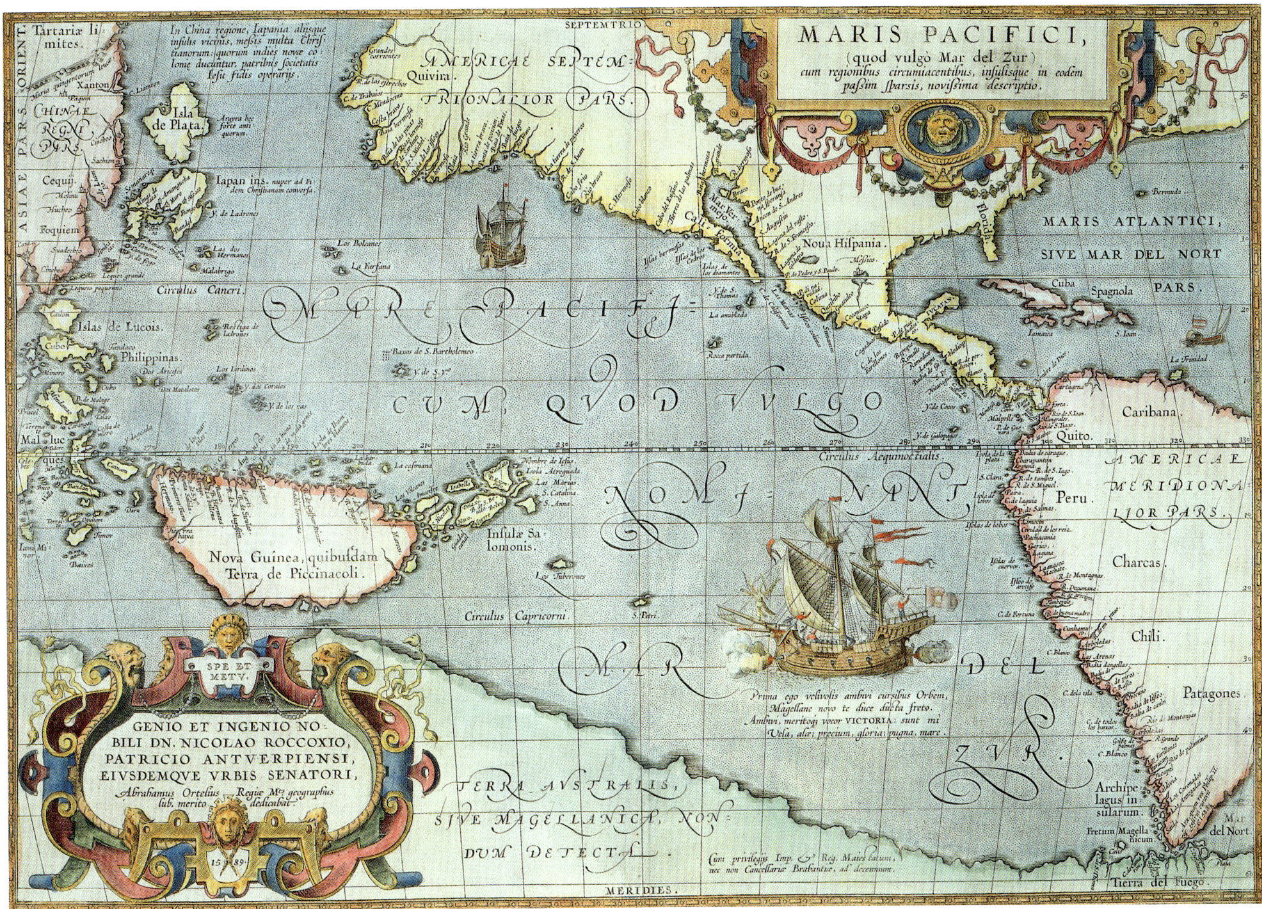

once attacked by the Great Khan but without success). The reliance on Marco Polo's testimony suggests his continuing influence on perceptions of Japan.

Variation in the rendering of geographical information was not particular to representations of Japan alone. Varying representations were characteristic for the Korean Peninsula, the northeastern portion of the Asian continent, Indonesia, and Java. It is most constructive to view these differences as the product of a Western understanding of the world that was undergoing great and rapid change as the exploration of distant lands and places occurred.

In the Latin-language version of *Theatrum* published in 1589, the plate *Maris Pacifici* (plate 18) was a new contribution to the 114 maps in the volume. Ortelius depicted Japan in the Dourado form (after the Portuguese chartmaker Fernao vaz Dourado), which shows only western Japan.[5]

It was not until the Latin-language edition of 1595 that *Theatrum* featured a map focusing solely on Japan (plate 19). Titled *Iaponiae Insulae Descriptio,* the map was made by the Portuguese cartographer Luís Teixeira. It is thought to have been modeled on a traditional Japanese map form that has been popularly attributed to the Japanese Buddhist priest Gyōki (668–749). Judging from the relative accuracy of the contours of peninsulas and coastlines, and the form of the islands of Kyūshū and Shikoku, it may be reasonable to assume that Teixeira's map was based on a more recent Gyōki-style map and produced after such maps had been brought to the West. The relationships among cities and the place names on the Teixeira map show a marked improvement in accuracy over earlier works.[6] And so, more than fifty years after the West encountered Japan in 1543, its image was presented for the first time to the Western world in a large-scale map. Teixeira's map of Japan remained in circulation for another forty or so years.

Around this time, Jodocus Hondius (1563–1612) produced his *Iaponia* (plate 20). Hondius had purchased the copperplates of Gerardus Mercator after his death in 1594. He based *Iaponia* and many other maps in his *Nieuwe atlas* (1606) on Mercator's versions.

PLATE 18
Abraham Ortelius
(Dutch, 1527–1598)

Maris Pacifici
(Pacific Sea)
from *Theatrum Orbis Terrarum,* Antwerp, 1589
Copperplate engraving: ink with hand color on paper
17½ × 22⅝ in.
(44.5 × 57.3 cm)
■

PLATE 19
Luís Teixeira
(Portuguese, 1564–1604)

Iaponiae Insulae Descriptio (Depiction of the Island of Japan)
from Abraham Ortelius, *Theatrum Orbis Terrarum*, Antwerp, 1595
Copperplate engraving: ink with hand color on paper
18½ × 21¾ in. (47 × 55 cm)

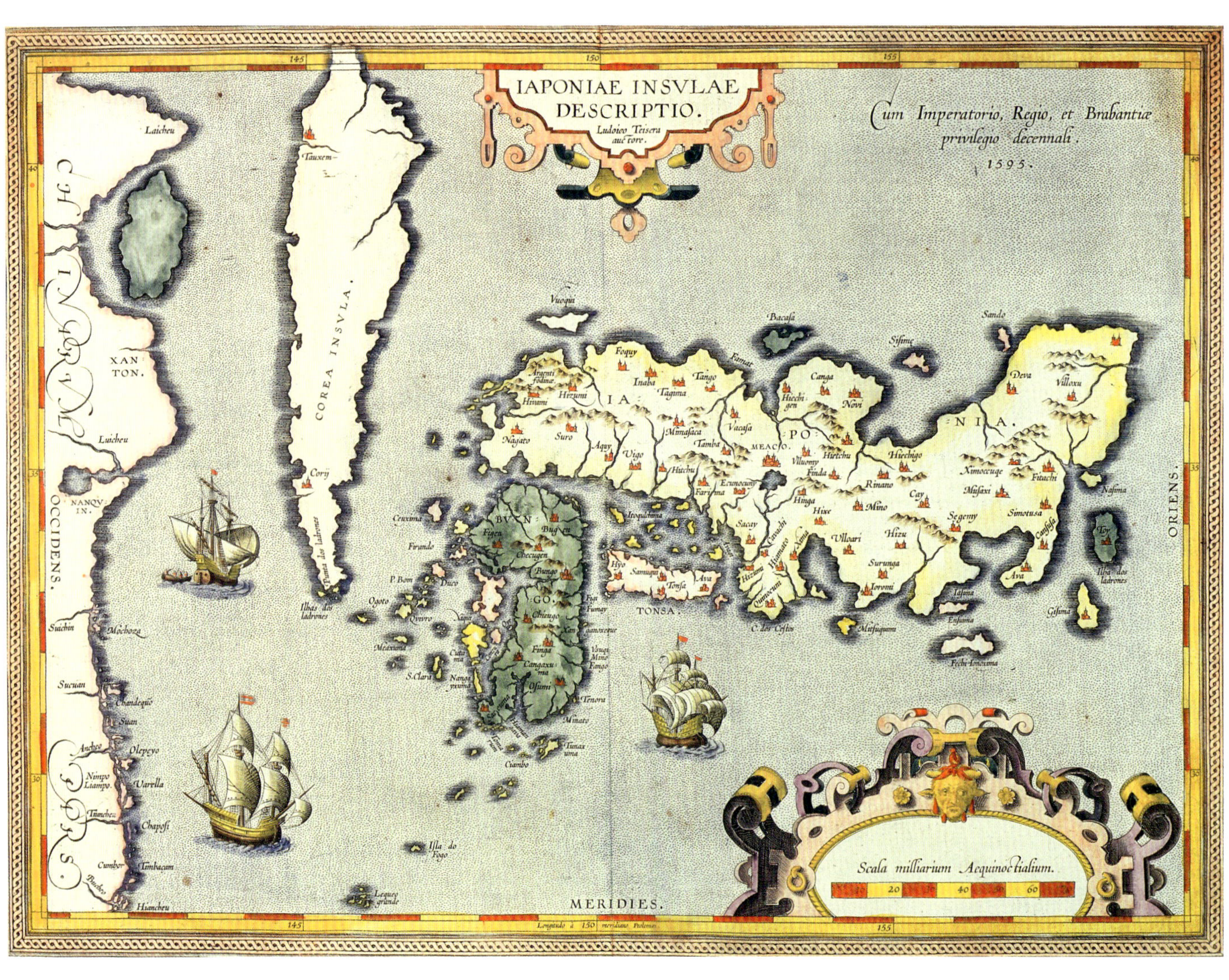

PLATE 20
Jodocus Hondius
(Dutch, 1563–1612)
Iaponia (Japan)
from *Nieuwe atlas*,
Amsterdam, 1606
Copperplate engraving:
ink with hand color
on paper
15¾ × 20⅝ in.
(40 × 52.3 cm)

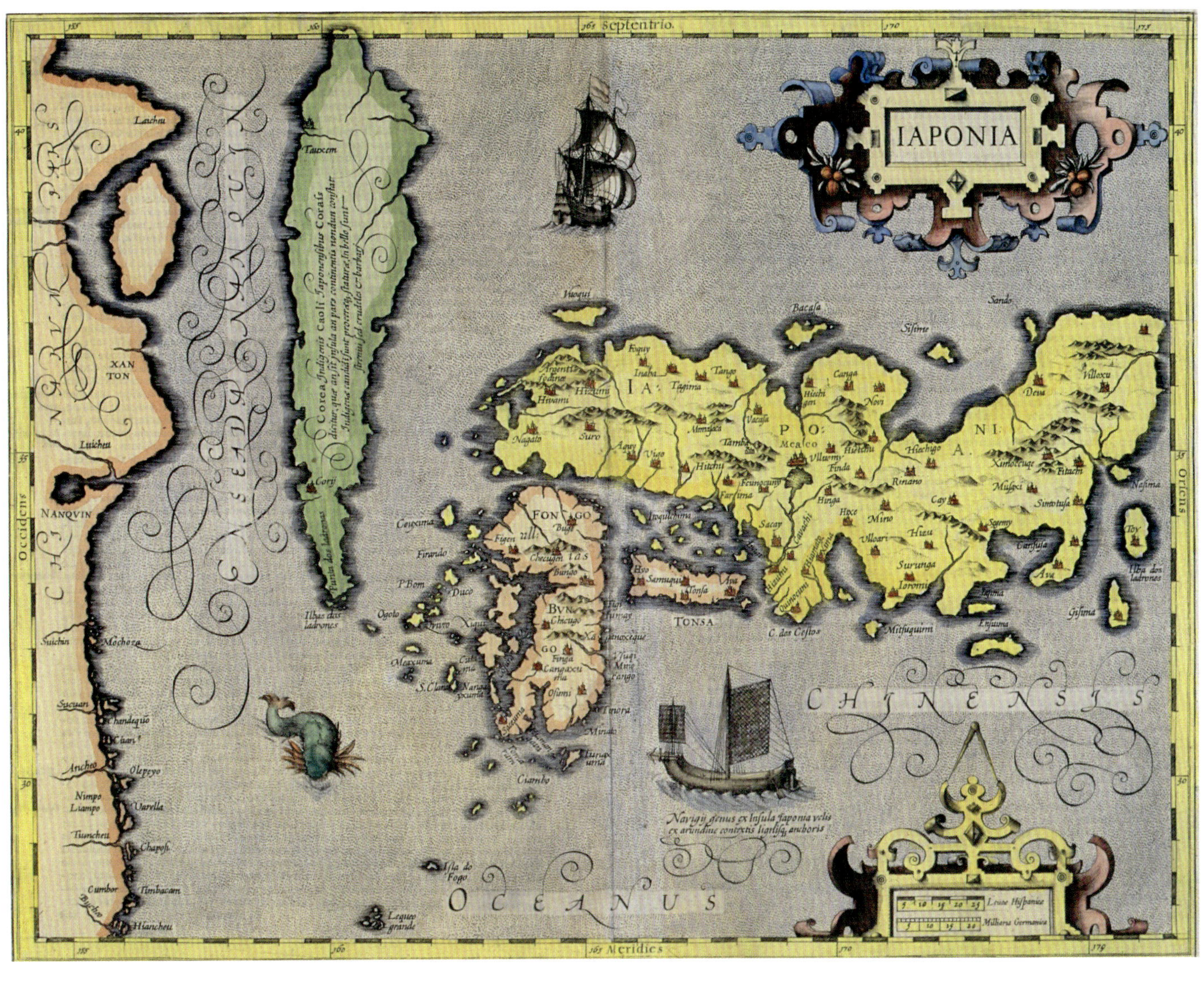

The meeting of East and West brought to Japan not only Christianity and guns but also an interest in world maps. One of the earliest documents reflecting this is a painted screen, *Yonto zu/Sekai zu* (Four Large Cities of the World/Map of the World, see plate 34a,b). The screen is an intriguing example not only of a world map but also of an early Western-style painting by a Japanese artist (for a discussion of this work, see the Introduction and Chapter 2 in this volume).

After the closure of Japan to the outside world in the mid-seventeenth century, Europe continued to influence and shape the imaginations of Japanese artists and mapmakers. The impact of Dutch maps can be clearly seen in a number of Japanese works, such as a late-eighteenth-century copy (plate 21) of the Dutch mapmaker Joan Blaeu's world map (revised by Nicholaes Visscher in 1678).[7] The most interesting example is perhaps a pair of folding screens, *Sekai yon-daishū zu/Yonjūhachi-ka-koku jinbutsu zu* (Regional Maps with Pictures of Forty-eight Foreign People, plate 22a,b), which on one screen features the continents of Europe and the Americas and, on the other, of Africa and Asia.

The unknown Japanese artist of this work took his main imagery directly from copperplate maps made by the Dutch cartographer Gerard Valck (c. 1650–1726). Valck was a popular Amsterdam publisher of maps with his son, Leonard Valck (1675–1755), and he also produced globes.[8] In comparing the continents of Asia and Europe from the screens with Valck's prints (plates 23, 24), we can immediately see that the Japanese artist carefully duplicated many compositional, geographical, and pictorial details, including the grid system. He also adorned the sides of his maps with smaller images of people in the costumes of the different regions of the continent concerned, and he ornamented the top border; in this, he was following the example of other of Valck's maps of the continents (fig. 8).[9] It is unknown how this style of map by Valck was introduced into Japan, but its influence on the screens is unmistakable, even with the changes the Japanese artist made.

For the top border of some of his maps of the continents, Valck repeated decorative motifs based on classical mythology—Atlas holding up the earth, and Apollo, the sun god, driving his chariot—which he placed in an undulating banner with the map titles. In the Japanese screens the title banner is absent, but the decorative program is generally consistent, with some exceptions. In the case of the map of America, for example, Atlas and Apollo have been replaced by Buddhist celestial beings (*apsaras*), a sun, and a moon (see detail, p. 47). Valck featured an assortment of animals in his top borders, and the Japanese artist did the same, but adding creatures of his choosing such as a rhinoceros and a full image of an elephant.

Similar transformations and adaptations were made to the other maps on the screens. Bordering Africa is a scene of Tartars hunting, and above Asia is a depiction of farming in the four seasons; both are traditional themes in Japanese painting. The border for Europe illustrates a somewhat incongruous view of a naval battle, which depicts mainly Dutch vessels. These decorative elements add a decidedly Asian feeling to the screens. The artist, by combining two of Valck's continents for each of his screens, made one unified composition incorporating Asian motifs. In doing this, he produced a unique aesthetic expression of East and West.

In addition to those world maps brought directly to Japan by Europeans, a number of important maps were introduced via China. Among the most significant is *Kunyu wanquo quantu* (J.: *Kon'yo bankoku zenzu,* Complete Terrestrial Map of All Countries, plate 25). The Italian Jesuit missionary Matteo Ricci (1522–1610) produced this map in Beijing in 1602 with the aid of a Chinese collaborator, Li Zhizao (1565–1630). More than twenty Japanese copies of it are extant, and at least ten of them were produced after the mid-eighteenth century, suggesting that, by then, Ricci's map was in wide circulation.[10] The resiliency of Ricci's map throughout the Edo period clearly demonstrates that Japanese artists and mapmakers, despite the introduction of Dutch maps and geographic information, regarded it as an important source of world knowledge. Because its labels were written in Chinese, it was more accessible to the Japanese, but even more appealing was the placement of China and Japan at its center.

Maps from Japan and Their Acceptance in the West

The circulation of Japanese maps in Europe and the West was closely guarded by the shogunate. The most famous example of how tightly the Japanese held geographic information is the Siebold Incident of 1828. Philipp Franz von Siebold (1796–1866), a German physician stationed at Nagasaki, was expelled from Japan for having obtained several forbidden maps of the country. At the heart of the controversy were some maps by Inō Tadataka and Mamiya Rinzō, but the presence of other Japanese maps in the Siebold Collection in Munich[11] suggests that maps widely available in Japan were brought abroad.

Maps of Japan were also published in the West. One European central to the early publication of Japanese maps is Adrien Reland (1676–1718), an Orientalist at Utrecht University. His monochrome *Le Japon divise en soissante-et-six provinces* (1715), attached to a collection of voyage narratives (*Recueil de voyages au nord*), was published by Jean-Frédérik Bernard. The subtitle to Reland's map indicates his source material was Japanese ("Cette carte est tirée des cartes des Japonois par monsieur Reland"). The probable prototype for it was likely the map style known as *Nihon kaisan chōriku zu* (maps of the seas and lands of Japan, plate 28), first issued in 1691 by Ishikawa Ryūsen. How Reland came to acquire the source material is related in a legend at the bottom of *Imperium Japonicum* (plate 26), a polychrome version of his map published by Guillaume Broedelet in 1715. The legend states that the Japanese prototype was in the personal collection of Benjamin Dutry, a senior officer of the Dutch East India Company.

In Reland's maps, place names are transliterated and given in Chinese characters, and cities, including castle towns, are indicated with the types of symbols often seen in Western maps. Reland's maps were the first to be published in the West with Chinese characters. Particularly interesting are the decorative paintings that border *Imperium Japonicum*. Above an area map at the lower right is a figure who can be identified as the Tokugawa shogun by his clan crest, the triple hollyhock. He wears a peaked cap rather than the topknot hairstyle common in Japan at that time, an indication that the Western mapmaker had not fully distinguished Japan from Qing China, and a Chinese quality prevails particularly in the decorative aspects of the map. A degree of fantasy exists in some motifs, as in the clothes and hairstyle of the woman in the space between the lower middle and right cartouches, or the shape of the ship behind her: these features are neither Asian nor Western, but most probably imagined.

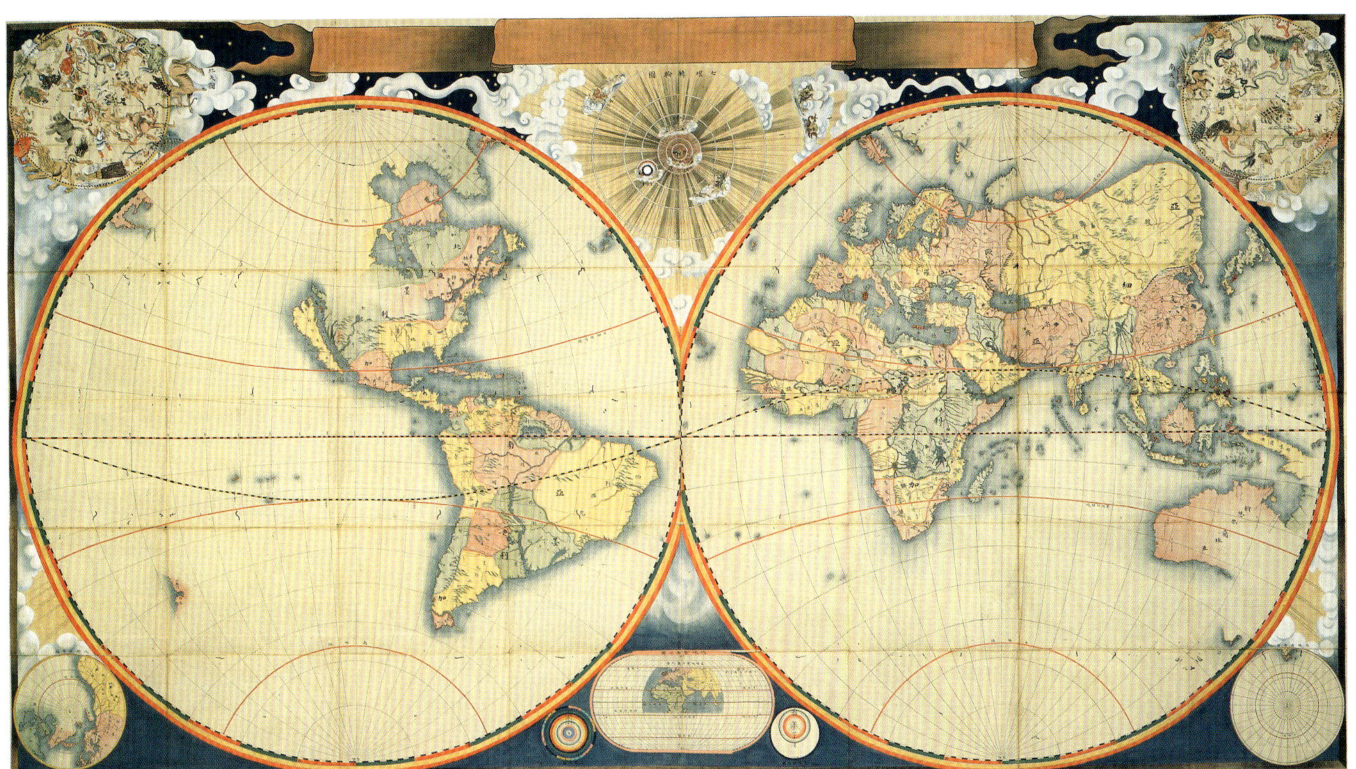

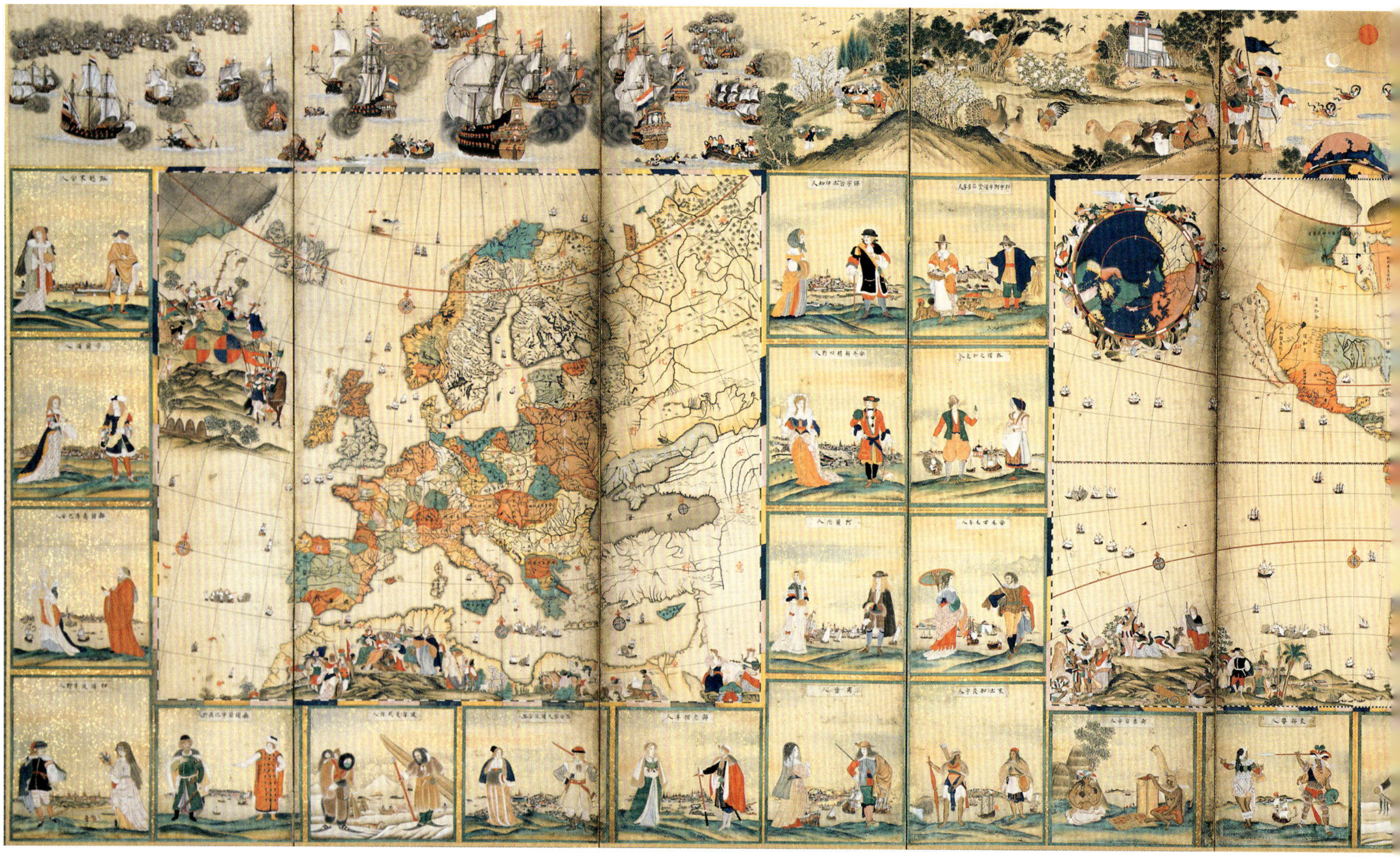

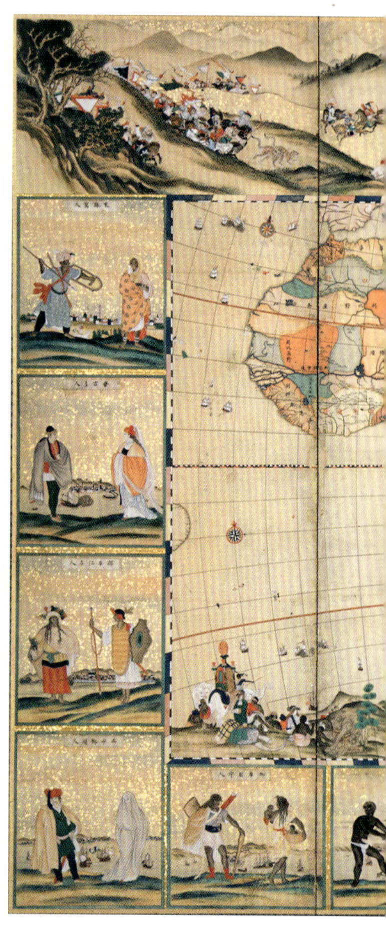

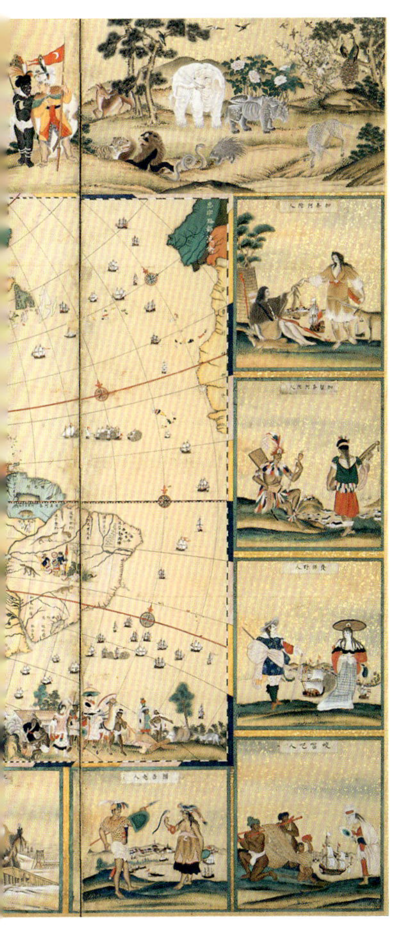

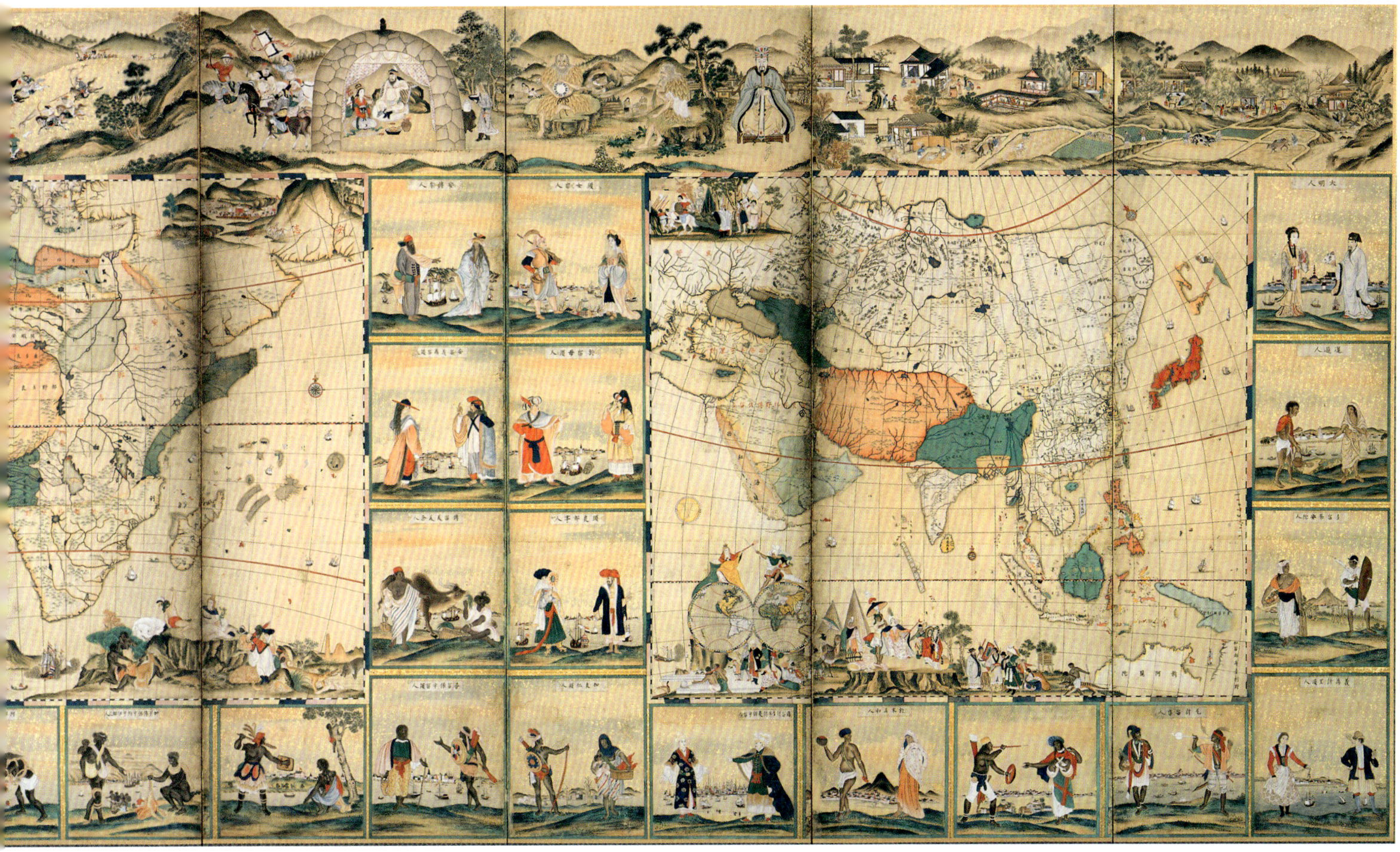

PLATE 22a,b
Japanese, unknown
artist
*Sekai yondaishū zu /
Yonjūhachi-ka-koku
jinbutsu zu* (Regional
Maps with Pictures
of Forty-eight
Foreign People)
Late 18th century
Pair of six-panel screens:
ink and color on paper
64½ × 143 in.
(163.8 × 362.8 cm) each

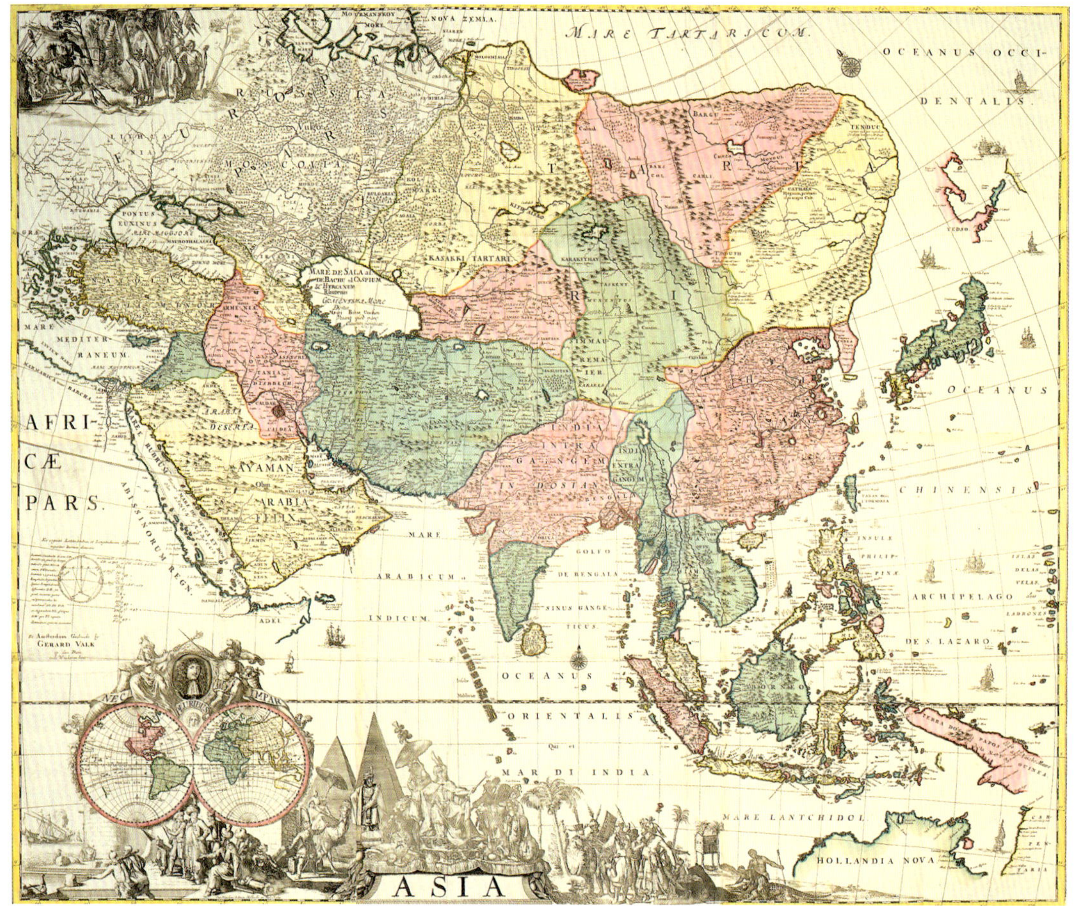

PLATE 23
Gerard Valck
(Dutch, c. 1650–1726)
Asia
Amsterdam, c. 1695
Copperplate engraving:
ink with hand color
on paper
40⅜ × 49½ in.
(102.6 × 125.6 cm)

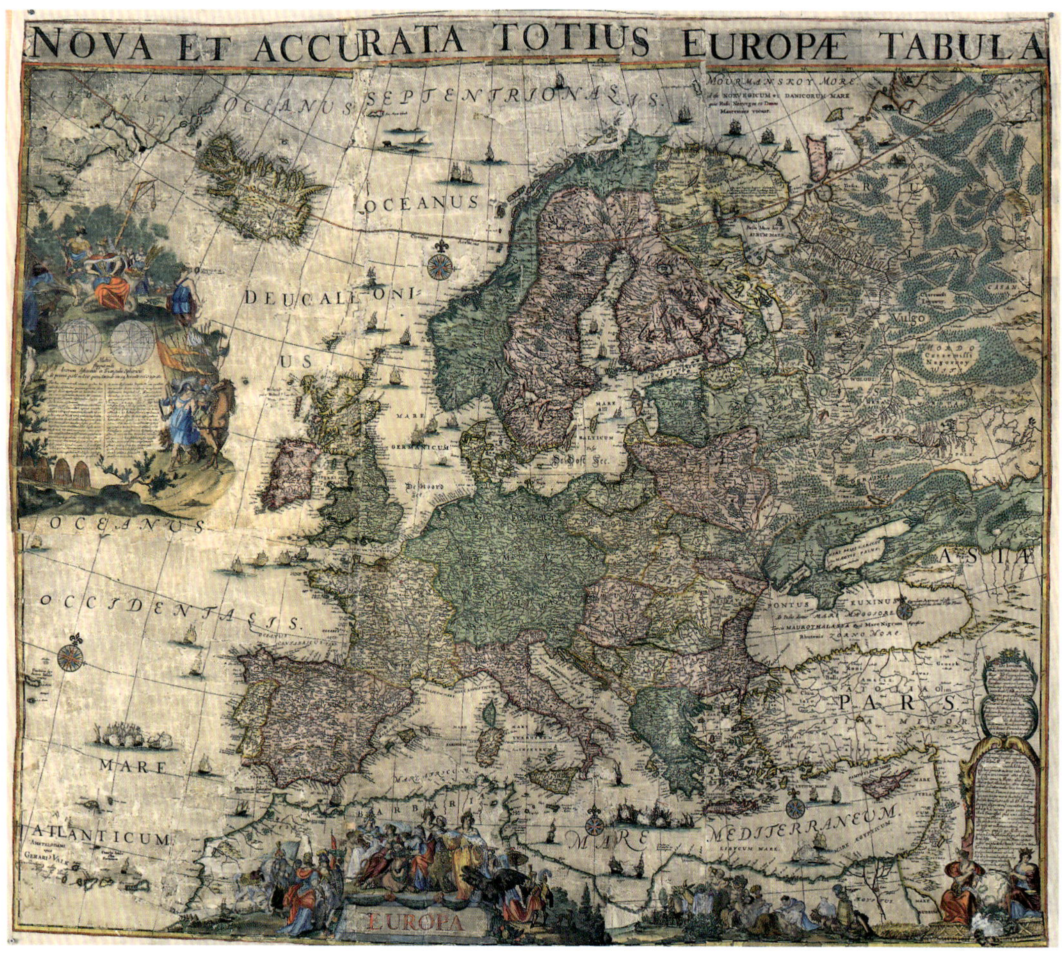

PLATE 24
Gerard Valck
(Dutch, c. 1650–1726)
*Nova et Accurata
Totius Europae Tabula*
[Map of Europe]
Amsterdam, c. 1695
Copperplate engraving:
ink with hand color
on paper
42⅛ × 48½ in.
(107 × 123 cm)

FIG. 8
Gerard Valck
(Dutch, c. 1650–1726)
Totius Americae Novior Accura Tabula [Map of North and South America]
Amsterdam, late 17th–early 18th century
Copperplate engraving: ink with hand color on paper
43⅜ × 58¾ in. (110 × 149 cm)
Národní Památkový Ústav, Castle Mnichovo Hradiště
Czech Republic
■

DETAIL
Border decoration above North and South America (plate 22a)
■

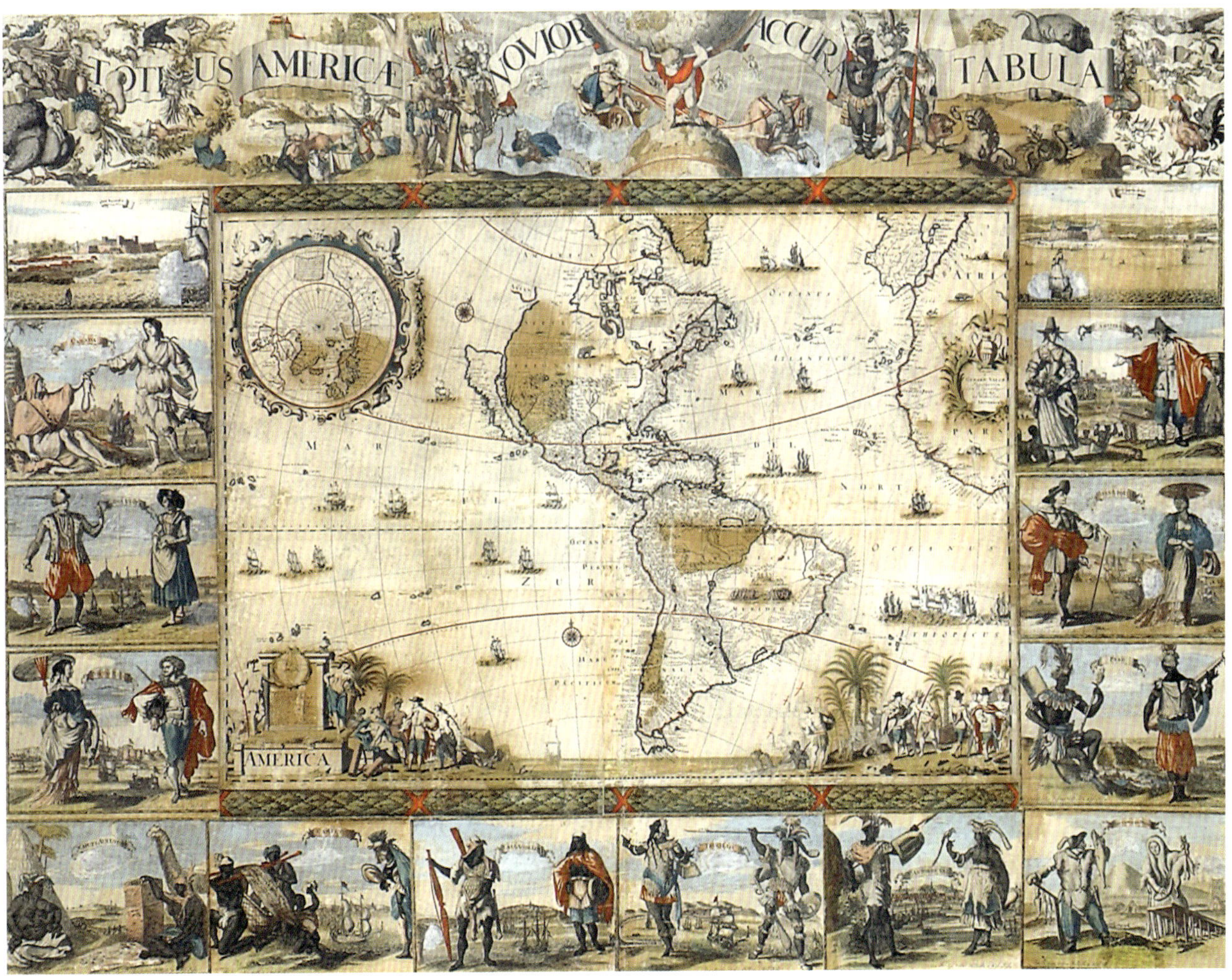

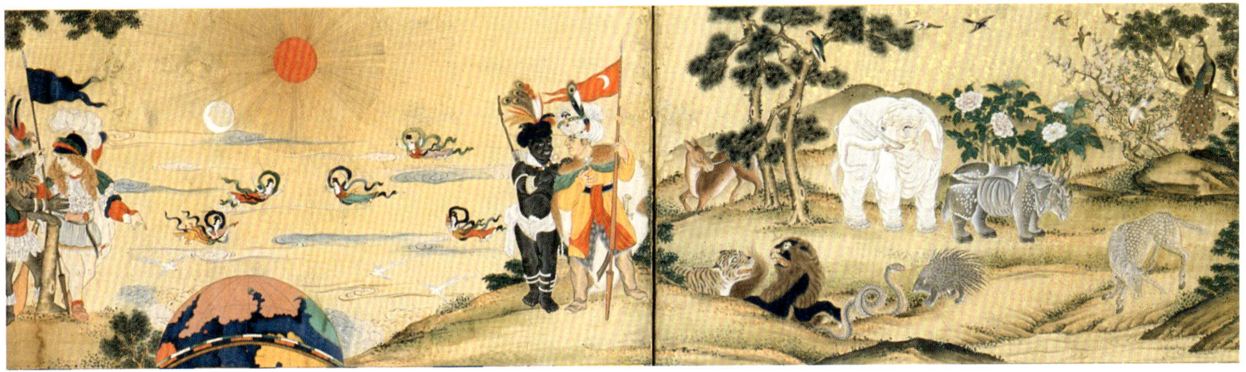

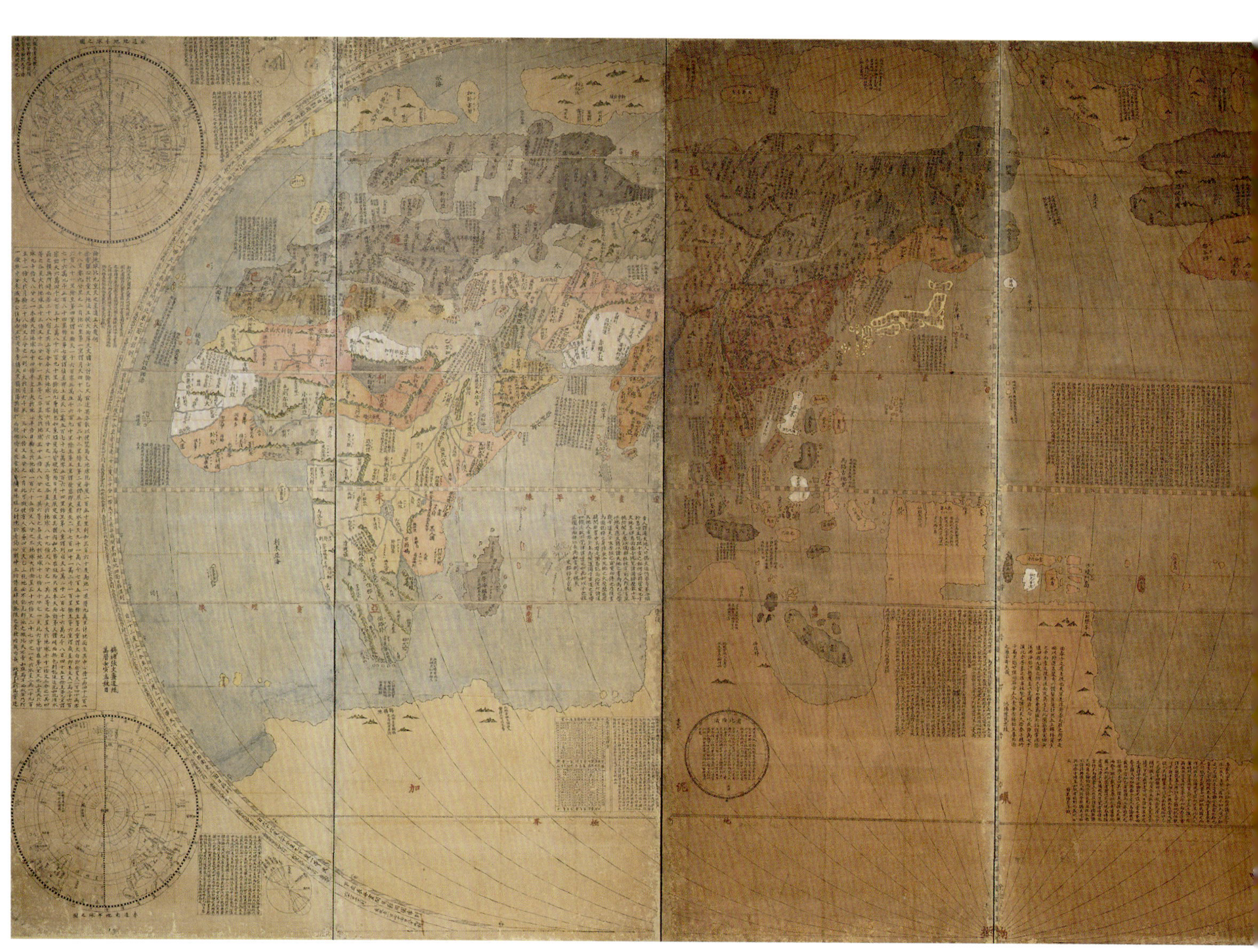

Maps of Japan of this type were published and republished in Europe until the middle of the eighteenth century.[12] In Japan, Ryūsen's work, the source for Reland's map, also continued to be published until the mid-eighteenth century. Similar works clearly were published and in circulation in both Japan and Europe at roughly the same time.

Another interesting example from this era is *Imperium Japonicum in Sexaginta et Octo Provincias Divisum* (plate 27) by Engelbert Kaempfer (1651–1716).[13] A German doctor serving the Dutch East India Company at Nagasaki, Kaempfer accompanied the director of the Dutch trading post to Edo in 1691 and 1692, and on these occasions he obtained a number of Japanese maps. Nine of them—three of Japan, two of Edo, one each of Kyoto, Osaka, and Nagasaki, and a route map between Edo and Nagasaki—are now at the British Library.[14] Kaempfer based his map on *Shinsen Dai-Nihon zukan* (plate 29), although differences in details are immediately apparent. For instance, in Kaempfer's map, Ezo (present-day Hokkaidō) is divided into two islands, "Matsumai" and "Jeso ga Sima," and the coastline is heavily scalloped. It is thought that such variations were introduced by Johann Scheuchzer, who published the first edition of Kaempfer's map in 1727, some eleven years after the doctor's death.[15]

At the lower edge of *Imperium Japonicum,* the presence of "Tofsitoku" (Fukurokuju), "Jebis" (Ebisu), and "Daikoku," three of the Seven Deities of Good Fortune, creates a distinctly Asian flavor. In both *Imperium Japonicum* and the Reland map, the figures representing the East (deities, in this case) suggest that European mapmakers intended to clearly differentiate Asia from the West and the rest of the world.

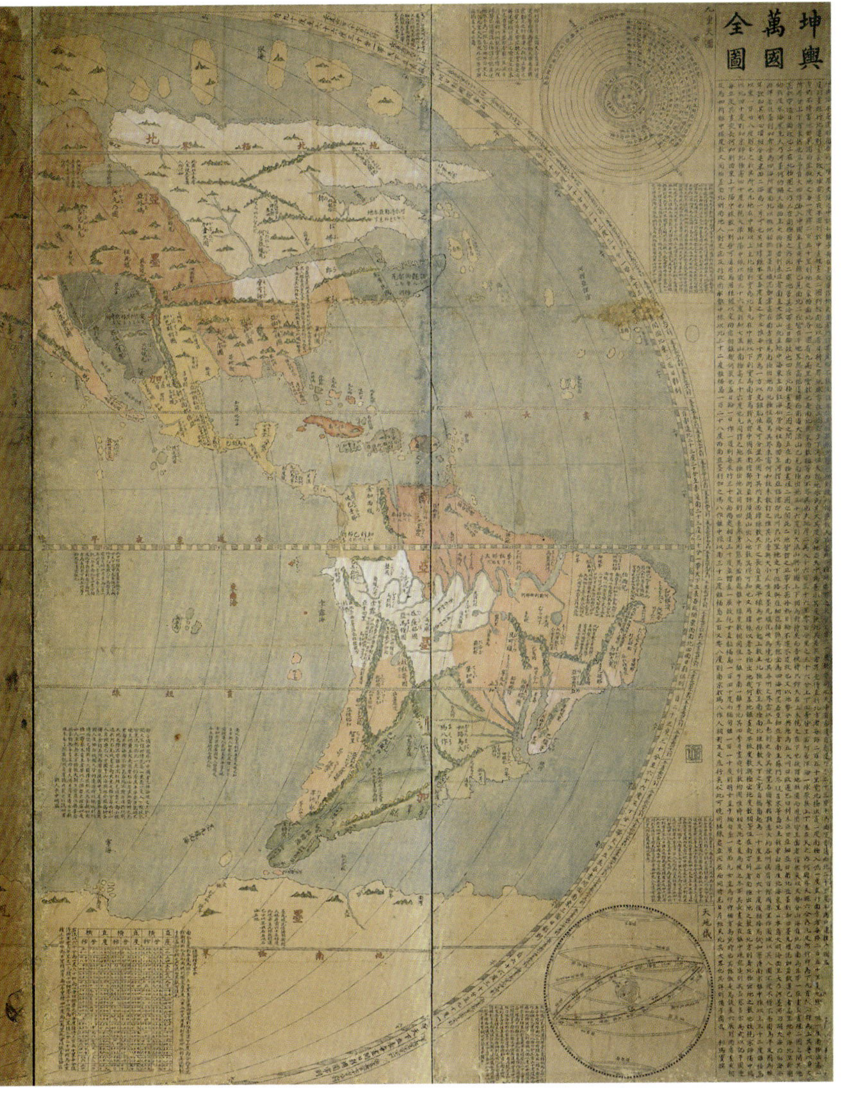

PLATE 25
Japanese, unknown artist
Copy of Kunyu wanquo quantu (Complete Terrestrial Map of All Countries)
Late 18th–19th century
After Matteo Ricci, Beijing, 1602
Six-panel screen: ink and color on paper
66 × 149¼ in. (167.5 × 379.1 cm)

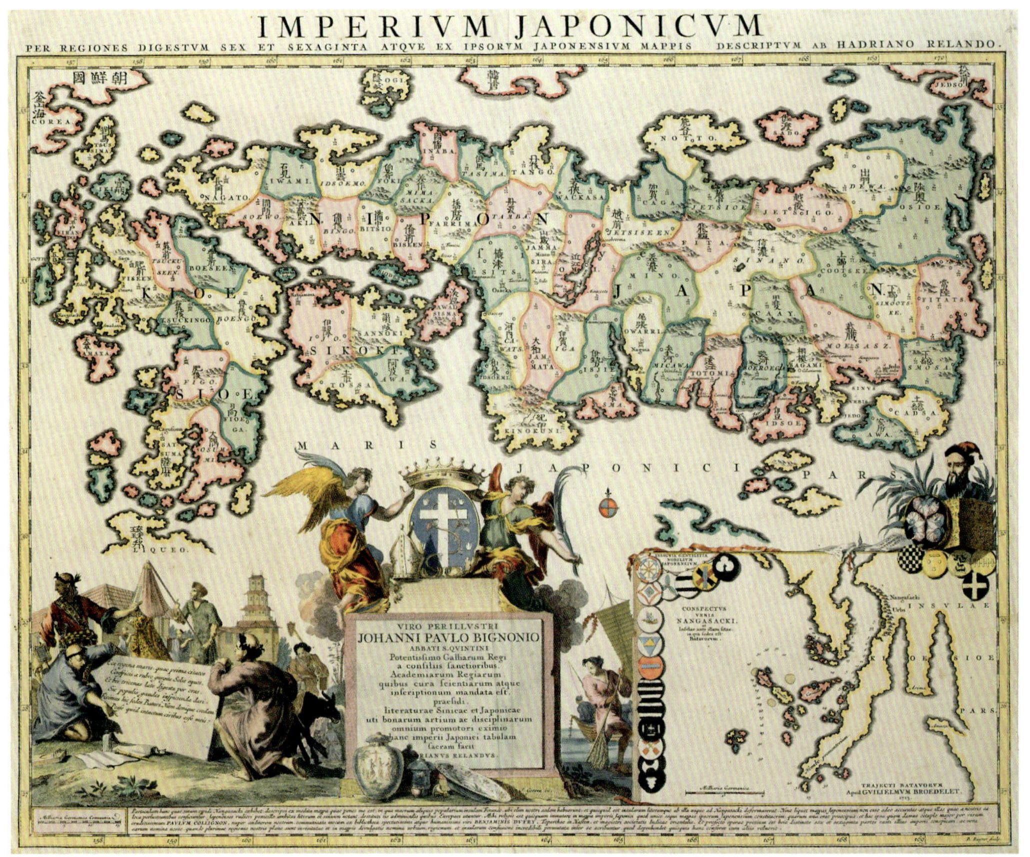

PLATE 26
Adrien Reland
(Dutch, 1676–1718)
Imperium Japonicum
(Empire of Japan)
from Guillaume
Broedelet, *Nieuwe atlas*,
Amsterdam, 1715
Copperplate engraving:
ink with hand color
on paper
21⅛ × 25 in.
(53.5 × 63.5 cm)

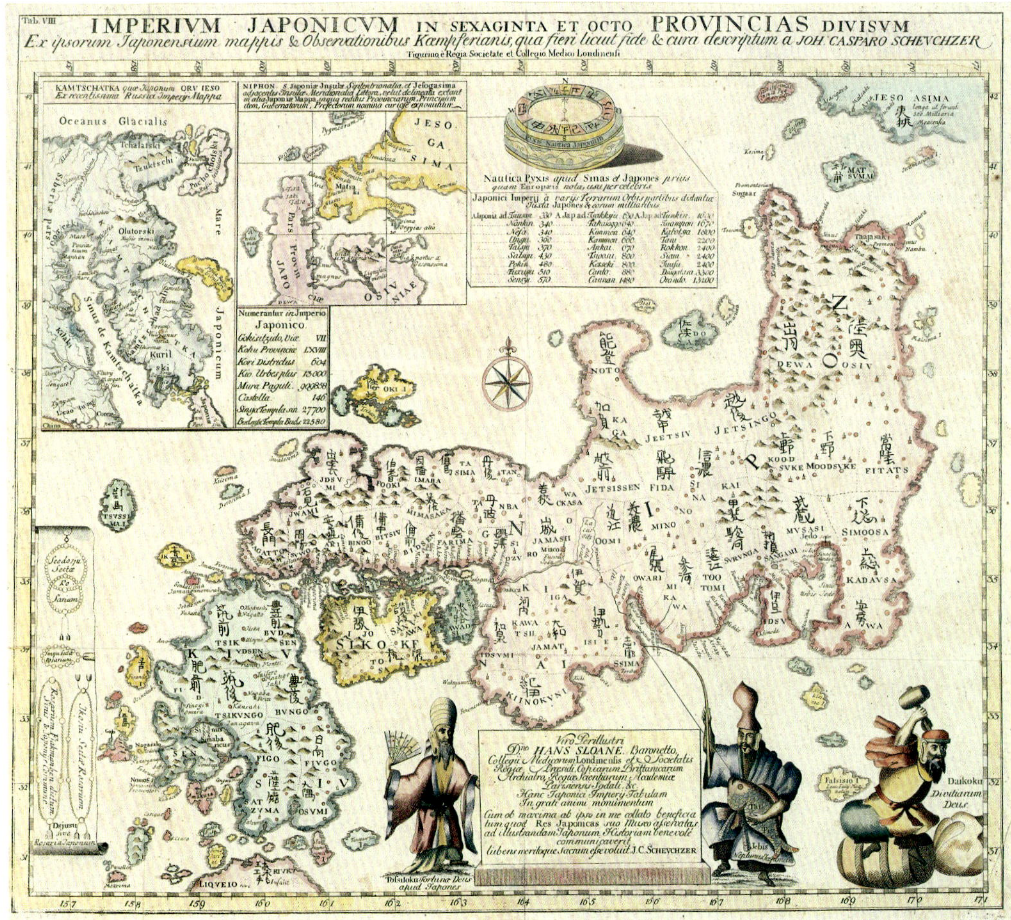

PLATE 27
Engelbert Kaempfer
(German, 1651–1716)
Imperium Japonicum
in Sexaginta et Octo
Provincias Divisum
(Empire of Japan
in Sixty-eight
Provinces)
from Christian Wilhelm
Dohm, ed., *Geschichte*
und Beschreibung von
Japan, Lemgo, 1777
Copperplate engraving:
ink with hand color
on paper
18⅜ × 21 in.
(46.6 × 53.3 cm)

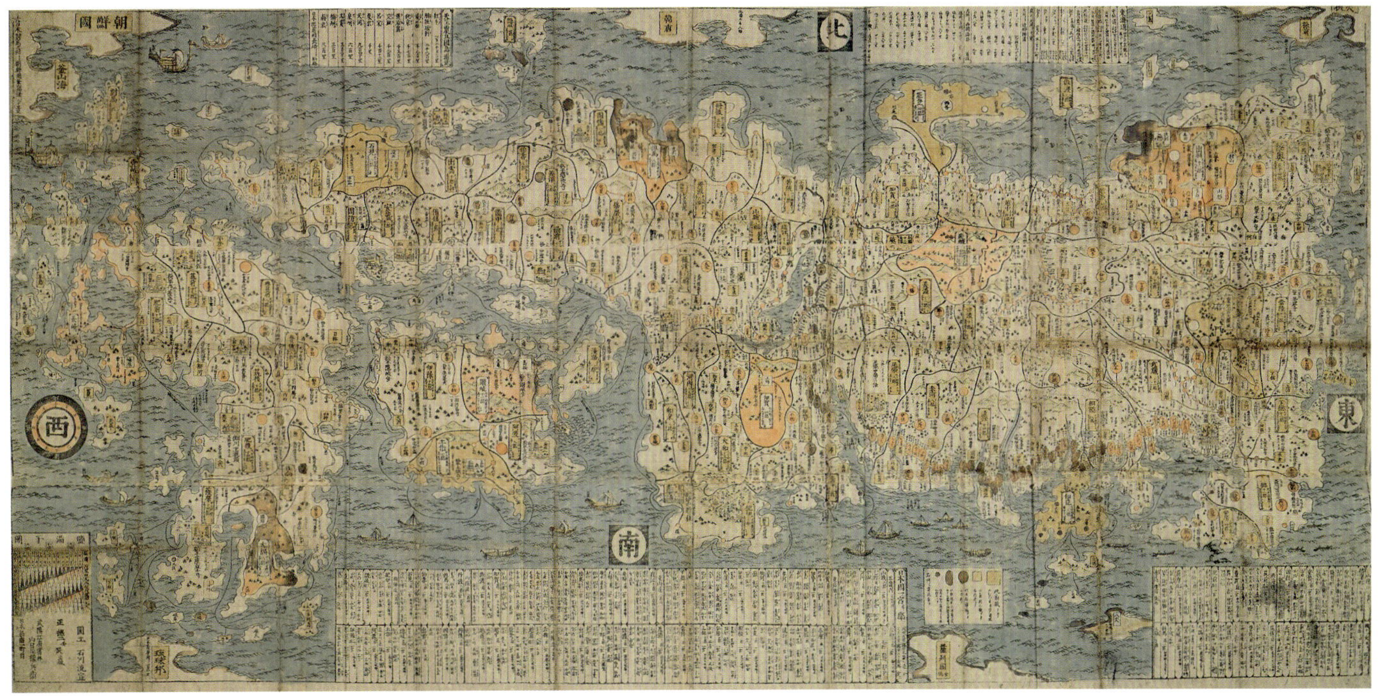

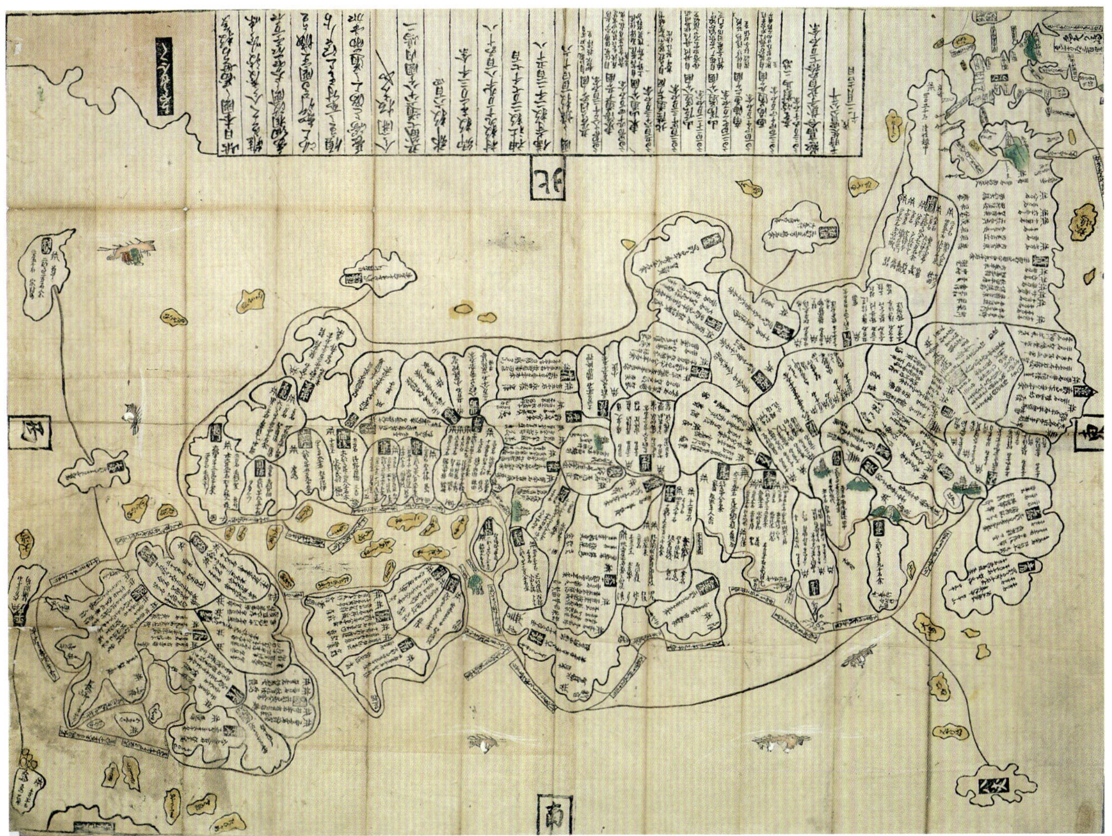

PLATE 28
Ishikawa Ryūsen
(Japanese, 1689–1713?)
Dai-Nihonkoku ōezu
(Map of Japan)
1712 (Shōtoku 2)
Woodblock print:
ink with hand color
on paper
35⅜ × 67⅛ in.
(89.9 × 170.4 cm)

PLATE 29
Japanese, unknown
artist
Shinsen Dai-Nihon zukan (Newly Revised Map of Japan)
1678 (Enpō 6)
Woodblock print:
ink with hand color
on paper
27 × 37⅛ in.
(68.5 × 94.3 cm)

PLATE 30
Copied by Kataoka
Yūchiku
(Japanese, dates
unknown)
Tenjiku no zu
[Buddhist
World Map]
1749 (Kan'en 2)
Hanging scroll: ink
and color on paper
65¾ × 52½ in.
(167 × 133.2 cm)

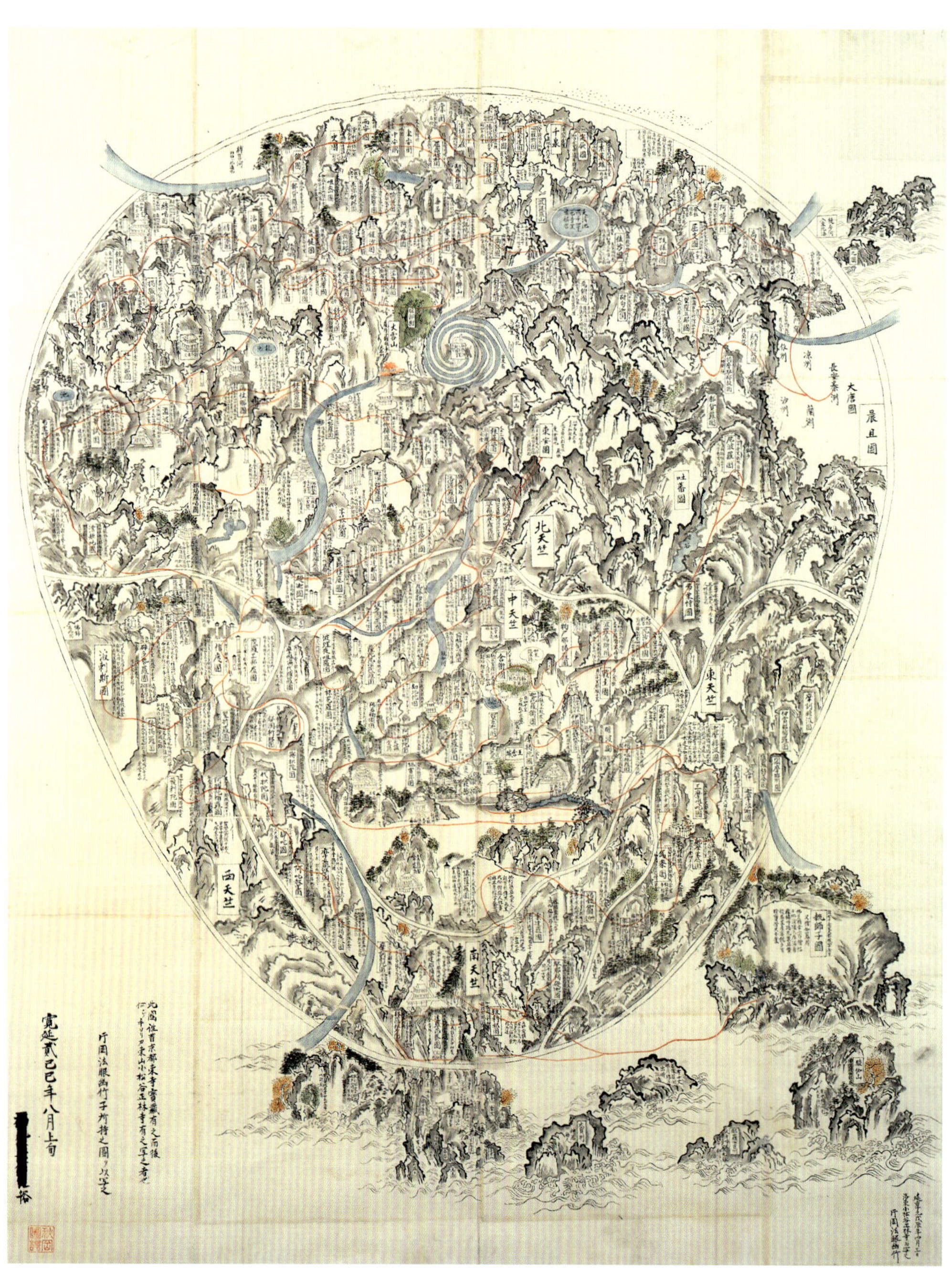

PLATE 31
Rōkashi
(Japanese, dates
unknown)
*Nansenbushū
bankoku shōka
no zu* [Buddhist
World Map]
1710 (Hōei 7)
Woodblock print:
ink with hand color
on paper
46¼ × 57⅛ in.
(117.3 × 145 cm)

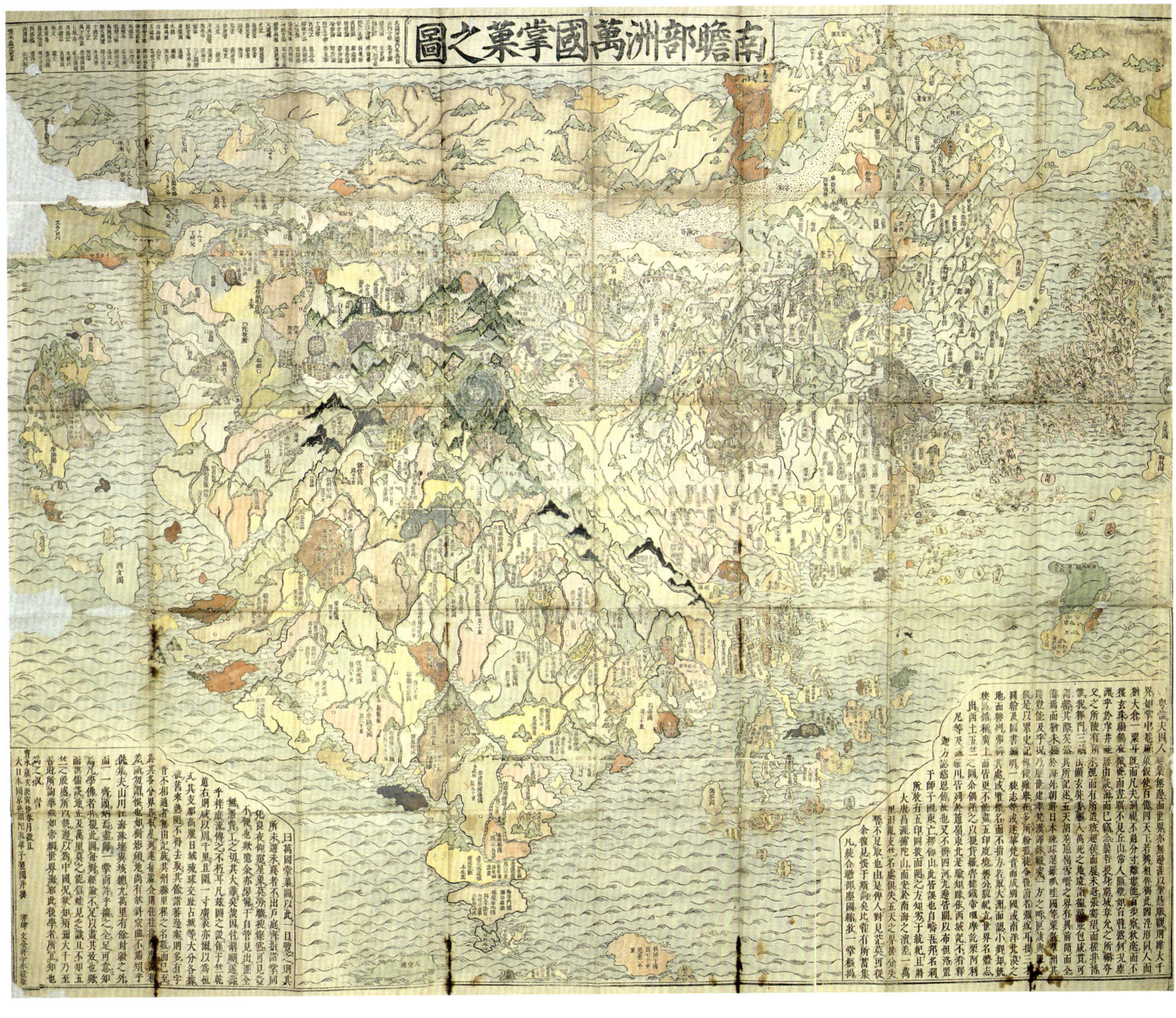

53

Conclusion

Until its encounter with the West, Japan appeared in maps as a place of legend and myth. Even after contact, perceptions changed slowly. As maps in Ortelius's *Theatrum* clearly show, the legendary notions about Japan were still dominant in the early stages of Europe's mapping of Asia and the world. As time passed, however, illustrations and maps gradually began to reflect a more precise knowledge of geography. While such maps remained inaccurate in many respects, they reflected the developing interaction and cultural exchange between the East and the West, and mark a significant transition in the cartography of Asia and Japan.

Like their Japanese counterparts, Western mapmakers freely made changes and added details where they saw fit, often copying from Japanese source materials. This acceptance and incorporation of Japanese forms and information to Western maps, albeit with the addition of cartouches and new decorative flourishes, clearly expresses the ambition of Western mapmakers to produce appealing, exotic, and saleable designs. But Western reception and interpretation were not straightforward, and a continuing tinge of prejudice and presumption reveals the deep entrenchment and prevalence of certain worldviews.

From medieval to premodern times in Japan, a great variety of maps and map forms, such as *Bukkyō-kei sekai zu* (Buddhist world maps, plates 30, 31), reflect the coexistence there of multiple worldviews. This contradicts, in many respects, the singularity of map forms and perspectives found in cartographic production in our era. Consequently, it is difficult to gauge exactly how individuals engaged with and interpreted these objects. But the existence of multiple worldviews in premodern society demonstrates a flexibility and open-mindedness that should be acknowledged.

NOTES

1. L. F. Benedetto, *The Travels of Marco Polo,* trans. Aldo Ricci (London: Routledge, 1931), 270–71.

2. E. G. Ravenstein, *Translations and Commentary on Martin Behaim's Èrdapfel* (London: Greaves and Thomas, 1994).

3. In Münster's map, Japan is labeled "Archipelagus 7448 Insularu" (7448 archipelago).

4. With regard to *Theatrum Orbis Terrarum* and Ortelius, see Cornelis Koeman, *The History of Abraham Ortelius and His Theatrum Orbis Terrarum* (Lausanne: Sequoia, 1964); its Japanese translation is *Kindai chizuchō no tanjō,* trans. Hasegawa Kōji (Kyoto: Rinsen Shoten, 1997).

5. The area that seems to be the Kii Peninsula is noted as "Bandel" (Bandō). The first Dourado-style Japanese map was the handdrawn *Nihon zu,* compiled into *Sekai chizuchō,* produced in 1568. The most well-known Dourado-style maps are those by J. H. van Linschoten, published in *Itinerario, Voyage ofte schipvaert* (1596).

6. With regard to the place names used in maps made in the West between the end of the sixteenth and the beginning of the seventeenth centuries, see Oda Takeo, *Kochizu no hakubutsushi* (Tokyo: Kokon Shoin, 1998).

7. Onoda Kazuyuki, "Rangaku no hattatsu to sekai chizu," in *Zusetsu sekai kochizu korekushon,* ed. Miyoshi Tadayoshi (Tokyo: Kawade Shobō Shinsha, 1999).

8. Extant Valck items imported into Japan at that time include world globes and celestial globes owned by the Matsura family in Hirado and the Nabeshima family in Takeo, in Kyūshū.

9. Valck's maps of Europe, America, and Asia with surrounding decoration have been kept at Mnichovo Hradiště, a castle in the Czech Republic, since 1921. The circumstances are not clear, but one or more of the maps reportedly was stolen when they were temporarily at Jemnište in 1992. I would like to thank Matsuda Kiyoshi, Kyoto University, and Günter Schilder, University of Utrecht, for this information. See also Matsuda Kiyoshi, "Ishikawa Tairō hitsu 'Seiyō hujin zu' no genryū," *Yamato bunka* 105 (2001), and Josef H. Billar, "Jemnist ist eine Reise wert: Kostbarkeiten holländischer Kartographie und Veduntenkunst in Böhmen," *Speculum Orbis* 1, no. 2 (1985: nos. 7–9).

10. *Kon'yo bankoku zenzu* can be found in Japan at the Tōhoku University Library, Miyagi Prefectural Library, and Kobe City Museum, among other locations; see Aoki Chieko, "Nihon ni denzon suru Kon'yo bankoku zenzu ichiran," in *Sekaizu yūran—Kon'yo bankoku zenzu to higashi Ajia* (Tsuchiura: Tsuchiura Shiritsu Hakubutsukan, 1996).

11. See, for example, Nagakubo Sekisui's *Kaisei Nihon yochi rotei zenzu* (Revised Route Map of Japan) in the Siebold Collection, Staatliches Museum für Völkerkunde, Munich, and found in Baba Akira's "Chizu no shoshigaku: Nagakubo Sekisui 'Kaisei Nihon yochi rotei zenzu' no baai," in *Chizu to ezu no bunkashi,* ed. Kuroda Hideo et al. (Tokyo: Tokyo Daigaku Shuppankai, 2001).

12. Publication in Europe of similar maps of Japan during this time include, among others, Henri Abraham Chatelain's *L'Empire du Japon, tiré des cartes des japonnosis,* in *Atlas historique* (1719), vol. 5; Reland's *Imperium Japonicum* (1715, c. 1720, c. 1745); and Matthaeus Seutter's *Imperium Japonicum* (c. 1740).

13. The map was attached to *The History of Japan,* a 1727 English-language translation by Johann Scheuchzer of Kaempfer's manuscript "Das Heutige Japan" (Japan of Today), which was not published in its original German until the 1770s. The 1729 Dutch translation of *History of Japan* indicates the distance between Nagasaki and Edo.

14. Lutz Walter, "Englebert Kaempfer and the European Cartography of Japan," in *Japan: A Cartographic Vision, European Printed Maps of Japan from the Early 16th to the 19th Century,* ed. Lutz Walter (Munich and New York: Prestel-Verlag, 1994), 61–68. Walter refers to two maps of Edo among those Kaempfer had brought from Japan. He describes one, made in 1681, as unknown and the other as Ishikawa Ryūsen's *Edo no ō-ezu* (cat. no. 88, pp. 160 and 198). Both of these maps are in the British Library, London. The former is *Zōho Edo zu,* made by an unknown mapmaker. The latter is properly titled *Edo on'ōezu zen* and was published by Hayashi Yoshinaga, as its inscription states: "Genroku ni tsuchinoto-mi no toshi go gatsu kichijitsu" (on a propitious day in the fifth month, second year of the Genroku era [1689]). Hayashi served in the shogunal map workshop. I am grateful to Hamish Todd, Head of Japanese Collections, Asia, Pacific and Africa Collections, The British Library, for his detailed confirmation of the nine maps of Japan in the library's Kaempfer Collection.

15. Scheuchzer likely referred to *Honchō zukan kōmoku* (Imperial Map of Japan), one of the maps Kaempfer had brought back from Japan and which is now in the British Library.

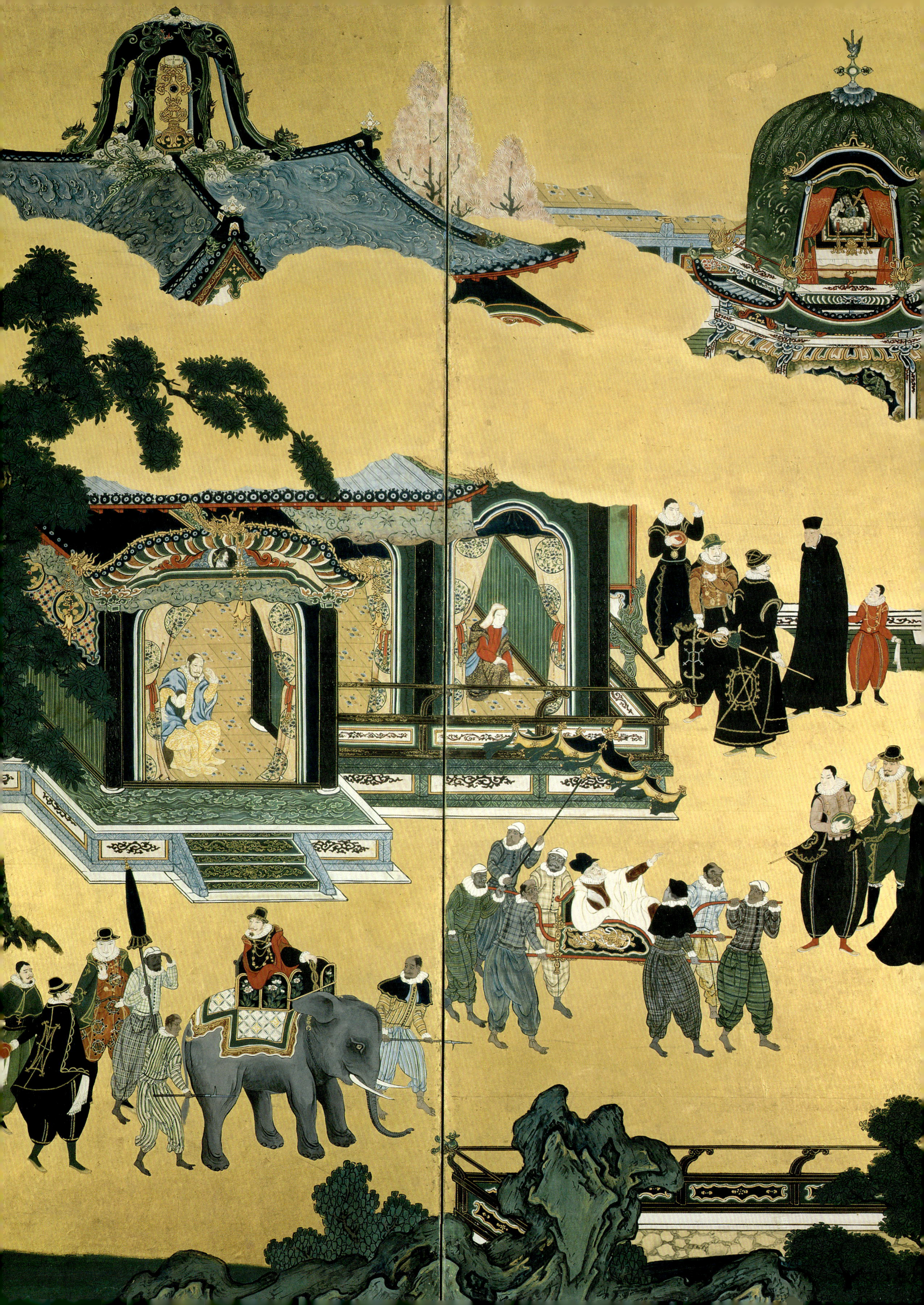

2

Narusawa Katsushi

Two Streams of Namban Painting

In 1492 Christopher Columbus "discovered" America. Although this fact is taught in schools, including those in Japan, many people today recognize the term "discover" as inappropriate. Still, this does not change the significance of the event, by which Europeans came to know that an unheard-of continent existed on the other side of the Atlantic. European "conquerors" came to this new world one after another as they expanded their colonies and developed trade relations. Intolerant of religions other than Catholicism, they endeavored to share the glory of their god with the indigenous people of North and South America. For those "discovered," it proved to be a difficult and complicated time.

A similar dynamic developed in sixteenth-century Japan, when a wave of great voyages from Europe surged toward Japan. With the arrival of a few Portuguese, who drifted ashore in a Chinese junk onto the outlying southwest island of Tanegashima in 1543, the West discovered Japan. In 1549 the first Western missionary, the famed Jesuit Francis Xavier (1506–1552), arrived in Japan. He landed at Kagoshima on Kyūshū and began evangelizing the Japanese people. Although he stayed but two years, Xavier remained a popular figure, and a number of early-seventeenth-century portraits of him by Japanese artists survive to this day (plate 32). For the next hundred years, Japan engaged in economic and cultural exchanges with Catholic Europeans, mostly from Portugal and Spain.

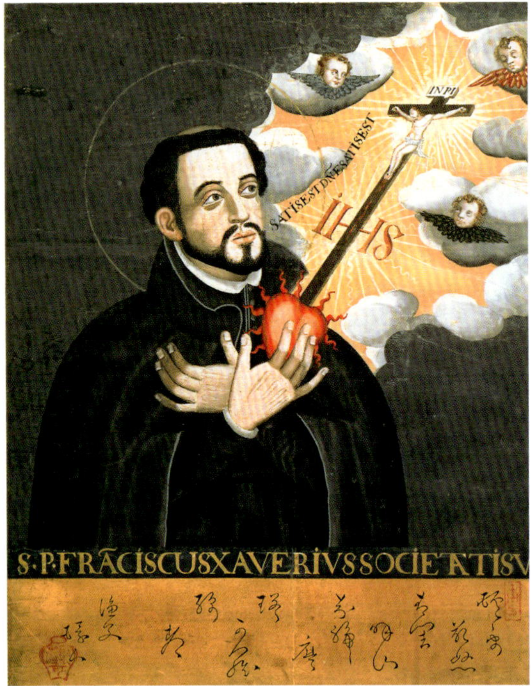

From the outset, the Japanese encounter with Europeans differed greatly from that of the native peoples of North and South America. The reasons for this include Japan's isolated location at the far reaches of European influence; the political upheaval raging in Japan at the time, during which a number of influential and powerful rulers consolidated power; and a unique cultural condition that fostered a high tolerance of other religions. As a result, the Japanese were exposed to and acquired aspects of European culture without submitting to colonization. In this process it can be argued that the Japanese "discovered" the West on their own terms, grounded in qualities inherent in their own culture, traditions, and art practices.

The artifacts known under the rubric of *namban* art (lit., art of the southern barbarians) were produced under these circumstances and initiated, in large part, by Japanese artists and their patrons. The term *namban* itself originated in the Chinese word for regions and people of the south, and the Japanese adopted it to refer to the Portuguese and Spanish who approached their country from the south. In art history, *namban* refers to Japanese art created from the late sixteenth to early seventeenth century under the influence of the subjects, designs, and techniques of Portuguese and Spanish arts.

Similar to the manner in which those who came from Portugal and Spain are categorized as

either Christian missionaries or laymen traders, *namban* art is divided into sacred and secular works. I propose two broad *namban* categories: art with religious or monarchial themes which carried an underlying purpose of learning from Western culture, and secular art, intended for the pure enjoyment of Western culture. Fundamentally speaking, however, it can be argued that the pursuit of learning often leads to pleasure, and with no clear differentiation between them, these purposes often were intertwined and can be difficult to tease apart.

The folding screen known as *Taisei ōkō kiba zu* (Foreign Emperors and Kings on Horseback, plate 33) is representative of the first category. Although the work appears as if it were completed in oil, scientific analysis has shown that only Japanese pigments were used.[1] The gold foil background demonstrates a close affinity to the Japanese painted screen tradition, but the artist directly appropriated *chiaroscuro* technique from Western painting to express and emphasize modeling of the human body. The figures featured on the screen were by and large borrowed, and enlarged forty times, from a large decorative map of the world, published in 1609 by the Dutch engraver Pieter van den Keere (Petrus Kaerius), which itself relied on a 1607 map by the Dutch chart maker Willem Janszoon Blaeu (fig. 9).[2] The Japanese work originally comprised a pair of eight-panel screens, each screen depicting four monarchs. The number of panels in the screen now at the Kobe City Museum was later refashioned from eight into four. Its mate, now in the collection of the Suntory Museum of Art, Tokyo (fig. 10), exists as a pair of four-panel screens.

From left to right, the monarchs on the Kobe screen are traditionally identified as the protector of the Catholic faith, the Holy Roman Emperor Rudolf II (r. 1576–1612); the Ottoman sultan; the grand duke of Moscow, czar of Russia; and the Great Khan, the nomadic Mongolian Tatar. The figures are faced off in two pairs, Western king against Muslim ruler. Clearly an intense battle is being waged between Western (Christian) and Islamic powers.

This combination of monarchial figures represents the realms and interests of long-standing enemies who repeatedly opposed one another as they battled for supremacy. At the time the screens were painted, in the early seventeenth century, the Hapsburgs and Ottomans were the

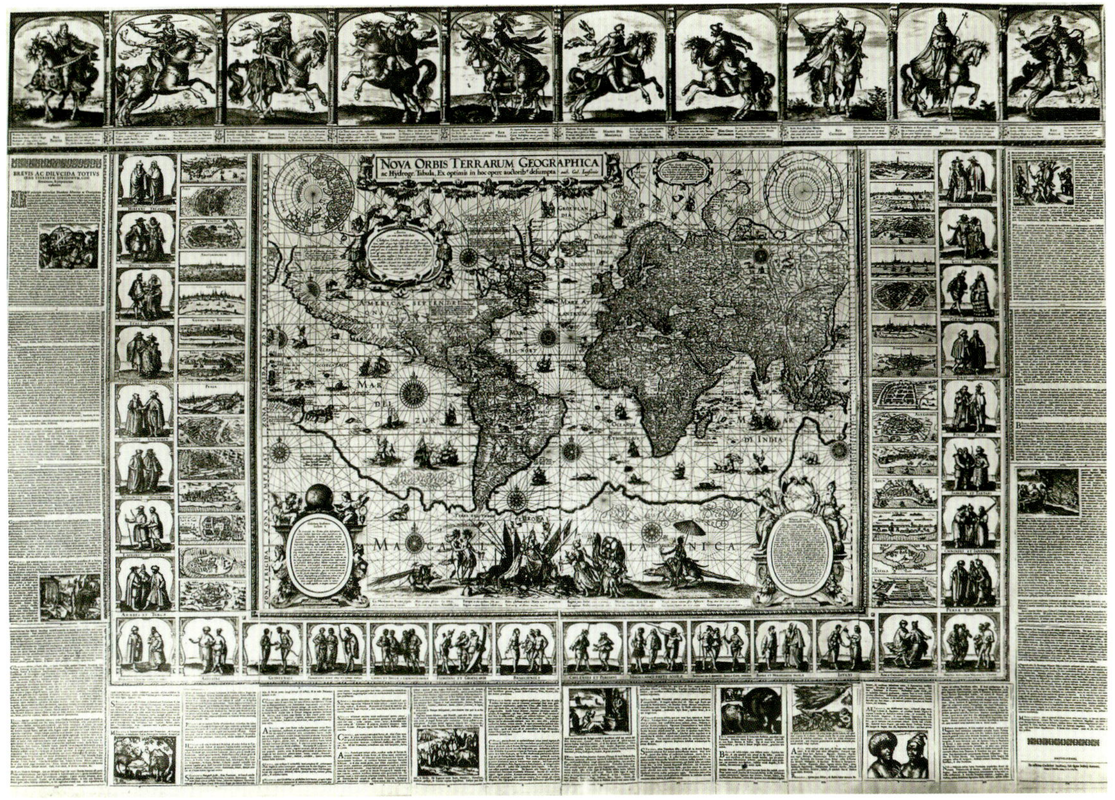

FIG. 9
Willem Janszoon Blaeu
(Dutch, 1571–1638)
Nova Orbis Terrarum Geographica [Map of the World]
Amsterdam, 1607
Copperplate engraving: ink with hand color on paper
56⅜ × 80⅜ in.
(143 × 204 cm)
courtesy Nederlands Scheepvaartmuseum, Amsterdam

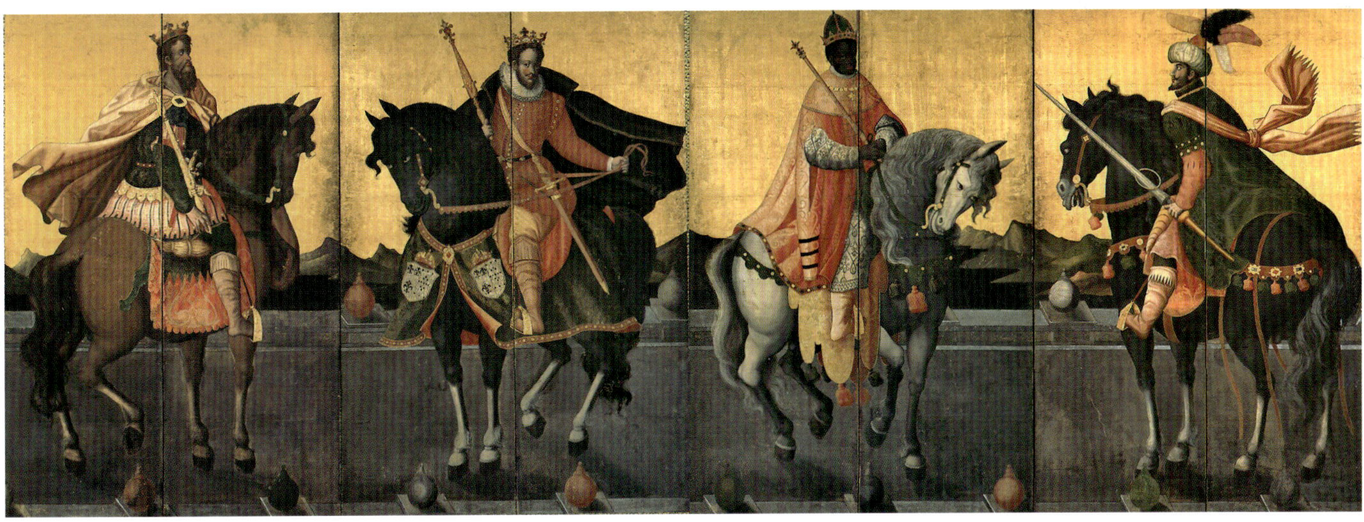

FIG. 10
Japanese, unknown artist
Taisei ōkō kiba zu (Foreign Emperors and Kings on Horseback)
Important Cultural Property
c. 1610s
Pair of four-panel screens: ink, color, and gold on paper
72½ × 96½ in.
(184 × 245 cm) each
Suntory Museum of Art, Tokyo

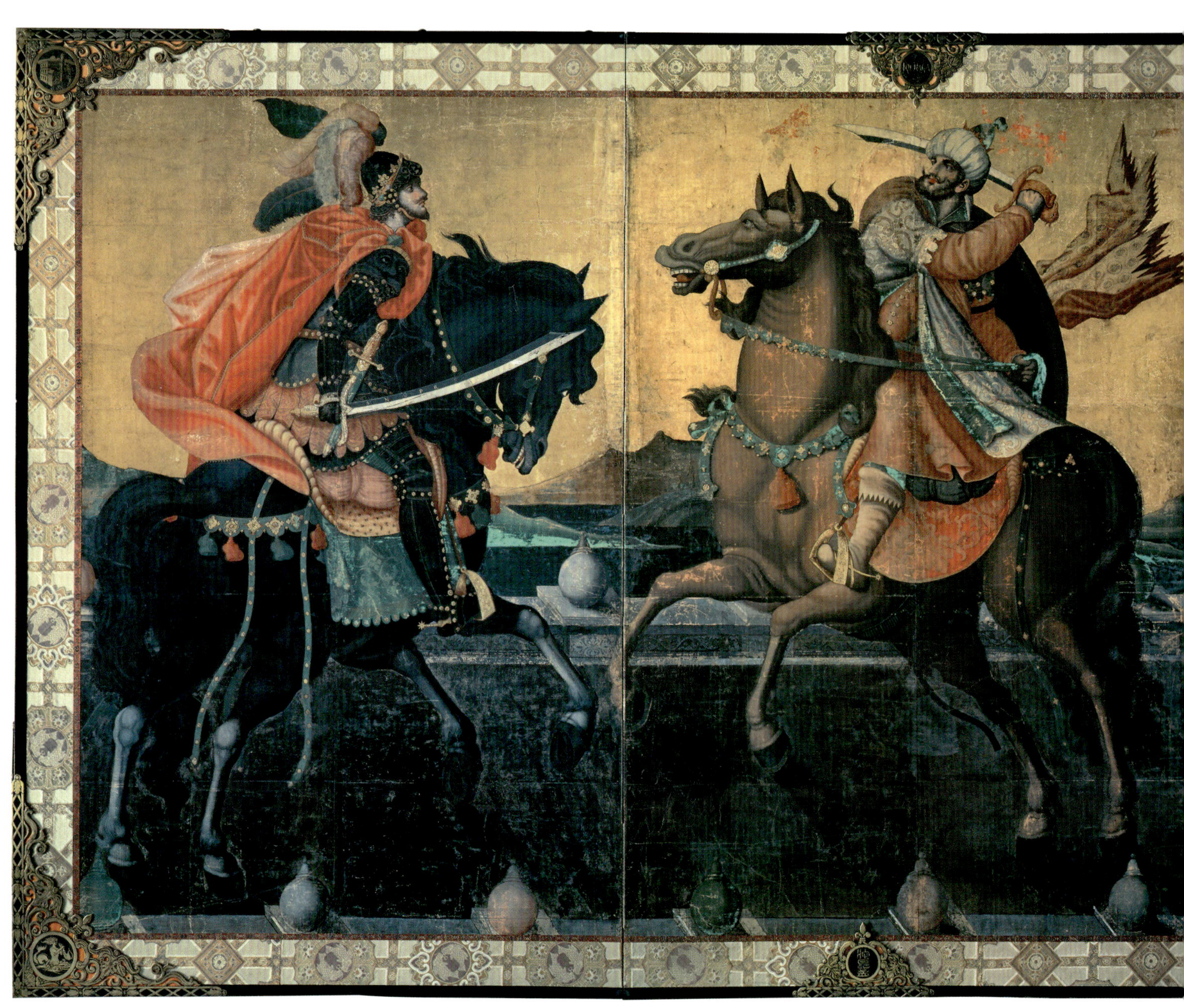

PLATE 33
Japanese, unknown
artist
Taisei ōkō kiba zu
(Foreign Emperors
and Kings on
Horseback)
Important Cultural
Property
c. 1610s
Four-panel screen: ink,
color, and gold on paper;
mounted by previous
owner, Ikenaga Hajime
65½ × 181¼ in.
(166.2 × 460.4 cm)

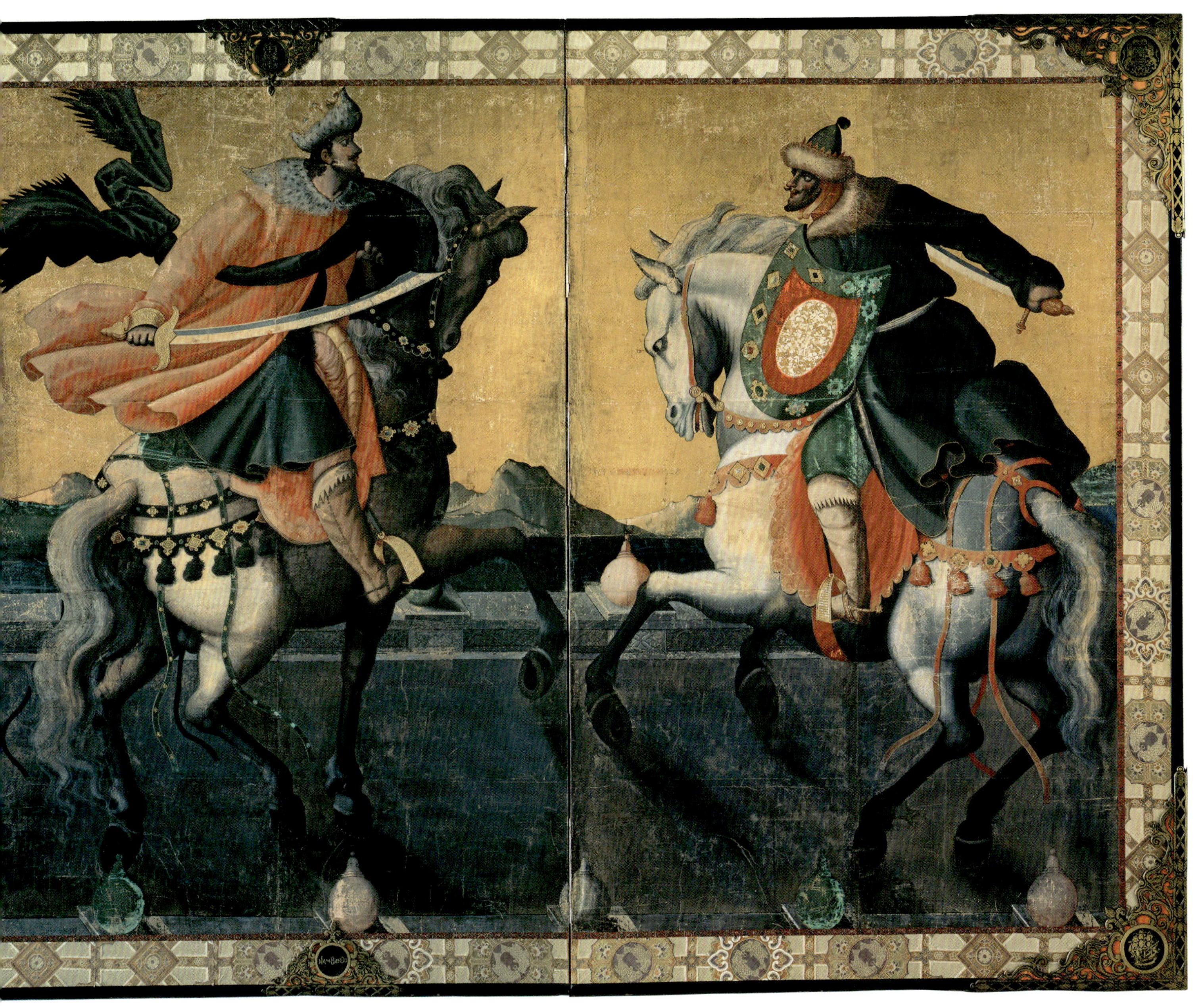

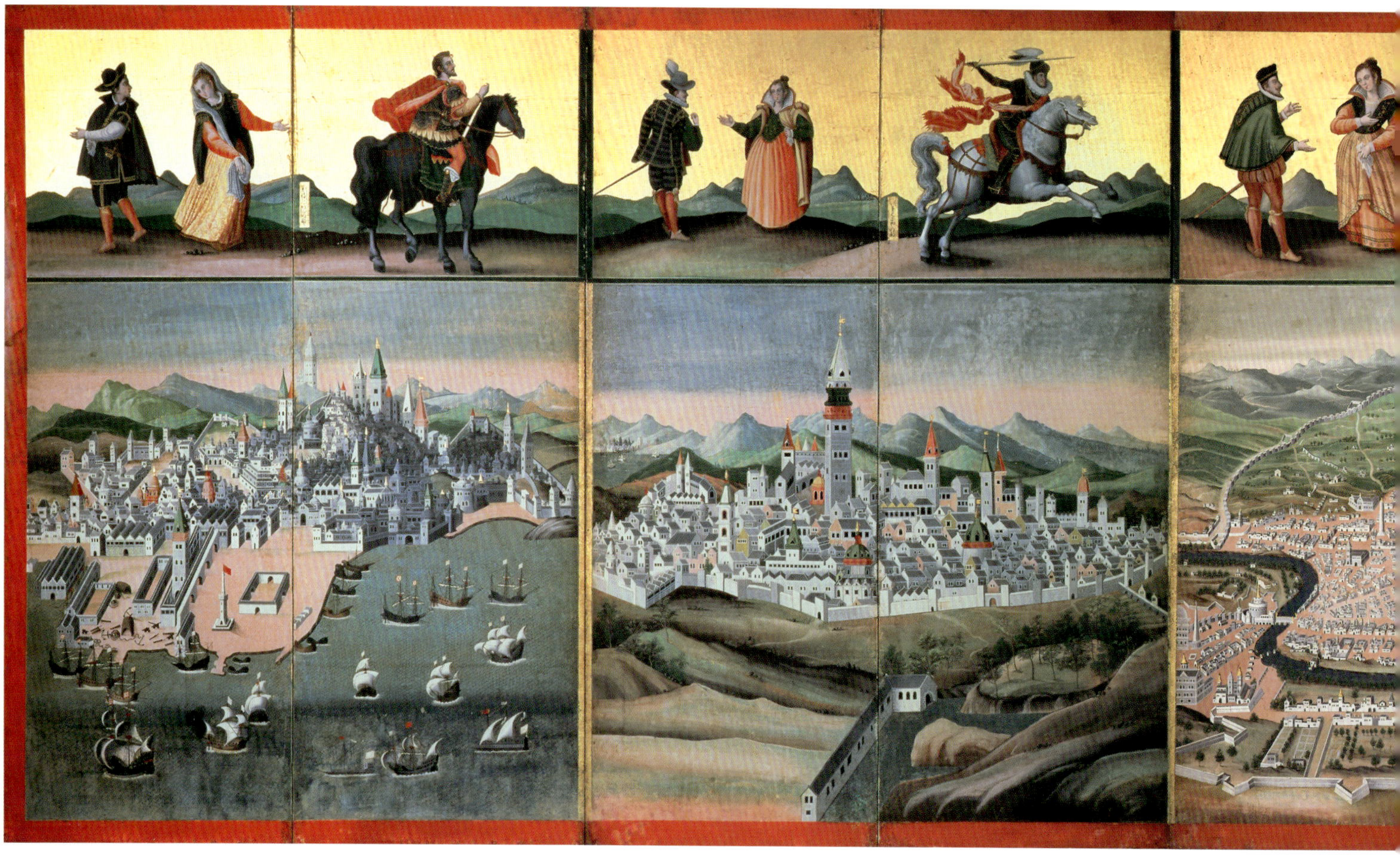

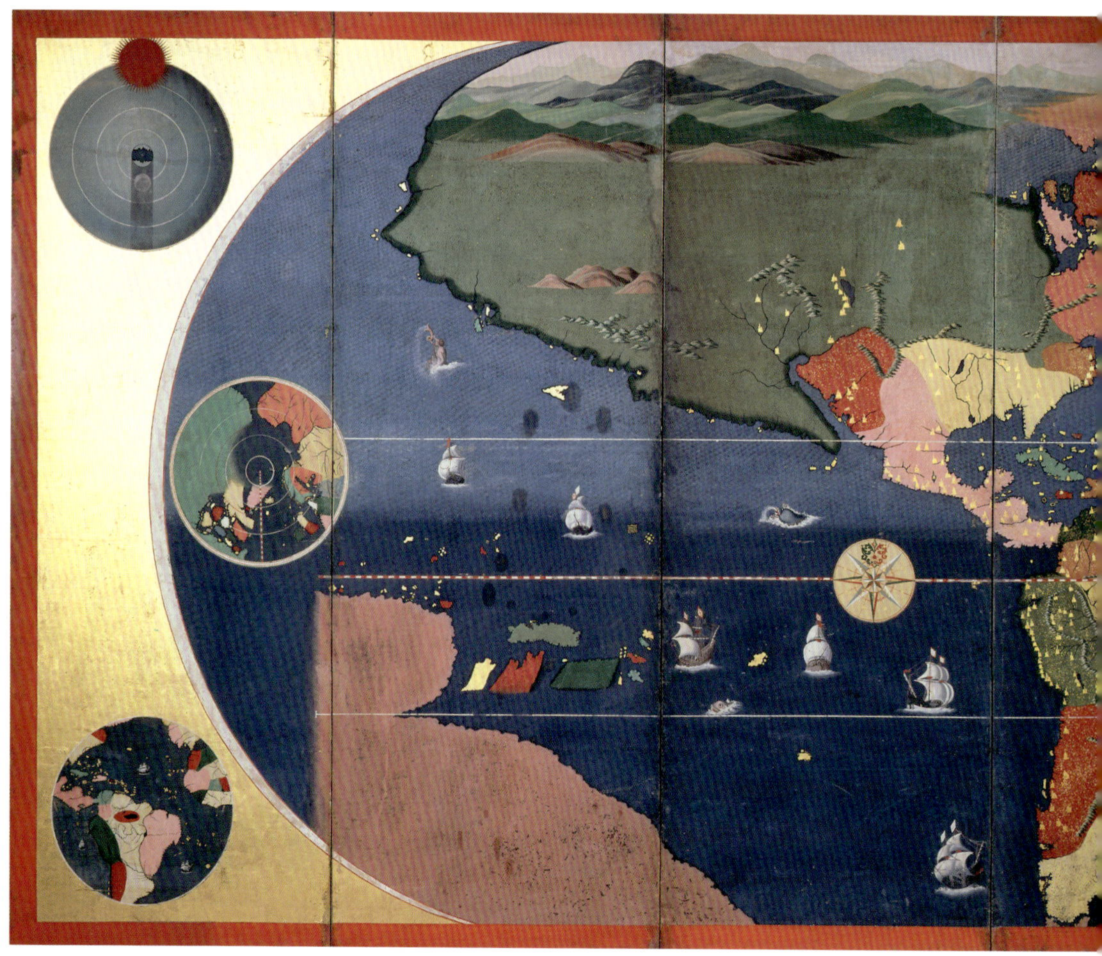

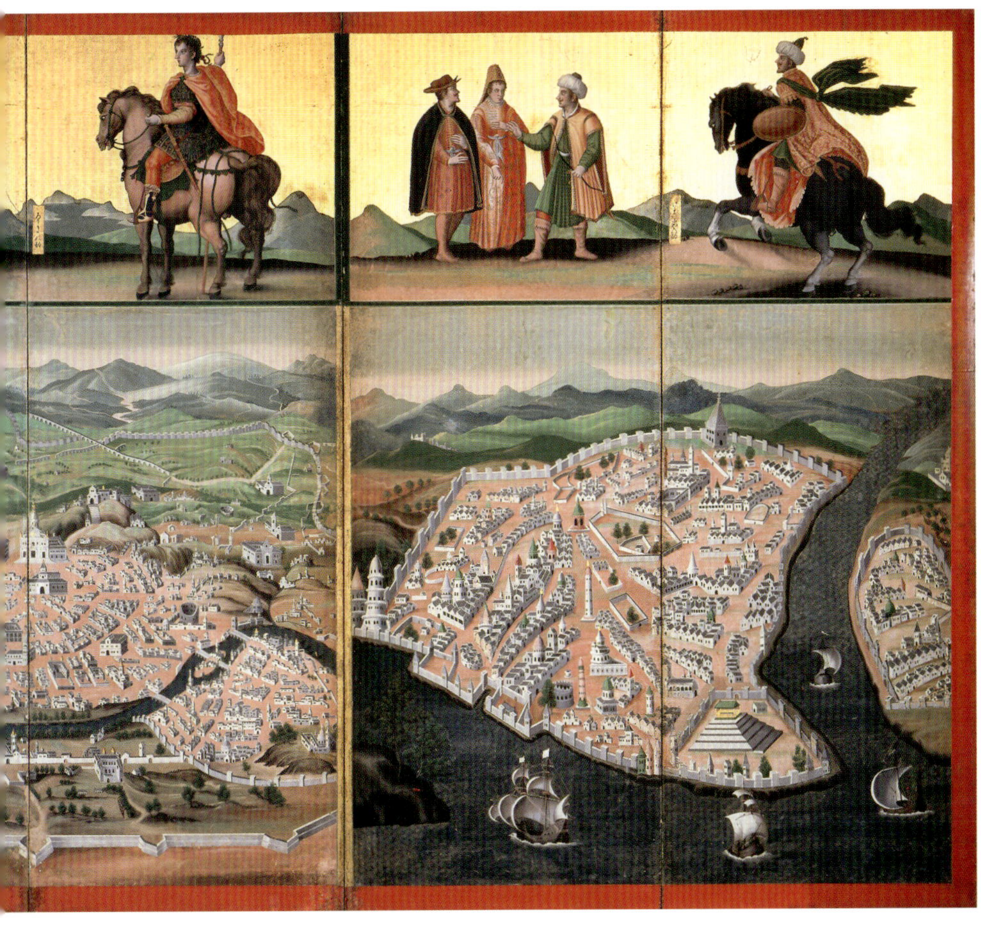

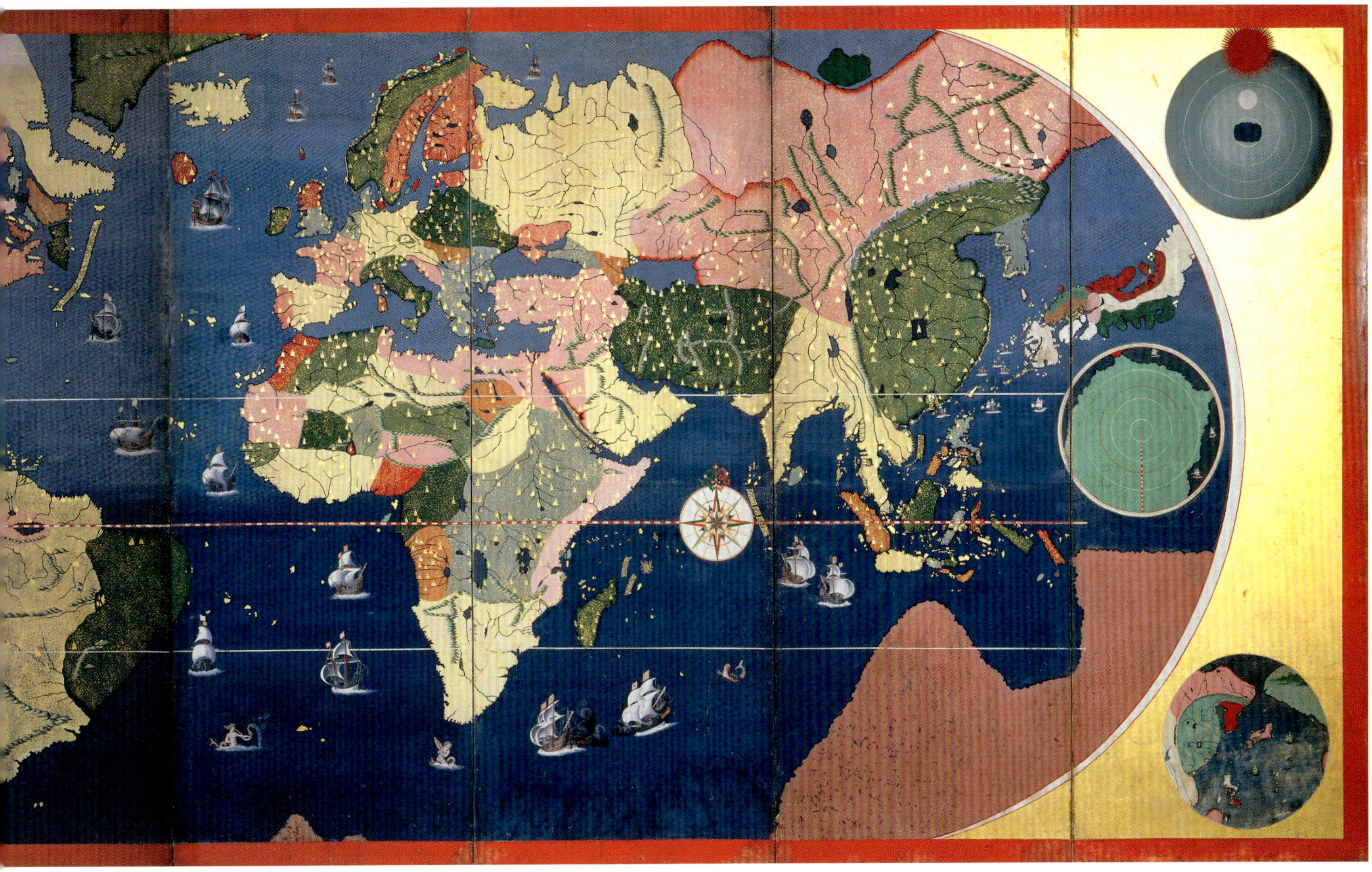

PLATE 34a,b
Japanese, unknown
artist
**Yonto zu / Sekai zu
(Four Large Cities
of the World / Map
of the World)**
*Important Cultural
Property*
Early 17th century
Pair of eight-panel
screens: ink, color,
and gold on paper
62½ × 188¼ in.
(158.7 × 477.7 cm) each

principal opponents in a conflict over East Central Europe (the so-called Long Turkish War, 1590–1606). Russia, under the leadership of Ivan the Terrible (1530–1584), had conquered the region of Tartary but skirmished with the Crimean Khanate, then under the protection of the Ottomans. Unlike the more didactic decorations on Van den Keere's map, the Japanese screen displays an aestheticized image of the religious struggles of four hundred years ago that continue to affect the world to this day.

The work was passed down through a leading daimyo family, the Matsudaira of the Aizu Wakamatsu domain, in present-day Fukushima prefecture in northeast Japan. Its provenance is exceptional: the first daimyo of the Aizu Matsudaira family was Hoshina Masayuki (1611–1673),

the younger brother of Tokugawa Iemitsu, the third Tokugawa shogun. In my view, because of parallels between it and a similar example at the Imperial Household Agency, Tokyo (see fig. 3a,b, pp. 24–25), this folding screen was likely produced in the 1610s for the Tokugawa family. Its intent was perhaps to demonstrate the current state of European affairs to Japanese rulers in clear and explicit pictorial terms. The outstanding quality of the screen surpasses any other Western-style Japanese paintings in both its monumental size and decorative aspects. Clearly the work was intended to express the important family status of its owner. This screen could be considered a Western-style interpretation of *Shutsujin ei*, a traditional pictorial subject in Japanese painting in which a sovereign is portrayed in elaborate attire

PLATE 35a–d
Georg Braun
(German, 1541–1622)
and Franz Hogenberg
(German, 1535–1590)

Four Cities
from *Civitates Orbis Terrarum*, Cologne, 1585
Copperplate engravings: ink on paper
17 × 11½ in.
(43 × 29 cm) at cover

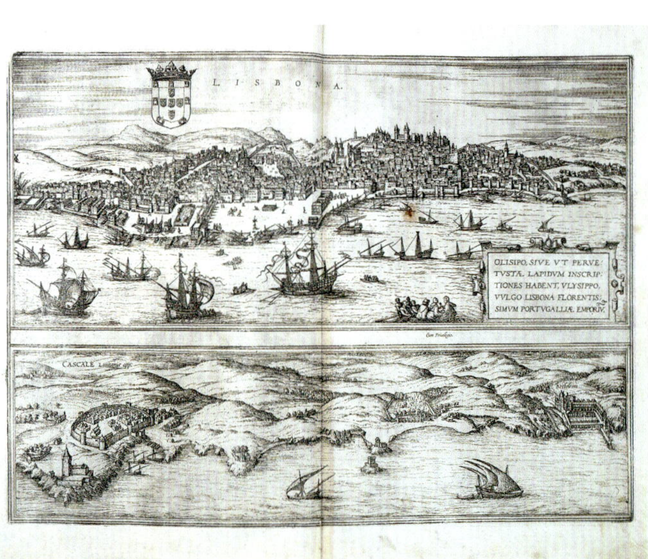

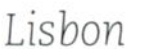

Lisbon

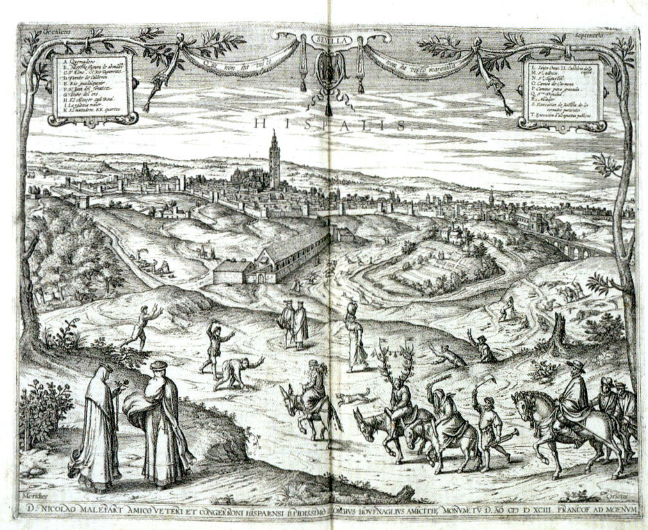

Seville

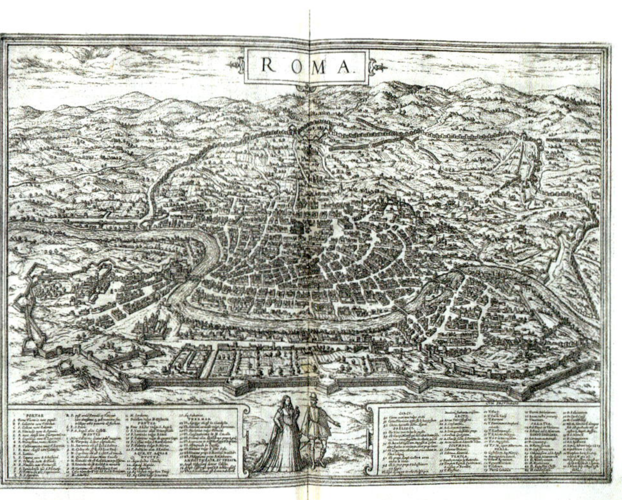

Rome

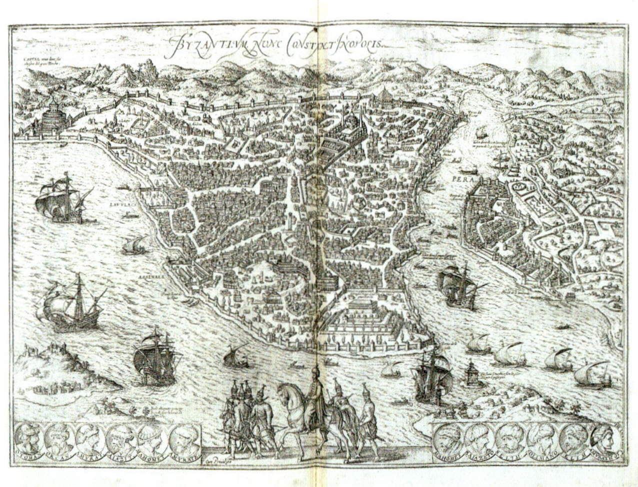

Constantinople

on his way to battle. The Japanese ruling elite must have appreciated this work with a sense of familiarity, as if they were witnessing these heroic monarchs—their counterparts—as they battled one another to gain control of the world.

Like *Taisei ōkō kiba zu,* the screens *Yonto zu/Sekai zu* (Four Large Cities of the World/Map of the World, plate 34a,b) were based on European geographical sources. When these sources were introduced to Japan and the history of the screens remain unknown; the screens themselves were only recently discovered in Spain.[3] The four cities represented on the left screen—Lisbon, Seville, Rome, and Constantinople—have antecedents in *Civitates Orbis Terrarum* (City Atlas, plate 35a–d), first published in 1572 by Georg Braun and Franz Hogenberg. For the view of Rome, the artist gave particular prominence to Il Gesú, the mother church of the Society of Jesus, a depiction thought to have been borrowed from an illustration in *Vita Beati Patris Ignatii Loyolae* (Antwerp, c. 1610) by Pedro de Ribadeneira (1526–1611), a Jesuit priest.[4] The featured cities were then the political and economic centers of the Mediterranean region, and here too, as in *Taisei ōkō kiba zu,* there is a suggestion of conflict between Christianity and Islam.

Again like *Taisei ōkō kiba zu,* the imagery for *Yonto zu/Sekai zu* (plate 34a,b) was taken from the 1609 Van den Keere world map. The end panels of the screen contain six illustrations: a solar eclipse, a lunar eclipse, images of the North and South Poles, a hemisphere with Japan at the center and another, with the reverse, showing Brazil in the center. It is possible that images such as these promoted the theory of the earth being round. In addition to employing knowledge gained from Westerners, the artist included detailed geographic information about Japan that would not have been known to Europeans. *Sekai zu* should be regarded as the most advanced expression of geographic knowledge at that time because of its synthesis of previously unrelated sources. The artist extended and curved the far eastern and western edges of the map, and Japan, at the far right, appears enormous and out of proportion in relation to the other land masses. This emphasis might have been the artist's expression of nationalism or an exaggerated effort to focus the viewer's attention. It is easy to imagine a viewer sitting on a *tatami* floor and examining this decorative interior screen, letting his imagination fly away to foreign lands. The splendid beauty of the screen must have induced great pleasure, and in this respect, the distinction between learning and enjoyment blurs, as it does in so many *namban* works.

Sunpuki, the history of Tokugawa Ieyasu (1542–1616), founder of the Edo shogunate, recounts an interesting episode that highlights the significance of such screens.[5] On the twentieth day in the ninth month, 1611, after examining a "Namban sekai zu byōbu" (Western-style world map screen), Ieyasu put various questions concerning foreign countries to Gotō Shōzaburō Mitsutsugu, who minted coins for the shogunate, and Hasegawa Sahyōe, a Nagasaki magistrate. These men were considered Ieyasu's closest advisers on foreign diplomacy, and at that time Ieyasu was striving to establish a trading route with Spain via Mexico (Nueva España). This incident exemplifies the usefulness to the ruling class of Japanese-produced folding screens with world maps in facilitating trade and foreign policy decisions.

Traces of the effort made by Japanese artists to instill their own creativity into images they adapted from Western models are particularly evident in a work such as *Rō shifu zu* (Portrait of a Reverend, plate 36). The painting clearly depicts a Western cleric, and its source appears to have been an iconic Christian image. But the artist rendered the hands of the man in a mudra configuration of Buddhist imagery. This clear attempt to obscure or disguise the painting's source is a reflection of the prohibitions against Christianity instituted by Japan's rulers in the late sixteenth and early seventeenth centuries. The precise and deft execution of the figure's facial features is exceptional when compared to the folding screens discussed earlier. Even so, the painter's rendering of the hands, for which he would not have had a Western model, is anatomically awkward. The Japanese artist Shiba Kōkan might have referred to this work when he made his oil painting *Kensu oshō zu* (Chinese Buddhist Monk Xianzi, plate 37), an image revered in Zen Buddhism in the late eighteenth century. In Kōkan's painting, the Chinese monk holds a shrimp, an attribute recalling Kensu's daily fishing.

While the former examples were created mainly as didactic aids for learning from Western culture, another type of foreign-inspired Japanese artwork, known as *seiyō fūzoku zu* (Western genre scenes), was contrived solely for the enjoyment

PLATE 36
Japanese, unknown
artist
Rō shifu zu
(Portrait of a
Reverend)
Early 17th century
Ink and color on paper
31 × 14½ in.
(78.7 × 36.8 cm)

PLATE 37
Shiba Kōkan
(Japanese, 1747–1818)
Kensu oshō zu
(Chinese Buddhist
Monk Xianzi)
1781–89 (Tenmei era)
Hanging scroll:
oil on paper
24 × 11 in.
(60.9 × 27.9 cm)

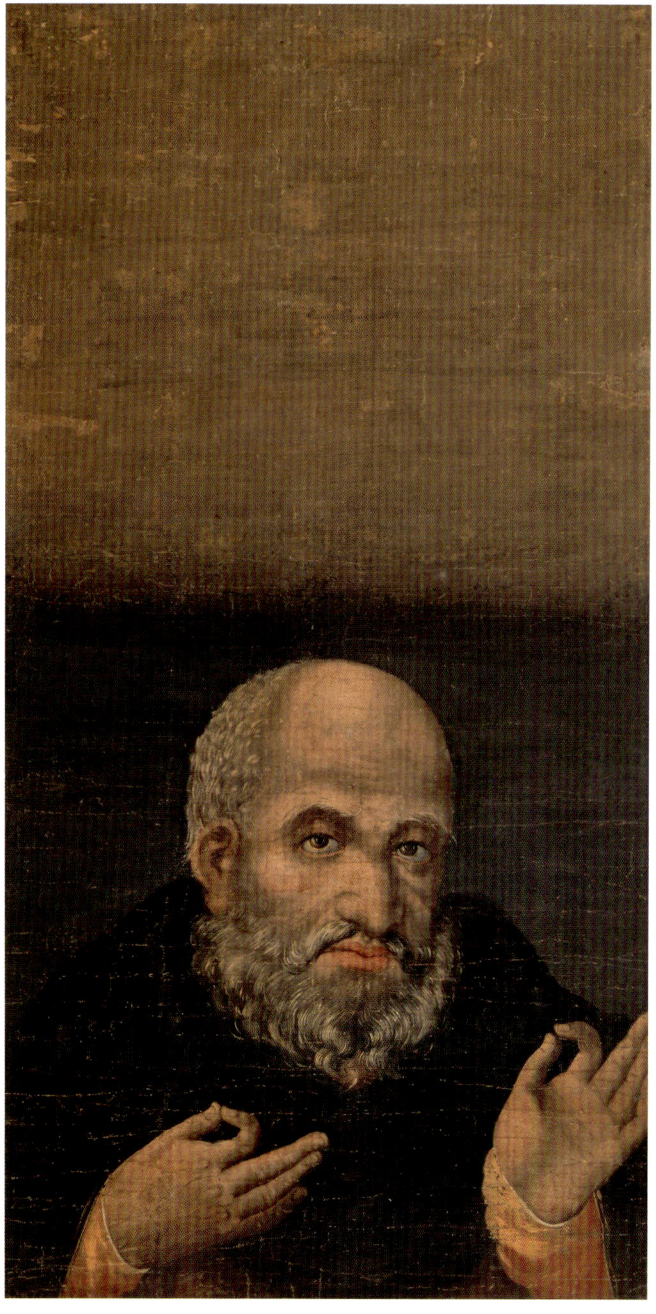

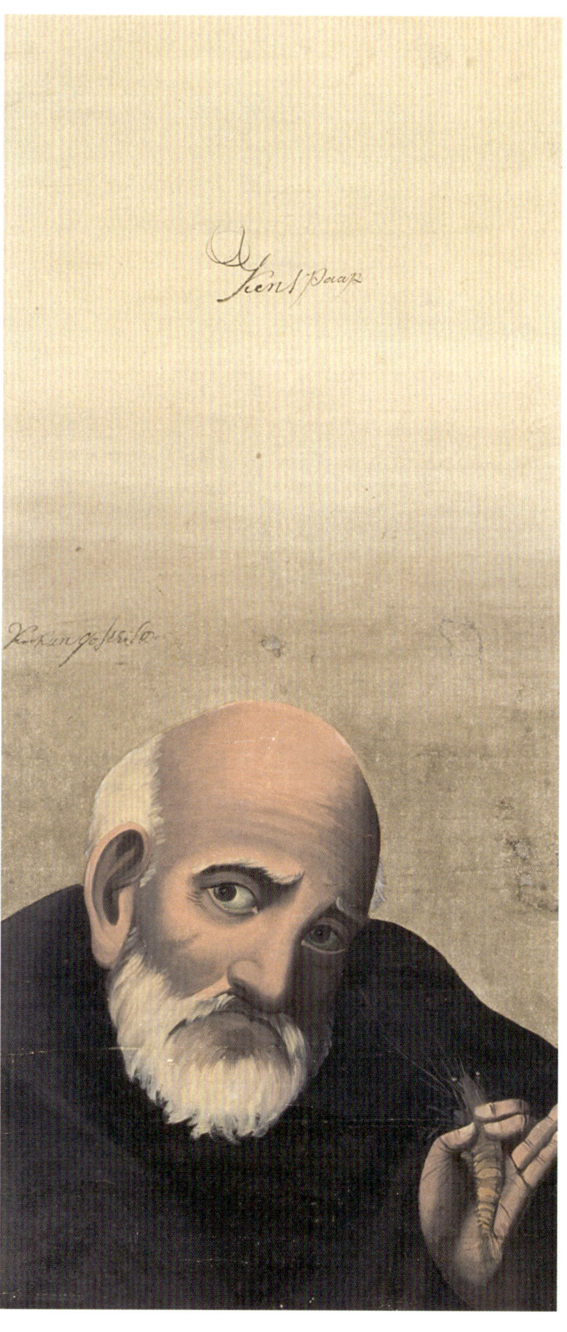

of Western culture. Displayed across the panels of a six-panel screen of this type are a variety of pastoral, contemplative, and genre scenes (plate 38a,b). In this, the work is comparable to contemporaneous genre painting in Japan. This particular pair of screens is commonly known as *Nanbu byōbu* for its provenance via the Nanbu family, the ruling daimyo of Iwate prefecture in northeastern Japan. The screens were discovered in 1882 inside a pagoda at Shōjuji, the temple of the Nanbu family located at Morioka in Iwate prefecture. The depicted figures are European, with the exception of one Japanese woman, whose robes and face are portrayed with the modeling and shading techniques of Western oil painting. This depiction is notable in the development of Western-style painting in Japan because no visual references existed for the rendering of a Japanese figure with these techniques. In this case, the Japanese artist had assimilated Western painting techniques with enough skill that he could apply it to a subject of his own.

PLATE 38a,b
Japanese, unknown artist
Seiyō fūzoku zu
(Western Genre Scenes)
Early 17th century
Pair of six-panel screens: ink and color on paper
46 × 121½ in.
(116.7 × 308.6 cm) each

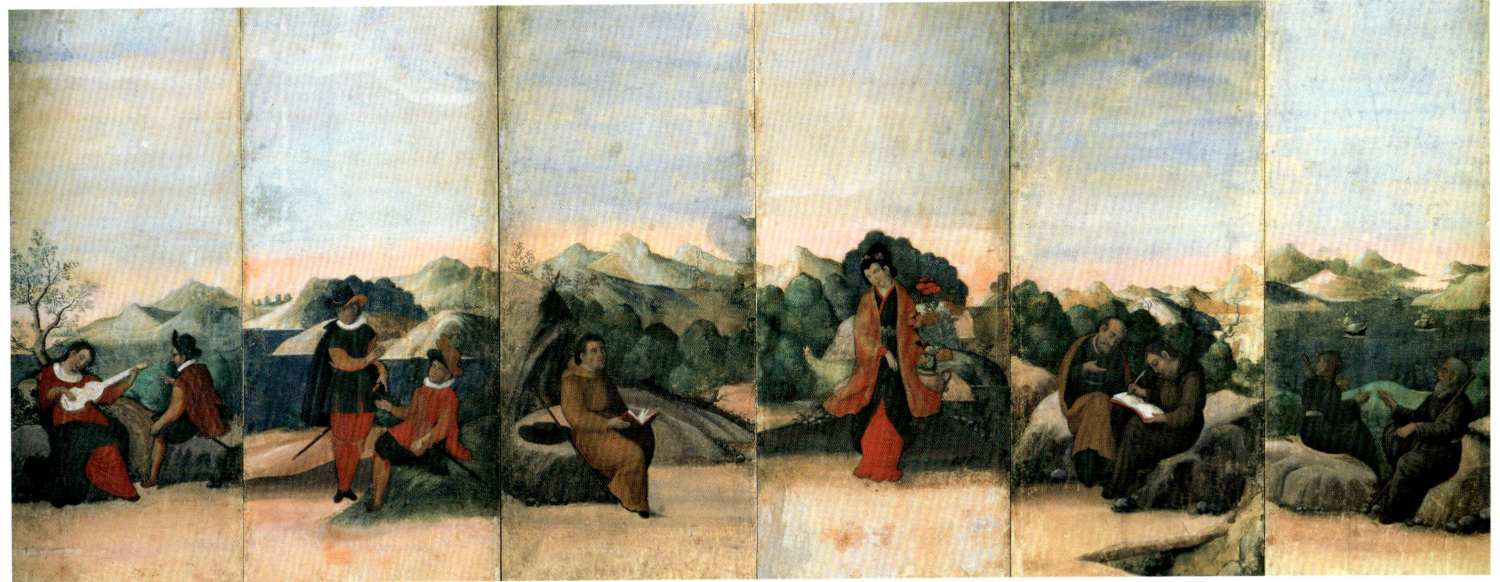

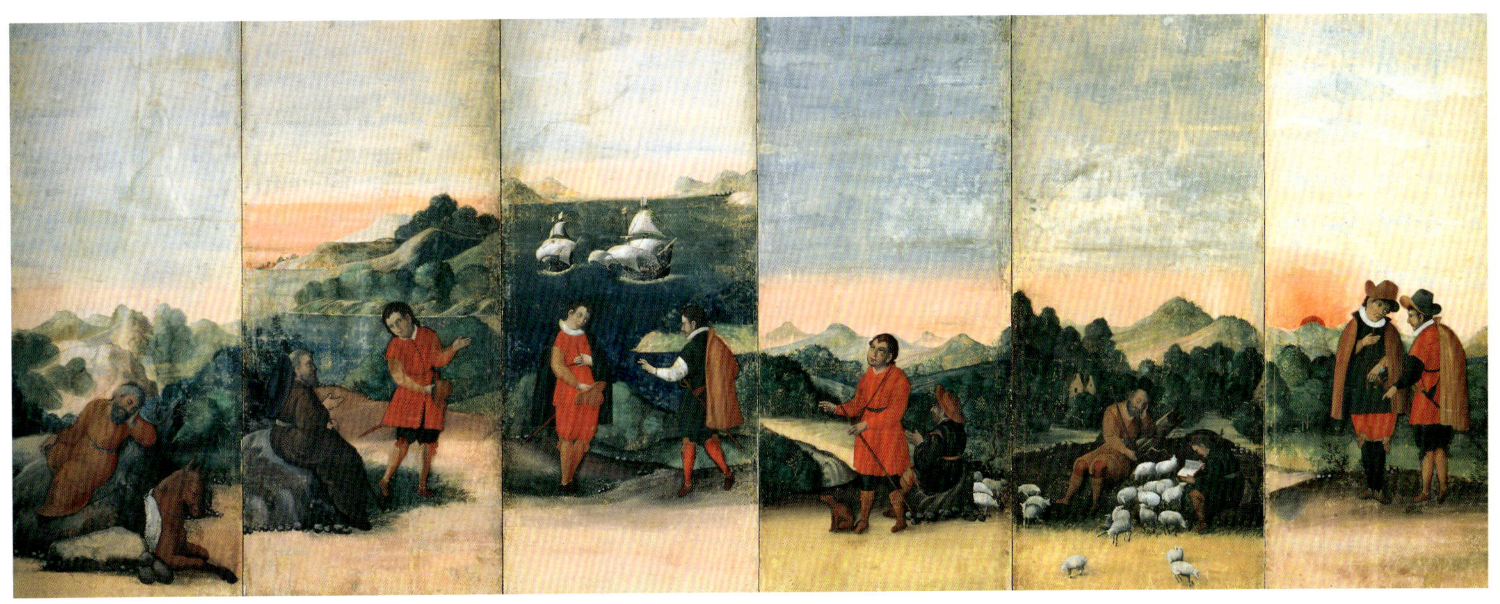

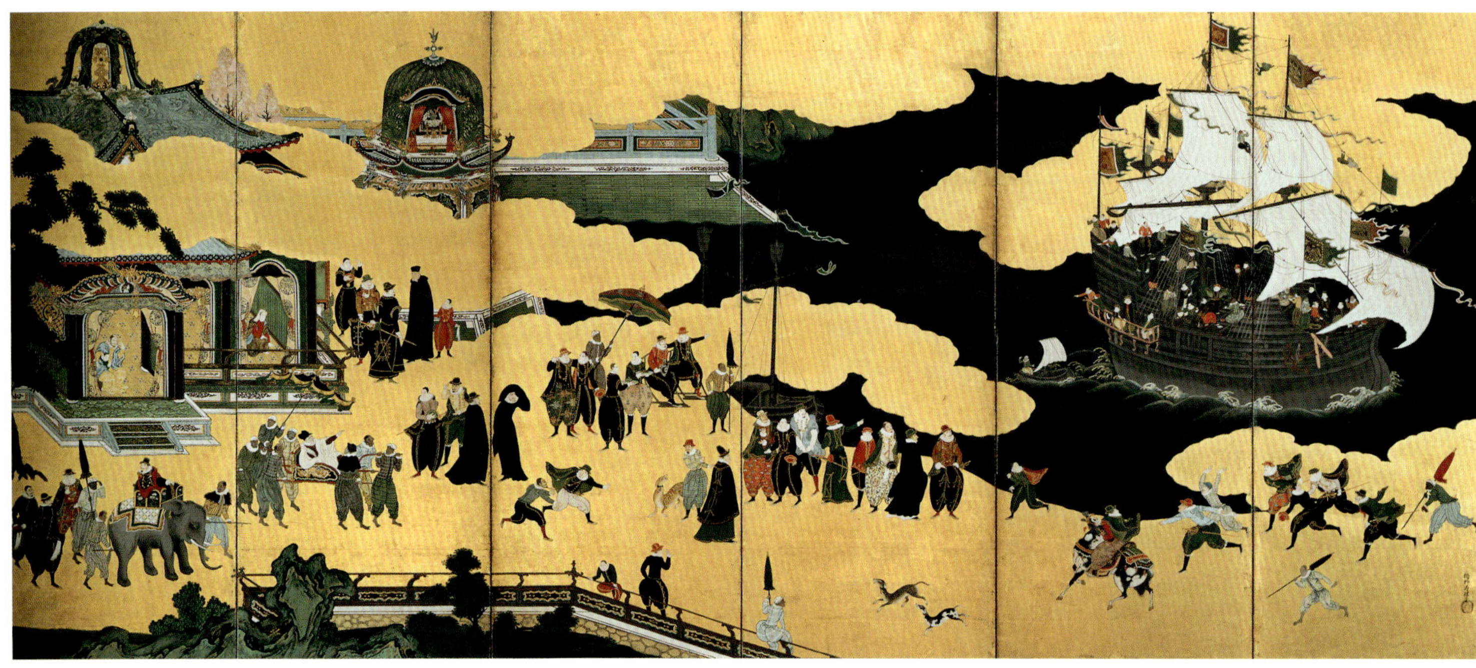

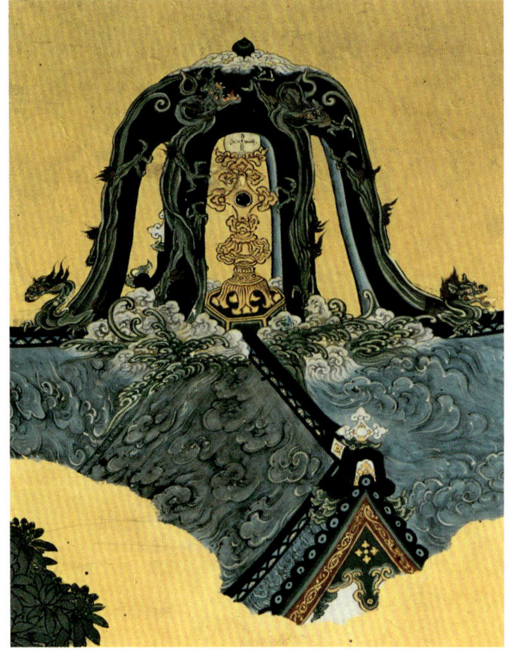

DETAIL
Building rooftop
embellished with
a monstrance
(plate 39a)

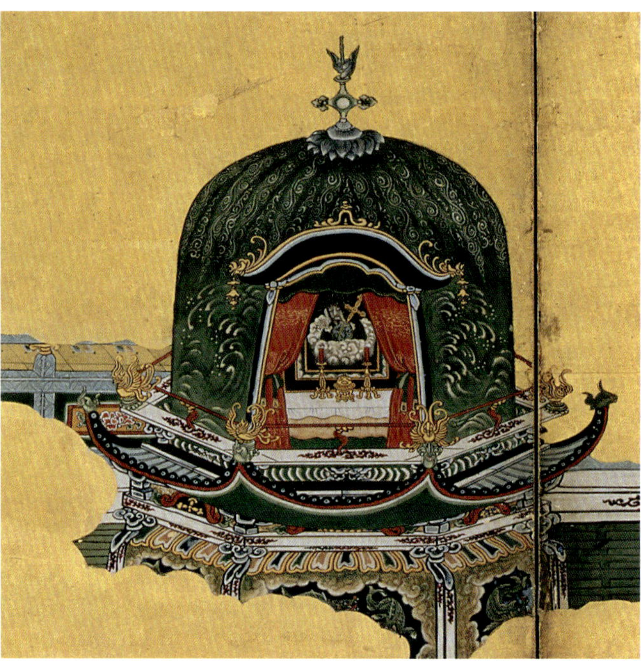

DETAIL
Domed building
with image of Christ
(plate 39a)

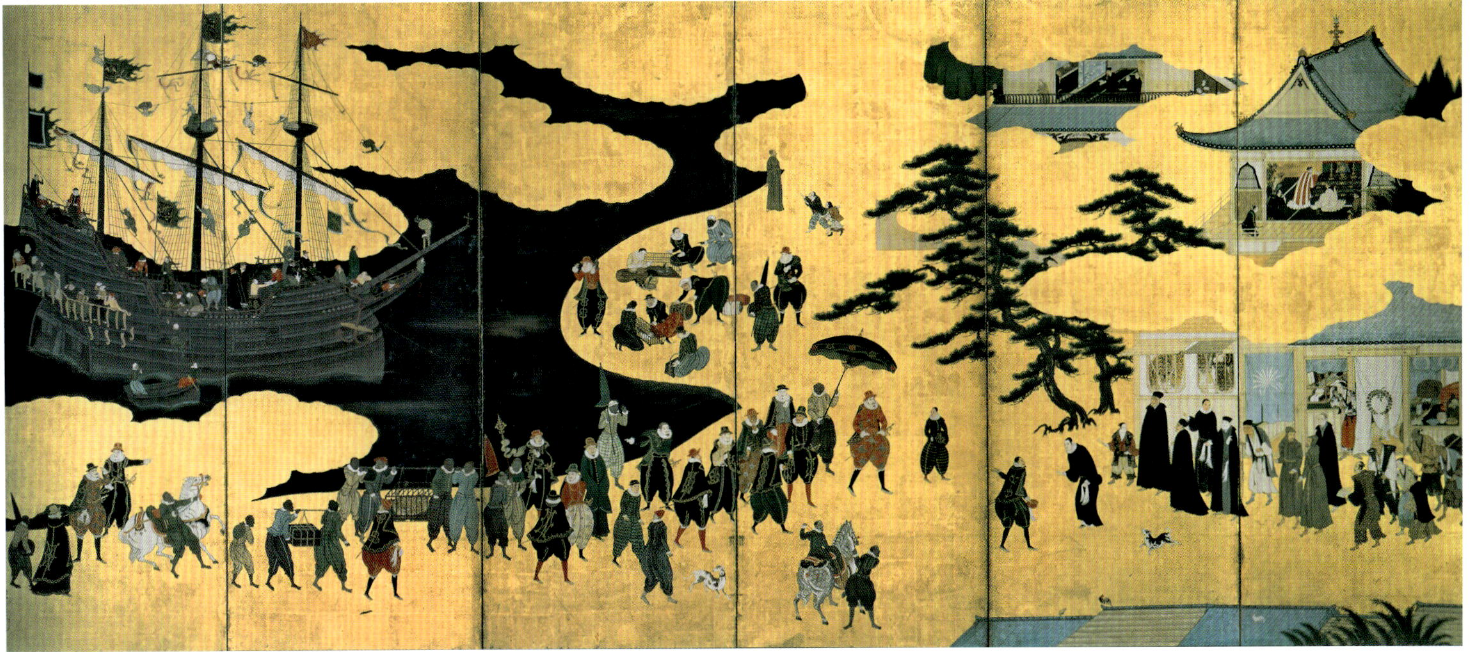

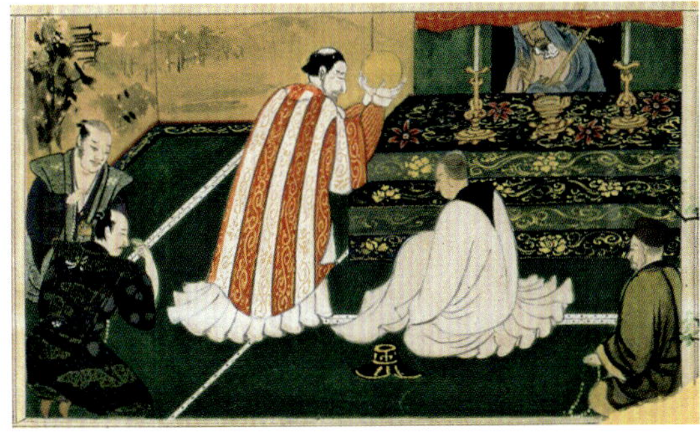

The Kano school artist Kano Naizen (1570–1616) produced a magnificent early pair of *namban* screens depicting two harbors, one foreign and one Japanese, and Western trading ships (plate 39a,b). This combination of foreign and Japanese harbor scenes is typical of early *namban* screens. In the left-hand screen, the ship departs from its Western port; on the right, it arrives at the Japanese harbor. In the departure scene, the artist cleverly employed a cloud pattern for the roof of the Chinese-style building, a device that emphasizes the foreignness of the unknown place.

A profusion of Christian imagery appears in the screens: a domed building on the left screen contains a devotional image of Christ as the Salvator Mundi, and in a building at the upper right of the right screen, a priest raises a golden orb toward a similar image of Christ. A flower pattern in the shape of a cross is seen under the eaves of the main building on the left screen, and the rooftop of the same building is embellished with a monstrance. While abundant, these Christian motifs do not necessarily indicate devotion to the Catholic faith. Such motifs were adopted as much or more for their intrinsic foreignness than for any religious significance.

Visible on these screens are imported greyhounds, hunting dogs that were treasured by Japanese warlords. On the left screen, a courtier rides an Arabian horse, prized for its remarkable ability and strength, especially when compared with the Mongolian horses typical in Japan. These animals were highly desirable prestige objects among the feudal lords struggling for political and social dominance.

At the lower left of the left screen, an elephant carries a nobleman on his back. This could be a sketch from life of the very elephant that was presented by a Spanish delegate in 1597 to the Japanese ruler Toyotomi Hideyoshi (1536–1598). Next to the elephant, a palanquin carries an individual of prominence; the model may have been the gift Hideyoshi received in 1591 from a Portuguese delegate in Kyoto. Historical documents indicate that Hideyoshi regularly used the palanquin throughout his life.[6] The elephant and the palanquin, special offerings that accrued exclusively to Hideyoshi on the basis of his royal authority, are symbols of his status and power, and by extension, this folding screen reflects Hideyoshi's interest and delight in things foreign. Considered in the context of Hideyoshi's invasion of Korea in the late sixteenth century and his ambitions on the continent, this painting might be interpreted as a visualization of his unfulfilled wishes.

A pair of *namban* screens by an unknown artist (plate 40a,b) depicts, on the left, a ritual or ceremony taking place in a foreign landscape and, on the right, a *namban* ship arriving at a Japanese harbor. This composition likely derived from a pair of screens attributed to Kano Sanraku (1559–1635) and in the collection of the Suntory Museum of Art, Tokyo.[7] The patterned rendering of the branches of the pines and the delineation of facial features in the Kobe screens suggest a connection with the Hasegawa School.

The Kobe screens were passed down through generations in a family long associated with the village of Asuka in Nara prefecture. The screens came there from Danzan Jinja, a Shinto shrine located nearby and dedicated to Nakatomi no Kamatari (614–699), founder of the Fujiwara clan. The shrine also placed special emphasis on the worship of the Dragon God. According to legend, a daughter of Kamatari married to a Chinese emperor wanted to dedicate a sacred jewel to her family temple in Japan, but the Dragon God, ruler of the seas, stole the jewel as it was being transported to Japan. It was only through the scheming of Kamatari, with the help of a woman diver, that the jewel was recovered. Murōji, another temple in Nara prefecture, is also associated with the legend of the Dragon God, and a *namban* screen is kept there. The relationship between the Dragon God and the Sacred Jewel legend offers a possible interpretation of these works. This idea will be further developed below.

On the right screen, the *namban* ship has just arrived in Japan, and its sail is lowered. At the stern, sailors amuse themselves by throwing dice and playing a board game. On shore, the head of the Western traders directs the unloading of goods from a smaller boat. A Christian church behind the Japanese buildings (on the second panel from the right), its doors and windows closed, is indicated by just its roof. Four Jesuit priests standing in front of the gate, one of them apparently greeting a trader, provide another allusion to Christianity. This follows a convention in which Japanese artists from the early seventeenth century depicted *namban* "temples" with their interiors hidden. With the prohibition of Christianity in 1612, artists began to eliminate overt Christian motifs from their works.

In the left screen, on a terrace stretching over a manmade canal, Westerners train horses. The walls of a Chinese-style palace building extend across the background, and at the far left,

PLATE 40a,b
Japanese, probably
Hasegawa School artist
Namban byōbu
(*Namban* Screens)
c. 1615–30
Pair of six-panel screens:
ink, color, and gold
on paper
58¾ × 139¼ in.
(149 × 353.3 cm) each

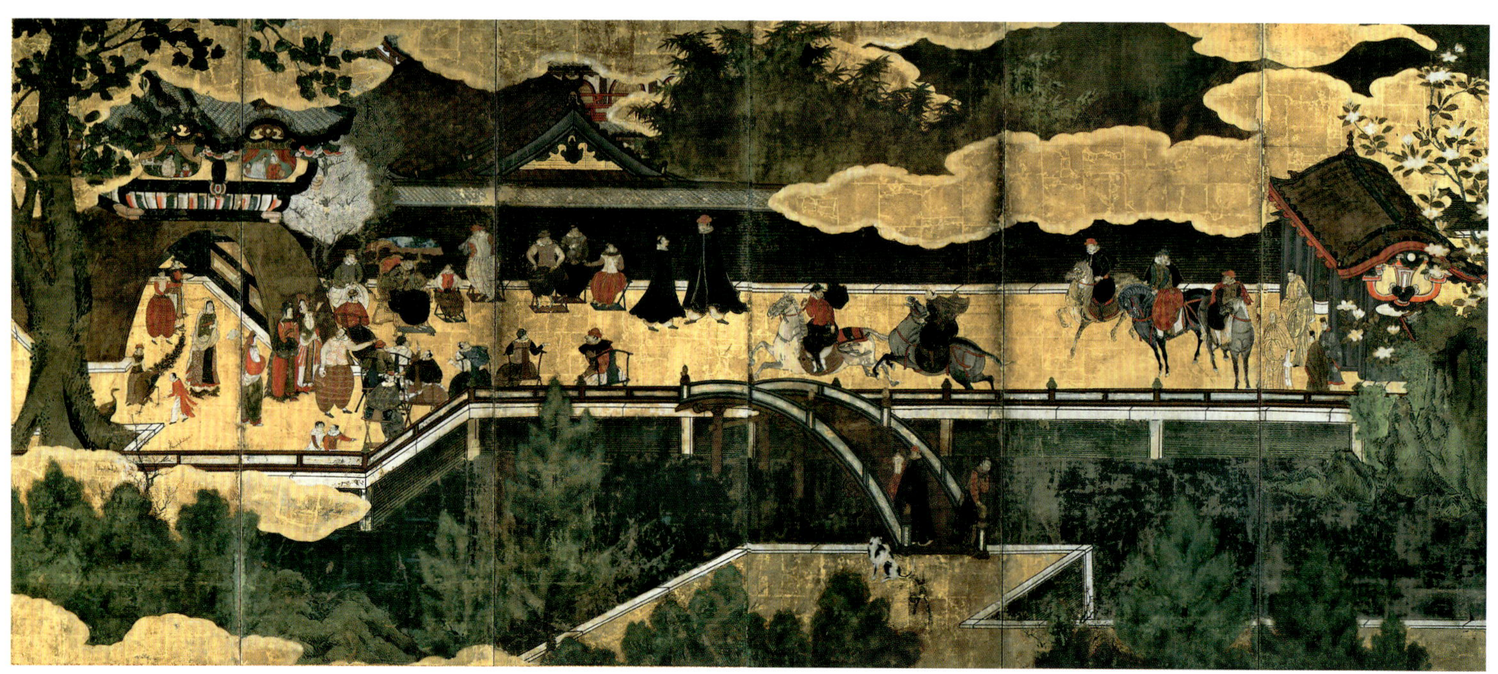

women pass through a tower gate, which is also in the Chinese style. They wear unusual outfits with skirtlike bottoms whose origin is uncertain, whether Chinese, exotic, or completely invented. From the watchtower, foreign women and children of high social class gaze down at the scene below; one of these women (at the far right) holds a golden globe in her lap. Interestingly, the same motif of a woman with a globe in a watchtower can be seen in the similar Suntory screen. Below the watchtower, a group of Westerners is seated on chairs, with one individual occupying the only chair with a sunshade. This man is likely the high captain of the traders or another person of power and position.

The overall meaning and significance of these scenes remain unclear, but they demonstrate the ways in which Japanese artists both adapted Western imagery and invented their own interpretations of foreign cultures and people. An item such as the orb raised by the priest in the Naizen *namban* screen, for example, finds a completely different context in this screen, where the woman holds a similar object on her lap. The Japanese artist recognized the sacred quality of visual symbols such as the orb and the monstrance when they appeared in a Christian context, much like the mirror in Shinto practice has a special symbolism and place. But it must be remembered that seventeenth-century Japanese people regarded *namban* ships as conveyors of riches, and it was natural for them to count the gleaming globe as one such (sacred) treasure. A direct comparison can be drawn to the well-known legend of the Dragon God and the Sacred Jewel, and it was likely through a traditional context such as this that the Japanese comprehended the Christian mission to their shores and its function in the late sixteenth and early seventeenth centuries.

As the *sakoku* policy of isolation instituted by the Tokugawa shogunate in the early seventeenth century took hold and foreigners were banished from Japan, screens featuring commercial and

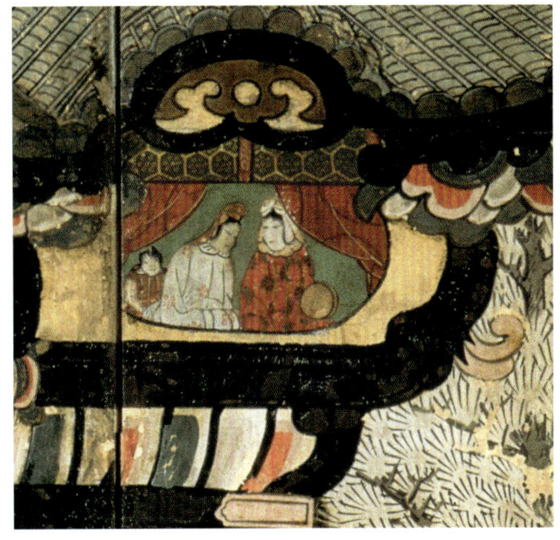

DETAIL
Woman with orb
(plate 40a)

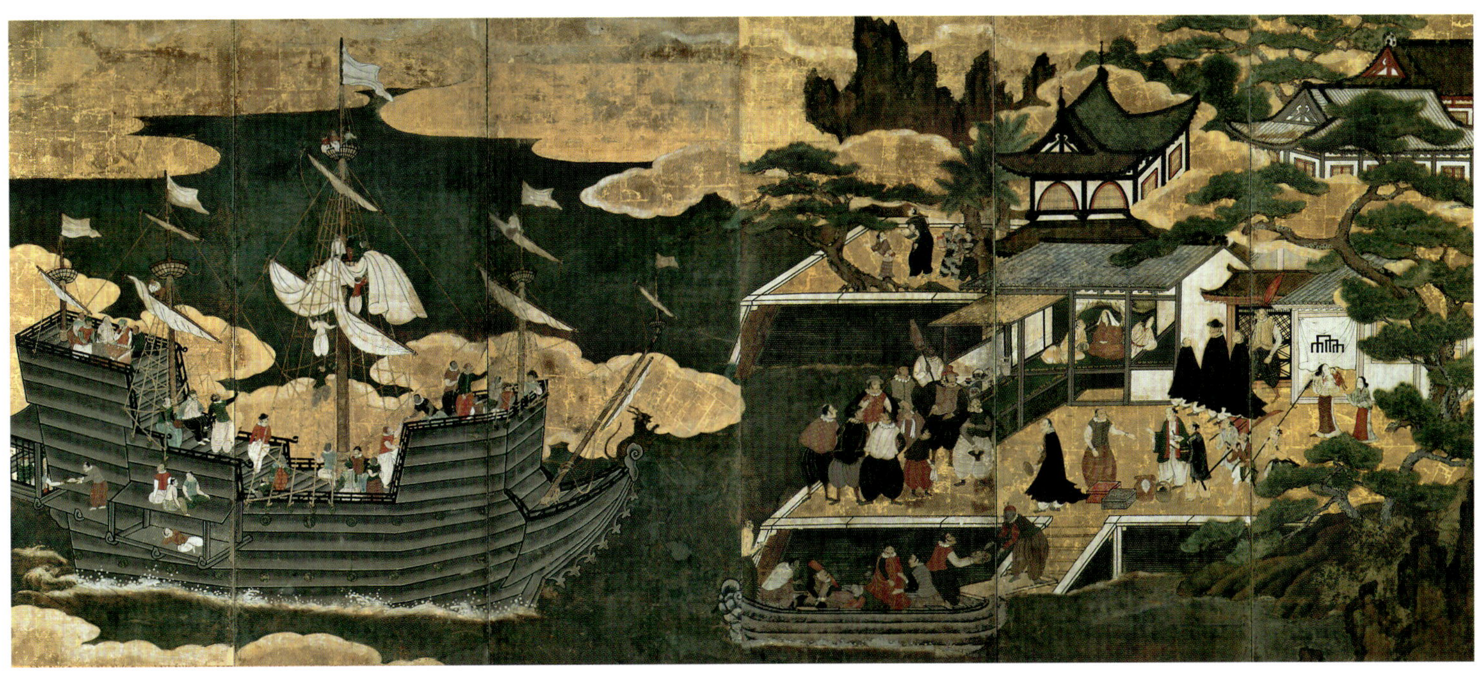

PLATE 41a,b
Japanese, Edo-Kano
School artist
Nambanjin kōeki zu
(Scenes of Trading
with Foreign
Merchants)
Late 18th century
Pair of six-panel screens:
ink and color on paper
56⅛ × 136 in.
(142.3 × 345.4 cm) each

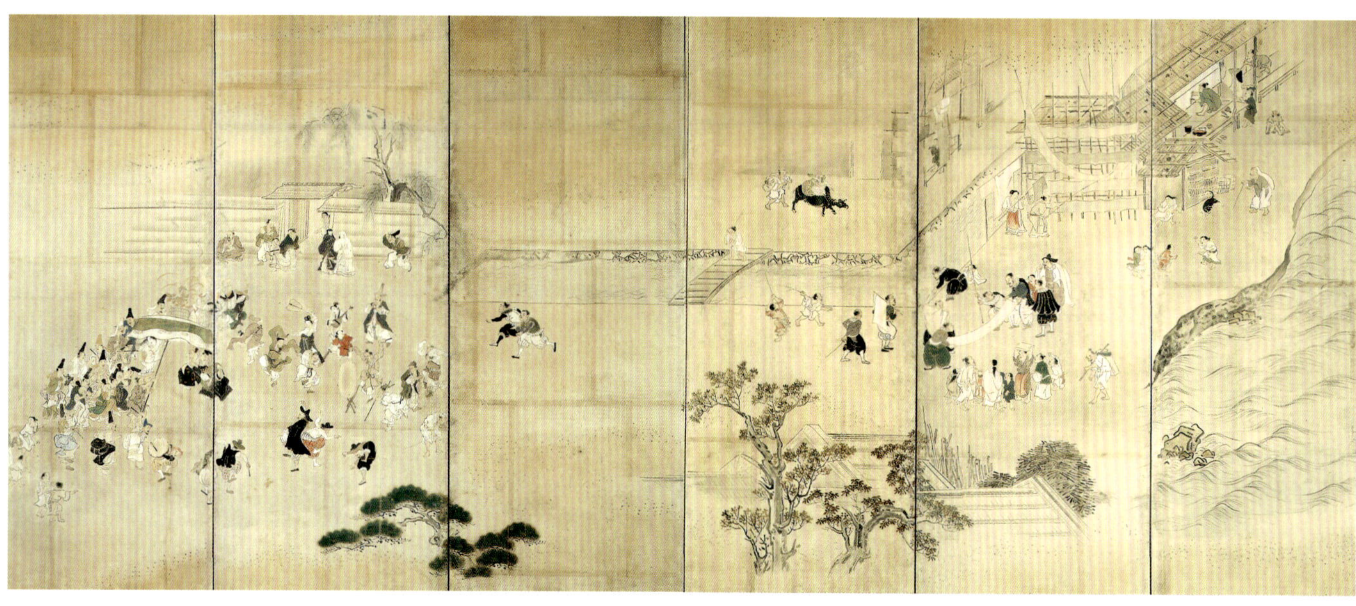

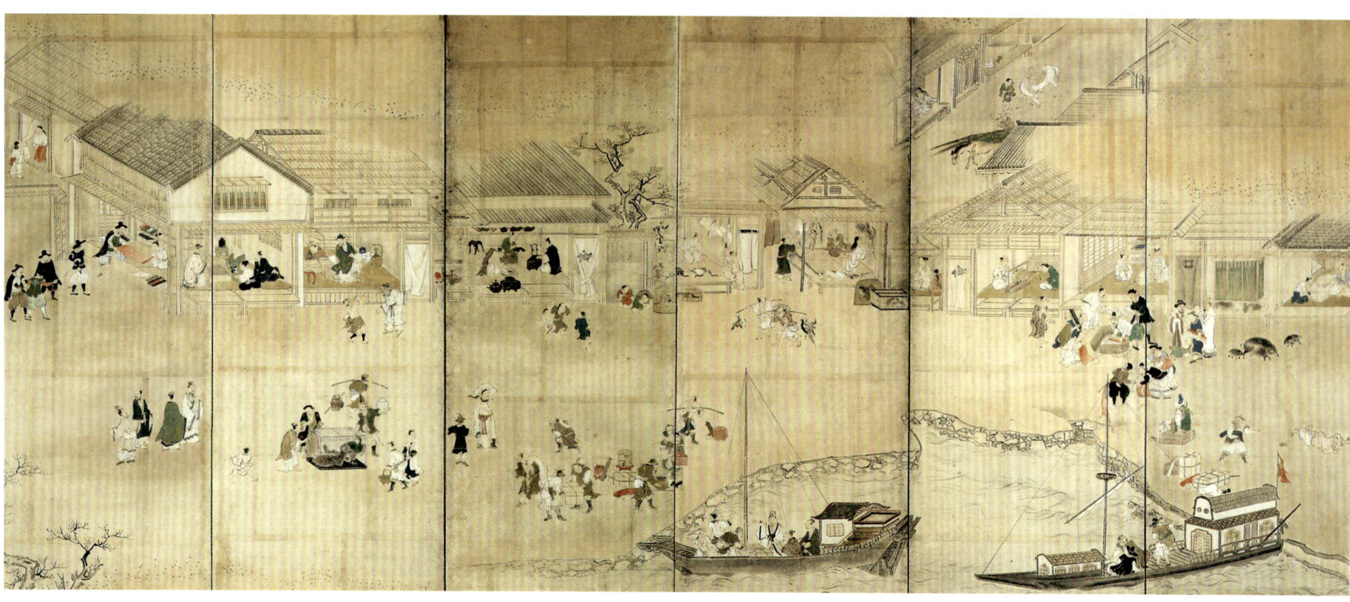

social exchanges with the *namban* traders (known as *nambanjin kōeki zu*) became popular. *Namban* screens of this era portray an idealized and friendly relationship between the people of Japan and Europe without the presence of religious motifs. In one such set of screens (plate 41a,b), the ships are not the black trading vessels that appeared in earlier *namban* images but Chinese-style ships. These lively paintings of commercial and trading activity include images not only of Europeans but also of people from other countries, including China and Mongolia. The artist probably constructed the screens with the special international trading city of Nagasaki in mind, likely basing his representation on hearsay about the new trading center of Dejima, the artificial island in Nagasaki harbor completed in 1636. Dejima was first developed to house Portuguese traders, but once the *sakoku* policy barred foreigners from entering Japanese harbors, it became the official enclave of the Dutch, who were moved there from Hirado in 1641. Operating from Dejima for the next two hundred years, the Dutch acted as Japan's sole trading representative in Europe.

Earlier *namban* screens captured the sense of wonder and curiosity with which the Japanese greeted the foreign cultures of Portugal and Spain. Now, however, there are fewer indications of this wonderment. The screen depicts a row of shops, and it is clear that the foreign ships bring rarities from abroad and take Japanese goods abroad. The theme of this picture is trade, and the export of goods is emphasized. Rather than focusing on foreign cultures and peoples as curiosities, these screens express a wish for good fortune and prosperity in international trading. Screens such as these can be interpreted as lucky charms that held the promise of great fortune in mercantile exchange. With references to Christianity removed and their subject matter transformed, *namban* screens survived in a new form as valued art objects.

NOTES

1. The National Research Institute for Cultural Properties, Tokyo, conducted this analysis in 1983, which was documented by NHK Osaka Television in a program aired January 3, 1984.

2. Van den Keere's 1609 version has not survived.

3. According to a 1955 catalogue published by Ikenaga Hajime, a previous owner of the screens, they had been in the possession of a Spanish nobleman. The screens were returned to Japan by the dealer Tomita Kumasaku, who purchased them in Paris in 1931. Ikenaga acquired them from Tomita in 1932.

4. See Sakamoto Mitsuru, "Namban bijutsu sōmokuroku," *Kokuritsu Rekishi Minzoku Hakubutsukan Kenkyū Hōkoku* 75 (1997): 62, for a reproduction of the source illustration (fol. 12 in the original volume). I would like to thank Matsuda Kiyoshi for providing detailed information about Ribadeneiro's book, a copy of which is held by the Jesuit Historical Institute, Rome.

5. For the *Sunpuki* (History of Tokugawa Ieyasu at Sunpu), see *Shiseki zassan,* vol. 6 (Tokyo: Gunsho Ruijū Kanseikai, 1995).

6. For Hideyoshi and his palanquin, see the correspondence for Luis Frois dated October 1, 1792, in Matsuda Kiichi, ed., *Jūroku/shichi seiki Iezusukai Nihon hōkokushu,* 1–1 (Kyoto: Dōbōsha Shuppan, 1987), 278–79, which translates the 1605 *De Rebus Iaponicis, Indicis, et Peruanis Epistolae Recentiores.*

7. *Namban byōbu* (*Namban* Screens), Important Cultural Property attributed to Kano Sanraku, Momoyama period, 1573–1615, pair of six-panel screens, ink, color, and gold on paper, 72¾ × 148⅜ in. (182 × 371 cm) each, Suntory Museum of Art, Tokyo.

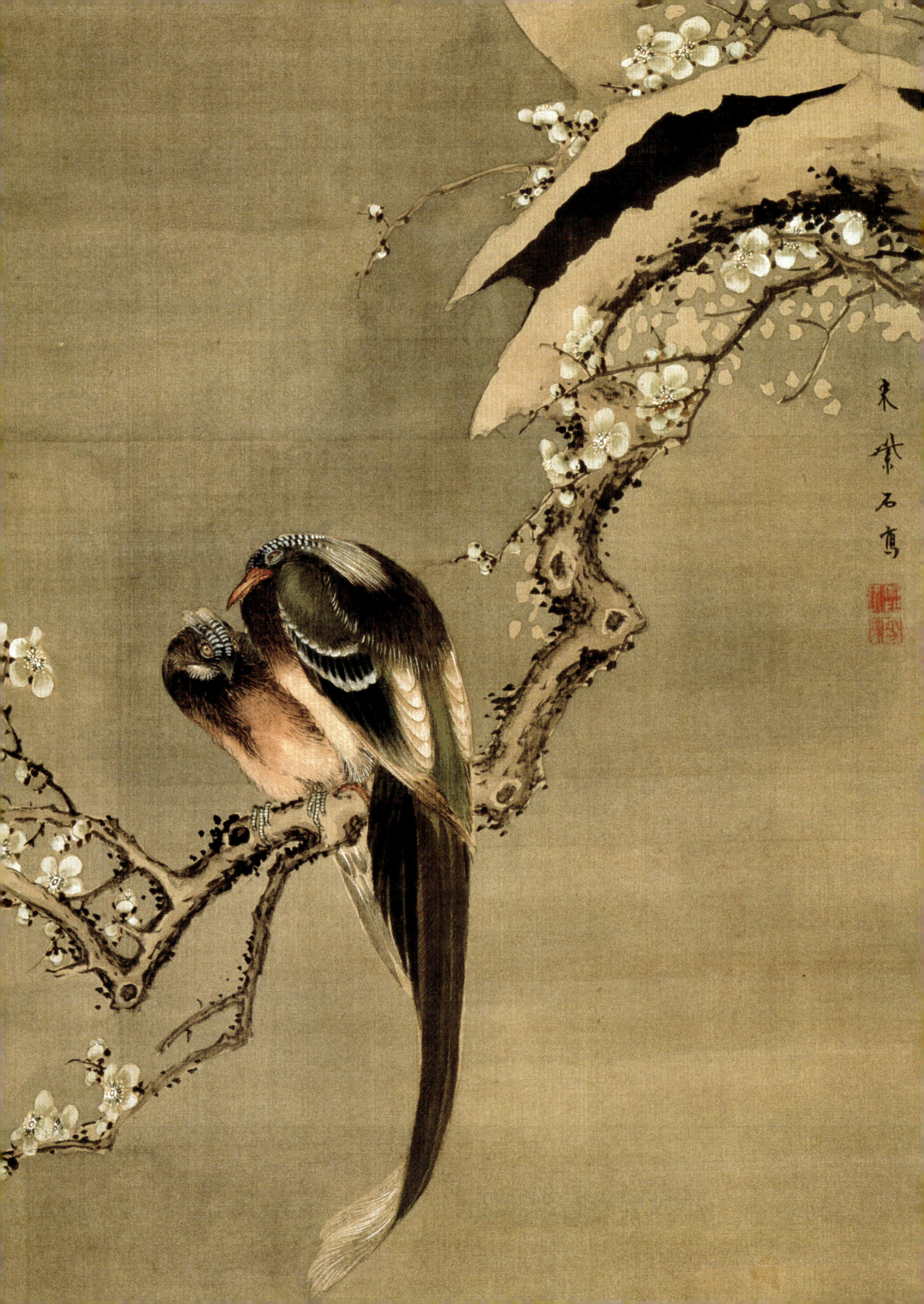

3

Narusawa Katsushi

The Art Scene in and around Nagasaki

A traveler stepping from the express train at Nagasaki's railroad station has reached the end of the line. There is no track leading to further destinations, only Nagasaki harbor and a widening view of the sea. Lingering there, one might recall the words from the 1572 epic poem "Os Lusíadas" by the Portuguese Luís de Camões: "Where the earth ends and the sea begins" (Onde a terra se acaba e o mar começa). This is the great appeal of arriving at Nagasaki by rail, an experience that cannot be matched by flying into its airport, some distance outside the city.

Japanese intellectuals of the Edo period dreamed about reaching Nagasaki with the single-minded intensity of an army of ants aiming toward the taste of sugar. Their desire to experience this place where "the sea begins" was much more acute than that of Camões, who witnessed the Atlantic from Cabo da Roca in Portugal, the westernmost point of the European continent. For the Japanese, who in this era were not allowed to travel abroad, Nagasaki was a pinhole-like oculus connecting them to foreign countries and the border—the sea—that could not be crossed.

In 1570 the Portuguese sought permission from the Japanese to found a port at Nagasaki, which lies at the head of a long, narrow bay. As can be seen in landscape views (plates 42, 43), the geography of the bay was ideal: mountainslopes contain the harbor and form a natural barrier from the waves of the East China Sea. Nagasaki flourished as a port, and by the early seventeenth century, the shogun Tokugawa Ieyasu (1542–1616) was actively promoting foreign trade. A magistrate (*bugyō*) appointed from Edo maintained direct control over the conduct of foreign affairs. After Ieyasu's death, however, Tokugawa foreign policy changed markedly. In 1639 ships from Spain and Portugal, countries that promoted Roman Catholicism, were banned from Japan's harbors, and the shogunate designated the Protestant Dutch as the only Western traders allowed in the country. They, and the Chinese, were permitted to enter Japan only through Nagasaki. At the same time, the shogunate prohibited Japanese citizens from traveling abroad.

PLATE 42
Kawahara Keiga
(Japanese, 1786–?)
Nagasakikō zu
(Nagasaki Harbor)
Early 19th century
Ink and color on silk
22⅛ × 31⅜ in.
(56 × 79.5 cm)

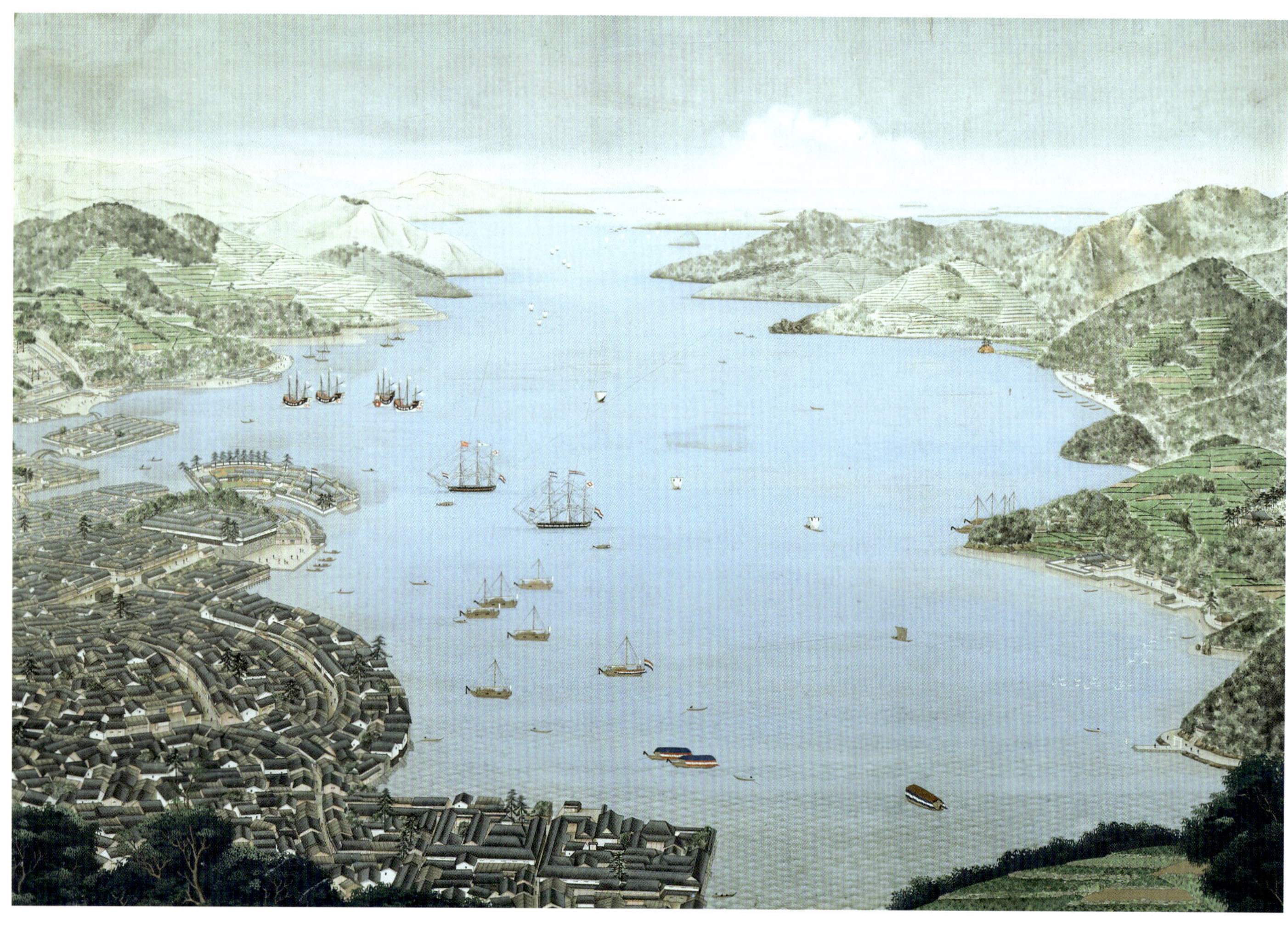

PLATE 43
Japanese, unknown
artist
Nagasakikō zu
(Nagasaki Harbor)
After Ishizaki Yūshi
(Japanese, 1768–1846)
Late 19th century
Hanging scroll: ink
and color on paper
19¼ × 28⅝ in.
(48.8 × 72.5 cm)

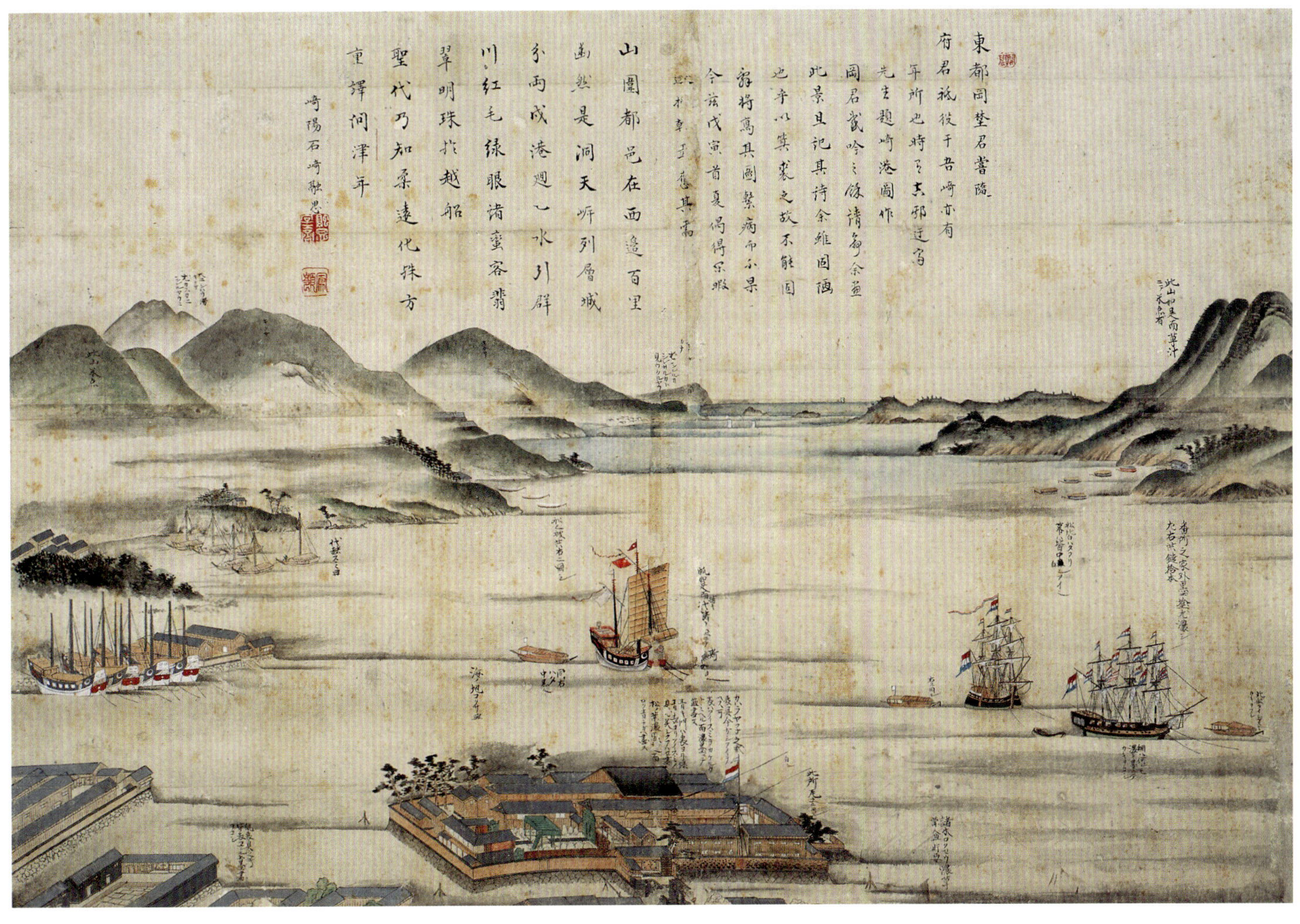

In 1641 the shogunate required the Dutch to move from Hirado to Dejima in Nagasaki harbor. This fan-shaped island of 15,500 square yards, including residences and warehouses, had been created from landfill and was linked to Nagasaki by only a single bridge. From this outpost, a small contingent of Hollanders operated the Japanese headquarters of the Dutch East India Company (Verenigde Oost Indische Compagnie, or VOC). Subjected to surveillance and various restrictions, the Dutch referred to their rented island as their national prison.[1] Dejima had been constructed in 1636 to contain Portuguese traders, and with their expulsion and the installment of the Dutch, the strict regulations concerning residence and interaction with the city of Nagasaki were now applied to the Dutch. Needless to say, the shogunate's purpose was to monopolize and regulate Dutch trading.

Unlike the Dutch, the Chinese were already a familiar presence in Nagasaki. A good number had settled there to avoid the political upheavals of late Ming and early Qing China. They conducted their trading business without restraint in the center of Nagasaki and were free to live where they liked. But in 1688–89 the shogunate extended its control by forcing the Chinese to live in a designated quarter called the *Tōjin yashiki*. The size of the *Tōjin yashiki*—approximately 35,000 square yards of residences only—gives evidence of the extent of the Chinese presence and business interests in Nagasaki.

Dejima and the *Tōjin yashiki* operated almost as foreign countries inside Japan. The Japanese were prohibited from entering either enclave, and the foreigners' access to Japanese areas was strictly regulated. The unique characteristics of the forbidden districts were matters of great curiosity to the Japanese. In 1697 the Nagasaki artist Watanabe Shūseki (1639–1707) was appointed the first *kara-e mekiki* to serve the magistrate at Nagasaki. The term literally means "inspector of Chinese painting," but in practice the *mekiki* inspected any imported paintings. Four families, including the Watanabe, came to assume an inherited lineage for this occupation in Nagasaki. Not only did they evaluate paintings on behalf of the government, they also made copies of them for the official files, almost like a staff photographer would. In this way, a record of unusual imported goods was created whose purpose, in part, was to inform the shogunate of objects it might want to acquire.

The city magistrate in 1699 ordered Shūseki to sketch a picture-map of Dejima and the *Tōjin yashiki*. The handscrolls *Nagasaki rankan zu*/*Nagasaki tōkan zu* (Scenes of Dutch Settlement and Chinese Settlement in Nagasaki) are thought to be a later replica of Shūseki's original sketch. In *Nagasaki rankan zu*, Westerners enjoy a meal, attend a performance of Western music (plate 44), and play badminton and billiards. In *Nagasaki tōkan zu*, we see a Chinese banquet, a performance of Chinese music (plate 45a), a Chinese-style shrine, stands selling alcohol and snacks, and Chinese people

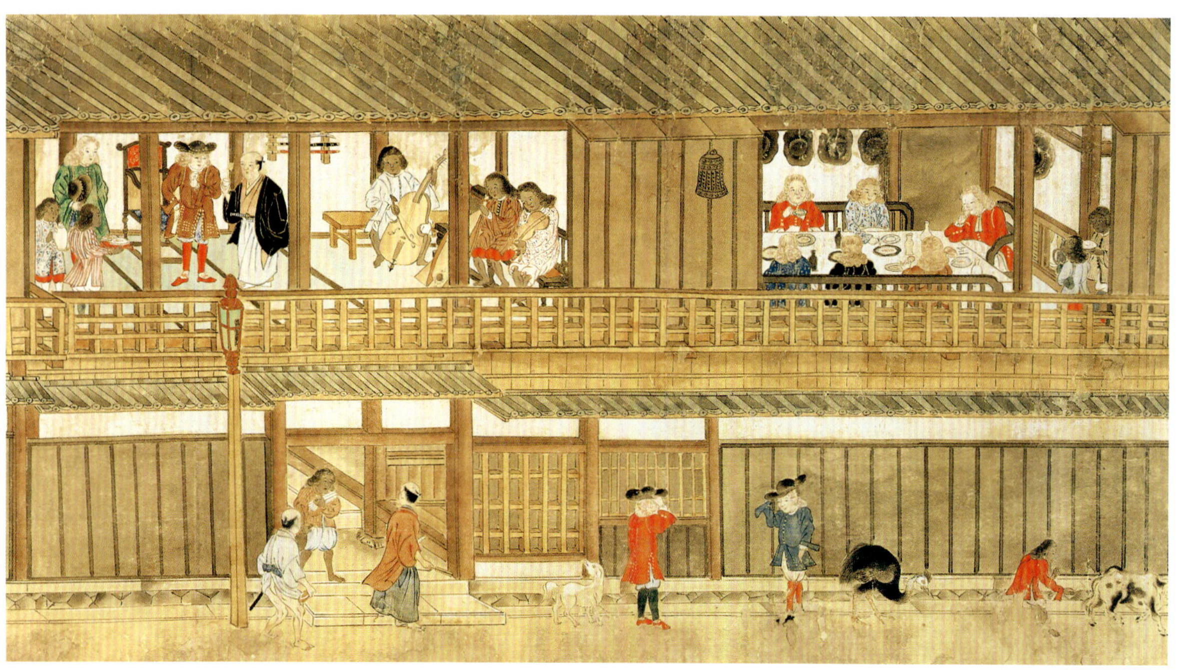

Section of *Nagasaki rankan zu* (Scenes of Dutch Settlement in Nagasaki)
Early 18th century
One of a pair of handscrolls: ink and color on paper
14⅛ × 192¼ in.
(35.8 × 487.7 cm)

PLATE 45a,b
After Watanabe Shūseki
(Japanese, 1639–1707)
**Sections of
*Nagasaki tōkan
zu* (Scenes of
Chinese Settle-
ment in Nagasaki)**
Early 18th century
One of a pair of hand-
scrolls: ink and color
on paper
14⅛ × 157¼ in.
(35.8 × 399.2 cm)

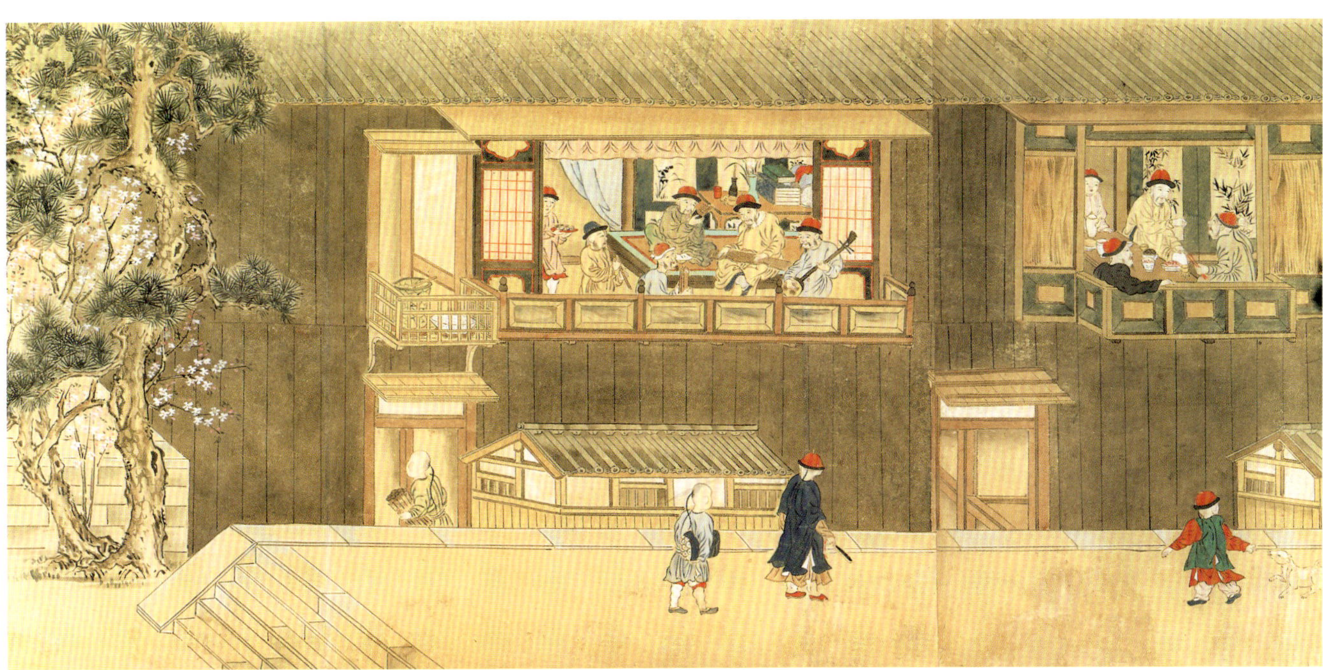

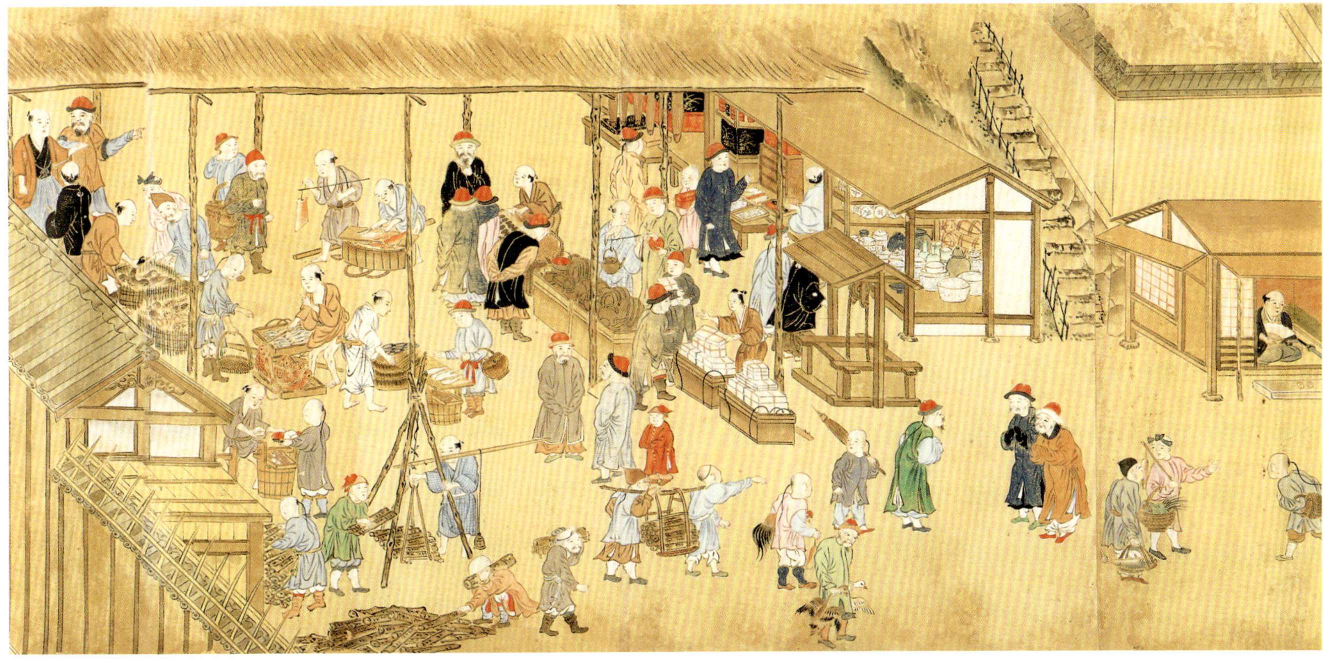

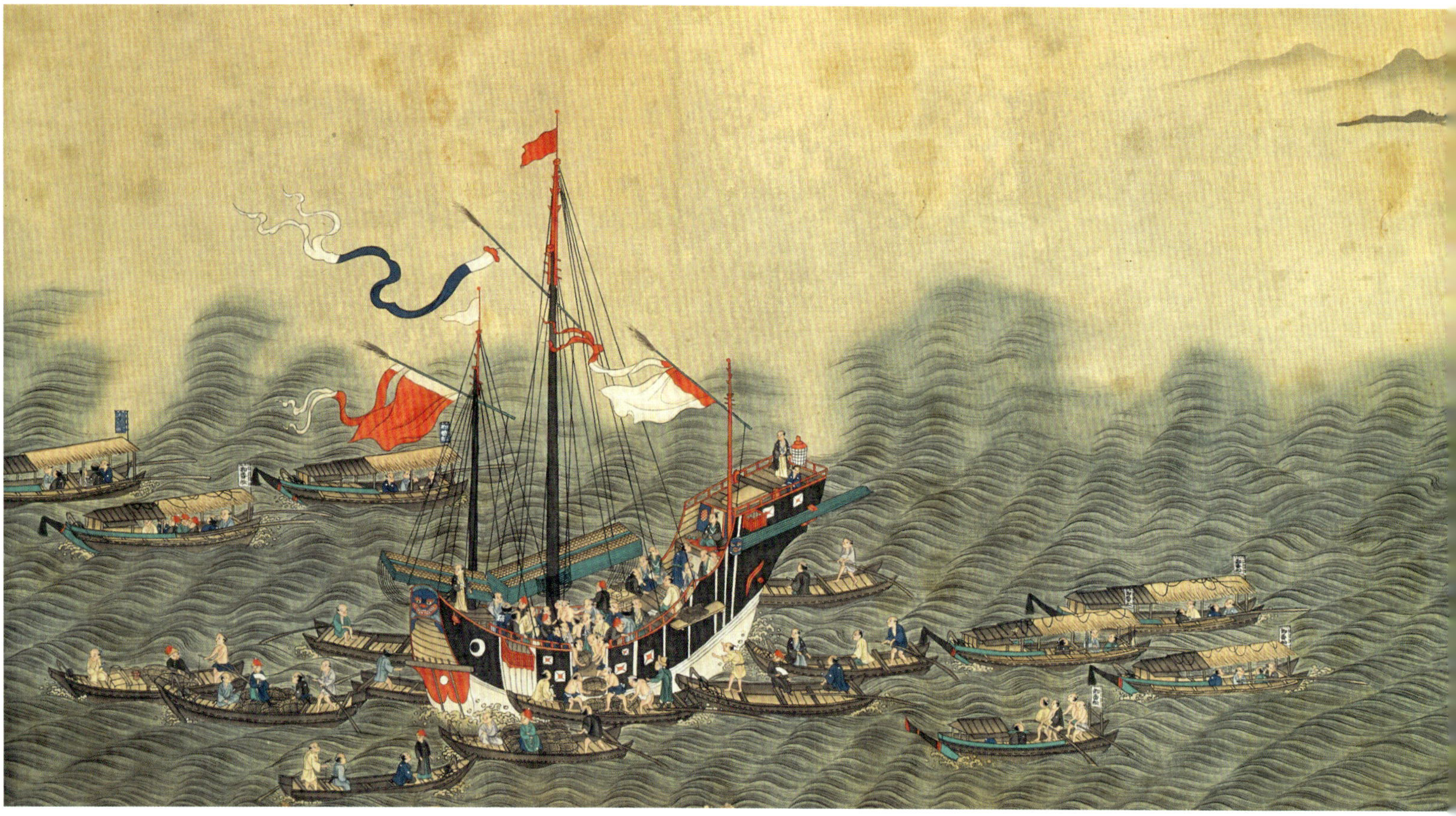

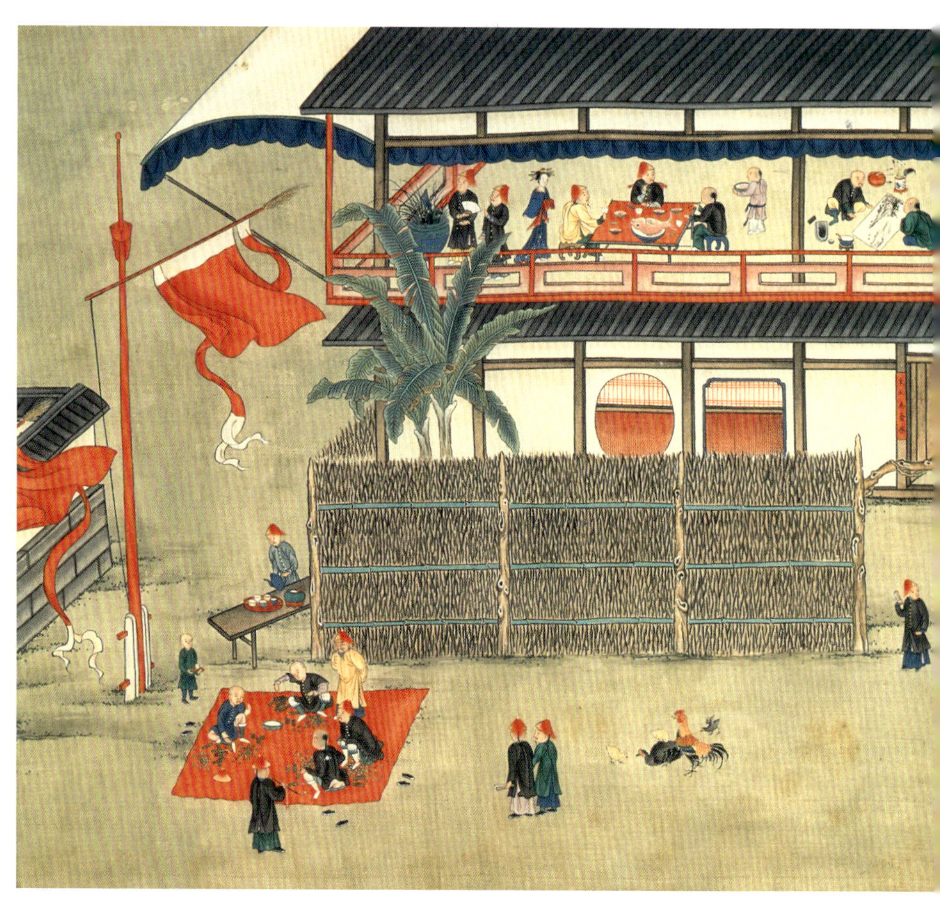

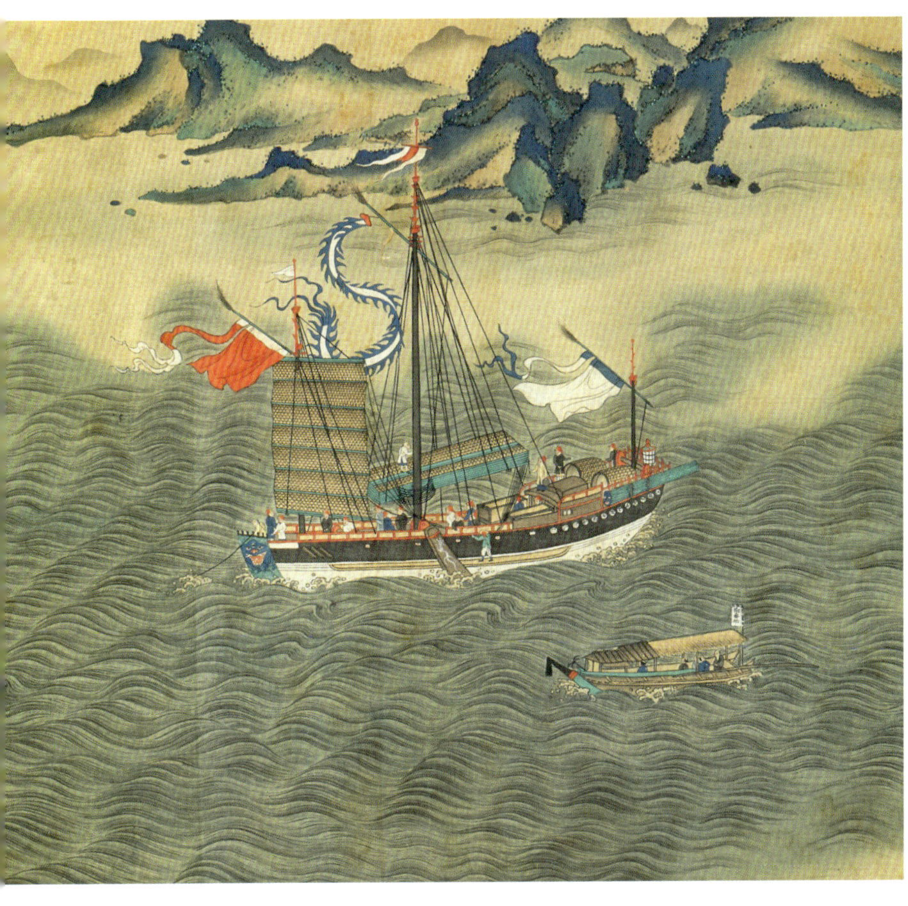

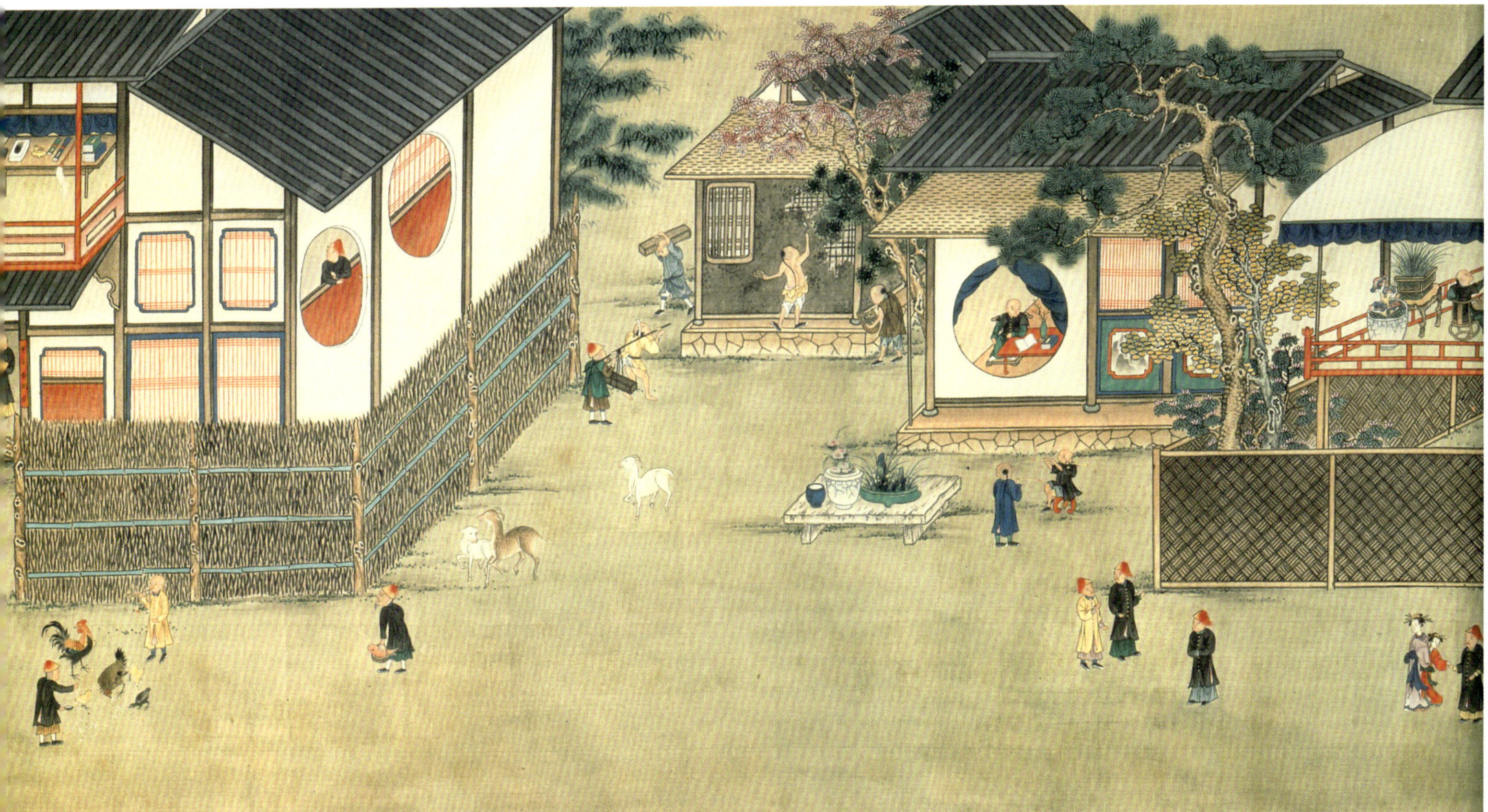

PLATE 46a,b
Watanabe Shūsen
(Japanese, 1736–1824)
**Sections of
*Nagasaki tōkan
kōeki zu* (Nagasaki
Scenes of Trading
with Chinese
Merchants and the
Chinese Settlement)**
Late 18th–early
19th century
Handscroll: ink
and color on silk
14⅜ × 306 in.
(36.4 × 776.9 cm)

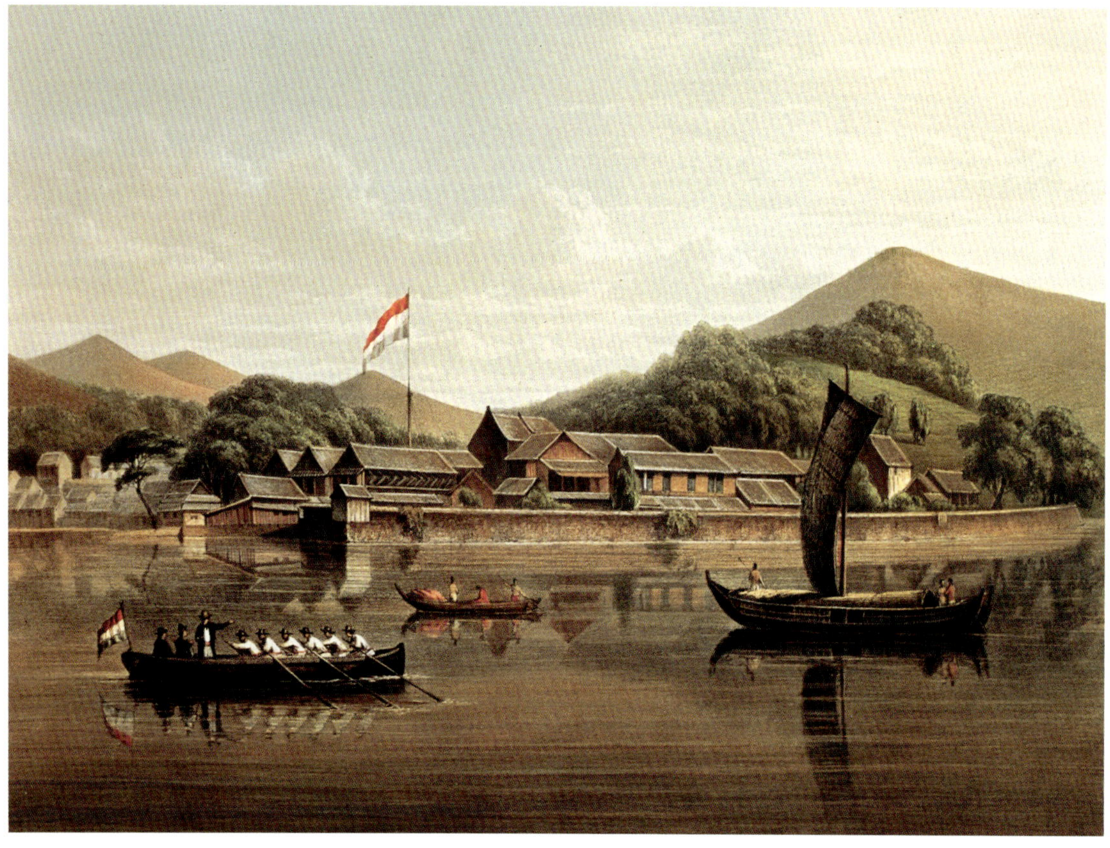

PLATE 47
J. M. van Lijnden
(Dutch, 1807–1864)
Desima (Dejima)
from *Souvenir du Japon*,
The Hague, 1860
Lithograph: ink and
color on paper
21⅜ × 28⅜ in.
(54.2 × 72 cm)

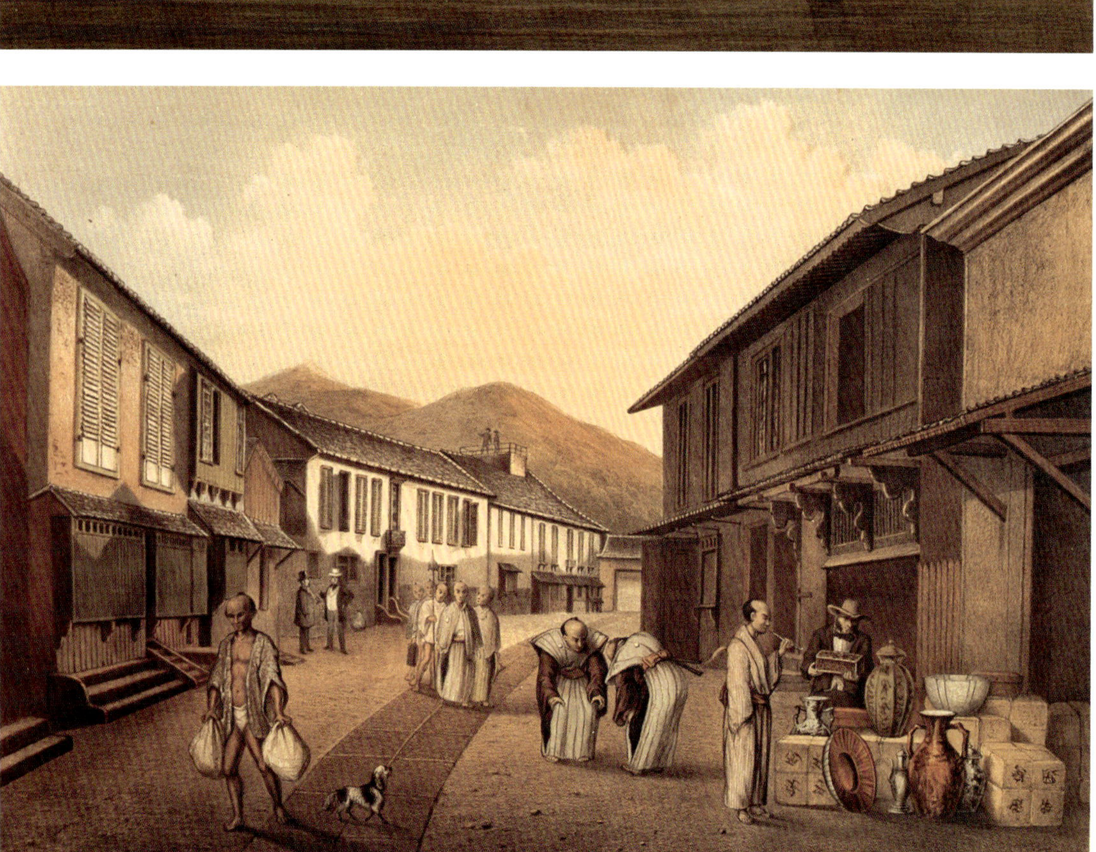

PLATE 48
J. M. van Lijnden
(Dutch, 1807–1864)
Une rue de Desima
(A Street in Dejima)
from *Souvenir du Japon*,
The Hague, 1860
Lithograph: ink and
color on paper
21⅜ × 28⅜ in.
(54.2 × 72 cm)

buying daily necessities and goods from approved Japanese dealers (plate 45b). Early picture-maps primarily illustrated foreign customs observed in the restricted areas, and they were meant to appeal to the curiosity of the ruling class for whom they were made.

As time passed, a new interest emerged in the portrayal of trade itself as well as where and how the foreigners lived. These depictions include foreign ships entering port and being unloaded and inspected. One handscroll with important illustrations is *Nagasaki tōkan kōeki zu* (Nagasaki Scenes of Trading with Chinese Merchants and the Chinese Settlement, plate 46a,b) by Watanabe Shūsen (1736–1824), the sixth descendant of Shūseki. Evidence of the prosperity of the Chinese can be found in this handscroll, for the simple buildings seen in earlier depictions of their settlement have been renovated in a sumptuous Chinese style. Such improvements would have been paid for by the Chinese.[2]

A number of extant landscapes depict Dejima from the perspective of Dutch visitors. When the Japanese portrayed the island, they did so from their natural vantage in the city. But foreigners arriving by sea saw Dejima from the opposite direction, and illustrations intended for Western audiences took this "reverse" viewpoint, as seen in an image from *Souvenir du Japon* by J. M. van Lijnden (plate 47). Van Lijnden, an envoy of the Dutch king Willem III, arrived at Nagasaki in 1855. Another illustration from the same book shows the main street of Dejima and focuses on what for the Dutch was a curiosity: the polite bows exchanged among the Japanese (plate 48).

One of the most exotic items to enter Japan via Nagasaki was the elephant. Records indicate that elephants were imported into Japan on four occasions before the implementation of the *sakoku* policy: in 1408, 1575, 1597, and 1602.[3] Over time, the animals died off, but the Japanese did not forget them. The elephant had appeared in Buddhist art in Japan from the earliest times as a vehicle for the well-known bodhisattva Samantabhadra, and images of the animal remained popular.

In 1728 the elephant returned to Japan. Shogun Tokugawa Yoshimune ordered a pair— one male, one female—brought from Vietnam so that he might assess the suitability of the gigantic animals for waging war. The female got no farther than Nagasaki before dying, but the male

was led to Edo, where it became clear that neither the shogun nor any human could easily manage or communicate with the sensitive beast on a battlefield. The elephant survived in Edo until its death in 1742.

A charming elephant painting (Zō zu, plate 49) is a reminder of a fascinating episode in the shipping trade history of the Far East. In 1795 Napoleon had occupied the Netherlands, which, as the Batavian Republic, became a vassal state of France. The British had reason to fear that every Dutch outpost might now be used to operate fleets against its territories and shipping interests. They ordered blockades of all the Dutch colonies in Asia, and from 1811 until 1816 the British dominated Java, where the Dutch East India Company had its Asian headquarters at Batavia. With their eyes on the Dutch-Japanese trade, the British formulated a plot to dispatch a Dutch crew with pro-British sympathies to Japan with the hope of gaining control of Dejima without disrupting the longstanding relationship between Nagasaki and Batavia. As part of this ruse, the British loaded onto one of the ships an elephant, which the British sympathizers planned to offer to the shogunate. The ships arrived at Nagasaki in the sixth month of 1813. The British had not anticipated the resolve of Hendrik Doeff, director of the Dejima trading post from 1803 to 1817, who firmly refused the British claim to Dejima and in the end turned the ship away. Doeff succeeded in protecting the Dutch flag flying over Dejima—the only place in the world, for the time, where it could be seen.

The intrigue and tension between Doeff and the British sympathizers was not known to the Japanese, for Doeff managed his dealings with them in secret. And the shogunate, having already learned from the 1728 experience, knew the elephant would not suit its purposes and declined the gift. As was the case with all imported objects of interest, sketches of the elephant were drawn by the *kara-e mekiki*; some of these were copied and refined into final versions. We know that several such drawings were made, for in addition to the example by Watanabe Kakushū (1778–1830) in the Kobe City Museum, a more precise version of the same composition is in the Rijksmuseum voor Volkenkunde, Leiden.[4] Kakushū's realistic depiction of the elephant surely would have evoked excitement in Japan about the arrival of the rare animal. But once landed at Dejima and sketched,

PLATE 49
Watanabe Kakushū
(Japanese, 1778–1830)
***Zō zu* (Elephant)**
c. 1813 (Bunka 10)
Hanging scroll:
ink and color on silk
16⅝ × 22¼ in.
(42.2 × 56.5 cm)
■

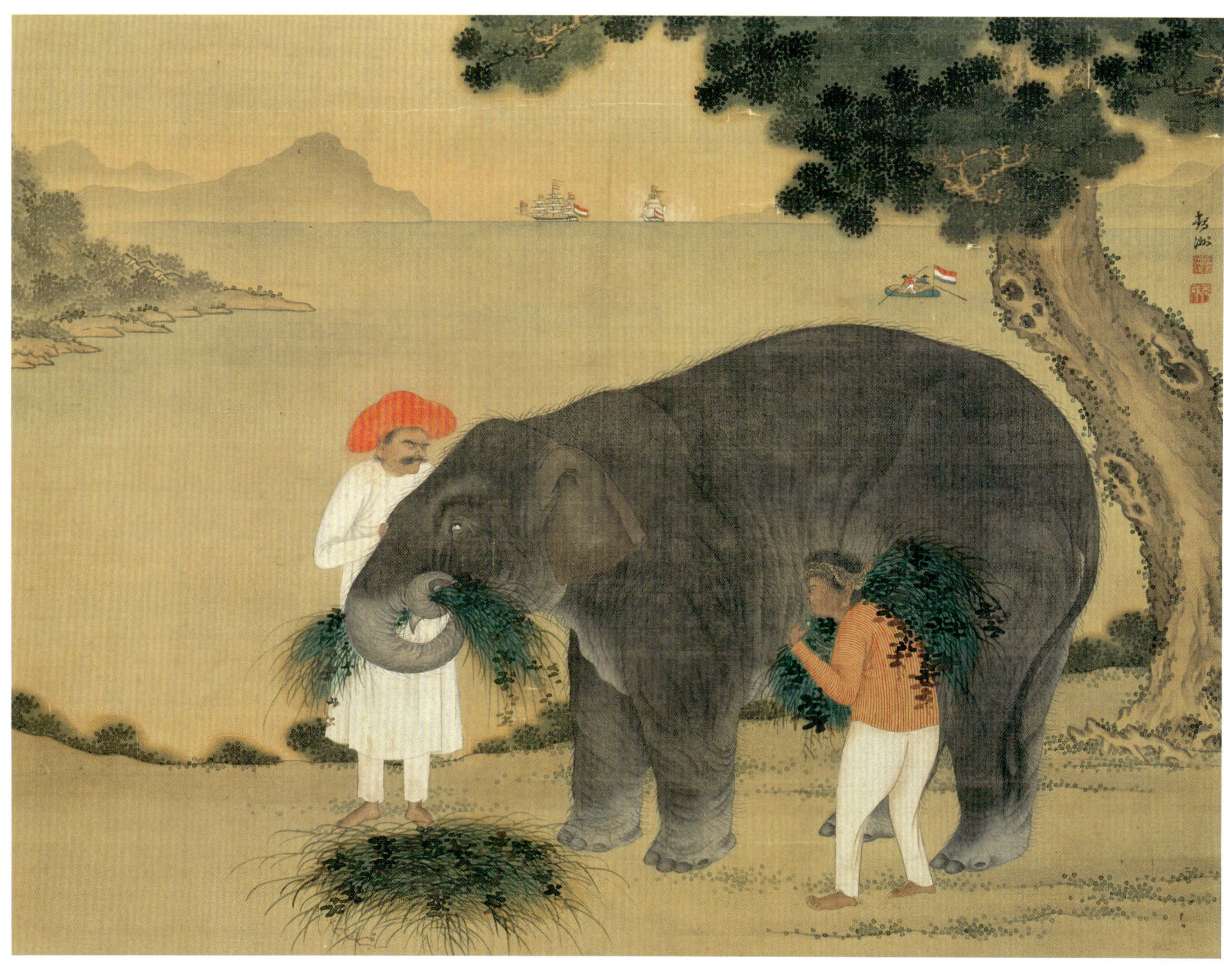

the elephant was returned to the ship, and it, and Britain's ambitions, disappeared.

Besides his directorship of Dejima, Doeff is well regarded for his role in editing the Japanese-Dutch dictionary, the *Doeff Halma*. A miniature portrait of him in his office (*Dwūfu zō*, plate 50) is deftly decorated with a mother-of-pearl inlay on a lacquer ground, a Nagasaki specialty. A Dutch inscription below the portrait image reads: "Hendrik Doeff Junior Opperhoofd van ao 1803 Tot Ao [ ]" (Hendrik Doeff II, Head from 1803 to [ ]). Because the closing date was not supplied, one can assume that the painting was made prior to 1817, the last year of Doeff's service at Dejima.[5] The artist, Kawahara Keiga (1786–?), was the only private painter from Nagasaki permitted access to Dejima.

The Japanese had some preliminary knowledge of the elephant from visual resources from ancient times, but the Western woman was a completely different matter. All Dutch employees at Dejima were men, and only twice, in 1817 and 1825, did any of their wives come to visit. In both instances, the shogunate promptly sent the women back home, much as it had earlier dispatched the elephant, claiming there was no precedent for allowing the traders' wives to land in Japan. In the end, the women, again like the elephant, left only their pictures behind.

In 1817 Jan Cock Blomhoff took over the directorship at Dejima. *Kōmōjin danjo zu [Buronhofu fusai shōyō zu]* (Dutch Couple on a Walk [the Blomhoffs], plate 51) was probably drawn from a painting of the family made when Blomhoff assumed his post (plate 52). The scene of the couple walking arm in arm would have been unfamiliar to the Japanese, who had no custom of expressing personal affection in public. A poem inscribed on the hanging scroll, written by a Chinese resident of the *Tōjin yashiki*, tells of the sorrow of a couple over their separation. The artist of the image, Taguchi Rokoku (?–1872), was the son of Kawahara Keiga, the portraitist of the Blomhoff family and Doeff.

In 1722 Shogun Tokugawa Yoshimune (1684–1751) ordered the Nagasaki magistrate to import Chinese masterpieces painted prior to the Ming Dynasty (1368–1644), and in 1726, he obtained five Dutch masterpieces, including a still life of flowers and birds by Willem Frederick van Royen which is now known only through copies (see fig. 12, p. 101, and plate 61). Chinese traders, however,

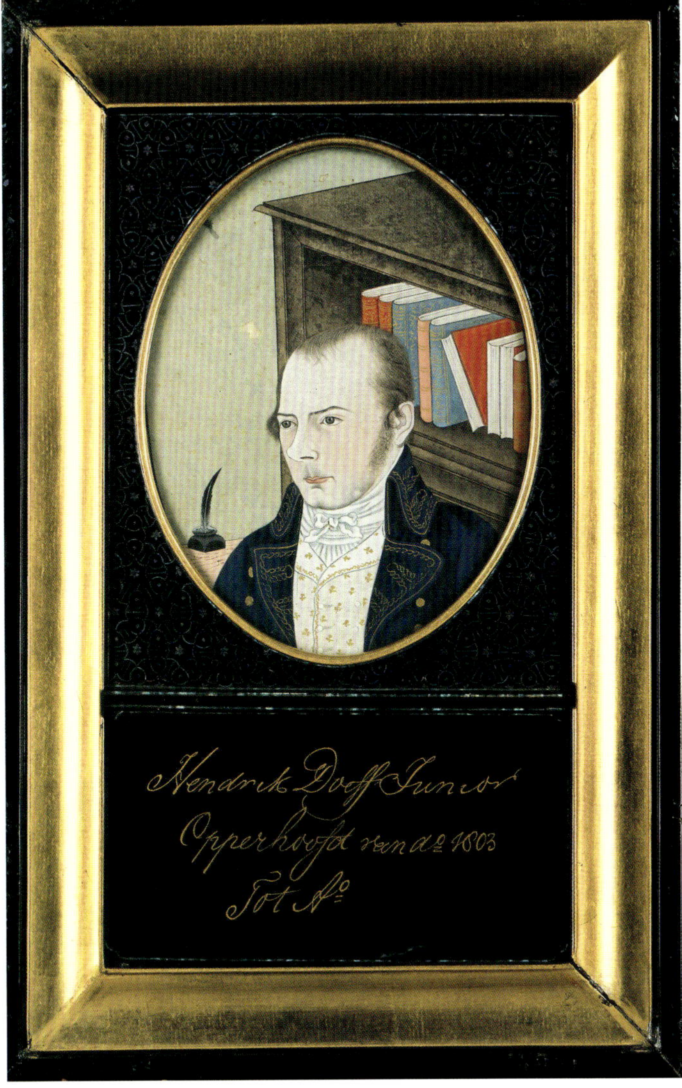

could not readily find any masterpieces for Yoshimune. Making the excuses that ancient paintings were too difficult to locate and too expensive to purchase, they instead presented Shen Nanpin (J.: Shin Nanpin, 1682–?), a professional painter from Zhejiang province in southern China who had a talent for producing works in the style Yoshimune desired. In fact, inscriptions on many of Nanpin's surviving works state the style of the predecessor or dynasty he had followed. Nanpin appears to have been able to satisfy the Japanese taste for painted works in the "old" style.

Nanpin arrived in Nagasaki in the twelfth month of 1731 on a trading ship from Nanjing. His stay was not long; he left Japan in the ninth month of 1733. But for Japanese artists his visit was momentous, for it was rare to see in the flesh a genuine painter from China—a place the Japanese revered for its artistic achievement. They paid close attention to Nanpin's style, and indeed, he greatly influenced Japanese artistic circles from that time.

Nanpin's first influence lay in the realism of his works. His paintings exhibited a style inherited from the bird-and-flower painters who served China's imperial court during the Northern Song Dynasty (960–1126). Extremely detailed and expressive, Nanpin's decorative works seemed hyperrealistic to the Japanese, as though his subjects—birds, flowers, and animals—were alive.

The popularity of Nanpin's innovative style did not reside in the serious, fastidious realism of the West, so famously expressed by Gustave Courbet: "Show me an angel, and I will paint one." At the root of Nanpin's appeal was his hyperrealism—a sense of constructed reality that transcended the real object even while acknowledging this illusion as "beauty." Such subtleties are difficult to verbalize, and a useful example can be found in comparing two works.

The painting known as *Matsu hinode shishi zu* (Lions Playing under a Pine at Sunrise) was made in the early eighteenth century and kept at Sōfukuji in Nagasaki (fig. 11). The unknown artist is thought to have been an early *kara-e mekiki* from the time before Shen Nanpin came to Japan. This image follows a conventional rendering of lions that would have been familiar to most Japanese. Contrasting this customary image is the utterly vivid, nuanced, and powerful *Shizi xi'er tu* (J.: *Shishi giji zu*, Lion and

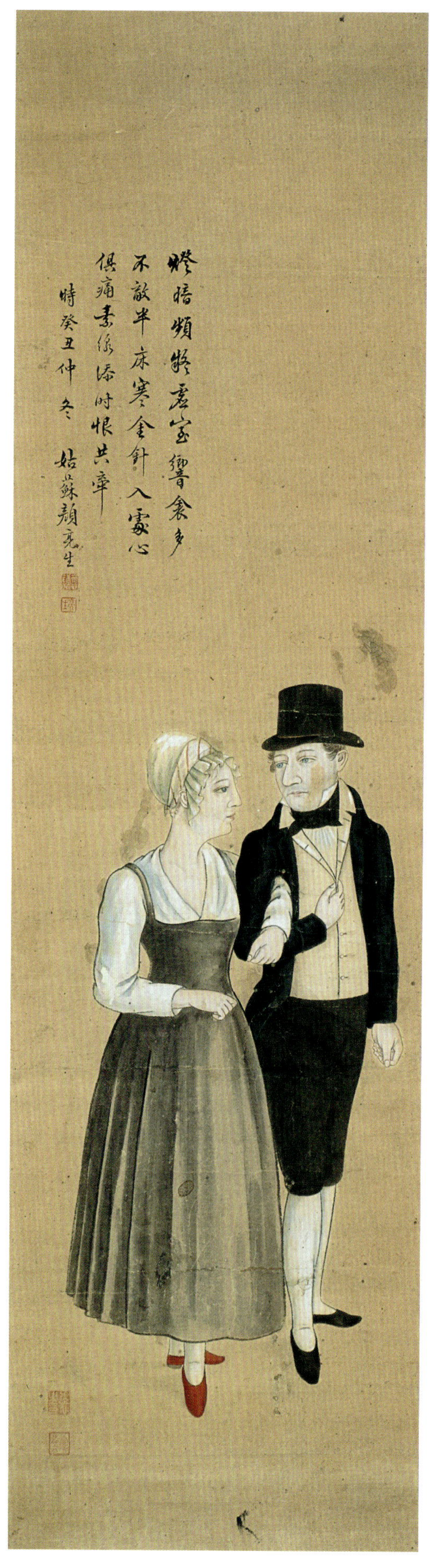

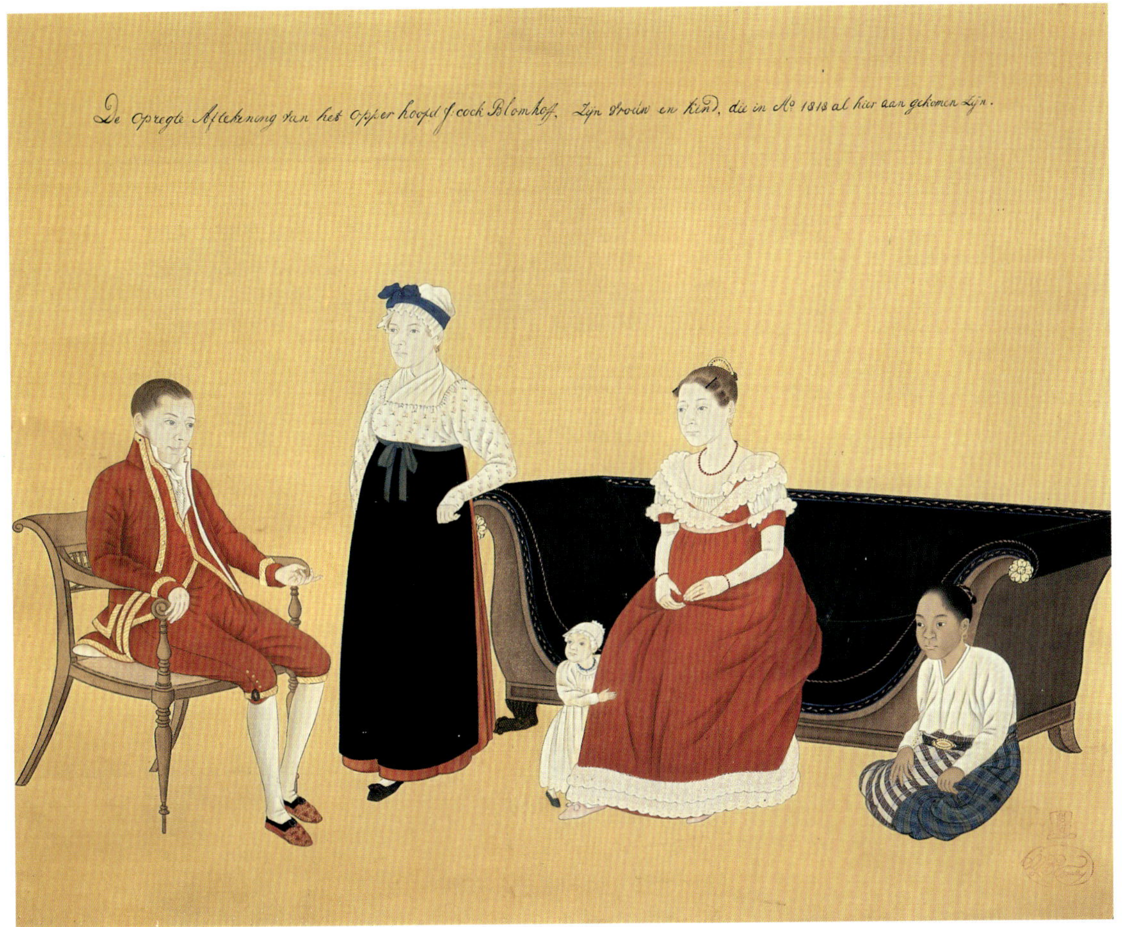

Cubs Playing in a Field, plate 53) by Nanpin. The obvious differences between these two images explain why Nanpin's work so captivated the Japanese. Fantasy in painted imagery had long been appreciated by them, and their aesthetic sensibility prepared them to indulge the illusion found in Nanpin's work as they relished the pleasant shock it induced.

Apparently Yoshimune was satisfied with Nanpin's production. Chinese traders imported twenty-three hanging scrolls by Nanpin at Yoshimune's request after the artist had returned to the continent, and of these, the shogun purchased twelve that employed rich colors.[6] Nanpin continued to receive orders in China from Japan, and many of the paintings he sent to Nagasaki were likely authored by his students.

Liang Ji (J.: Ryō Ki, act. 1774–81), who painted *Changchun fugui tu* (J.: *Chōshun fūki zu*, Peonies and Pot Marigolds as Symbols of Wealth and Longevity, plate 54), was probably one such student. Little is known of him, and he was perhaps a student in the generation after Nanpin. Few of his works remain in Japan, and we do not know whether he ever visited there. Liang Ji executed his paintings in a style softer than that of Nanpin, formulating objects in the *mokkotsu* (boneless) method that deemphasizes line and depicts planes through color.

Another factor contributing to Nanpin's success in Japan was his clever use of motifs that doubled as auspicious metaphors. The Japanese and Chinese could communicate to some degree through writing because they shared many of the same characters, or *kanji*. In ancient times, the Japanese had appropriated certain characters from the Chinese with somewhat similar pronunciations. They created two phonetic syllabaries—*hiragana* and *katakana,* known collectively as *kana*—that were derived from various *kanji*. The combination of *kanji* and *kana* established the basis of the Japanese language. Because *kanji* are ideographic, they carry different meanings depending on context even though particular pronunciations are the same. Nanpin's *Shizi xi'er tu* once again offers an instructive example.

This painting with a parent lion and its cubs might be expressed in *kanji* as 大獅、小獅 (big

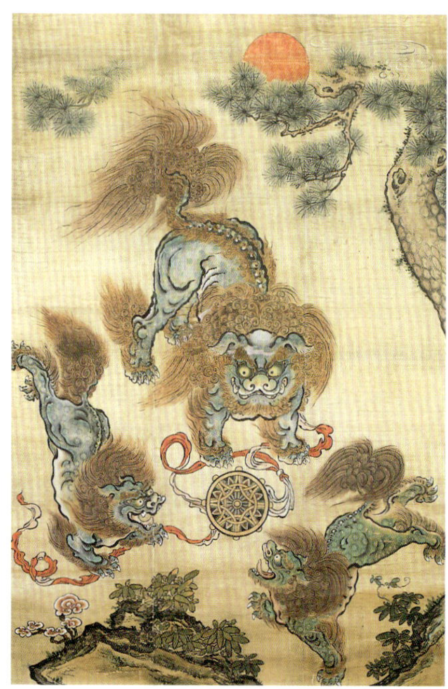

FIG. 11
Japanese, unknown
artist
*Matsu hinode shishi
zu* (Lions Playing
under a Pine
at Sunrise)
Early 18th century
Hanging scroll: ink
and color on silk
99⅛ × 67⅛ in.
(251.7 × 170.5 cm)
Sōfukuji, Nagasaki

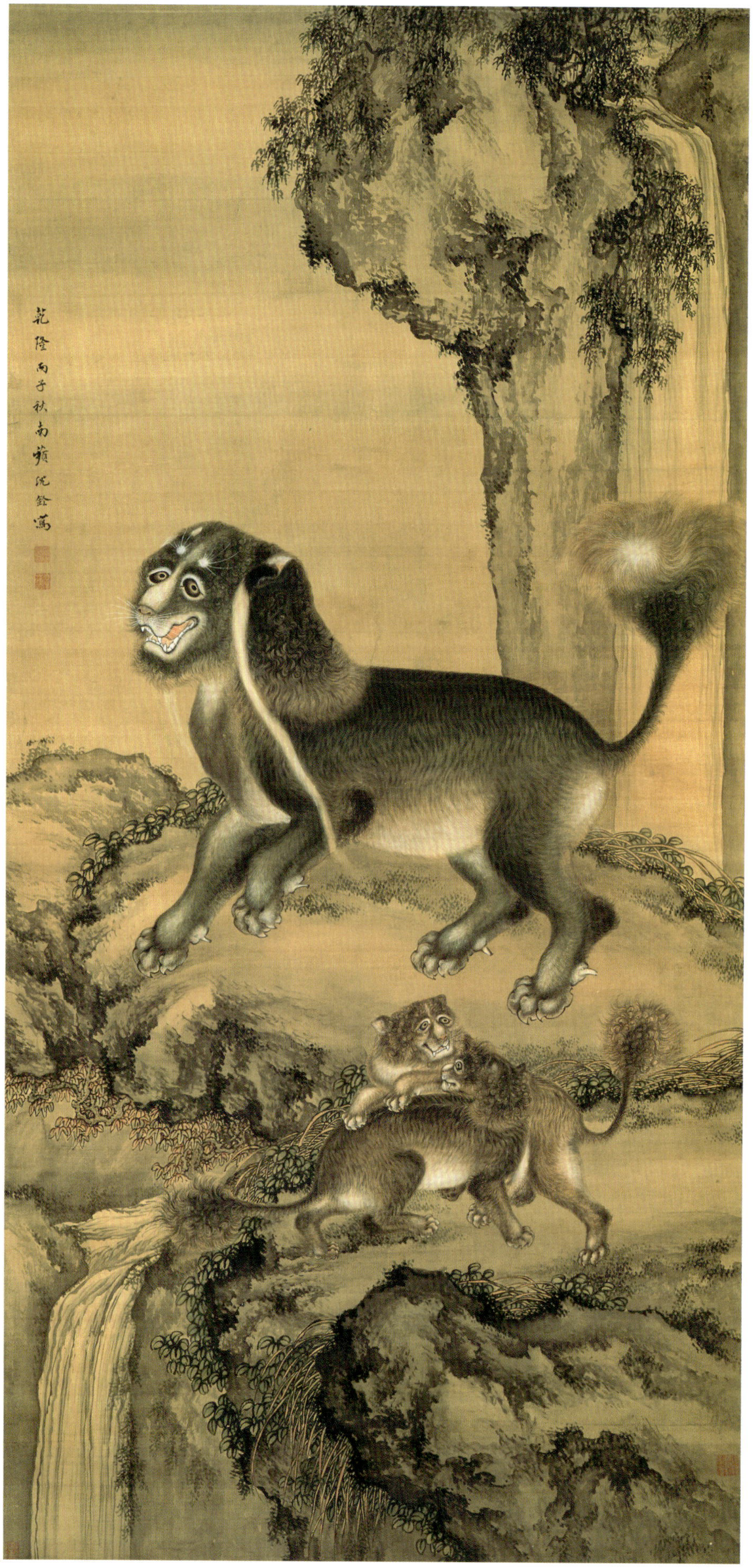

PLATE 53
Shen Nanpin
(Chinese, 1682–?)
Shizi xi'er tu
(J.: *Shishi giji zu;*
Lion and Cubs
Playing in a Field)
1756 (Qianlong 21)
Hanging scroll: ink
and color on silk
77¼ × 38⅛ in.
(196 × 96.6 cm)

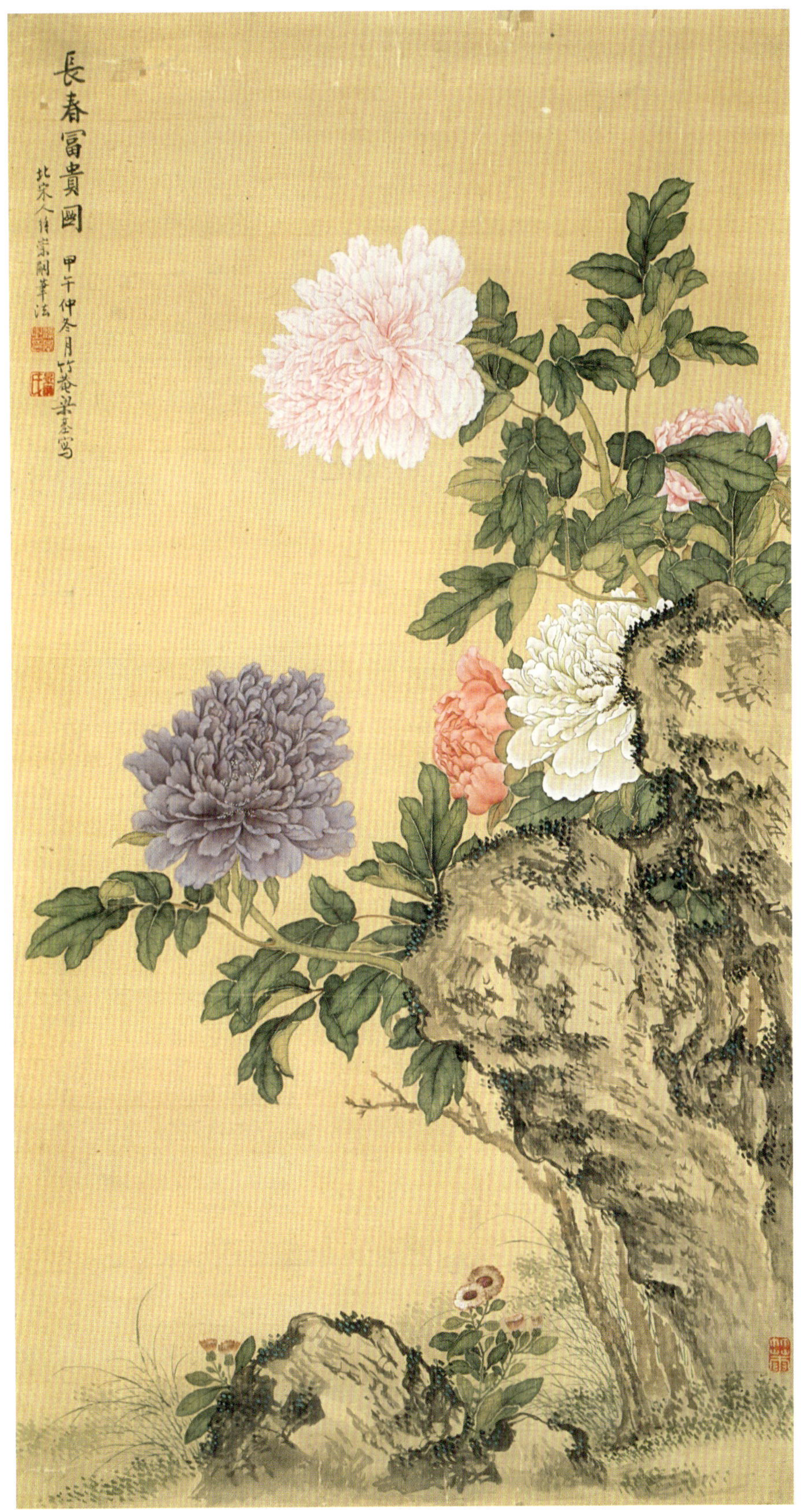

PLATE 54
Liang Ji
(Chinese, act. 1774–81)
Changchun fugui tu
(J.: *Chōshun fūki zu*,
Peonies and Pot
Marigolds as
Symbols of Wealth
and Longevity)
1774 (Qianlong 39/
An'ei 3)
Hanging scroll: ink
and color on silk
36⅛ × 19¾ in.
(91.6 × 50 cm)

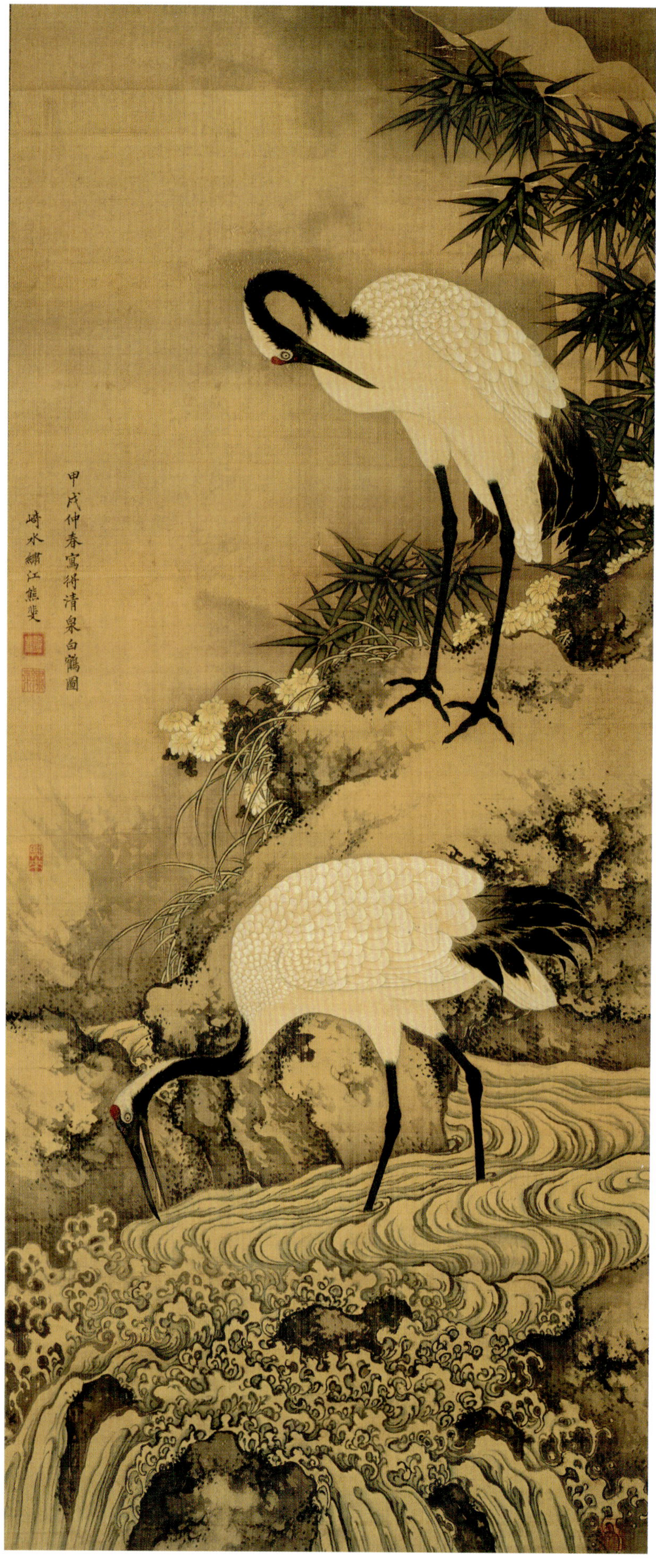

PLATE 55
Yū Hi
(Japanese, 1712–1772)
Seisen hakkaku zu
(Two Cranes at
Clear Stream)
1754 (Hōreki 4)
Hanging scroll: ink
and color on silk
45¾ × 19⅞ in.
(116 × 50.4 cm)

lion, small lion). The kanji '獅' would indicate "lion" and be pronounced *shi*. In China, the terms indicating the official ranks of the imperial court were 太師、少師 (Grand Tutor, Junior Tutor). The *kanji* meaning "tutor" is also pronounced *shi*. Thus *shi* could connote both "lion" and "tutor." The pronunciation embodied an auspicious connotation signifying a high-ranking adviser of the emperor and a wish that future generations would continue in this rank and remain prosperous.[7]

Some might consider this mere word play. But even today it is undeniable that this sort of riddle and nuance provide a pleasureful dimension to aesthetic appreciation, regardless of the quality of the work itself or of the viewer's ability to assess it. Japanese intellectuals found an almost indescribable, titillating appeal in the delight made possible through the medium of *kanji,* the shared component of the Japanese and Chinese languages. It enabled the Japanese, who had nurtured their culture under the model of China's, to experience a pleasing affinity with the country they admired.

One inheritor of the Shen Nanpin painting style was Yū Hi (1712–1772), a Nagasaki painter (plate 55). No Japanese would think he was Japanese by looking at his name. Yū Hi's principal occupation was as a Chinese interpreter for the Nagasaki magistrate. For the sake of convenience at work, interpreters had names in both Japanese and Chinese. Yū Hi used this, his Chinese name, when signing his artwork; his Japanese name was Kumashiro Hikonoshin. Because of his proficiency in Chinese, Yū Hi was able to learn directly from Nanpin, and he played an important role in transmitting Nanpin's style to other Japanese artists.

Yū Hi's allegorical *Ōbo kenju zu* (Xi Wangmu's Peaches of Immortality, plate 56) embodies a good omen associated with a folk belief rooted in Chinese Daoism. The painting represents the peach of eternal life, which is said to have been presented to Emperor Wu of the Han Dynasty by the Chinese goddess Xi Wangmu (J.: Seiōbo). Such peaches flourished only once every three thousand years. The picture is even more interesting when one considers that the peach also symbolizes Xi Wangmu, ruler of all female immortals.

Yū Hi's many students helped to spread the Nanpin style throughout Japan. Among them, the Edo painter Kusumoto Kōhachirō (1715–1786),

popularly known by the Chinese name Sō Shiseki, was the most influential. He studied with Yū Hi in Nagasaki during the 1750s and with the Chinese painter Song Ziyan (J.: Sō Shigan, ?–1760), who was said to have been a student of Nanpin's. It was from this teacher that Sō Shiseki adopted his artist's name. It was a popular trend among Japanese intellectuals and artists at that time to take a Chinese-style name. As his paintings *Kanbai jutaichō zu* (Pair of Red-Billed Blue Magpies on Plum Tree, plate 57) and *Budō zu* (Grapes, plate 58) clearly show, Shiseki's unique style can be located in his focus on a foreground motif and his use of pastel color to create a translucent painted surface. With a distinguishing skill that took him beyond Nanpin or Yū Hi, Shiseki became Edo's most popular artist.

Unlike the inroads made by Chinese culture, the influence of Western painting in Nagasaki had yet to appear. The severing of ties to the outside world in the first half of the seventeenth century prevented any easy revitalization of interest in Western painting. Nagasaki, as Japan's only open port, was tightly guarded throughout the Edo period to prevent any infiltration of Christian influence. *Fumie*—the act of forcing Japanese citizens to step on Christian images to demonstrate their apostasy—was an infamous ceremony that for years took place as a New Year's event. It is not hard to imagine that such currents bred a cautionary attitude toward Western culture and discouraged painters from taking risks.

Only in the second half of the eighteenth century, after Yoshimune had eased restrictions in 1720 on the importation of Chinese translations of Western books, did those cautious artists begin painting openly in oil, a medium they had denied themselves. Artists in Edo, such as Shiba Kōkan, were the first to move toward oil painting, with artists in Nagasaki lagging a little behind.

The two great Nagasaki artists specializing in Western painting were Wakasugi Isohachi (1759–1805) and Araki Jogen (1765–1824). Isohachi was an amateur painter who worked at the Nagasaki Trade Association, the commercial agency that controlled foreign trade on behalf of the government. His exotic, almost tropical use of color in *Hanakago to chō/Kachō no Oranda fūkei zu* (Flower Basket with Butterflies/Dutch Scenery, plate 59a,b) is reminiscent of the naïve art of Henri Rousseau.

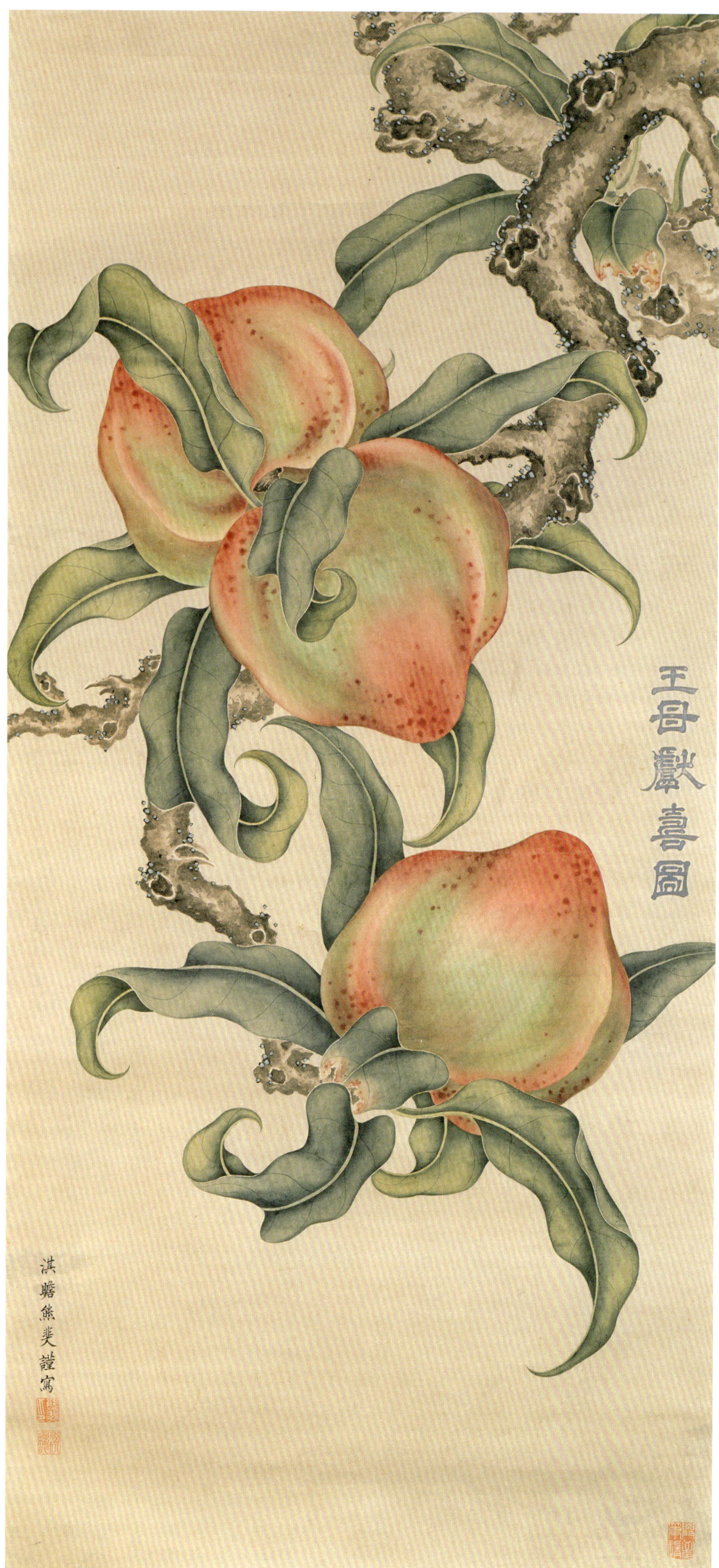

PLATE 56
Yū Hi
(Japanese, 1712–1772)
Ōbo kenju zu
(Xi Wangmu's
Peaches of
Immortality)
Mid-18th century
Hanging scroll: ink
and color on paper
52⅝ × 24⅞ in.
(133.5 × 63.1 cm)

PLATE 57
Sō Shiseki
(Japanese, 1715–1786)
Kanbai jutaichō zu
(Pair of Red-Billed
Blue Magpies
on Plum Tree)
1764–81 (Meiwa–
An'ei era)
Hanging scroll: ink
and color on silk
39¾ × 15⅝ in.
(101 × 39.6 cm)

PLATE 58
Sō Shiseki
(Japanese, 1715–1786)
Budō zu (Grapes)
1764–81 (Meiwa–
An'ei era)
Hanging scroll: ink
and color on silk
74⅞ × 19¾ in.
(190 × 50 cm)

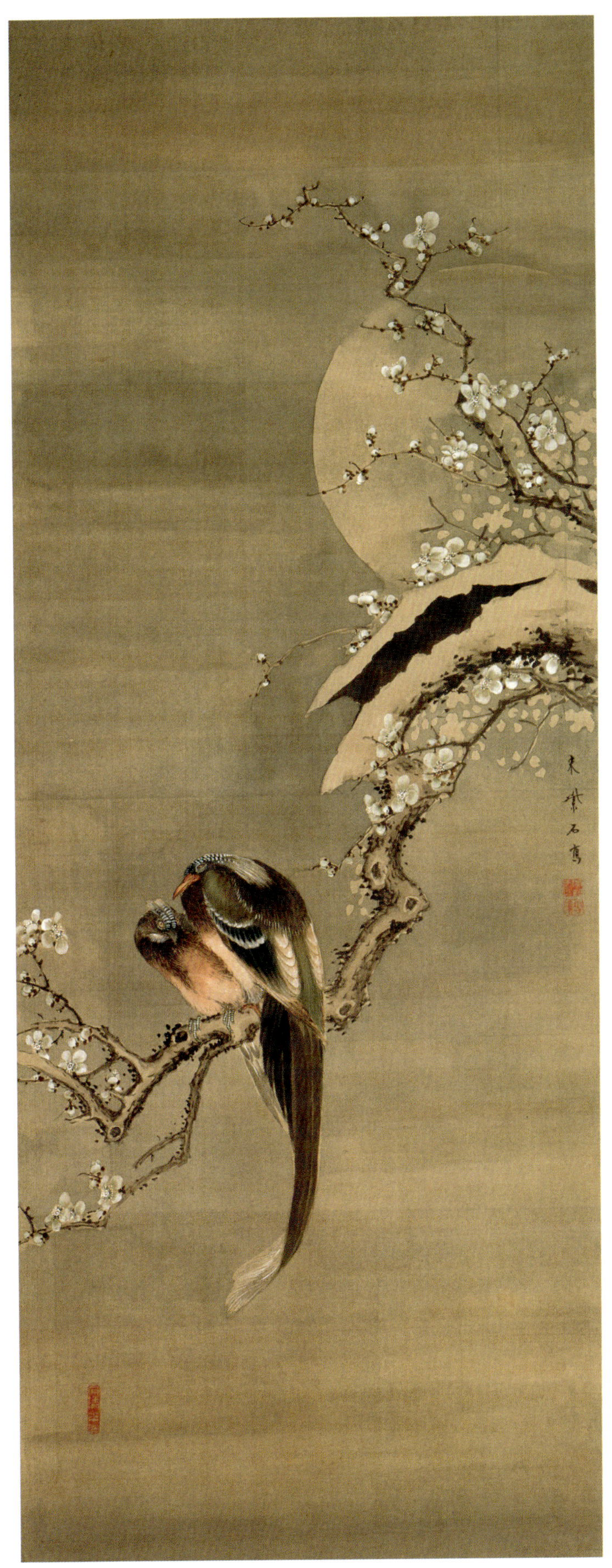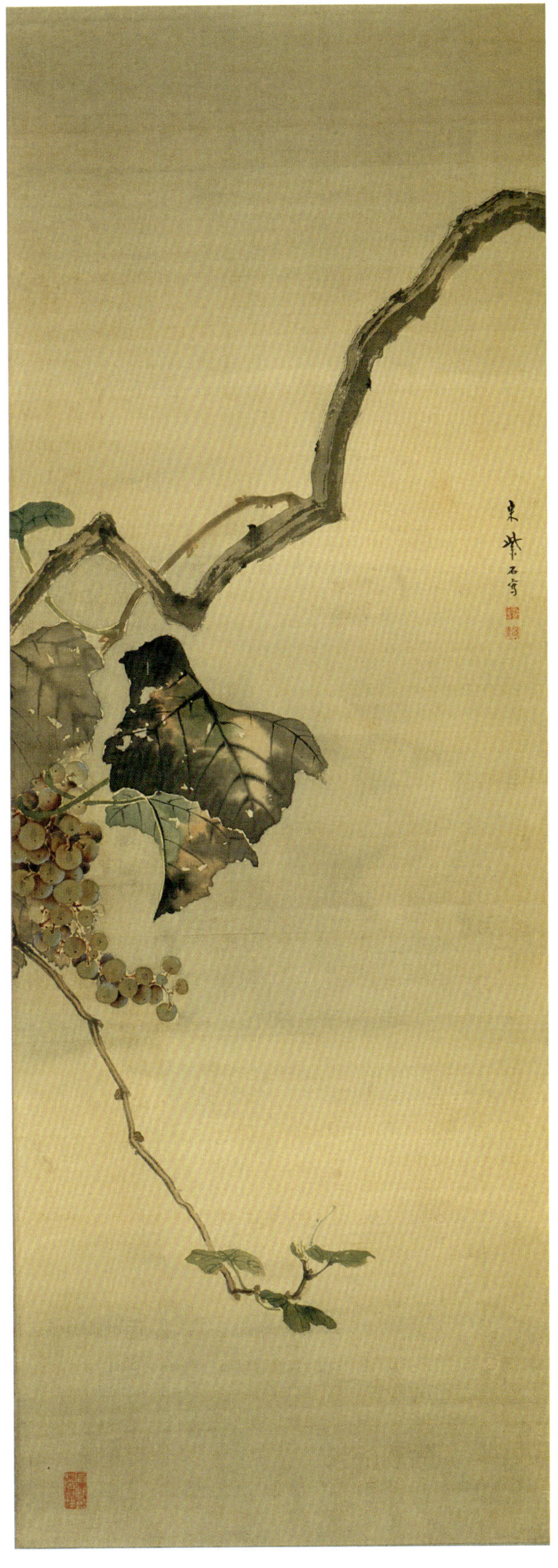

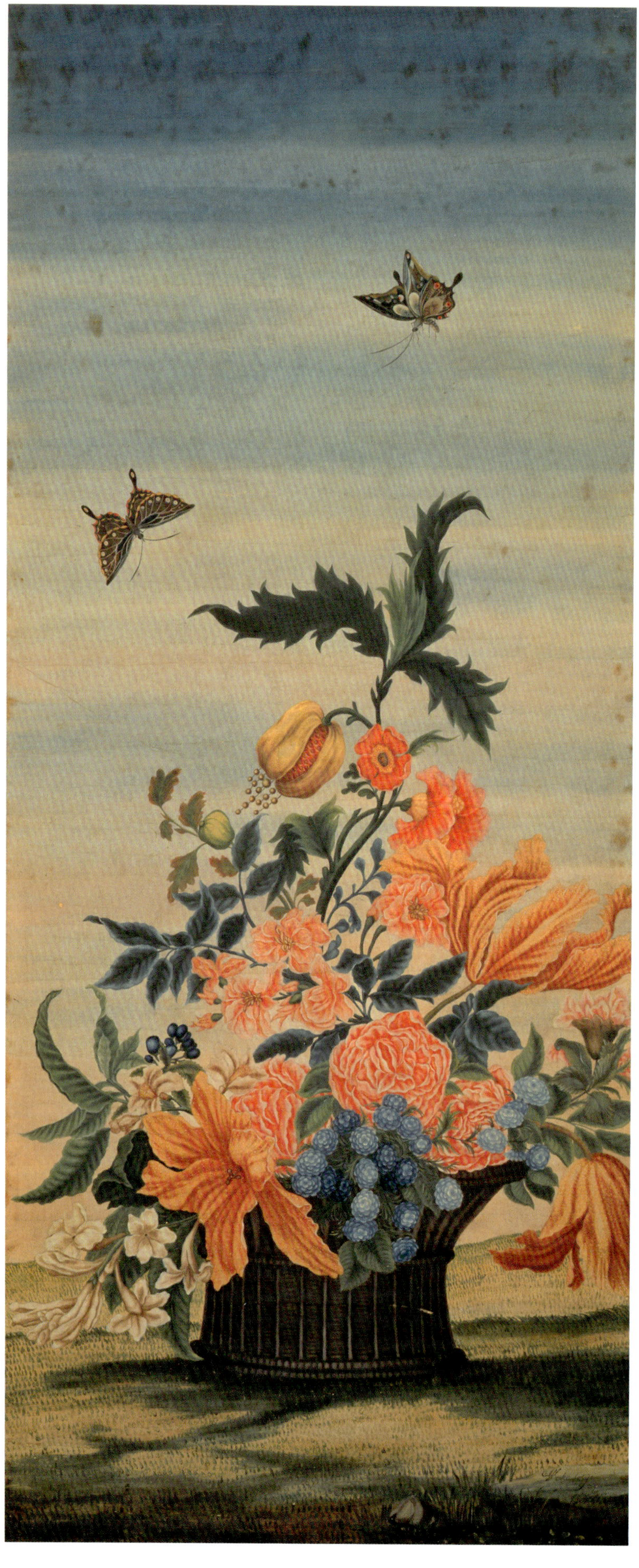

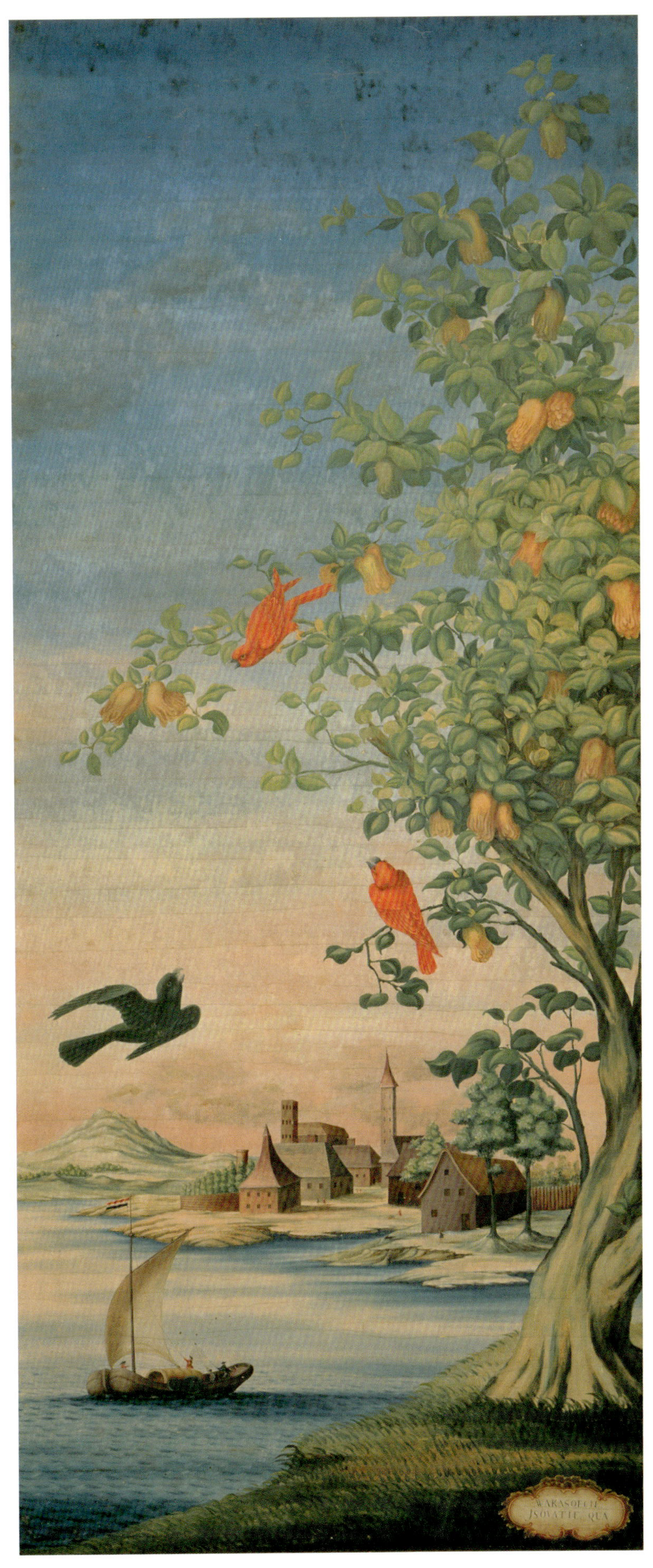

WARASOLUI
ISOVATIEQUA

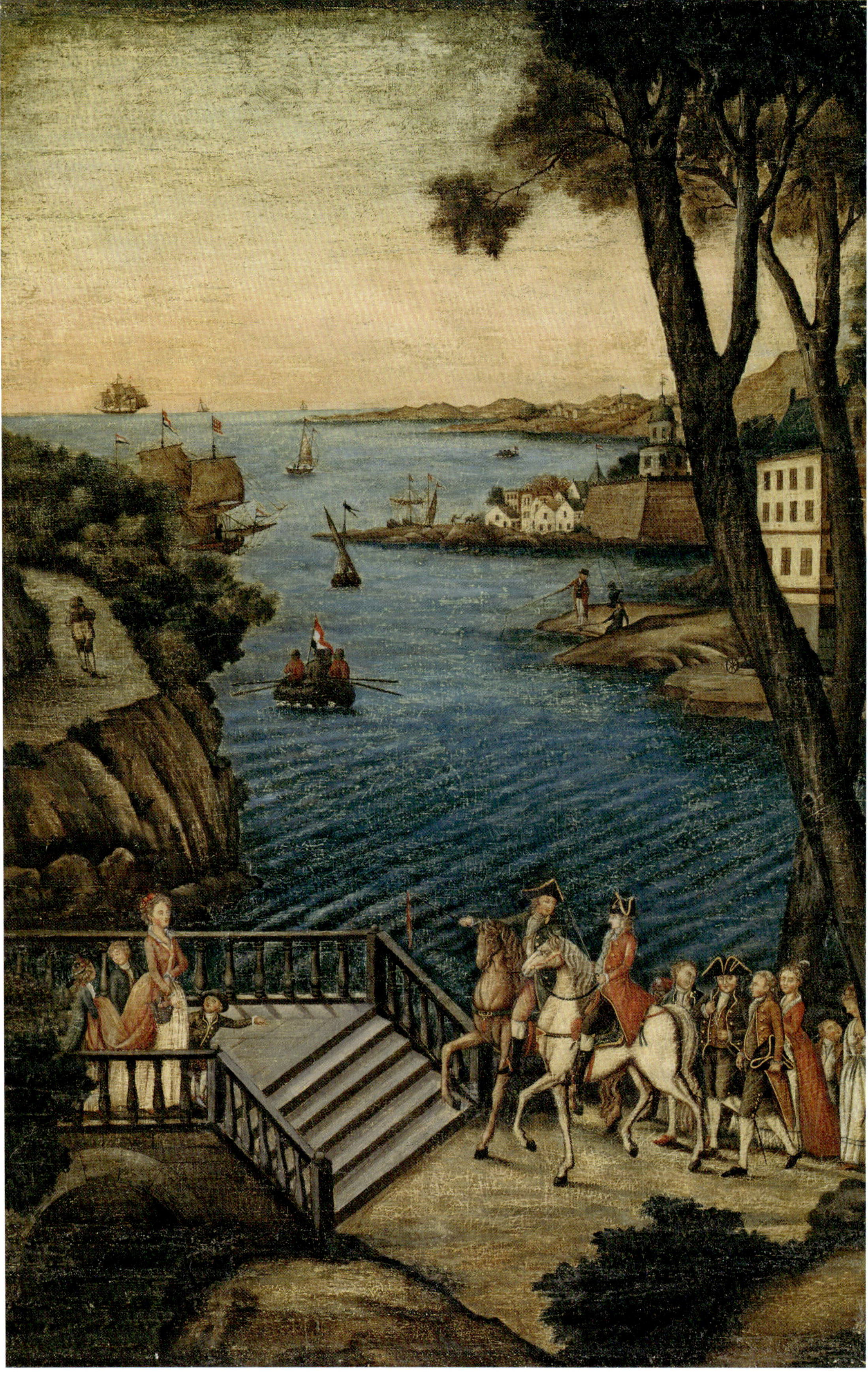

PLATE 60
Araki Jogen
(Japanese, 1765–1824)
Hinkai tojō zu (Port
City in Europe)
First quarter
19th century
Oil on canvas
35⅛ × 23¼ in.
(89.2 × 58.9 cm)

On the other hand, Jogen was a professional artist who had been adopted into the Araki family, themselves *kara-e mekiki*. The advantage this status afforded him—giving him access to art supplies and art reference books—is apparent in his *Hinkai tojō zu* (Port City in Europe, plate 60). His technique is of such a high standard that one might mistake his work for a Western painting.

The influence of foreign culture on Japan during the Edo period was overwhelmingly Chinese in nature. Because Japan steadfastly turned away from Asia and toward the Western world from the late nineteenth century, many Japanese have forgotten this fact. The study of the impact of Western culture on that of Japan receives more attention today, yet the need for a comprehensive analysis of other influences should not be overlooked.

NOTES

1. Two German physicians stationed at Dejima—Englebert Kaempfer in his *History of Japan* (1727) and Philipp Franz von Siebold in his *Nippon* (1897)—used the word "prison" to refer to the island, and likely many other residents shared their sentiment. See Siebold's use of "staatsgefängnisses" (state prison) in *Nippon*, vol. 1 (Leipzig, 1897), 250.

2. Ōba Osamu, ed., *Nagasaki tōkan zu shūsei*, Kinsei Nicchū kōshō shiryō shū 6 (Suita: Kansai Daigaku Shuppanbu, 2003).

3. See Isono Naohide, *Nihon hakubutsushi nenpyō* (Tokyo: Heibonsha, 2002).

4. The Leiden work, titled *Vijfjarige Ceylonese olifant en zijn twee begeleiders gezien tegen de baai van Nagasaki* (A Five-year-old Ceylonese Elephant and Its Attendants at Nagasaki Bay), was added to the collection of the Rijksmuseum voor Volkenkunde in 1999 (ink and color on silk, 16¾ × 22⅛ in. [42.4 × 56.2 cm], inv. no. 5964-1).

5. Kaneshige Mamoru, *Shīboruto to machieshi Keiga*, Nagasaki shinbun shinsho 8 (Nagasaki: Nagasaki Shinbunsha, 2003).

6. A record of the twenty-three imported hanging scrolls is found in an authentification written by Mori Ransai and attached to the hanging scroll *Ichiro kōmyō zu* (White Heron and Gray Starling) by Shen Nanpin (private collection); see *Hana to toritachi no paradaisu*, exh. cat. (Kobe: Kobe City Museum, 1993), 74 and 89. Exactly when the scrolls were imported is unknown, but it must have been between 1733 and 1755 (Yoshimune's death).

7. Zhou Ji-yin and Jin-teng Xiu-shi (Kondō Hidemi), *Shen Quan yan jiu* (Nanjing: Jiangsu Art Press, 1997).

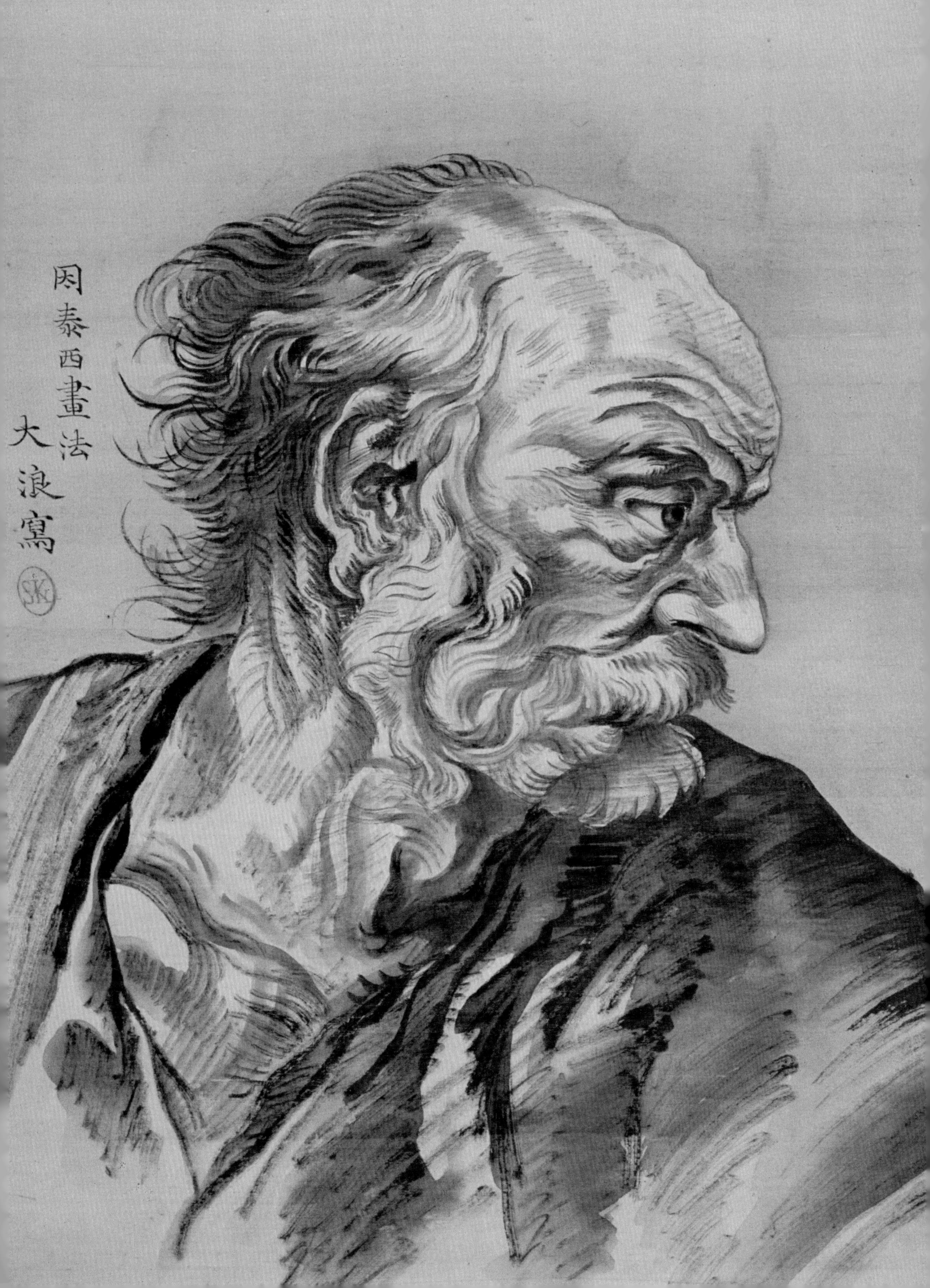

因泰西畫法
大浪寫

4

Katsumori Noriko

The Influence of Ransho on Western-style Painting

Western-style paintings from the Edo period (1615–1868) have a close relationship with *rangaku,* the study of Western (Dutch) learning. This term is often employed in critiques of Western-style painting from that time, but to what extent have the ties between Western studies and Western-style paintings been fully understood?

Scholars of Japan's premodern era have tended to focus on Dutch-related materials and give less weight to empirical analyses of Japanese studies and culture, on which China exerted a great influence. But as the Japanese historian Ōba Osamu has observed, the easy recitation of historical matters in textbooks has contributed to a common misconception about *rangaku* and its development.[1] A typical summation of *rangaku* achievements might highlight the following publications and occurrences: Nishikawa Joken's 1659 *Kai tsūshō kō* (Thoughts about Commerce between China and Foreign Countries); Arai Hakuseki's 1715 *Seiyō kibun* (Record of Things Heard about the West) and his 1748 *Sairan igen* (Overview of World Features), based on his interviews with the Italian missionary Giovanni Battista Sidotti, famously confined to an Edo prison; relaxation in 1720 of a longstanding ban on certain foreign books by Shogun Yoshimune, who also ordered the scholars Aoki Konyō and Noro Genjō to learn the Dutch language; and Sugita Genpaku's 1774 *Kaitai shinsho* (New Book of Anatomy).

This catalogue of well-known scholarly efforts—based on various Western sources—is often repeated and has contributed to the mistaken idea that the foreign books famously restricted in Japan in 1630 and then allowed in 1720 were *ransho,* or books in the Dutch language. In fact, these policies applied only to Chinese translations of Western books. Books in Dutch, presented as gifts from foreign visitors, had been preserved over the decades in the shogunal library but were largely disregarded. When the bibliophile shogun Yoshimune opened the library again in 1720, Japanese scholars had the opportunity to reencounter and study *ransho* firsthand.

My strategy for gaining a full understanding of *rangaku,* and correcting misled impressions of it, is to examine empirical evidence. I have analyzed the relationship between Western-style painting and *rangaku* by looking at *ransho* themselves. For this reason, I have chosen to use the term "*ransho*" rather than the more prevalent "*rangaku*" for the title of this essay.

Yoshimune's Scholarly Pursuit

On the thirtieth day in the fourth month, 1716, following the death of Tokugawa Ietsugu, who left no heir, the Kishū Tokugawa lord Yoshimune (1684–1751) became Japan's eighth shogun. In a policy known as the Kyōhō Reform, Yoshimune reorganized the structure and bureaucracies of his government and instituted economic reforms. The Kyōhō Reform had its roots in Yoshimune's intellectual curiosity, for he loved books. It had a great impact on his thirty-year reign and on the subsequent development of the arts and sciences in Japan. The shogunate began managing its collection of books and public documents through cataloguing and acquisitions, and government agencies produced maps of Japan, conducted a census, and researched medicinal plants and regional products. These activities eventually led to the establishment of academic studies such as herbal medicine and natural history, and provided an important basis for the emergence of Western-style painting in Japan.

Over the years, enforcement of the 1630 ban on importing Western books written in or translated into Chinese was inconsistent. It was up to the Nagasaki magistrate (*bugyō*) and the shogun's senior councillor (*rōjū*) to decide which books might be allowed, and in 1685 they set a particularly restrictive standard. But Yoshimune had a strong interest in astronomy and calendrical science, and he both obtained related books and promoted these areas of study. In 1720 he reasserted that the ban on Western books translated into Chinese applied only to works on Christianity. Approximately twenty categories of books were now expressly allowed into Japan, including those on science and technology, poetry and prose, and geography.

This loosening of restrictions would have some influence on Western-style painting. For example, it was now possible to obtain reference works such as Giulio Aleni's *Zhifang waiji* (Record of Areas beyond the Tribute States), which had been published in 1623 in China. When Satake Shozan, the lord of the Akita domain, introduced Western painting concepts and technique in his *Gato rikai* (Understanding Paintings, 1778), his statements were guided by the objective basis of Aleni's natural history. Aleni's work was so respected that the scholar and Western-style painter Ishikawa Tairō chose his professional name, Tairō, from it (based on the Chinese translation of Tafel Berg, or Table Mountain, located in South Africa).

Yoshimune was fascinated by animals and plants not found in Japan, and he pressed for the cataloguing of the shogunal collection. A number of valuable zoological and botanical texts were brought to light and translated, including Johannes Jonstonus's *Beschryving van de natuur* (Picture Book of Animals, 1660 ed.) and Rembertus Dodonaeus's *Cruydt-boeck* (Picture Book of Plants, 1618 ed.). With this growing interest in Western sciences, increased attention was paid to the Dutch books found on the trading vessels that came to Nagasaki.

Yoshimune also enjoyed paintings and calligraphy. In 1722 he ordered the acquisition of both Chinese (*kara-e*) and Dutch (*kōmō-e*) paintings. The Chinese artist Shen Nanpin (1682–?) came to Japan in 1731 expressly to provide paintings in the classical Northern Song Dynasty style,[2] and in 1726, five Dutch oil paintings were shipped to Japan, two of which were displayed at Gohyaku Rakanji, a Buddhist temple in Edo.[3] It would not be an exaggeration to say that Yoshimune almost single-handedly planted the seeds for the development in Japan of *rangaku,* natural history, and Western-style paintings.

Two Copies of Flowers-and-Birds by Willem Frederick van Royen

In 1796 the brothers Ishikawa Tairō (1762–1817) and Mōkō (1763–1826)[4] made repeated visits to Gohyaku Rakanji to copy one of the paintings exhibited there, a floral still-life by the Dutch artist Willem Frederick van Royen (fig. 12). Another copy of the same painting by Tani Bunchō (1763–1841) is also well known (plate 61). Apart from a difference in the inscriptions on them, the versions appear to be identical, and one might assume that both were made directly from the original oil

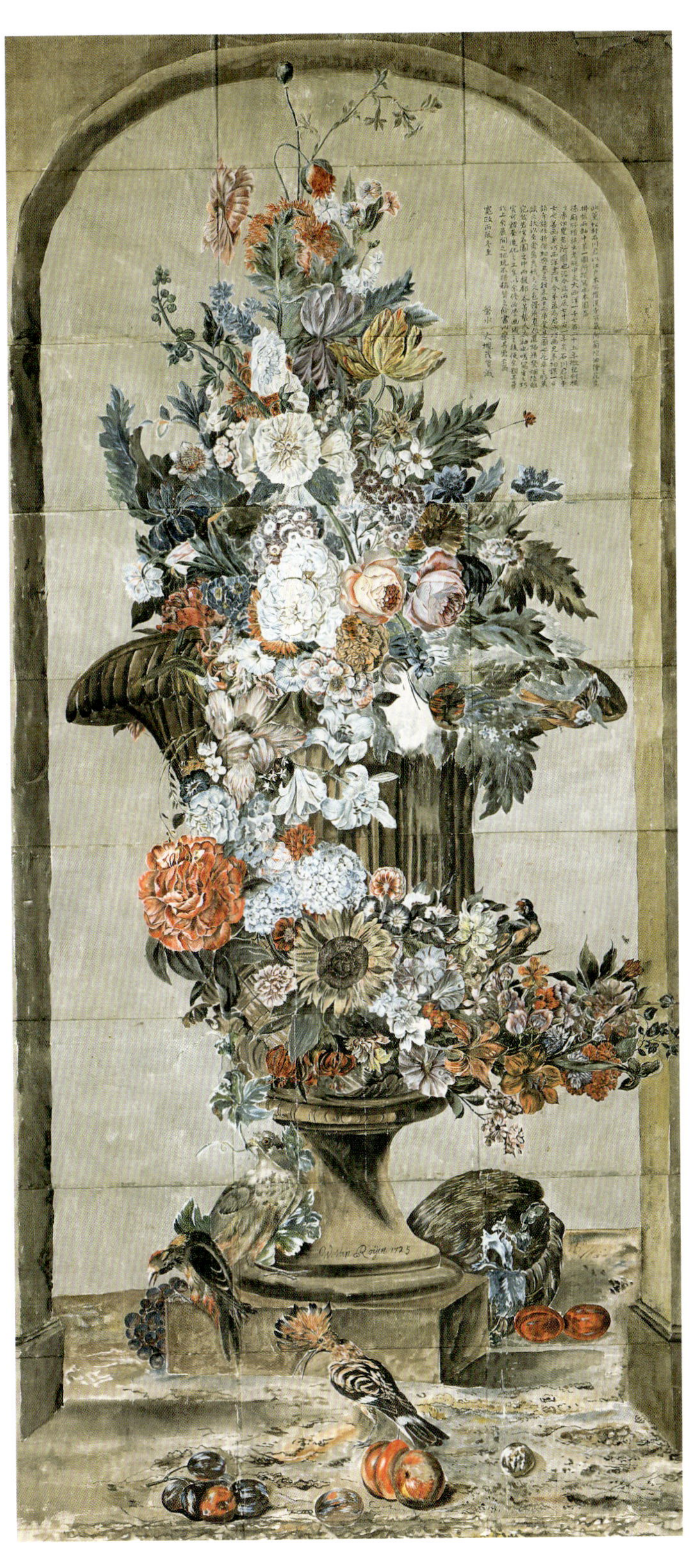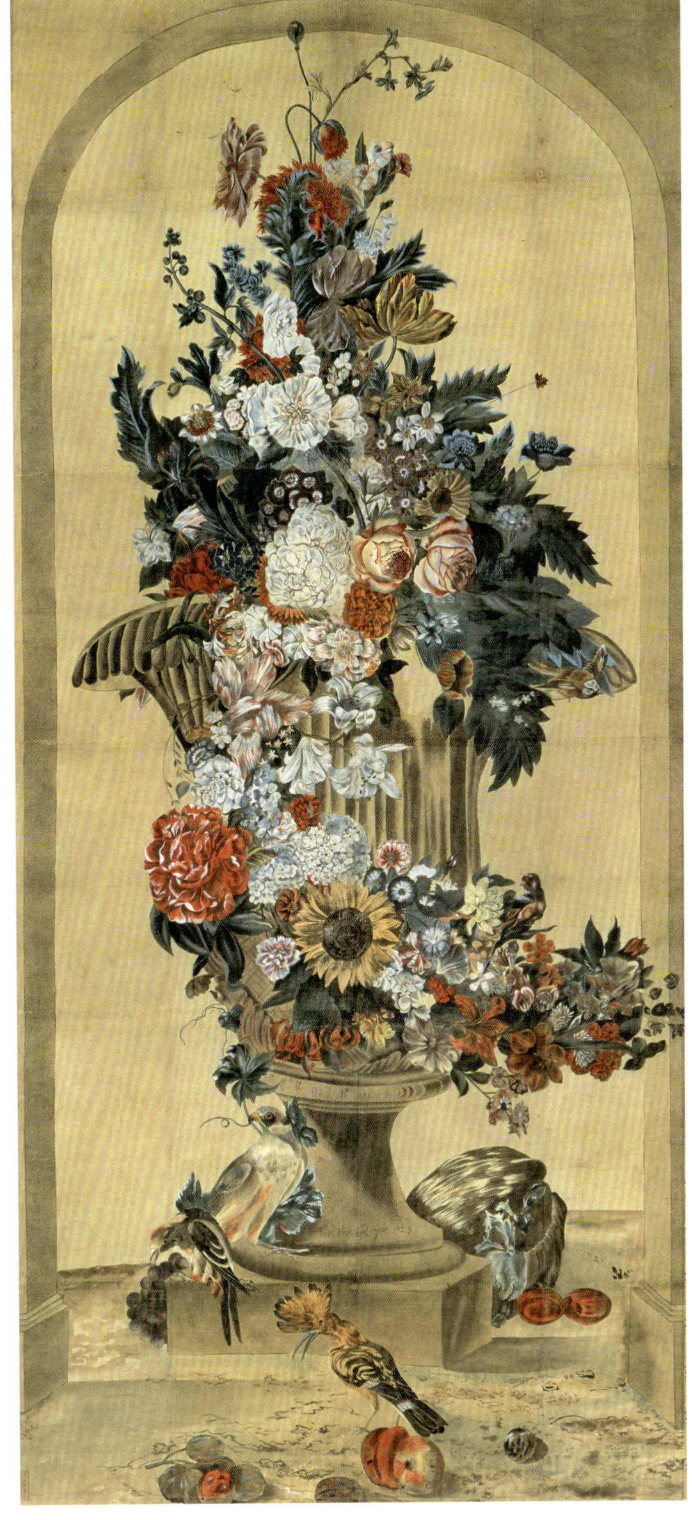

painting. But on close comparison, one can begin to see that they were created with distinct intentions and techniques.

In Tairō and Mōkō's version, there is a strong emphasis on the direction of light, whose source can be located at the left side of the picture plane. We can see that the brothers attempted to render shadow and create a sense of spatial depth by using dark and light colors as well as ink and white highlights. They were also attentive to the modeling of three-dimensional form in depicting petals and leaves. It is clear they wanted not only to copy the pictorial motif of the original but also to replicate its manner of representation, namely, its Western style. Bunchō, in his version, gave more weight to duplicating the motifs accurately. He first outlined the contour of a petal or leaf with a thin black line of ink, and then colored it in. Because the rendering of details is somewhat vague and some areas of shadow do not make sense pictorially, it is natural to conclude that Bunchō created his picture not from the original but from Tairō and Mōkō's copy.

At the time he made his version of the Van Royen still-life, Bunchō was studying and copying various old paintings and calligraphic works stored in temples and shrines around Japan, a project he undertook at the order of Matsudaira Sadanobu (1759–1829), a senior councillor to the Tokugawa shogunate. Bunchō's copies would be published in *Shūko jisshu* (Ten Categories of Collected Antiques, 1800), and many speculate that he copied the Van Royen as part of this endeavor. In *Bunchō gadan* (Discussions on Painting by Bunchō and Others, c. 1811), Tairō explained Western rules of perspective and shading by referring to the Dutch painter and theoretician Gérard de Lairesse's *Het groot schilderboek* (Great Book of Painting), whose 1707 edition he owned. This book was later passed on to Bunchō,[5] who came to revere Tairō as a master of Western painting. The two versions of *Copy of Flowers-and-Birds by Willem Frederick van Royen* highlight the relationship created between Tairō and Bunchō in learning the technique of Western painting.

Rangaku *Meets Western Painting*

In 1771 the physician Sugita Genpaku (1733–1817) witnessed the dissection of a human body. He had with him, for reference, a copy of the 1734 Dutch translation of Johannes Kulmus's anatomy, known in Japan as *Tafel anatomie*.[6] Inspired by its accuracy, Genpaku and others determined to translate Kulmus's work. Published in 1774 as *Kaitai shinsho* (New Book of Anatomy) and based on research into and comprehension of Western sciences, it is recognized as the first true product of *rangaku*.

Odano Naotake (1749–1780), a retainer of the Akita domain, produced the book's illustrations. Naotake had acquired a knowledge of Western-style painting techniques from Hiraga Gennai (1728–1779), an Edo-based naturalist and student of Western studies who visited Akita in 1773 as an adviser on the development of mines. In that same year, Naotake was sent to Edo on domain business. He began his artistic training with Gennai in Edo, and was asked to copy the copperplate engravings in Kulmus's book and reprint them as the woodblock illustrations of *Kaitai shinsho*.

Although *Kaitai shinsho* is foremost a translation of Kulmus's anatomy, it refers to other Dutch books as well. Explanatory notes list five bibliographical sources for its illustrations and six others for its annotations. Although no source is given for the frontispiece (plate 63), Juan de Valverde's *La anatomia del corpo humano* (1560) likely served as the model.[7] Illustrations of the hand and foot are thought to be either copies from Govard Bidloo's *Anatomia Humani Corporis* (1685), or Bidloo's illustrations as copied by William Cowper in his *Anatomy of Human Bodies* (1698). The illustrations for Bidloo's book were done by Lairesse (plate 62), whose exquisite draftsmanship brings a sophistication to the images which is imparted still in Naotake's illustrations (plate 64). Considering that *Het groot schilderboek* was the guiding authority for the theory of Western painting at the time, it is pleasing to note that drawings based on Lairesse appear in *Kaitai shinsho*, the product of the first encounter between *rangaku* and Western-style painting.

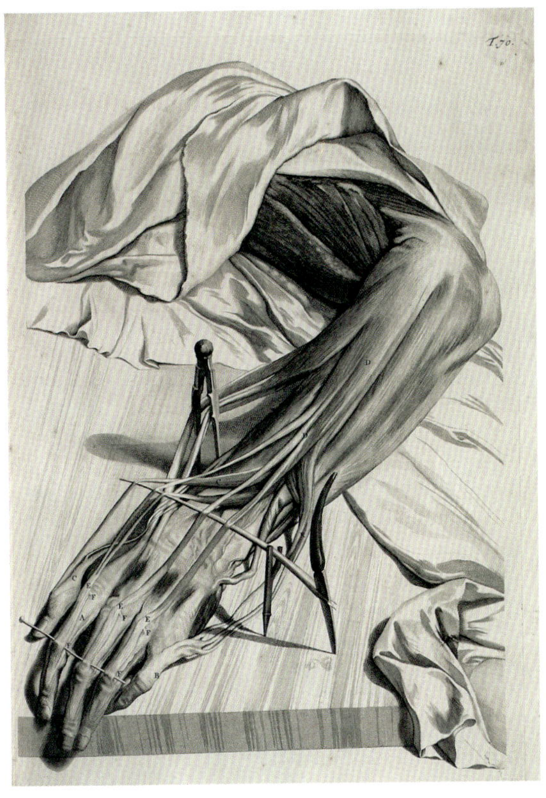

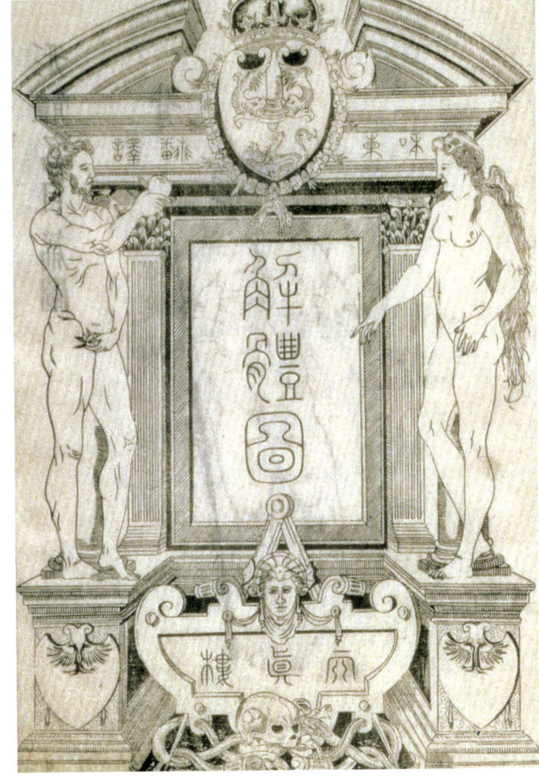

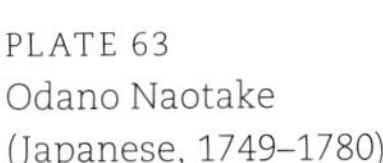

PLATE 62
Gérard de Lairesse
(Dutch, 1640–1711)
Dissection of Arm
from Govard Bidloo,
*Ontleding dea
menschelyken lichaams*,
Utrecht, 1728
Copperplate engraving
and etching: ink
on paper
20¾ × 14⅜ in.
(52.5 × 36.5 cm) page

PLATE 63
Odano Naotake
(Japanese, 1749–1780)
Frontispiece
from Sugita Genpaku
et al., *Kaitai shinsho*,
Edo, 1774 (An'ei 3)
Five books bound
in Japanese style
Woodblock print:
ink on paper
10½ × 7⅛ in.
(26.5 × 17.9 cm) page

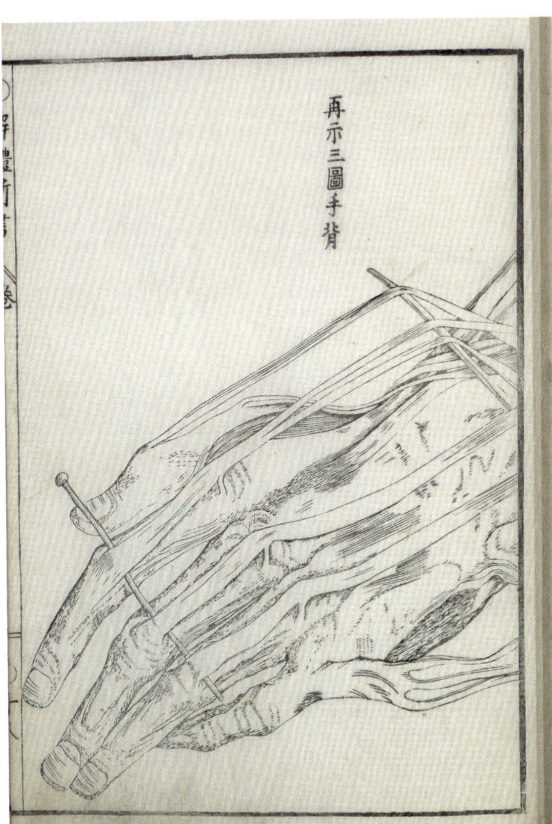

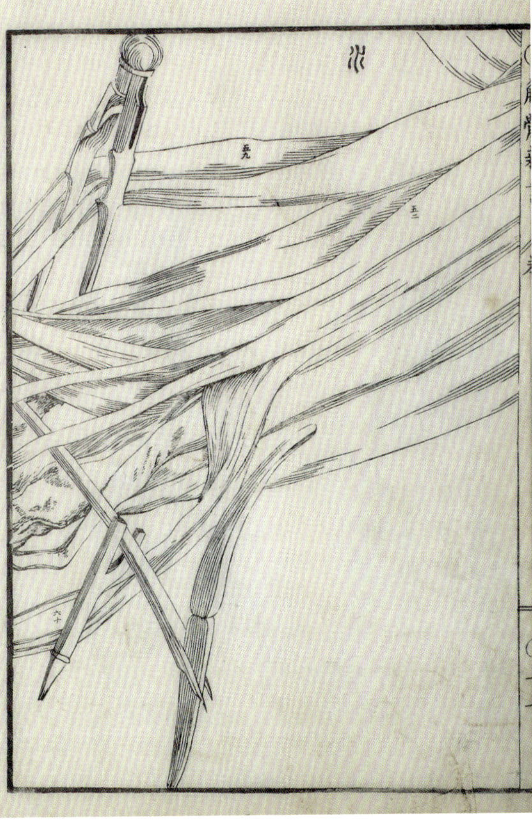

PLATE 64
Odano Naotake
(Japanese, 1749–1780)
Dissection of Arm
from Sugita Genpaku
et al., *Kaitai shinsho*,
Edo, 1774 (An'ei 3)
Five books bound
in Japanese style
Woodblock print:
ink on paper
10½ × 7⅛ in.
(26.5 × 17.9 cm) page

Gennai's Western Painting Practices

The artificial paint pigment known as Prussian blue (*Berlijn blauw*) was manufactured in Europe for the first time in 1704, and by the second half of the eighteenth century, it was being exported to Japan.[8] The first reference to Prussian blue in Japan occurs in *Butsurui hinshitsu* (Classification of Various Materials, 1763), where Hiraga Gennai noted the meritoriousness of its deep blue color. *Seiyō fujin zu* (A Western Lady, plate 65) is his only surviving oil painting, and the circumstances of its production remain unclear. Gennai studied painting in Nagasaki in 1770, when he is thought to have acquired the techniques of Western painting. Analysis of the pigment used in *Seiyō fujin zu* has shown that Gennai applied Prussian blue for the woman's collar, and combined indigo and yellow pigment for the green of the leaves.[9] The importation of Prussian blue during the Meiwa (1764–72) and An'ei eras (1772–81) has been confirmed through contemporaneous records, yet *Seiyō fujin zu,* thought to have been created in 1770–73, is significant as an actual early example of an oil painting that employed the pigment. Although his artistic skill is not highly regarded, Gennai is seen as the leading theorist of Western-style painting during his time. Given the seemingly close relationship between the reception of the new blue pigment and the dissemination of the principles of Western-style painting, Gennai's tenure in Nagasaki deserves further study.

Satake Shozan (1748–1785), who inherited Gennai's theory, wrote in detail about Prussian blue in a technical note about pigments (*tainseibu*) in his *Gato rikai,* and he used the pigment in his work. In *Kakitsubata ni hasami zu* (Irises and Western Scissors, plate 66), Shozan employed the traditional pictorial motif of a flowering plant while modeling the vase with chiaroscuro and rendering the flowers and leaves with detailed brushwork. A pair of Western-style scissors adds an exotic feel to the image. The picture has a seal with an inscription in Dutch. Shozan colored the flowers with light blue, and for another work in the same series (*Kakitsubata ni naifu,* Irises and a Knife; Akita Senshū Museum of Art), he chose dark purple for the flowers. Analysis of the pigments has shown that in both paintings he used Prussian blue. Similarly, analysis has shown that Naotake employed Prussian blue in his works.[10]

Naotake is thought to have broadened his study of Western painting by copying images from books, referring to such volumes as Jonstonus's *Beschryving van de natuur* and Johann Elias Ridinger's *Türkischer Pferdsaufbuz samt einem die nöthigen Anmerkungen hierzu enthaltenden Brief* (Augsburg, 1752), a picture book of horses and riders from various countries. From the illustrations he learned how to render distant views with the detailed line characteristic of copperplate prints. This is a typical feature of *Akita ranga,* the school of Western-style painting to which Shozan, Naotake, and Gennai are assigned. With Gennai as its theoretical guide, the art of *Akita ranga*—with its naturalistic detail and illusionistic methods—paved the way for the development of Western-style painting in the Edo period.

In Naotake's *Hasu zu* (Lotus, plate 67), which is based on a 1777 sketch, the title flower dominates the foreground. Its sophistication stems from the lively brushwork and low vantage point with a distant background view, a compositional type common in *Akita ranga.* In a peculiar twist, after Gennai in 1779 accidentally wounded two people, one of whom died, Naotake was ordered back to Akita. As if to follow Gennai, who died in prison in the twelfth month of 1779, Naotake himself died a year later.

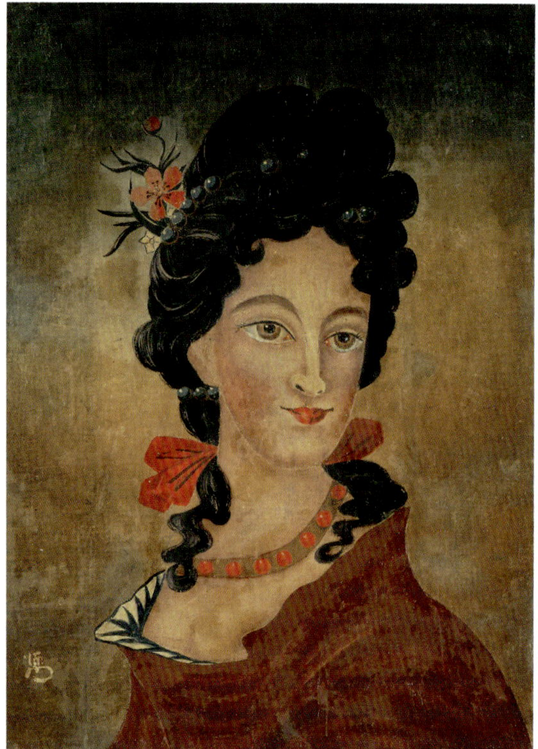

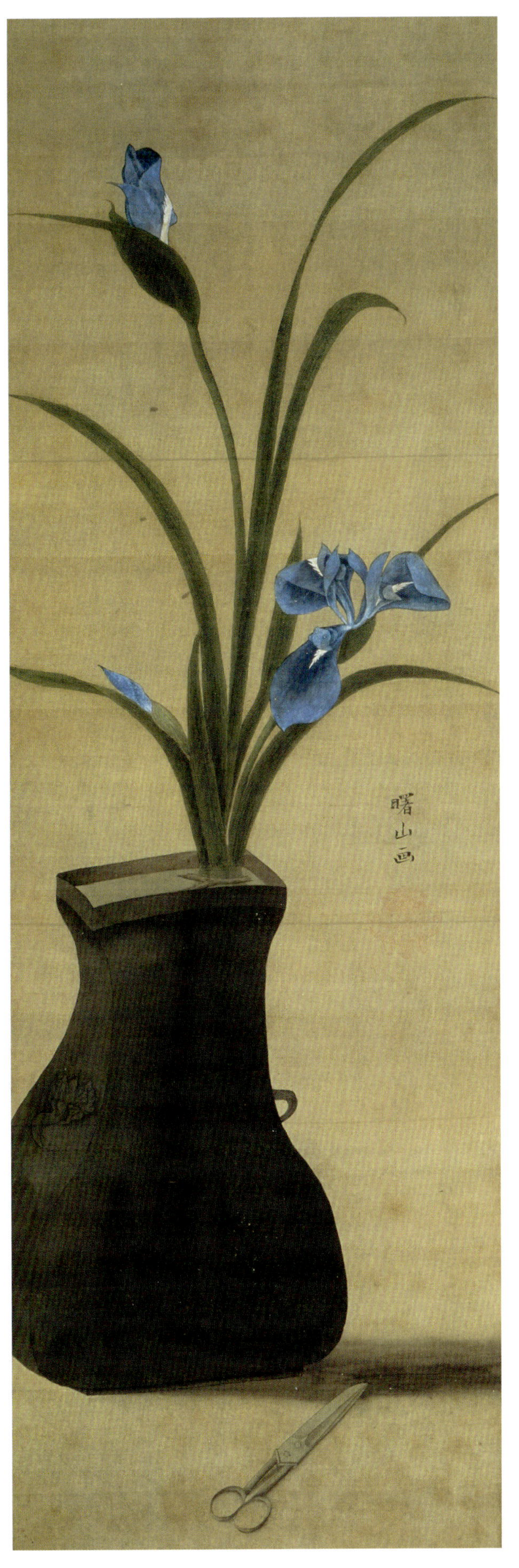
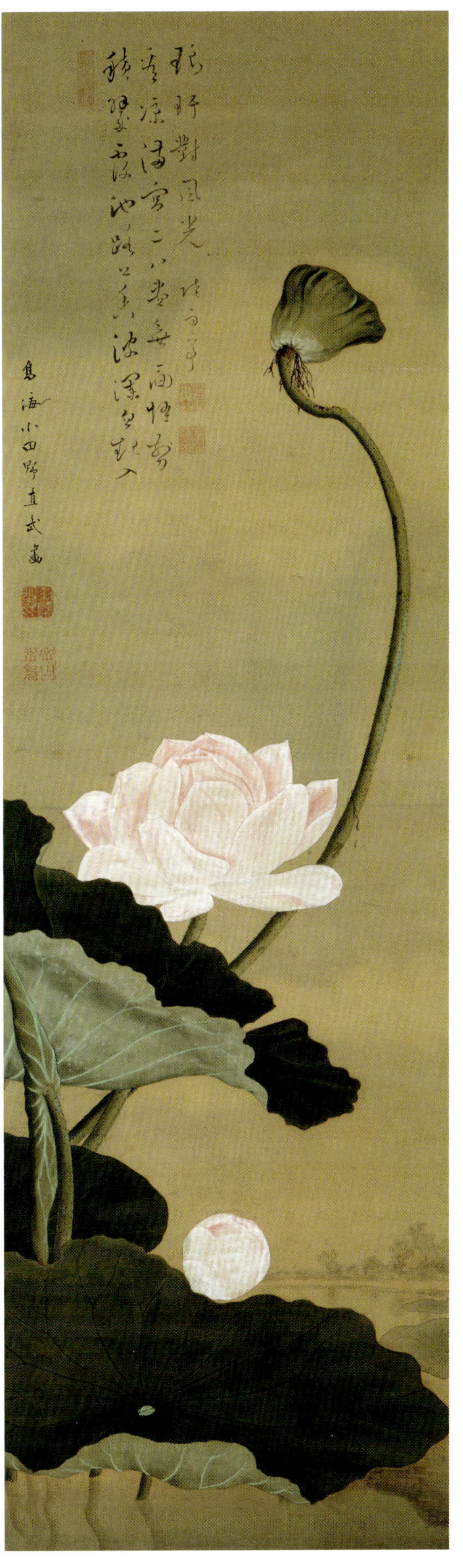

A Portrait of Hippocrates

Ishikawa Tairō (1762–1817) came from a line of direct retainers to the shogun, and from 1788 until his death, he served in the Great Guard of the Tokugawa shogunate. With responsibilities at Osaka and Nijō castles as well as at Edo, he made repeated long visits to Osaka and Kyoto. Tairō's elegant *Kōmō fujin zu* (A Dutch Lady, plate 68) demonstrates his skillful handling of ink, especially in the *chiaroscuro* seen in the pleats of the woman's dress and the shading of her face. He made effective use of colored pigment in the red applied to her lips. On the roller attached to the upper end of the hanging scroll is an inscription reading "A Dutch lady drawn by Ishikawa Tairō" and an ownership seal of Kimura Kenkadō (1736–1802), a well-known collector. According to correspondence between the men, Tairō produced this painting and presented it to Kenkadō in 1801 at his request.[11] The relatively large and exquisite Dutch signature is one that Tairō used from the end of the Kansei (1789–1801) and throughout the Kyōwa (1801–4) eras.

In 1799, at the behest of Ōtsuki Gentaku, a Confucian and Western scholar, Tairō copied a portrait of Hippocrates from the Dutch translation of Johann Gottfried's *Historiche chronyck*, a book known in Japan as the *Koruneiki*. Tairō's picture was the first accurate reproduction of a portrait-type of Hippocrates then popular in Europe. The original made for Gentaku cannot be located, but a similar version from the same year is extant (fig. 13); in this case Tairō produced the image at the request of Yoshikawa Sōgen, a doctor of Western medicine and a *rangaku* scholar. He must have considered Tairō a special painter to select him for this commission. The same could be said of Kitayama Kangan (1767–1801), who probably modeled his *Heisuteru zō* (Portrait of Lorenz Heister, M.D., plate 70) after an image appearing in an imported medical text. Heister, a physician, was a highly regarded figure among those Japanese doctors who practiced Western medicine.

Tairō produced another portrait of a man now identified as Hippocrates (plate 69),[12] but this time based on Gilles Demarteau's copperplate engraving of François Boucher's *Head of a Man*.[13] A Japanese inscription next to the head reads "Made using Western painting technique, copied by Tairō" (Taisei no gahō ni yoru, Tairō utsusu), and

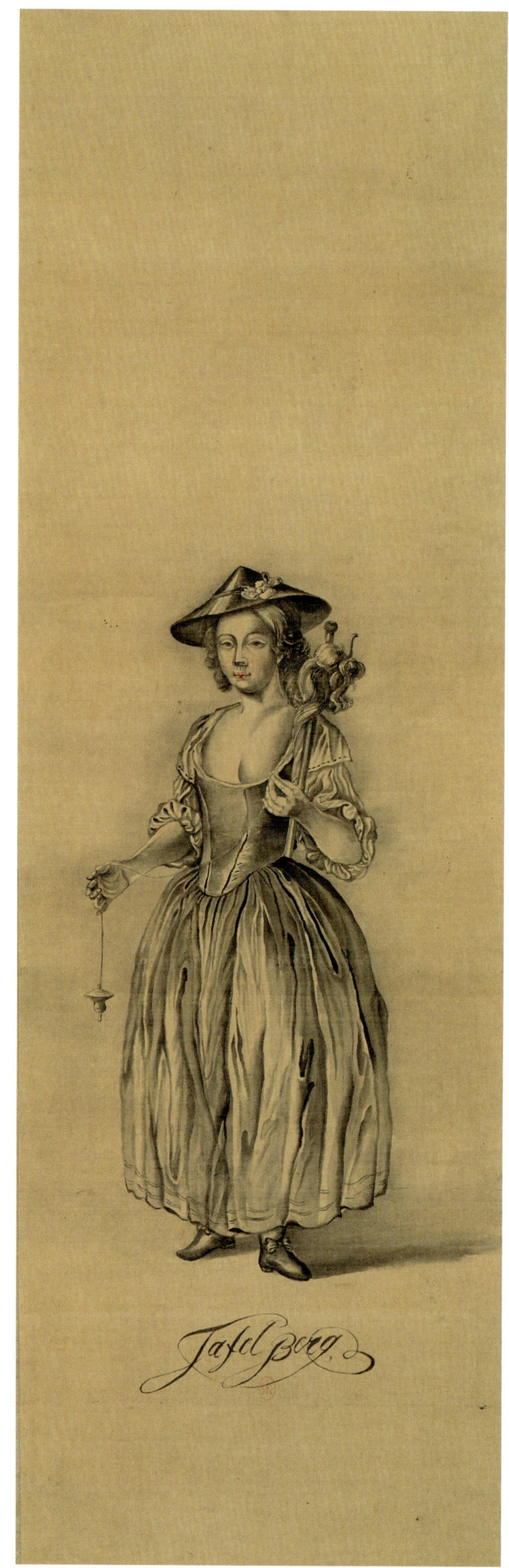

PLATE 68
Ishikawa Tairō
(Japanese, 1762–1817)
Kōmō fujin zu
(A Dutch Lady)
1789–1801 (Kansei era)
Hanging scroll:
ink and color on silk
38⅛ × 12¾ in.
(96.6 × 32.4 cm)

FIG. 13
Ishikawa Tairō
(Japanese, 1762–1817)
Hipokuratesu zō
(Portrait of
Hippocrates)
1799 (Kansei 11)
Hanging scroll:
ink on silk
26⅞ × 14⅝ in.
(68.3 × 37.1 cm)
Koga City Museum of
History, Ibaraki

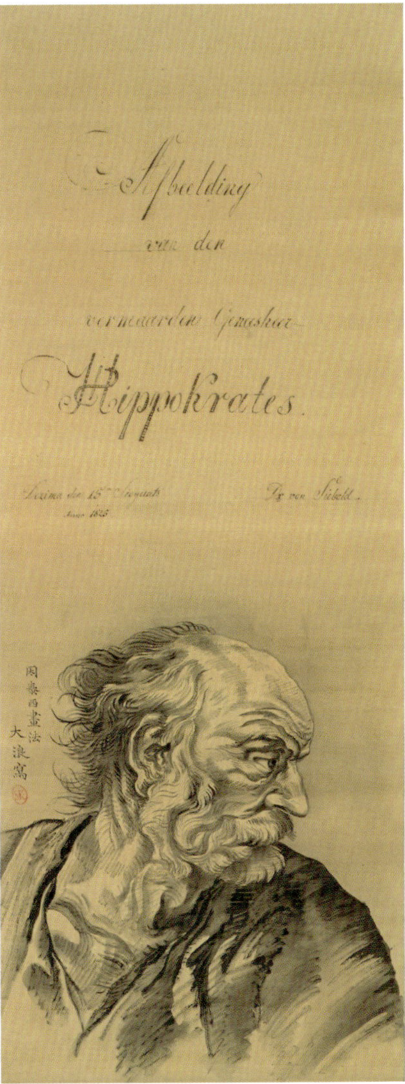

PLATE 69
Ishikawa Tairō
(Japanese, 1762–1817)
Hipokuratesu zō
(Portrait of
Hippocrates)
Early 19th century
Hanging scroll:
ink on silk
31½ × 12⅜ in.
(79.9 × 31.4 cm)

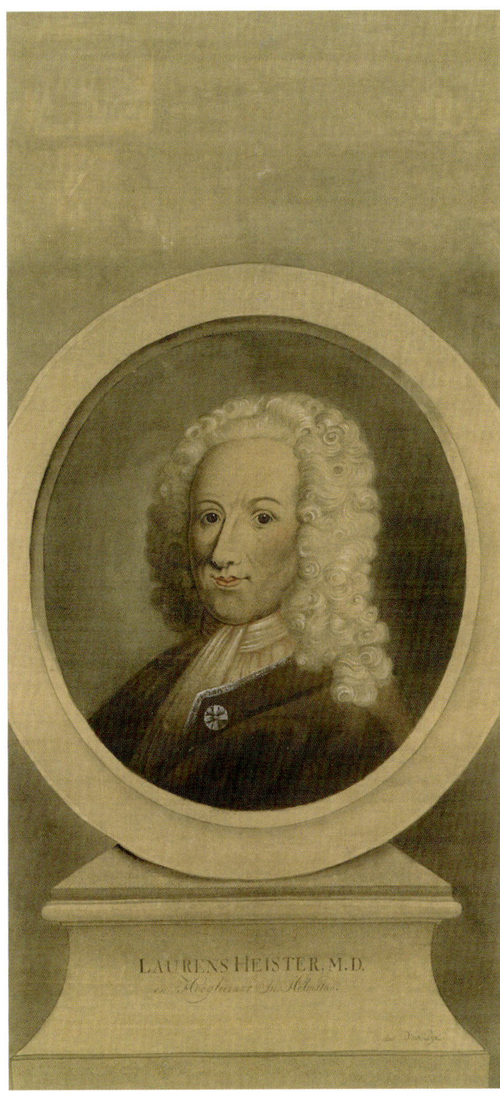

PLATE 70
Kitayama Kangan
(Japanese, 1767–1801)
Heisuteru zō
(Portrait of Lorenz
Heister, M.D.)
Late 18th century
Hanging scroll:
ink and color on silk
33 × 15¾ in.
(83.6 × 39.9 cm)

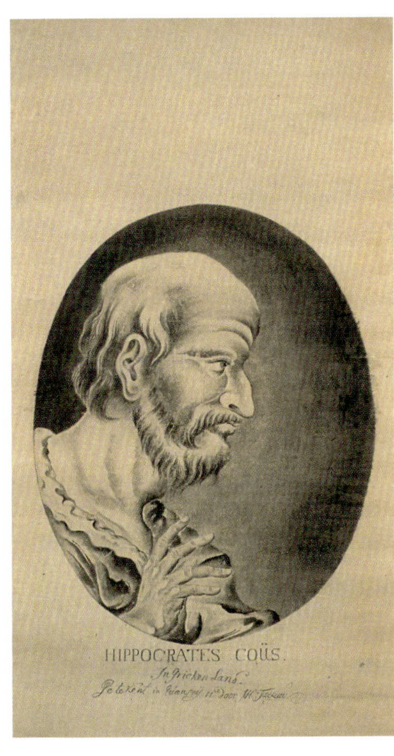

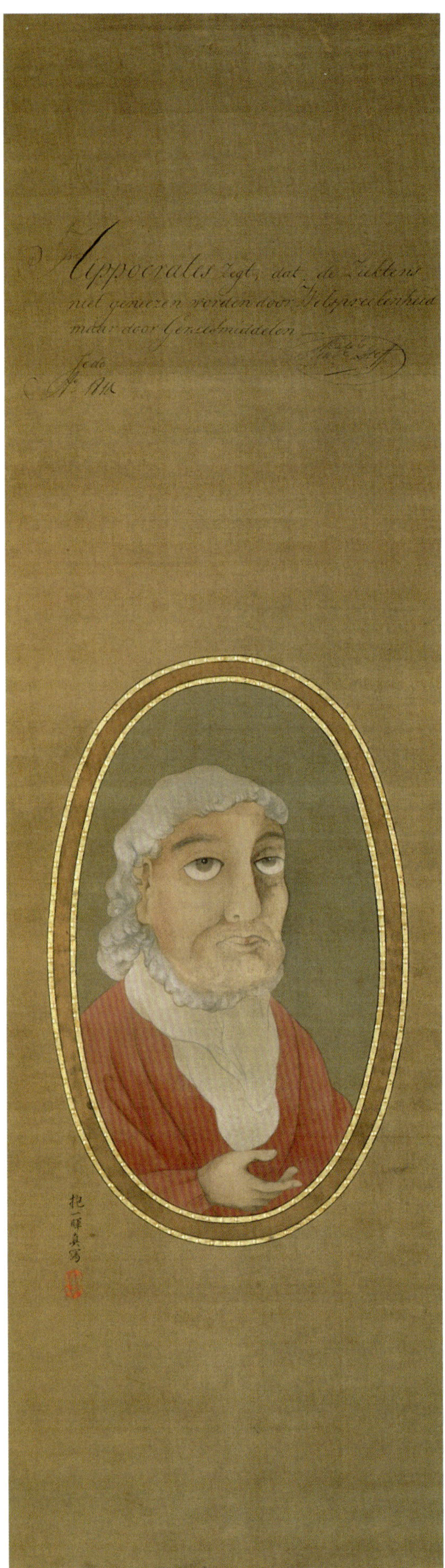

beneath it is a seal in Roman characters. Attached to the back of the portrait is a provenance written by Tani Bunchō in 1818, the year after Tairō's death. It is thought that the piece was made to commemorate the time during which Tairō instructed Bunchō in the techniques of Western painting.

It was the wish of many Japanese doctors practicing Western medicine at the time to own a portrait of Hippocrates, and various versions were produced by many different artists.[14] One that stands out among them is *Hipokuratesu zō* (Portrait of Hippocrates, plate 71) by the famous Rimpa-school artist Sakai Hōitsu (1761–1828). The picture bears the name of Hendrik Doeff (1777–1835), the director of the Dutch trading post at Dejima in Nagasaki (for a portrait of Doeff, see plate 50). An aphorism in Dutch reads: "Hippocrates says, sickness is healed not by eloquence but by medicine." Although ascribed to Hippocrates, this maxim can be attributed to Celsus, a Roman author of medical treatises. Two grammatical mistakes in the Dutch inscription[15] and traces showing that some letters were re-formed point with near certainty to Japanese authorship. The signature, however, is in a different hand, and it is possible that it was written by Doeff himself, though further examination is required. The combination of the Rimpa style and the subject of Hippocrates may seem incongruous, but Hōitsu was, along with his elder brother Sakai Tadazane, close friends with Katsuragawa Hoshū (1751–1809), a *rangaku* scholar.[16] Hōitsu took a subject very popular among Japanese doctors of Western medicine and infused it with his unique artistic sensibility. This is evident in his carefree line and the decorative treatment of the roundel, formed by applying a layer of gold to a coating of powdered shell (*gofun*).

From Tairō to Kuniyoshi: The Reception of Ransho

As we have seen, the illustrations in Western books were a rich trove of source material for Japanese artists, and their varied responses to and incorporation of the images need careful study. Here I will point out just a few of these influences and appropriations.

Joan Nieuhof's *Gedenkwaerdige zee en lantreize door de voornaemste landschappen van West-en Oostindiën* (Voyages and Travels into the Provinces of the West and East Indies, plate 72a,b), which Tairō owned, provided the most up-to-date information on other countries in its time. Tairō relied on it for his illustrations for *En roku* (All about Tobacco), written by Ōtsuki Gentaku and published in 1806. Nieuhof's text was translated and studied by Yamamura Saisuke (1770–1807) as *Shinyaku tōzai kiyū*. The *ukiyo-e* print artist Utagawa Kuniyoshi (1797–1861) also found sources in Nieuhof's work for images such as *Chūshingura, jūichi danme, Youchi no zu* (Act Eleven: The Night Attack, from "The Forty-Seven Loyal Retainers of Akō," plate 73) and *Nijū-shi-kō dōji kagami, Taishun* (Shun the Great, from the series "Twenty-four Paragons of Filial Piety," plate 74). Another of Kuniyoshi's prints (plate 75) took inspiration from an illustration of the shipwrecked sailor of Daniel Defoe's *Robinson Crusoe*.[17] The inspiration for Kuniyoshi's *Ōmi no yūfu Okane* (The Brave Woman Okane of Ōmi Province, plate 76), which startlingly renders Okane in traditional Japanese style against a Western-style background, can be located in another book owned by Tairō, a French edition of *Aesop's Fables* (plate 77).[18] Most likely the Nieuhof and the Aesop volumes came into Kuniyoshi's possession after Tairō's death.

How remarkable that two artists of such different characters—Tairō, a painter in the shogun's service, book collector, and *rangaku* scholar, and Kuniyoshi, a craftsman of popular art with the urbane temperament of a native of Edo—found inspiration in the same books. Each artist made use of Western books in his own way, based on his unique personality and nature. For Tairō, the books were not only source materials for pictorial motifs; he to some extent could grasp the meaning of the texts and work with those themes that interested him. For Kuniyoshi, on the other hand, the content had absolutely no significance; he used the books simply as design manuals. With his genius, Kuniyoshi infused the illustrations with new life, and today the resulting artwork is held in high regard.

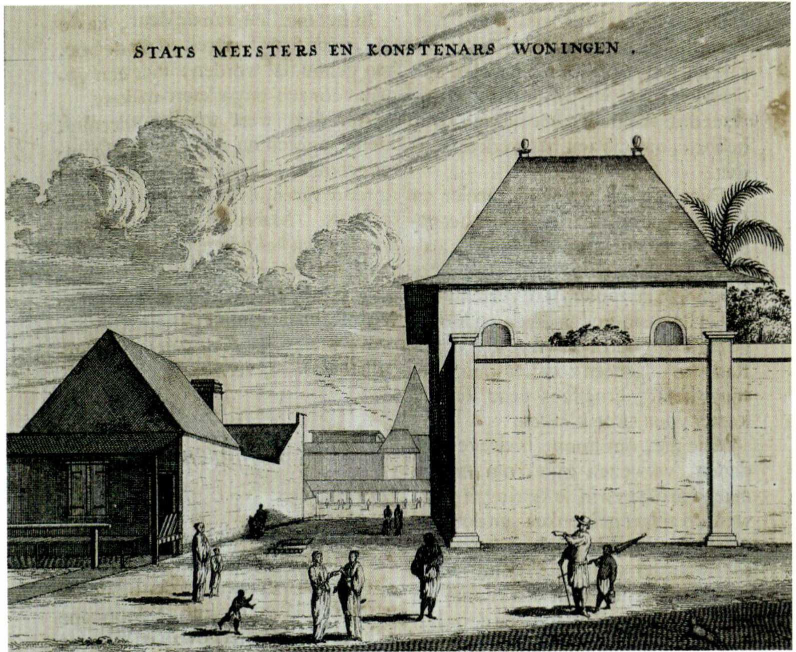

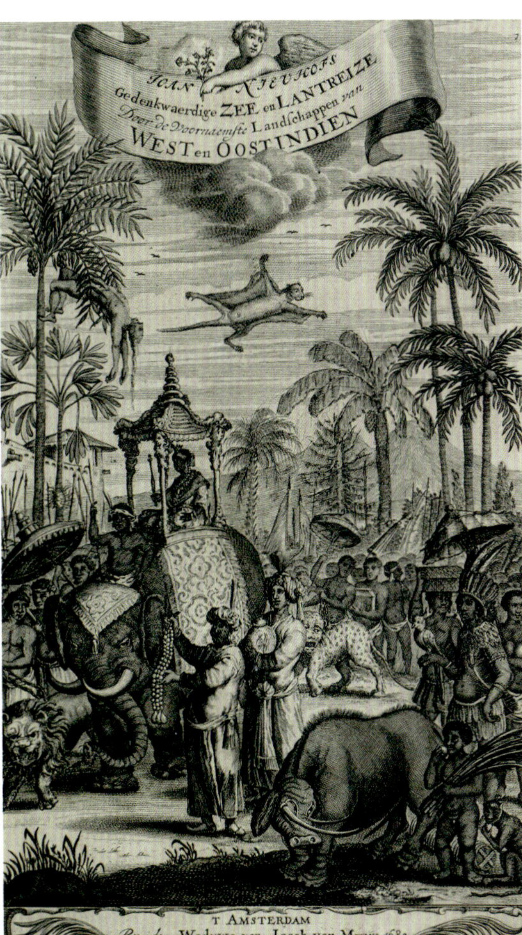

PLATE 72a,b

Houses Belonging to Artisans and to the City Official in Batavia

Frontispiece

from Joan Nieuhof, *Gedenkwaerdige zee en lantreize door de voornaemste landschappen van West-en Oostindiën*, Amsterdam, 1682
Copperplate engravings: ink on paper
15⅜ × 9⅞ in. (39 × 25 cm) at cover

PLATE 73
Utagawa Kuniyoshi
(Japanese, 1797–1861)
*Chūshingura,
jūichi danme,
Youchi no zu* (Act
Eleven: The Night
Attack, from "The
Forty-Seven Loyal
Retainers of Akō")
c. 1831 (Tenpō 2)
Ō-ban woodblock print:
ink and color on paper
10⅜ × 15⅛ in.
(26.3 × 38.2 cm)

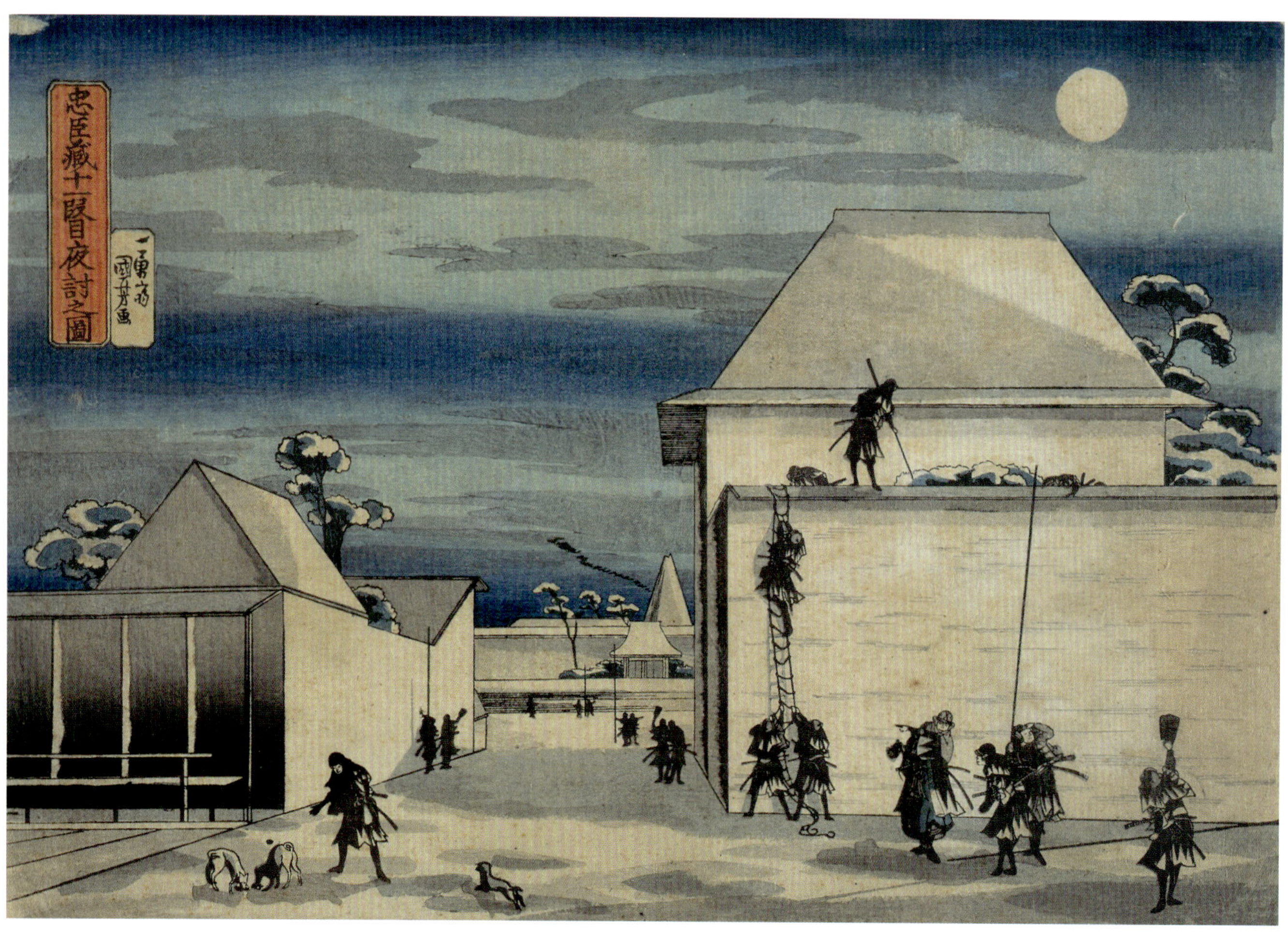

PLATE 74
Utagawa Kuniyoshi
(Japanese, 1797–1861)
Nijūshi-kō dōji kagami, Taishun
(Shun the Great, from the series "Twenty-four Paragons of Filial Piety")
Published by Wakasaya Yoichi
c. 1843–44 (late Tenpō–early Kōka era)
Ō-ban woodblock print: ink and color on paper
10¼ × 14⅞ in. (25.8 × 37.6 cm)

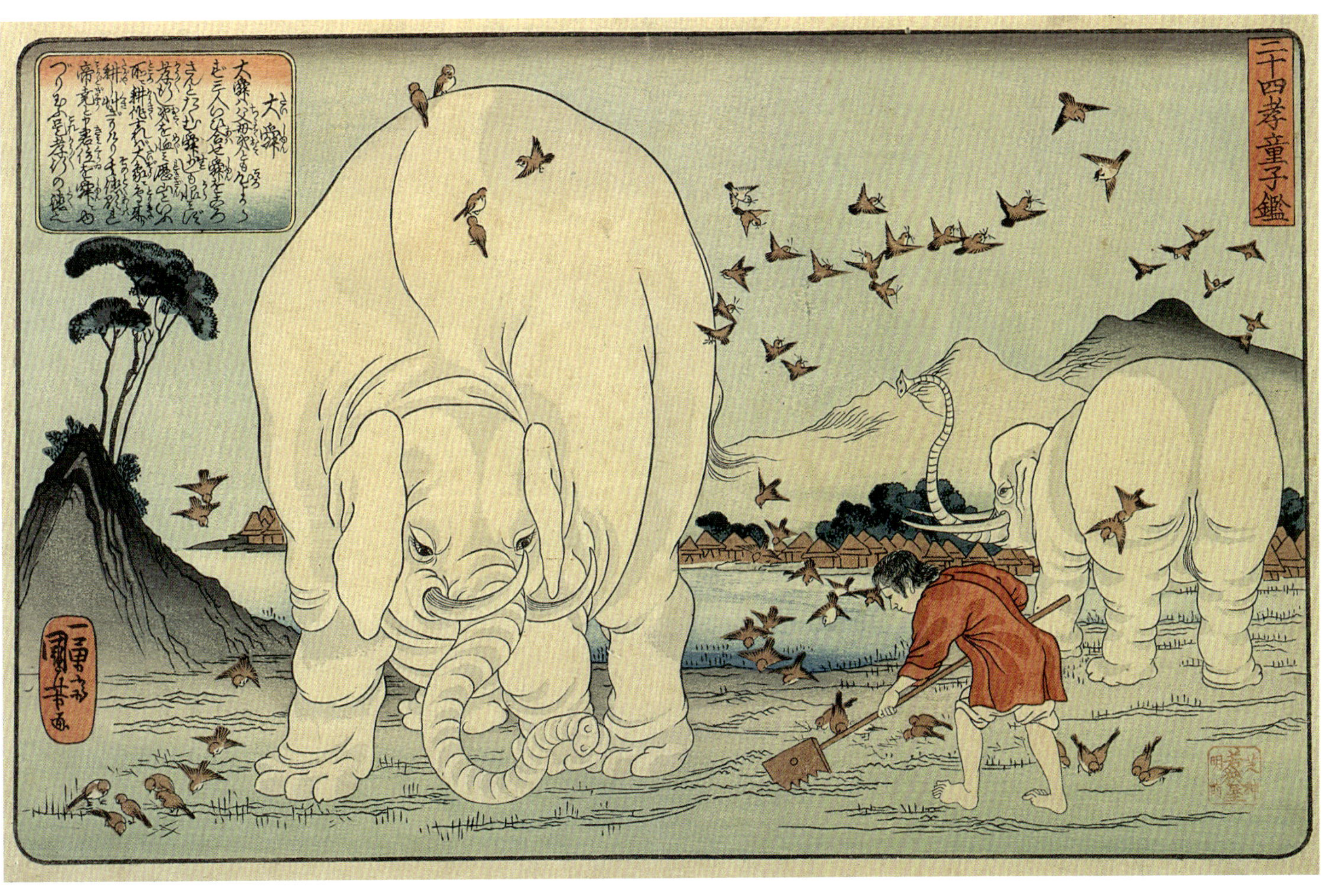

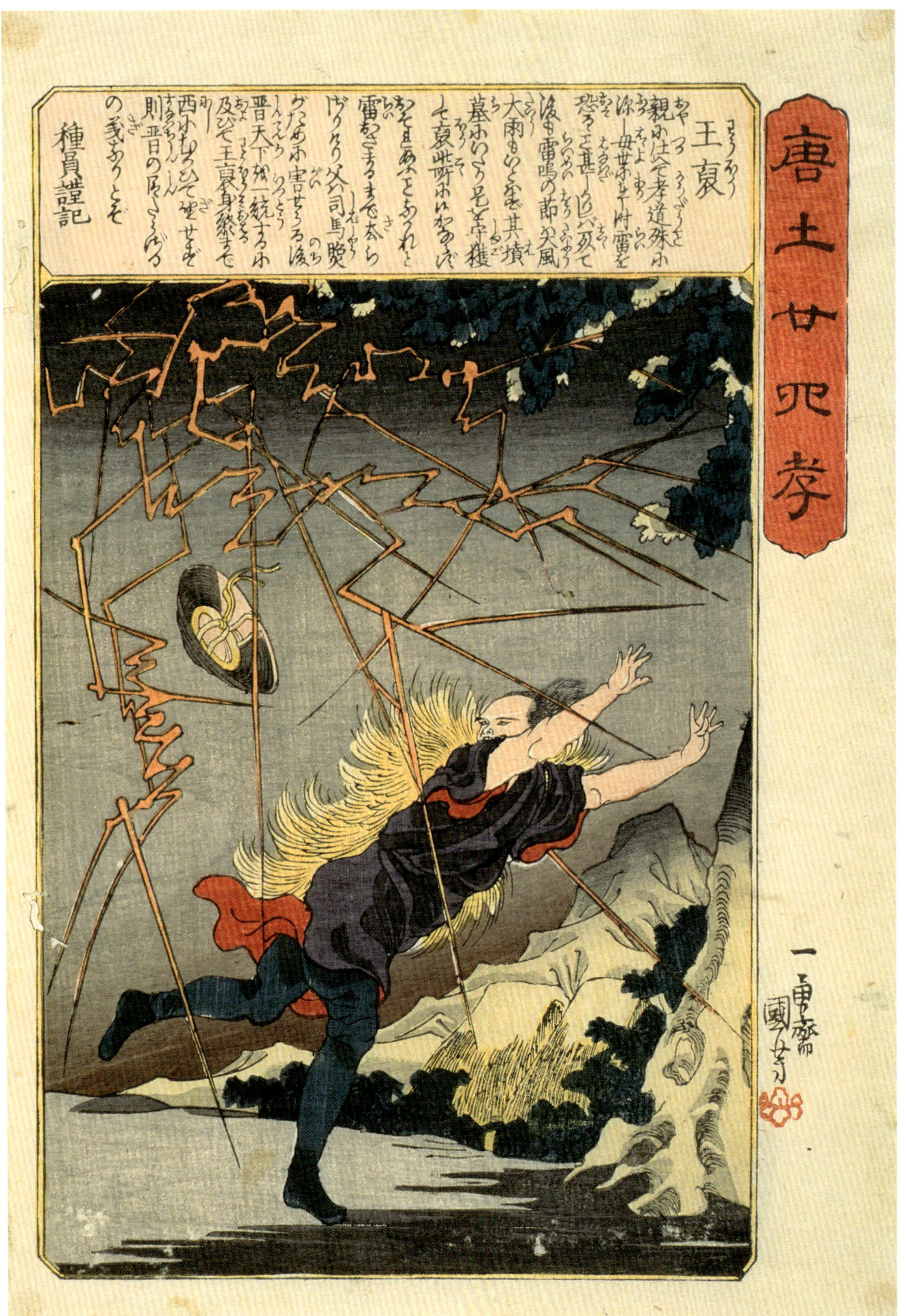

PLATE 75
Utagawa Kuniyoshi
(Japanese, 1797–1861)
Tōdo nijūshi-kō, Ōhō
(Wang Pou, from the
series "Twenty-four
Chinese Paragons
of Filial Piety")
Published by Tsutaya
1853 (Kaei 6)
Chū-ban woodblock
print: ink and color
on paper
10¼ × 7⅜ in.
(26.0 × 18.5 cm)

PLATE 76
Utagawa Kuniyoshi
(Japanese, 1797–1861)

Ōmi no yūfu Okane
(The Brave Woman
Okane of Ōmi
Province)
Published by
Yamaguchiya Tōbei
c. 1831 (Tenpō 2)
Ō-ban woodblock print:
ink and color on paper
10⅜ × 14¼ in.
(26.2 × 36.2 cm)

PLATE 77
Le cheval et le lion
(The Horse and the
Lion)
from *Fables d'Esope*,
Paris, 1810
Copperplate engraving:
ink on paper
10⅛ × 7⅜ in.
(25.5 × 18.6 cm) at cover

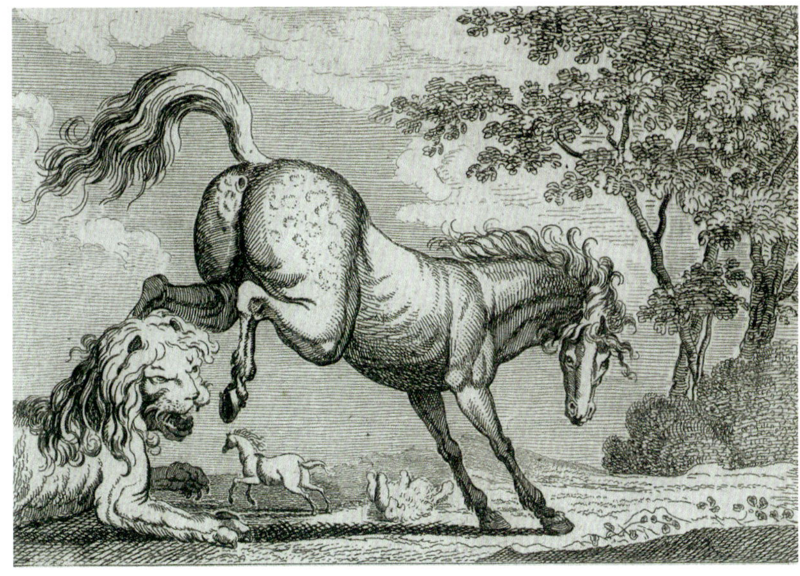

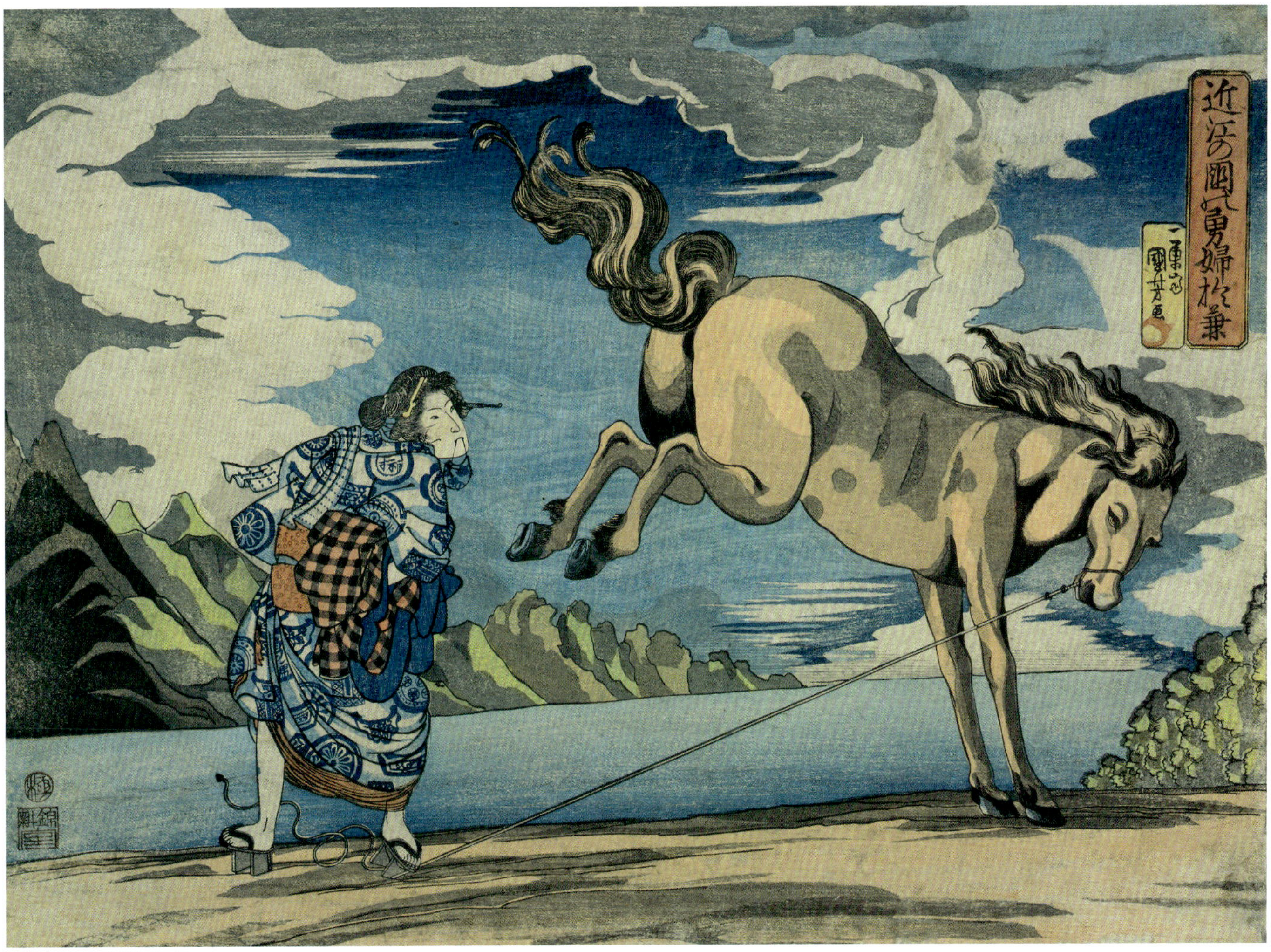

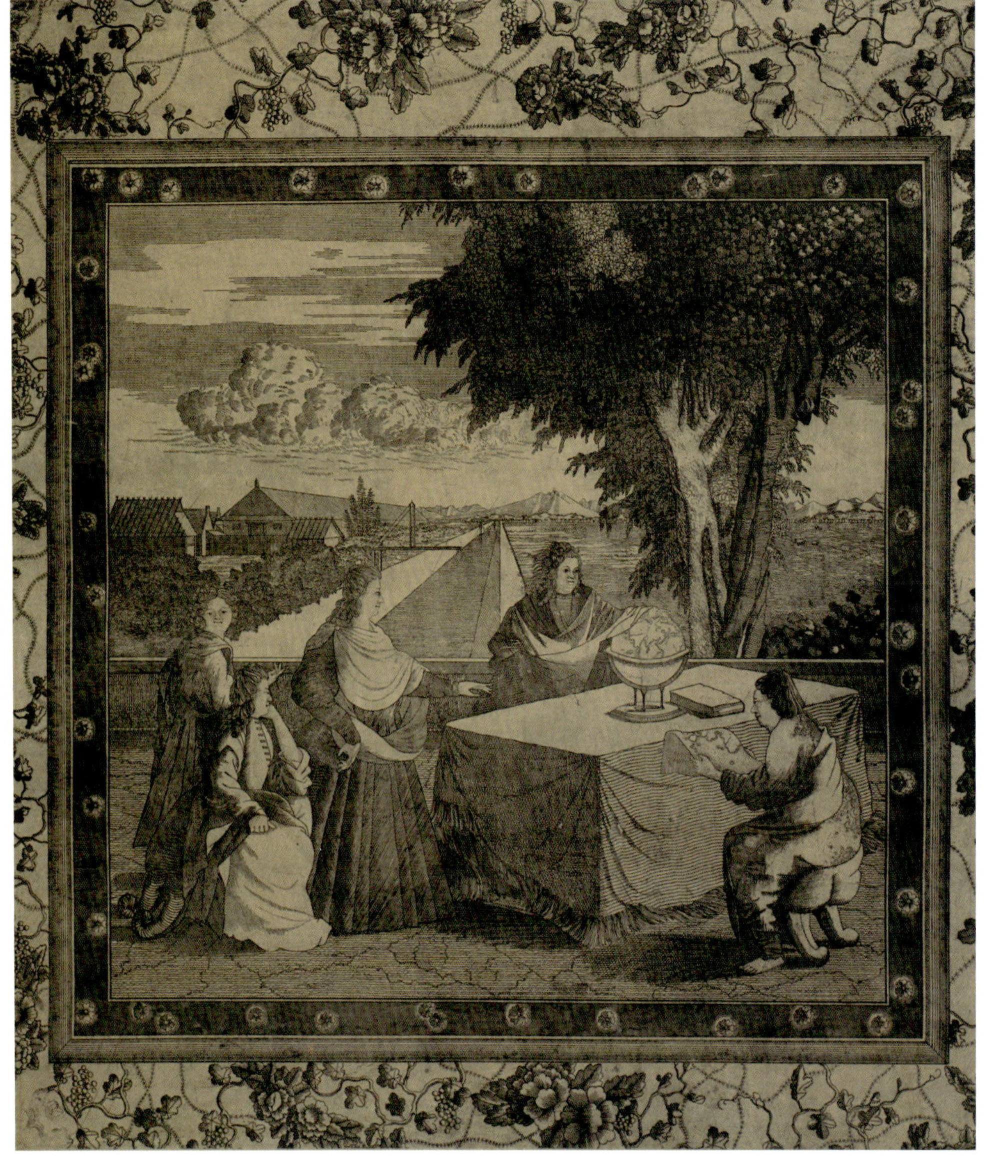

PLATE 78
Aōdō Denzen
(Japanese, 1748–1822)
Koronbusu ekken zu
(An Audience
with Columbus)
Early 19th century
Part of a hanging scroll
Etching: ink on paper
15¾ × 13¾ in.
(40 × 34.8 cm) image

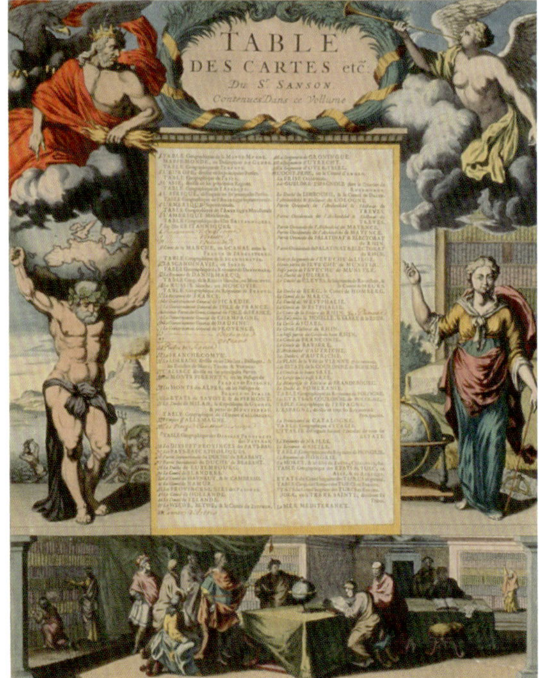

FIG. 14
Nicolas Sanson
(French, 1600–1667)
Table des cartes
(List of Maps)
from *Atlas nouveau,*
Paris, 1692
Copperplate engraving:
ink and color on paper
25¼ × 19⅞ in.
(64 × 50.3 cm) at cover
Ishikawa Prefectural
Library

Aōdō Denzen and An Audience with Columbus

Finally, I would like to introduce some new discoveries regarding Aōdō Denzen (1748–1822) and his access to European books. As an official painter to Matsudaira Sadanobu, Denzen participated in the production of *Shintei bankoku zenzu* (Newly Revised Map of the World, see plate 164), and he is thought to have possessed a high level of geographical knowledge. We know that for source material he used a version of the *Nieuwe atlas* produced by the Dutch firm Covens & Mortier and brought to Japan in 1789.[19]

Recently the source for Denzen's copperplate print *Koronbusu ekken zu* (An Audience with Columbus, plate 78) was identified with a copperplate illustration that decorates a page of Nicolas Sanson's *Atlas nouveau,* published in 1692

(fig. 14).[20] Isaac Titsingh (1745–1812), a director of the Dutch trading post at Dejima, presented a copy of this atlas in 1780, according to its dedication, to Kuchiki Masatsuna, the lord of Fukushiyama. It eventually came to the Maeda family of the Kaga domain (present-day Ishikawa prefecture). Denzen's rendering of hairstyles, clothing, and props in *Koronbusu ekken zu* is detailed and original, with shadows, light effects, and shading. The artist produced a work with a strong exoticism by depicting a world which is wholly distinct from that portrayed in the original.

When, where, and from whom did Denzen obtain a view of this valuable atlas? Denzen's contact with the Kaga domain can be traced through his contributions to the 1808 *Ihan teikō naishō dōhan zenzu* (Copperplate Illustrations for an Anatomical Atlas, plate 79), a collection of illustrations appended to the text of *Ihan teikō*

PLATE 79
Aōdō Denzen
(Japanese, 1748–1822)
Untitled (Internal
Organs)
from Udagawa Genshin
and Fujii Hōtei,
*Ihan teikō naishō dōhan
zenzu,* Edo, 1808
(Bunka 5)
Folded book in
Japanese style
Etching and woodblock
print: ink on paper
12 × 8¼ in.
(30.3 × 20.7 cm) at cover

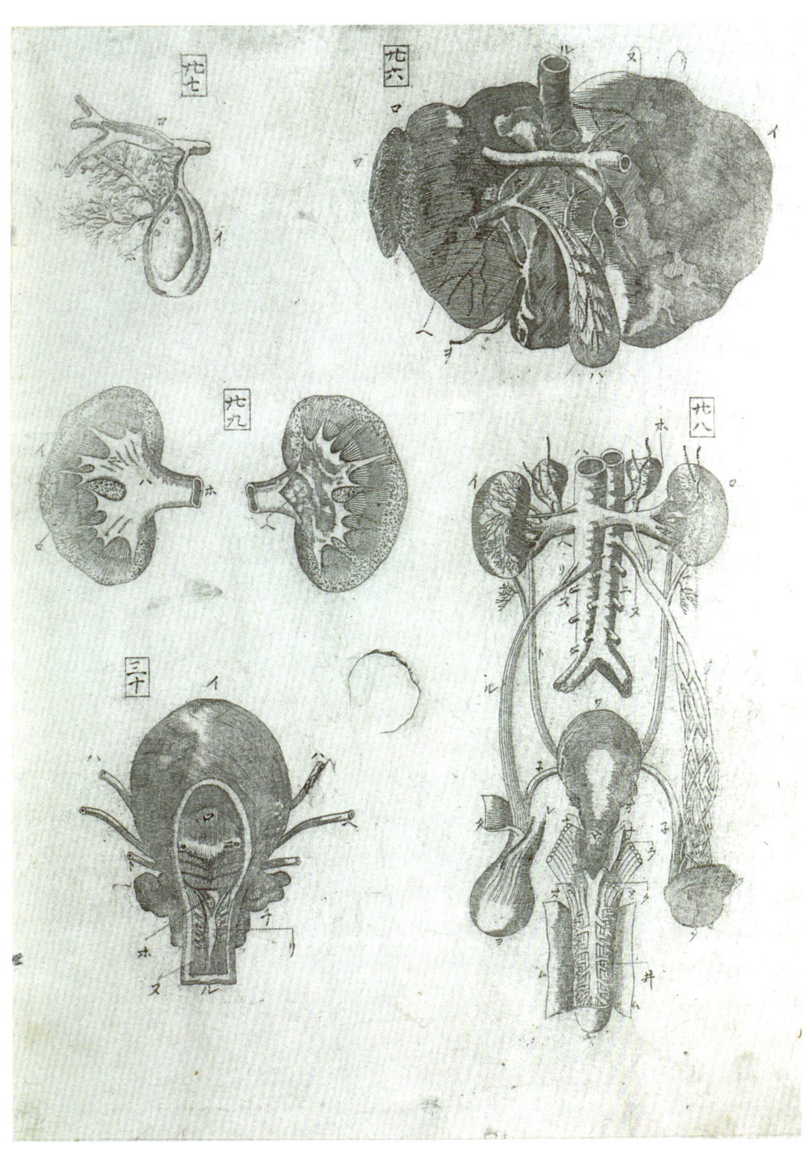

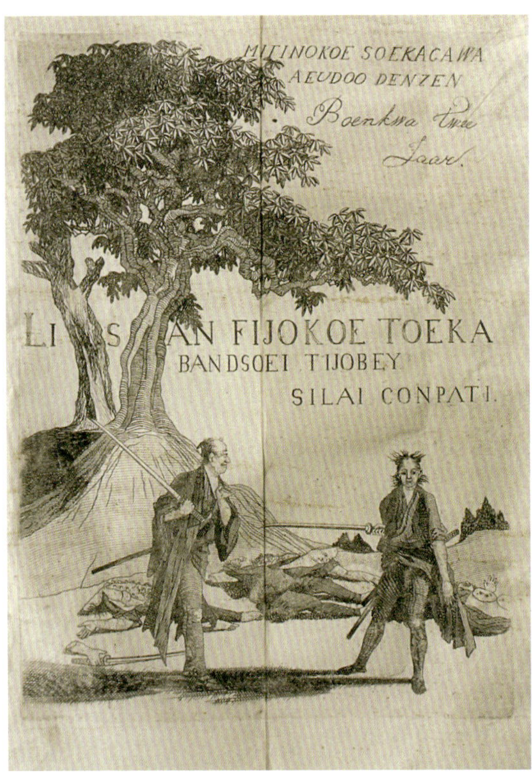

FIG. 15
Aōdō Denzen
(Japanese, 1748–1822)
Meguro hiyokuzuka
(Lovers' Tomb
at Meguro)
1805 (Bunka 2)
Etching: ink on paper
10¼ × 7⅝ in.
(26.0 × 19.2 cm)
Sukagawa City Museum,
Fukushima

(Elements of Medical Science), itself first published in 1805. Fujii Hōtei (1778–1845), who in 1809 had become the first doctor of Western medicine practicing in the Kaga domain, played a leading role in selecting Denzen as the artist in charge of the copperplates for this book. When Hōtei was appointed the official doctor in Edo in 1809, he took up residence in the Kaga domain's estate in nearby Sugamo. It is thought that Denzen gained the opportunity to copy *Atlas nouveau* through Hōtei, who had the utmost trust of the Kaga lord.

Another image of interest is Denzen's 1805 *Meguro hiyokuzuka* (Lovers' Tomb at Meguro, fig. 15). The exact purpose for which it was made is unknown, but it was inspired by a literary work of the same title which was performed at *bunraku* and *kabuki* theater. Denzen depicted a famous scene from the story, in which the lead character commits murder. Two men face one another, their swords drawn. Behind them, two splayed corpses, heads and arms severed, lie on the ground. One is split open to reveal bones and internal organs. In the same year, Denzen had begun his preparatory work for the *Ihan teikō* atlas, using as his references six Western books of anatomy by Verheyen, Blankaart, Kulmus, Palfyn, Bidloo, and Browne.[21] One can only assume that Denzen's study of their detailed anatomical illustrations of the human body had a great influence on the creation of *Meguro hiyokuzuka*.

Clearly the act of copying Western book illustrations played out differently for different artists, depending on individual temperaments, work environments, and patronage. The relationship between Western-style painting and *rangaku* is more complex than once thought, and only additional research will produce a full understanding of the proper place of *ransho* in this equation.

NOTES

1. Ōba Osamu, *Nihon kōryū shiwa* (Osaka: Nenshōsha, 2003).

2. For the impact of Shen Nanpin's arrival in Japan, see Chapter 3 in this volume.

3. That the Dutch paintings were presented before 1729 can be inferred from the inclusion of copies of the two paintings displayed at Gohyaku Rakanji in *Gazu hyakkachō*, a five-volume treasury of art reproductions published in that year. The copies were made by a painter named Zaiga; see plate 9.

4. *Koga bikō (1845–50)*, ed. Asaoka Okisada, lists Mōko's name, artist name, and position (Oguri godayū, gō Tōgaku, Nibangumi Ō-onban), and goes on to say that "he painted well, and is a contemporary of Tairō."

5. Tairō's copy of Lairesse's book is now at the Kyoto University Library. Its provenance can be traced in a signature and label in it. See Matsuda Kiyoshi, *Yōgaku no shoshiteki kenkyū* (Tokyo: Rinsen Shoten, 1998).

6. Kulmus's 1722 *Anatomische Tabellen* had been translated into Dutch in 1734 (*Ontleedkundige tafelen*) by Gerard Dicten.

7. The Akita domain sent its doctor, Inami Buei, to Nagasaki in 1727, and he could have then obtained the Valverde book, which has been passed down in the Inami family. It is likely that Naotake obtained access to the book through his connection to the domain and Inami.

8. Sasaki Sēichi, "Kinsei (18 seiki kōhan ikō) no Ajia ni okeru purushan burū no tsuiseki," in *Tama bijutsu daigaku kiyō* 2 (1985).

9. Katsumori Noriko, "Wakasugi Isohachi Kenkyū," and Kuchitsu Nobuaki, "Wakasugi isohachi no sakuhin ni mochiirareteiru ganryō no tokuchō ni tsuite—tokuni seishoku ganryō no dōtei kara—," *Kobe shiritsu hakubutsukan kiyō* 21 (2005).

10. The test was conducted in June 2006 by Katsumori Noriko for the Pola Foundation for the Arts 2006 Research Scholarship. The measurement was taken by Kuchitsu Nobuaki of the National Institute for Cultural Properties, Tokyo.

11. Katsumori Noriko, "Kenkadō no shūchin shumi," in *Kitani Yoshinobu sensei koki kinen ronshū* ([Osaka]: Kitani Yoshinobu Sensei Koki Kinen Ronshū Kankōkai, 2006).

12. Thought to be a later addition, the Dutch inscription above the figure's head translates "A portrait of the admirable doctor Hippocrates"; beneath it is the signature of Philipp Franz von Siebold, dated in the fifteenth day of the first month, 1825, at Dejima. It is not clear when the painting came to be recognized as a likeness of Hippocrates.

13. Utilizing his copperplate printing technique, Gilles Demarteau (1722–1776) published a compilation of works by famous painters to be used by art students in Paris. Matsuura Seizan (1760–1841), lord of the Hirado domain, obtained this book and published it as *Furansu gachō wakai* (Understanding French Paintings, c. 1786) after attaching a translation by Motoki Yoshinaga; see the comments by Matsuda Kiyoshi in *Edo dai-tenrankai—mono zukuri Nihon*, exh. cat. (Tokyo: Kokuritsu Kagaku Hakubutsukan, 2003). It is thought that Tairō's decision to use *Head of a Man* was based on his acquaintance with this book, which was used as a textbook for Western painting.

14. Ogata Tomio, *Nihon ni okeru Hipokuratsesu sanbi* (Tokyo: Nihon Iji Shinpōsha, 1971).

15. I would like to thank Torii Yumiko of Ōita University for this information.

16. Imaizumi Genkichi, *Rangaku no ie Katsuragawa no hitobito* (Tokyo: Shinozaki Shorin, 1965).

17. Since its first publication in London in 1719, *Robinson Crusoe* has been published in many languages with assorted illustrations. Kuniyoshi most likely had an opportunity to see one of these many editions. The Japanese translation of the novel is based on a 1721 Dutch version.

18. Katsumori Noriko, "Tairō kara Kuniyoshi e—bijutsu ni miru ransho juyō no katachi—," *Kobe shiritsu hakubutsukan kiyō* 16 (2000).

19. Katsumori Noriko, "Aōdō Denzen to ransho—'Sekai yondaishū shinchizuchō' to Wainman 'Kenka shokubutsu zufu' wo megutte—," *Nichiran gakkai kaishi* 52 (2004).

20. Katsumori Noriko, "Aōdō Denzen sen 'Koronbusu ekken zu' wo megutte," *Kobe shiritsu hakubutsukan kiyō* 22 (2006).

21. These were a 1711 Dutch translation of Philippe Verheyen, *Corporis Humani Anatomia* (1693); Stephen Blankaart, *De nieuw hervormde anatomie* (3rd ed., 1696); Gerard Dicten, *Ontleedkundige tafelen* (1734, a Dutch translation of Kulmus's anatomy); Johan Palfyn, *Heelkonstige ontleeding van 's menschen lichaam* (1718 or 1733 ed.); Govard Bidloo, *Anatomia Humani Corporis* (1685); and John Browne, *Myographia Nova sive Musculorum Ominium* (1694). See Frederik Cryns, *Edo jidai ni okeru kikairon-teki shintaikan no juyō* (Kyoto: Rinsen Shoten, 2006).

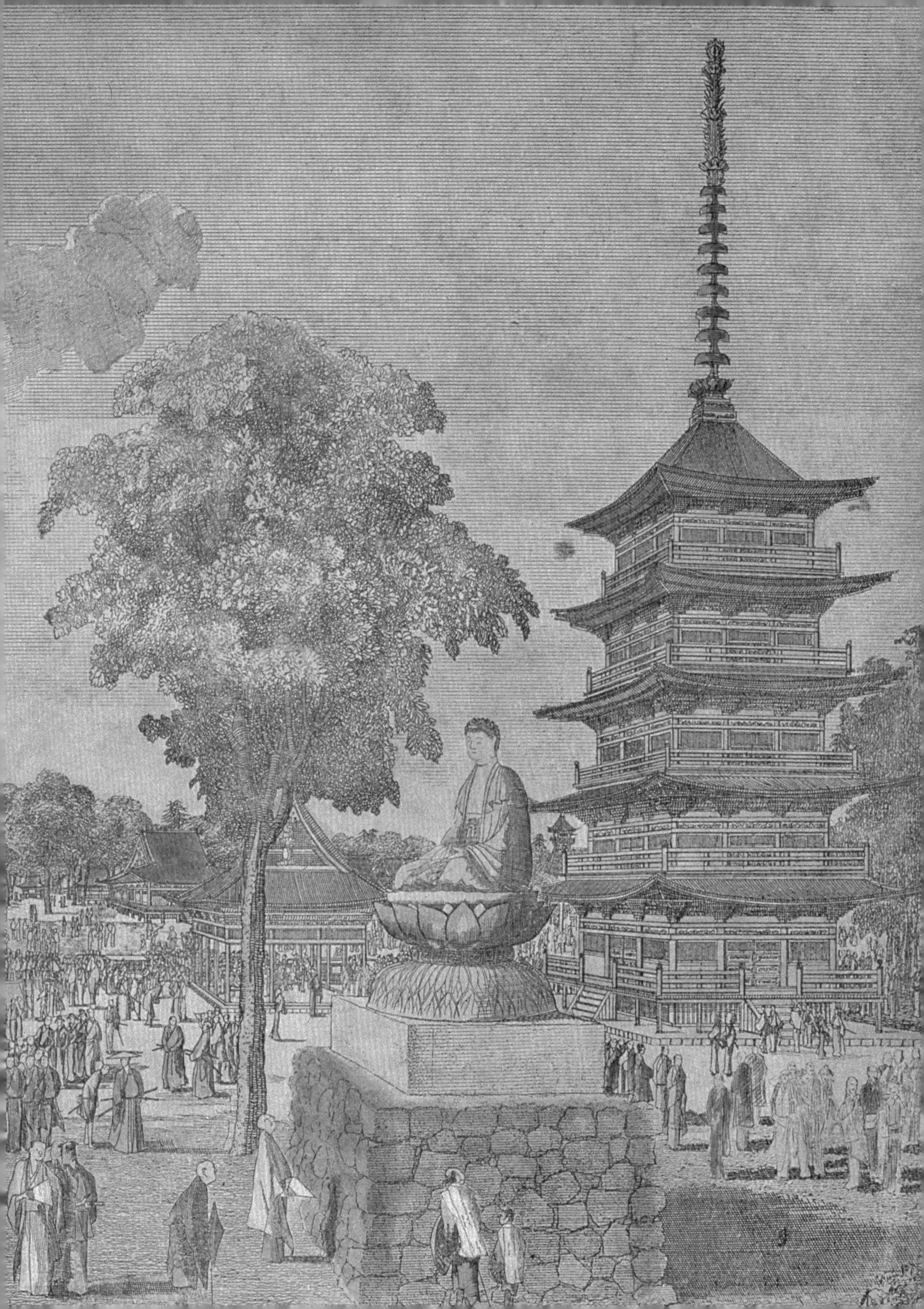

5

Tsukahara Akira

The Early Copperplate Prints of Shiba Kōkan and Aōdō Denzen

Until the middle of the nineteenth century, Chinese and Japanese attitudes toward the West differed markedly. The Chinese located themselves at the conceptual center of the civilized world and perceived Western countries as peripheral, inhabited by barbarians whose culture was strange and peculiar. Many Japanese, however, believed that Western civilization transcended their own, and some regarded the West with awe and some nervousness. Perhaps no group was more representative of this mind-set than the scholars associated with the *rangaku* (Dutch learning) movement that emerged in Japan in the middle of the eighteenth century.

The artists Shiba Kōkan (1747–1818) and Aōdō Denzen (1748–1822) were closely associated with the *rangaku* scholars and their activities. Today, historians consider them among the most important of the late Edo-period artists who worked in the Western style. Because their periods of production overlapped—Kōkan active from the 1780s to 1810s, and Denzen from the 1790s to 1810s—there is a commonly held belief that the two artists had a master-apprentice relationship. But when their backgrounds are examined more closely, it is clear that their personalities, as well as the circumstances and contexts in which they produced their artwork, differed greatly. In exploring a number of works by Kōkan and Denzen, this essay highlights many important aspects concerning the significance of visual culture during this fascinating moment in Japanese art history.

Shiba Kōkan is popularly identified as a man of samurai stock, but in fact he was born into a family of wealthy merchants or craftsmen in Edo. In an inscription found on a portrait of his mother, Kōkan wrote that his father, identified as Maruya Ichirobei, passed away when he was about fourteen years old, and from that time, his inheritance quickly gone, his mother struggled greatly in raising him. While this inscription suggests a straitened upbringing, Kōkan could only have become an artist with access to the personal connections necessary to obtain adequate training and to open avenues into the art world.

Kōkan struggled financially to establish himself as an artist, and to survive, he moved away from the Chinese-inspired Kano school style in which he was trained. He instead made paintings in the popular *ukiyo-e* style, a number of which imitated the works of Suzuki Harunobu (c. 1725–1770), the leading artist of the genre at the time. Some historians have hypothesized that Kōkan was drawn into the *ukiyo-e* industry through a family tie. A man named Maruya had published Harunobu's works, and since this surname may be a derivation of that used by Kōkan's father, Kōkan and the publisher may have been related. This idea is further supported by the fact that the Maruya family, prominent hardware wholesalers in the Fukagawa area of eastern Edo, were patrons of the temple at which Kōkan was later buried.

That Kōkan might have been born into a family of hardware merchants is particularly intriguing given his later fame as a copperplate artist. Such a background would have provided him with early exposure to the general trade of metalwork and to the specific techniques and methods of metal processing. In his essay *Shunparō hikki* (c. 1811), Kōkan revealed that before deciding on a career as a painter he had intended to become a maker of swords or decorative sword fittings. But the extremely high level of craftsmanship already practiced by sword metalworkers and decorators discouraged him from believing he could excel in this field, and he turned to painting.

Kōkan's familiarity with the techniques of metal engraving for sword decoration is crucial in our understanding of the impressive etchings he produced in the 1780s. Etching requires specialized knowledge and skills in handling sheet metal, applying corrosives, and operating a printing press. Kōkan's mastery of the necessary skills was a signifcant accomplishment, given the further technical expertise required for copperplate etching—polishing the plate, applying an acid-resistant ground, delicately etching with a metal point or stylus, and using acid to create an intaglio printing plate. One must remember that woodcut was the only printing technology widely available to the Japanese. In this context it is interesting to note the Japanese technique known as *kusara-kashi* (corrosion), which was used in the decoration of sword guards (*tsuba*) and fittings. This process parallels the preparation of copperplates for printing, in which craftsmen created designs by corroding areas of metal that were not protected by an acid-resistant paint. The similarities between *kusarakashi* and Western copperplate etching are close enough that Kōkan could have readily made the transition from one technique to the other.

Kōkan's motivation for turning to Western artistic methods derived not only from his technical expertise but also from his association with the *rangaku* scholars in Edo. One individual who exerted great influence on Kōkan was the naturalist and writer Hiraga Gennai (1728–1779). Gennai was acquainted with two artists, Suzuki Harunobu and Sō Shiseki (1715–1786, see plates 57, 58), whose painting styles Kōkan had emulated early in his career (plates 80, 81). In *Shunparō hikki,* Kōkan wrote that Gennai had shown him prints from his private collection, including imported Western-style copperplate prints from a richly illustrated encyclopedia of animals (1660) by Johannes Jonstonus.

Gennai himself did not specialize in Western learning, but he was a close friend of Sugita Genpaku (1733–1817), an influential physician and scholar who in 1774 produced *Kaitai shinsho* (New Book of Anatomy, see plates 63, 64), the earliest Western-style anatomical work to be published in Japan. Through Gennai, Kōkan subsequently became acquainted with the first generation of *rangaku* scholars, gaining access to illustrations found in Dutch academic publications and furthering his keen interest in the minutely detailed, fine expression possible with copperplate etching. With technical information available only in Western books, and himself inadequate in the Dutch language, Kōkan could not on his own have understood and learned the

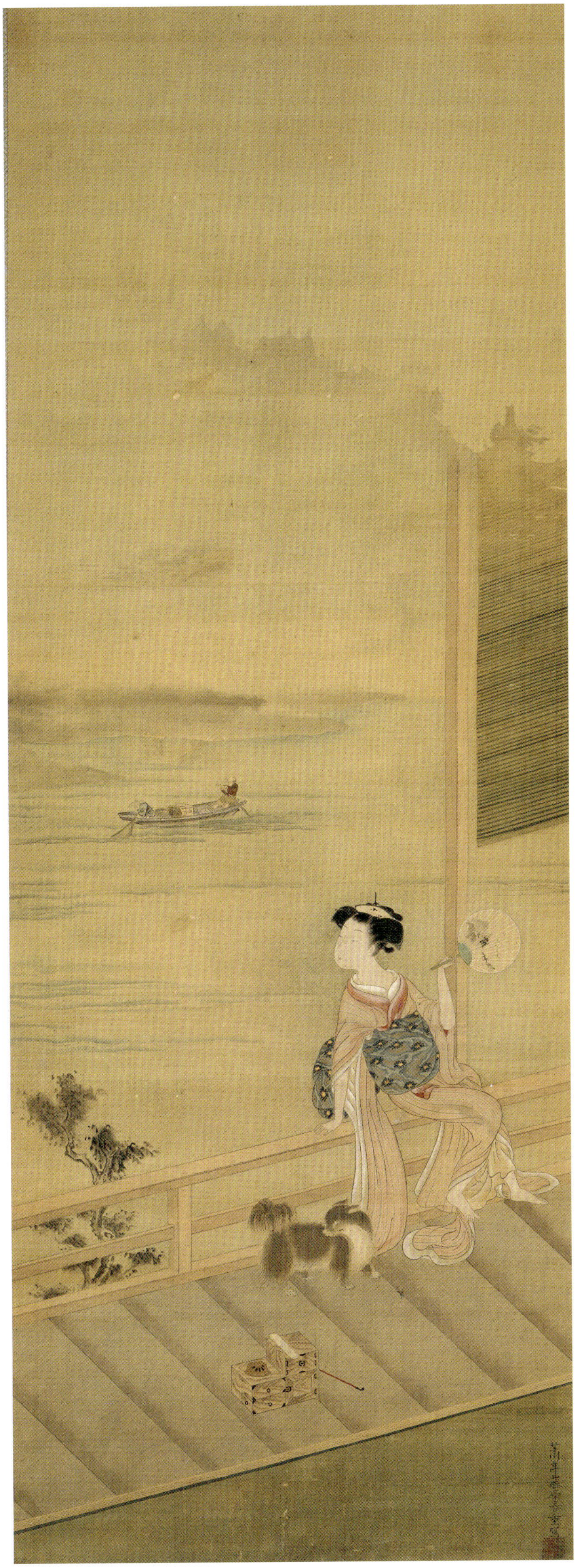

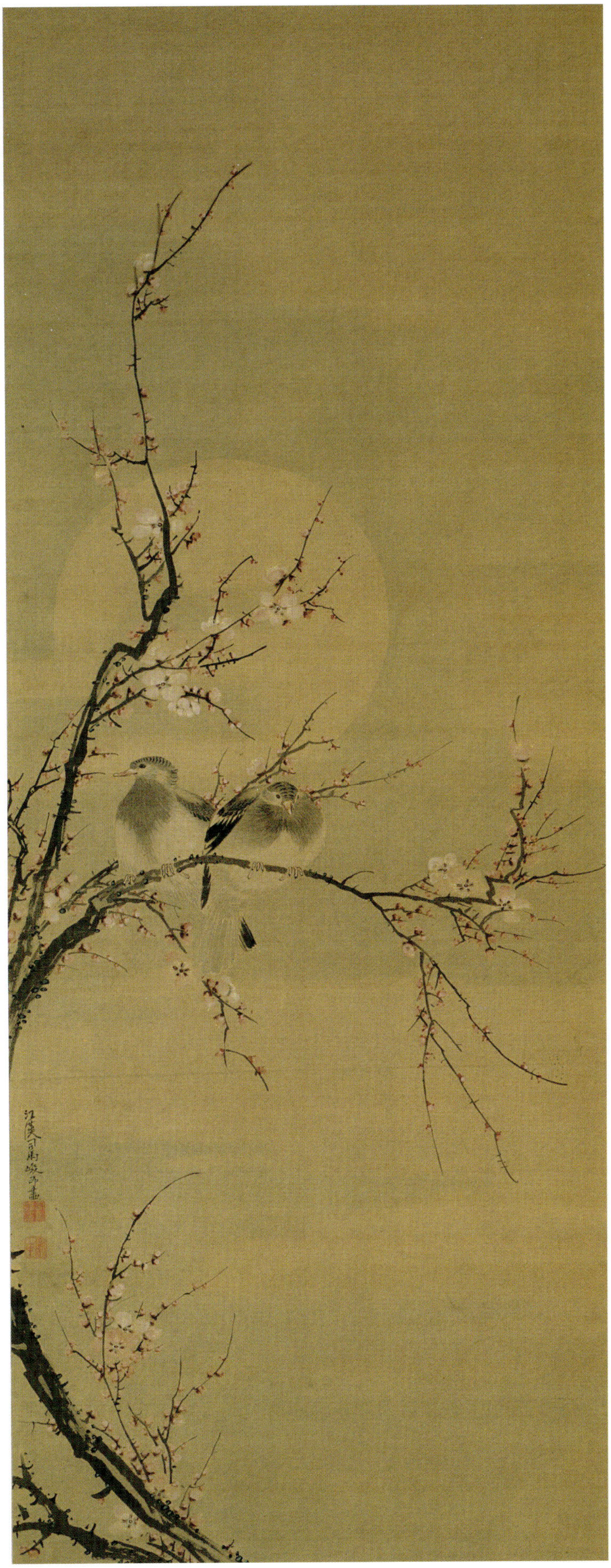

PLATE 82
Shiba Kōkan
(Japanese, 1747–1818)
Mimeguri no kei
**(View of Mimeguri
in Edo)**
1783 (Tenmei 3)
Etching: ink with
hand color on paper
11⅛ × 16 in.
(28 × 40.4 cm)
■

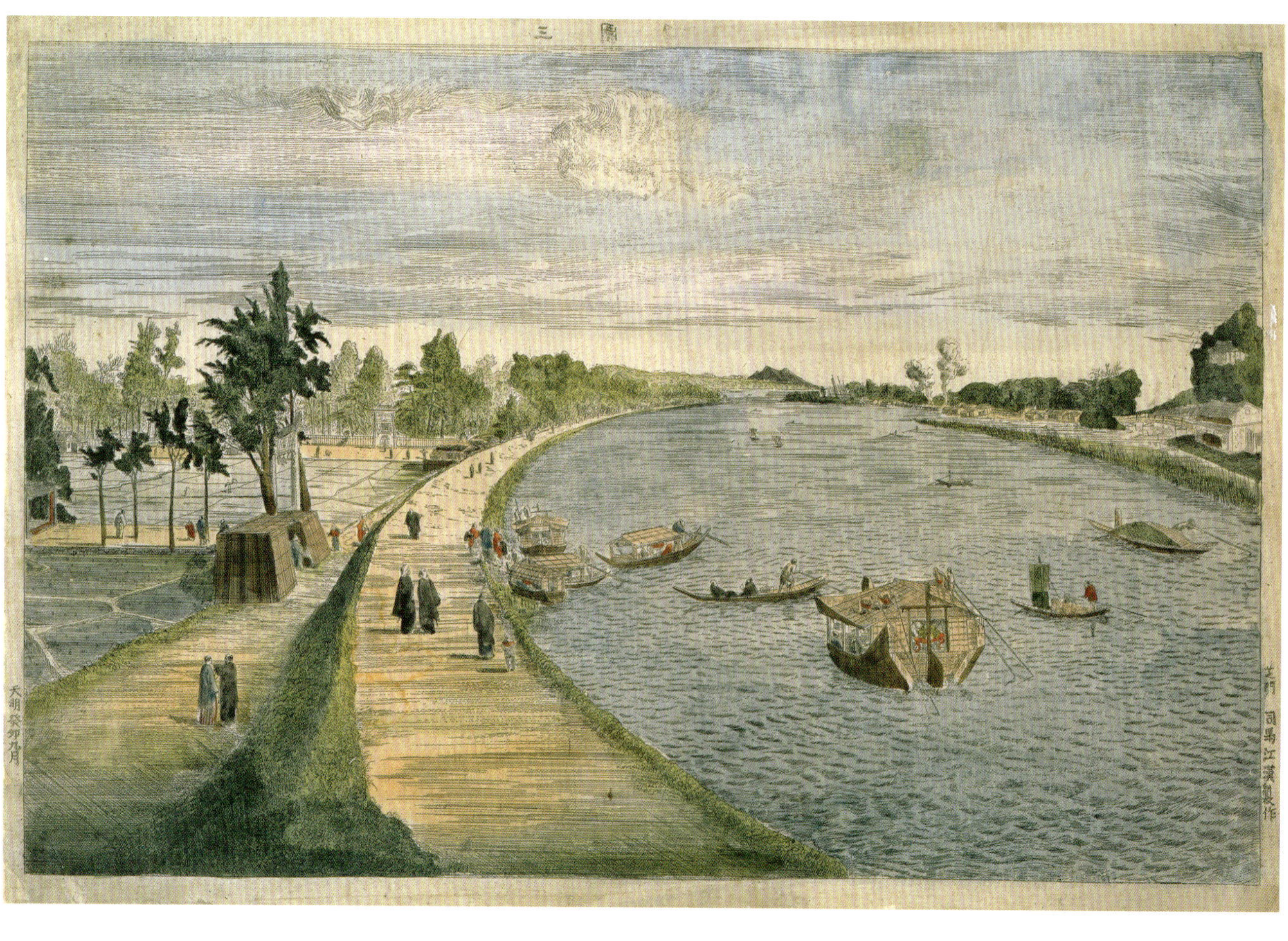

techniques of copperplate printing. He gained this crucial knowledge with the aid of the *rangaku* scholar Ōtsuki Gentaku (1757–1827), who had translated a Dutch version of *Dictionnaire oéconomique* (1709) by Noël Chomel. In this encyclopedic work, Kōkan likely was able to access a full explanation of copperplate printing technology and methods.

With this new knowledge, Kōkan in 1783 succeeded in producing Japan's first copperplate etching, *Mimeguri no kei* (View of Mimeguri in Edo, plate 82), a view of the Sumida River. It was the first of many *megane-e* (optical paintings viewed through a special device) illustrating famous places in Edo that Kōkan would produce (plate 83). The technical achievement of these works was not lost on Kōkan, who throughout his thirties and forties was known to openly boast of being the first Japanese to create a copperplate print. His enthusiasm for these small printed works diminished after the 1790s, when he began to make larger-scale oil paintings and printed maps of the world (see plate 163) that expressed his interest in world geography and the Copernican system of heliocentricity.

When compared to Western works, Kōkan's oils appear technically simplistic, despite some attempts at overpainting and layering. Kōkan termed his oil works *rōga* (wax painting), and although he never provided exact details about the materials and techniques he used, scholars believe he bound his pigments with oil extracted from sesame seeds, a technique employed at that time in the production of oiled paper and paper umbrellas. Japanese artists were using this type of paint by the middle of the eighteenth century.

Kōkan produced large-scale oils on a variety of subjects, and a main theme concerned Europeans engaged in work and labor (plates 84a,b, 86). The model for this motif was Jan and Kaspar Luyken's *Spiegel van het menselyk bedryf* (Book of Trades), first published in Amsterdam in 1694 (plate 85). This book illustrated one hundred vocations, each of which was associated with a moralistic admonition. Kōkan admired Europeans for their history, culture, and advanced scholarship, technologies, and social systems. He insisted that this higher civilization was sustained by industrious, capable citizens who were guided by didactic works such as *Spiegel van het menselyk bedryf*.

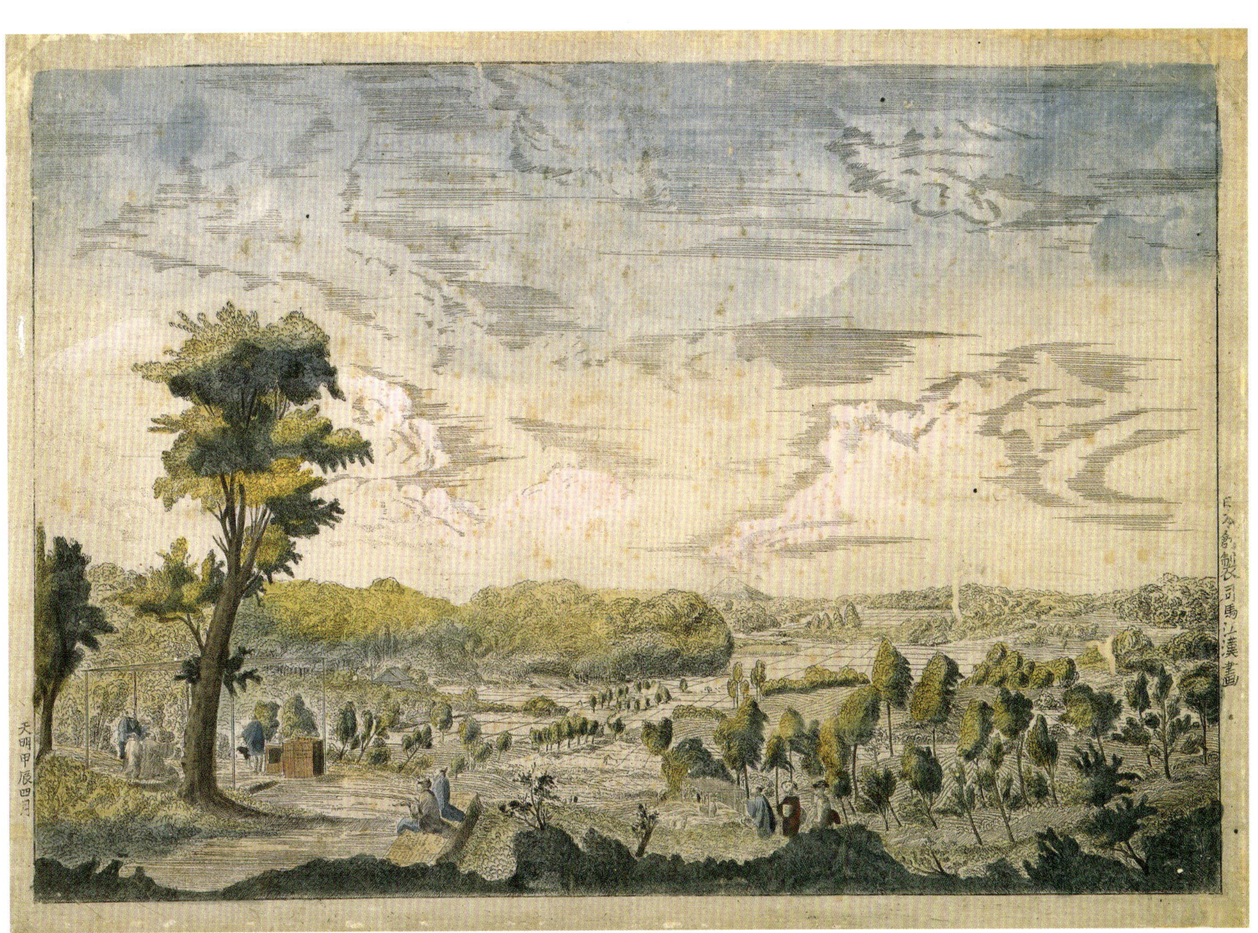

PLATE 84a,b
Shiba Kōkan
(Japanese, 1747–1818)
Ikoku fūkei jinbutsu zu (European Landscapes with Figures)
1790s (Kansei era)
Pair of hanging scrolls: oil on silk
45¼ × 21⅞ in. (114.9 × 55.6 cm) each

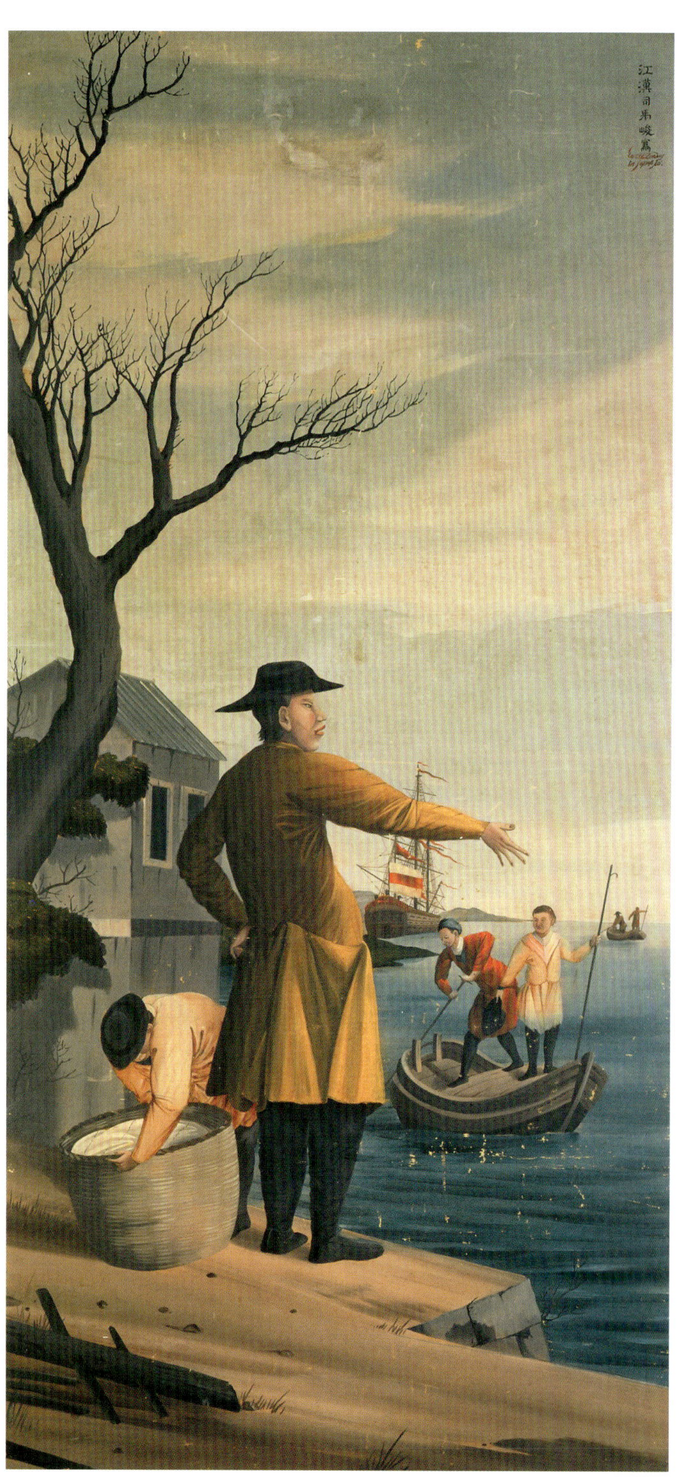

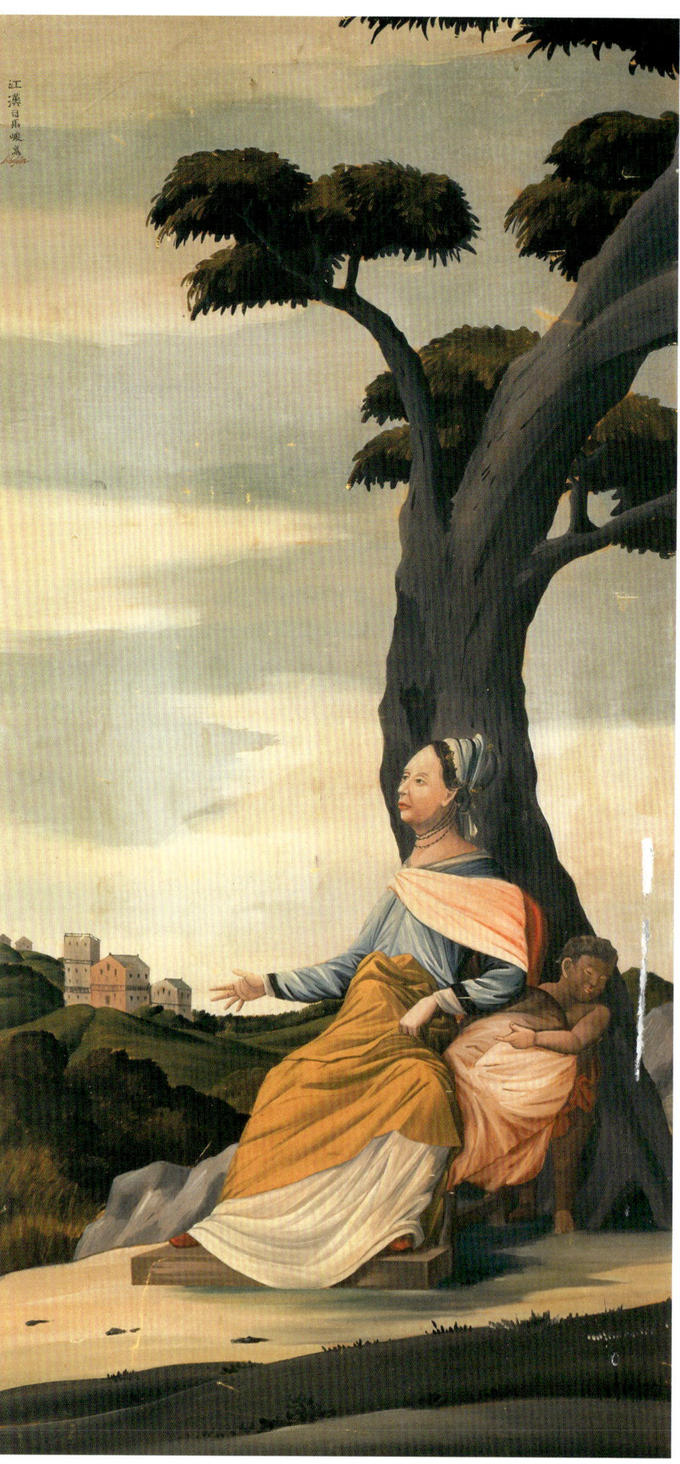

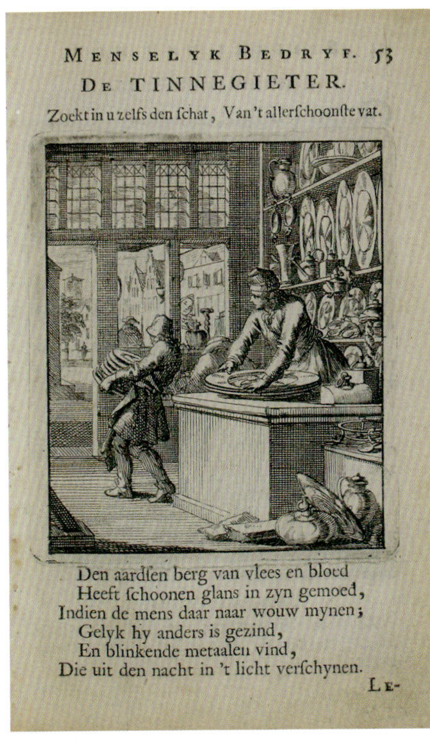

PLATE 85
Jan Luyken
(Dutch, 1649–1712)
and Kaspar Luyken
(Dutch, 1672–1708)
De tinnegieter
(The Tinsmith)
from *Spiegel van het menselyk bedryf*, Amsterdam [n.d., first ed. 1694]
Etching: ink on paper
6¼ × 4 in.
(15.7 × 10 cm) page

PLATE 86
Shiba Kōkan
(Japanese, 1747–1818)
Ikoku kōjō zu
(Scene in a Foreign Factory)
1790s (Kansei era)
Hanging scroll: ink and color on silk
25¼ × 50⅝ in.
(64 × 128.6 cm)

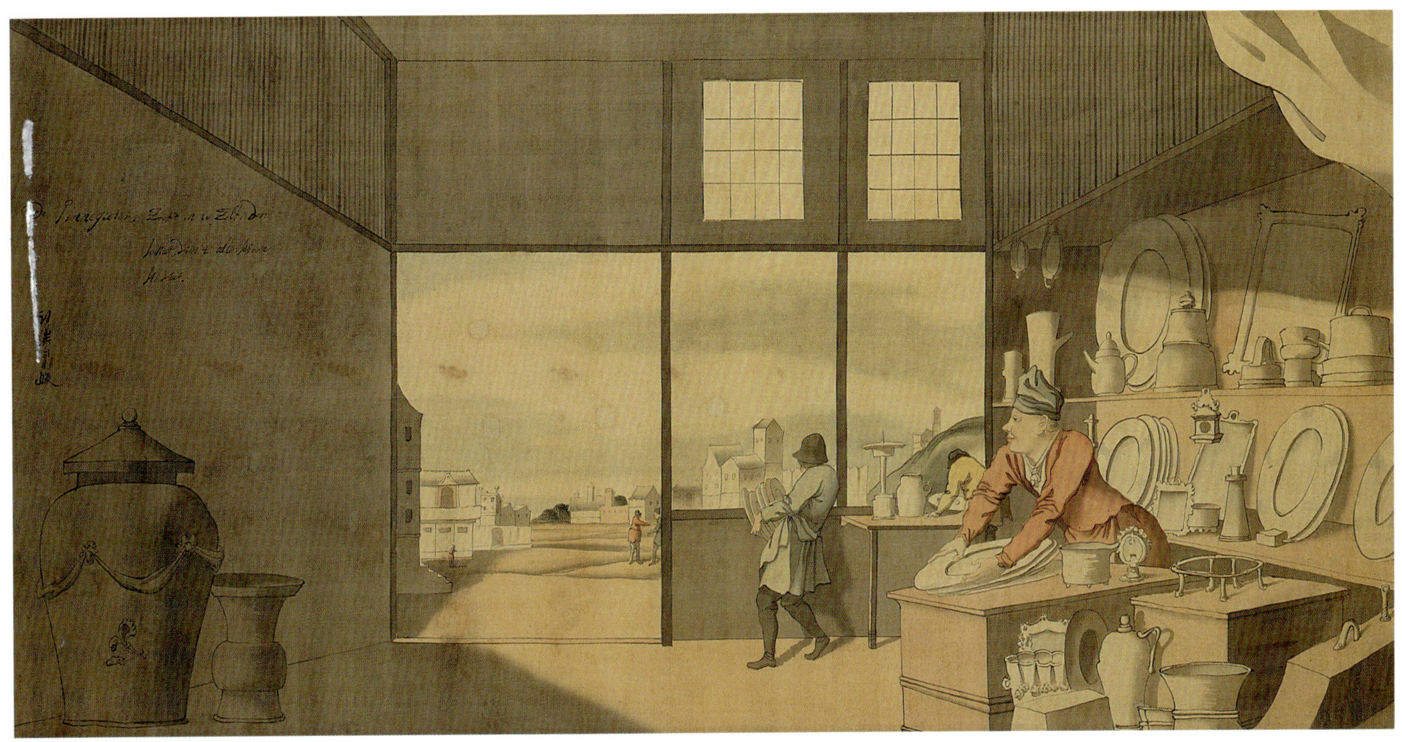

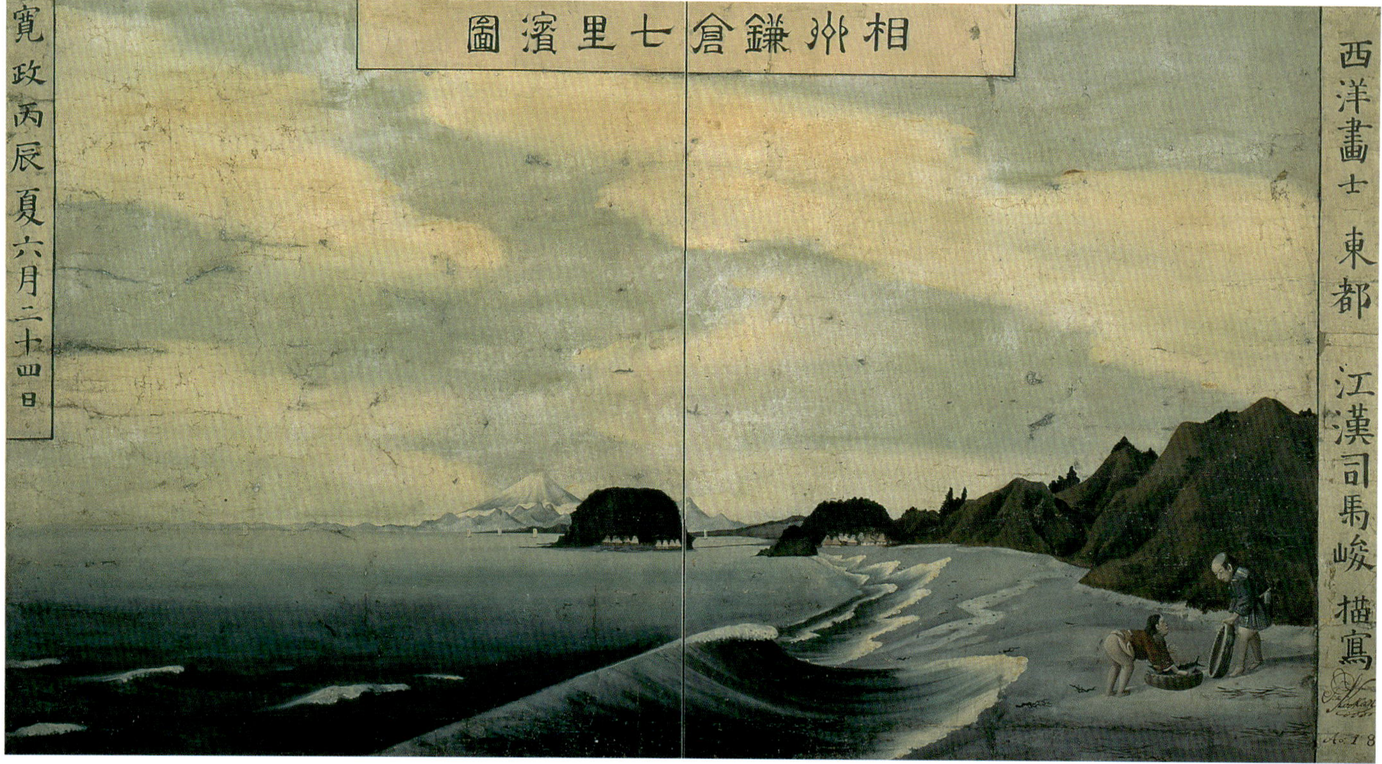

Despite his admiration of Western culture and civilization, Kōkan produced more illustrations of Japanese than Western scenes. Traveling to Nagasaki in 1788, Kōkan made a number of highly naturalistic and accurate paintings of Mount Fuji and the surrounding areas. The mountain became the core motif of his later work, which earned him the nickname "Painter of Mount Fuji." During the 1790s Kōkan developed his grandest artistic project. He created a number of large landscape oil paintings, which he dedicated to temples across the country, and he strongly encouraged their public display (plate 87). Kōkan's desire to be recognized as the greatest Western-style painter in Japan at that time was implicit in his self-promotion.

Yet in 1809 Kōkan expressed his intention to cease painting landscapes in oil. He returned to the more traditional painting forms of ink and wash (plate 88). But he did not turn his back entirely on Western ideas of art production. In his views of Mount Fuji, for example, Kōkan incorporated light effects as well as aerial perspective.

Shiba Kōkan is clearly an important figure in the history of Japanese art, although he operated solely in the private sphere, without public acknowledgment or official patronage for his projects. Moreover, Kōkan had few students of his own and did not leave a successor or establish a painting school in his style. While some critics have observed that Kōkan was concerned only in furthering his own interests, others have come to regard him as a significant artist born of the merchant class who should be recognized for his creativity and his challenges to the orthodox, established modes of art production in Japan.

PLATE 87
Shiba Kōkan
(Japanese, 1747–1818)
Sōshū Kamakura Shichirigahama zu
(Shichirigahama Beach at Kamakura, Sagami Province)
1796 (Kansei 8)
Two-panel screen: oil on paper
37¾ × 70⅜ in.
(95.7 × 178.7 cm)

PLATE 88
Shiba Kōkan
(Japanese, 1747–1818)
*Sunshū Kashiwabara
Fuji zu* (View of
Mount Fuji from
Kashiwabara,
Suruga Province)
1812 (Bunka 9)
Hanging scroll: ink
and light color on silk
15½ × 28½ in.
(39.3 × 72.3 cm)

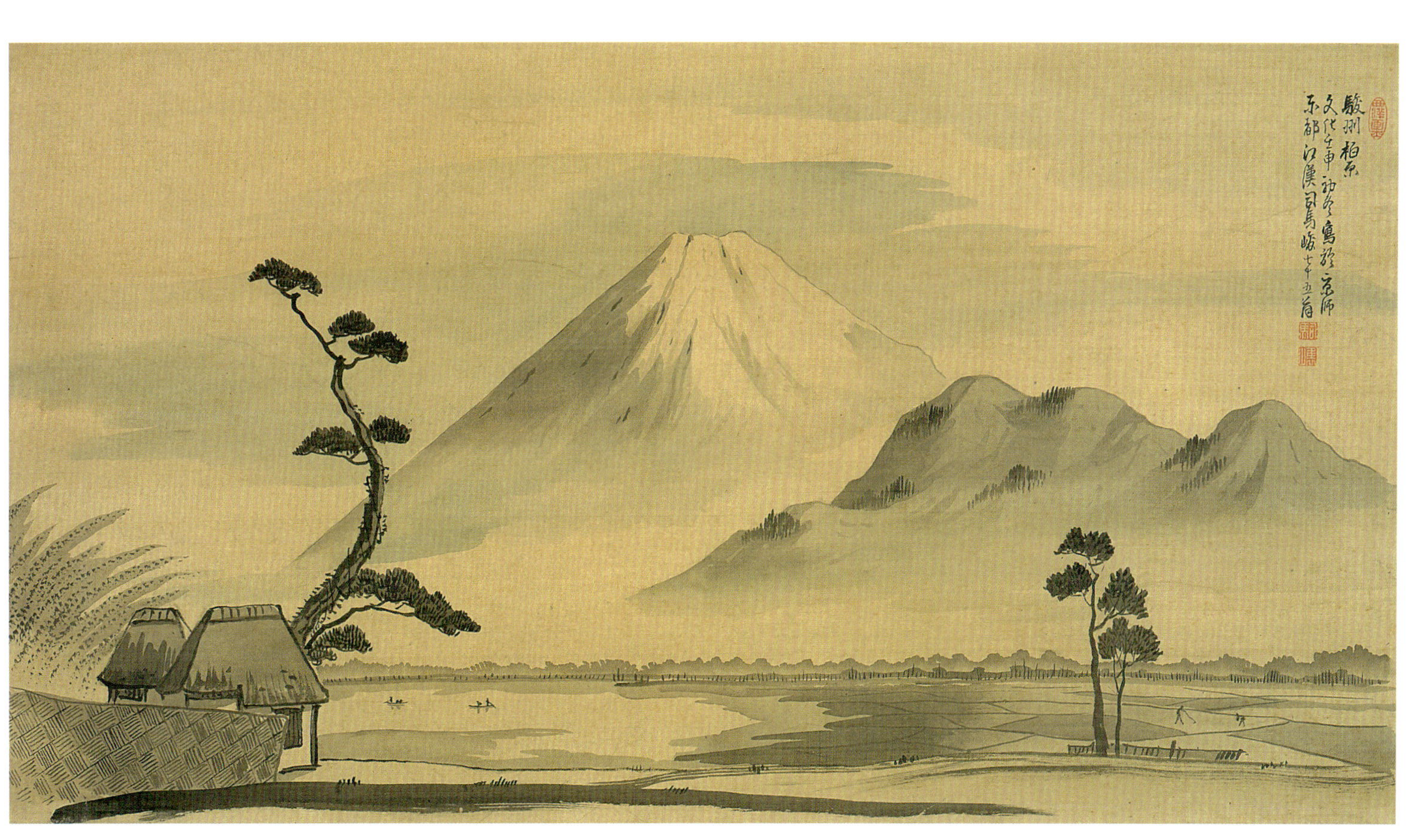

Aōdō Denzen

Matsudaira Sadanobu (1759–1829), an influential senior councillor (*rōjū*) to the Tokugawa shogunate, regarded the popularization of Western learning and cultural forms as represented by Shiba Kōkan with great suspicion. In his essay *Taikan zatuwa* (1797–1800), Sadanobu warned that the technological information and innovations outlined in Western books, while perhaps convenient, were neither beneficial nor desirable for Japan. Nonetheless, Sadanobu did not entirely reject European civilization. Notable among the technologies he approved was that of copperplate printing, whose depth of detail surpassed existing indigenous methods. Sadanobu was instrumental in developing Japanese copperplate print technologies from its earliest days.

The 1792 Russian expedition to Japan under the leadership of Adam Erikovich Laxman occurred amid a growing shogunal interest in world affairs. It was in this context that Shiba Kōkan completed his important 1792 *Yochi zenzu* (Map of the Earth), the first copperplate-printed world map produced in Japan. Kōkan had hoped to gain favor with Sadanobu in this endeavor, but, disappointed by the quality of Kōkan's map, the influential official turned to other copperplate specialists.

In 1794 Sadanobu summoned Aōdō Denzen (whose given name was Nagata Zenkichi), a dye shop owner and painter who lived in Sukagawa, Iwashiro province (now Fukushima prefecture), a domain under Sadanobu's control. Sadanobu appointed Denzen as his official painter and arranged for him to study under the noted painter Tani Bunchō (1763–1841), who was also in the councillor's service. How Denzen came to excel in Western-style painting is not known, but he became so proficient that Sadanobu bestowed upon him the pseudonym "Aōdō," which translates roughly as "Studio of Asia and Europe." With official support and patronage, the artist established a public career, leading a life very different from his contemporary Shiba Kōkan, who worked free of ties to the government.

A better understanding of Sadanobu's negative reaction to Kōkan's work, as well as what he probably desired, can be achieved by comparing examples of copperplate prints by Kōkan and Denzen. Kōkan's 1783 *Mimeguri no kei* is extremely important for being the first copperplate etching produced in Japan and for its accurate perspectival treatment, especially in relation to what was commonly seen in Japanese works at the time. When this image is closely examined (detail, lower left), however, one can see that the perspectival effect comes mostly from the painted colors Kōkan added later, and not via etched line. Furthermore, the etching lines appear at a rate of two or three per millimeter and are inconsistent, creating the effect of a rough sketch more than of a unified, finished print. We can contrast this with an enlarged detail from one of Denzen's large-scale landscape copperplate prints, in which the etched lines, occurring at a rate of four to five per millimeter, are stable and uniform, a result possible only through Denzen's

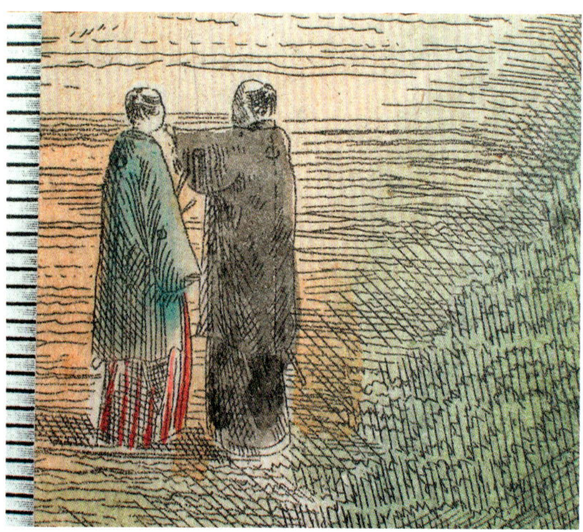

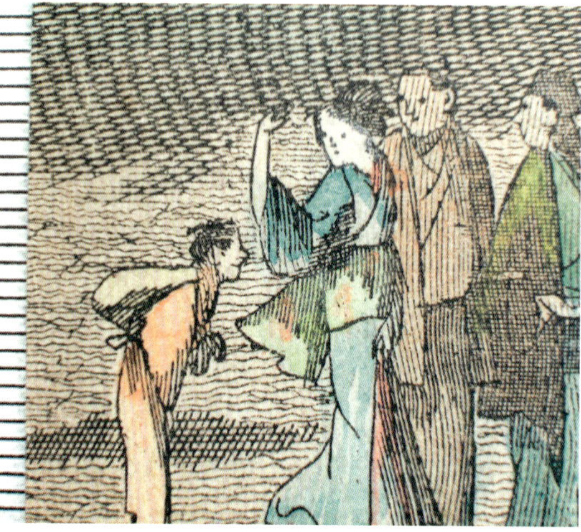

DETAIL (left)
Etched lines in Kōkan's *Mimeguri no kei* (plate 82)

DETAIL (right)
Etched lines in Denzen's *Dai-Nihon Kinryūzan no zu* (plate 89)

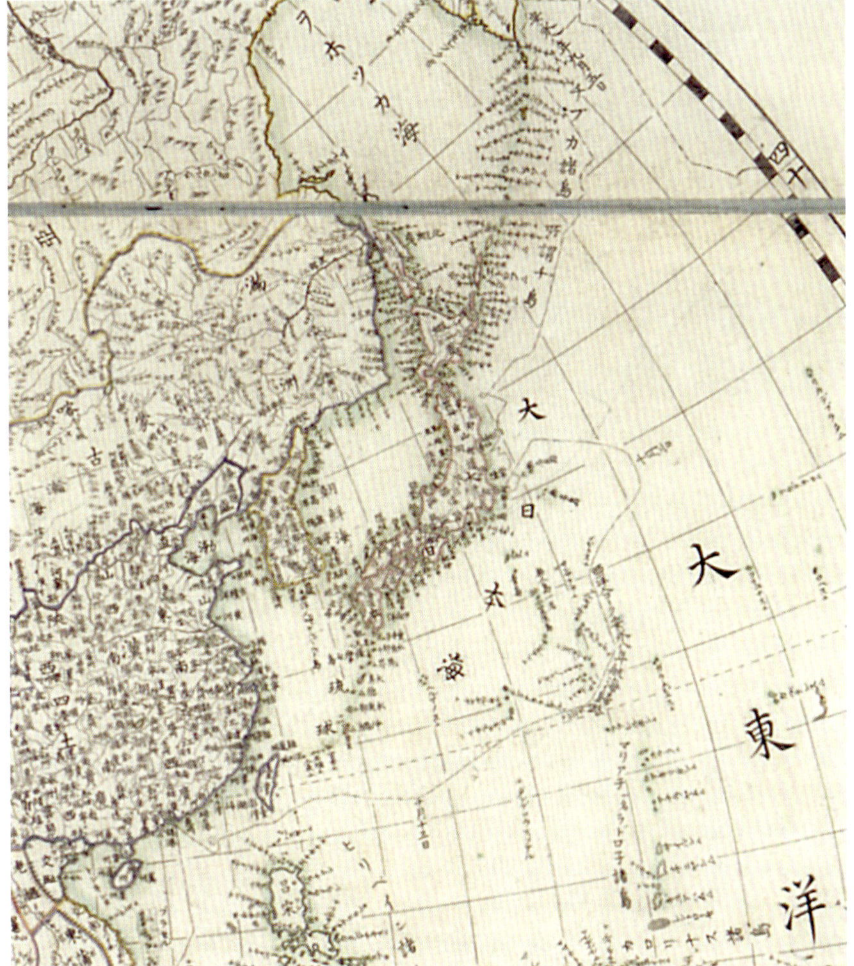

mastery of the technical process (detail opposite, lower right).

Kōkan himself is said to have acknowledged Denzen's ability, calling him "a Dutchman born in Japan." Denzen began producing copperplate prints prior to 1797, and they greatly exceeded those of Kōkan in detail and scope. Furthermore, through his relationships with leading *rangaku* scholars, Denzen came to exert great influence over the development and evolution of later Western learning and copperplate printing in Japan. For example, Denzen was responsible for the 1808 illustrated atlas appended to *Ihan teikō* by the *rangaku* scholar Utagawa Genshin and his students (see plate 79). This work is especially significant because it contains the first copperplate illustrations of anatomical subjects produced in Japan. In addition, in about 1816 Denzen prepared a printed version of *Shintei bankoku zenzu* (Newly Revised Map of the World), which had been designed in 1810 by Takahashi Kageyasu, the shogunate's minister of astronomy (see detail above and plate 164). Historians value the accuracy and detail of this work, finding it to be on par with world maps produced elsewhere around the globe at the time. Because of the quality of his output, Aōdō Denzen is regarded as a premier illustrator who excelled in collaborative projects with *rangaku* scholars.

The success of Denzen's copperplate etchings cannot be attributed simply to the stability and consistency of his line. He was able to subtly express both shadow and three-dimensionality through the careful and calculated control of the thickness and spacing of line. This ability separates his work from that of Kōkan.

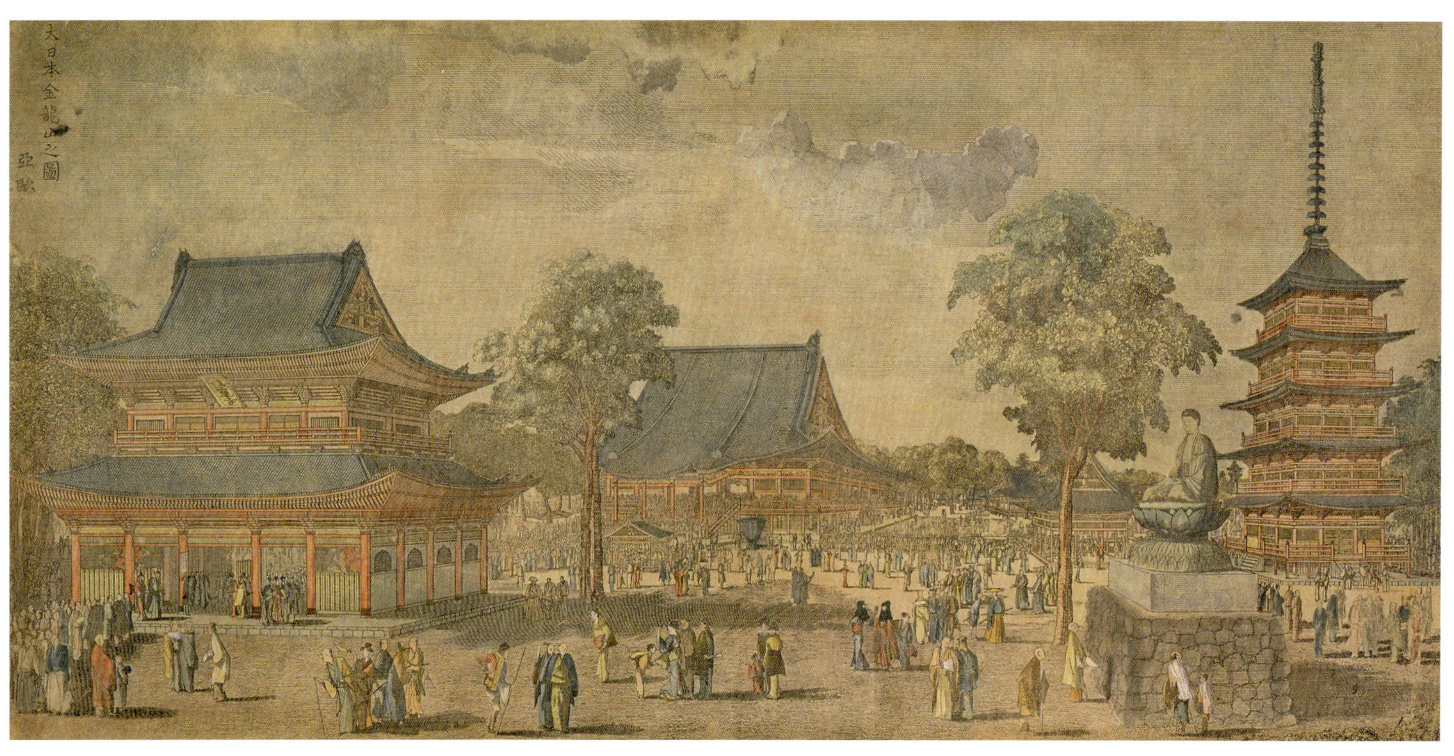

PLATE 89
Aōdō Denzen
(Japanese, 1748–1822)
*Dai-Nihon Kinryūzan
no zu* (View of Japan:
Sensōji at Kinryūzan)
c. 1809 (Bunka 6)
Etching: ink with
hand color on paper
10¼ × 21⅛ in.
(26 × 53.4 cm)

Denzen was not only talented in scientific or highly detailed subjects such as medical illustrations and maps. He also excelled at landscape scenes. The extant works attributed to him today range from larger-scale views exceeding 20 inches in width, including *Dai-Nihon Kinryūzan no zu* (View of Japan: Sensōji at Kinryūzan, plate 89) and *Zerumania kakuchū no zu* (View of a European Plaza, plate 90), to much smaller pieces. Of the latter, twenty-five works are known, with the smallest being a set of famous views of Edo that gained great popularity. Evidence of Denzen's hand can be seen in other printed works such as *ukiyo-e* by Utagawa Kuniyoshi and the copperplate prints produced by the Gengendō school of printmakers in Kyoto. Such diversity and range demonstrate Denzen's versatility and appeal across different genres and regions in Japan.

Because many imitations and atelier works exist under the name of Aōdō, much needs to be clarified in his oeuvre. Problems arise not only with copperplate etched prints of nonscientific subjects but also oil paintings that carry Denzen's signature and seal. The style of these works varies, with some reminiscent of those by Kōkan, and little is known about their attribution and provenance. There is no disagreement, however, that *Imado kawarayaki zu* (Producing Tiles at Imado, plate 91), is the finest and most reliable example of Denzen's oil painting.

PLATE 90
Aōdō Denzen
(Japanese, 1748–1822)
Zerumania kakuchū no zu (View of a European Plaza)
1809 (Bunka 6)
Etching: ink on paper
11⅞ × 22⅛ in.
(30.1 × 56.1 cm)

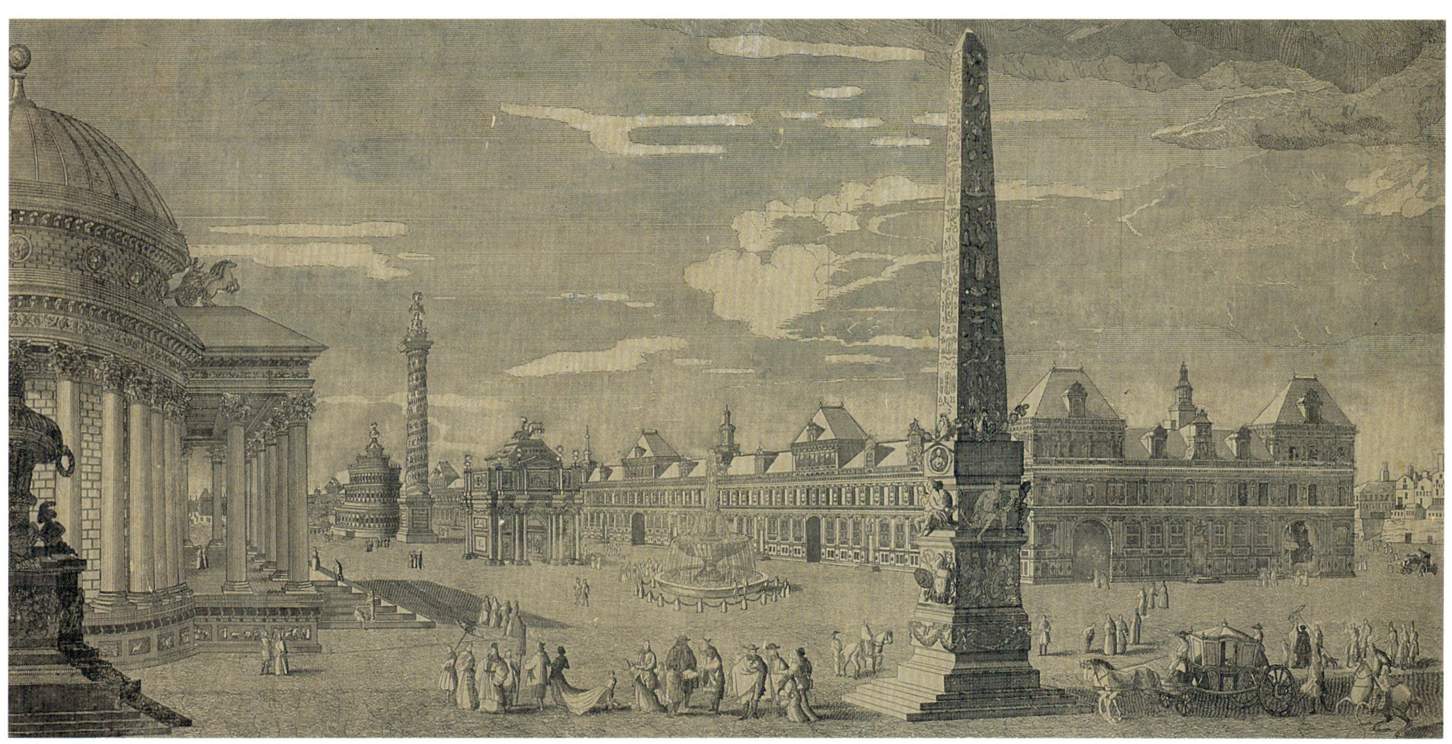

PLATE 91
Aōdō Denzen
(Japanese, 1748–1822)
*Imado kawarayaki
zu* (Producing
Tiles at Imado)
1800–10
Hanging scroll:
oil on silk
16⅛ × 25⅞ in.
(40.8 × 65.6 cm)

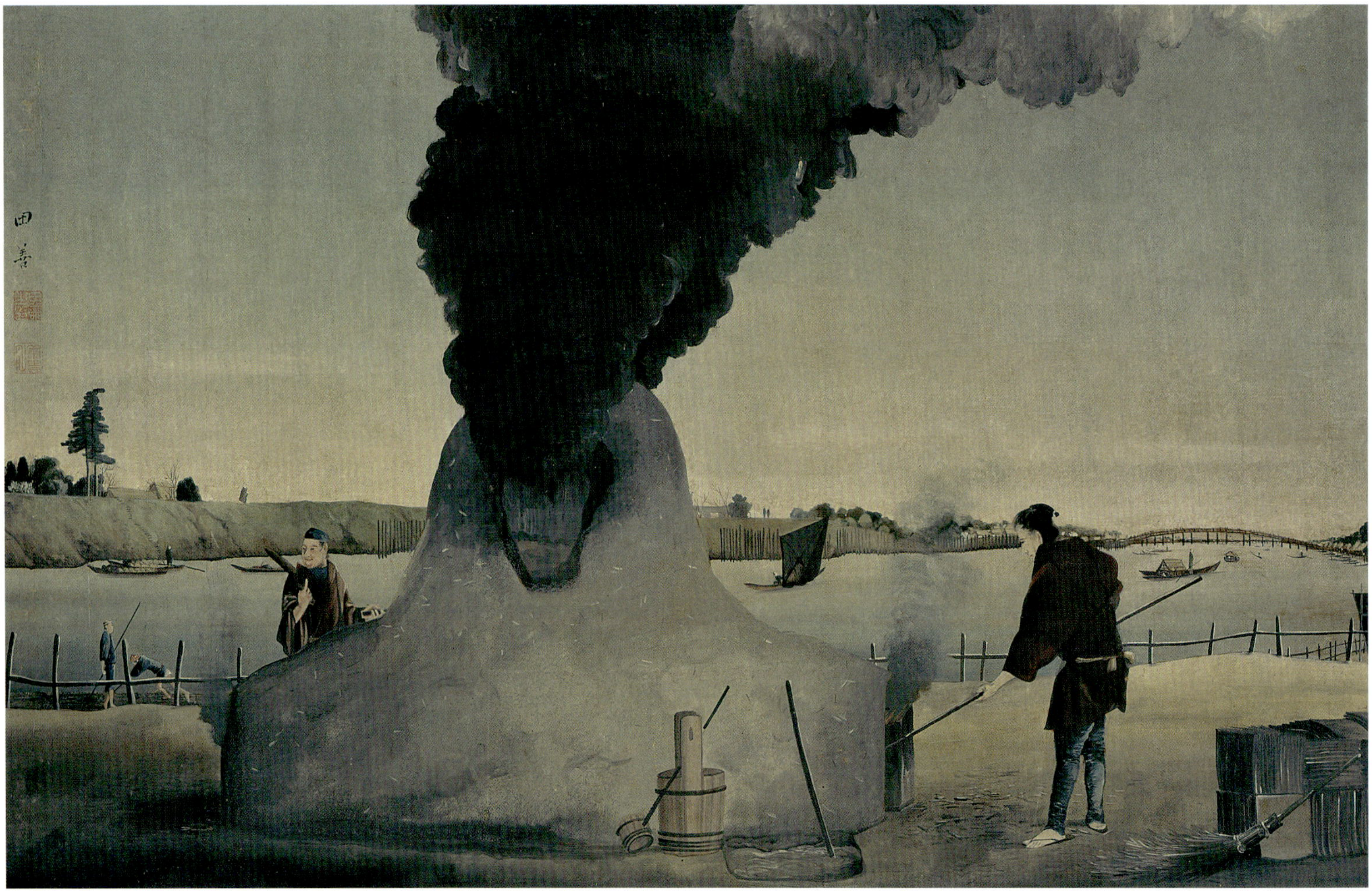

Copperplate technology carried an important political and scientific power throughout late Edo Japan, and given the pressure on him in this regard, it would be fascinating to better understand how Denzen approached and viewed his landscape and nonscientific images. While Kōkan expounded his views and opinions in numerous surviving essays and letters, Denzen left us no such material by which to gain deeper insights into his concerns and beliefs.

Shiba Kōkan and Aōdō Denzen were very different individuals and artists. Kōkan was in many respects an innovator, while Denzen was the consummate artisan. Neither man established a school to ensure that his style and artistic concepts would be perpetuated. Yet the founder of the Gengendō school, Matsumoto Yasuoki (1786–1867), the printmaker Yasuda Raishū (documented 1814–58), and others produced works that were clearly influenced by Kōkan. Gengendō II (Matsuda Ryokuzan, 1837–1903) and Okada Shuntōsai (documented 1842–60) made prints in a manner that appears inspired by Aōdō Denzen. While Kōkan and Denzen left no institutionalized legacy, the techniques of copperplate printing which they established and developed in Japan were passed on and maintained up to the Meiji period.

REFERENCES

Asakura Haruhiko et al., eds., *Shiba Kōkan zenshū,* 4 vols. (Tokyo: Yasaka Shobō, 1992–94).

Naruse Fujio, "Shiba Kōkan no katei-kankyo to ningen-sei," in *Shiba Kōkan hyakka jiten,* exh. cat. (Kobe: Kobe City Museum and Machida City Museum of Graphic Arts, 1996).

Oka Yasumasa, *Megane-e shinkō—ukiyoe-shi ga nozoita seiyō* (Tokyo: Chikuma Shobō, 1992).

I would like to thank Ad Stijnman, a copperplate etcher, for suggesting the relationship between Kōkan's etching and sword decoration.

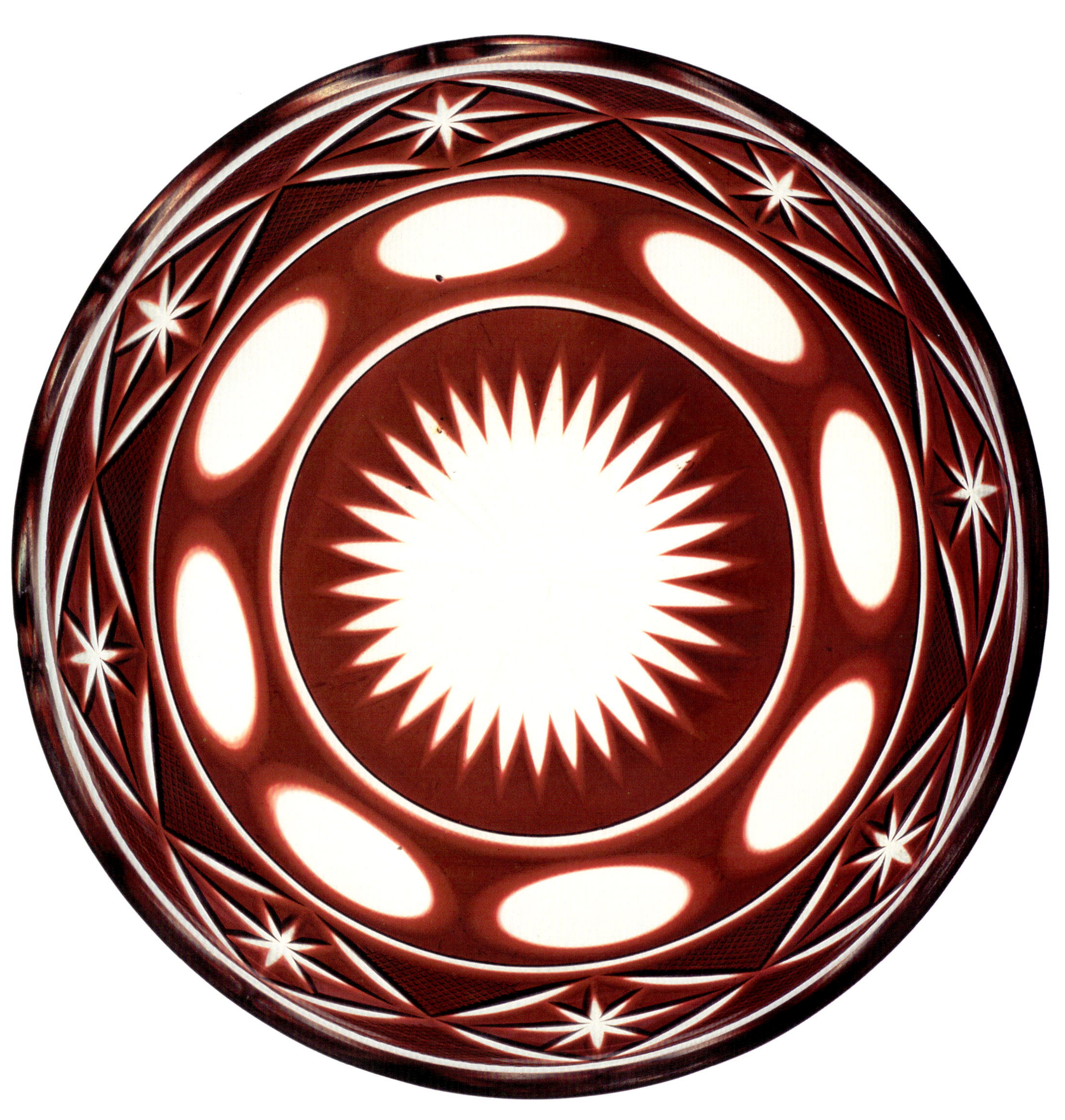

6

Hollandisme in Japanese Craftwork

Oka Yasumasa

The influence of the Japanese aesthetic on artwork produced in Europe in the late nineteenth century is captured by the words *japonisme* and *japonaiserie*. During this time, European and American artists responded enthusiastically to the enormous volume of art and craftwork exported from Japan, including *ukiyo-e* prints, paintings, and the porcelain known as Arita ware. The Japanese as a people, meanwhile, were striving to absorb and use Western knowledge, social systems, and technology. They had been interested in the West before the opening of Yokohama harbor in 1859 brought an end to the Tokugawa shogunate's *sakoku* (isolationist) policy, which had endured in varying degrees since 1639. Even during the *sakoku* period, Dutch and Chinese vessels had imported various foreign goods: silks from China, wool from Europe, cotton and ivory from India and Indonesia, sugar and medicines processed in Europe. After the eighteenth century, European books, metalwork, glasswares, and ceramics increasingly were brought to Japan. Today, Japanese academics generally agree that Japan was not entirely closed off from the outside world during *sakoku* but had been gathering material information about other countries even within this restrictive system.

Even while exporting Arita porcelain from Nagasaki to fill requests from the Dutch East India Company (Verenigde Oost Indische Compagnie, VOC), the Japanese themselves were importing Dutch ceramics, which they treated as special treasures (plate 92). European craftwork brought to Japan under *sakoku* included, in 1656, Dutch earthenware ordered from the VOC by the daimyo of the Kurume domain (Kyūshū),[1] and VOC records from the mid-seventeenth century show Japanese orders for stoneware vases from Cologne as well as for Dutch jugs, bowls, and dishes.[2] The Japanese found the quality of these items to be commensurate with the aesthetics of the tea ceremony, and they gave detailed specifications for the shape and decoration of the imported objects.

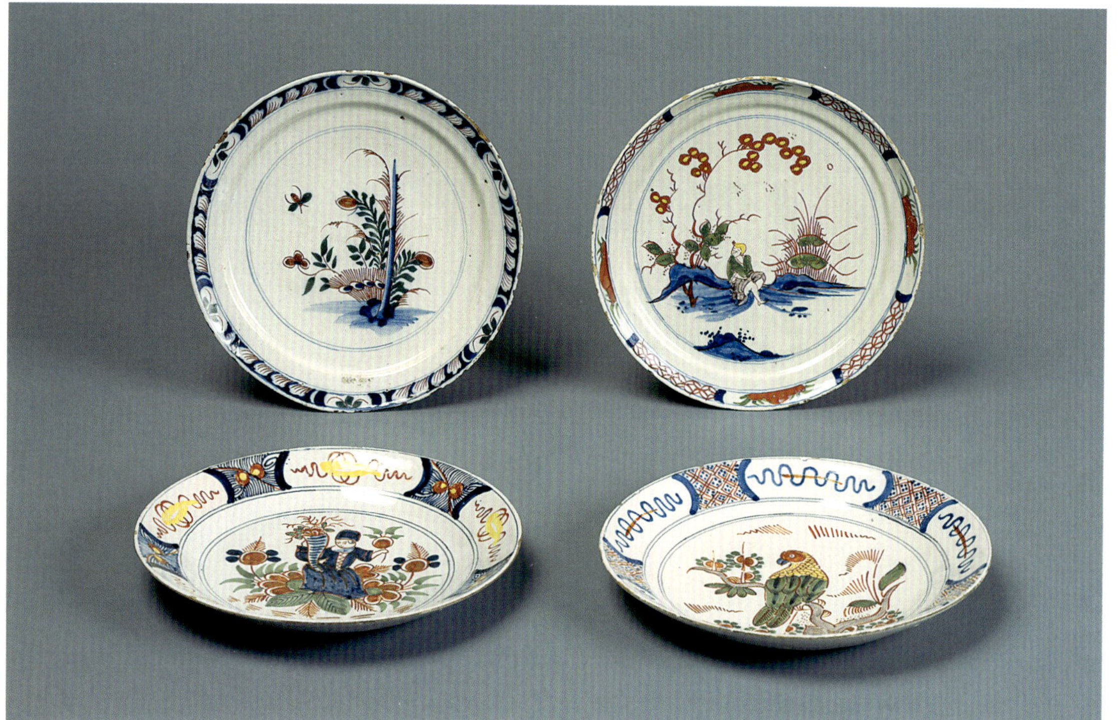

**Plates with
Various Designs**
Holland, early
18th century
Delftware, tin-glazed
earthenware with
polychrome decoration
h. 1⅛ × diam. 9¼ in.
(2.8 × 23.3 cm) each

The Japanese interest in European products rose steadily from a limited following among the daimyo and high officials in the shogunate to a swell of popularity among Japanese intellectuals, including the samurai and merchant classes. One can trace this widening attraction through the travelogues of two German physicians who served the Dutch East India Company in Japan: Engelbert Kaempfer, posted at Dejima from 1690 to 1692, and Philipp Franz von Siebold, resident from 1823 until 1829.[3]

At the end of the seventeenth century, when Western craftwork had only a limited cachet, Kaempfer recognized a stoneware spittoon made in Cologne displayed at a Japanese inn as a rare and precious decoration: "I took notice once, that there was an earthen pot of Cologne . . . with all the cracks and fissures carefully mended . . . it being esteem'd a very great rarity, because of the distant place it came from."[4]

By the end of the eighteenth century, wealthy Japanese expanded their interest to European glasswork, and by the early nineteenth century Siebold could report that a senior town official named Itō Mokunojō, from Shimonoseki in Yamaguchi prefecture, was an ardent collector of Dutch materials.[5] Itō showed Siebold the cabinet of curiosities he had created in his house, a room filled with European furniture, clothes, teaware and dinnerware, pocket watches, clocks, books, and pictures. One could enter the room only by crawling through a small passageway, which Siebold gamely did. It is notable that such a dedicated collector of curiosities could be found among the class of townspeople.

PLATE 93
Keisai Eisen
(Japanese, 1790–1848)
*"Ranji-waku Edo
meisho" Edo
Nihonbashi yori
Fuji wo miru zu*
(View of Mount Fuji
from Nihonbashi,
from the series
"Famous Places
of Edo Framed by
Dutch Alphabet")
Published by Ezakiya
Kichibei
1830–44 (Tenpō era)
Ō-ban woodblock print:
ink and color on paper
10⅜ × 15⅜ in.
(26.2 × 38.9 cm)

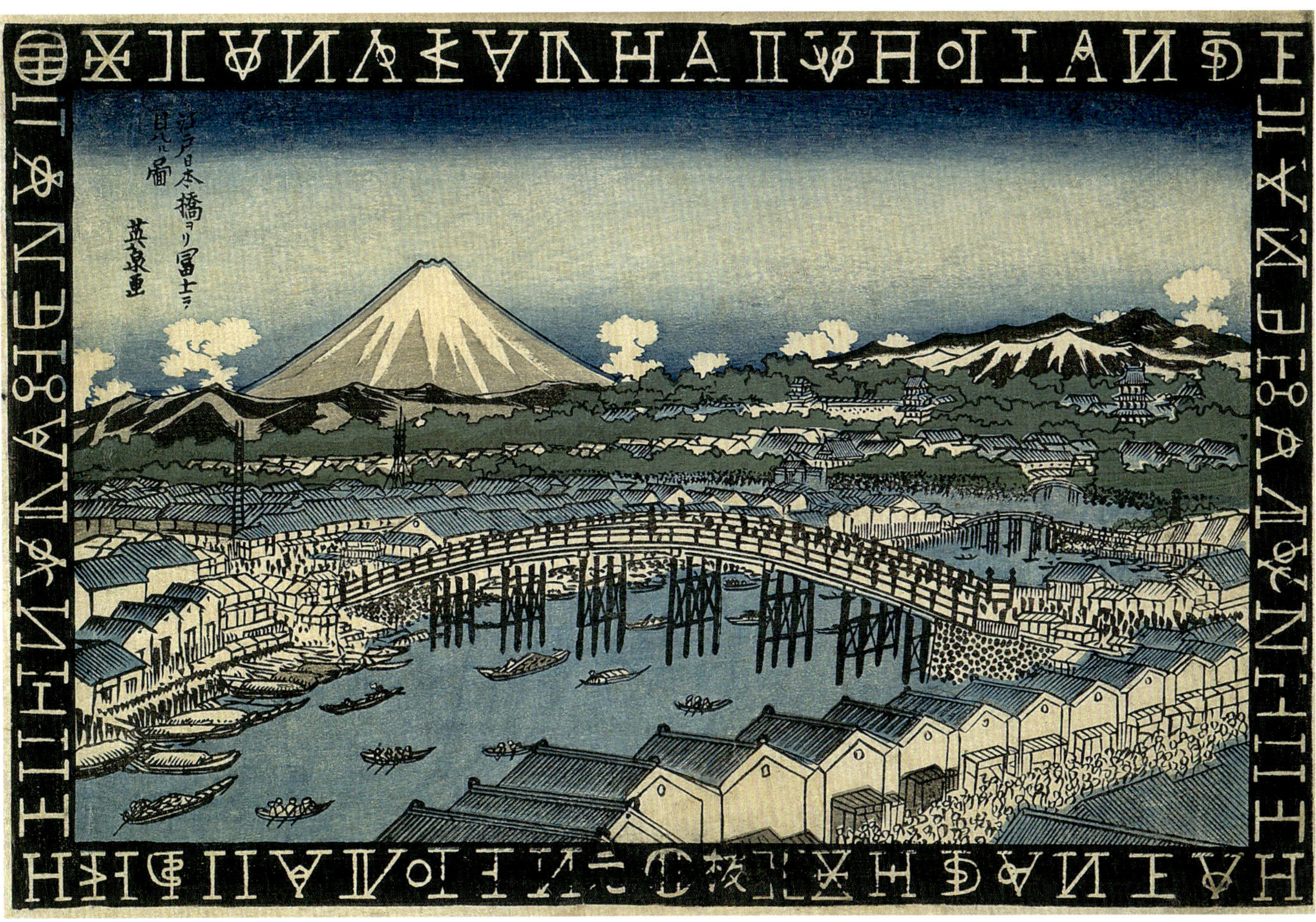

Wallet with Floral
Design
17th–18th century,
assembled in Japan
early 19th century
Imported gilded leather
(*kinkarakawa*), string,
and metal fitting
5½ × 8¼ in.
(13.9 × 21 cm)

Coin Purse with
Greek Goddess Diana
Late 17th century,
assembled in Japan
early 19th century
Imported gilded leather
(*kinkarakawa*)
3⅛ × 4½ in.
(7.9 × 11.3 cm)

Tobacco Pouch with
Elephant Design
17th–18th century,
assembled in Japan
early 19th century
Imported gilded leather
(*kinkarakawa*), cord,
stone, and metal fittings
3⅛ × 4¾ in.
(7.8 × 12.1 cm)

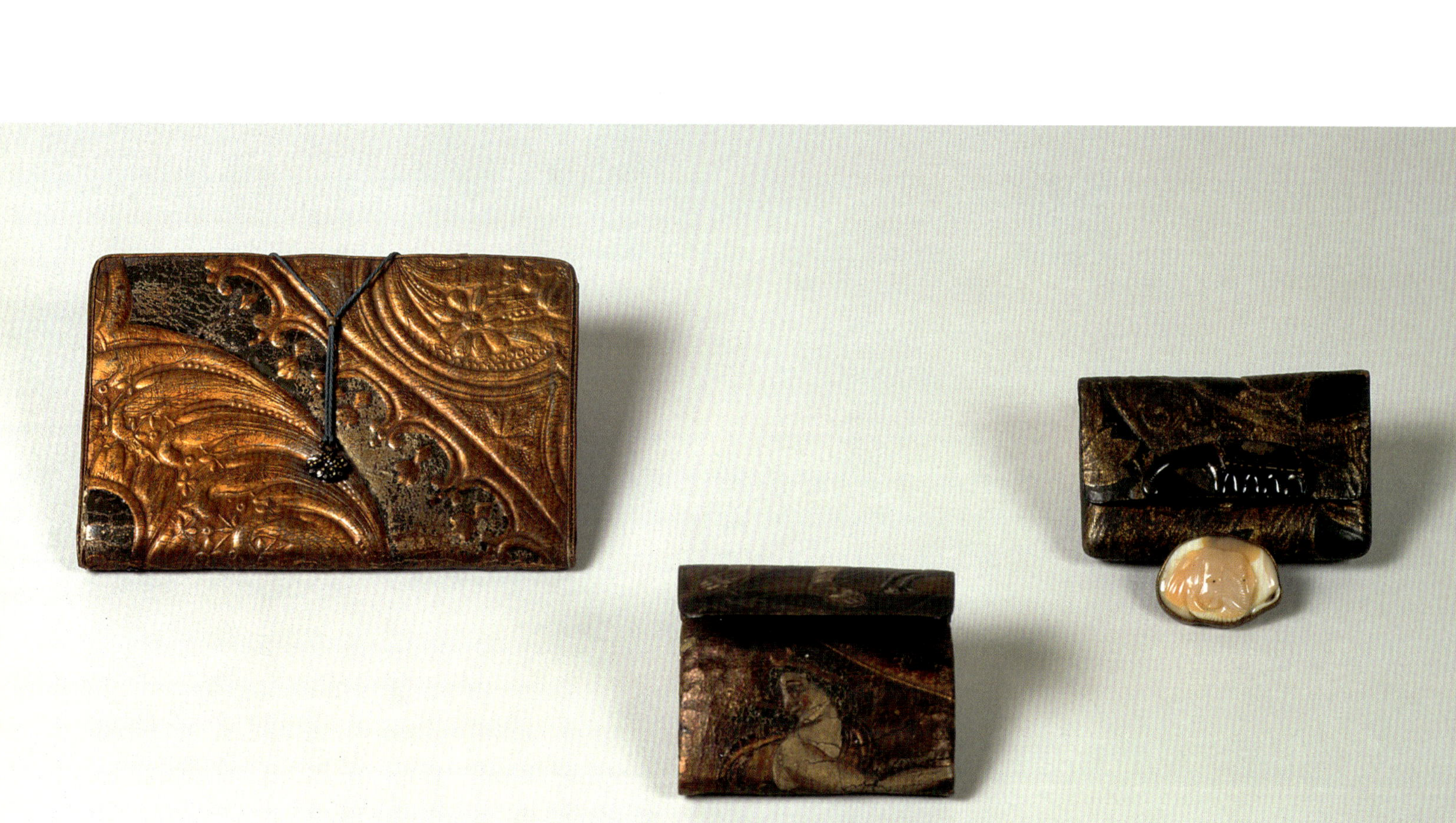

Itō Mokunojō's special room dedicated to products and things from foreign lands resembled the cabinets of curiosities popular in the seventeenth century among the affluent class in Holland. Although altogether more modest, Itō's prideful display shared the same purpose as the collections assembled by European nobility, such as the sumptuous Porcelain Cabinet of Augustus I, Elector of Saxony, in Dresden. It parallels also the decorating practice popular among the nineteenth-century English and French bourgeoisie, who adorned their drawing rooms with pictures and artifacts obtained from Islamic regions, China, and Japan. The peoples of Western Europe and the Far East were each fascinated by the exoticism of the pictures and crafts the other culture produced, and they displayed these objects to flaunt their wealth and refined taste.

Itō's position as a town official brought him in direct contact with the Dutch when they passed through Shimonoseki on the way to Edo to greet the shogun, but even common Japanese people sought Western items in the late eighteenth and nineteenth centuries. This interest is evident in the brisk market for Western-style paintings by Japanese artists (see plates 84a,b, 86) and *ukiyo-e* prints that featured Western subjects or motifs (plate 93). European ceramics, glass, metalwork, and textiles became popular, as did Dutch and German *cuoi d'oro* (*kinkarakawa*), leatherwork pouches decorated with silver leaf (plate 94). This innocent penchant for things foreign undoubtedly originated in the Japanese trait to particularly treasure foreign goods that were transported on ships.

The craze for Western items inspired the development of a wide range of Japanese products, and not all of these were accessible to common people. Japanese glassmakers in the Edo period tried to create shapes similar to Western examples, although they were hindered by their Chinese-based materials and processes, which resulted in a soft and fragile product with a lead content of 50 percent (called *bīdoro*). In the early nineteenth century, technological advances finally made it possible to produce a thick crystal glass known as *giyaman* (plate 95). Glassworkers in Satsuma (Kagoshima prefecture, Kyūshū) developed the marvellous hand technique of *Satsuma kiriko* (Satsuma cut glass), in which they overlaid cut crystal with colored glass (plates 96, 97). Because its production was labor intensive, Japanese cut glass, especially *Satsuma kiriko,* was even more expensive than imported European glassware. It was most often bestowed as a gift of the highest quality by members of the Satsuma clan to individuals of the daimyo class.

Another beautiful, fragile object with exotic appeal was the telescope. The general public would have had access only to domestic models, but their quality was inconsistent and imported telescopes were preferred.[6] The marvelous example in the Kobe City Museum required such skilled glassworking technique to produce that it was long thought to have been made outside Japan (plate 98).[7] The tiny cylinder is embellished with a European landscape and figures achieved by painstakingly applying paint to the reverse side of the glass (*garasu-e* technique); the cylinder exterior was chased with a flower-and-bird decoration that was filled with brilliant pigments. Such supremely beautiful telescopes drew the attention of Westerners too. J. A. Stutzer, a Swedish surgeon based at Dejima in 1787–88, purchased six Japanese glass telescopes and later presented them to Catherine the Great of Russia.[8]

The motifs of Christianity, if not their meaning, were among the Western designs that crossed over to Japanese products. Daimyo and generals in the 1590s could be found wearing rosaries and Christian medals purely as exotic fashions. One of the early Western motifs to be adopted by the Japanese was the Chi-rho monogram formed by the Greek letters *chi* and *rho* (X and P), the first two letters of the name of Christ. A roughly shaped Oribe-type tea bowl with thick black glaze bears an incised decoration with some resemblance to the monogram (plate 99). Another tea bowl with a cross design was produced at Shōdai kiln in Kumamoto, Kyūshū (plate 100). The bowl's white slip decoration (*punch'ŏng*) reveals the influence of the Korean potters who worked at Shōdai. Bowls of this type have an interesting link as vessels for purified water: they were used in Korean Confucian rituals to offer sacred water to ancestors; bowls with a cross design held blessed water at Christian services; and finally the Japanese adopted them as fresh water jars for tea gatherings.

PLATE 95
**Three-tiered
Food Container
in Lattice Pattern**
Japan, mid–late
19th century
Cut glass
h. 7½ × diam. 4⅞ in.
(18.8 × 12.2 cm)

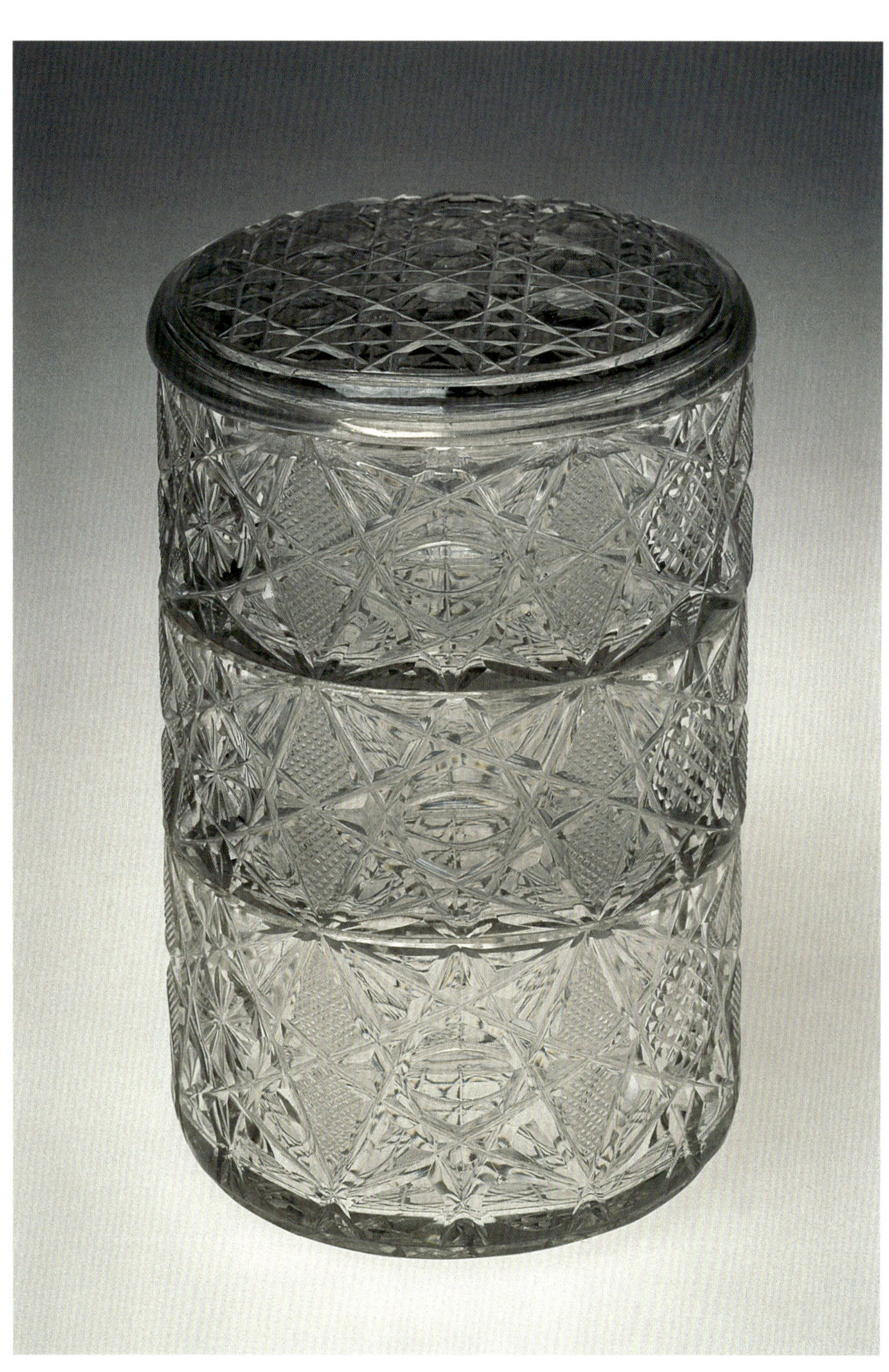

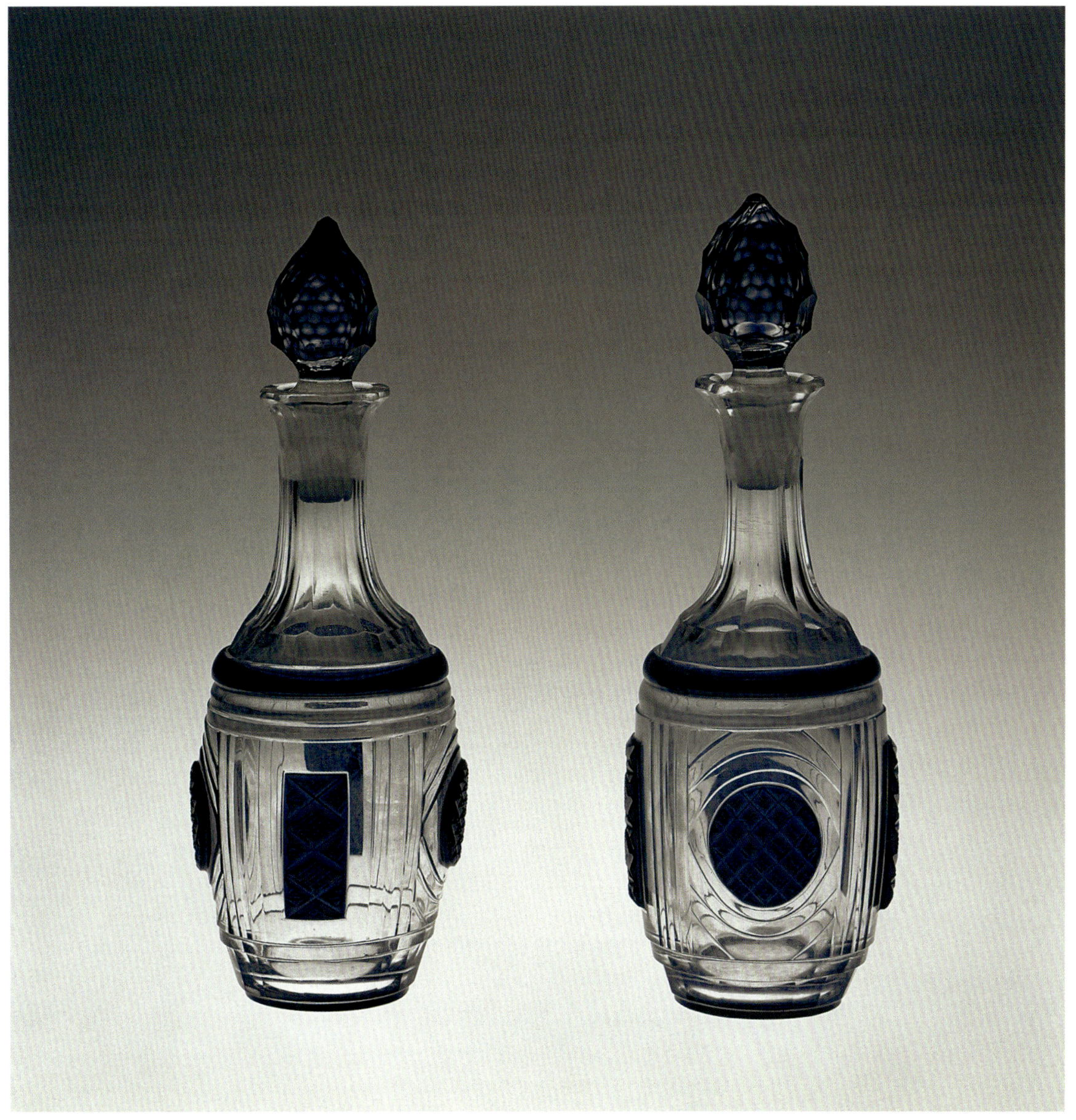

PLATE 96
Pair of Decanters
Japan, 1850–82
Cut glass with
cobalt blue overlay
(*Satsuma kiriko* method)
h. 6⅞, 6¾ × diam. 2½ in.
(17.3, 17.1 × 6.3 cm)

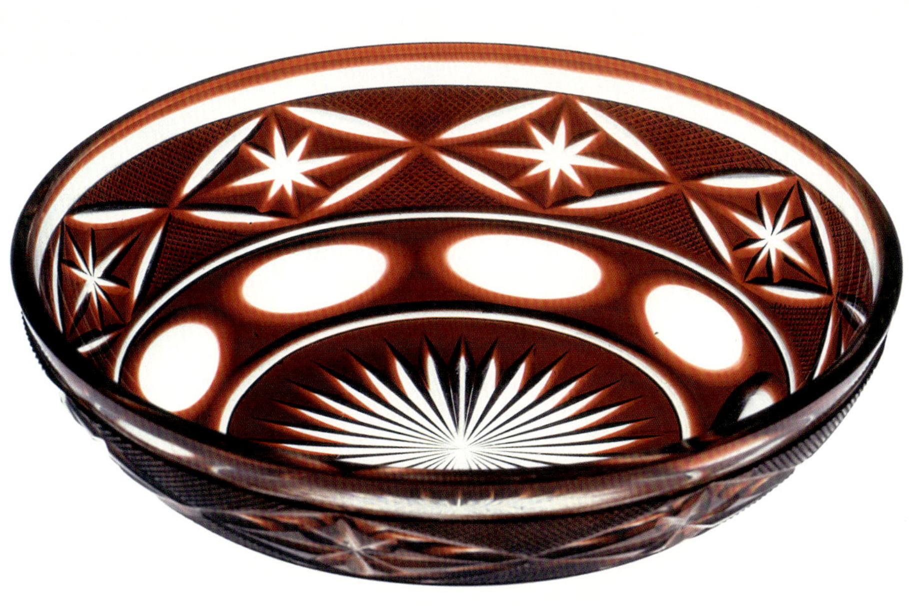

PLATE 97
Bowl with
Geometric Design
Japan, 1850–82
Cut glass with
copper red overlay
(*Satsuma kiriko* method)
h. 2 × diam. 6⅞ in.
(4.9 × 17.5 cm)

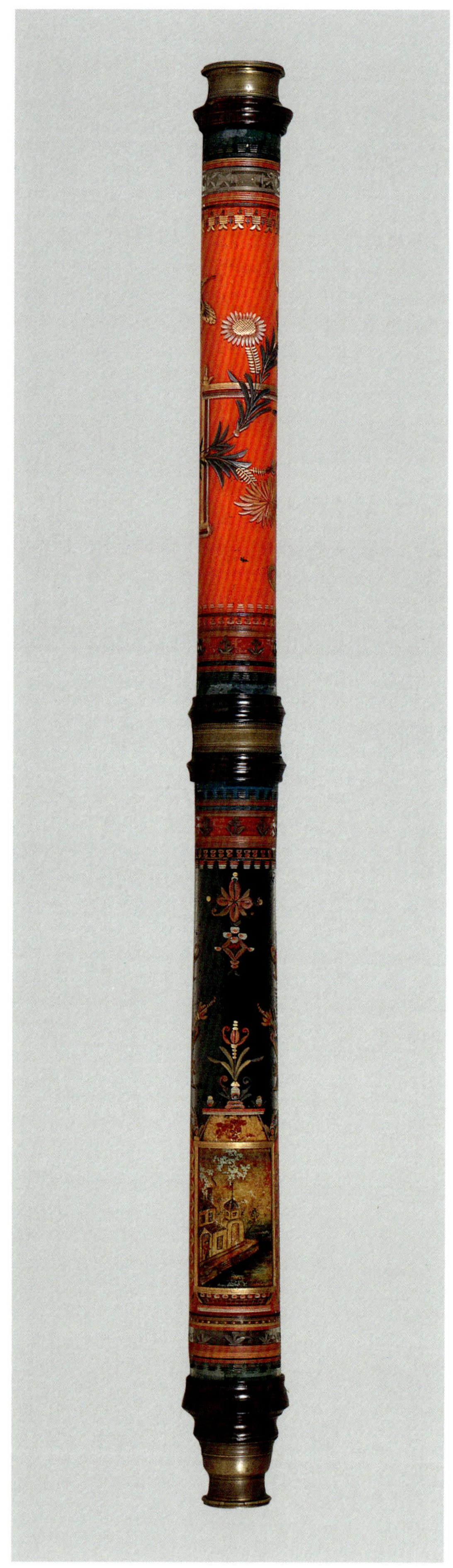

Telescope Decorated with European Motifs

Japan, late 18th century
Gravure-chased glass
with pigment, lenses,
and metal fittings
l. 23¾ × diam. 2 in.
(60.2 × 5 cm)

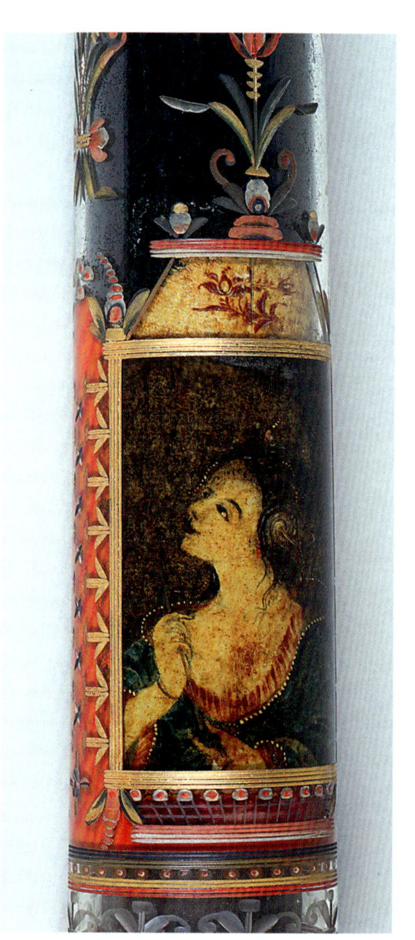

Figural decoration
(plate 98)

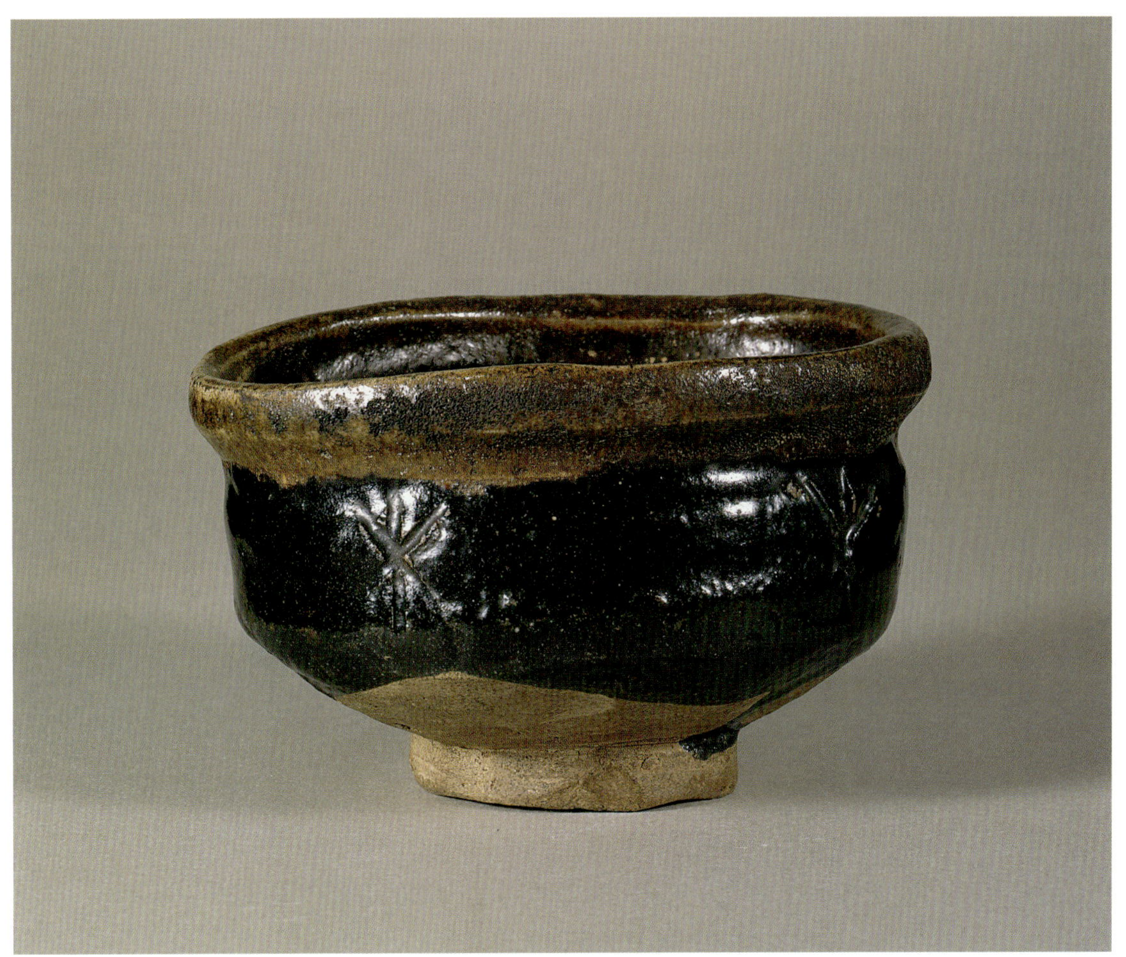

PLATE 99

**Clog-shaped
Tea Bowl with
Monogram Design**
Japan, late 16th–early
17th century
Mino ware, *oribe-
guro* type, glazed
earthenware
3¼ × 5⅜ × 4¼ in.
(8 × 13.4 × 10.7 cm)

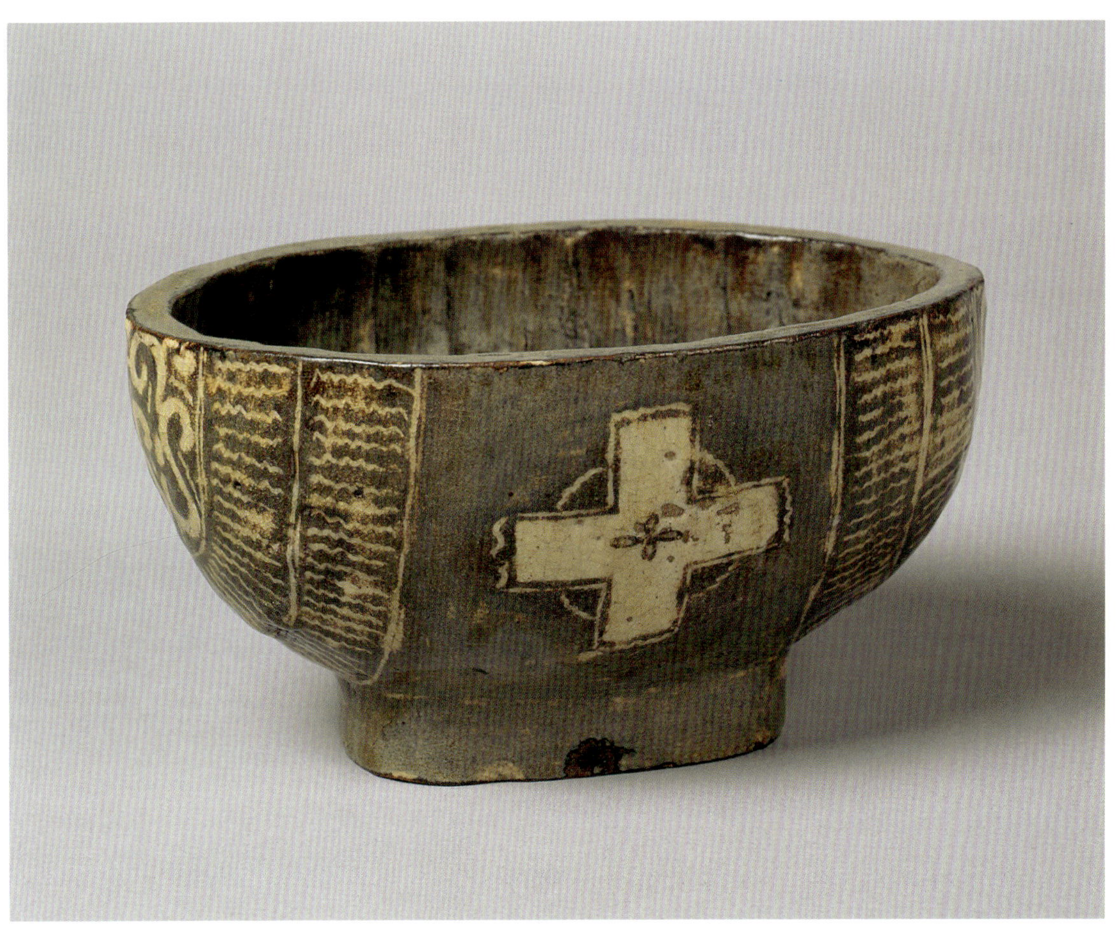

PLATE 100

**Bowl with
Cross Design**
Japan, 17th century
Shōdai ware, earthen-
ware with inlaid
white slip
4⅛ × 8 × 6⅛ in.
(10.3 × 20.2 × 15.6 cm)

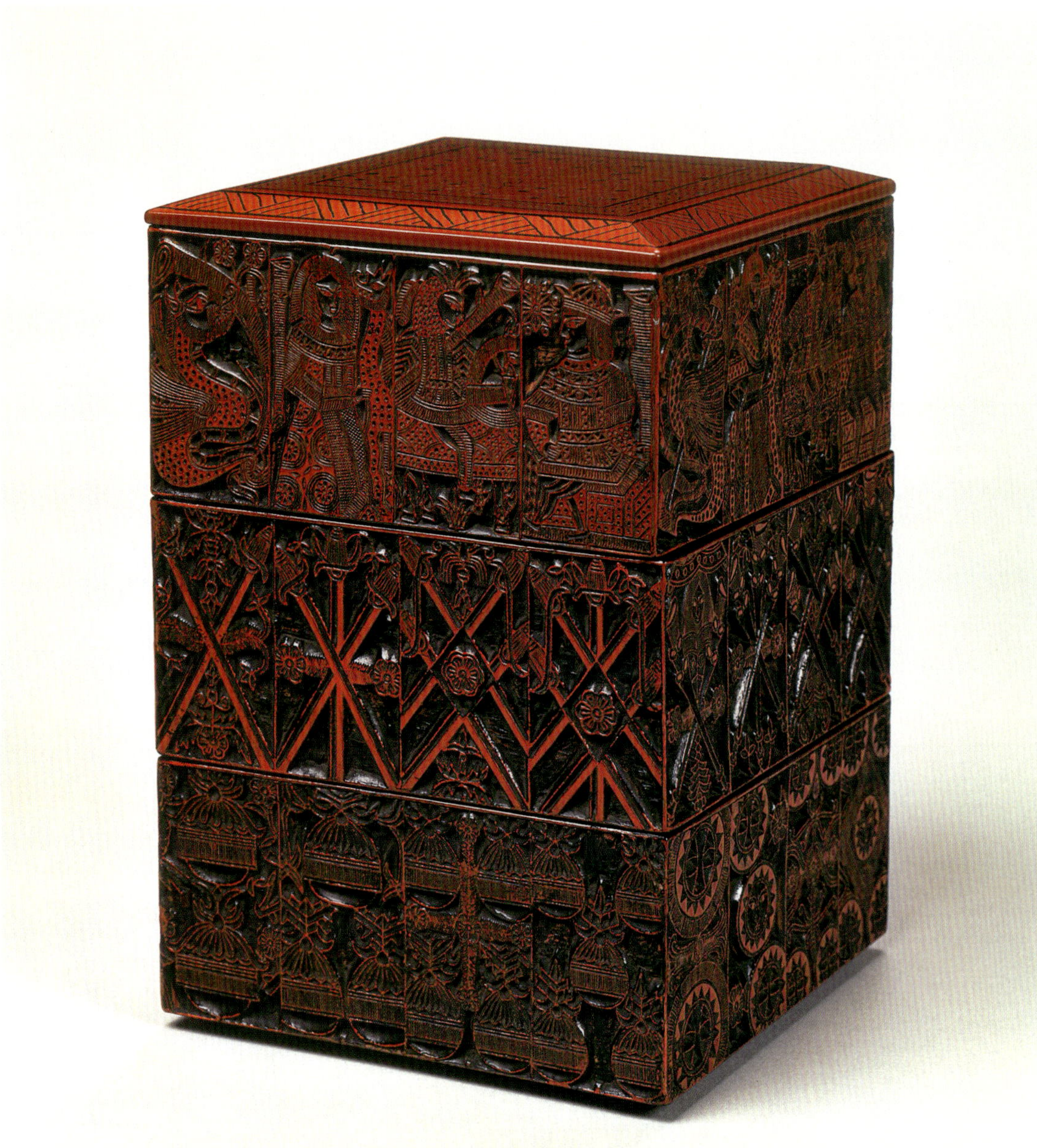

PLATE 101
Three-tiered
Food Container
Japan, late 16th–early
17th century, assembled
mid-19th century
Lacquered *tenshō karuta*
woodblocks, lacquered
wood cover and bottom
8 × 5¾ × 5¾ in.
(20.1 × 14.4 × 14.4 cm)

PLATE 102
Playing Cards
(tenshō karuta)
re-created from
woodblocks
in plate 101

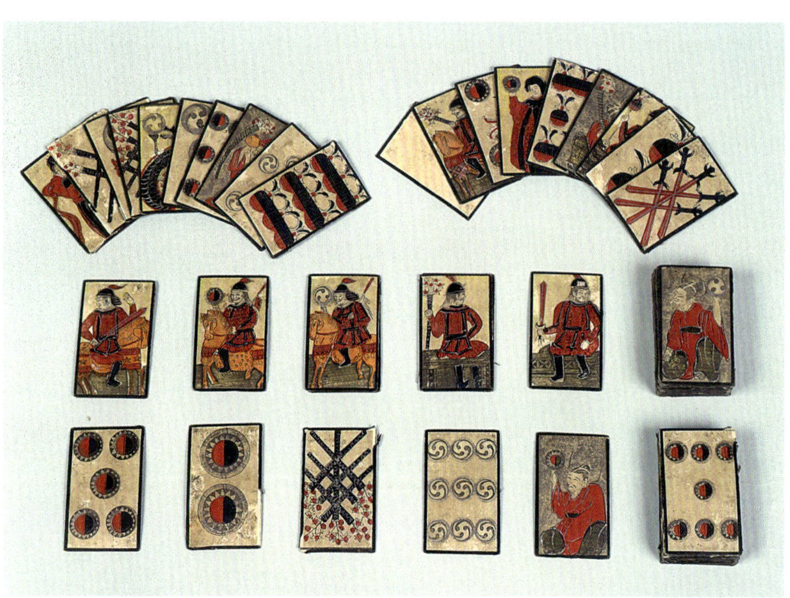

The Portuguese introduced playing cards to Japan, and sets of cards, called *tenshō karuta*, were made locally via woodblock printing. A delightful food container was ingeniously crafted from the woodblocks used in printing such cards (plate 101). It must have been great fun to assemble the woodblocks, coat them with red lacquer, and then add a cover and bottom to make this three-tiered box. The process had the fortunate effect of preserving the woodblocks, and a set of *tenshō karuta* was recently recreated by making rubbings of the box's surface (plate 102). In the late Edo to early Meiji periods, the motifs of the king and queen found on playing cards were adopted in Japanese lacquerware.

From the late eighteenth century until the middle of the next, Arita ware tea cups, bowls, and plates offered many examples of foreign motifs applied to Japanese objects, and a significant number of these items are extant (plates 103–105). In addition, by the mid-nineteenth century, Japanese people were familiar users of English and Dutch mass-produced transfer-print tableware. It is thought that small cups were imported into Japan especially for the drinking of green tea (*sencha*), a practice that had become popular in the late Edo period (plate 106). These mass-produced items differed from the thick-bodied Dutch ceramics used during the seventeenth century for powdered green tea (*maccha*). Sets of imported English and Dutch ceramic plates and bowls have survived in old Japanese boxes dating from the mid-nineteenth century. Inscriptions on those boxes read "Dutch ceramic plates" (Oranda yakimono zara) or "Dutch dessert plates" (Oranda kashi ki) and give the number of dishes in the set. Clearly Japanese merchants who specialized in the trading of overseas goods were ordering and selling a large volume of imported tableware from Holland (*Oranda watari*).

This desire for Western things among the common class—apart from the interest of the wealthy class of daimyo and merchants, or scholars and doctors of Western medicine who sought scientific knowledge—and the influence of Europe on Japanese art can be summed up in a word I have coined, "*hollandisme*." I have designated this term as a counterpart to the similar notion of *japonisme*.

In *Rangaku kaitei* (A Guide to Dutch Studies, 1788), the Japanese Dutch-studies scholar Ōtsuki Gentaku (1757–1827) lamented the surge of fake

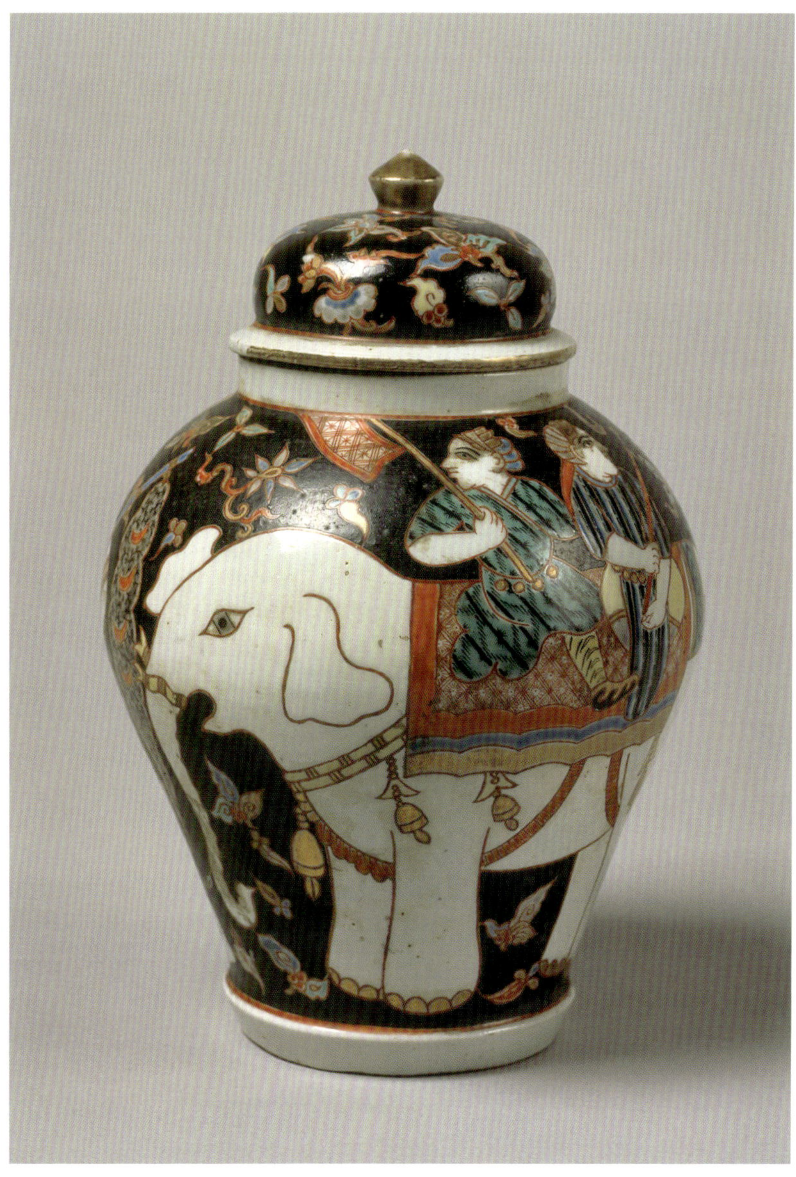

Covered Jar with Elephant and Indian Figures
Japan, late 18th century
Arita ware, porcelain with polychrome decoration
h. 9½ × diam. 6⅝ in. (24 × 16.8 cm)

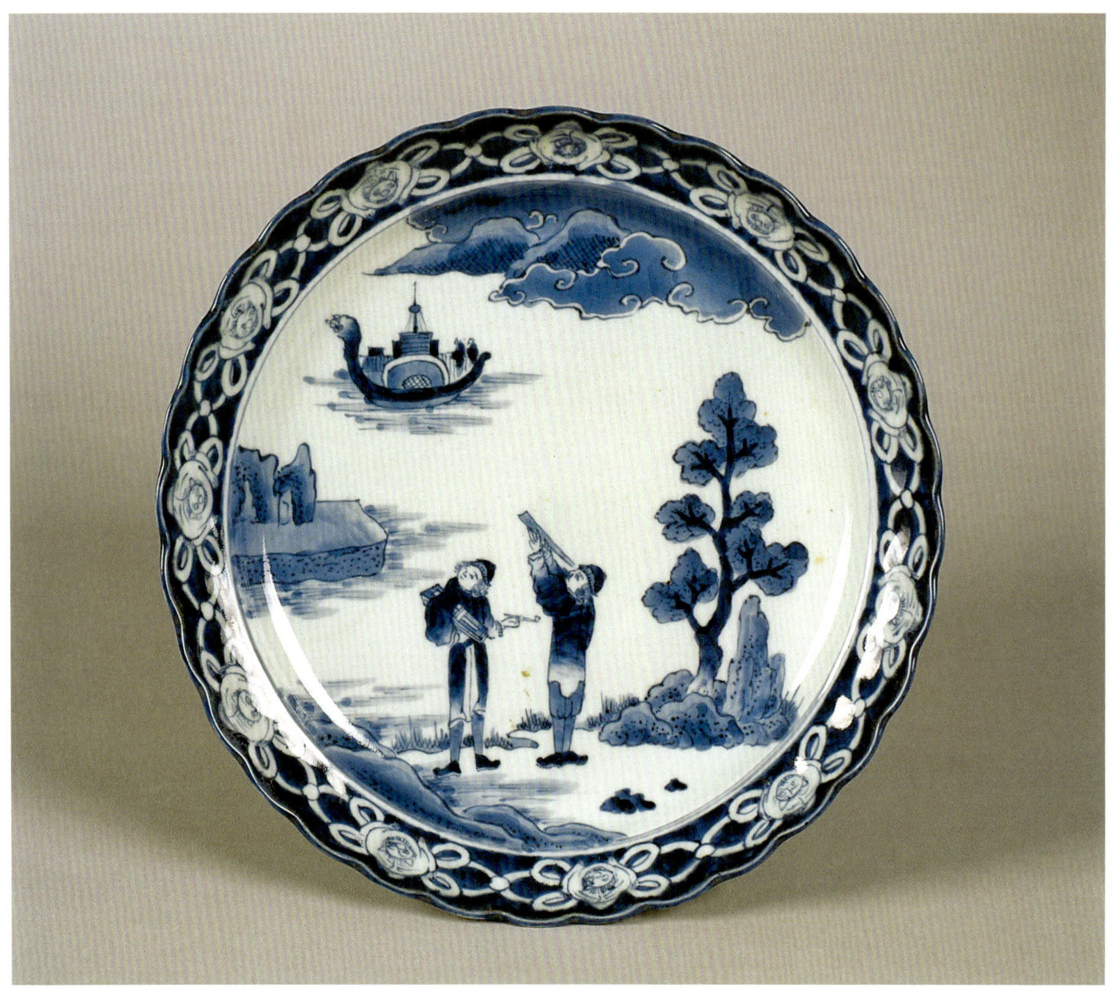

PLATE 104

**Plate with Scene
of Two Dutchmen**
Japan, early
19th century
Arita ware, porcelain
with underglaze cobalt
blue decoration
h. 2⅛ × diam. 12⅛ in.
(5.4 × 30.6 cm)

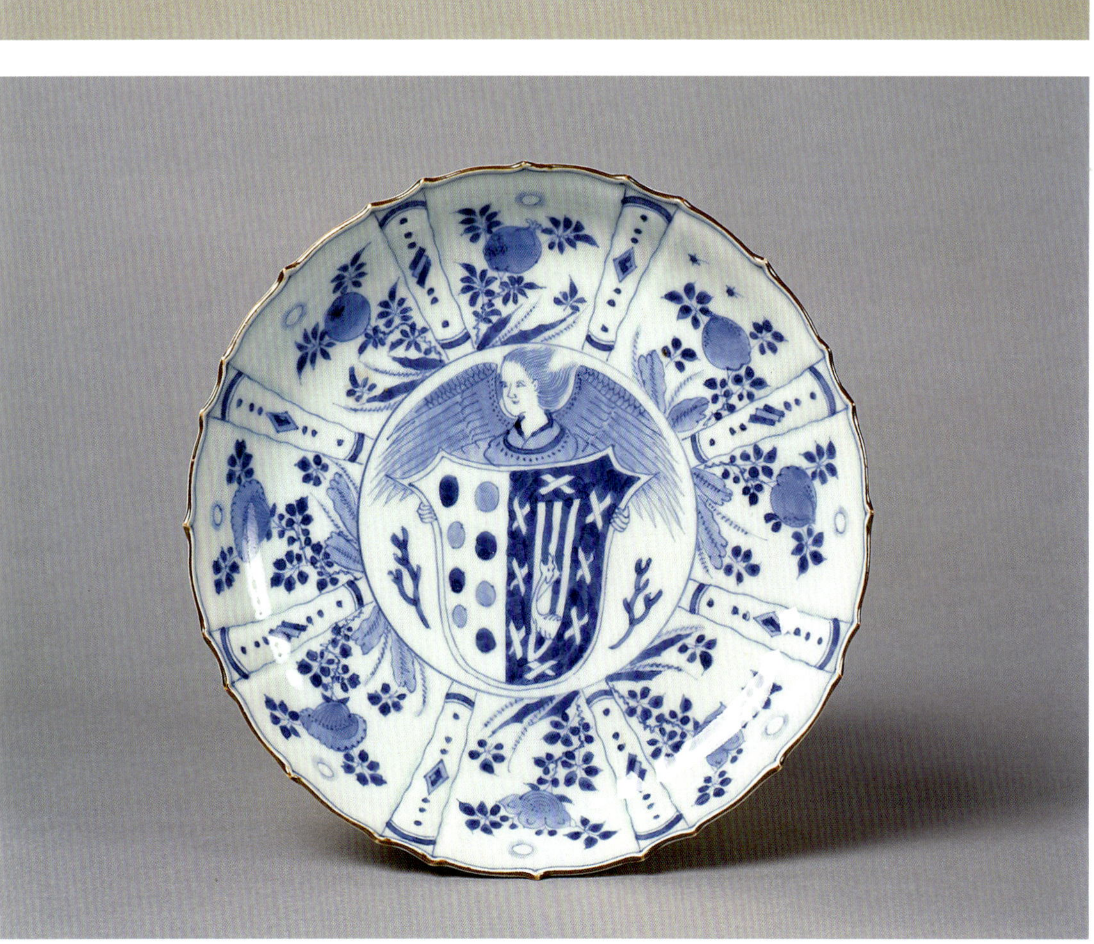

PLATE 105

**Kraak-style Plate
with Emblem Design**
Japan, c. 1781–89
(Tenmei era)
Arita ware, porcelain
with underglaze cobalt
blue decoration
h. 1½ × diam. 9⅛ in.
(3.8 × 23 cm)

Dutch products in the marketplace, but even these imitations are signs of *hollandisme*. Ōtsuki wrote that anything unusual, skillfully crafted, or pleasing in appearance was labeled Dutch (*Oranda*), much to the delight of shoppers. Such commodities ranged from medicines to trinkets, and Ōtsuki bemoaned the fact that so many traders were profiting by selling fake Dutch goods.

This inundation of imitation Dutch products in late-eighteenth-century Edo took full advantage of the Japanese tendency to be dazzled by things from foreign countries. A craze developed for a type of landscape painting (*megane-e*) viewed with a special device (*nozoki megane* or peep-show box, plates 107a,b, 108). What was new and Western about such paintings was the incorporation of perspective, which gave the viewer a feel for the spatial depth of the depicted landscape as he or she looked through the lens installed in the viewing box. Including the word *Oranda* on the viewing box signaled the foreignness of it, even though it was made in Japan. One box from 1788, for example, is inscribed "*Oranda megane-e*" (see plate 7). Such viewing tools played a large role in introducing perspective to Japanese painting. The technique of trompe l'oeil, which creates the illusion of spatial depth, and the very encounter with this pictorial structure, which had its origin in the West, were new encounters, the experience of which the Japanese regarded as "*Oranda*."

Sencha Set
in Dutch Design
*Charcoal heating
pot, teapot, water pot, and
tea caddy cover*
Japan, early
19th century
Kyoto ware and style,
earthenware and
stoneware with various
decoration and glazes;
imported cotton (*sarasa*)

—

Cups with Landscape
Design
England, late
18th century
Caughley ware, earthenware with lead glaze and
cobalt blue decoration
Heating pot: h. 4¾ in.
(12.1 cm); teapot:
h. 4⅛ in. (10.3 cm);
water pot: h. 4 in.
(10 cm); cups: h. 1⅛ in.
(2.7 cm)

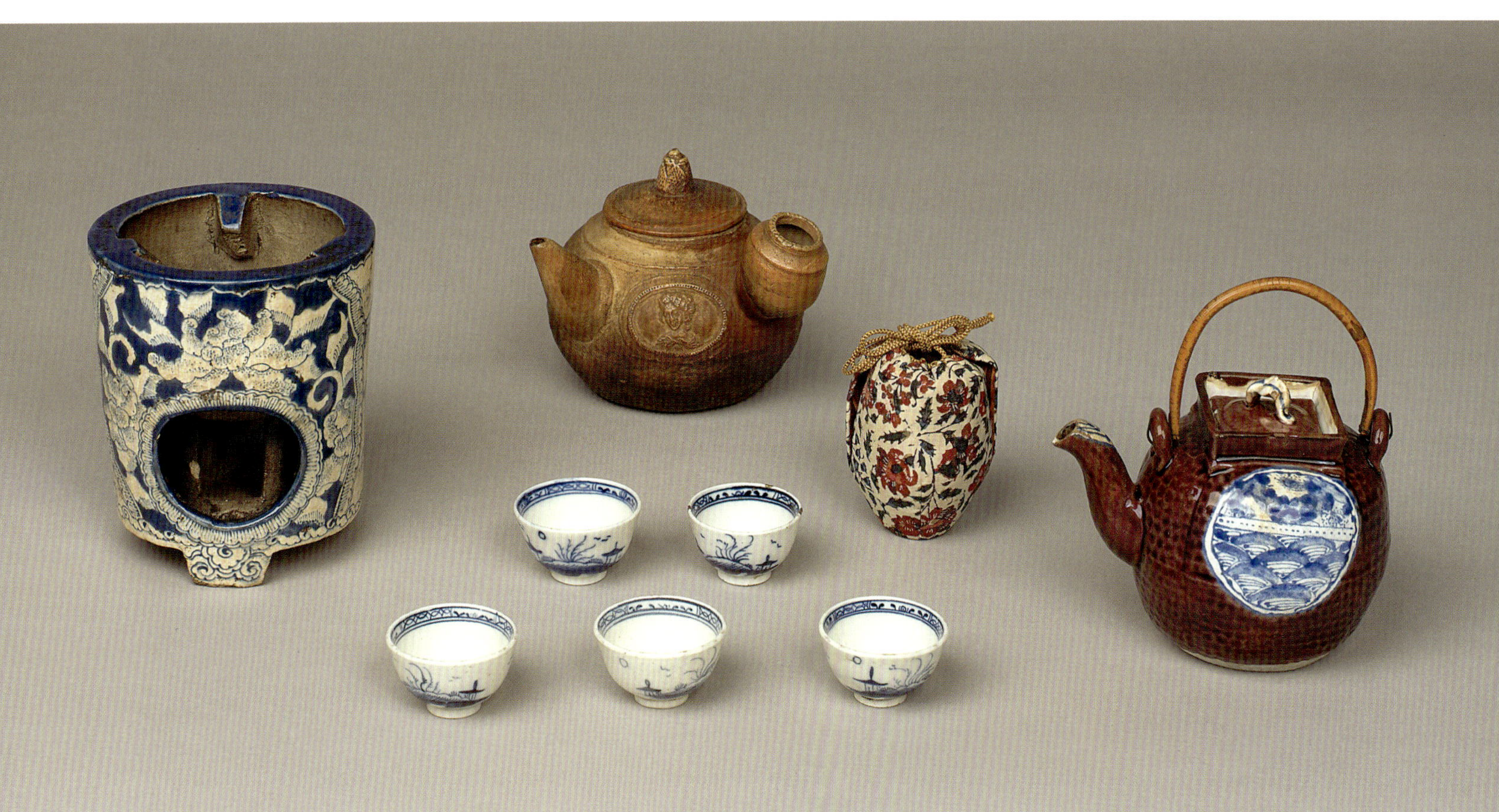

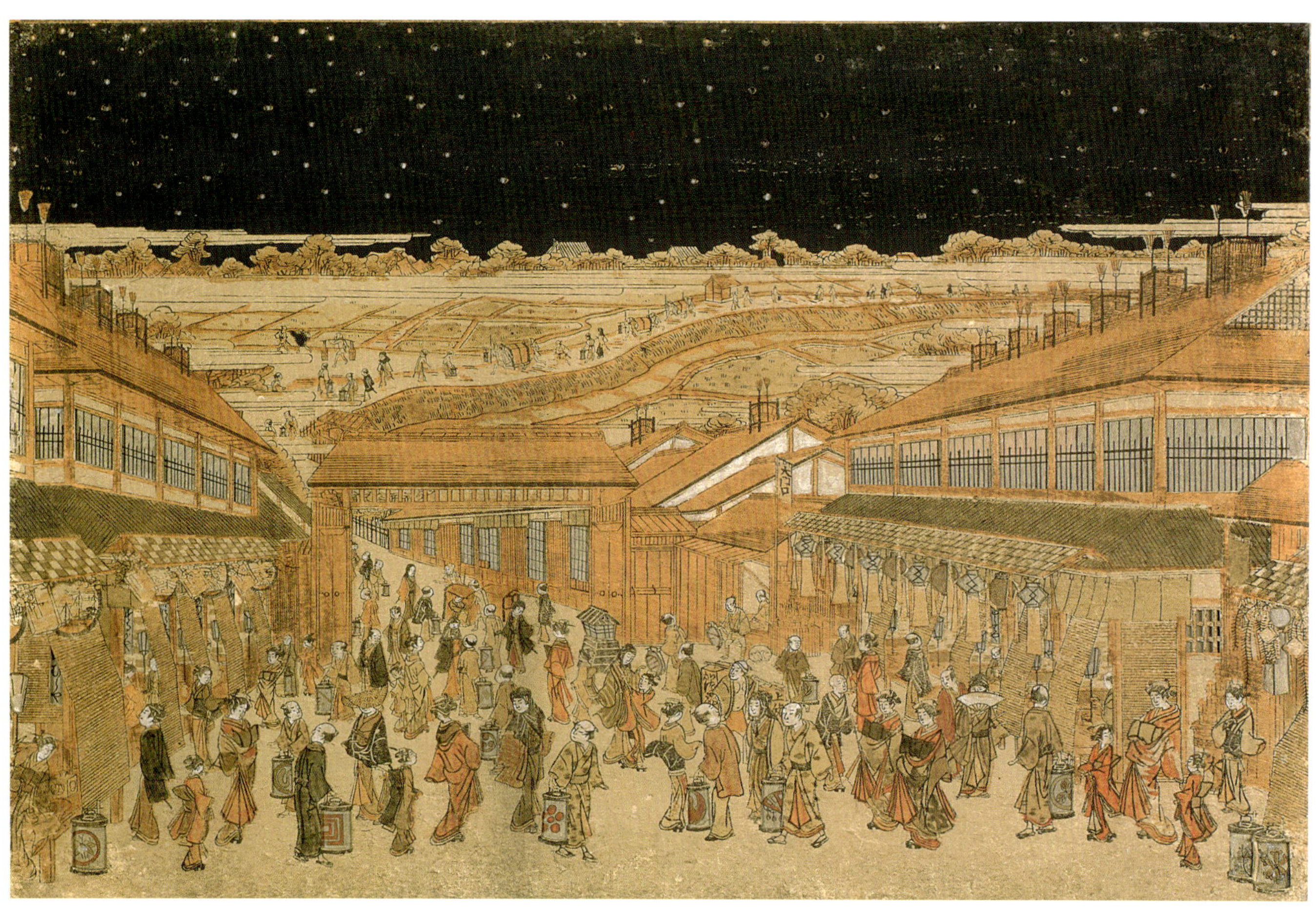

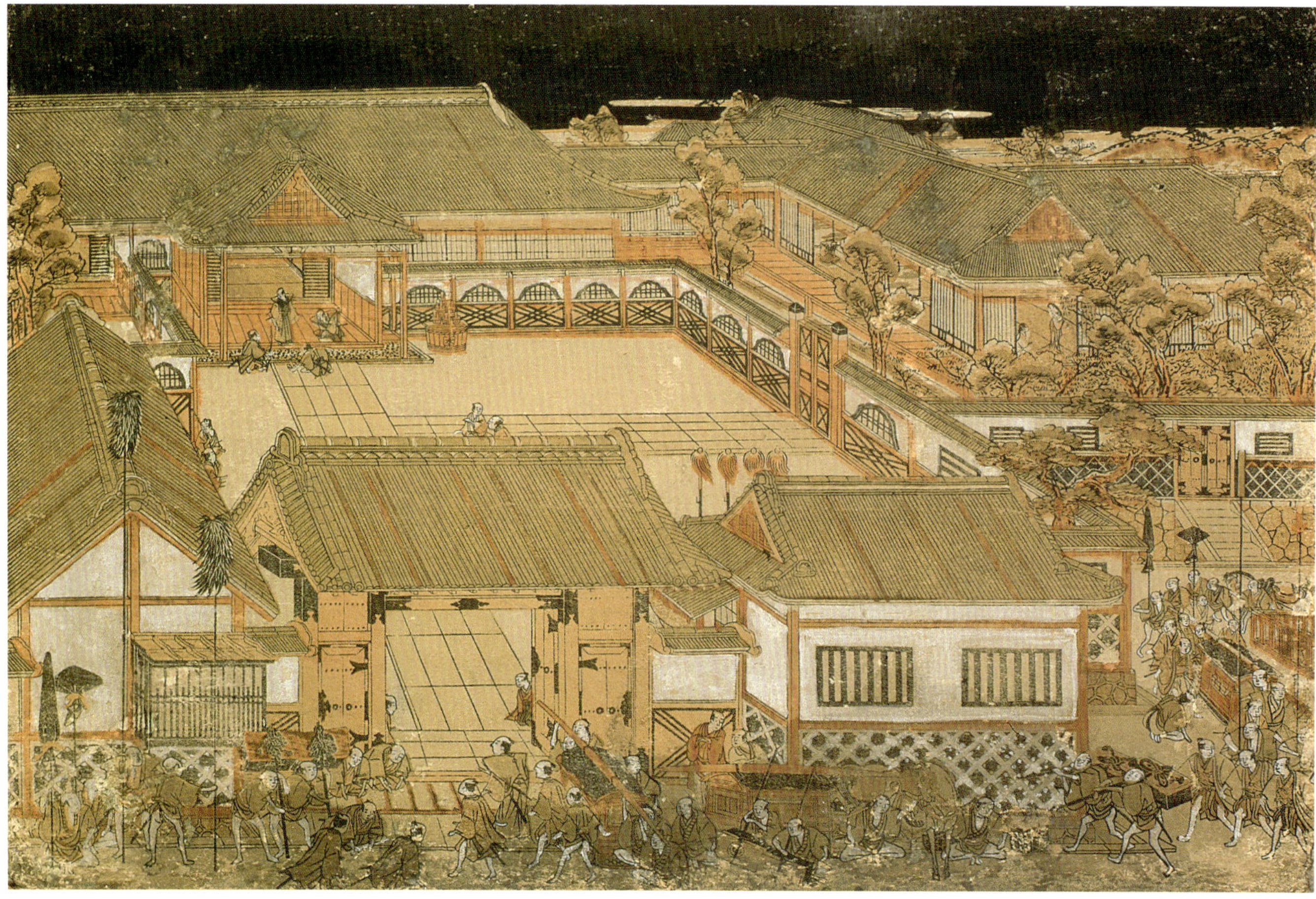

PLATE 107a,b
Utagawa Toyoharu
(Japanese, 1735–1814)
*Wakoku keiseki
Shin'yoshiwara
Nakanomachi
no zu* (View of
Nakanomachi at
Shin'yoshiwara)

Daimyō yashiki
(Daimyo Residence)
c. 1764–81
(Meiwa–An'ei era)
Uki-e woodblock prints:
ink and color on
punched paper
9⅜ × 14¼ in.
(23.7 × 36 cm) each
■

PLATE 108
Nozoki megane
(Peep-show Box)
Japan, c. 1764–81
(Meiwa–An'ei era)
Lacquered wood,
convex lens, and paper
10½ × 15⅝ × 15½ in.
(26.7 × 39.7 × 39.2 cm)
box

Shown in *Nozoki megane*:
Utagawa Toyoharu
(Japanese, 1735–1814)
*Oranda yukimi no
zu* (Snowy View
of Holland)
Uki-e woodblock print:
ink and color on paper
9⅜ × 14¼ in.
(23.7 × 36 cm)
■

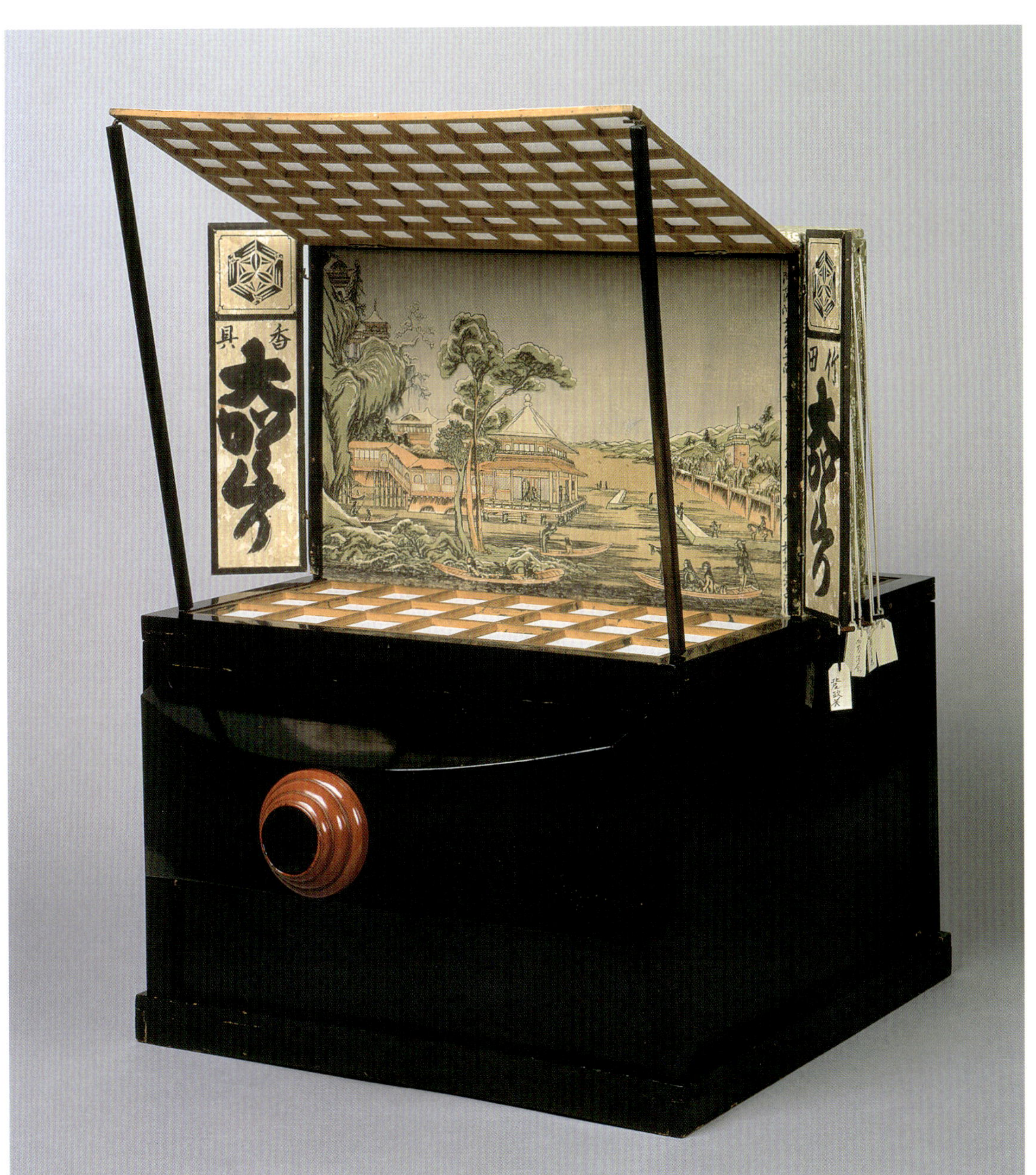

Exotic Designs in Craftworks

Arita ware produced for the domestic market from the late eighteenth to mid-nineteenth century with Dutch figural motifs provides significant examples of the *hollandisme* that appealed to ordinary Japanese. What was behind this decision to incorporate portraits of foreigners on high-quality tableware? The practice of applying Western pictorial motifs to craftwork has a precedent in lacquerware produced for domestic consumers from the late sixteenth to the seventeenth century, including writing boxes, letter boxes, and saddles with gold or silver lacquer pictorial designs. Some motifs depict ships from Portugal or Spain arriving in Kyūshū, including at Nagasaki, as well as their crew members and African or Indian servants. These pictures were applied to saddles (plate 109) and even to metal stirrups, suggesting that their users regarded foreigners from faraway countries across the ocean not simply as novel but also as being in possession of special powers. Otherwise, why select these motifs as decorative designs on military implements?

One compelling example is a hand drum (*tsuzumi*) with motifs of matchlock guns arranged on its lacquered body (plate 110). This is not merely a case of employing an uncommon motif; the design embodies a wishful pun that the drum would "sound well" as a percussive instrument. The pictorial design selected for a given item embodied some meaning that reflected its user's aspiration. One cannot help supposing that a saddle with a motif depicting a Portuguese was made with the hope that it would induce the fortunes of war to favor its user. Likewise, we can imagine that an image of a foreigner applied to sword guards (*tsuba*) or carved toggles (*netsuke*) probably had a talismanic function such as warding off evil spirits (plates 111–113).

Imagery of foreigners began to appear on Arita ware in the late eighteenth century, and as far as

PLATE 109

Saddle with Design of European Figures

Japan, 1604 (Keichō 9)
Makie lacquered wood with metal and leather
h. 10⅞ (front) × w. 15 in.
(27.5 × 38 cm)

PLATE 110

Hand Drum Cylinder with Design of Matchlock Guns

Japan, late 16th–early 17th century
Makie lacquered wood
h. 11 × diam. 4⅜ in.
(27.8 × 11.1 cm)

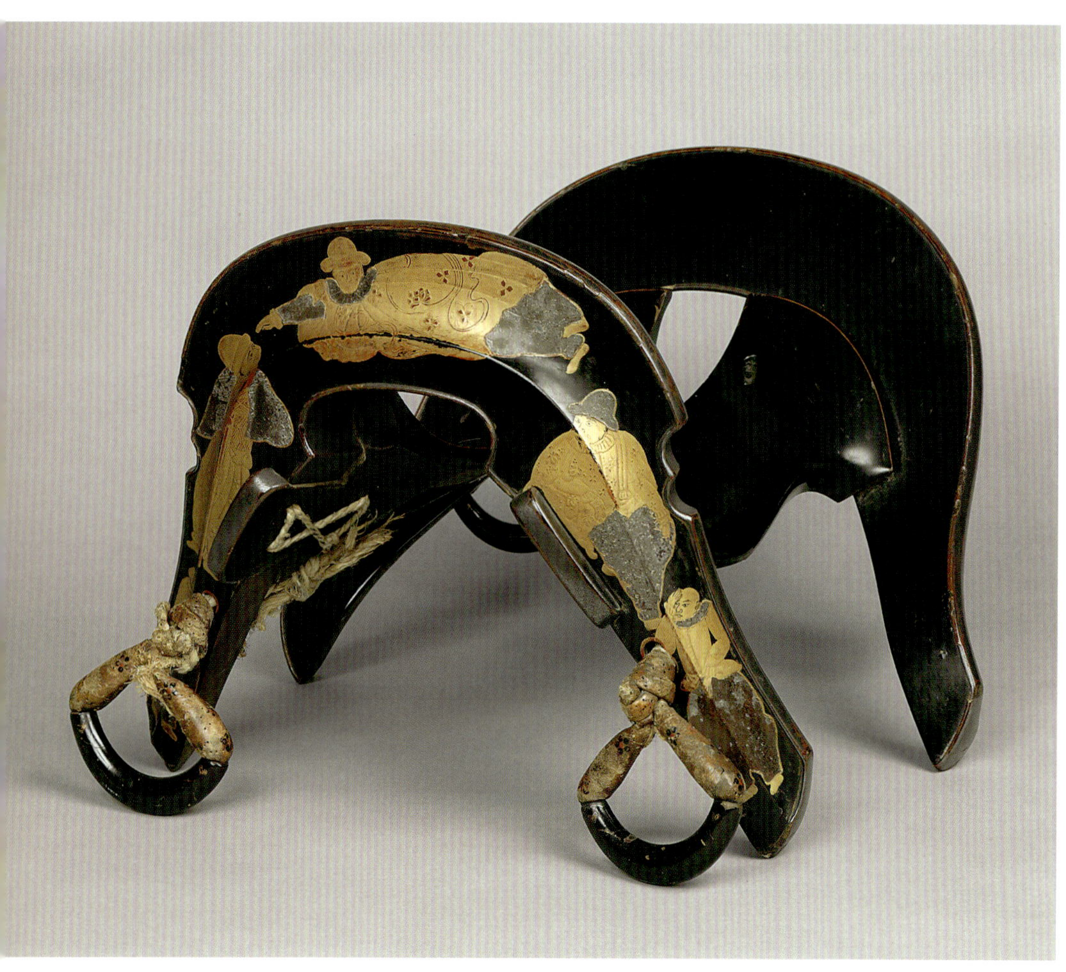

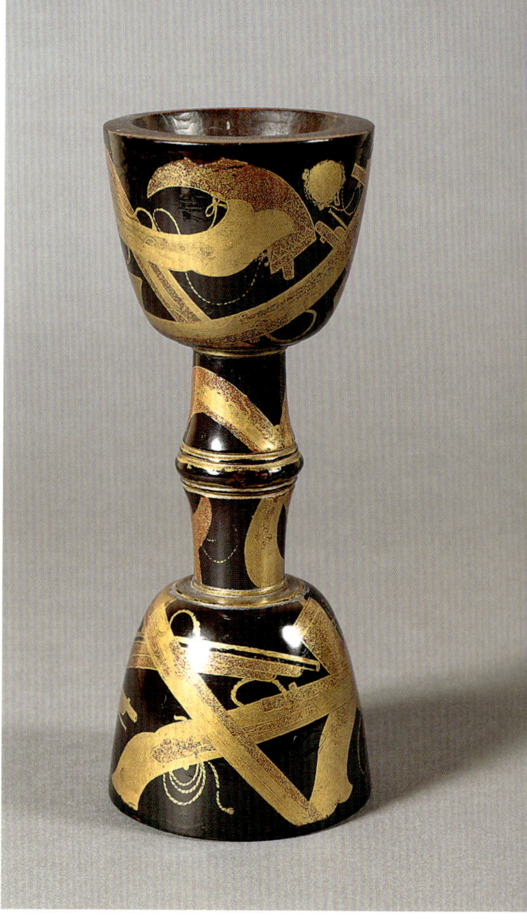

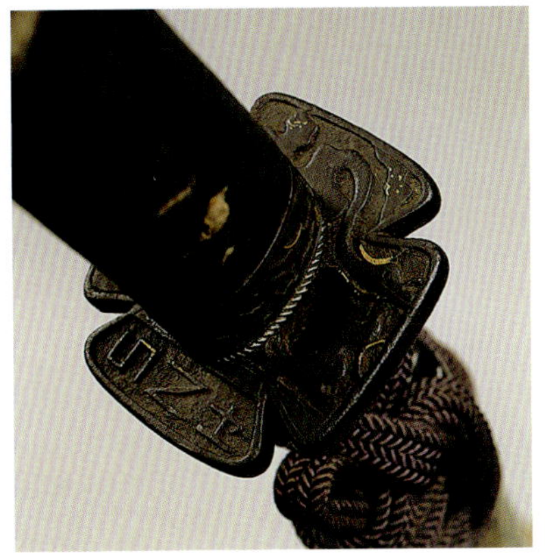

DETAIL
Sword guard
mounted on sword

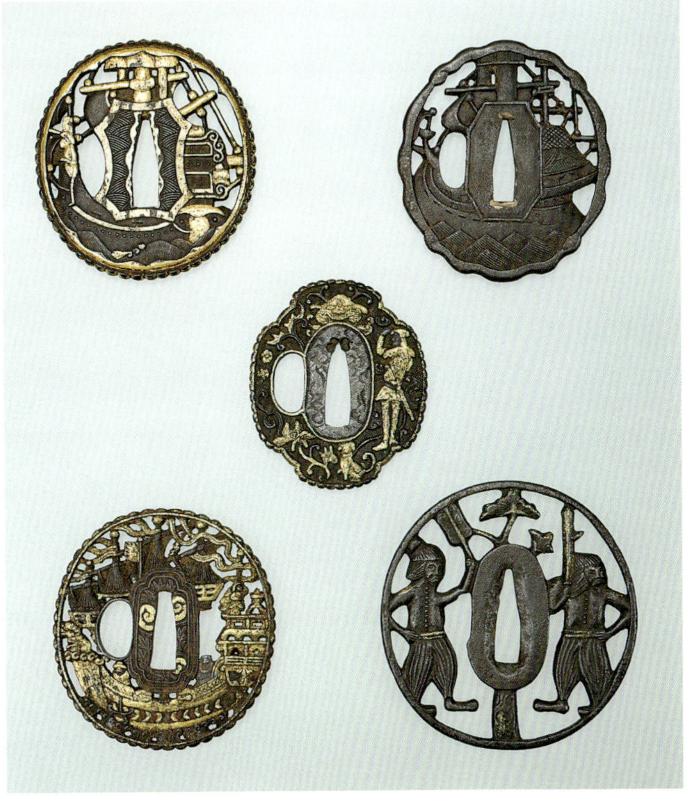

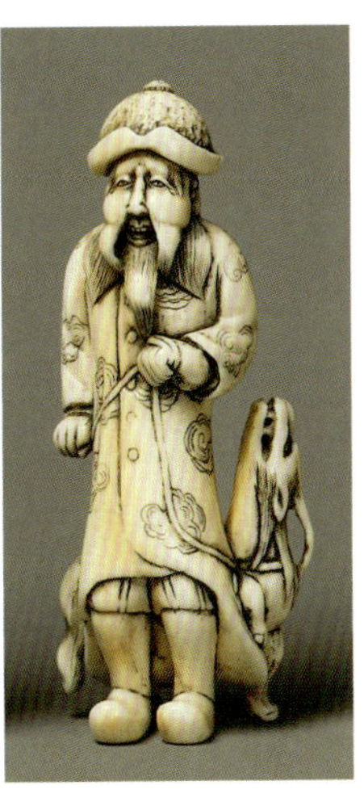

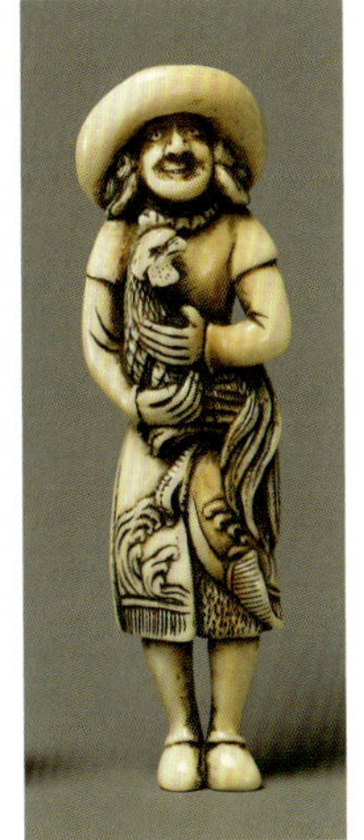

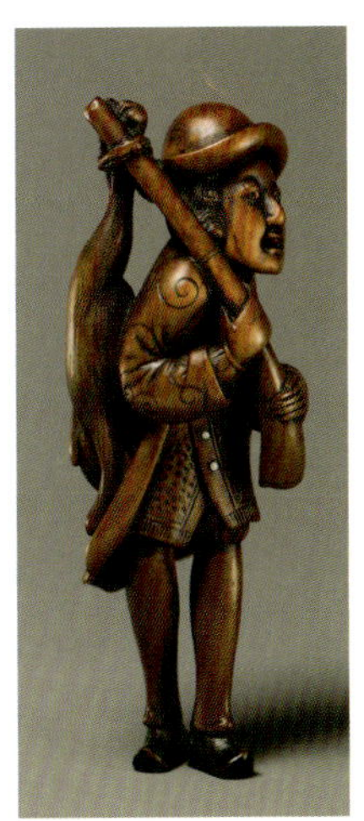

PLATE 114

**Five Covered Bowls
in Five Ships Design**
Japan, late 18th century
Arita ware, porcelain
with polychrome
decoration
h. 2¾ × diam. 5⅛ in.
(7 × 12.8 cm) each

DETAIL (left)
Dutch figures
(plate 114)

DETAIL (right)
Dutch ship
(plate 114)

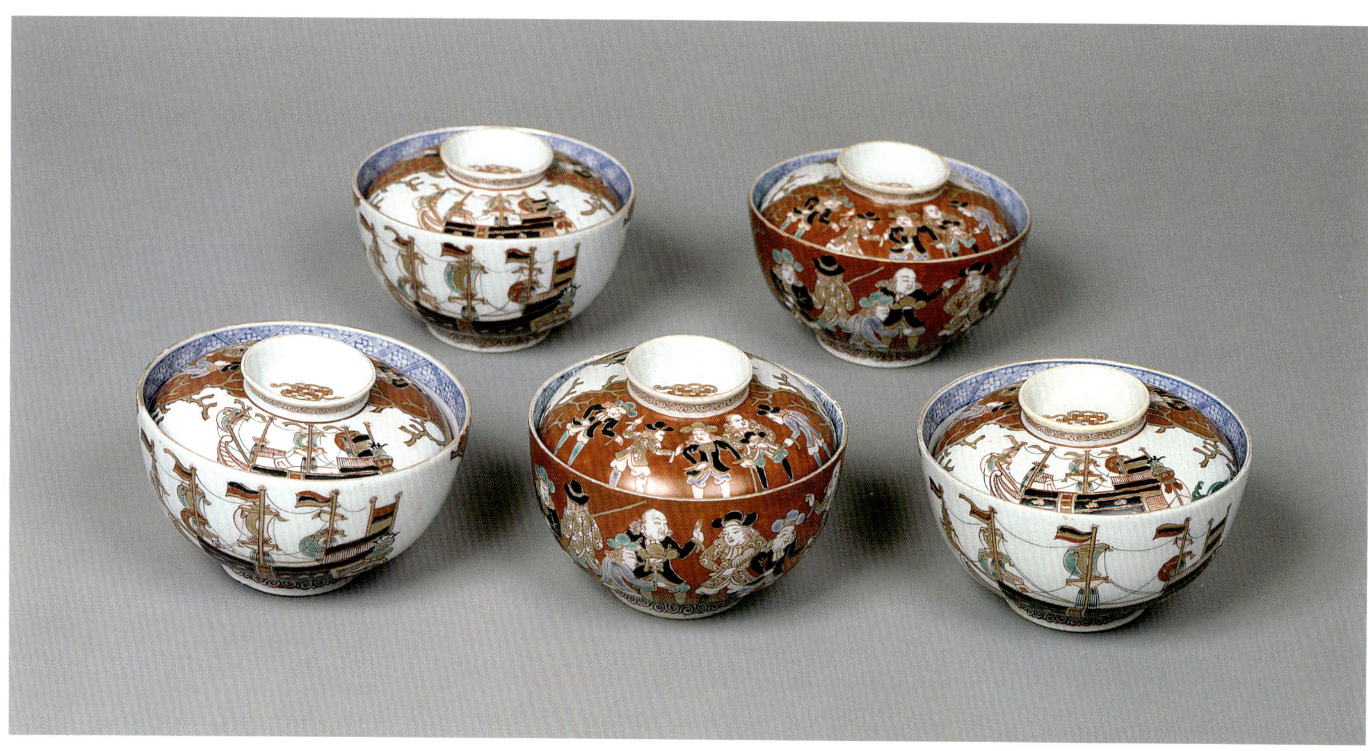

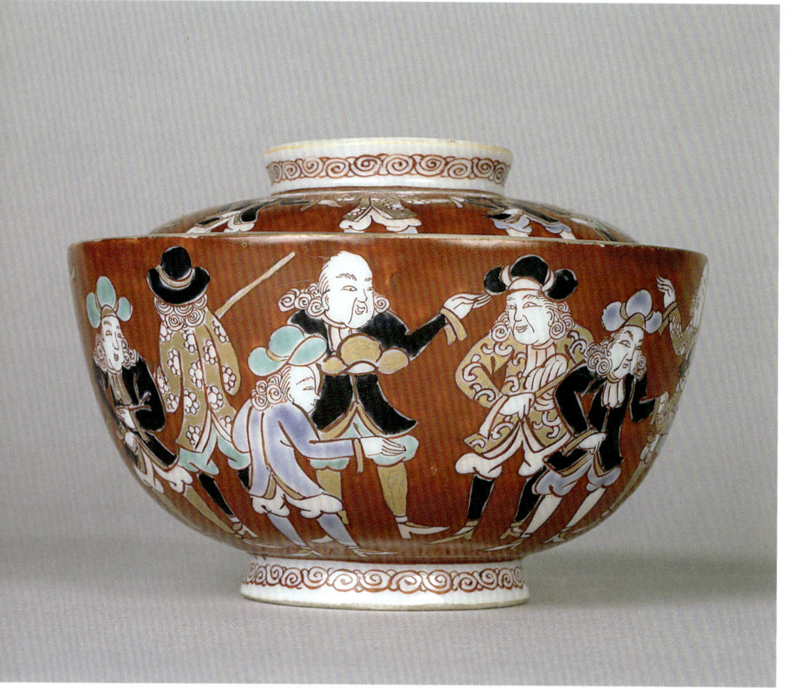

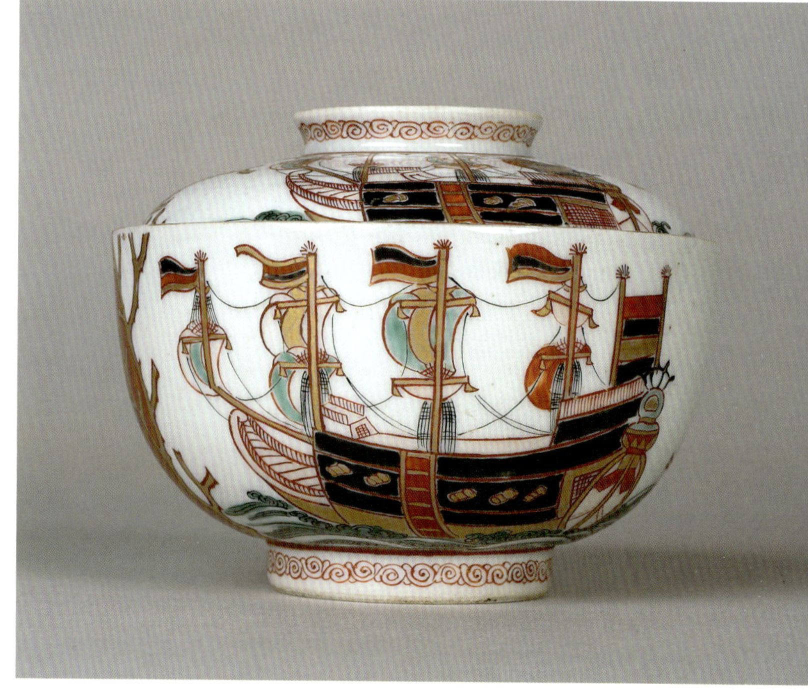

I know, the figures were exclusively Dutch. There are no known examples depicting the Portuguese. There are two basic types of Dutch figural motifs. One has its roots in the Arita ware Five Ships design, which was applied to high-quality polychrome porcelain in the late eighteenth century (plate 114). The other motif featured Dutch figures wearing capes and originated in the designs for porcelain and enamelware produced in China at Jingdezhen (see plate 119 for a Japanese example).[9]

Responding to the *chinoiserie* prevalent at the time, European artists of eighteenth-century Meissen porcelain or English blue-and-white ceramics came to incorporate Chinese figures in their designs. Similar to the way in which Arita ware imitated the design of Chinese porcelain made at Jingdezhen, European craftsmen employed motifs from Chinese and Japanese porcelain in emulation of the original. Behind this practice was their interest in the Far East and a taste for rare, expensive products.

The use of Dutch figural motifs in Arita ware was similarly a response to the demands of the domestic market, but it extended beyond a simple interest in the West. There is no doubt that the Dutch living at Dejima were a curious and fascinating presence for the Japanese. Yet surely this could not have been the only reason to feature them on tableware. Furthermore, depictions of foreigners occur in objects suitable for festive or special occasions (*hare*), not daily life (*ke*), for reasons I will examine below.

The Chinese ideology of Sinocentrism placed their country at the center of the world; the foreign places in the four cardinal directions around it were considered the lands of barbarians. This concept had been introduced and taken root in Japan in ancient times, and the Chinese figures depicted on porcelain made at Jingdezhen during the Ming (1368–1644) and Qing (1644–1912) dynasties were considered neither barbaric nor foreign. What is more, they became standard pictorial motifs for Arita ware, for example, in such typical images as the Eight Legendary Immortals (*Hassennin*) or scenes of Chinese children at play (*karako asobi zu*). The Japanese regarded these and other Chinese motifs, some borrowed from the teachings of Daoism, as auspicious, and thus the Arita artisans adopted them, and the Japanese people fully accepted them. Western figures had no such longstanding familiarity. In their foreignness, they were regarded as possessing special magical powers. It was likely for such reasons that Dutch figural motifs came to be depicted on Arita ware.

It would be well to remember here the Japanese belief in *raihōshin*, gods from an unknown land beyond the sea who bring happiness. Aspects of this belief are seen still in the form of festivals held annually in seaside areas along the Sea of Japan and in Okinawa. A typical example is the *namahage* festival, held annually on Oga Peninsula in Akita prefecture. Young village men disguise themselves wearing masks with the devil faces of *namahage*, the fierce-looking messengers of the *kami*, sacred Shinto spirits. They go from house to house, uttering threats and carrying wooden kitchen knives. The head of a family welcomes and pacifies them with sake and food. A visit from the *namahage* gives a blessing for happiness in the household and for a rich harvest in the New Year.

There are several origins given for this festival. Popular legend relates it to Emperor Wu of the Chinese Han dynasty (206 BCE–220 CE), who is said to have arrived at Oga Peninsula from the air, accompanied by five bats; others relate it to mountain practitioners of Buddhism (*shugenja*). Most notably, *namahage* are thought to refer to big, red-haired, blue-eyed foreigners who were imagined to be gods from the eternal lands beyond the sea, bringing happiness and prosperity. These periodic visitors from afar aroused some trepidation, but they were welcomed for their perceived benefit as gods of good fortune.

In the early days of their visits, the Portuguese and Spanish from the faraway southern sea were identified as the "southern barbarians" (*nambanjin*). This notion became fixed in the tradition of *namban* screen painting. After the *sakoku* policy was set in place, this image was projected upon the Dutch who arrived at Nagasaki. Even after *namban* vessels disappeared from screen paintings, they and Dutch vessels were seen as treasure ships that brought wealth. Such perceptions lasted into the early nineteenth century, as seen in a woodblock print by Utagawa Sadatora, *Hizen Nagasaki zu* (Nagasaki, Hizen Province, plate 115). At the top, there is a fan with a scene of a Dutch vessel entering a port, beside which an inscription reads: "arrival of a treasure ship" (Ōminato takara no nyūsen). In considering why Arita ware includes Dutch motifs among traditional symbols of wealth such as coral, money pouches, or jewels, it seems evident that the Dutch vessels had come to be associated with the traditional auspicious symbol of the treasure ship.

Another interesting example comes in the form of a tobacco container (plate 116). Its decoration of a foreign ship mixes aspects of the vessels of the *nambanjin* with those of the Koreans, whose missions came to Japan twelve times between the sixteenth and eighteenth centuries.

Japanese fishermen who lived by the sea regarded *yorimono*—things carried by the current and washed ashore—as sacred objects. These included driftwood and large fish, as well as whales, sharks, and dolphins that might approach the shore and, sometimes, corpses. In places facing the Pacific Ocean, such as Tosa on Shikoku Island, bodies that drifted ashore from afar were laid to rest with the utmost care and enshrined as deities known as *yorigami*. It was thought that the tremendous spiritual power possessed by those who died by drowning could be transformed into a positive energy that would bring fishermen a big catch. Fishermen, whose livelihood depended on luck, prayed for a rich haul to these deities, generally called *ebisu*. This form of worship was based on the idea that a different world existed beneath the sea. The term *ebisu* was applied strictly to foreigners and not to the Japanese. The 1603 *Nippo*

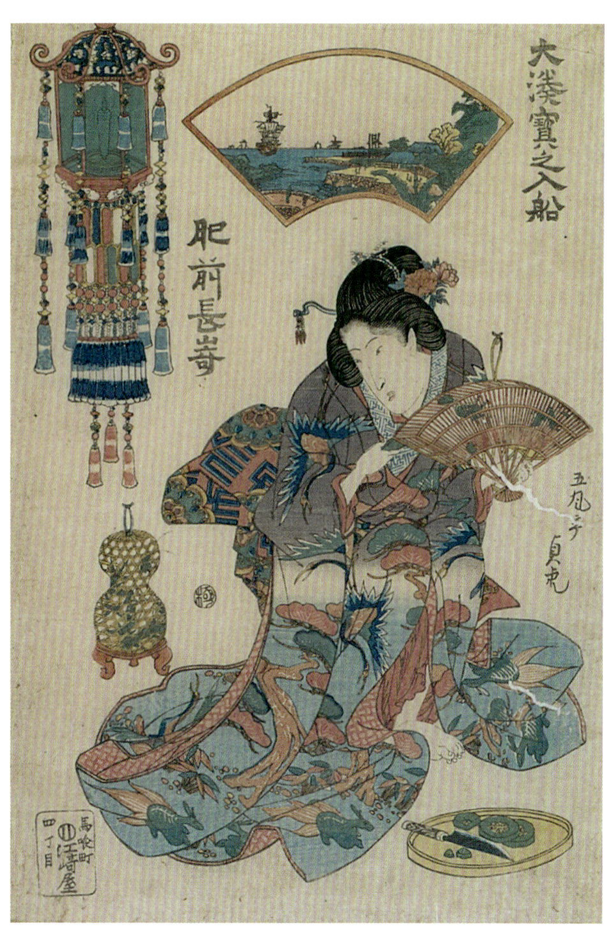

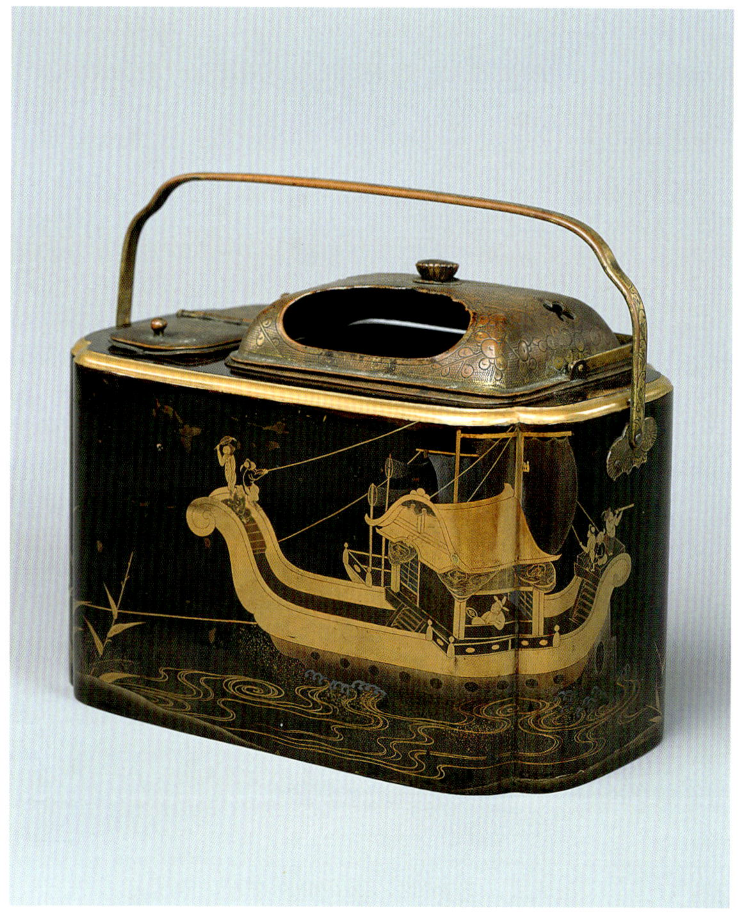

jisho or *Vocabulario da lingoa de Iapam* (Japanese-Portuguese Dictionary) published in Nagasaki and thought to have been edited by a Jesuit priest, defines *ebisu* as "barbarians" and "fishermen's idols."

Ebisu possessed magical power because they came from an unknown land, and with this power, they came to be worshiped as deities. The Tartars to the north, the Portuguese and Spanish "southern barbarians," and the red-haired, blue-eyed Dutch were all grouped together as *ebisu*. Underlying this categorization was the Japanese folk belief that sought to be favored by magical powers. The more foreigners the Japanese could designate as *ebisu*, the better the chances of being touched by good luck. Taking these beliefs into account, we can begin to understand the appeal of Dutch figures as a design motif.

The production of Arita ware began only in the early seventeenth century, and the southern barbarian motif was not employed in its designs. In lacquerware and metalwork, however, the *namban* motif can be found from the sixteenth century. Some of the high-quality polychrome porcelain made for the domestic market in the

late eighteenth century incorporates images of Dutch vessels and people. Eventually Dutch figural motifs were also applied to blue-and-white porcelain tableware intended for daily use. Thus, by the first half of the nineteenth century, a significant number of Dutch figural motifs had been created.

The Dutch motifs sometimes were combined with symbols of prosperity such as jade and ancient Chinese bronze vessels, creatures of Chinese legend such as the *kirin* (a mythical beast), or animals with spiritual connotations such as elephants and camels. In 1821 and 1824, the Dutch brought camels to Japan and put them on display. To stir up interest, a circular advertising the characteristics of the camels was prepared: "Their hair can be used as a charm that cures smallpox and wards off evil spirits. Both the male and the female are gentle by nature, and they make an extremely good pair" (plate 117). The painters of Arita ware depicted camels alongside Dutch figures because of their novelty and auspiciousness (plate 118).

Another example, an eight-sided bowl, once again imparts auspiciousness to a Dutch motif

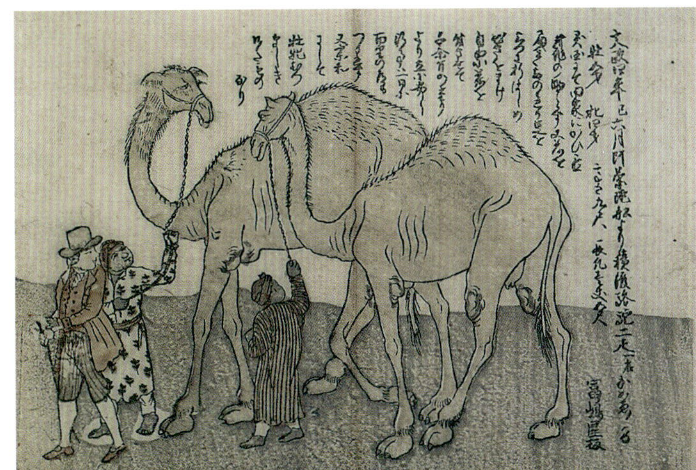

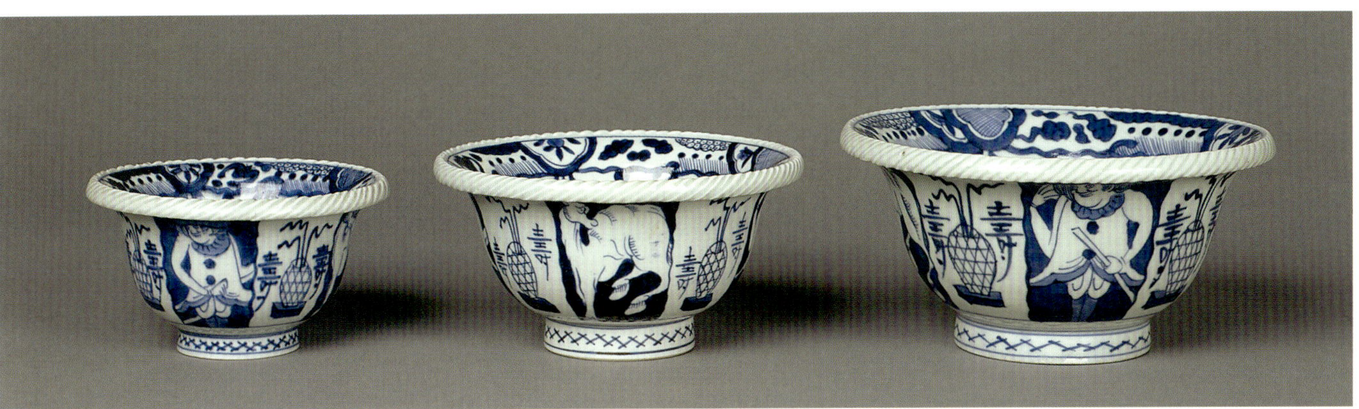

155

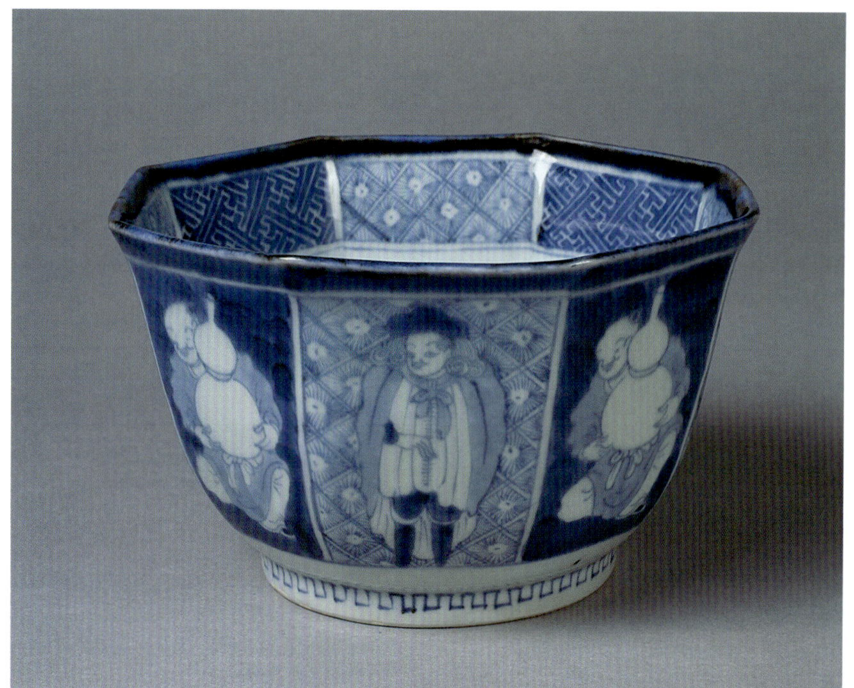

by pairing it with a traditional symbol (plate 119). The bowl bears alternating panels depicting a standing Dutchman wearing a mantle and a Chinese figure holding a large gourd, which suggests he is a legendary immortal. We can speculate that common people regarded the Dutch figural motif as favorable, bringing good luck to their activities, and not incongruous even when juxtaposed with a traditional Chinese immortal. From the late Edo period, it was not unusual to mark special occasions by setting a table with plates and bowls with Dutch motifs.

These Dutch figural designs are not indicative of the extent of Westernization among ordinary Japanese people, and they were not vehicles by which the Japanese incorporated Western culture into their own. Rather, these motifs document the particular attitude held by the Japanese toward foreigners as bringers of good fortune, a viewpoint that had been prevalent since the sixteenth century.

Significance of Dutch-style Japanese Ceramics

During the *sakoku* period, Dutch, English, and German ceramics were brought to Japan, but in far fewer numbers than the porcelain exported from Arita. Imported ceramics were rarities treasured by leisured members of the wealthy class who indulged a desire for foreign things, which they reserved for use on special occasions.

Inspired by these European ceramics, a completely new type of ware came to be produced in Japan from the eighteenth century. This type, known as Kyoto ware, had an earthenware base covered with a white slip and painted decoration, often in cobalt pigment (plates 120, 121). Its motifs frequently combine Eastern and Western elements, including landscapes, flowers, and arabesque patterns. It is clear that Kyoto ware took as its point of departure the tin-glazed earthenware (faience) made in Delft. The aesthetic maturity and sophistication of these precious pieces were intended to satisfy the refined tastes of practitioners of the tea ceremony and drinkers of green tea (*sencha*). It is notable that the makers of Kyoto ware preferred low-fire earthenware resembling Delftware, even though it was possible to create hard-paste porcelain in Arita.

Kenzan II (Ihachi, act. mid-18th century) and his successor Kenzan III (Gosuke, act. 1818–44) worked in Kyoto and produced this type of

PLATE 120
Large Plate with
European Landscape
Design
Japan, c. 1804–44
(Bunka–Tenpō era)
Kyoto ware style,
earthenware with
white slip and cobalt
blue decoration
h. 3 × diam. 19⅜ in.
(7.5 × 49.1 cm)

PLATE 121
Two-tiered Food
Container with
Foreign Landscape
Design
Japan, c. 1804–44
(Bunka–Tenpō era)
Kyoto ware style,
earthenware with
white slip and poly-
chrome decoration
5½ × 7⅜ × 7⅜ in.
(14 × 18.7 × 18.7 cm)

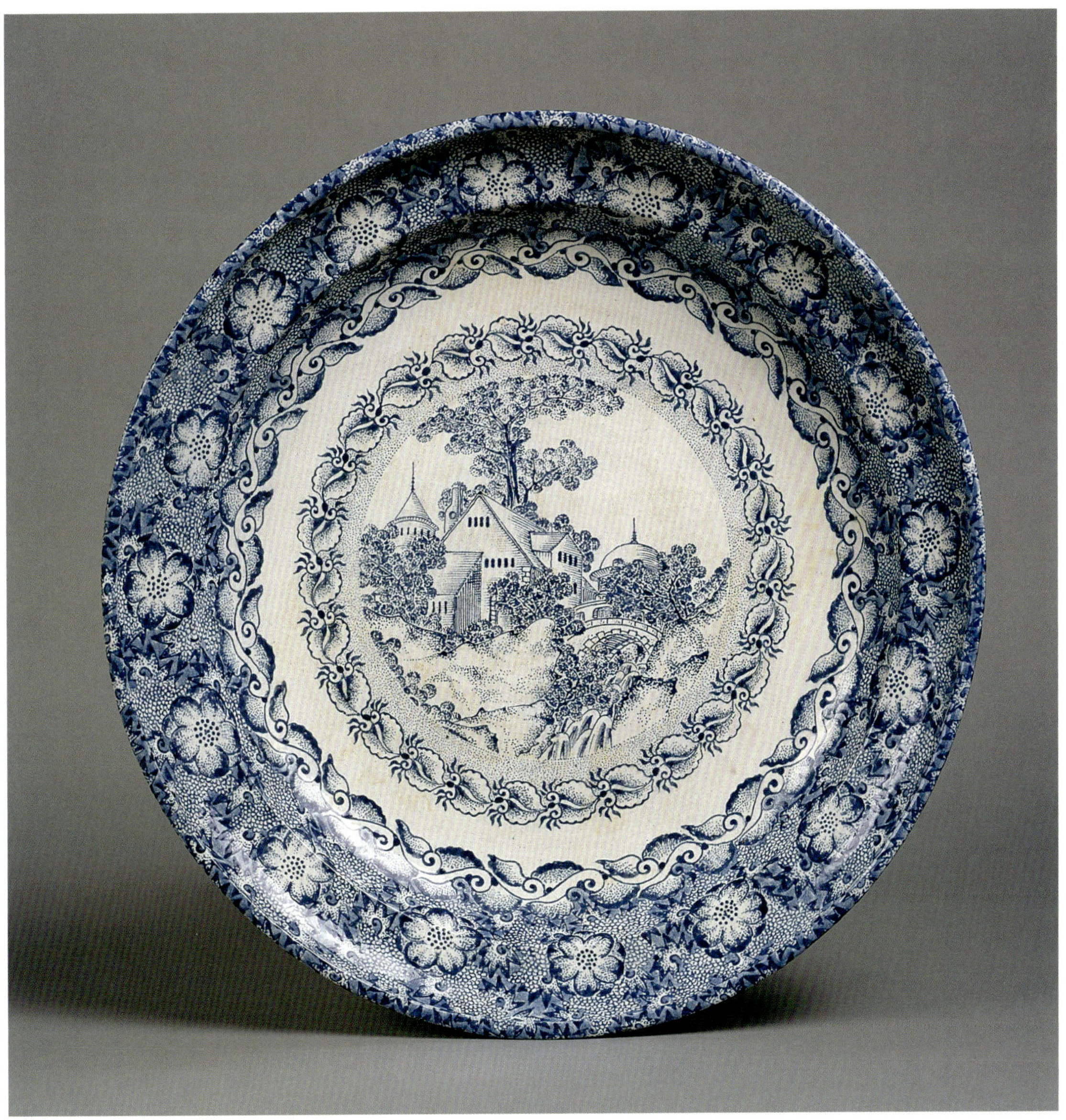

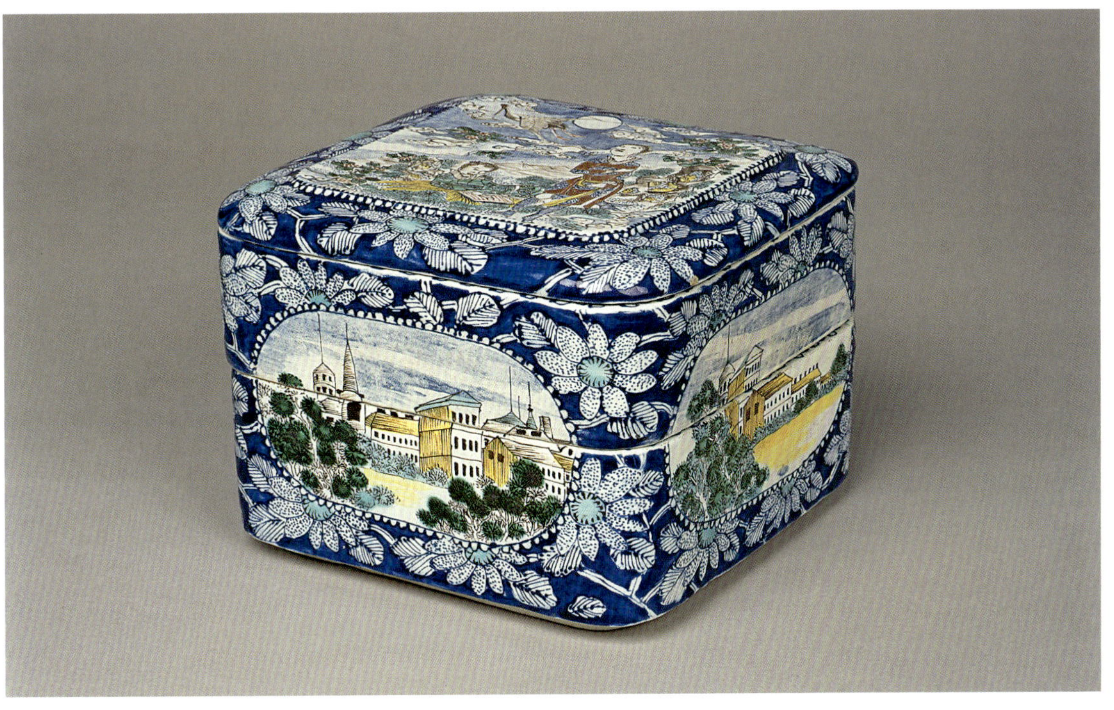

157

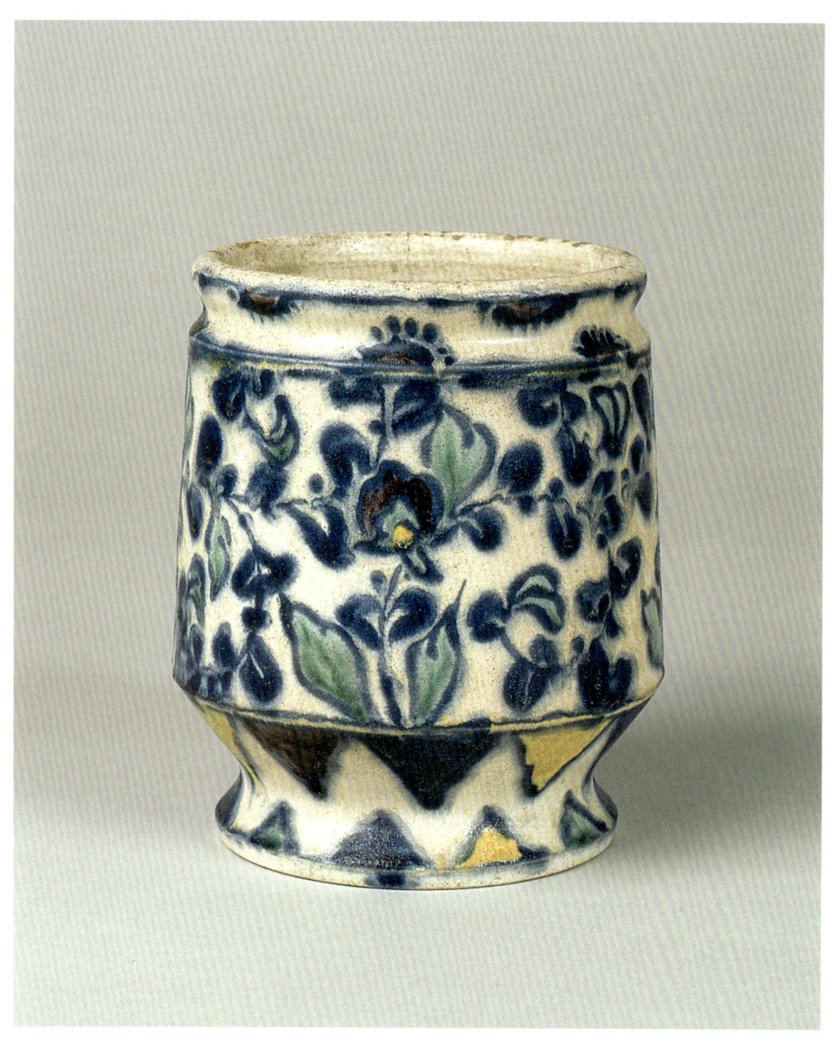

PLATE 122
Attributed to Ogata
Kenzan II
(Japanese,
act. mid-18th century)

**Charcoal Container
with Dutch Floral
Design**
Signature: Kenzan
18th century
Kyoto ware, earthen-
ware with white slip
and polychrome
decoration
h. 5¼ × diam. 4⅛ in.
(13.3 × 10.5 cm)

PLATE 123
Attributed to Ogata
Kenzan III
(Japanese,
act. 1818–44)

**Six Square Plates
with Floral Design**
Signature: Kenzan
Early 19th century
Kyoto ware, earthen-
ware with white slip
and cobalt blue
decoration
1¾ × 4⅝ × 4⅝ in.
(4.4 × 11.5 × 11.5 cm)
each

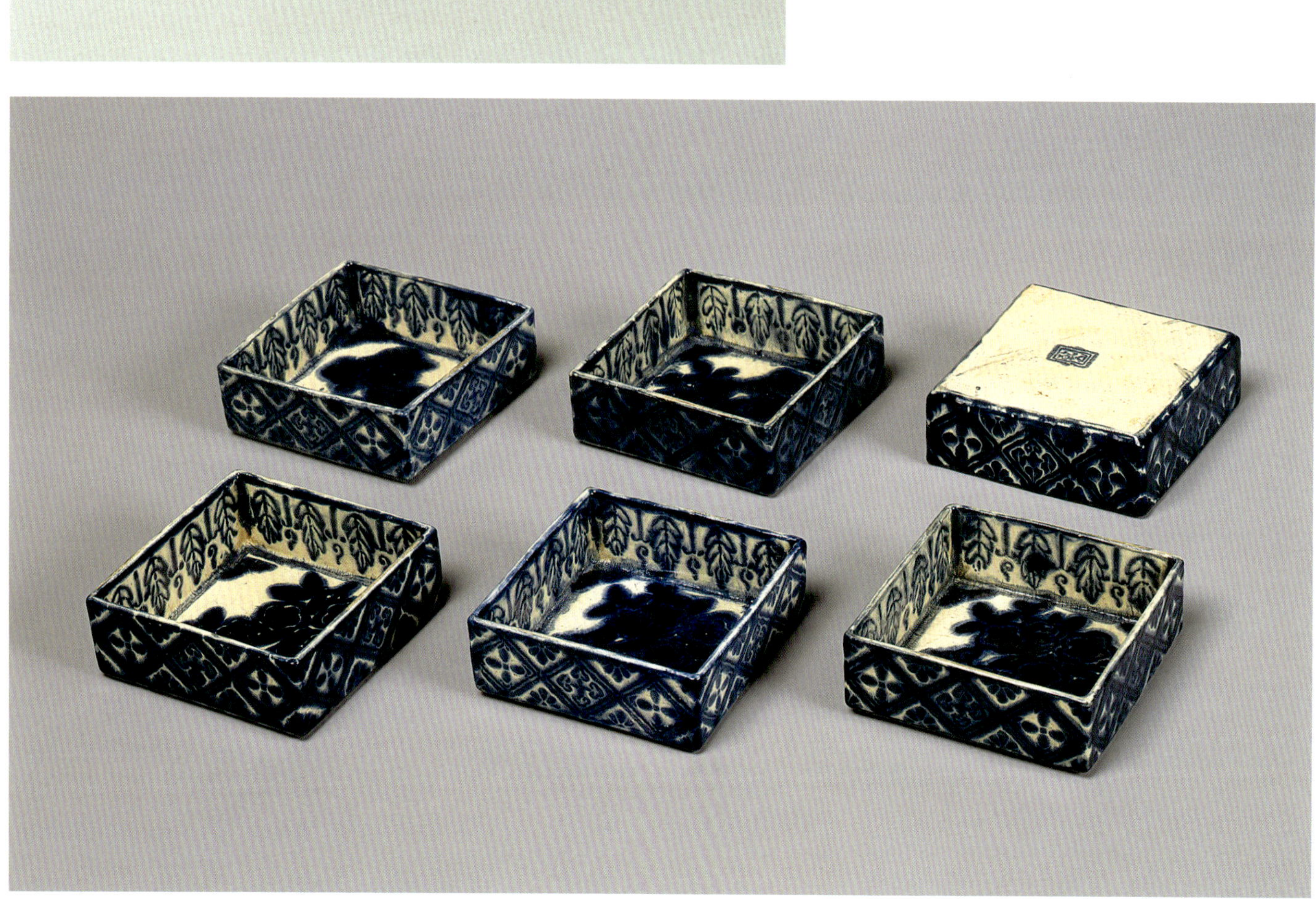

ceramic during the early stages of its development (plates 122, 123). Kyoto artists such as Ninnami Dōhachi (1783–1855), Ogata Shūhei (1788–1839), and Mashimizu Zōroku (1822–1877) also made and decorated the ware (plate 124). Similar work can be found among high-quality Iga ware, made in Mie prefecture and influenced by Kyoto ware and the products of the Edo ceramist Ida Kichi-roku (1792–1861).

An interesting example of this ceramic that combines elements of East and West is a Kyoto-ware sword holder with a European town design (plate 125). The imaginative village scene includes numerous strolling figures and towers rendered with the use of perspective. The edges of the land-scape are decorated with flower and arabesque patterns, and a decorative border in the lower part of the holder effectively employs a pointillis-tic pattern that resembles the designs of imported European calico. The shadows behind the figures in the landscape show that the artist recognized the white blank produced by the glaze as a three-dimensional space. This piece is thought to be by an artisan at the Awataguchi kiln in Kyoto and produced some time during the Bunka (1804–18) or Tenpō (1830–44) era. A top-quality, one-of-a-kind piece, the sword holder undoubtedly was made in response to a special order.

Judging from the stances of the depicted fig-ures, the artist probably used a European cop-perplate print from the mid-eighteenth century as a model for the hand-painted village scene. The detailed rendering of the flower borders and the pleasant pictorial gradation accom-plished through stippling have some of the feel of a copperplate print. These characteristics dif-ferentiate the decoration from that applied to Delft ceramics, which relied on line rather than

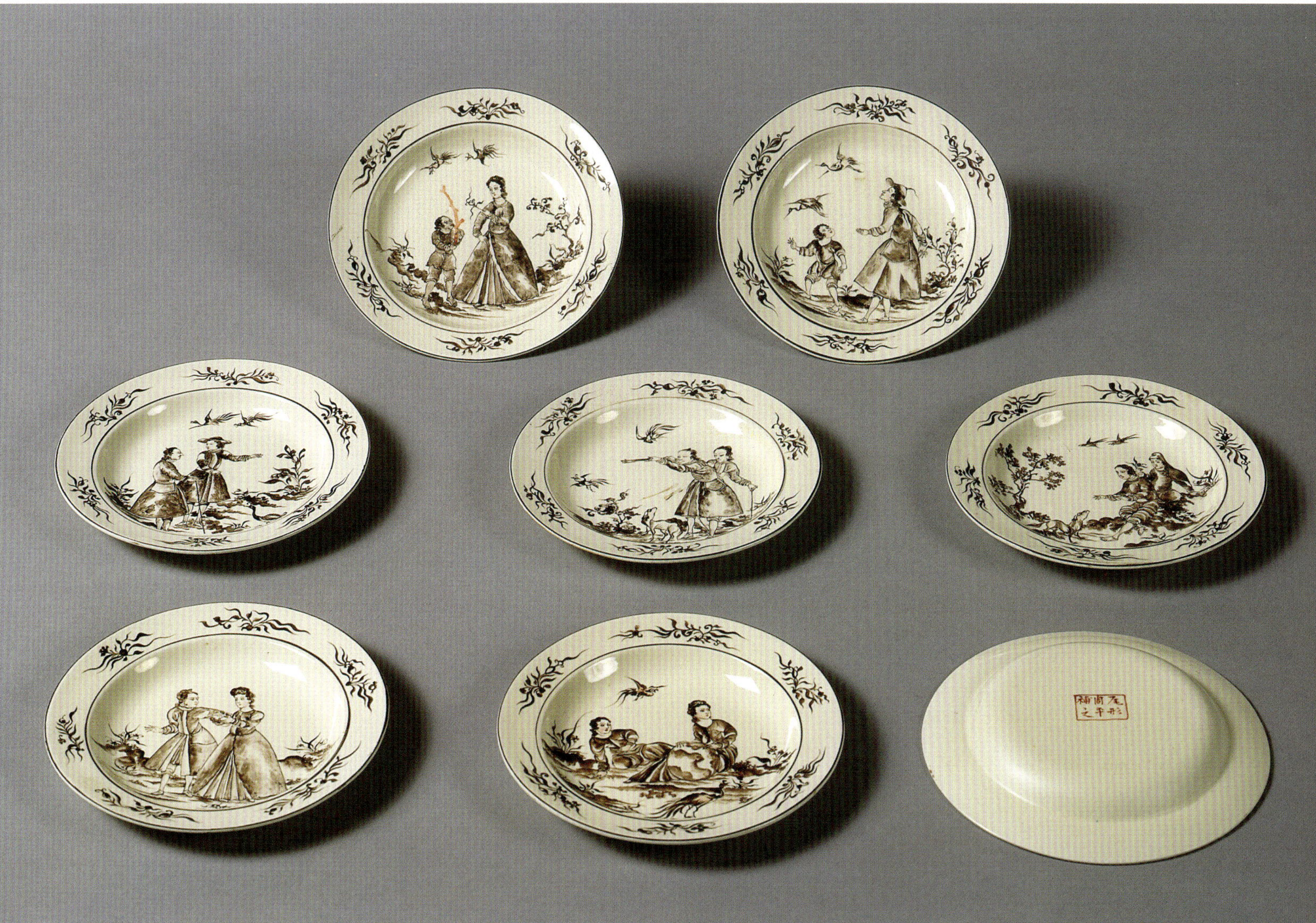

stippling and blurring effects. The pictorial program of the sword holder is much more sophisticated than the simple Dutch figures depicted
on Arita ware. This Dutch-style Japanese earthenware produced in Kyoto reveals, in an extrava-
gant form, the history of the Japanese reception
of shapes and designs of European ceramics from
the seventeenth to nineteenth centuries. In contrast, the Arita porcelain decorated with Dutch
figural motifs as auspicious symbols were rendered in a conventional Japanese fashion. The

Dutch-style Kyoto earthenware is equivalent to
Western-style Japanese painting and printmak-
ing, while Arita porcelain can be compared with
namban screens. Whereas the former employed a
Western style of expression, whatever the subject
might have been, the latter used a Japanese form
to depict a Western subject.

From where did the inspiration for the sword
holder's detailed landscape scene in cobalt blue
decoration come? A likely model would be the
work of the great Delft landscape painter Frederik

PLATE 125

Sword Holder with
European Landscape
Design

Japan, c. 1804–44
(Bunka–Tenpō era)
Kyoto ware style,
earthenware with
white slip and cobalt
blue decoration
16 × 15 × 8⅛ in.
(40.5 × 37.9 × 20.5 cm)

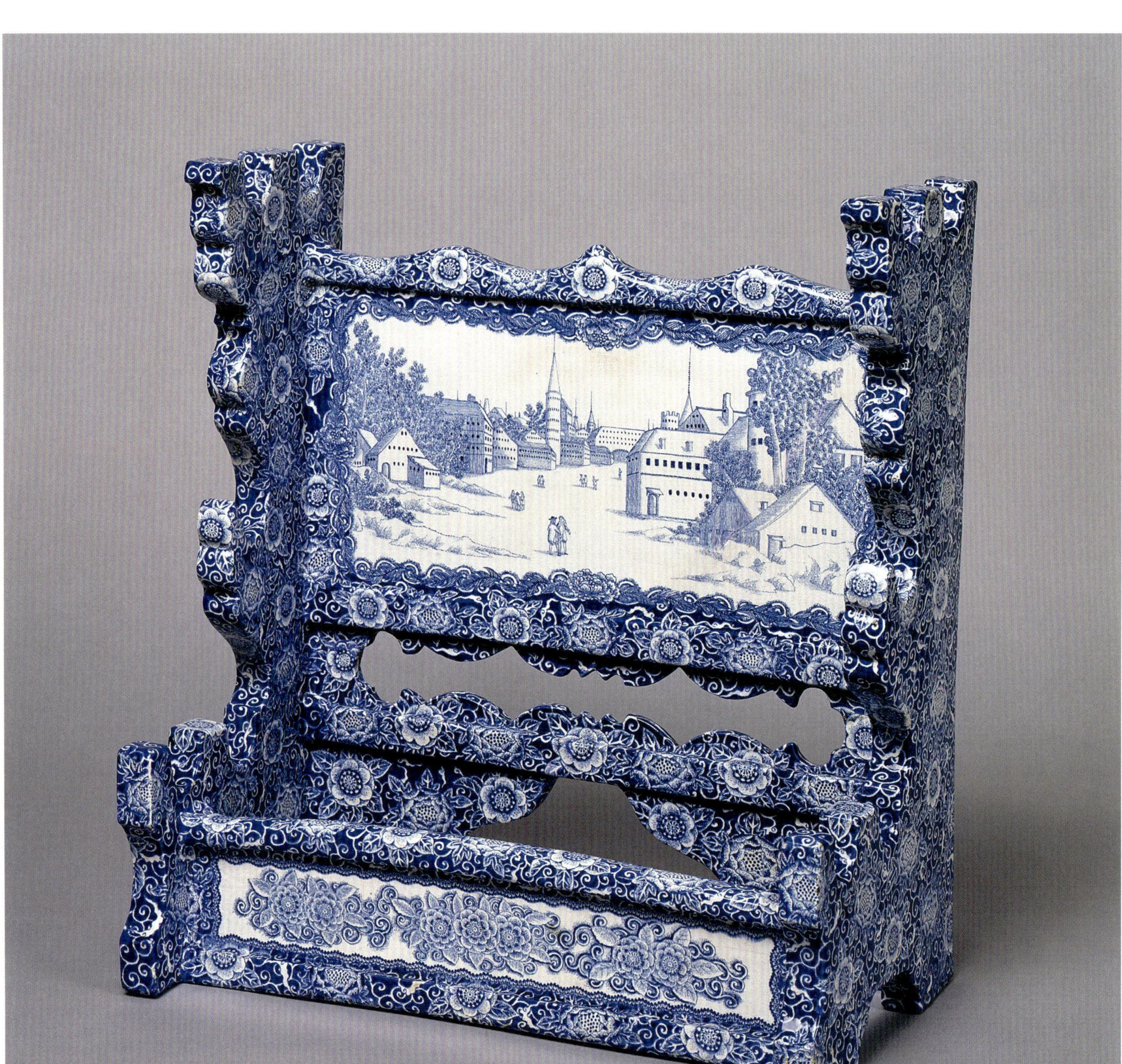

van Frijtom (c. 1632–1702).[10] The artist who decorated the sword holder must have at least seen a detailed landscape painted on a Delftware dish, plate, or tile made under Van Frijtom's influence (fig. 16). The surrounding flower pattern, however, takes its source from transfer-printed decoration, such as the wild rose pattern seen on the border of an English plate with a Philosopher design (fig. 17). This design is seen frequently in the tableware that was mass-produced in Staffordshire in northern England in the first half of the

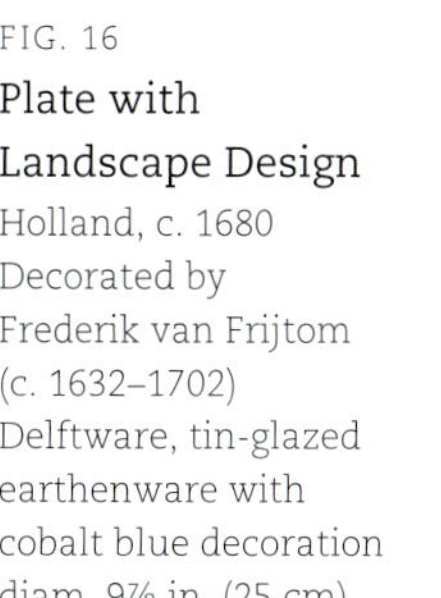

Plate with Landscape Design

Holland, c. 1680
Decorated by
Frederik van Frijtom
(c. 1632–1702)
Delftware, tin-glazed
earthenware with
cobalt blue decoration
diam. 9⅞ in. (25 cm)
Rijksmuseum, Amsterdam (BK. 1984-28)
■

Plate with Philosopher Design

England, early
19th century
Delftware, tin-glazed
earthenware with
cobalt-blue transfer
printed decoration
h. 1⅛ × diam. 10 in.
(2.7 × 25.2 cm)
Private collection
■

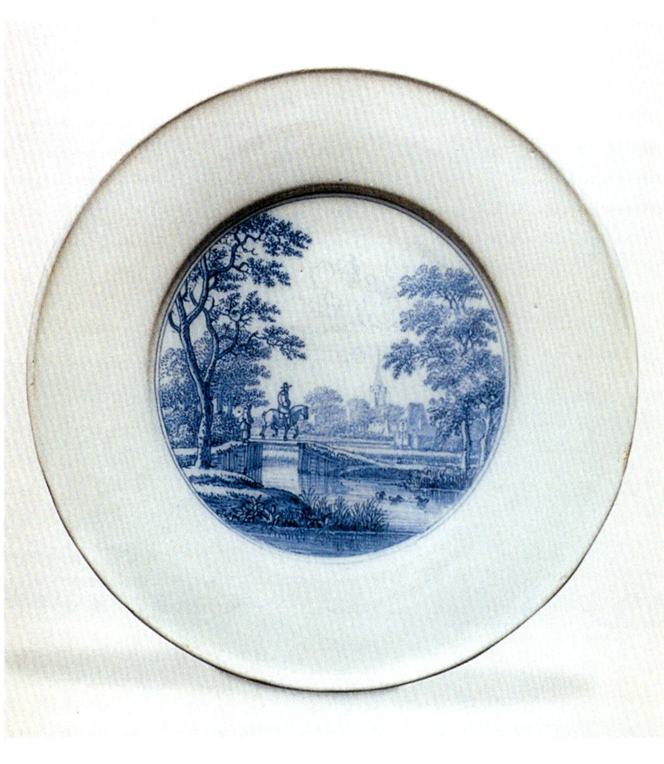

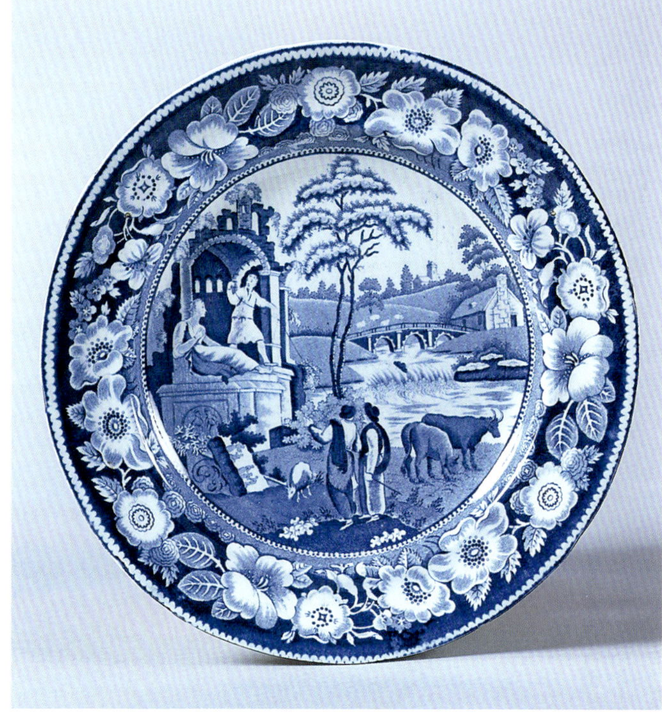

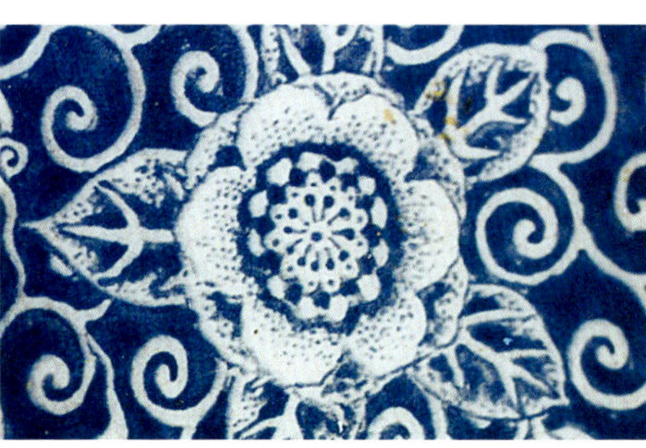

DETAIL
Flower and
arabesque design
in hand-stippled
technique
(plate 125)
■

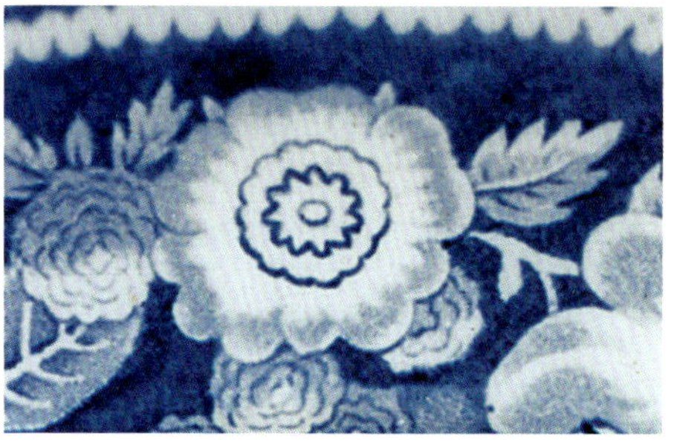

DETAIL
Transfer-printed
wild rose pattern
(fig. 17)
■

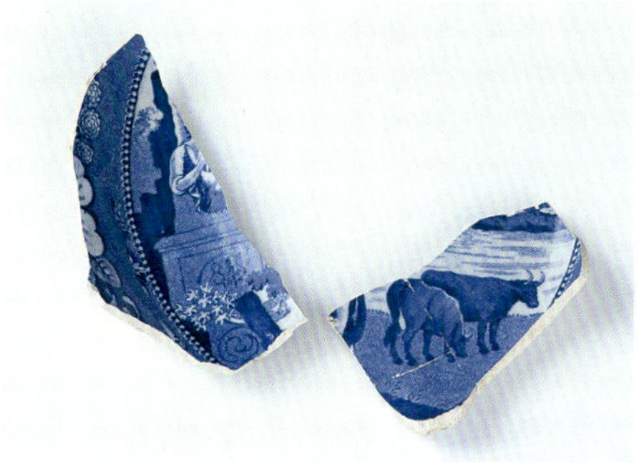

FIG. 18
Shards of a
Philosopher plate
excavated at
Dejima, 2001
Nagasaki
City Board of
Education
■

PLATE 126
**Undergarment
with Hexagonal
Patchwork**
Cloth imported
c. 1830–60, sewn in
Japan late 19th–early
20th century
Sarasa (imported cotton)
l. 54¾ × w. 51¼ in.
(139 × 130 cm)

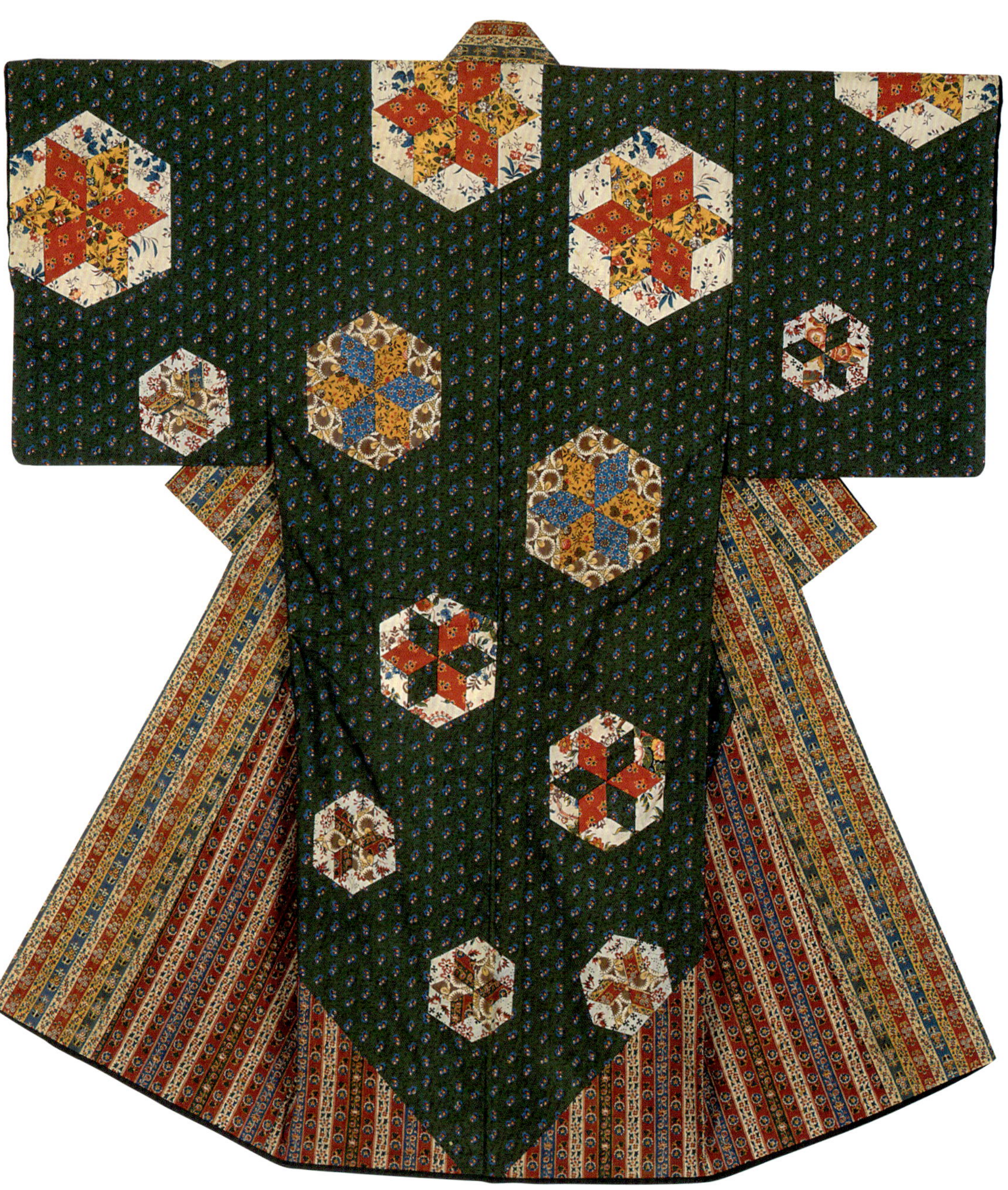

nineteenth century and sold in Europe, America, and Canada. The Dutch trading post at Nagasaki sold it to the Japanese, popularizing the product as *Oranda yaki*. Plate fragments of the Philosopher design with the wild rose border have been recovered at Dejima, Nagasaki (fig. 18). The flower pattern of the sword holder clearly was influenced by the stippling common in transfer-printed ceramics. Another influence could be the printed textiles made in Holland at the time and exported to Japan, where they were fashioned into traditional garments (plate 126).

Sometimes Dutch figures or characters of the Roman alphabet were added to Dutch-style Japanese ceramics to emphasize their Western feel. The origin of other motifs cannot always be easily recognized because Japanese artists freely interpreted them in their traditional style. Because these ceramics were not for daily use but prized as precious objects, their decorative, rather than practical aspects, were emphasized.

In sum, they reveal in three-dimensional form the essence of a "foreign country," as created and imagined by the potter, the painter, and the purchaser from the upper echelons. In this I see a synthesis of the Japanese, Chinese, and Western elements that characterized Japanese culture of the *sakoku* period.

In Dutch-style Japanese ceramics, we see Western-style depictions of Western landscapes, rendered with the use of perspective and painted in cobalt blue. But they take shapes that are uniquely Japanese, such as that of a sword holder or a bowl for rinsing sake cups. This type of ceramic is saved from becoming an imitative Dutch craftwork—in other words, kitsch—because we find in them a sophisticated artistic creativity propelled by *hollandisme*. Because the Japanese characteristically practiced an accommodating receptivity toward other cultures, they were able to regard a foreign landscape as a "paradise" that brings happiness.

NOTES

1. The order was for "ten or twelve dishes of Dutch earthenware of different sizes and fine Dutch clay, white, 'and the painting various'"; see T. Volker, *Porcelain and the Dutch East India Company as Recorded in the Dagh-registers of Batavia Castle, Those of Hirado and Deshima and Other Contemporary Papers, 1602–1682,* Mededelingen van het Rijksmuseum voor Volkenkunde, no. 11 (Leiden: Rijksmuseum voor Volkenkunde, 1971), 124.

2. Reports related to Japanese orders of Western ceramics are found in the years 1636, 1640, 1645, and 1652. Ibid., 119, 122, 124, 125.

3. Kaempfer left his excellent *History of Japan* (1727), and Siebold's *Nippon* (1897) was published posthumously.

4. Englebert Kaempfer, *History of Japan,* trans. J. G. Scheuchzer (Glasgow, James McLehose and Sons, 1727), vol. 2, 322.

5. Philipp Franz von Siebold, *Nippon* (1897, Oshabrück: Biblio Verlag, 1969), 116–17.

6. Peter Abrahams, "The History of the Telescope in Japan," http://www.europa.com/~telscope/tsjapan.txt (accessed March 13, 2007).

7. A measurement of lead content executed in 1990 by the author on a similar glass cylinder proved it was made at Nagasaki (though a lens and metal fittings could have been imported).

8. In 2004 Yoshihiro Kaieda, Chief Curator, Cultural Promotion Division, Nagasaki Prefectural Government, confirmed the presence of six glass Japanese telescopes at the Kunstkamera, St. Petersburg. Four are inscribed "Japan 1788," and all are made to the standard of Nagasaki glass engraving. I express my sincere gratitude to Kaieda for providing me this information.

9. Oka Yasumasa, "Ishō to shiteno Oranda," in *Orandae imari to bīdoro giyaman,* exh. cat. (Fukuyama Shiritsu Fukuyamajō Hakubtsukan, 1998), 7.

10. For the relation between Van Frijtom and Arita ware, see Christiaan J. A. Jörg, "Oranda muke no Nihonsei shikki ni tsuite," in *Eikō no Oranda kaiga to Nihon,* exh. cat. (Osaka: Asashi Shinbunsha Bunka Kikakukyoku Osaka Kikakubu, 1993), 142–43.

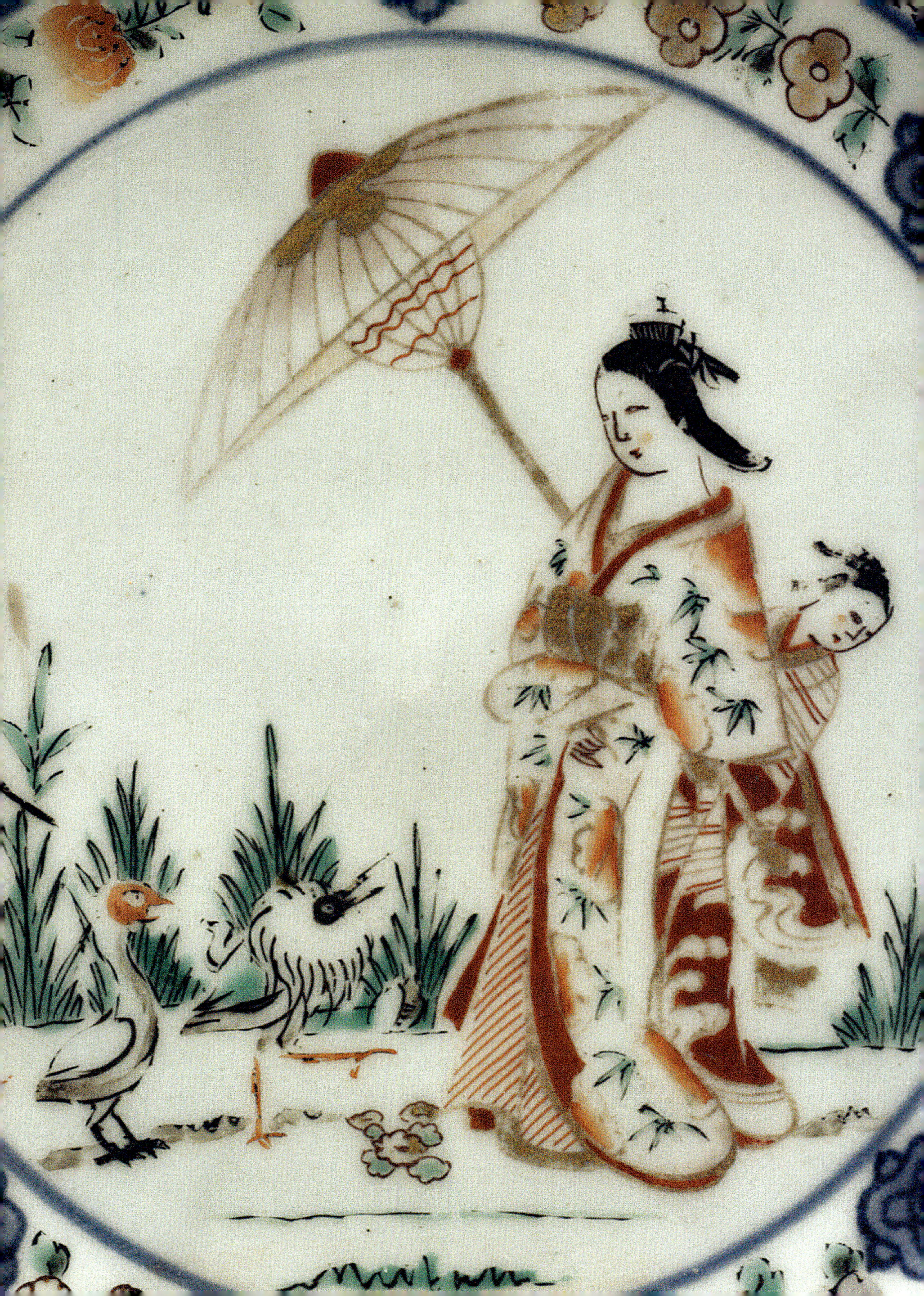

7

Christiaan J. A. Jörg

Japan and the West
Export Porcelain and Lacquerware

The Dutch enjoyed a special relationship with Japan from their chance arrival in 1600 until the opening of Japan in the mid-nineteenth century. Dutch merchants provided the Japanese with European and Asian commodities and after the 1630s, during the period of *sakoku*, the closing of Japan, with information about the rest of the world. These merchants sold cloth, spices, and Chinese silk, and brought Western books, instruments, glass, and Delft faience. Dutch cargoes included Japanese copper and gold, paper, porcelain, and lacquer, and the Japanese kimono influenced Dutch fashionable dress. This essay focuses on porcelain and lacquer, commodities representative of the much wider field of interaction in decorative art between Japan and the Netherlands.

Porcelain

Porcelain manufacturing techniques were introduced to Japan at the beginning of the seventeenth century by Korean potters who arrived in the wake of Toyotomi Hideyoshi's campaigns in Korea (1592–98). The potters settled on Kyūshū, in Arita, where suitable porcelain stone deposits were available and nearby harbors facilitated transport of finished products to other parts of Japan.[1]

Production during the first half of the century was small scale, and Arita potters had to compete with the well-established Japanese stoneware kilns. The advantage of *shoki*-Imari (early Imari) over stoneware was the material: the white porcelain body, decorated in underglaze blue, was similar to the fashionable Chinese porcelain imported into Japan since the 1620s. The affluent merchant class in Edo, Kyoto, and elsewhere admired Chinese porcelain and used it in the tea ceremony and for special meals. The Arita product competed successfully and created its own niche.[2]

A short excursion to China is needed to explain how and why Japanese porcelain came to be associated with the Dutch. Since the Yuan dynasty (1279–1368), Chinese porcelain decorated in underglaze cobalt blue, produced at Jingdezhen, the center of porcelain production in Jiangxi province, was widely exported to markets in southeast Asia, India, Iran, and the Middle East. A special export type was being developed in the second half of the sixteenth century, typified by the serial production of large quantities with scant attention to detail and finish. Intended to meet a growing overseas demand, porcelain was transported by Chinese junks to the main trade centers in southeast Asia whence it was distributed by Arab, Malay, Indian, and other merchants to various destinations. The Portuguese, too, participated in this inter-Asian porcelain trade and also shipped it to Lisbon but did not re-export it to northern Europe.

The name for these wares is Kraak porcelain, a Dutch word derived from *caracca,* a merchant ship frequently used by the Portuguese in their Asian trade. These porcelains are thinly potted and often have irregularities in the shape or the glaze. They are painted exclusively in a brilliant underglaze blue with confident, quick strokes and washes. Decorations comprise traditional landscapes, water scenes, animals, and flowering plants—neutral motifs that were acceptable to a wide public. Human figures occur less often because Islamic customers did not buy pieces with such representations. The sides and/or the rim are divided into repeating wide and narrow panels filled with lucky symbols, jeweled pendants, or geometric designs. The outlines of these panels usually follow similar paneling in low relief, achieved by molding the clay body. Bowls, saucers, and dishes, including very large dishes of about 20 inches in diameter, came in sets of different sizes, each fitting into the other and designed for efficient storage aboard ships.[3]

When the Dutch arrived in Asia around 1600, they learned that Chinese porcelain—rare in northern Europe—was a potentially profitable commodity. Merchants of the Dutch East India Company (Verenigde Oost Indische Compagnie, VOC) actively bought it as part of their trade assortment for Asia and the Netherlands. In fact, porcelain was so successful on the home market that within a few years it became a common exotic element in many Dutch interiors and even was featured in still-life paintings of the period.

After the death of Emperor Wanli (r. 1573–1619), a further diversification of Chinese porcelain production occurred. The court ceased ordering large quantities of porcelain from the major factories in Jingdezhen, and potters had to find new outlets for their wares. The upcoming class of affluent merchants became an important target for the domestic market, as did overseas clients like the Dutch, who were able to purchase in huge quantities. A new type was developed, now called Transitional porcelain, the name relating to the period in which the Ming dynasty (1368–1644) was succeeded by the Qing dynasty (1644–1912) of the Manchus. This porcelain is thicker than Kraak, and the body consists of a very fine, smooth porcelain paste. Well made and finished, the pieces have an impeccable shape and glaze. The decorations in a beautifully nuanced underglaze blue cover the entire available surface, with no paneled sections, and are often based on woodblock prints illustrating Chinese romances and novels.

The Dutch, based in Taiwan from 1621, started ordering specially commissioned pieces from 1634 onward—for instance, beer mugs, candlesticks, and mustard pots—modeled after earthenware, pewter, glass, or wood examples provided to Chinese middlemen by VOC merchants. Such fashionable tablewares in Western shapes were a great success and yielded good profits; more ordinary dishes, cups, and saucers continued to be made as Kraak. Apart from some rare exceptions, neither Kraak nor Transitional porcelain was decorated in European style because Chinese motifs made them more exotic and desirable to Dutch customers.[4]

A different attitude toward decorative style characterizes the porcelain made to order in Jingdezhen for Japan in this period. These wares, called Ko-sometsuke, not only have Japanese shapes but Japanese-style decorations as well. Contrary to the export wares for the Dutch, these porcelains usually have a Kraak-type body and are painted in underglaze blue as well as in overglaze enamels.[5]

Matters changed again during the 1640s. In China, the shift from the Ming to the Qing dynasty caused fierce uprisings and turmoil. Production in Jingdezhen stagnated, and transport from the kilns to the harbors in the east and south became more and more difficult. Foreign clients such as the Dutch and the Japanese faced mounting problems when attempting to buy their typical quantities, and exports from China largely ceased around 1650.

In Japan, the shortage of Chinese porcelain stimulated the Arita potters to expand their output and produce more sophisticated wares. The quality of the body was improved and the variety of shapes increased to include larger objects such as dishes and bottles. The decorations became more elaborate and displayed a typical Japanese style in composition, subject, and ornamentation.

The Dutch dealt with the shortage in two ways.[6] First, the earthenware industry in Holland made imitations of Chinese porcelain. To this end, they refined the clay, made a thinner body, and covered their pieces, front and back, with a white, nontranslucent tin-oxide glaze. In this way, the objects, although made of soft earthenware, had the appearance of porcelain. This faience, as it is called, was decorated in cobalt blue with Chinese-style motifs closely copying the original Kraak and Transitional porcelain. Delftware—most faience factories were concentrated in the town of Delft—was an immediate success, not only because it so closely resembled Chinese wares but also because it was much cheaper. It was exported throughout Europe and may be regarded as one of the artistic accomplishments of the Dutch Golden Age.

The Dutch found a second solution to the shortage of porcelain in Japan. The Dutch East India Company, based at Hirado, was forced by the Japanese government to move to Dejima in Nagasaki harbor in 1641. This fan-shaped artificial island had been built for the Portuguese in the 1630s, but they had been expelled from the country for proselytizing. Apart from the Chinese, the Dutch were the only foreigners allowed to continue trading, but they were strictly controlled. Nevertheless, they had a monopoly much envied by other Westerners.

The Dutch must have known about the porcelain production in nearby Arita, but had paid little attention to it beyond occasionally buying a piece of *shoki*-Imari as a souvenir or gift. Now things were different, and in the 1650s the VOC, by way of experiment, started ordering small quantities of Japanese porcelain for the apothecary shop in Batavia (modern Jakarta), the company's headquarters on the island of Java. The bottles, salve pots, and jars proved suitable, and from 1658

onward the VOC placed substantial annual orders for thousands of pieces of porcelain to be sold in Asia and in the Netherlands.

At first, the Arita potters copied Kraak and Transitional wares from China because these types were familiar to the Dutch, and thus they would sell well in the Netherlands. The potters struggled, however, to produce the large quantities ordered by the Dutch. Compared to the facilities in Jingdezhen, their workshops were smaller, their production process more individual, and, importantly, their basic material was different. Porcelain stone from the Izumiyama quarry in Arita was of good quality and, unlike the clays in China, did not need additions after preparation, but its plasticity necessitated the use of supports or spurs placed under the bases of larger dishes to prevent horizontal sagging during firing. The marks these spurs left in the glaze are unique to Japanese export wares.

Generally speaking, Japanese wares are slightly thicker and heavier than Chinese wares, and the glaze on Arita wares contains many tiny air bubbles, which do not allow for sharp contours or painting as finely detailed as that on Chinese wares. Decorations were painted in a blue derived from cobalt oxide which was less refined than its Chinese equivalent and fired darker with a grayish hue. The greatest novelty that Japanese wares offered was color. Chinese Kraak was exclusively painted in underglaze blue and Transitional wares largely so. Japanese potters had developed a range of bright, opaque enamel colors for application on the glaze and successfully used them on the new export wares. From the very beginning the VOC traded in underglaze blue as well as in enameled Japanese porcelain, creating an interest in both types that would last almost a century.

The development outlined above is well illustrated by three examples. One is a large Chinese Kraak dish with the unusual design of a curling dragon in the center and the characteristic paneled division of the sides and rim (plate 127). Four wide panels are filled with a branch of peaches, a symbol of immortality, but named "sunflowers" by the Dutch, who knew nothing of the symbolic meaning. The other four wide panels show auspicious symbols such as the artemisia leaf, the sun disk, and a scroll; the eight narrow panels have a pendent jewel. The Japanese traditionally call this type of Chinese export porcelain *fuyō-de* (hollyhock or rose-mallow type) because it resembles the shape of this flower. The second piece is a Japanese Arita dish with fruit-bearing pomegranate branches in the center and paneled sides and rim in Kraak style, although the designs have been simplified and exhibit a Japanese style (plate 128). The third object is a Dutch Delftware dish, made of earthenware and decorated in blue with a *jardiniere* with flowers on a fenced terrace and two butterflies on either side (plate 129). Here, too, the border shows the typical Kraak division into eight wide and eight narrow panels. The decoration closely copies designs on Kraak wares, and to the seventeenth-century observer this Delftware dish must have looked, at first sight, like its Chinese model when hung or placed on a mantel.

After buying Chinese wares decorated in underglaze blue for half a century, Dutch customers were keen to have the new, fashionable enameled Japanese pieces in their homes. Therefore, this type underwent several changes, most likely stimulated by Dutch demand. For about twenty years, the initially opaque-enameled pieces (known as the Early Enamels) became more translucent and refined, showing a wider range of color shades. Eventually, two main varieties emerged, Kakiemon wares and Imari wares.

Kakiemon porcelain is named after a kiln complex in Arita owned by the Kakiemon family, which is still operational. Much of its production was destined for export, partly for the Dutch, but probably in even larger quantities for the Chinese, who resold these wares to French and English customers in Canton (modern Guangzhou). Kakiemon ware can be decorated with a combination of underglaze blue and enamels (or just in underglaze blue), but it is rightly famous for its refined designs in enamels only. Flowering plants, blossoming prunus branches, birds, and mythical animals were popular subjects on Kakiemon, elegantly painted with great attention to detail and often asymmetrically placed with much white space around the designs. A special clay was exclusively used by this kiln, resulting in the creamy white *nigoshide* body, and superior wares were made between 1680 and 1720. Stimulated by the success of Kakiemon, other Arita factories copied the style, and it is not always easy to distinguish these Kakiemon-style pieces from the genuine product.

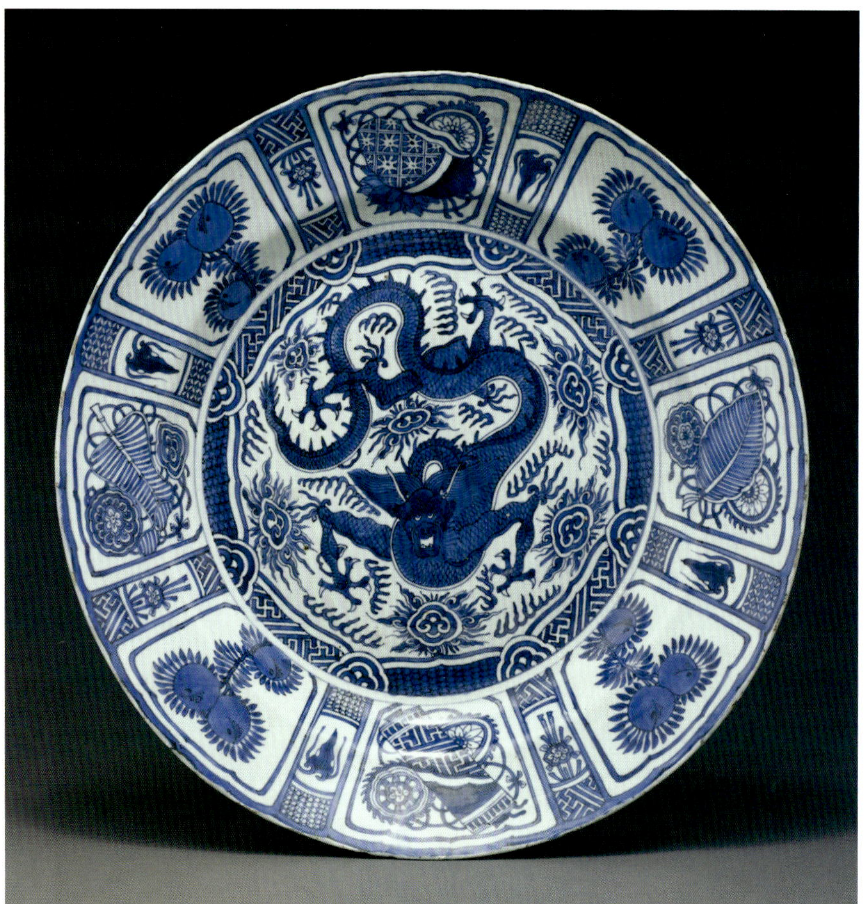

PLATE 127
Kraak Plate with Dragon Design
China, early
17th century
Jingdezhen ware,
porcelain with under-
glaze cobalt blue
decoration
h. 3 × diam. 20¼ in.
(7.6 × 51.4 cm)
Seattle Art Museum,
bequest of Joan Louise
Applegate Dice, 91.40

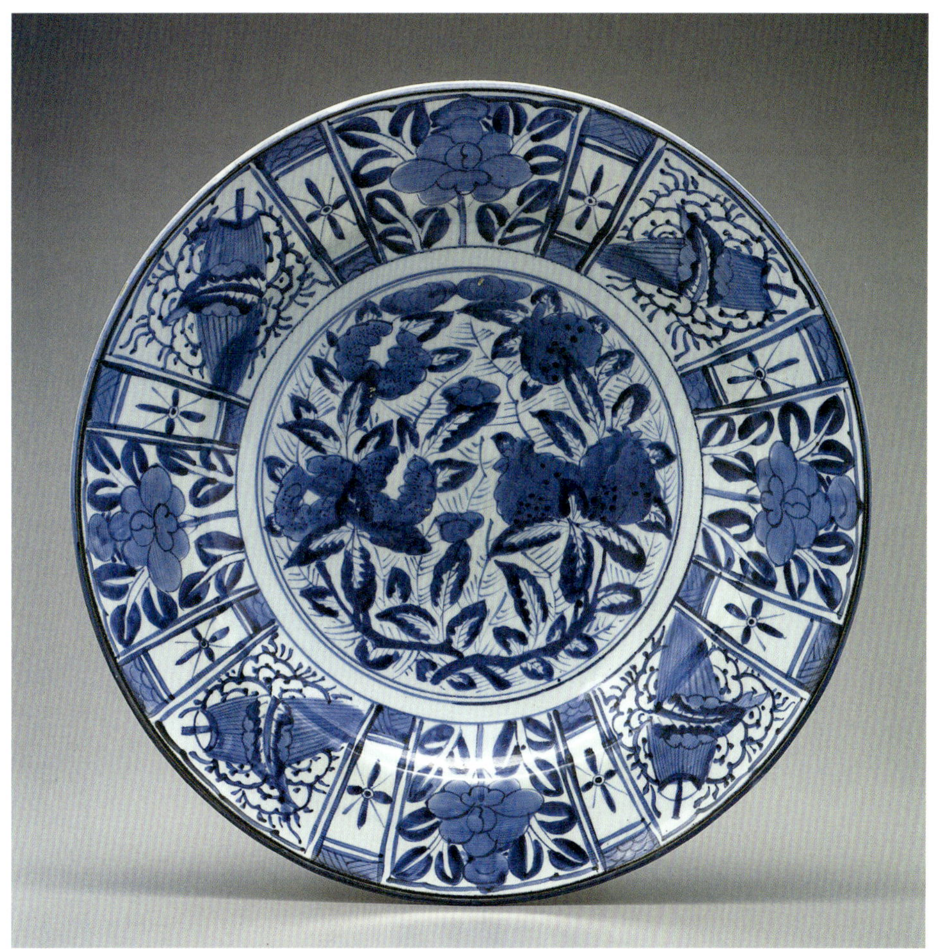

PLATE 128

Kraak-style Plate with Pomegranate Design

Japan, 1650–60
Arita ware, porcelain with underglaze cobalt blue decoration
h. 4⅛ × diam. 23¼ in. (10.5 × 59.1 cm)
Seattle Art Museum, Floyd A. Naramore Memorial Purchase Fund and by exchange, 76.63
■

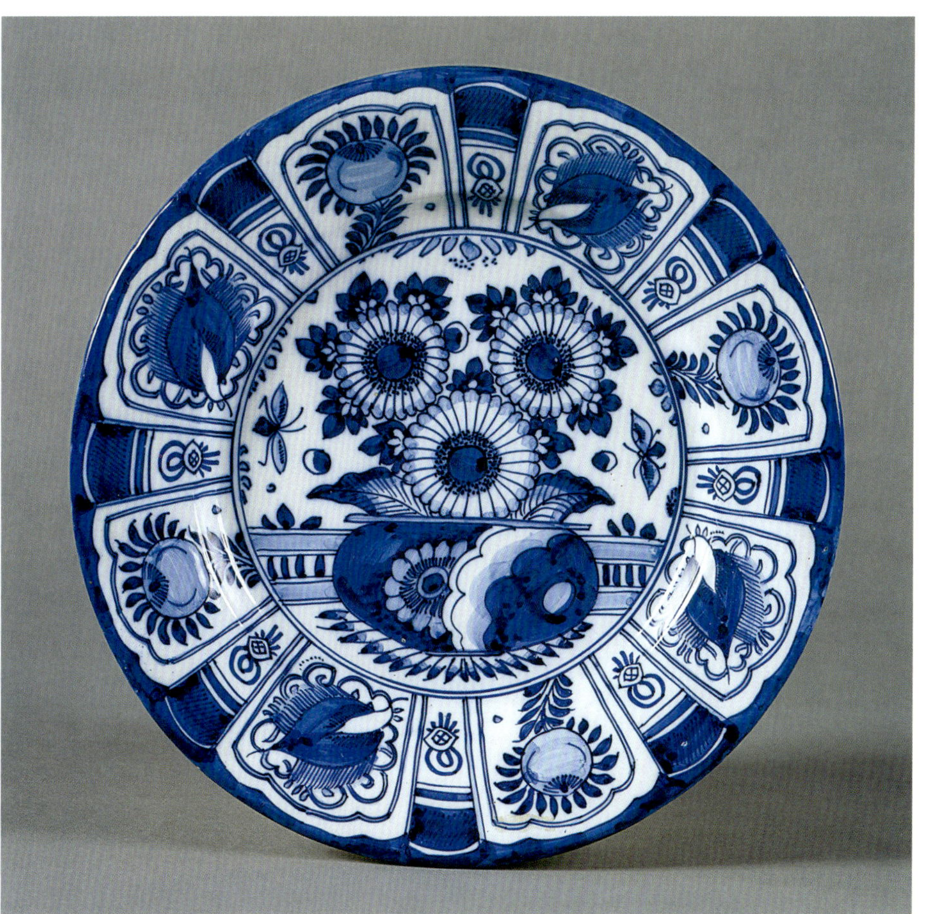

PLATE 129

Kraak-style Plate with Design of Vase of Flowers on a Terrace

Holland, late 17th century
Delftware, tin-glazed earthenware with cobalt blue decoration
h. 1⅞ × diam. 13 in. (4.6 × 32.8 cm)
■

An octagonal bowl, its sides painted with flowering plants, is an excellent example of good Kakiemon (plate 130). A similar decoration is seen on an octagonal, two-handled cup and matching saucer made about 1730 in the Meissen factory near Dresden, Germany (plate 131). It copies the Kakiemon design very closely, but the shape is different: cups with handles were never made in Japanese ceramics and are a typical Western addition. This imitation illustrates how popular the Japanese style had become in Europe, because it was precisely the Oriental quality that made these Meissen porcelains—the first real hard-bodied porcelain manufactured in Europe—so desirable.

After the arcanum, or secret, of porcelain production had spread throughout Europe, other factories copied Kakiemon designs. Another Meissen dish is decorated in iron red and gold with two phoenixes circling each other, the sides painted with two dragons and two clusters of ribbons (plate 133). It more or less copies a Kakiemon dish with a lobed rim and a similar center design that shows two dragons emerging from waves, chasing the Buddhist Sacred Jewel symbolizing purity and the fulfillment of wishes (plate 132).

The other enameled variety is called Imari, which is a rather confusing name. In Japan, it often denotes Arita porcelain in general; in the West,

it indicates porcelain decorated in underglaze blue combined with overglaze red and gold, less often with additional black, aubergine, and green enamels. Imari is also the name of the harbor from which much Arita porcelain was shipped to other destinations in Japan. Like Kakiemon, the Imari style matured around 1680, but it was popular for much longer—Imari was still being produced on a large scale for the West at the end of the nineteenth century. It was made for export in the seventeenth and eighteenth centuries in

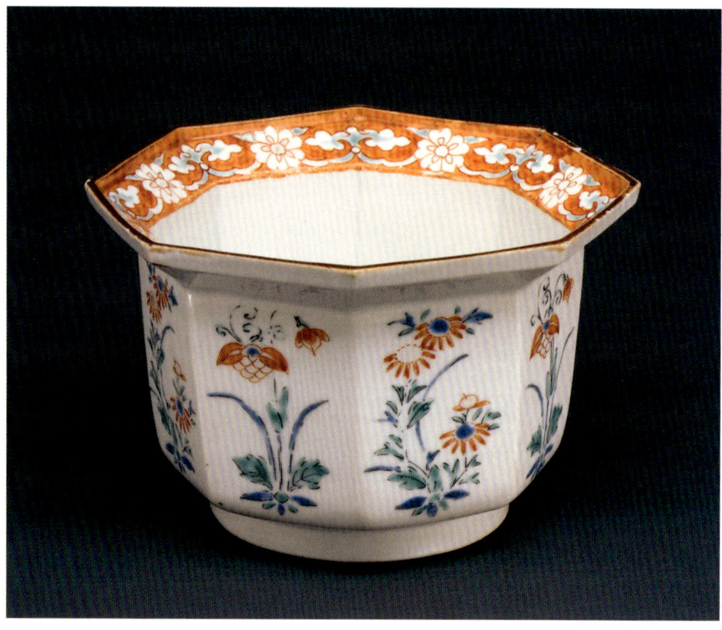

Octagonal Bowl with Floral Design

Japan, c. 1670–90
Arita ware, Kakiemon style, porcelain with overglaze polychrome enamels
h. 3 × diam. 4¼ in. (7.6 × 10.8 cm)
Seattle Art Museum, gift of Martha and Henry Isaacson, 76.97

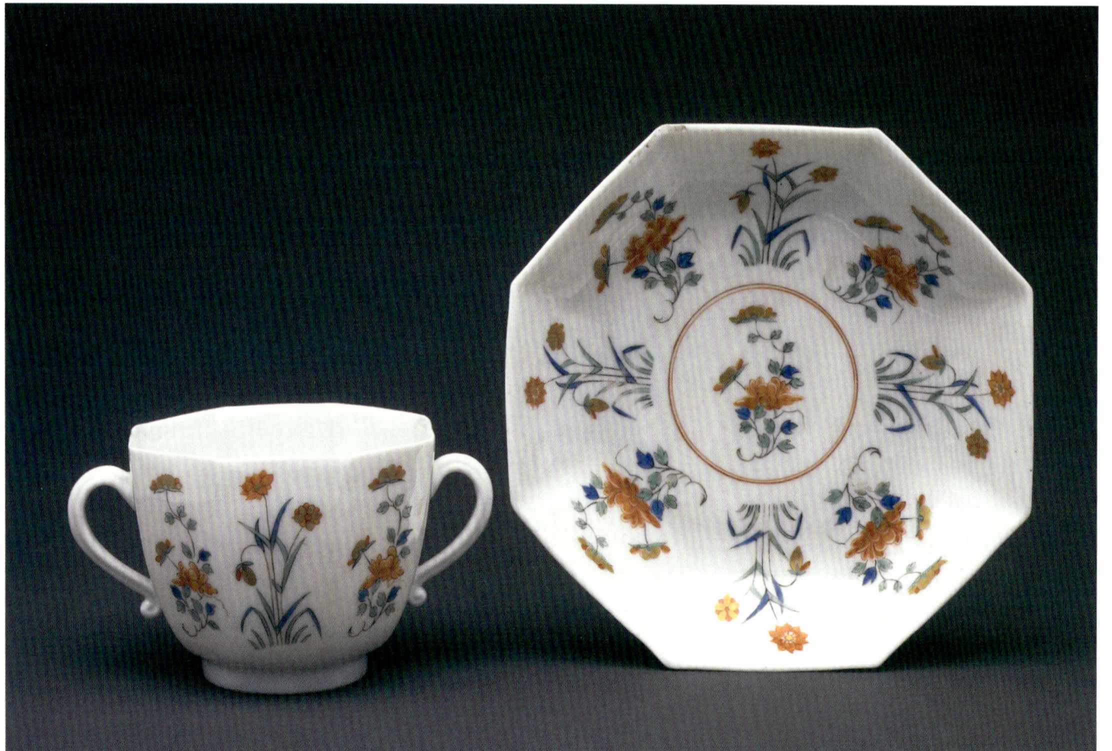

Two-handled Cup and Saucer with Floral Design

Germany, c. 1730
Meissen manufactory, porcelain with overglaze polychrome enamels
Cup: h. 2⅜ × diam. 4⅛ in. (6 × 10.8 cm); saucer: h. 1³⁄₁₆ × diam. 5⅝ in. (3.2 × 14.3 cm)
Seattle Art Museum, gift of Martha and Henry Isaacson, 61.75

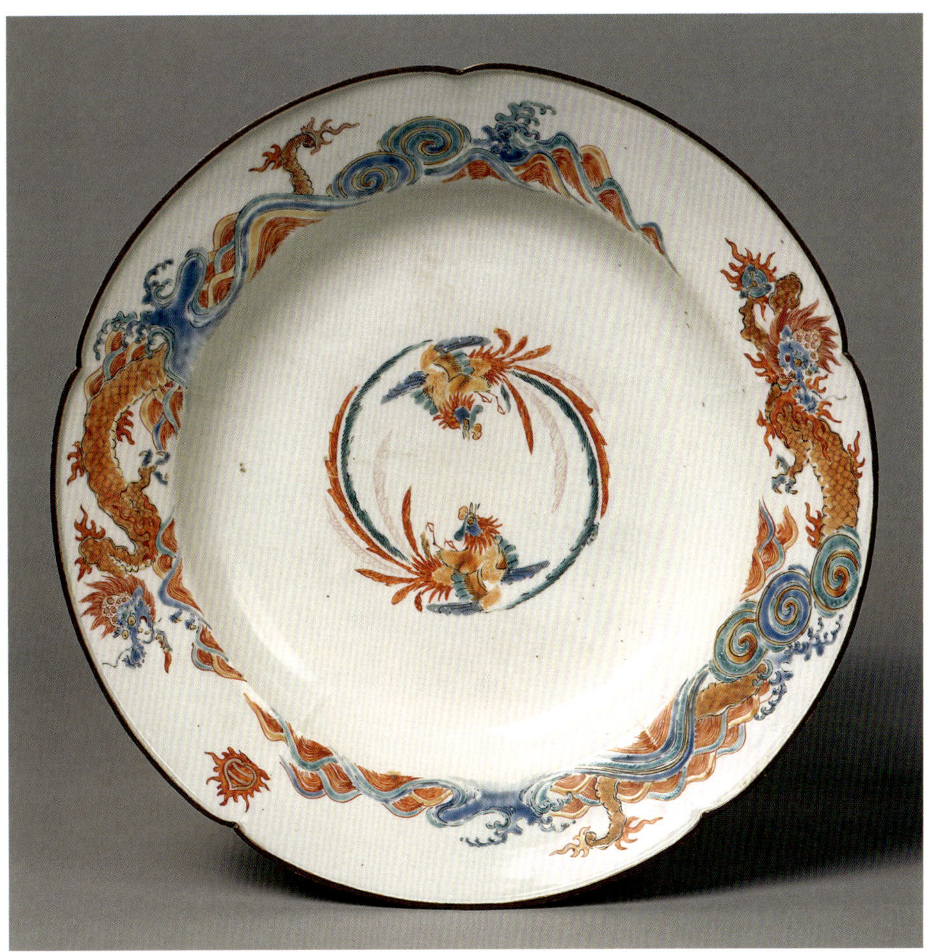

PLATE 132
Dish with Phoenix
and Dragon Design
Japan, c. 1670–90
Arita ware, Kakiemon
style, porcelain with
overglaze polychrome
enamels
h. 1⅞ × diam. 9⅞ in.
(4.6 × 25 cm)
■

PLATE 133
Dish with Phoenix
and Dragon Design
Germany, c. 1734–39
Meissen manufactory,
porcelain with iron
red and gilt
h. 2 × diam. 11¾ in.
(5.1 × 29.9 cm)
Seattle Art Museum,
gift of Martha and
Henry Isaacson,
69.199
■

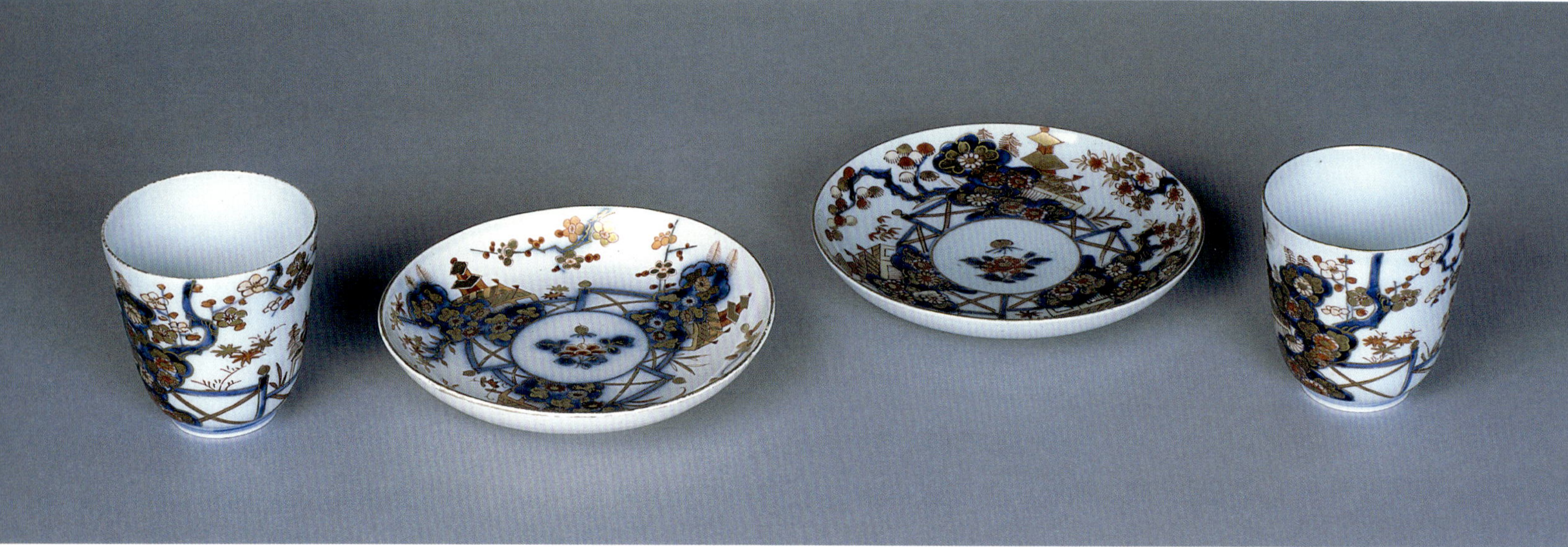

several specialized, largely anonymous workshops, and archaeological excavations are sometimes the only aid to identifying the output of a particular factory.

Decorations on Imari pieces are crowded, and border designs are often complex, appealing to European baroque taste. This, and the color combination, creates a "heavy" impression overall, especially when compared to Kakiemon. Western shapes such as cuspidors, goblets, coffee pots, or beer mugs are far from rare, and there is a profusion of variously modeled tewares, dishes, and plates. Uniquely Japanese are the tall chocolate cups and saucers (plate 134), undoubtedly made to Western order and unknown in Chinese export porcelain. Chocolate, a newly fashionable drink in Europe at the end of the seventeenth century, was prepared with a head of beaten foam, hence the taller height of its serving cups. The cups usually had covers but these were frequently lost in the succeeding years.

Another excellent example of Japanese export porcelain in a Western shape is the shaving or barber's bowl (plate 135). It was made after a Dutch brass, pewter, tin, or earthenware model with the typical semicircular cutout at the lower end. This fitted around the neck of a man being shaved or around a patient's arm during bloodletting by a doctor. A cord threaded through the two holes at the top was tied around the client's neck; when not in use, the bowl hung on a wall. This example has the typical Imari decoration in underglaze blue and overglaze iron-red and gold of a richly

filled flower vase on a terrace. The rim has several sections filled with flowerheads; its reverse is decorated with two blossoming prunus sprays. The base has the abovementioned spur marks. Other examples in Western shapes for drinking or dining are known, but curiously, unlike their Chinese counterparts, eighteenth-century Japanese potters never seem to have made extensive dinner sets with matching pieces.

Imari probably had more appeal than Kakiemon—at least in the Netherlands, where it is still abundant—and it is not surprising that it was copied in Delftware from the late seventeenth century. A fine example of this so-called Delft Imari is a plate produced around 1700 at either the factory De Drie Klokken (The Three Bells) or Het Hart (The Heart).[7] The color scheme in predominately blue, red, and yellow (as a cheap imitation of gold) marks this piece as Delft Imari (plate 136). The motif of large flowering plants, an angled fence, and two flying birds is not based on Japanese models but loosely copies Chinese blue-and-white export wares of the period. It indicates that Dutch clients were no longer very discriminating. In fact, such pieces appealed to a general interest in the Far East, and it did not really matter if Japanese and Chinese characteristics were combined, as long the effect was exotic. Nowadays we call such a decoration, a mixture of Oriental motifs rendered in a Western way, *chinoiserie*.

Delftware potters were certainly not the only ones to copy and use Imari colors and decorative

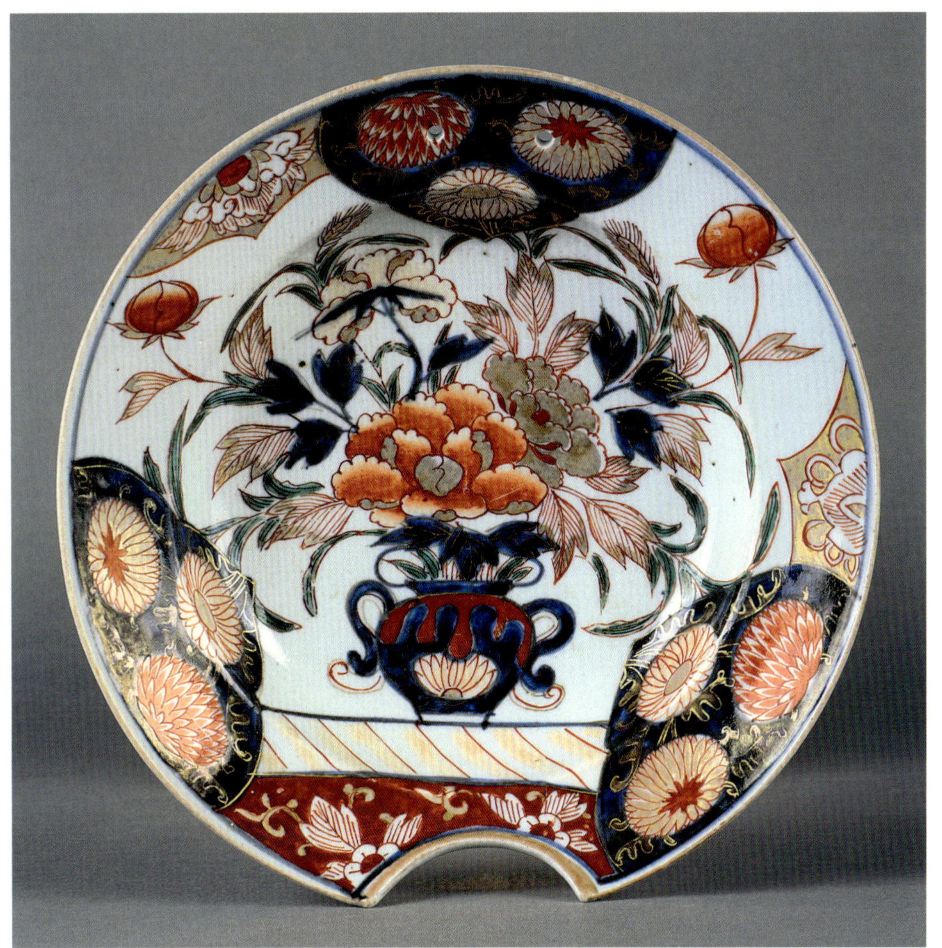

PLATE 135

**Shaving Basin
with Design of
Vase of Flowers
on a Terrace**
Japan, early
18th century
Arita ware, Imari type,
porcelain with poly-
chrome decoration
h. 2⅝ × diam. 10½ in.
(6.5 × 26.5 cm)
■

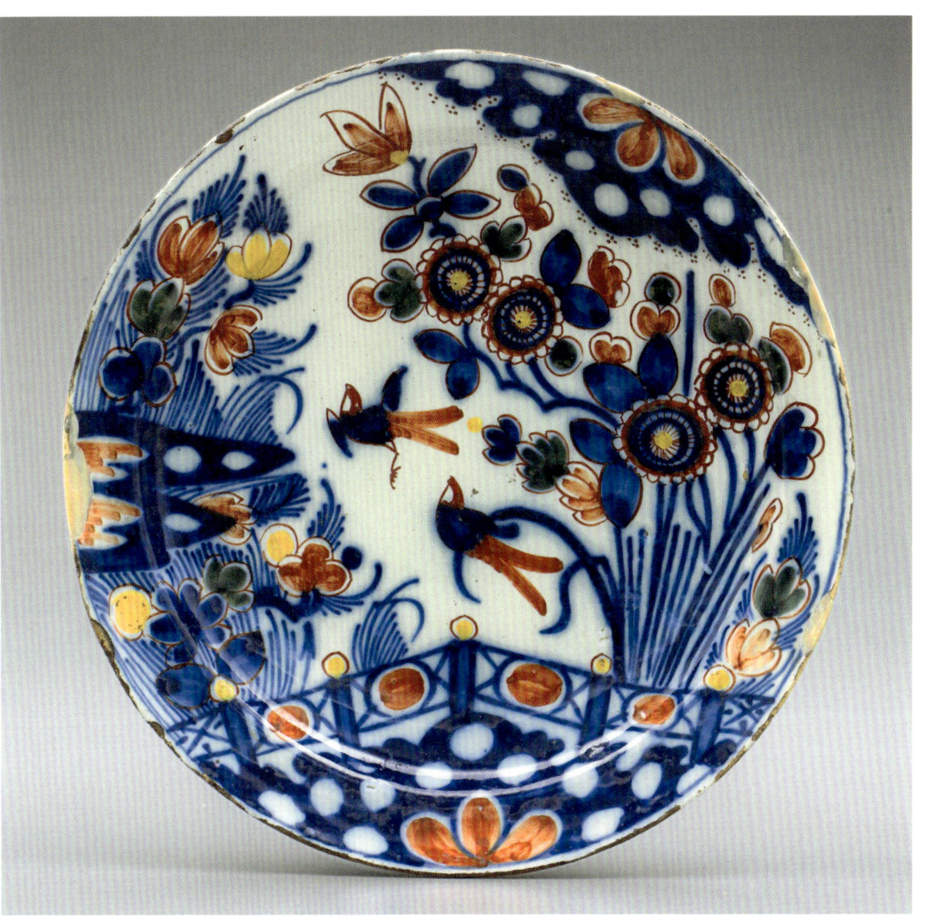

PLATE 136

Plate with Flower
and Bird Design
Holland, c. 1700
Delftware, De Drie
Klokken or Het Hart
manufactory, tin-glazed
earthenware with
polychrome decoration
h. 1¾ × diam. 10½ in.
(4.5 × 26.7 cm)
Seattle Art Museum,
purchased with funds
from the Decorative Arts
Acquisition Fund and
the Floyd A. Naramore
Memorial Purchase
Fund, 83.64
■

motifs. Imitation Imari was produced throughout Europe, in either faience or porcelain, testifying to the widespread popularity of this type; see, for instance, the beautiful lobed dish of soft-paste porcelain made in the mid-1750s at the Chelsea factory in England (plate 137). Its shape and decoration closely copy a Japanese Imari dish of about 1700. The lobed shape resembles the Japanese *kiku,* the stylized chrysanthemum symbolizing fertility and wealth. *Kiku* flowerheads are scattered at random over the border, which is divided into panels with flowering plants, while the lobed center (again shaped as a *kiku*) has a curling chrysanthemum twig placed asymmetrically in the blank space. Thus, this elegant design has several layers in which the *kiku* is prevalent: the outer contour, the border, the contour of the center, and the center decoration create a pleasing complexity and suggestion of depth.

Imari-style decorations initially served to exploit the popularity of the Japanese model and to promote faience or porcelain manufactured in Western factories. When the Chinese saturated the market with their own imitations of Imari, European producers moved away from Asian styles and successfully developed all kinds of Western decorations. Between circa 1750 and 1850, however, close copies were sometimes still made, such as the saucer in Imari style made in Vienna by the Du Paquier factory (see plate 134). In my opinion these copies are not the expression of a revival of interest in the Far East but were usually made as additions to Chinese or Japanese sets, or as replacements for broken pieces. Of course, things changed in the second half of the nineteenth century when Far Eastern porcelain became fashionable again. Collections were formed, and factories such as Samson in Paris made good profits with their eclectic "re-creations."

Returning to Japanese export wares, porcelain figures of animals and Japanese men and women were much appreciated in the West. Although fragments have occasionally been found during archaeological excavations in city dwellings in Japan, the figures seem primarily to have been made for export. In particular, figures from the Kakiemon kiln are famous, but several other Arita kilns made them as well, some inspired by the Kakiemon pieces, others produced in Imari style. A good example of this latter category is a

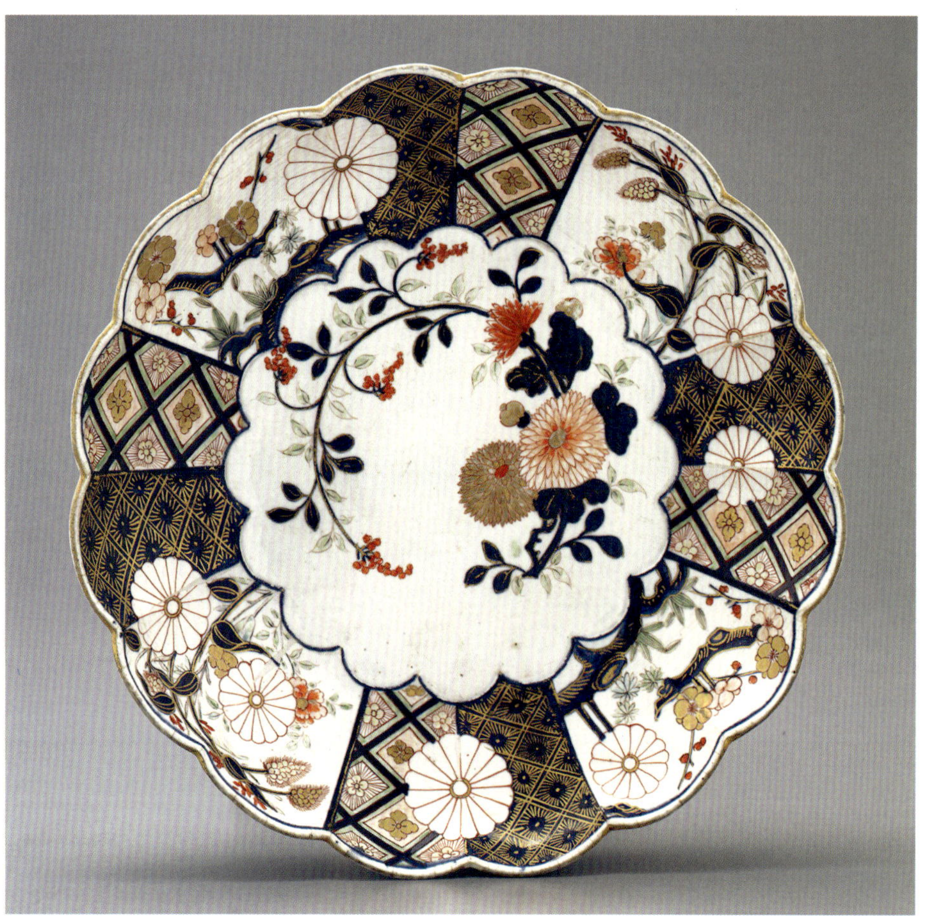

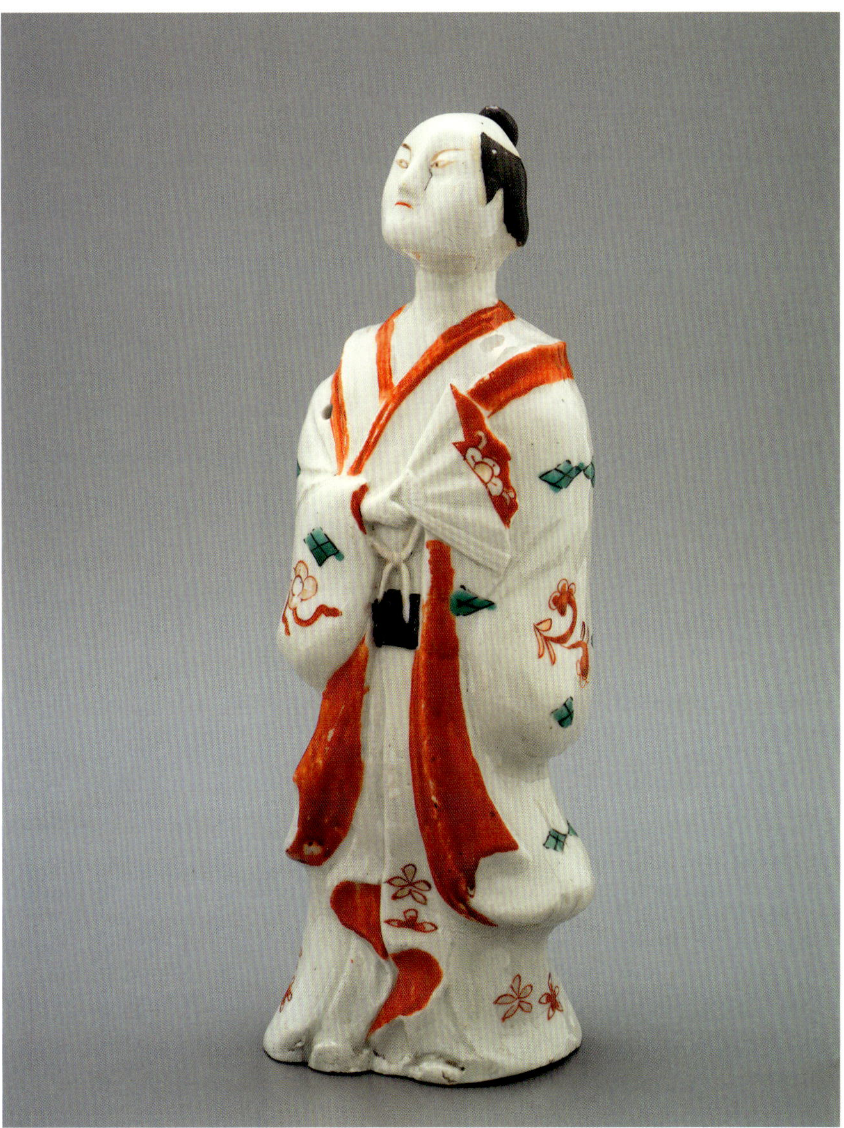

figure of a standing man wearing a kimono and holding a fan (plate 138). Details on his garment are in overglaze green and iron red, and his hair and obi are painted in shining black enamel. Traditionally, such a figure is called an "actor," but he might be the idealized image of a Japanese conforming to the Western concept of the exotic, destined to be an eye-catcher on a mantelpiece or in a porcelain cabinet in a Dutch, German, or English interior.

A specific group of Japanese export ceramics challenges this European exoticism because their decoration is not in Japanese style but is based on Western prints, drawings, or other models, and thus hides its Japanese origin at first sight. It is possible, however, that such pieces were regarded as even more exotic. A European landscape by Japanese painters on Japanese porcelain was truly something remarkable! In Japan such *commande* porcelain, as the style is called, is much rarer than in China, where porcelain with Western designs was frequently made to order.

Several examples of Japanese *commande* are included here. Two dishes in underglaze blue have borders with six very wide and six very narrow panels, and although these have been simplified, the Kraak origin is still obvious (plates 139, 140). In each case, the center is decorated with the initials of the VOC, carefully copied from a model. One of the dishes was over-decorated later with iron red, probably in Holland. Such dishes (and the much rarer bowls) were used by company officials throughout Asia at formal occasions in their lodges and factories, or by officers aboard VOC ships.

A much more elaborate example of *commande* is a plate decorated in underglaze blue with a Western-style landscape of a Dutch village with

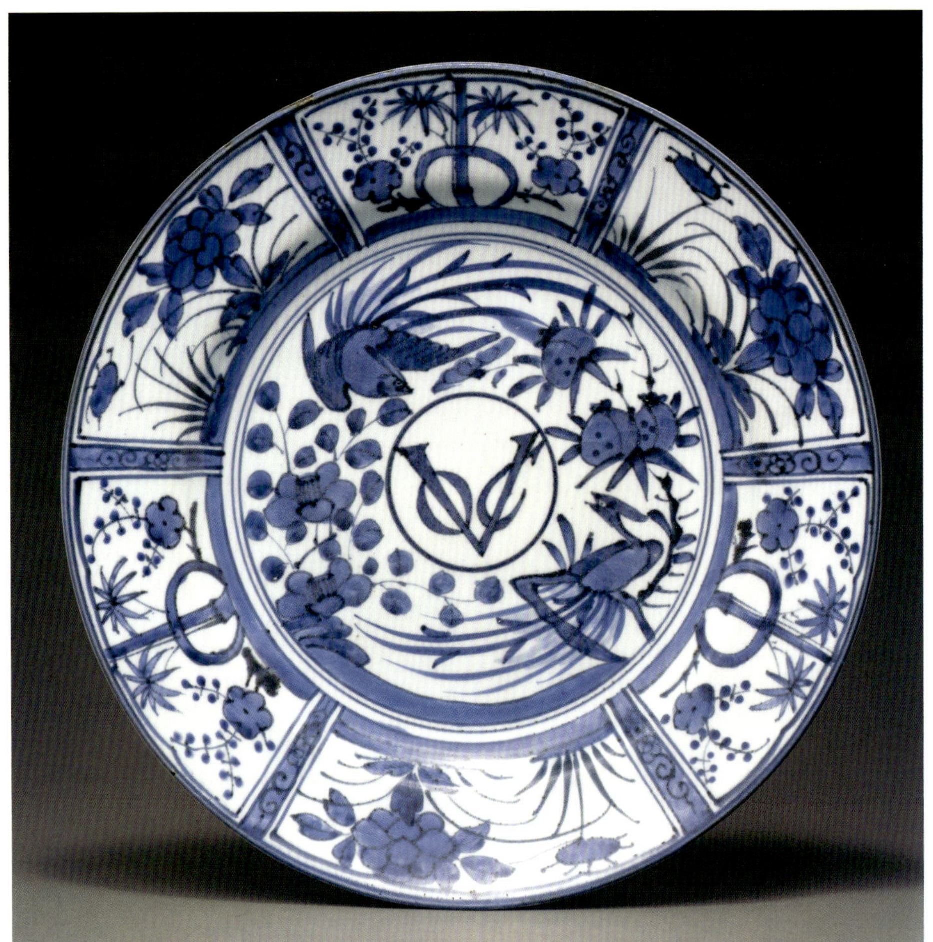

**Kraak-style Plate
with VOC Initials**
Japan, 1690s–early
18th century
Arita ware, porcelain
with underglaze cobalt
blue decoration
h. 2⅜ × diam. 15⅜ in.
(6 × 39.1 cm)
Seattle Art Museum,
Floyd A. Naramore
Memorial Purchase
Fund, 75.78

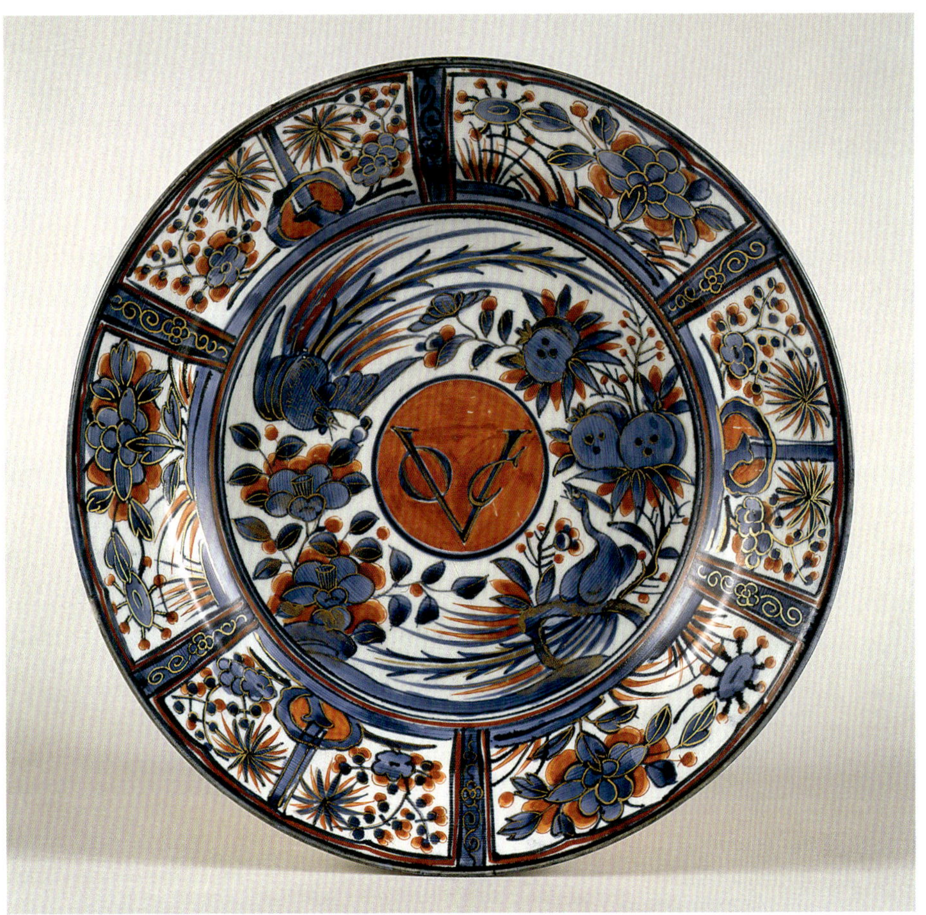

**Kraak-style Plate
with VOC Initials**
Japan, 1690s–early
18th century
Arita ware, porcelain
with underglaze cobalt
blue decoration (over-
glaze iron red and gilt
added probably in
Holland)
h. 2½ × diam. 15⅝ in.
(6.4 × 39.5 cm)

a church tower, rooftops, ships' sails, and coastal sand dunes with a fire beacon (plate 142). On the hilly foreground are a fence post, a man leading a cow, and two travelers wearing hats. Curiously formed clouds with curlicue outlines float in the air; the frilled rim has a continuous pattern of waves. This decoration is known as the Scheveningen design after the coastal village of that name near The Hague.[8] Many variations on this decoration were made in Arita for the Dutch in the early eighteenth century, initially closely copying a print or a piece of Delft faience, but becoming more Japanized over time. Interestingly, the decorations were so popular that the Chinese copied them on their own export wares for the Dutch (plate 141), thus establishing a Dutch-Japanese-Chinese-Dutch connection.[9]

A Dutch-Chinese-Japanese-Dutch connection is exemplified by two so-called Pronk plates that carry a design with a story.[10] In 1734 the VOC directors asked the Dutch artist Cornelis Pronk (1691–1759) to draw models and decorations for porcelain teaware, dinner sets, garnitures, and ewers with matching basins to be made in China. His first attempt—over the years he made four different designs—was a *chinoiserie* showing a Chinese lady at a waterfront with reeds; she watches four approaching birds while a servant holds a parasol above her. The rim has four rows of chamfered rectangles in which eight cartouches are reserved. Four are filled with birds, the four smaller ones with either the lady or the parasol bearer. The reverse of the rim shows eight large insects. Sets of drawings with this design were sent to Batavia in 1735; miraculously, two

originals have survived and are now in the collection of the Rijksmuseum, Amsterdam.

The next year, orders for porcelain with this design were sent to China and Japan. The Chinese produced the required porcelains in three versions: underglaze blue, Chinese Imari (underglaze blue, iron red, and gold), and overglaze enamel colors. But the costs were enormous, and although the public reacted very favorably, the company stopped ordering this design after two shipments to Holland in 1737 and 1738. A Chinese plate now in Kobe (plate 143) is a fine example of the underglaze-blue version of the Parasol Ladies, as this decoration is commonly called, and can be dated precisely to 1737. Interestingly, the reverse differs from the original drawing in that seven, not eight, insects are depicted, and only three birds, not four, approach the woman.

In Japan, representatives of the porcelain factories quoted even higher costs and according to company documents, VOC merchants did not order such porcelain. But Japanese plates decorated with the Parasol Ladies do exist and therefore must have been ordered privately by one or more Dutch employees, using the drawings sent from Batavia. These Japanese examples were made in two versions, in underglaze blue (very rare) and in Imari colors (plate 144). The Japanese porcelain painter changed the figures of the Chinese ladies into two Japanese *bijin* (beauties) wearing kimono and with typical Japanese hairstyles in black. Like the Chinese plate, the reverse shows seven insects. These two plates perfectly illustrate the interaction in ceramics between the East and the West.

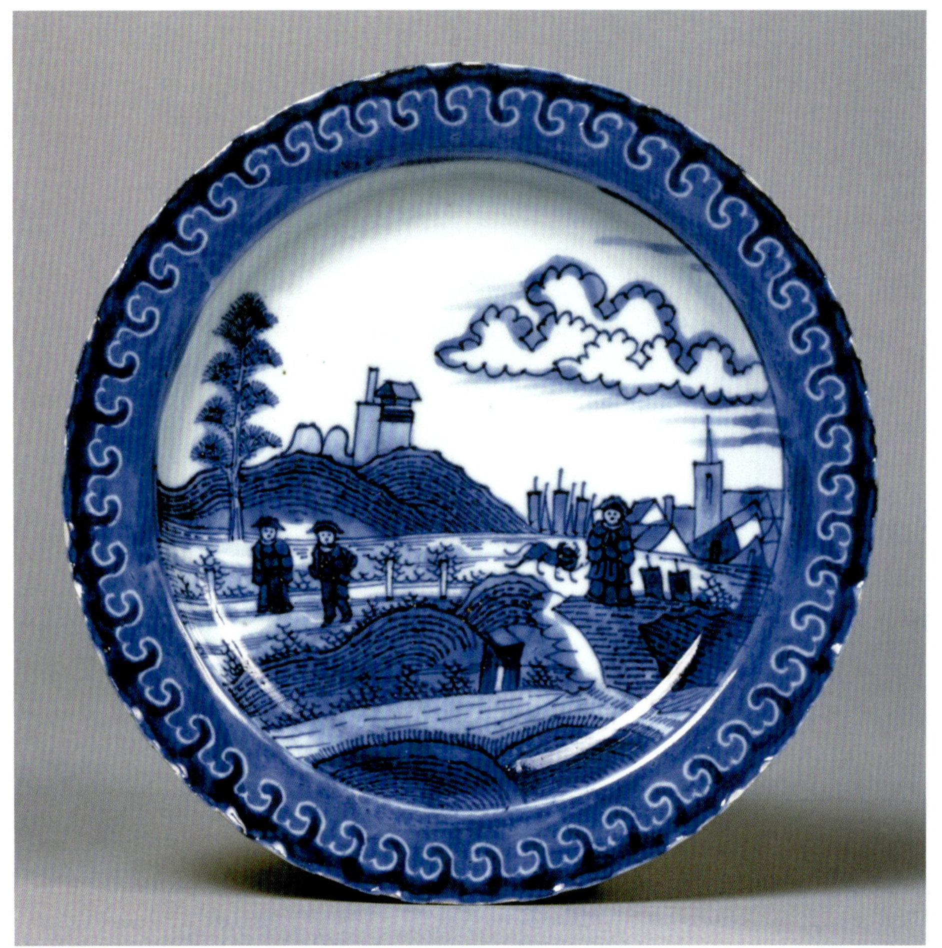

PLATE 141
Plate with
Scheveningen Design
China, c. 1725
Jingdezhen ware,
porcelain with
underglaze cobalt
blue decoration
h. 1 × diam. 8 in.
(2.4 × 20.2 cm)
■

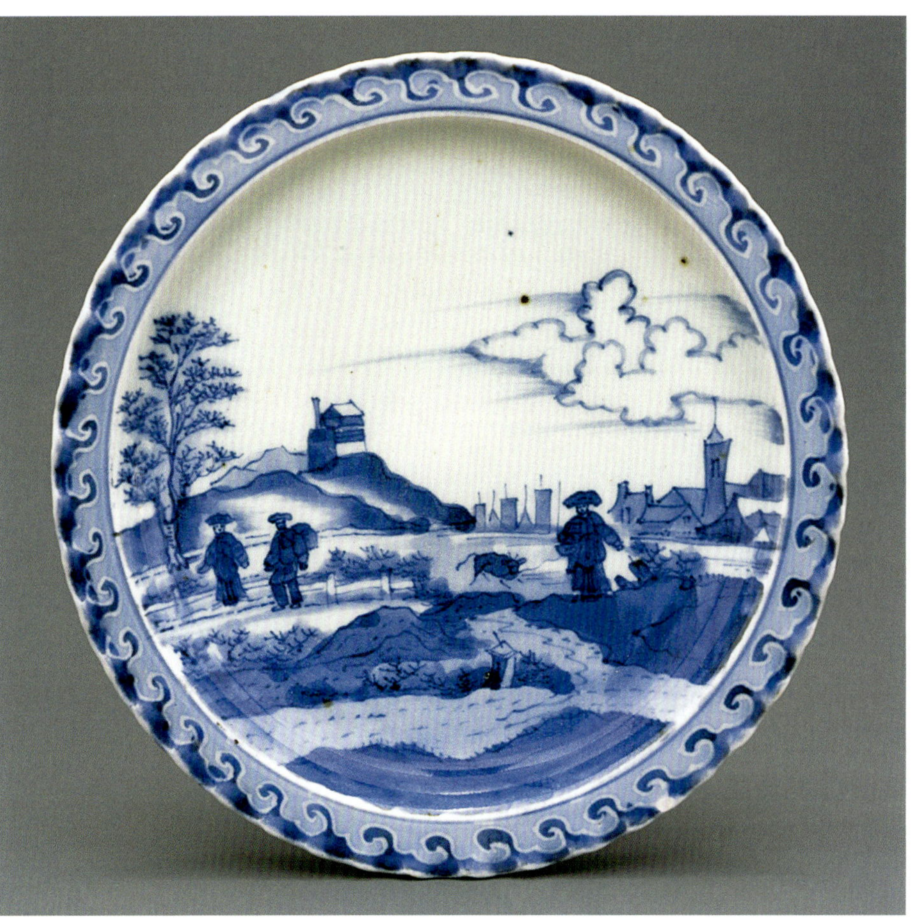

PLATE 142
Plate with
Scheveningen Design
Japan, c. 1700–25
Arita ware, porcelain
with underglaze cobalt
blue decoration
h. 1 × diam. 7½ in.
(2.5 × 19.1 cm)
Seattle Art Museum,
gift of Frank Stout,
92.47.5.1
■

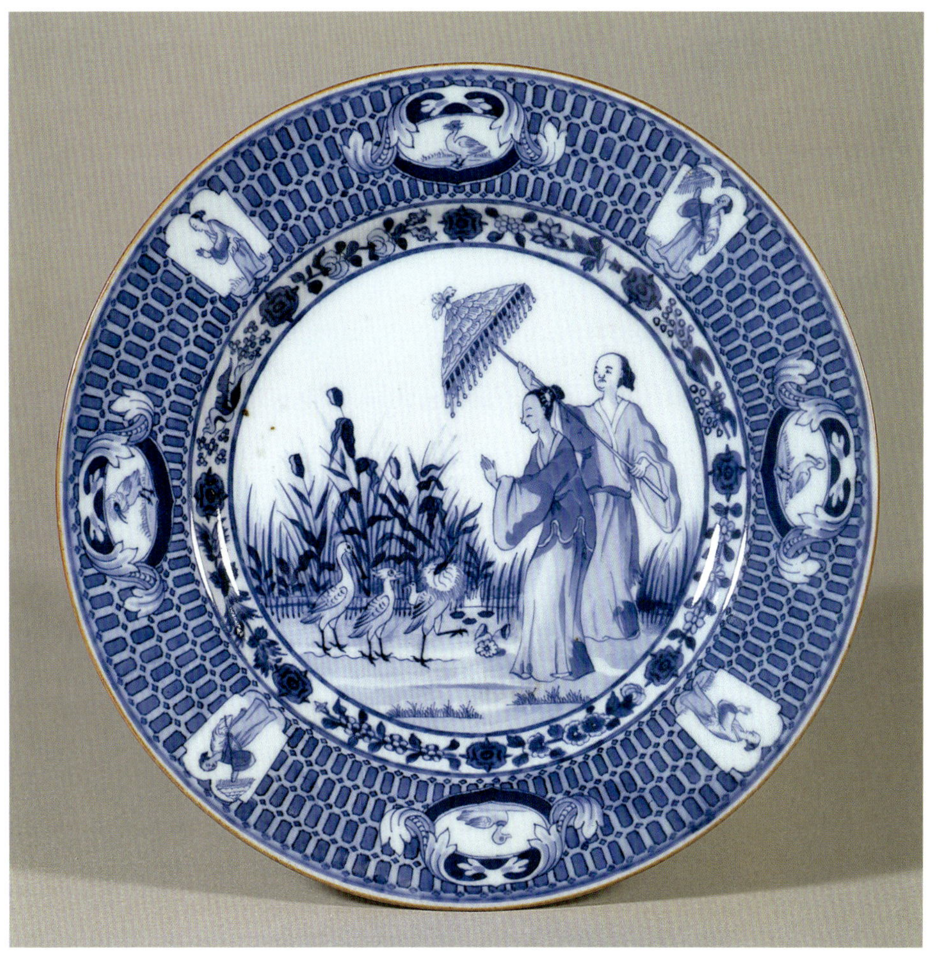

**Plate with Parasol
Ladies Design**
China, 1737
Jingdezhen ware,
porcelain with under-
glaze cobalt blue
decoration
h. 1⅛ × diam. 9 in.
(2.8 × 22.8 cm)

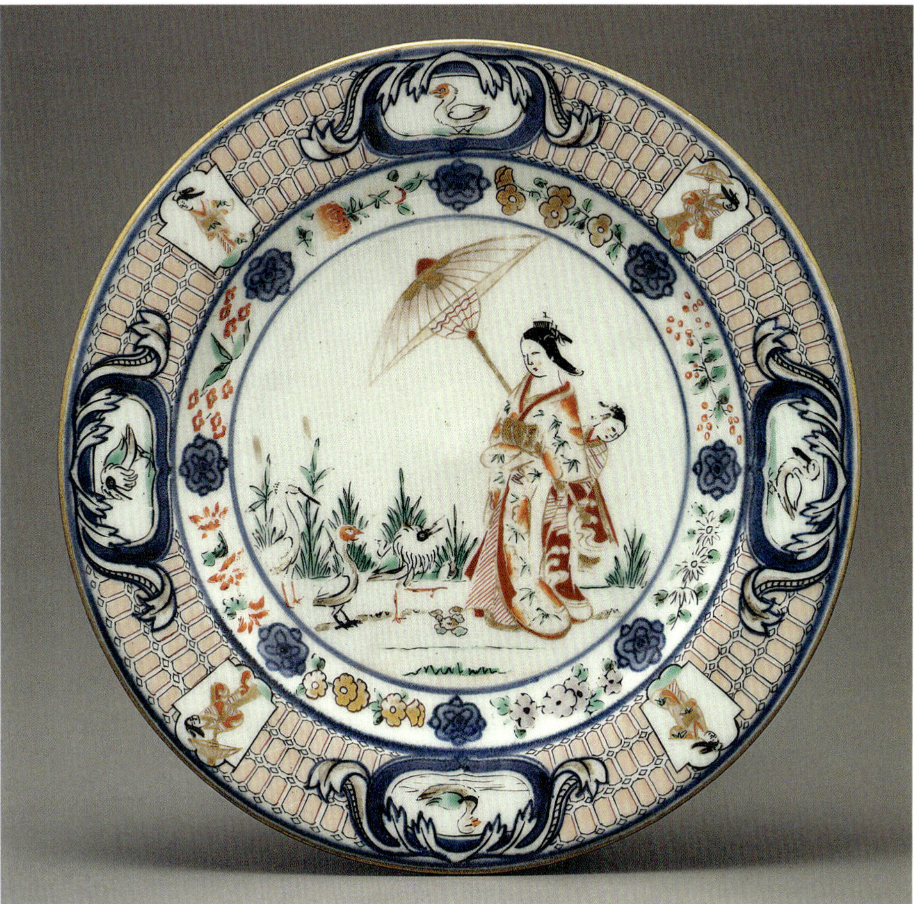

**Plate with Parasol
Ladies Design**
Japan, c. 1737
Arita ware, Imari type,
porcelain with poly-
chrome decoration
h. 1 × diam. 9¹⁄₁₆ in.
(2.5 × 23.2 cm)
Seattle Art Museum,
gift of Victor and
William Staadecker
in memory of their
sister, Elizabeth
Staadecker, 74.4

Lacquerware

Lacquer is a natural product that gives an object a smooth, shiny, and impregnable coating.[11] The Chinese and the Koreans made beautiful lacquerware, but Japanese craftsmen were regarded as the best. From the second half of the sixteenth century, Portuguese traders in Japan ordered all kinds of lacquered objects, including in Western shapes such as traveling cabinets, retables, coffers, and folding tables. Usually these export wares have a layer of thick, black lacquer on a wooden core, decorated with painted gold lacquer and small pieces of inlaid mother-of-pearl in dense compositions of flowering plants, twigs with leaves, birds, deer, and other animals; human figures are rare. Geometric patterns form complex borders, while sectioned parts of the main decoration are divided by bands, imitating the iron or leather straps on Portuguese models. It is assumed that examples of Gujarati japanned work inlaid with mother-of-pearl, or woodwork inlaid with ivory, made to order on the west coast of India, served, in part, as models.

Japanese export lacquer of this type is called *namban,* from the Japanese word meaning "foreign."

Although primarily made for export, it is possible that some *namban* lacquerware was sold on the Japanese domestic market, where it was regarded as exotic. A small coffer from the collection of the Kobe City Museum is a fine example of *namban* lacquer dating to the early seventeenth century (plate 145). It has an overall decoration of a flower-and-leaf pattern with mother-of-pearl inlays cut in the shape of flowerheads. The copper mounts and lock, originally brightly gilded, follow the European type but were made in Japan.

Dutch seamen chanced upon Japan in 1600, and by 1609 the Dutch had established a trading post in Hirado, on Kyūshū, competing with the Portuguese and the English, the latter arriving shortly after the Dutch. The VOC tried to market lacquered goods, but the first shipment, arriving in the Netherlands in 1610, was not a commercial success, and lacquer buying in Japan ceased almost immediately. Privately, however, Dutch employees in Hirado continued to collect lacquer, and pieces circulated in Batavia and in the Netherlands. Apparently, Japanese lacquerware also fetched good prices at local auctions, and after some hesitation the VOC directors began ordering lacquerware again in 1634. By this time

PLATE 145

Coffer with Design of Flowering Trees, Birds, and Deer
Japan, 1620–40
Makie lacquered wood with mother-of-pearl inlay, metal fittings
12½ × 17⅜ × 9⅝ in. (31.7 × 44 × 24.3 cm)

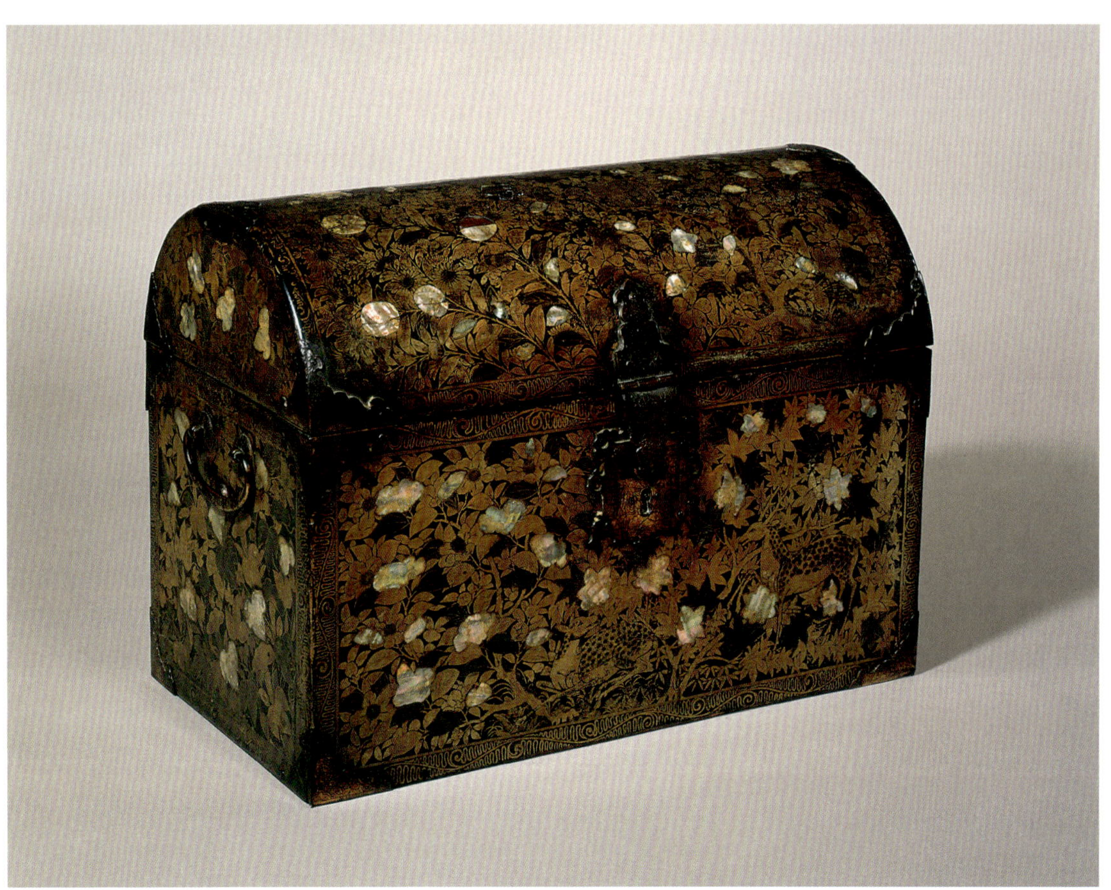

Portuguese trade with Japan had diminished, and by placing large, expensive orders, the Dutch took the initiative in the purchasing and thus in the production of export lacquer, which was made in Kyoto.

The decorations in *namban* style are rather crowded and with mother-of-pearl inlays that are sometimes coarse and unsubtle. They were not popular with the Dutch, and a new, more naturalistic and detailed style was gradually introduced, known as the Pictorial style. Painted decorations gradually replaced mother-of-pearl, which eventually fell out of use. Banded sections disappeared, the broad geometric borders became smaller, and the surface intended for the main decoration increased at the expense of the background. The decorations also display a remarkable development. Initially schematic, they became detailed naturalistic renderings of mountainous landscapes, flying or swimming birds, mythical and other animals, and figural scenes with pavilions, humans engaged in various activities, or groups of travelers. In fact, this style is much more in keeping with lacquer decorated for the domestic market in Japan and harks back to earlier styles.

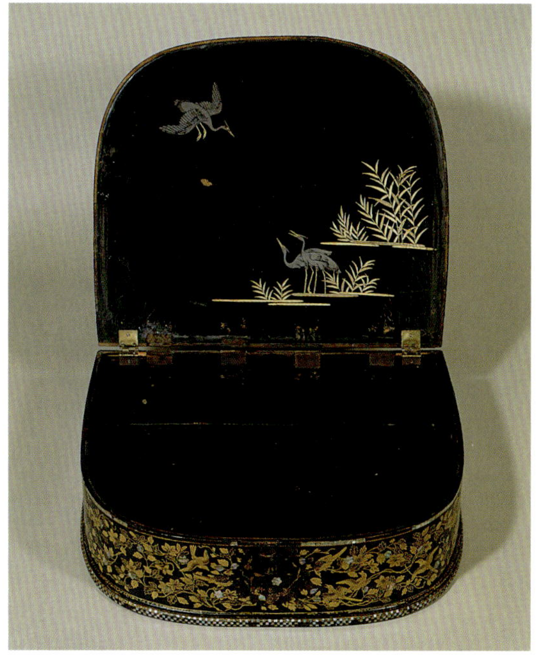

A transitional phase from circa 1630 to 1650 is discernable as *namban* decorations were supplanted by more pictorial designs. An early example of this Transitional style is a unique pouch-shaped box (plate 146), which is a fine amalgamation of a Western shape and typical

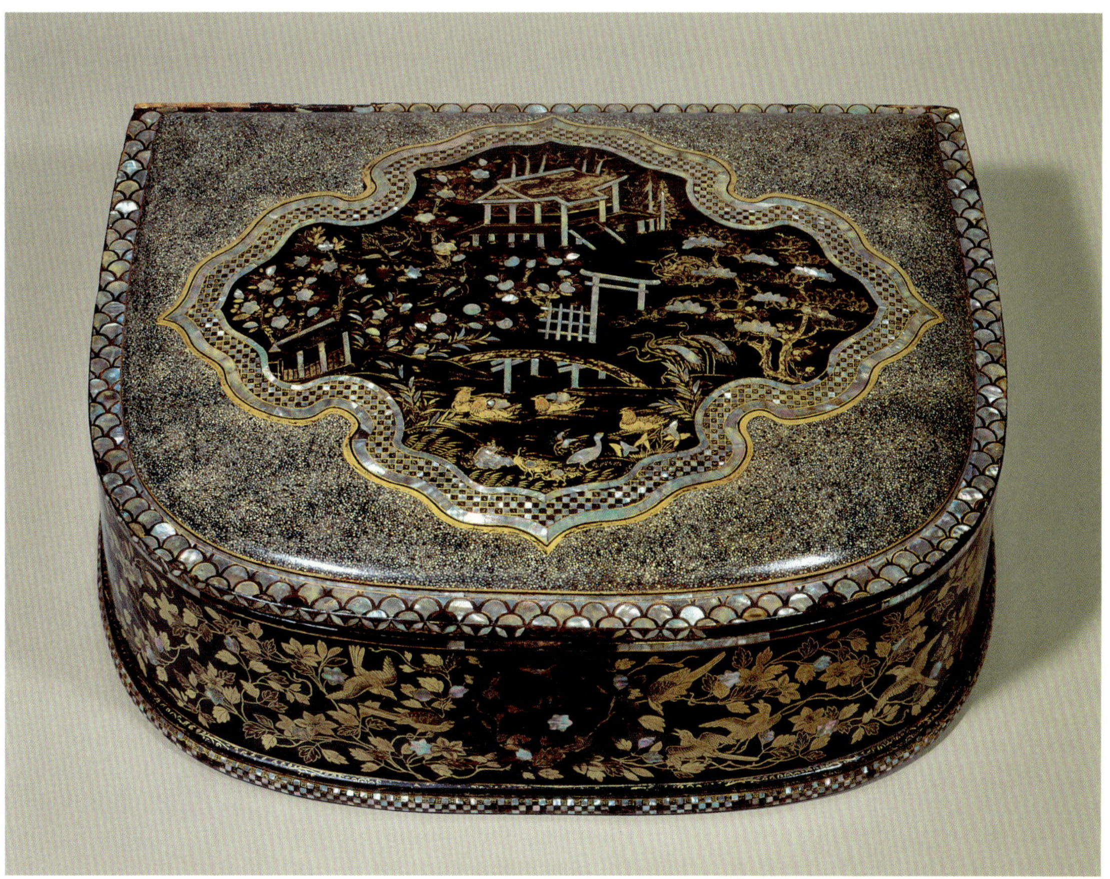

PLATE 146

Box in Saddlebag Shape with Design of the Sumiyoshi Shrine

Japan, 1630–50
Makie lacquered wood with mother-of-pearl inlay, metal fittings
7⅛ × 21¾ × 19 in. (18 × 55 × 48 cm)

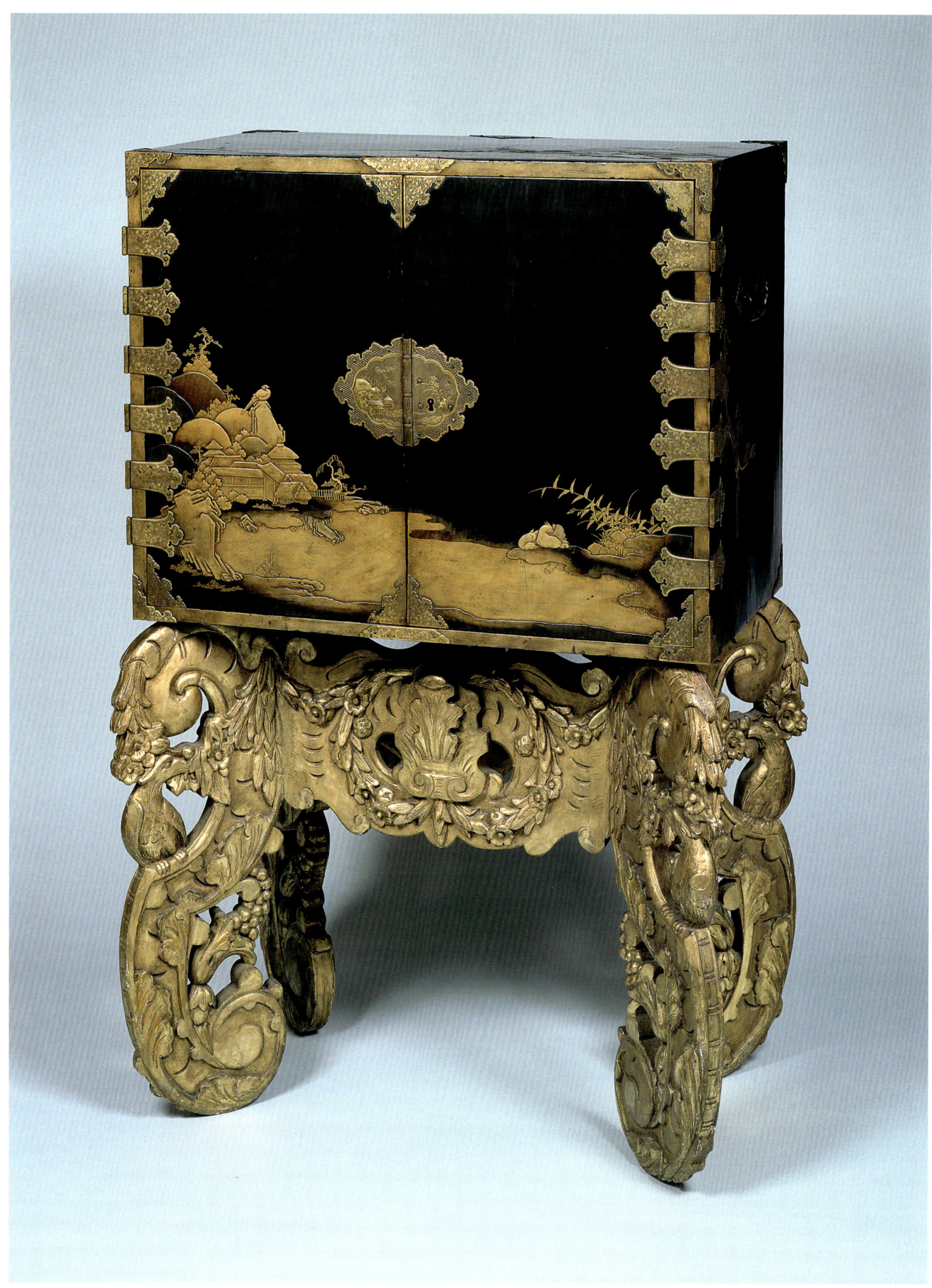

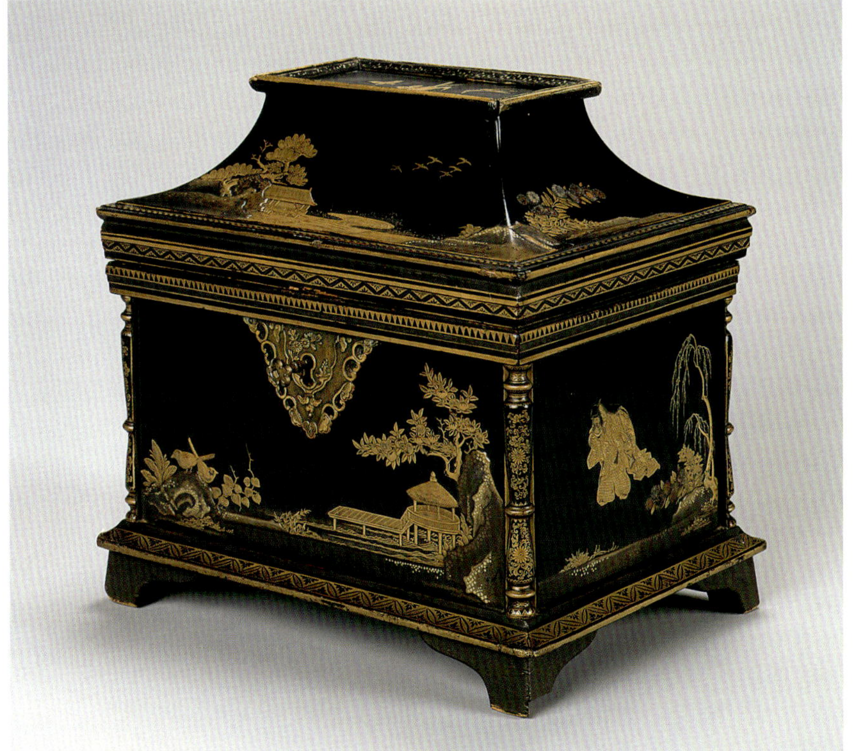

Japanese motifs. The sides still have the dense flower-and-leaf pattern of *namban* lacquer, but the large, elaborately shaped cartouche on a ground of prepared ray skin has a figural scene set in a landscape with the Sumiyoshi Bridge, inlaid birds and animals, and a border of a small, mother-of-pearl checker pattern. The interior has a sketchy gold lacquered painting of egrets and reeds on a black lacquered ground.

The Dutch had virtually monopolized the trade in Japanese export lacquer by the middle of the seventeenth century, and the Pictorial style blossomed. Large cabinets, called *comptoirs,* were very popular among wealthy Dutchmen who displayed them prominently in the interiors of their homes. *Comptoirs* usually have two hinged side-doors that reveal several small drawers when opened. Painted borders are small or have completely disappeared from the doors, which provided a shining black surface for elaborate decorations of mountainous landscapes, fowl, or figures, rendered in detail with gold lacquer. Such scenes often have slightly raised parts, further emphasizing the naturalistic elements. In the West, the cabinets were placed on finely worked stands (these were never made in Japan, but could, of course, have been japanned in Europe) and held treasured curiosities such as collections of shells, minerals, coins, or jewels. A *comptoir*

on a richly carved and gilded stand, dating to the second half of the seventeenth century, is an excellent representative of this type (plate 147).

Another fine example is a jewel box with pilasters at the corners (plate 148). It has a complex construction that prevents opportunistic theft of the treasures stored within. One side of the body can be raised when the lid is open, revealing a secret drawer running along the entire width under the floor of the casket. The lid hinges at the back; its sides slope upward in a concave profile to the top, which projects slightly all around. This top slides to one side, revealing a compartment. In some cases—but not here—the interior of the lid has a mirror, and so the casket could function not only as a jewel box but as a beauty case as well.

In about 1690 the VOC encountered setbacks, and luxury goods were partly removed from its orders. Chinese and Japanese export porcelain for the home market was no longer bought, nor was Japanese lacquerware. Private individuals took over but could not advance the large sums needed to order Japanese lacquered furniture such as *comptoirs* and chests. Instead, they requested smaller objects such as dishes and plates, cups and saucers, knife boxes, shaving bowls, boxes, and so forth. For most of the eighteenth century, such lacquer was appreciated as gifts, souvenirs, or private merchandise and was almost invariably decorated in a reduced—and therefore cheaper—Pictorial style. It is remarkable that, unlike Japanese *commande* porcelain, Western depictions do not occur on lacquerware, apart from occasional dishes and ceremonial shields with the armorials of Dutch families. There is no explanation for this, because, had they so wished, the Dutch could have had all kinds of Western scenes and motifs applied by the Japanese lacquer craftsmen.

Then, suddenly, about 1785, this gap was filled by an extraordinary range of decorative oval medallions and rectangular plaques that would have been valued as collector's items at the time. We do not know much about their unexpected appearance, but J. F. Baron van Reede tot de Parkeler, who served as the head of Dejima in 1786 and 1788–89, was one of the first to order such medallions. They are lacquered in black and gold on a copper base and have a hanging ring at the top. The very slightly raised decorations show portraits of statesmen, artists, kings and queens, popes, scholars, philosophers, and other famous Europeans, with either a surrounding inscription mentioning their name or a text in gold lacquer on the back. The portraits and texts were carefully copied from engravings in *L'Europe illustré,* a six-volume work by Dreux du Radier (Paris, 1755–65) that met the widespread international demand for illustrated compilations of famous people, sights, and events. Apart from the above-mentioned series, of which several must have been made, other sets featured Roman emperors, Dutch VOC governors-general in the East Indies, and Chinese emperors, among others. Sizes vary occasionally—most are about 5 inches high—and a few rectangular variants exist, some with inlaid mother-of-pearl instead of gold lacquer. The eleven medallions from the Kobe City Museum depict various famous persons from Western history (plates 149a–j, 150). Most have the names of their subjects written in capitals, but on two rare examples a running script was used. The large medallion showing

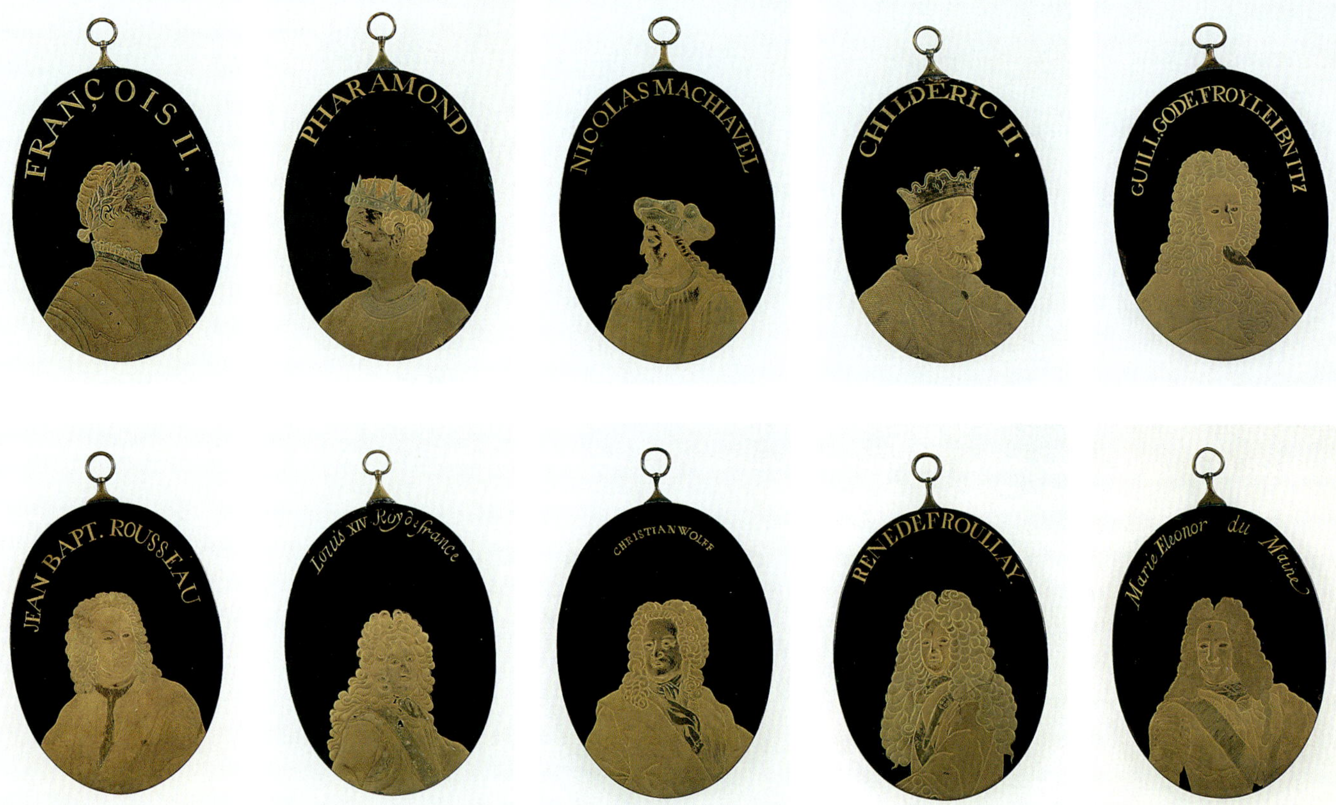

the Italian artist Polidore Caldara (c. 1492–1543) may have been part of a separate, larger format series (plate 150).

Much rarer, but made as part of the same interest in the famous, are rectangular plaquettes showing cityscapes (in particular of Rome), scenes from antiquity, and sea battles, also in gold and black lacquer on a copper base. Two plaquettes from the Kobe City Museum depict scenes from sea battles that attracted much attention at the time, namely the meeting of Dutch and English ships at Dogger Bank and near Cadiz in 1781. Originally part of a series of four plaquettes, each depicts a decisive moment in the conflict, copied by the Japanese lacquerworker from prints by Mathias de Sallieth published in 1782. Different versions of the plaquettes exist: with a long explanatory text below the scene on the front (plate 151), with a short text below (plate 152), or with text on the back. The first example is particularly interesting because below the text is inscribed "Verlakt bij Sasaya in Japan Ao. 1792"

(Lacquered by Sasaya in Japan in 1792). Unfortunately, the figure of Sasaya remains elusive; he is mentioned in VOC documents in connection with lacquer ordered for the Dutch in Nagasaki as well as in Kyoto. Lacquerware is very rarely dated, but in this case we know that it took ten years before the sea battle at Dogger Bank was commemorated on lacquer in Japan.

The Napoleonic Wars in Europe (1803–15) interrupted Dutch trade in the East, and Dejima was isolated for more than a decade, until 1816. By then, fashions had changed, and American merchants from the Boston area, sailing under the Dutch flag to Nagasaki between 1797 and 1803, had introduced Japanese lacquered furniture with restrained decorations in neoclassical style and featuring inlaid mother-of-pearl. Such inlays became more dominant in the first half of the nineteenth century, their effect often heightened by very thin, colored metal foil placed beneath the inlay. Because the production of these wares initially was done in Kyoto but shifted to

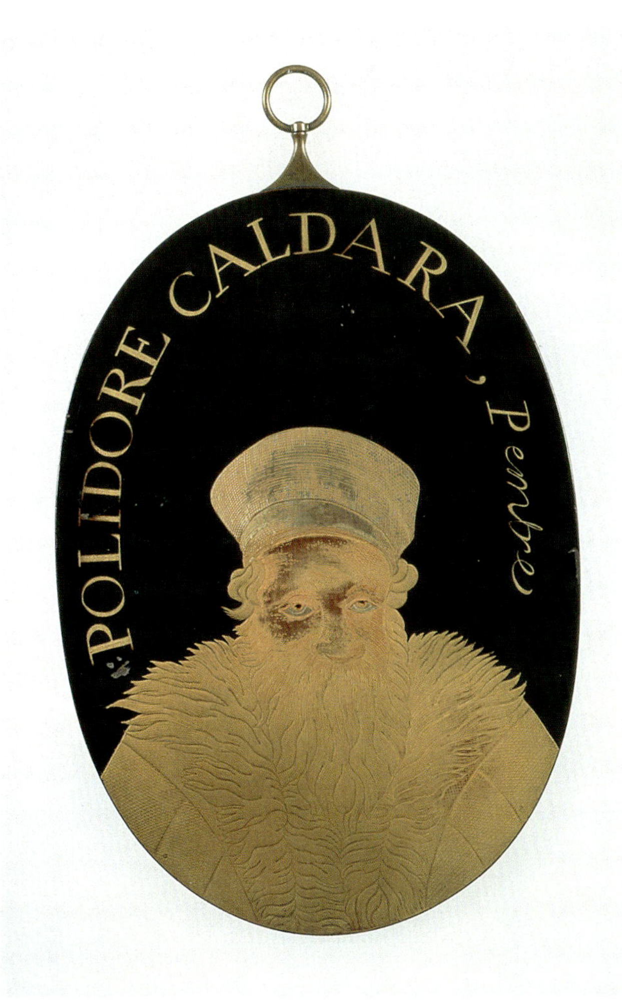

185

**Plaque of
Naval Battle
near Cadiz**

Japan, Sasaya, 1792
(Kansei 4)
Makie lacquered copper
plate (frame added in
Holland or England)
11⅞ × 17½ in.
(30 × 44.5 cm)

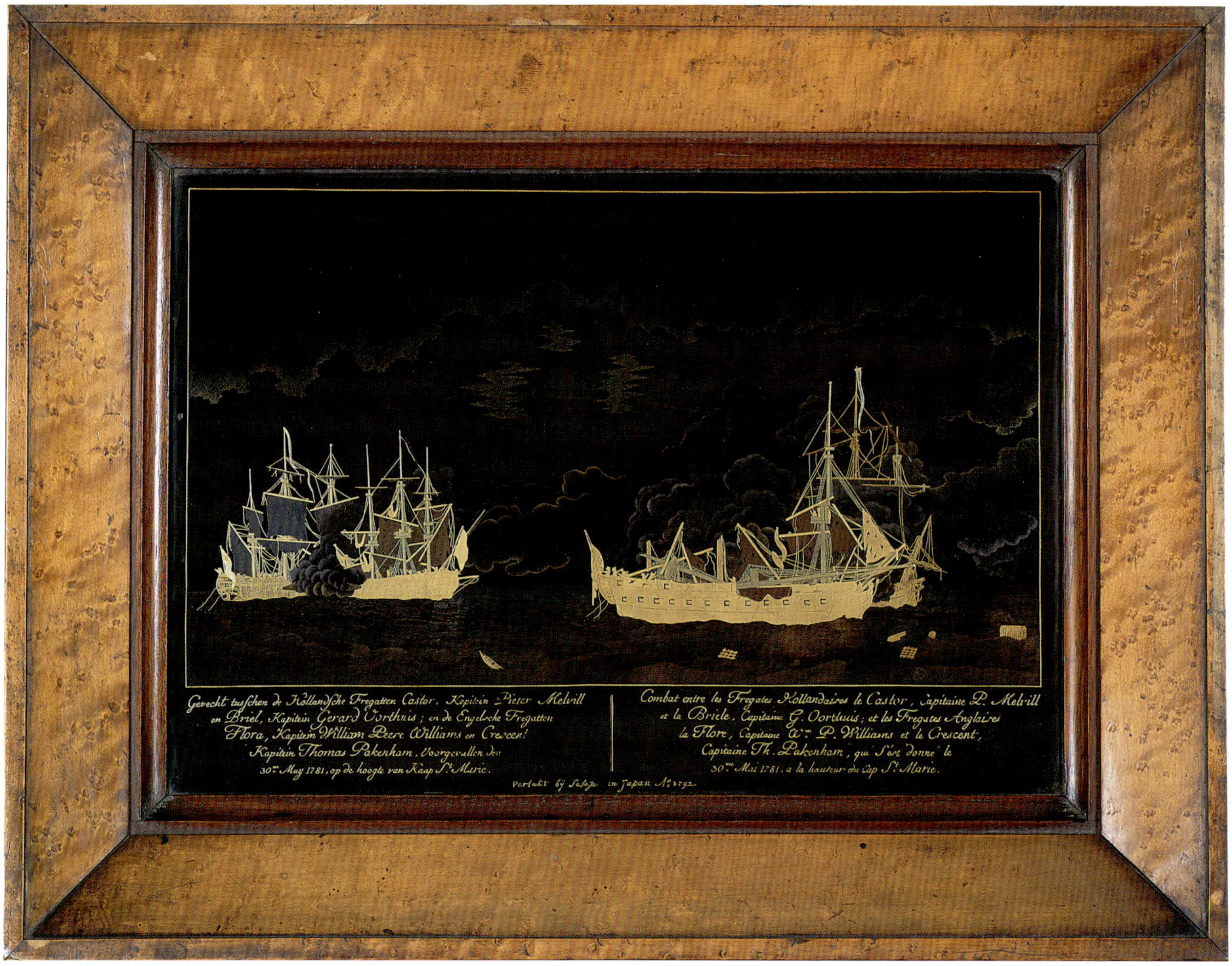

PLATE 152
Plaque of
Naval Battle
off Dogger Bank
Japan, Sasaya, 1792
(Kansei 4)
Makie lacquered copper
plate (frame added in
Holland or England)
11⅞ × 17½ in.
(30 × 44.5 cm)

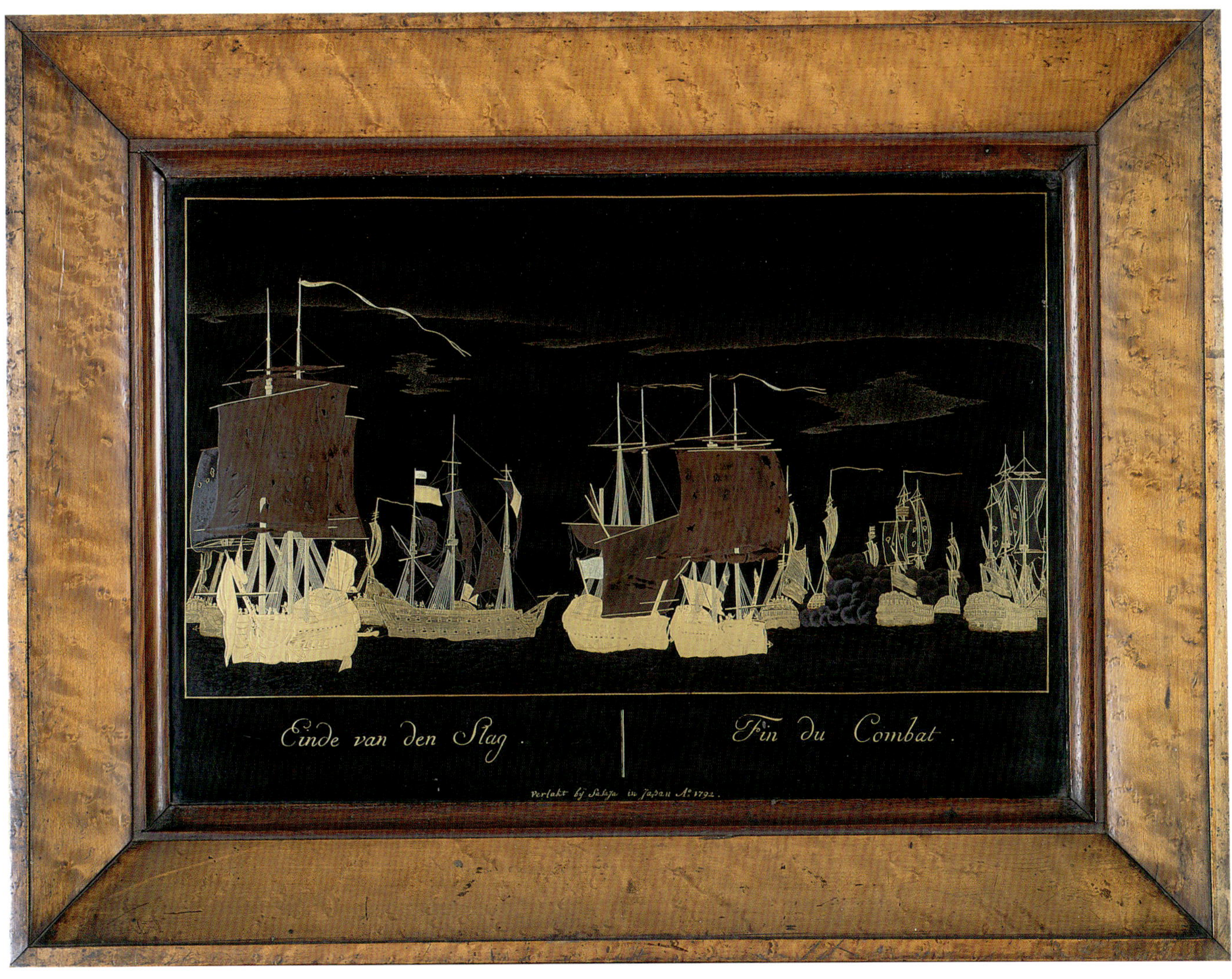
Einde van den Slag.
Fin du Combat.
Verlakt by Sasaja in Japan A.° 1792.

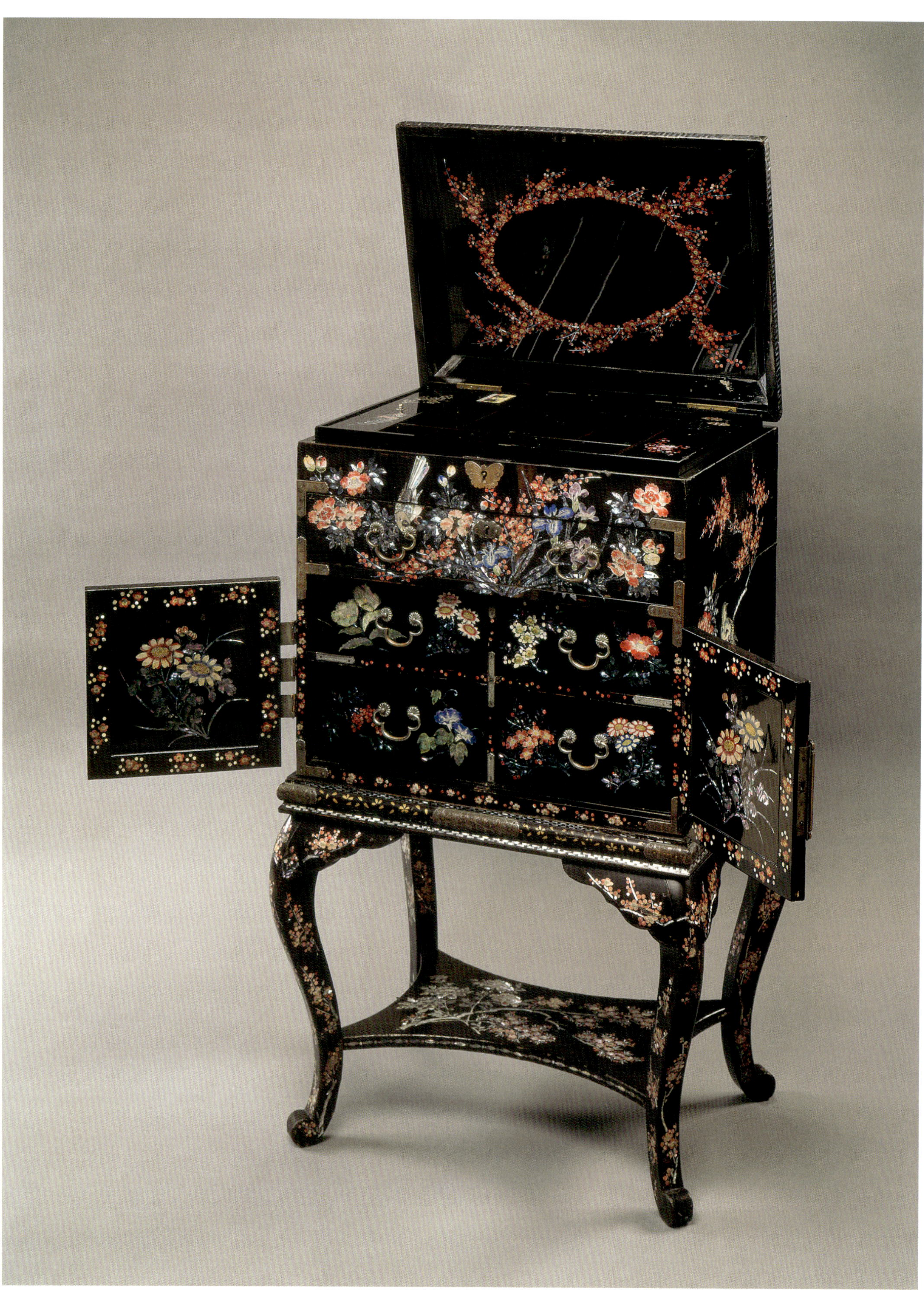

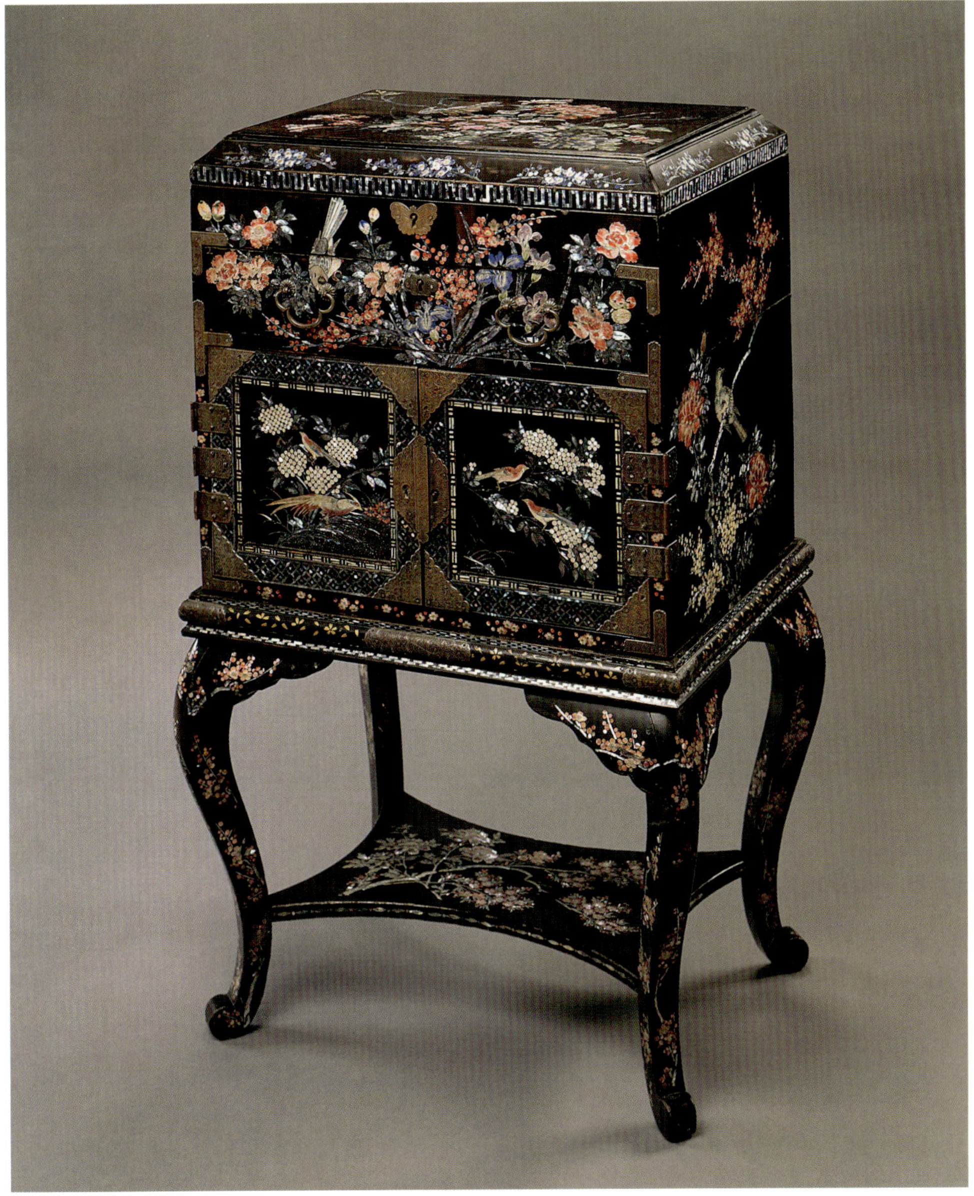

Nagasaki when the Dutch resumed orders, it was called the Kyoto-Nagasaki style, and later simply the Nagasaki style.

A beautiful example in the Nagasaki style is a cabinet on a matching stand with cabriole legs connected by an indented plateau (plate 153a,b). It has four drawers behind two doors, a wide drawer above, and a hinged top that lifts to reveal a compartmented interior. In fact, it is an adapted, more complex version of the seventeenth-century cabinets or *comptoirs* made to order for the Dutch. Interestingly, a comparable cabinet can be seen on an engraving in the *Illustrated London News* of February 4, 1854, depicting Japanese objects shown at an art gallery exhibition on Pall Mall in London (fig. 19).[12] Another example in the Nagasaki style is a sewing table with lyre-shaped side

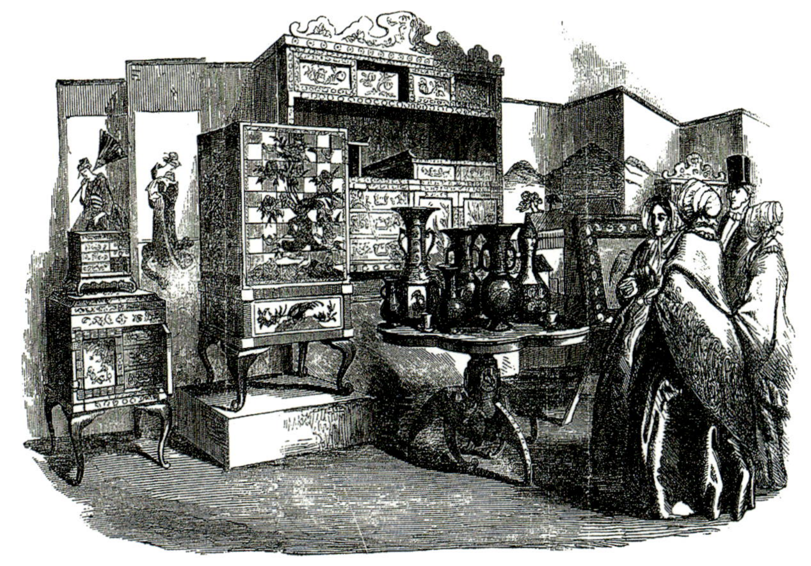

legs and a tray top (plate 154). A textile bag, used to store all kinds of sewing materials, would have been suspended from a drawer-frame under the wide drawer. The table is exuberantly decorated with scattered flowers and garlands of inlaid mother-of-pearl, and the top shows a naturalistic scene of birds at a pond, grasses, and a blossoming prunus. Such relatively small pieces of furniture were quite popular in the West, but larger, more expensive objects such as *secrétaires,* tables, and chairs were less frequently ordered.

Affordable and popular were game, sewing, and writing boxes, often decorated with Western scenes, wholly or partly executed in mother-of-pearl (plate 158). A subcategory is formed by tobacco boxes or snuffboxes, which usually were rectangular with flattened corners and decorated in mother-of-pearl, and gold and black lacquer on a copper base. Ordered for private use or as special gifts for relatives and friends, some such boxes have an inscription in Dutch on the inside of the lid, copied in gold lacquer by the

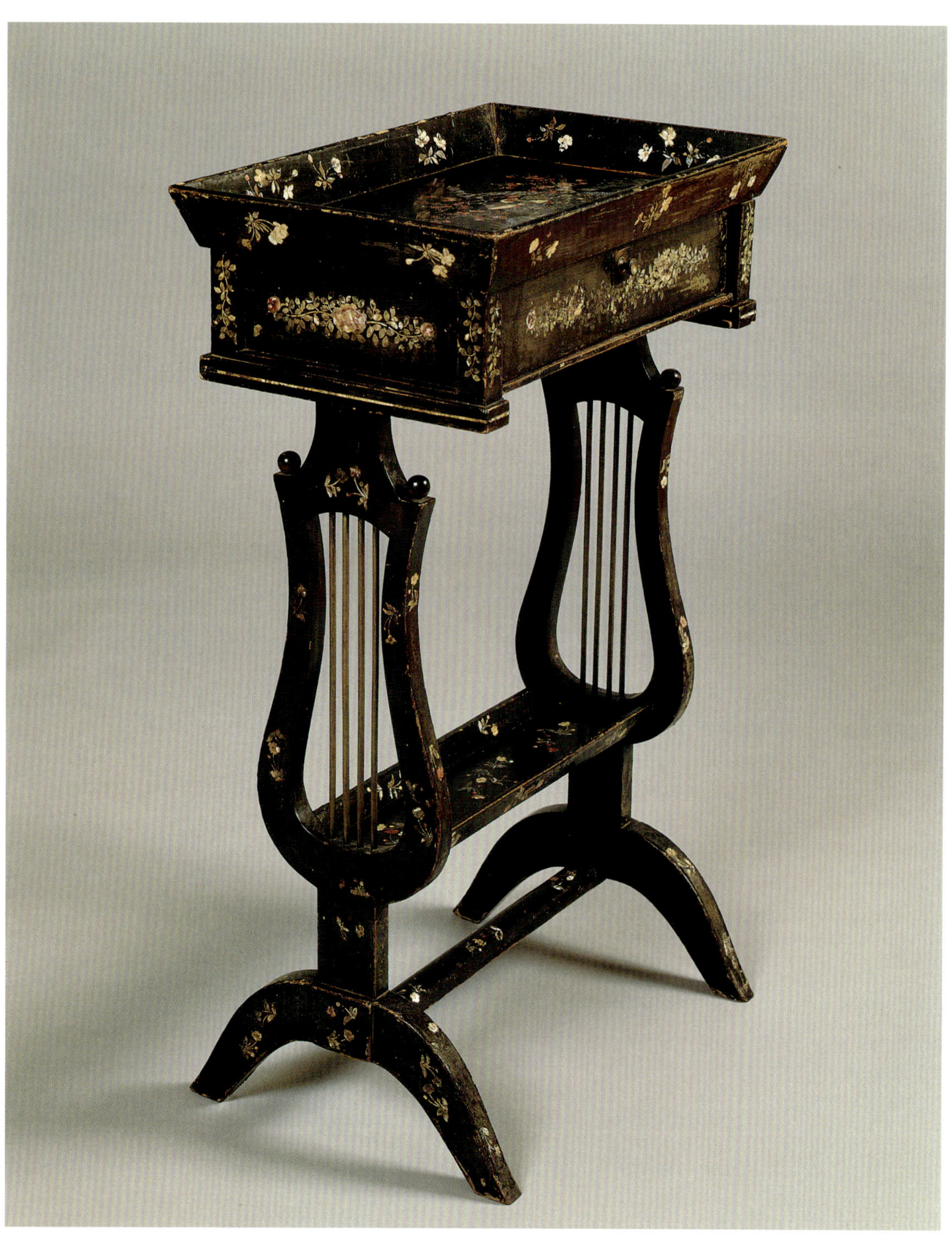

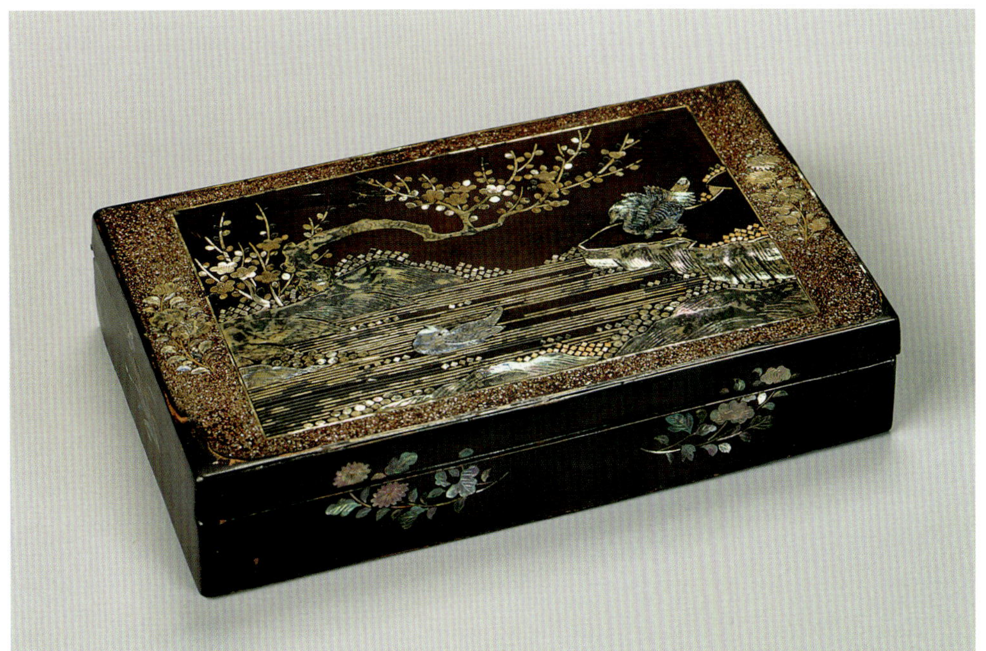

PLATE 155

Tobacco Box with Landscape Design

Japan, late 18th–early 19th century
Lacquered copper plate with mother-of-pearl inlay, metal fittings
1 × 5¼ × 3⅛ in.
(2.5 × 13.3 × 7.9 cm)

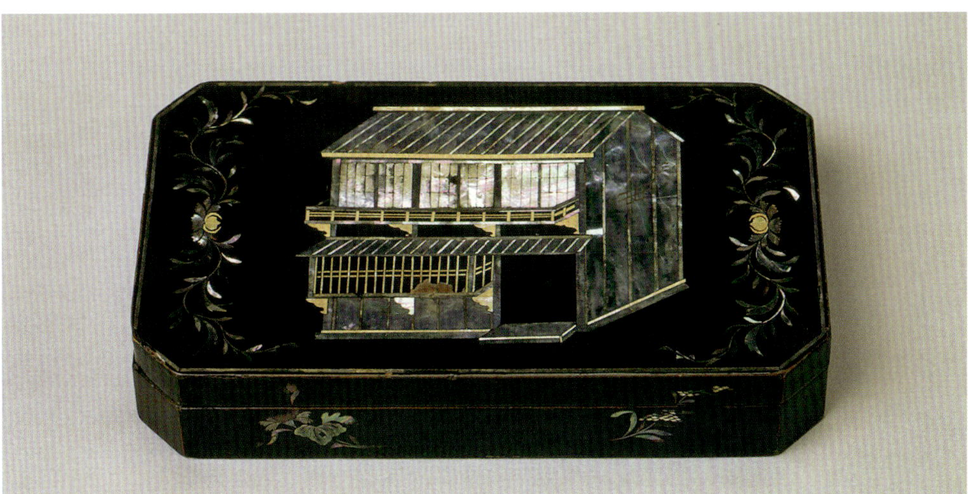

PLATE 156

Tobacco Box with Design of Dejima House

Japan, late 18th century
Lacquered copper plate with mother-of-pearl inlay
1 × 5⅞ × 3⅜ in.
(2.2 × 14.7 × 8.6 cm)

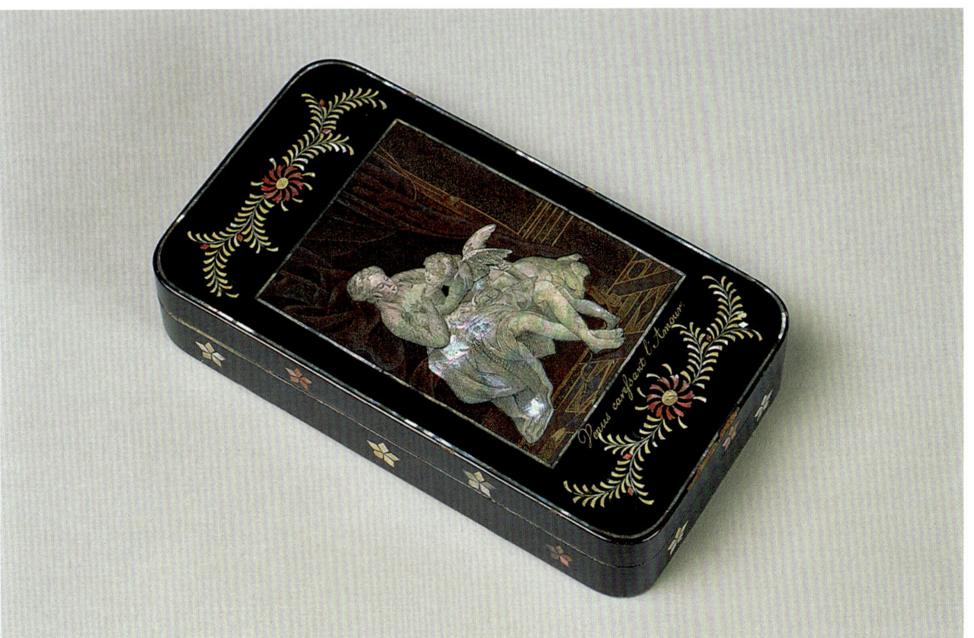

PLATE 157

Tobacco Box with Design of *Venus caressant l'Amour*

Japan, 1790s–early 19th century
Makie lacquered copper plate with mother-of-pearl inlay
1 × 5⅜ × 3 in.
(2.4 × 13.5 × 7.6 cm)

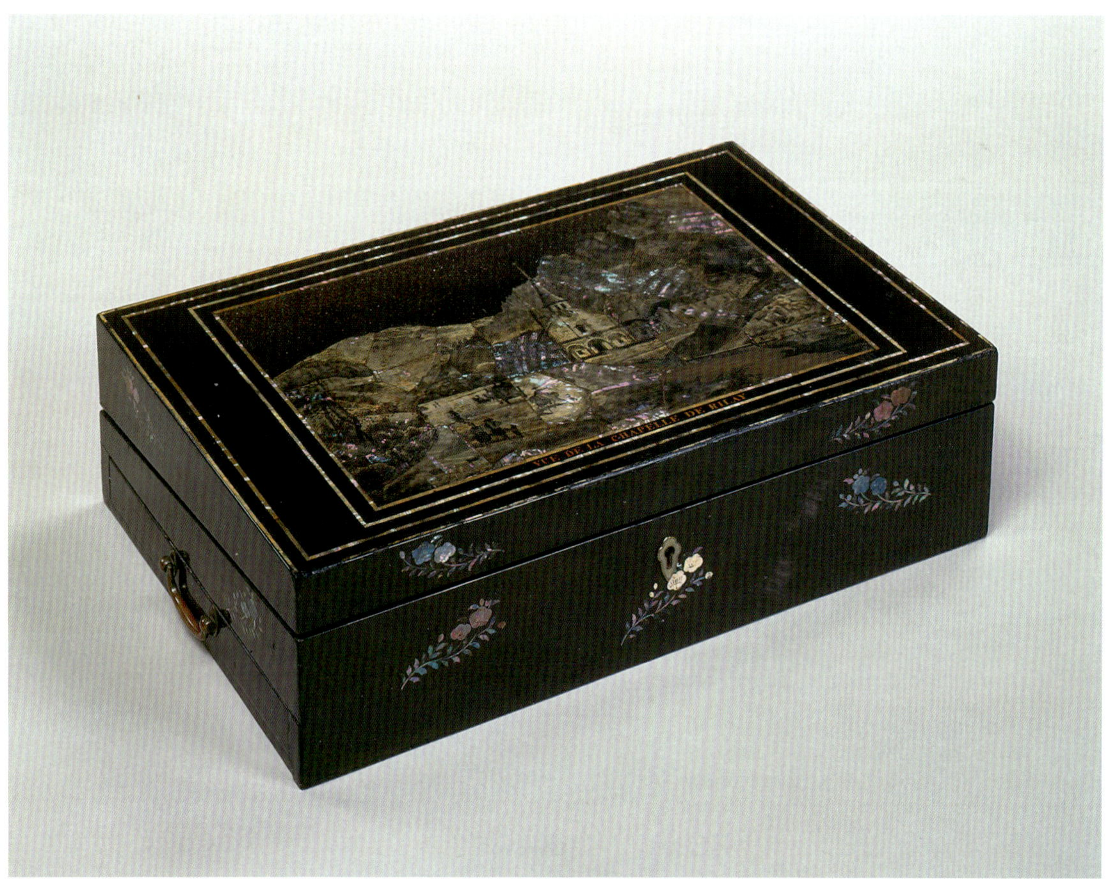

PLATE 158

**Box with Design
of *Vue de la
chapelle de Rilay***

Japan, c. 1854–60
(Ansei era)
Lacquered wood with
mother-of-pearl inlay,
metal fittings
4⅛ × 15 × 9⅝ in.
(10.4 × 38 × 24.3 cm)

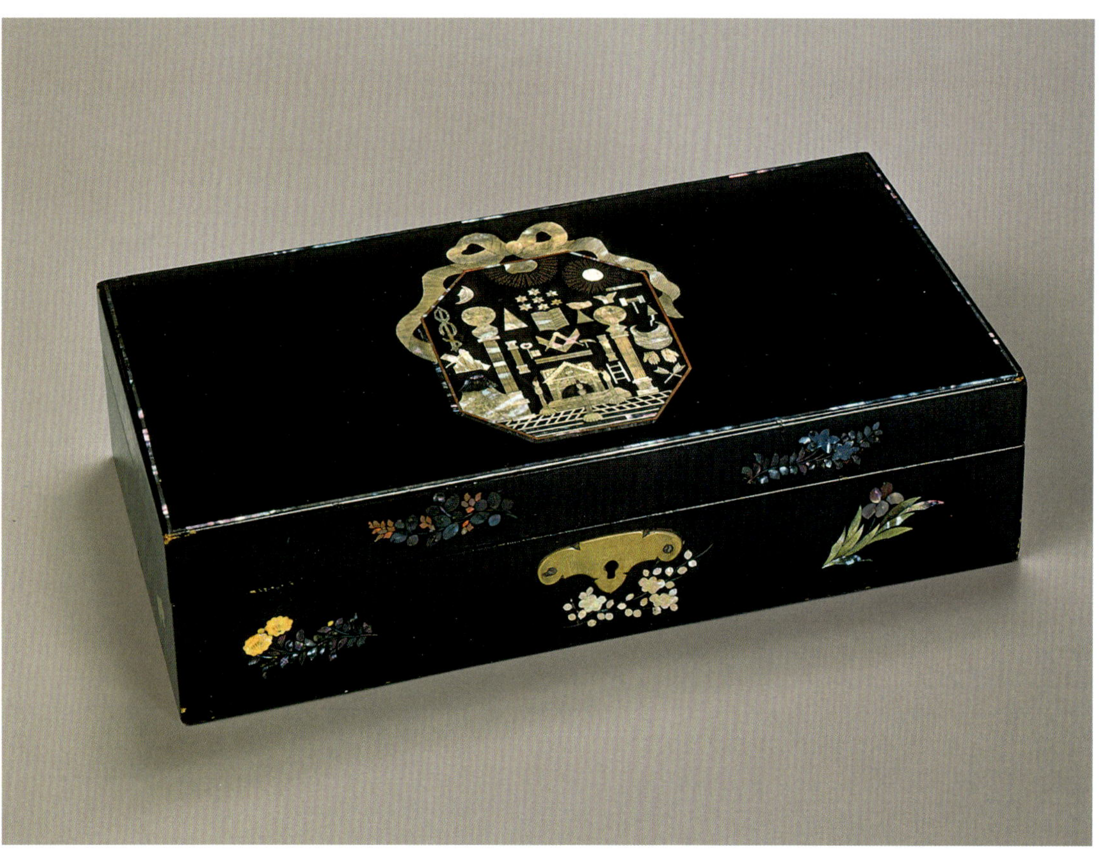

PLATE 159

**Box with Masonic
Emblems**

Japan, c. 1820–40
Lacquered wood with
mother-of-pearl inlay,
metal fittings
3¼ × 12⅝ × 6⅝ in.
(8 × 32 × 16.6 cm)

Japanese craftsman from a written model. One tobacco box shows a Japanese landscape with cherry blossoms (plate 155); another, depicting a house on Dejima, is clearly a souvenir ordered by a Dutch employee (plate 156). An interesting box with a classical theme is inscribed "Venus caressant l'Amour" (Venus caressing Cupid), the scene copied from an as-yet unidentified European engraving (plate 157).

Finally, there are boxes with Masonic decoration. Dutch and English merchants commonly became members of a Freemasonry lodge, of which there were several in Asia. Some of the special objects needed for their rituals were ordered in the Far East, such as embroidered textiles from China and lacquered boxes from Japan. The characteristic Masonic emblems—the pillars of the Temple of Solomon and various tools—on one such box (plate 159) were taken from an engraving and copied in mother-of-pearl, inlaid in black lacquer.[13] These and other boxes with Western shapes and/or Western designs can be dated between circa 1820 and 1840. Lacquer orders seem to have dwindled until the opening of Japan by the Americans in the 1850s, which reinvigorated lacquer production and led to the stunning export lacquerware of the later nineteenth century.

NOTES

1. I would like to refer the reader to the general sources I consulted on Japanese export porcelain: Oliver Impey, *Japanese Export Porcelain: Catalogue of the Collection of the Ashmolean Museum, Oxford* (Amsterdam: Hotei, 2002), and Christiaan J. A. Jörg, *Fine and Curious: Japanese Export Porcelain in Dutch Collections* (Amsterdam: Hotei, 2003).

2. The only monograph thus far on *shoki*-Imari in a Western language is by Oliver Impey, *The Early Porcelain Kilns of Japan: Arita in the First Half of the Seventeenth Century* (Oxford: Clarendon Press, 1996).

3. The standard work on Kraak porcelain is by Maura Rinaldi, *Kraak Porcelain: A Moment in the History of Trade* (London: Bamboo Publications, 1989).

4. For a survey of export wares made for the Dutch in the seventeenth and eighteenth centuries, see Christiaan J. A. Jörg, *Chinese Ceramics in the Collection of the Rijksmuseum, Amsterdam* (London: Philip Wilson, 1997); for a survey of VOC documents relating to the VOC porcelain trade in the seventeenth century, see T. Volker, *Porcelain and the Dutch East India Company as Recorded in the Dagh-registers of Batavia Castle, Those of Hirado and Deshima and other Contemporary Papers, 1602–1682* (Leiden: E. J. Brill, 1954, 1971).

5. Julia B. Curtis, *Trade, Taste & Transformation: Jingdezhen Porcelain for Japan, 1620–1645*, exh. cat. (New York: China Institute Gallery, 2006).

6. Christiaan J. A. Jörg, *Interaction in Ceramics: Oriental Porcelain & Delftware*, exh. cat. (Hong Kong: Hong Kong Museum of Art, 1984).

7. The dish, of a shape the Dutch call a *pannekoekje* ("pancake"), has no footring and was fired on pins in a cassette. It is marked on the back with the initials "IVL" for Jan van der Laan or Jan Jansz. van der Laan, a masterpotter who worked at the factory De Drie Klokken (where he is mentioned in 1675) as well as at Het Hart (where he is mentioned in 1693). The Mesch family owned both factories. We have no further information on this potter. See C. H. de Jonge, *Delfts Aardewerk* (Rotterdam/The Hague: Nijgh and Van Ditmar, 1965), 205.

8. In older literature the scene is sometimes called "Deshima" after the Dutch settlement in Nagasaki harbor, but the landscape and buildings are obviously Dutch, not Japanese. Interestingly, the catalogue of an auction held in Amsterdam in 1778 already refers to this type of dish as a "Scheveningen plate"; see Christiaan J. A. Jörg, "To the Highest Bidder: The Auction of a Porcelain Shop in Amsterdam in 1778," *Transactions of the Oriental Ceramic Society* 65 (2001): 67.

9. Several Chinese dishes of different shapes decorated with this design were salvaged from the *Ca Mau* wreck by the Vietnamese Salvage Company in 1998–99. The wreck contained some Yongzheng-marked pieces and can be tentatively dated to about 1725. See Nguyên Dinh Chiên, *The Ca Mau Shipwreck, 1723–1735* (Hanoi: Ca Mau Department of Culture and Information/The National Museum of Vietnamese History, 2002), 108–9, ills. 27–30.

10. Christiaan J. A. Jörg, *Pronk Porcelain: Porcelain after Designs by Cornelis Pronk*, exh. cat. (Groningen: Groninger Museum, 1980).

11. For a general survey of export lacquer, I refer the reader to Oliver R. Impey and Christiaan J. A. Jörg, *Japanese Export Lacquer, 1580–1850* (Amsterdam: Hotei, 2005).

12. Ibid., fig. 516.

13. Most Japanese Masonic lacquer has this type of emblem. It is copied from the frontispiece of the publication *Jachin and Boaz, or An Authentic Key to the Door of Free Masonry, Both Ancient and Modern*. One edition was printed in 1797 in Albany; see ibid., n. 11, p. 63, fig. 105.

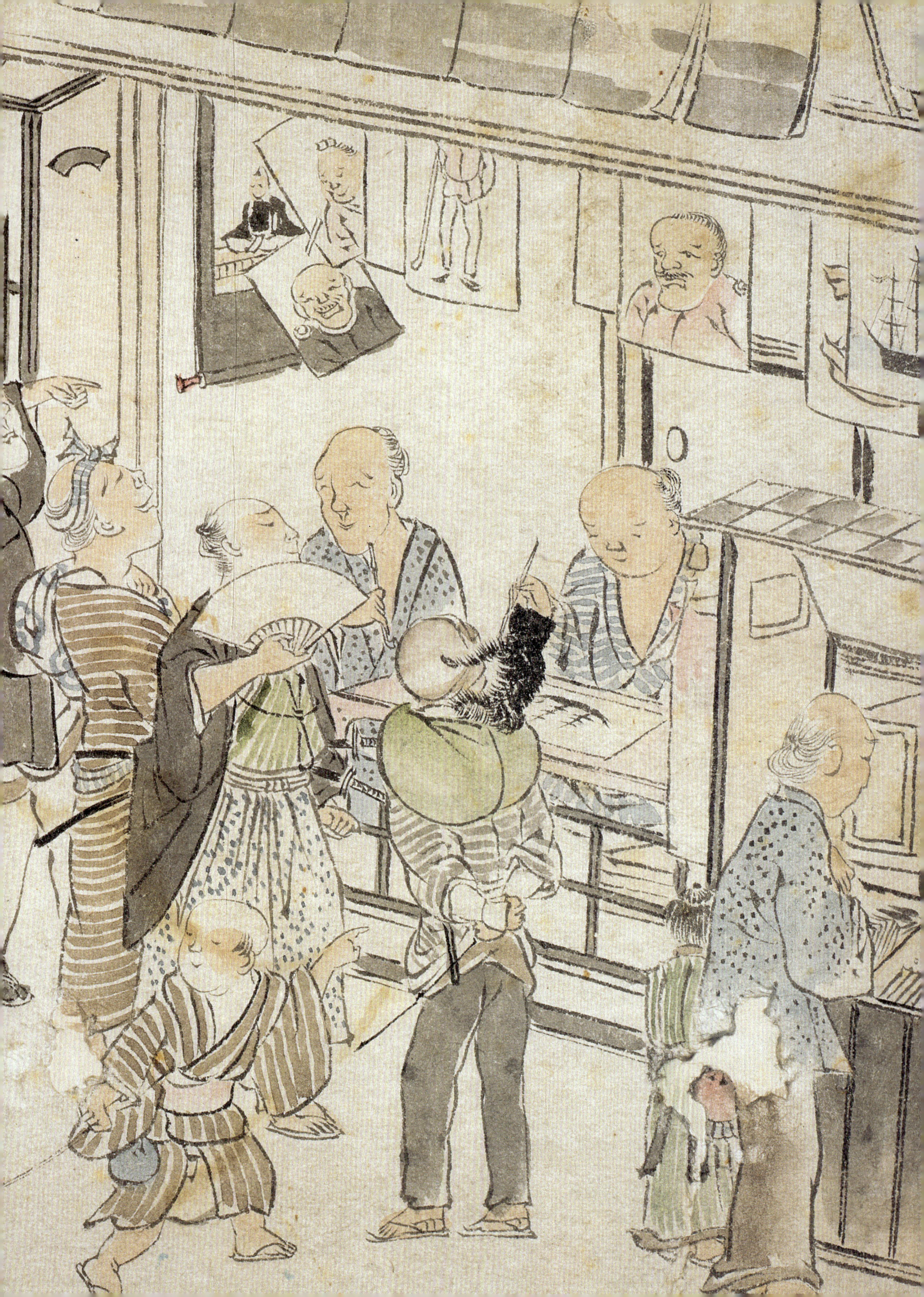

8

Tsukahara Akira

The Opening of Japan and Its Visual Culture

In 1853 and again in 1854, Commodore Matthew C. Perry (1794–1858) guided the ships of the American East India Squadron into Edo Bay. Representing the interests of the United States, Perry demanded a number of concessions from the Japanese shogunal government. These included permission to obtain supplies and coal to sustain American ships of trade in the Pacific, protection for American seaman who might drift onto the country's shores, and the establishment of commerce and trade relations with Japan. Many Japanese—even today—have interpreted this momentous historical event as shattering a peaceful state of unfettered isolation. Having lived more than two hundred years under the exclusionary policies of *sakoku* (lit., closed country), the Japanese people understood virtually nothing of the world around them. With the sudden appearance of the American steamship fleet, the Japanese leadership could do little to prevent the Americans from opening their country to outside influences. The Americans had, indeed, come to Japan well prepared and apparently were willing to use force to accomplish their aims. Among the American ships that came to Japan, two (and three in 1854) had a displacement fifteen to twenty times greater than that of the largest existing Japanese ship at the time.

The Tokugawa shogunate was caught off-guard by the entrance of the American ships into Japanese waters even though the Dutch traders established at Nagasaki had anticipated their arrival in the 1852 *Betsudan fūsetsu gaki* (Special Annual Report on Foreign Events) presented to the Nagasaki magistrate and forwarded to the shogunate. Because of poor communication, however, the shogunate was slow to plan for the eventual appearance of Americans on their shores. Nonetheless, despite their lack of preparation, Japanese officials conducted peaceful discussions and negotiations with the Americans. The Japanese, through various sources, already had an indication of the state of American naval and ship technology and power. They had gathered this information through a series of encounters with Americans over the past half-century, although exactly when the first of these interactions occurred is not clear. It may have been as early as 1791, when a foreign ship—possibly the American vessel *Lady Washington* or

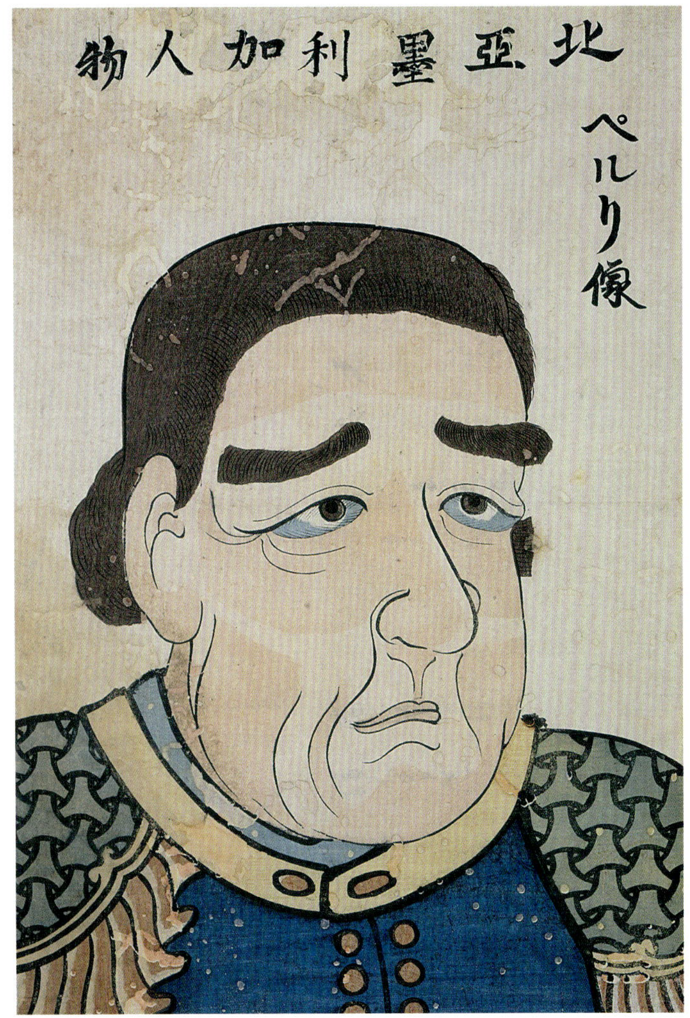

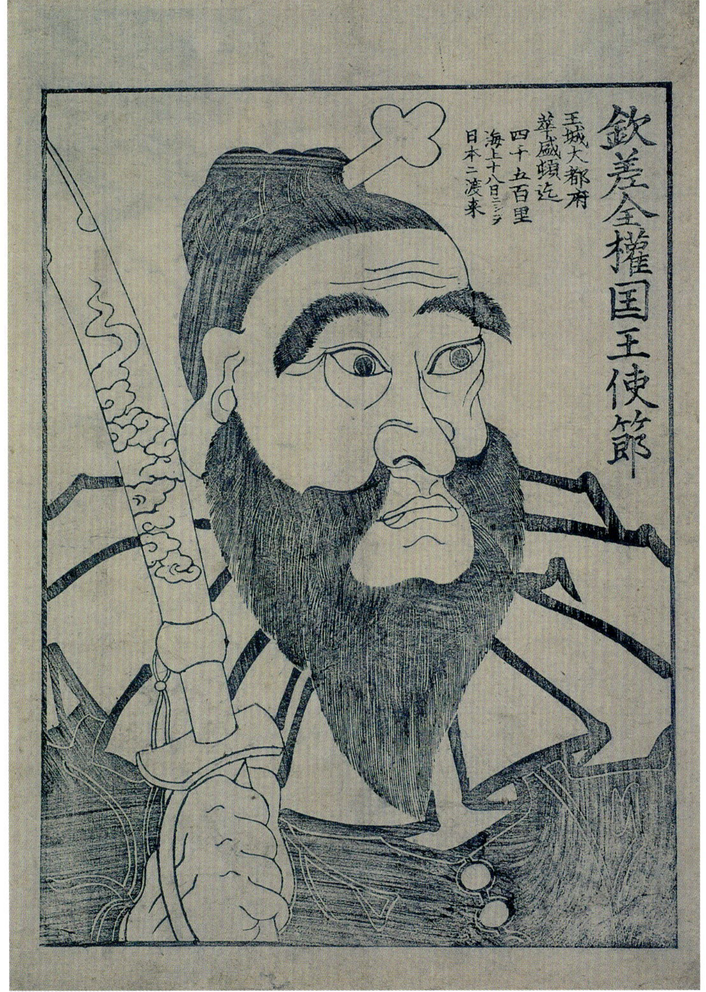

Grace—drifted ashore in Kishū province (present-day Wakayama prefecture). The first documented arrival of an American ship in Japan took place in Nagasaki several years later. Indeed, archival sources clearly indicate that Americans had visited Japan on a number of occasions from the end of the eighteenth century.

The work of the intellectual and artist Shiba Kōkan (1747–1818) provides some useful details concerning early Japanese recognition of the physical nature and topography of the United States. As will be discussed further, Kōkan was one of the few Japanese individuals outside the shogunate who could consult the *Oranda fūsetsu gaki* (Annual Report on Foreign Events). Although a diplomatic document, the Japanese translation of it circulated among *rangaku* (Dutch-learning) scholars, and such access provided Kōkan with a better understanding of world affairs.

In laying out his 1792 *Yochi zenzu* (Map of the World; revised edition published probably in 1793 as *Chikyū zu,* plate 163), Kōkan had little information with which to accurately render the geographical features of the North American continent. The cities of Boston and New York are not identified, and neither is the territory east of the Mississippi River, the area settled by the 1783 Treaty of Paris as comprising the United States. Consequently, the young country is not clearly expressed as an independent or recognizable political entity. Even the *Oranda fūsetsu gaki* is silent on the United States and its recently gained independence. The Japanese ruling elite were unaware of the new nation's growth in power and influence, especially in the Pacific region.

In a letter addressed to Kimura Kenkadō of Osaka, dated the twenty-second day of the seventh month, 1798, Shiba Kōkan wrote, "It appears that a small Dutch boat has arrived in Nagasaki. But we hear rumors that those who arrived were British, not Dutch. I cannot vouch for the truth of this. I have yet to read the *Oranda fūsetsu gaki,* but I will have to make efforts to verify this."[1] Nothing

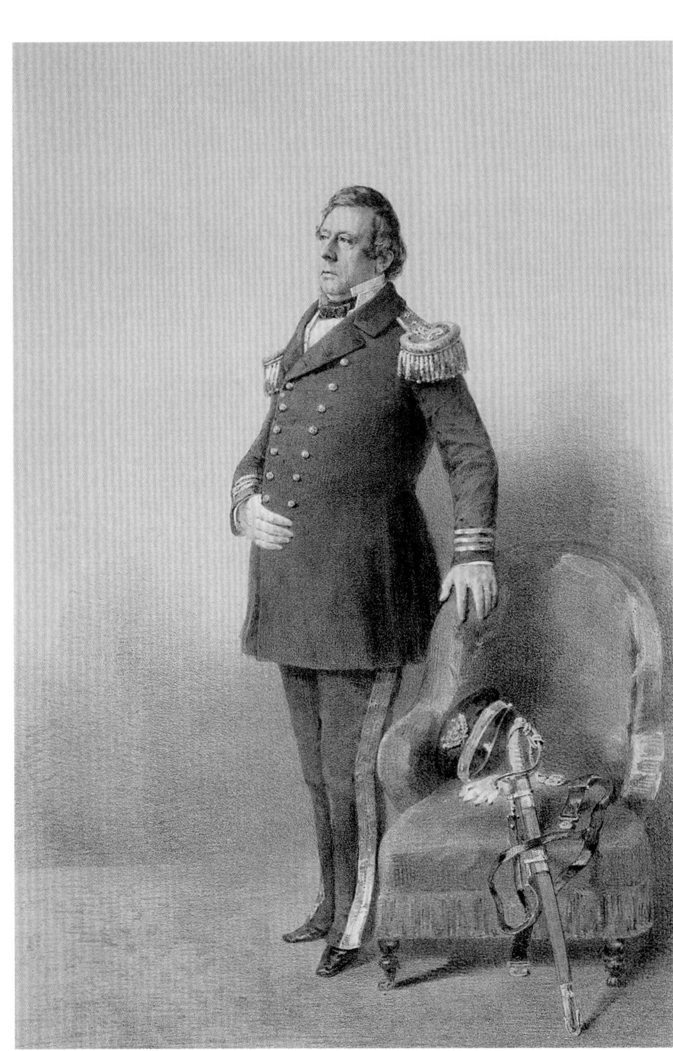

in the letter suggests that those on the ship were American or connected to the United States. But the rumor is indicative of the complicated state of Japanese perceptions of international relations and the delicacy with which information was transmitted in the time leading up to the first American-Japanese contacts.

The close of the eighteenth century in the Western world marked an era of revolution and upheaval. At the time Holland, which since 1795 had been under the control of the French, was the only European state that maintained trading relations with Japan. The English, seeing an opportunity amid hostile relations with the French, moved to occupy Dutch colonies and to disrupt Dutch shipping. Under these circumstances, the Dutch could barely sustain their colony of Batavia (present-day Jakarta, Indonesia), whose inhabitants feared British attack. To maintain the movement of goods, the Dutch chartered neutral ships to ply the Dutch-Japanese trade route. The United States took part in this enterprise.

Although the nationality of the ship and its captain need to be verified, it is known that a ship recognized as American by the Dutch at Batavia and Nagasaki bore the name *Eliza of New York* and traveled between those ports in the sixth month of 1797 and 1798. Why, then, did the rumor reported by Kōkan in 1798 identify the ship in Nagasaki harbor as British and not American? Given that only Dutch ships were allowed to moor in Japanese waters, it must have been a shock for the Japanese to see the *Eliza*, which was a smaller ship than those typically at Nagasaki. They must have puzzled over why the crew did not speak Dutch, despite the fact that the ship flew the Dutch colors. Some *rangaku* scholars with access to the *Oranda fūsetsu gaki* knew that British ships were appearing in the waters around Japan and had heard of the British threats to the Dutch, their colonies, and their trade routes. Japanese interest in British ships was consequently high.

The Japanese who interacted with the Dutch apparently had some recognition of the differences in European languages, and they may have been able to identify the language spoken by the crew of the *Eliza* as English. Because the Japanese did not know of America's independence until at least the early nineteenth century, it is likely that the Japanese mistook the *Eliza* as a British ship. Additionally, at the turn of the nineteenth century, Japanese authorities did not believe the

British posed a great threat to the Dutch-Japanese trade. Given the importance and the benefits of trade with Europe, they did not pursue a clearer identification of the *Eliza* and simply treated its crew as if they were indeed Dutch. So although this American ship visited Nagasaki in 1797 and 1798, the rumors circulating among the intellectual and ruling elite in Osaka and Edo had the British, not Americans, coming to Japan.

In 1800 the American ship *Massachusetts* arrived without proper authorization in the port of Nagasaki. A crew member named William Cleveland kept a diary, which is considered today one of the earliest accounts of Japan written by an American.[2] When a number of Japanese laborers at Nagasaki came aboard to assist in pulling the anchor, Cleveland observed that they were not as tall as Europeans but extremely well built and good looking, and even clearly looked down on the Americans. One asked Cleveland if America was about the same size as Nagasaki. When a world map illustrating America's true size in relation to Holland was shown to him, the Japanese appeared astonished. Cleveland, in many respects, was surprised by the Japanese response. In his diary he speculated that the Dutch, the only Europeans allowed to maintain relations with Japan, had likely manipulated information to create a negative image of their potential rivals.

It cannot be confirmed whether the Dutch actively conveyed misinformation about the geographic importance of North America as a means of minimizing American political or economic clout and significance. According to Cleveland, another Japanese sailor stated his intention of visiting America, but clearly the provisions of *sakoku* would have prevented him from doing so. However the Dutch might have manipulated intelligence, *sakoku* exclusionist policies restricted individuals and ships from traveling abroad and censored the flow of information.

This lack of knowledge of the growing power of the United States in world affairs at the turn of the nineteenth century is exemplified by the vagueness of Kōkan's world map discussed above. A new map made about 1816, the *Shintei bankoku zenzu* (Newly Revised Map of the World), etched by Aōdō Denzen (1748–1822), would capture a greatly changed representation of America and one much more accurate by modern standards (plate 164).

Takahashi Kageyasu (1785–1829), an astronomer and geographer who worked for the shogunate,

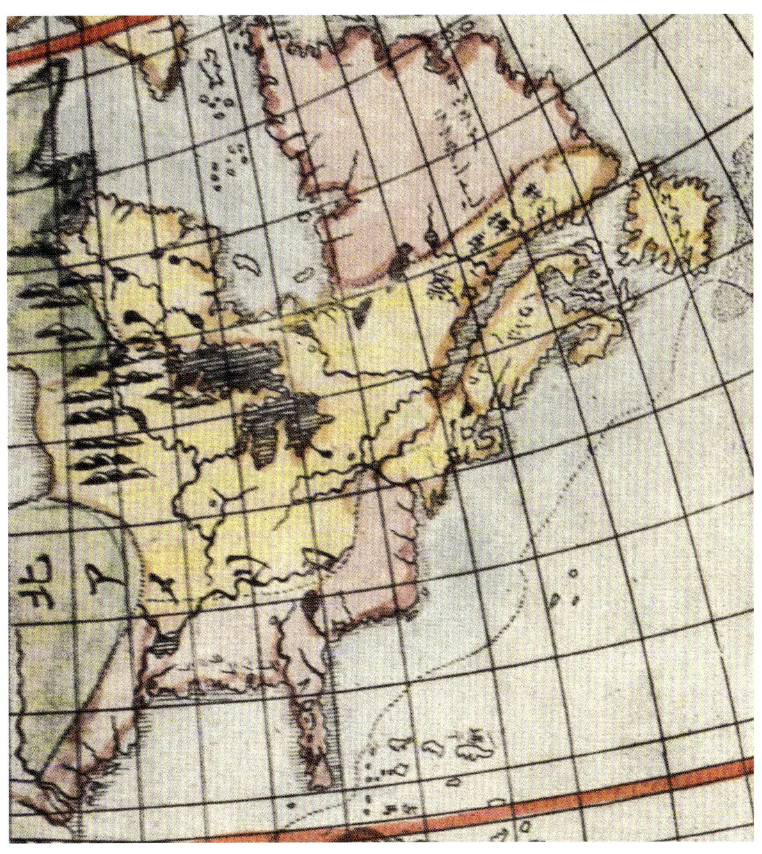

DETAIL
East Coast
of America,
from *Chikyō zu*
(plate 163)

PLATE 163
Shiba Kōkan
(Japanese, 1747–1818)
**Chikyū zu (Map
of the World)**
c. 1793 (Kansei 5)
Etching: ink with
hand color on paper
21⅞ × 34 in.
(55.4 × 86.4 cm)

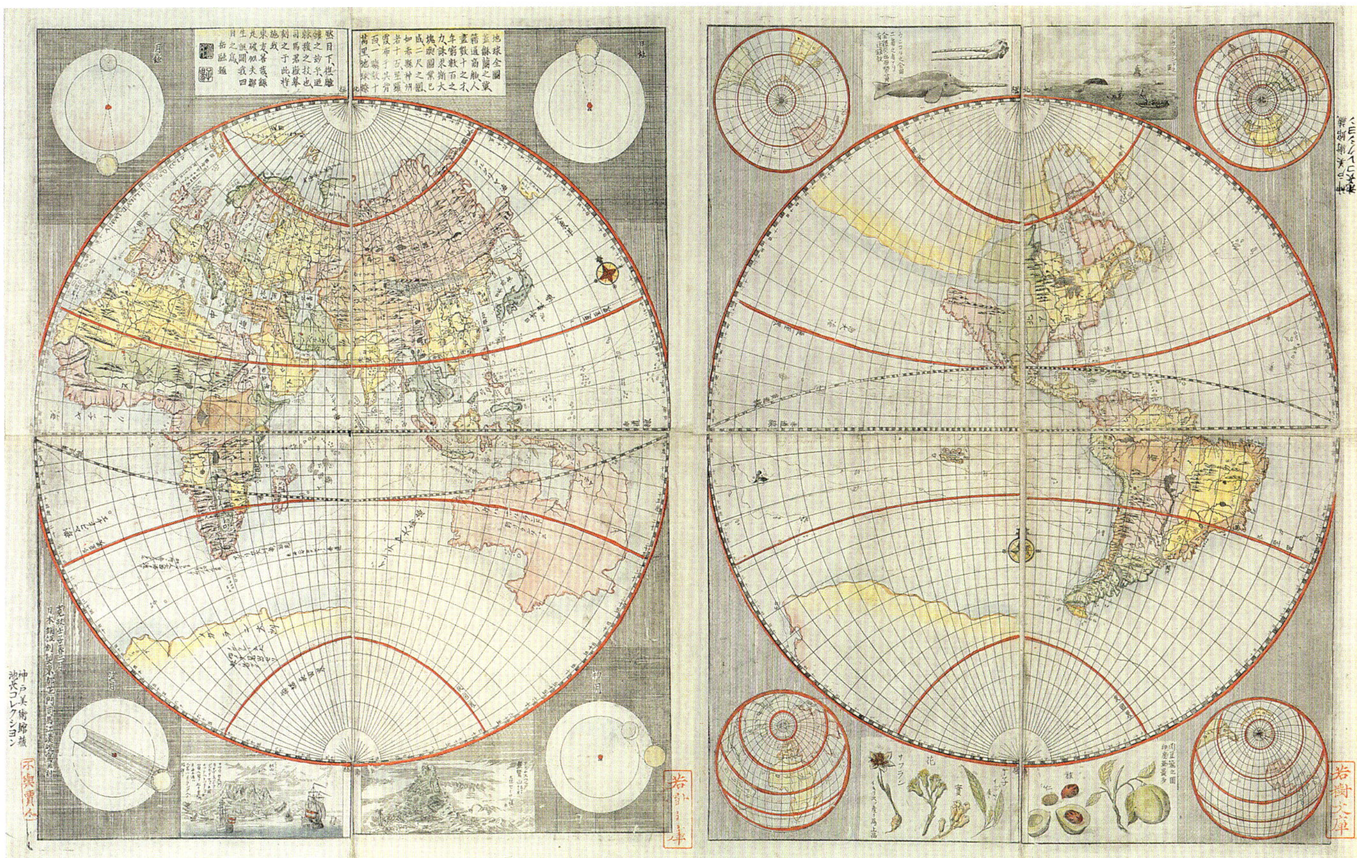

had completed the original map in 1810. His map fully embraced shogunal interests in drafting and cartographic methods while accurately reproducing geographic information. Kageyasu clearly indicated the American territory east of the Mississippi acquired via the Treaty of Paris in 1783. The names of a number of regions and cities are also found, demonstrating a heightened understanding of American geography. While there is no label for the United States of America, Takahashi's and Denzen's maps acknowledged the new political and social entities within North America.

The Japanese encountered Americans and America in a number of other instances prior to 1853. In 1803 Captain William Robert Stewart entered Nagasaki harbor in a ship flying an American flag and tried, unsuccessfully, to establish commercial relations with the Japanese. American whalers rescued a Japanese seaman, John Nakahama Manjirō, from the 1841 shipwreck of a Japanese fishing boat; Manjirō was taken to the United States and not returned to Japan until 1851. Other encounters include the shipwrecking or intended landing in Japan of the American Ranald MacDonald, who came to Rishiri Island at the north side of Hokkaidō in 1848, and the attempted opening of Japan by Commodore James Biddle, who in 1846 approached the Uraga Channel at the mouth of Edo harbor with the warships *Columbus* and *Vincennes* but was turned away. While these events were important in establishing contact, none was widely documented in Japan.

Although produced at the beginning of the nineteenth century, the *Shintei bankoku zenzu* was not widely available, most likely a consequence of its large size (46 × 78 inches) and reliance on the latest copperplate printing technology.[3] When Perry arrived in 1853, Kōkan's world maps, though indistinct and inaccurate, were still widely popular. In fact, the shogunal officers responsible for protecting Japan from the outside world still believed that America was an English colony. The Japanese perception of the United States in the mid-nineteenth century remained incomplete and unclear.

It was around this time that the outcome of the Opium War of 1840–42, fought between Great Britain and China, greatly affected how the Japanese regarded Europeans and Americans. The defeat of Chinese Qing forces and the humiliation of the Nanjing Treaty were conveyed to the shogunate through the *Betsudan fūsetsu gaki*. Almost immediately, the news filtered throughout Japanese society and created a heightened sense of danger and apprehension.

Awareness of the Opium War and its import for Japan grew further in 1849 with the publication in Japan of *Kaigai shinwa* (New Stories from Overseas) by Mineta Fūkō. It combined a detailed Chinese description of the war with Chinese and Western images. The shogunate immediately censored it, but a number of copies remained in circulation. The book and its illustrations, depicting pitched battles with foreign forces (plate 165a), significantly changed Japan's perception of its place in international relations and the balance of power between the East and the West.[4]

The many fine illustrations in *Kaigai shinwa*, besides conveying the horrors of the war, gave new information on recent Western technology including vessels such as the steamship, whose large smokestack and paddle wheel can be seen in one print (plate 165b). But even prior to the Opium War, the steamship began appearing in Japanese visual imagery. It is not clear how this early knowledge of the steamship was transmitted, but informal interactions with foreigners are thought to have played a part. For example, in 1838, the scholar and painter Watanabe Kazan (1793–1841), a serious student of Western learning, had an opportunity to meet with the director of the Dutch trading post, and from Kazan's record of their conversations, we know that steam engines and steamships were discussed. Whatever the impetus, by the 1830s, the steamship was appearing as a motif in ceramic ware (plate 166), and woodblock prints bearing the title *sutōmu bōto* (steamship) could be found. Interest in the steamship as a battleship grew in Japan after the Opium War and spread further through illustrations in publications such as *Kaigai shinwa*. A world map included in this book is of additional interest for the label "kyōwa seiji" visible on the American continent (plate 165c), a reference to the country's republican form of government.

The Opium War greatly affected China's perception of the world and differentiated the English, who were detested for their policies and practices, and the Americans, who were widely admired for their independence from England. Immediately after the war, in 1842, the Chinese historian and geographer Wei Yuan (J.: Gigen, 1794–1857) published *Haig guo tu zhi* (J.: *Kaikoku*

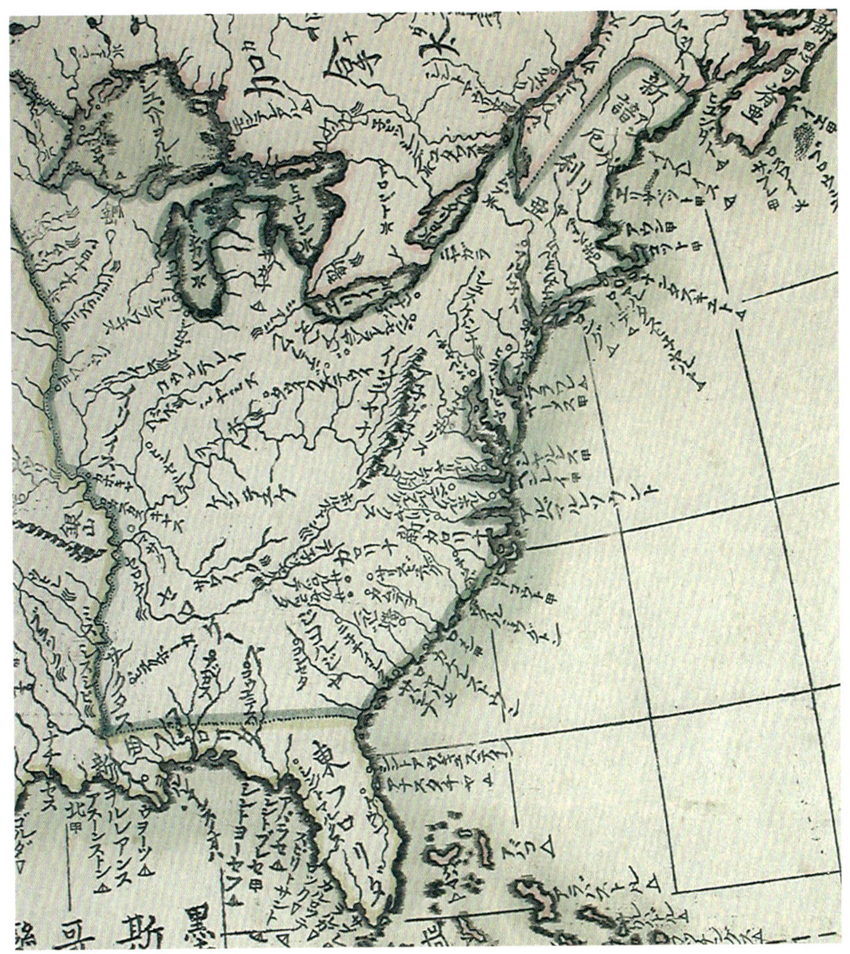

DETAIL
East Coast of America,
from *Shintei bankoku
zenzu* (plate 164)

PLATE 164
Aōdō Denzen
(Japanese, 1748–1822)
*Shintei bankoku
zenzu* (Newly
Revised Map
of the World)
c. 1816 (Bunka 13)
Etching: ink with
hand color on paper
45¼ × 77⅞ in.
(114.8 × 197.7 cm)

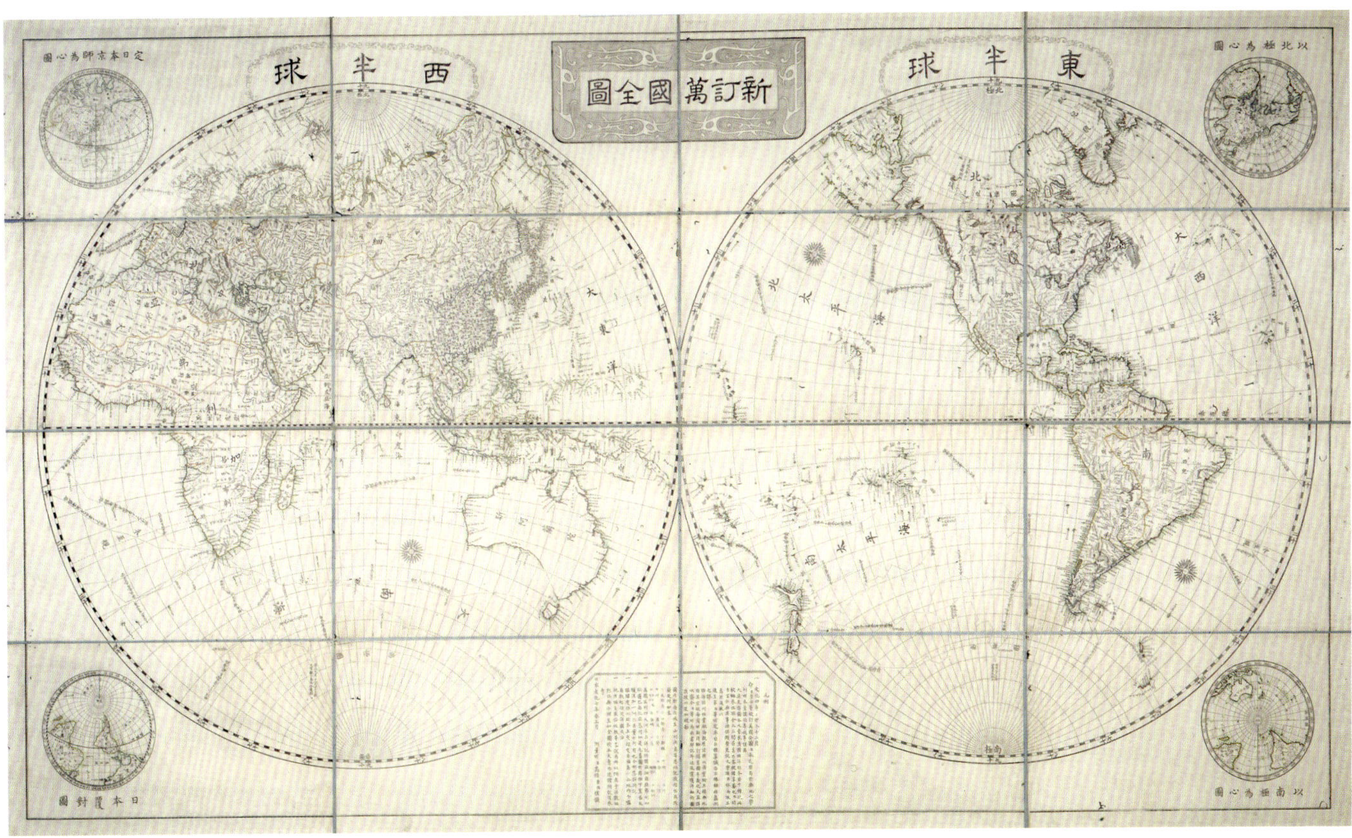

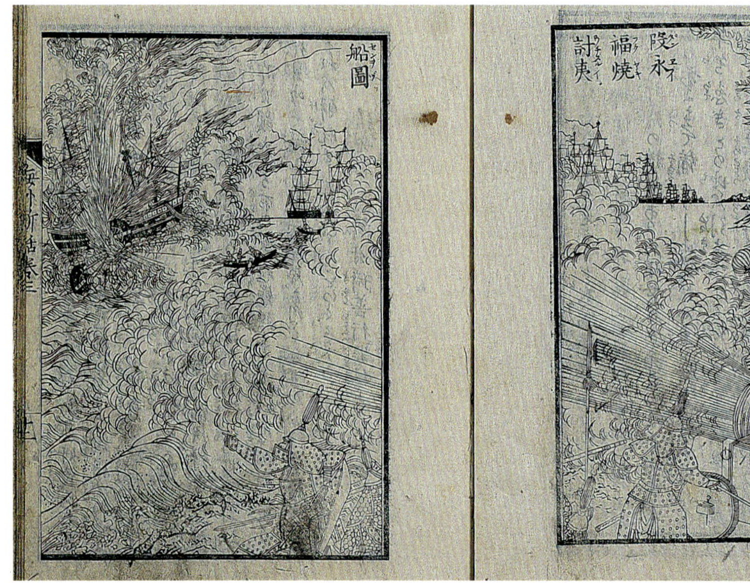

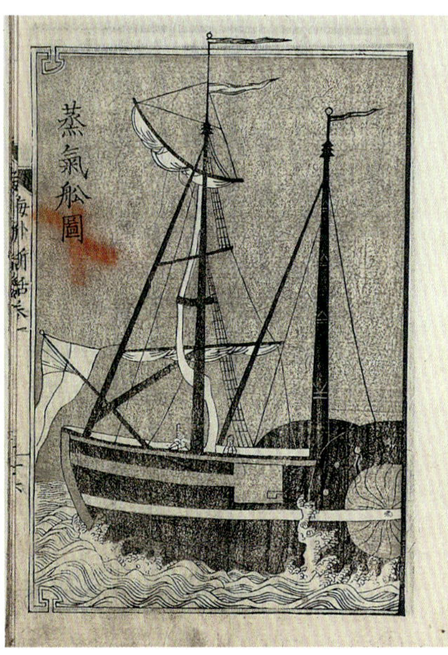

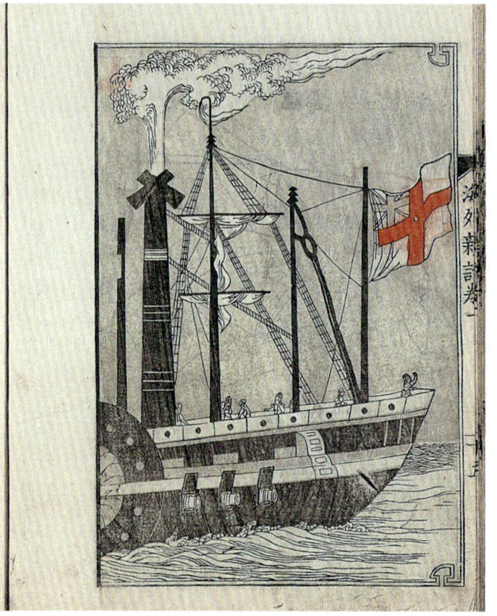

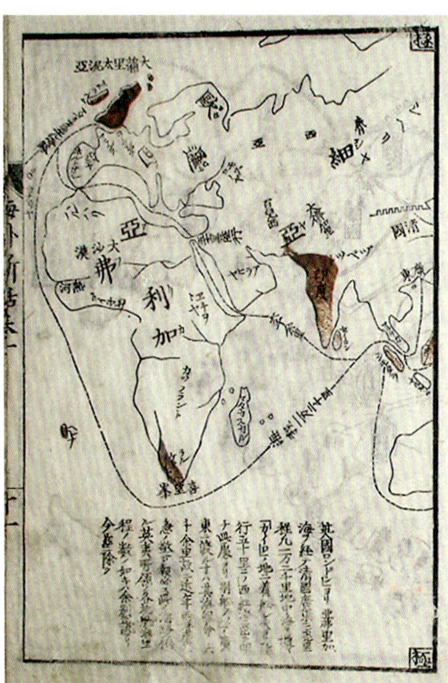

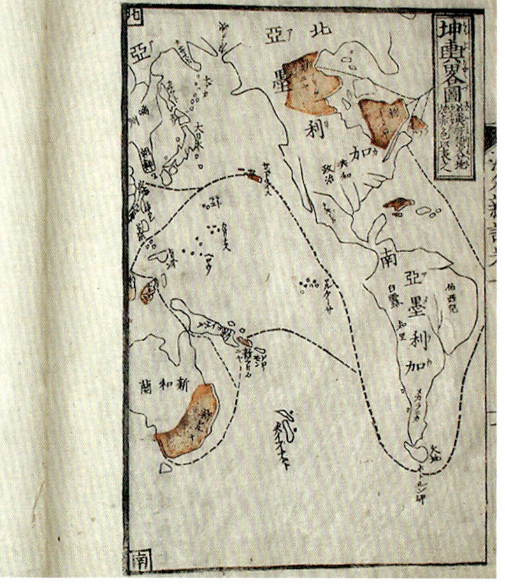

PLATE 165a–c
Japanese, unknown artist

Dan Eifuku isen wo yakiuchi suru zu
(Scene of Chinese Firing on British Ships)

Jōkisen zu
(Steamship)

Konyo ryakuzu
(Map of the World)
from Mineta Fūkō, *Kaigai shinwa*, Edo, 1849 (Kaei 2)
Five books bound in Japanese style
Woodblock prints: ink and color on paper
10¼ × 7⅛ in. (26 × 17.9 cm) at cover

202

zushi, Illustrated Gazetteer of the Maritime Countries). This influential work, which brought new attention to the threat of Western powers and issues of maritime defense, was brought to Japan by 1851. Written in Chinese, the text had a much more immediate impact than earlier reports about the Western world that had filtered into Japan via the *rangaku* scholars. It drastically changed Japanese awareness of the United States and its people. Whether or not informed by this work or others brought to Japan from China during the 1840s—most notably the *Kaigai shinwa*—from this time the Japanese clearly adjusted their perceptions of the United States and their response to it.

On July 12, 1853, the initial official diplomatic exchange between Japan and the United States was completed on the flagship *Susquehanna* in Uraga harbor. Kayama Eizaemon, a Japanese representative of the Uraga magistrate, participated in the proceedings. When he was shown a globe after the meeting, he pointed immediately to the locations of Washington and New York, apparently knowing that these were the two largest cities in the United States. He quickly identified a number of European countries and locations as well.[5] Kayama's party inspected the ship's steam technology, guns and muskets, and some daguerreotypes.[6]

During the initial meeting, an American official commented that the Japanese were "not only well-bred, but not ill-educated."[7] This positive affect of the Japanese was important in facilitating negotiations and encouraged the Americans to respond accordingly, leading to the successful signing of a treaty of peace and cooperation. In many respects, the information about the United States that the Japanese had gradually attained over a half-century of contact had prepared them for this historic moment.

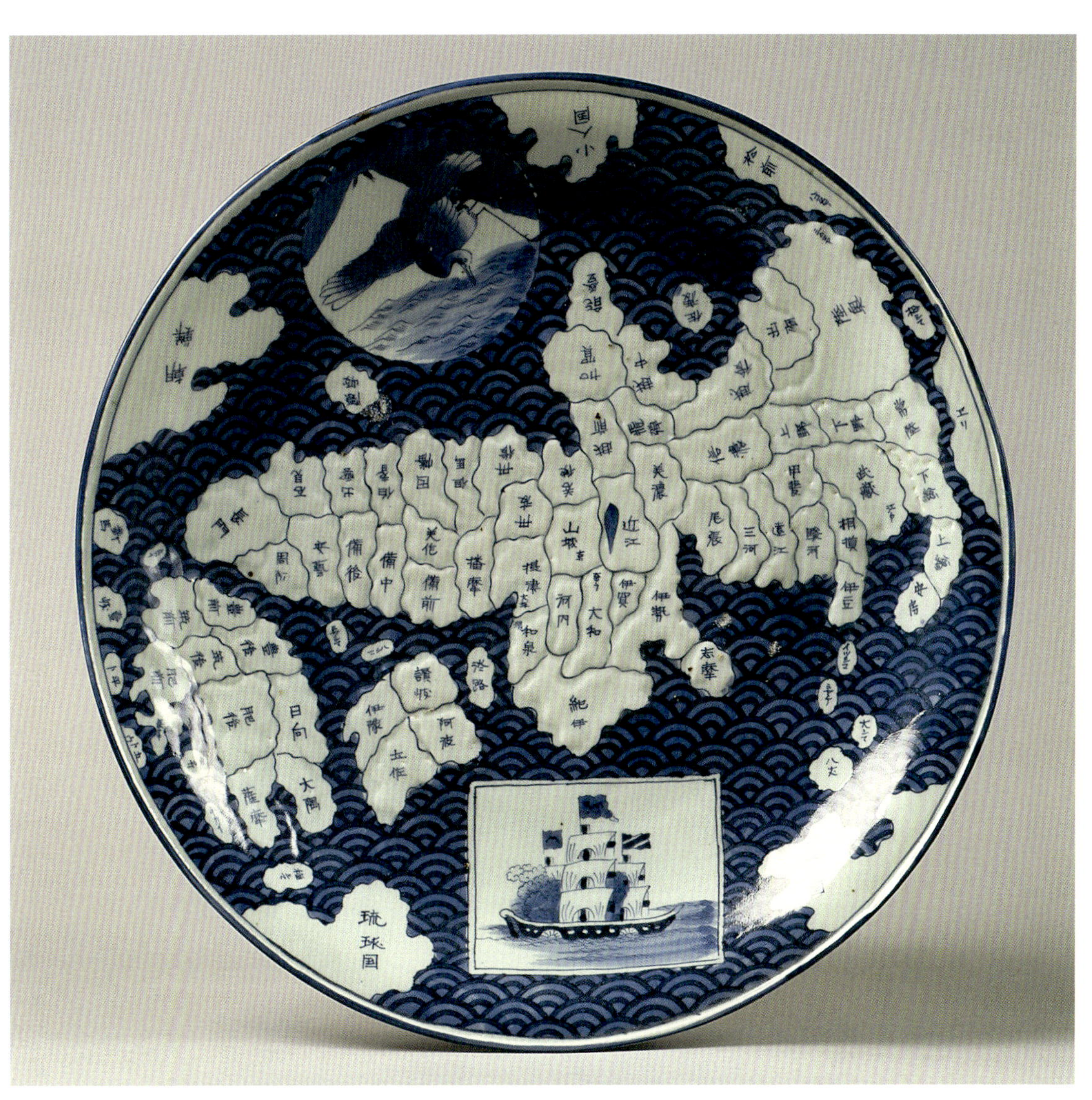

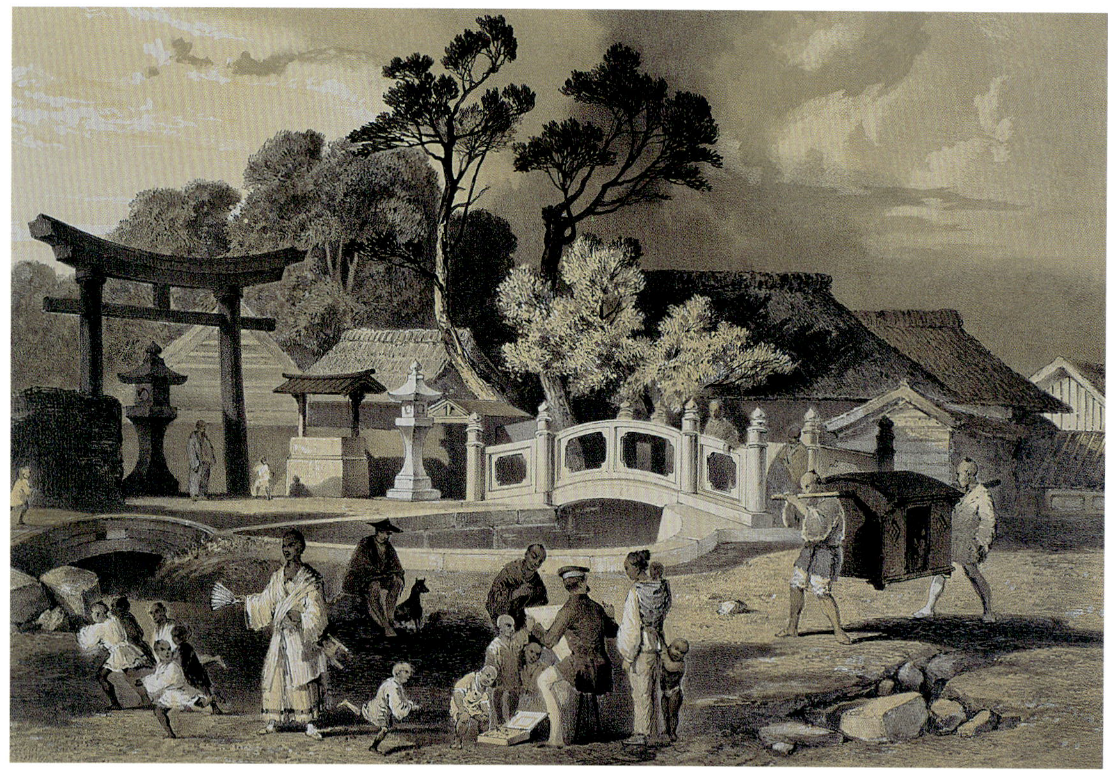

PLATE 167a,b
Wilhelm Heine
(German, 1827–1885)
Bridge at Shimoda

**Graveyard and
Temple at Shimoda**
from *Graphic Scenes
in the Japan Expedition*,
New York, 1856
Lithographs:
ink and color on paper
14⅞ × 20⅜ in.
(37.6 × 51.5 cm) page

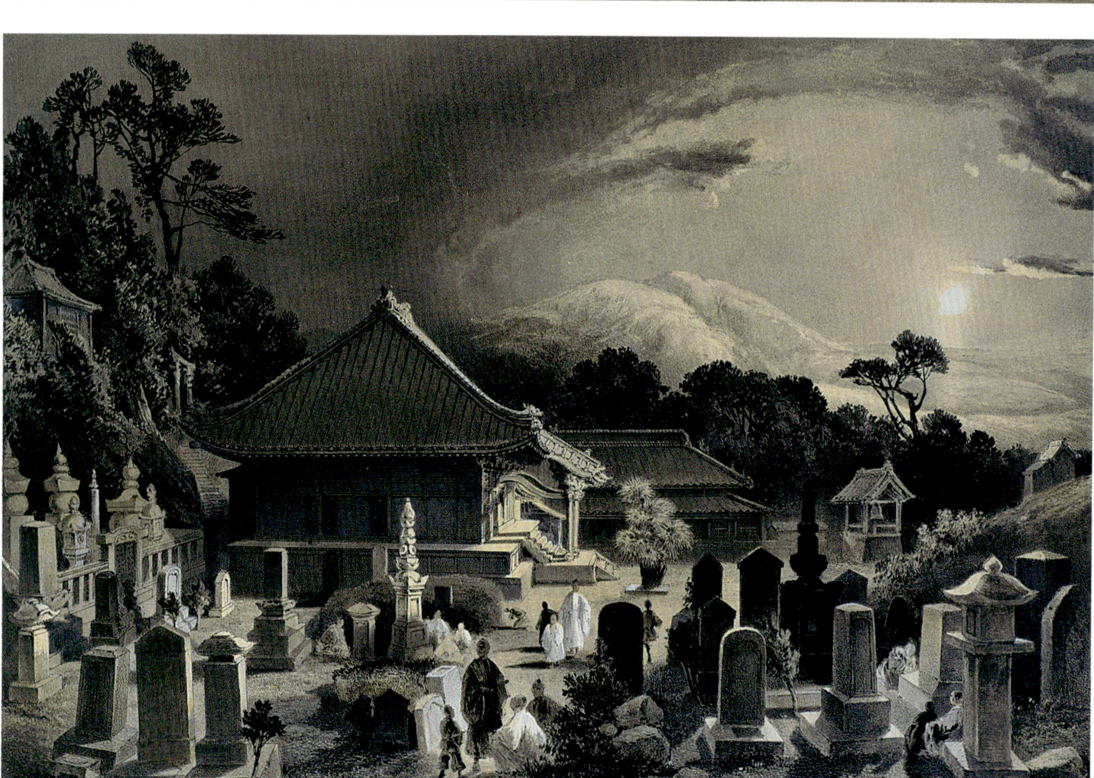

Japanese Reaction to Perry's Visit

The news that American ships had anchored in Japanese waters in 1853 quickly spread throughout the city of Edo and beyond. People regarded the visit as an extraordinary occurrence, different from earlier events or shipwrecks involving foreign peoples. Some Japanese were wary of the Americans, but most were curious about them, their culture, and the technology they brought with them. S. Wells Williams, an American interpreter, wrote in his diary that he found the Japanese extremely hospitable. He noted that many local Japanese in smaller launches and boats attempted to examine the American steamships more closely even as Japanese officials warned them to keep away. In general, Williams gives the impression that the Japanese were a good-natured people who were ruled by cowardly authorities.[8]

A view of the Japanese who attempted to gain a closer glimpse of the Perry fleet is captured in the handscroll *Bakumatsu fūzoku zukan* (Genre Scenes of the Last Days of the Tokugawa Regime,

plate 168a–g). The scroll provides a clear idea of the visual scene in and around Edo and Yokohama during the time of Perry's second visit in 1854. In one charmingly casual scene, the artist illustrated individuals of all social backgrounds and ages at the shore's edge as they jockey for a better view of ships in a harbor (plate 168a). In another scene (plate 168b), a man attempts to climb over a barrier, mocking an official sign that warns "it is forbidden to observe the foreign ships" (isen kenbutsu muyō). The festive mood of the citizenry is contrasted by the guarded poses of the samurai, who are ready to charge forward on horseback to protect their country (plate 168c).

At least one controversial incident may have sparked the ire of those guards. In an episode described in Perry's expedition narrative, the Japanese and Americans were both taken aback to find that curiosity had propelled E. C. Bittinger, the chaplain on the steamer *Susquehanna*, to set out on foot toward Edo.[9] Perry summoned him back in some alarm. A popularized Japanese version of Bittinger's foray describes the chaplain as

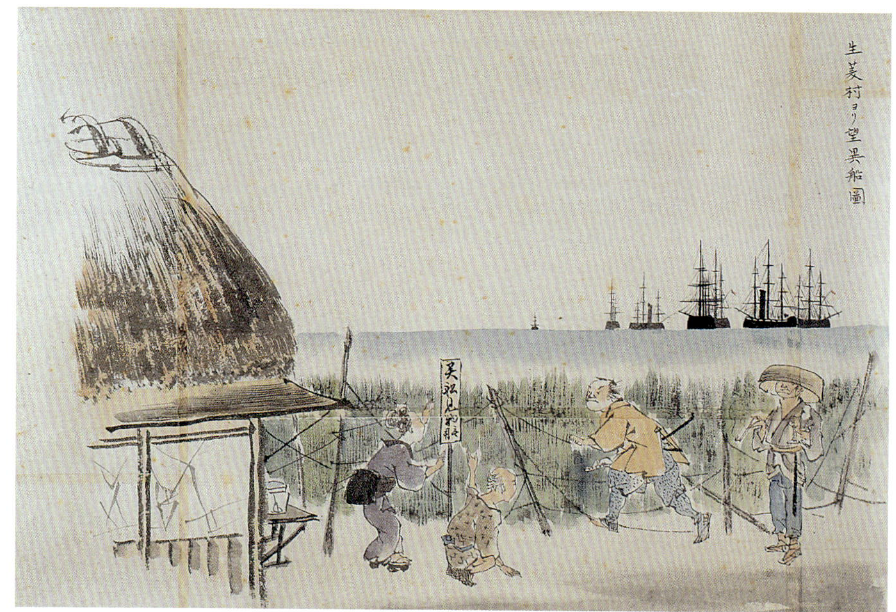

PLATE 168b
*Namamugimura
yori isen wo nozomu
zu* (Viewing the
Black Ships from
Namamugi Village,
Kanagawa)

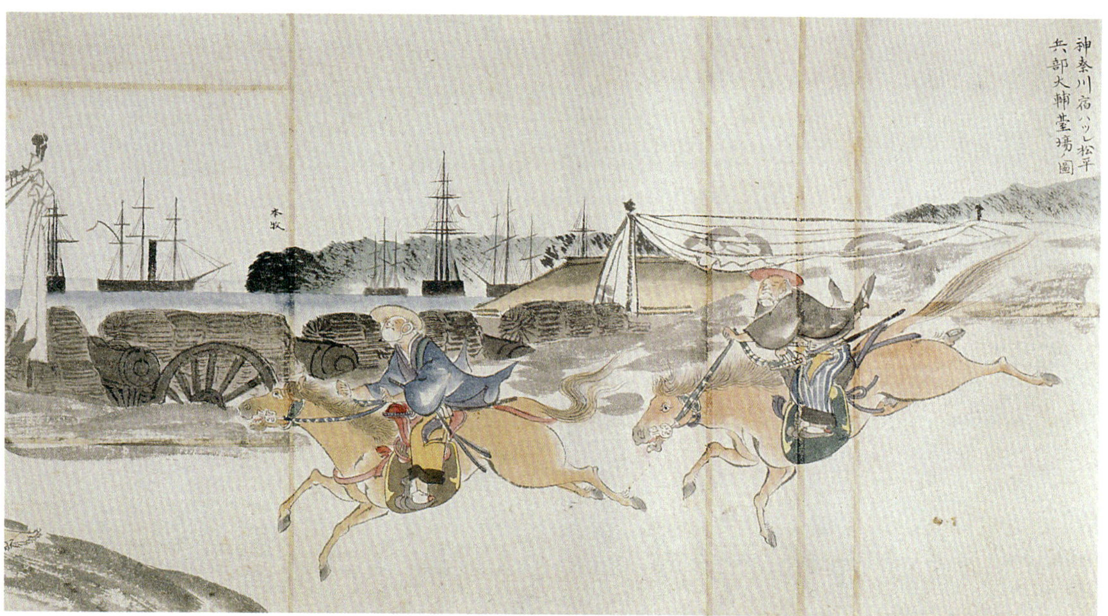

PLATE 168c
*Kanagawa shuku
hazure Matsudaira
hyōbudayū daiba
no zu* (Fortress
Managed by Military
Officer Matsudaira,
from Kanagawa Station)

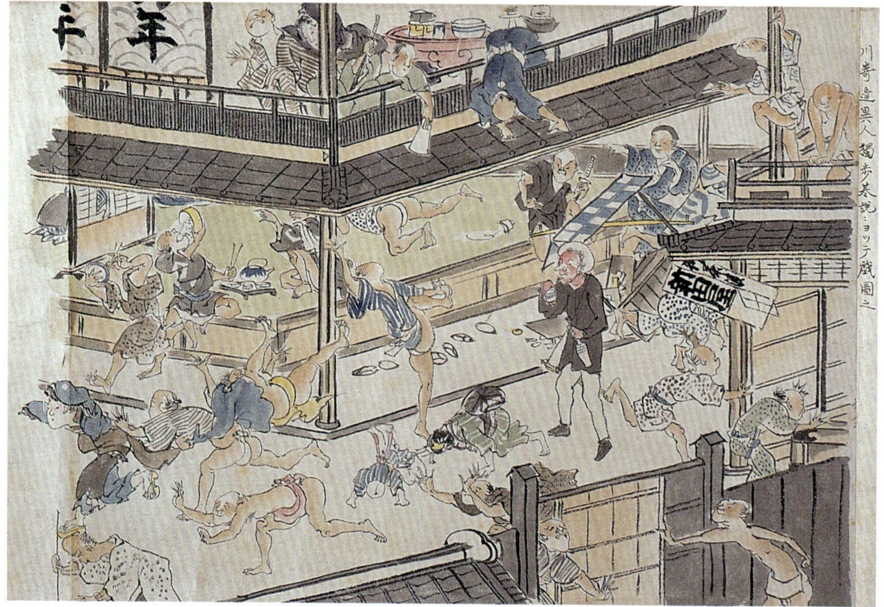

PLATE 168d
*Kawasaki atari
ijin doppo no
kōsetsu niyotte kore wo
gizu su* (Caricature Based
on a Rumor of Drunken
Chaplain Bittinger Stag-
gering around Kawasaki
Town)

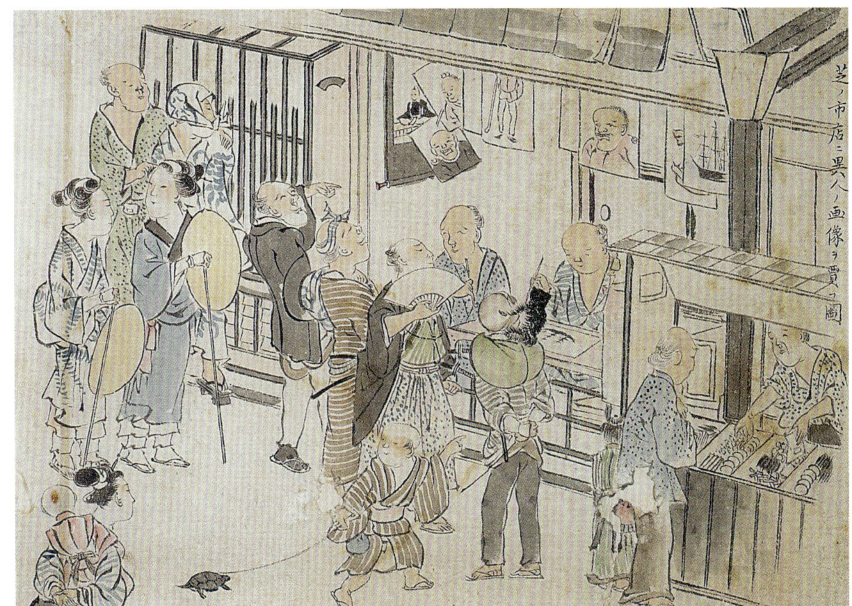

PLATE 168e
Shiba no ichi mise ni ijin no gazō wo kau zu (Purchasing Portraits of Foreigners at Market in Shiba)

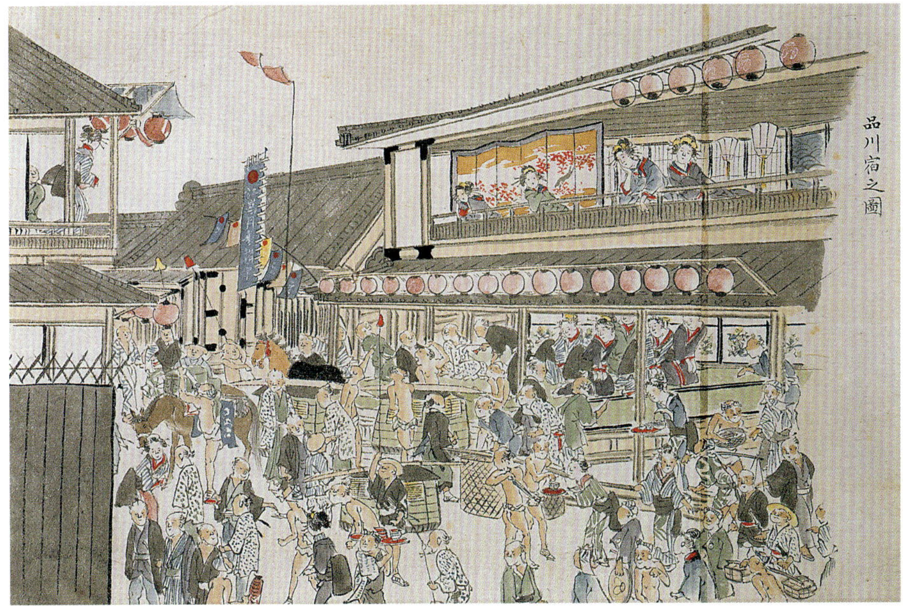

PLATE 168f
Shinagawajuku no zu (Shinagawa Station)

staggering on his way, drunk and with sake bottle in hand. The illustration of this hearsay account in *Bakumatsu fūzoku zukan* conjures an innocent stranger more than a threatening or frightful intruder (plate 168d).

The people of Edo, inspired by their encounter with the Americans, showed unusual ingenuity and business sense. Shinagawa Station at the southern entrance to Edo teemed with traffic moving toward Yokohama (plate 168f). Japanese merchants and artists quickly took advantage of the popularity and spectacle of the American visit and began producing souvenirs and themed goods such as those portrayed in the *Bakumatsu fūzoku zukan,* where portraits and straw dolls of the foreigners and prints of their ships can be seen for sale in a stall on a shopping street (plate 168e). These products were clearly intended as popular merchandise to catch the public fancy.

Other depictions of the Americans seem to reflect the easy attitude of the shogunate toward the visitors. In the woodblock print and sketch *Amerikajin shinsha* (Portraits of Two Americans, plate 169a,b), Perry and Captain Henry A. Adams take on devil-like personas, but they do not inspire fear. *Ukiyo-e* prints—mass-produced, popular, and affordable—were particularly well suited for expressing official sentiment. The portraits of the two Americans appear to have been produced as part of an album immediately after Perry's fleet returned in 1854. Included with them were lists of crew members on each warship and gifts offered to the Japanese shogunate. Perry's second visit, the text describes, came about because the American people thought so highly of Japanese virtue that they returned bearing gifts as tribute from a vassal country.

The *Bakumatsu fūzoku zukan* illustrates the impressive range of gifts that Perry's fleet gave to the shogunate (plate 168g) Among the presents carried to Edo Castle at the settlement of the treaty between the United States and Japan

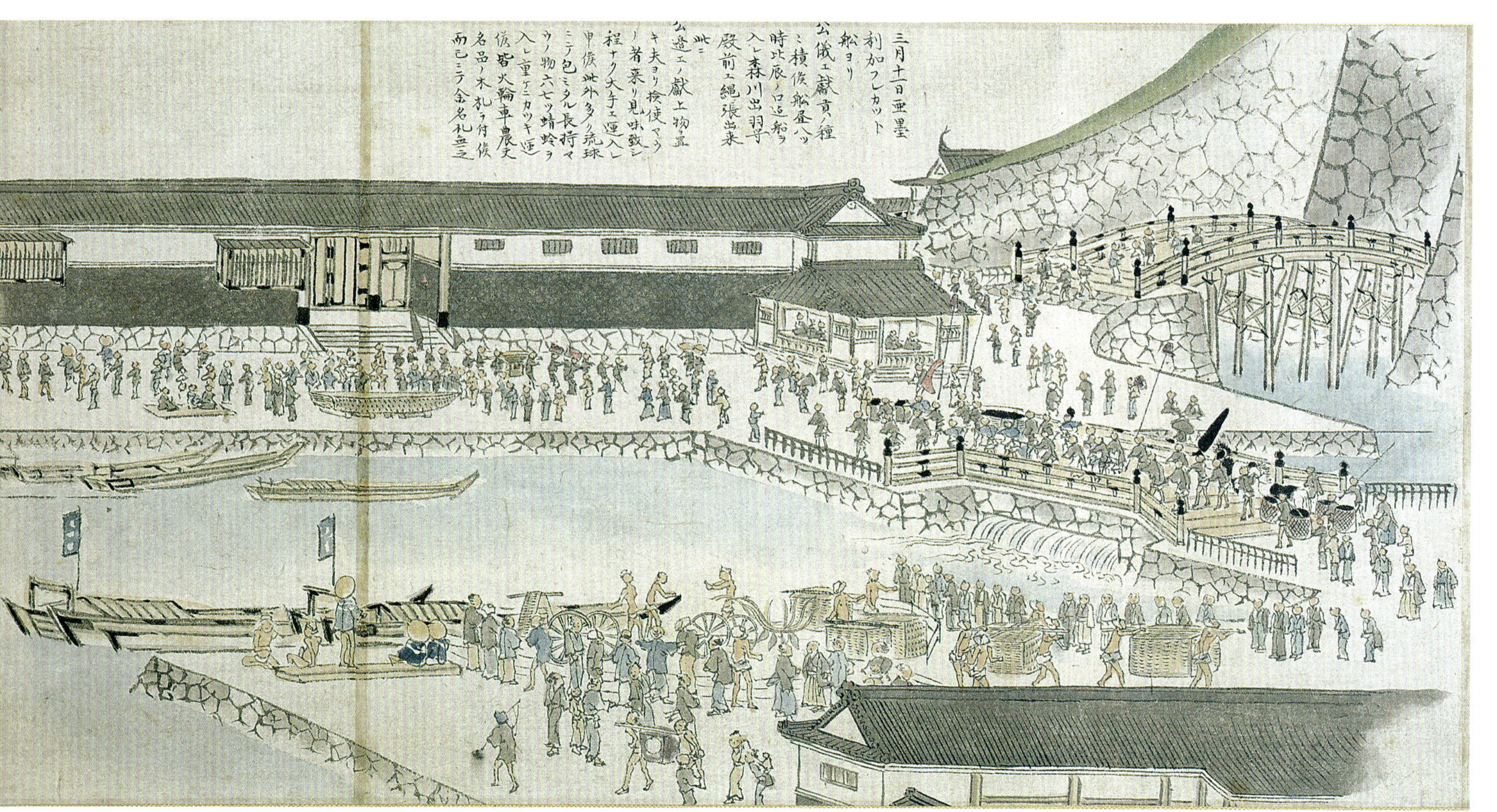

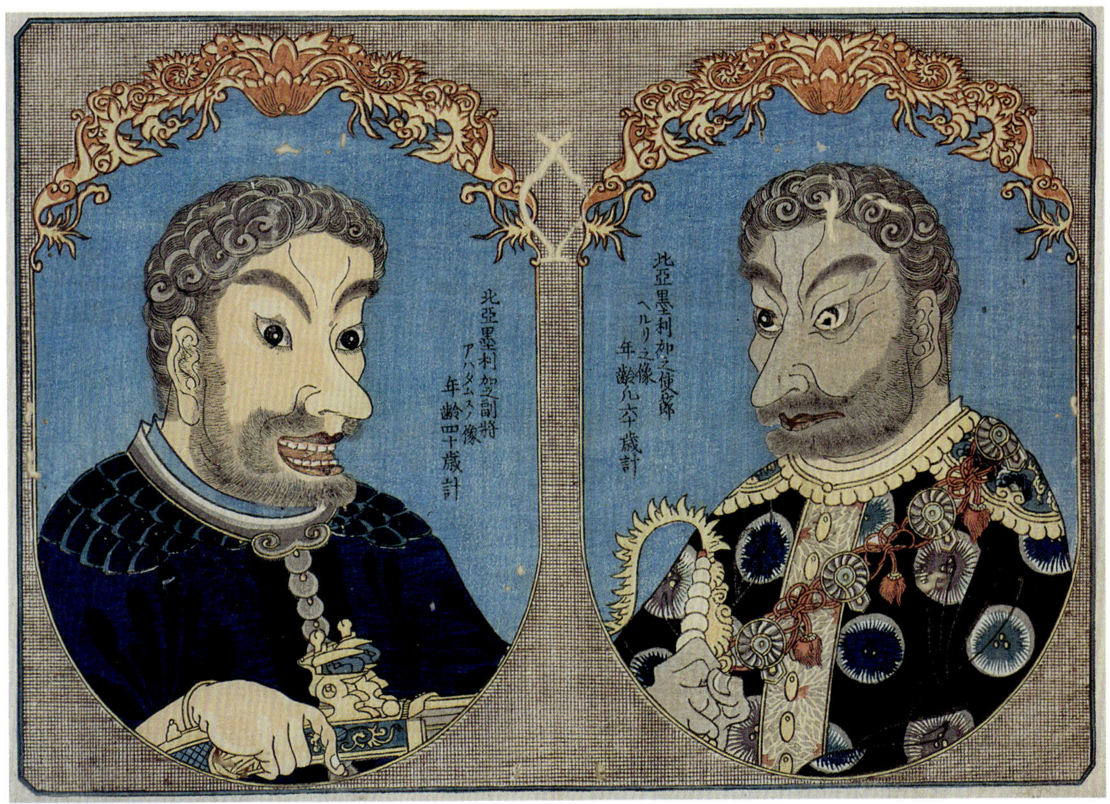

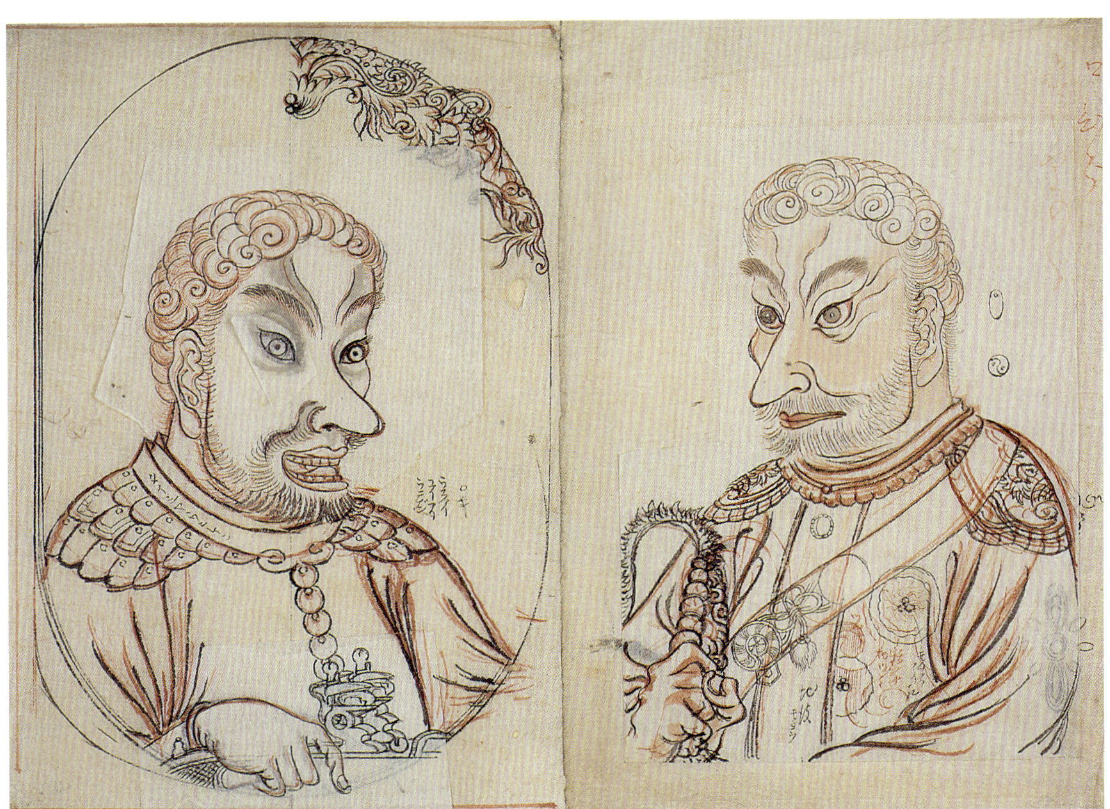

PLATE 169a,b
Attributed to Hasegawa
Sadanobu
(Japanese, 1809–1879)
"Amerikajin shinsha"
Peruri no zō /
Ahadamusu no zō
(M. C. Perry / Henry A.
Adams, from
"Portraits of Two
Americans")
published by Inda Rōzō
1850s
Album with woodblock
prints and sketch: ink
and color on paper
6½ × 9⅜ in.
(16.5 × 23.7 cm) each

were a miniature steam locomotive, a working telegraph system, and lithographic images of the Mexican-American War. The Americans clearly gave such objects to express the advanced state of their civilization, military power, and technology. The implications of the presents could not be fully appreciated by everyday Japanese, who were unaware of circumstances overseas.

After Perry's return in 1854, events in Japan developed and changed quickly. The conclusion of the 1858 Treaty of Amity and Commerce between the United States and Japan intensified the conflict between supporters and opponents of the *sakoku* exclusionist measures. In 1859 Yokohama harbor was opened to foreign trade, and the last of the artwork featuring exoticized Westerners or Western objects—commonly called Yokohama prints (*Yokohama ukiyo-e*)—were produced.

The Yokohama prints showed in great detail the vibrant activity of the new international port and the foreigners living there. *Ukiyo-e* artists and publishers may have been catering to public demand but one cannot rule out government pressure on these same artists and publishers to emphasize the benefits of overturning *sakoku* policies and supporting new relations with the West.

Many Yokohama prints went beyond reality and into the realm of fantasy. In a number of works that name major cities in Western countries, the scenes are of faraway places with imaginary or utopian qualities. Steamships, locomotives, and hot air balloons fill these advanced and idealized lands (plates 171, 172). In one example, the Japanese artist Utagawa Yoshikazu (act. 1848–54) simply appropriated a southern European location from an image published in the *Illustrated London*

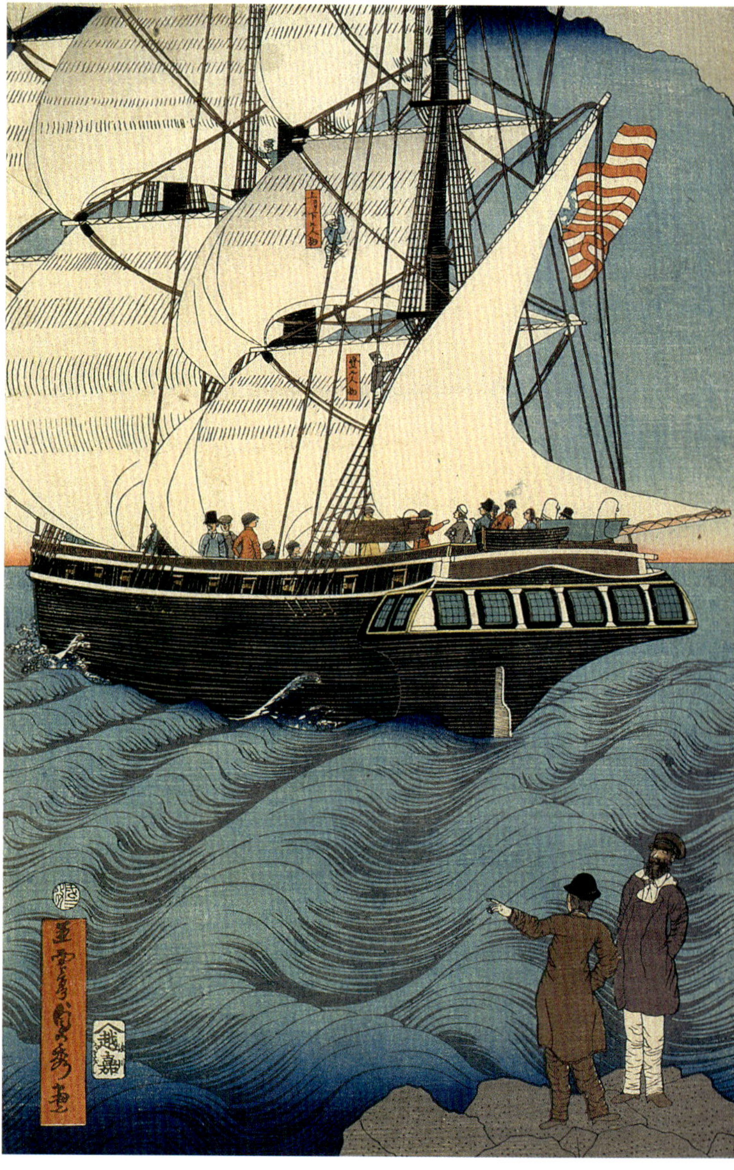

PLATE 170
Gountei Sadahide
(Japanese, 1807–1879?)
*Amerika Kari-
foruniakō shuppan
no zu* (Scene of
Departing Ship,
Port of California)
Published by Chōki
1862 (Bunkyū 2)
Ō-ban woodblock
triptych: ink and color
on paper
14⅞ × 30¼ in.
(37.7 × 76.6 cm)

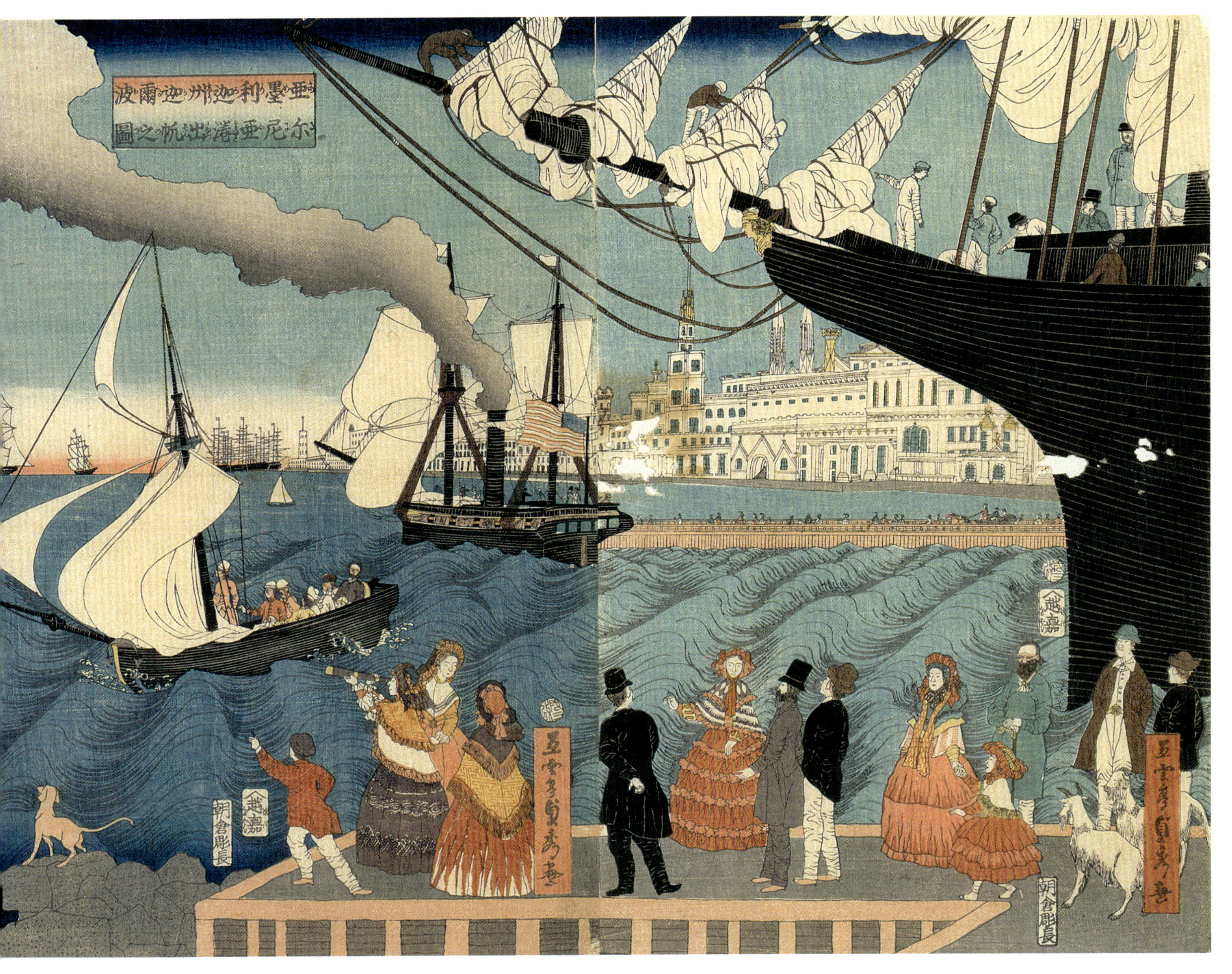

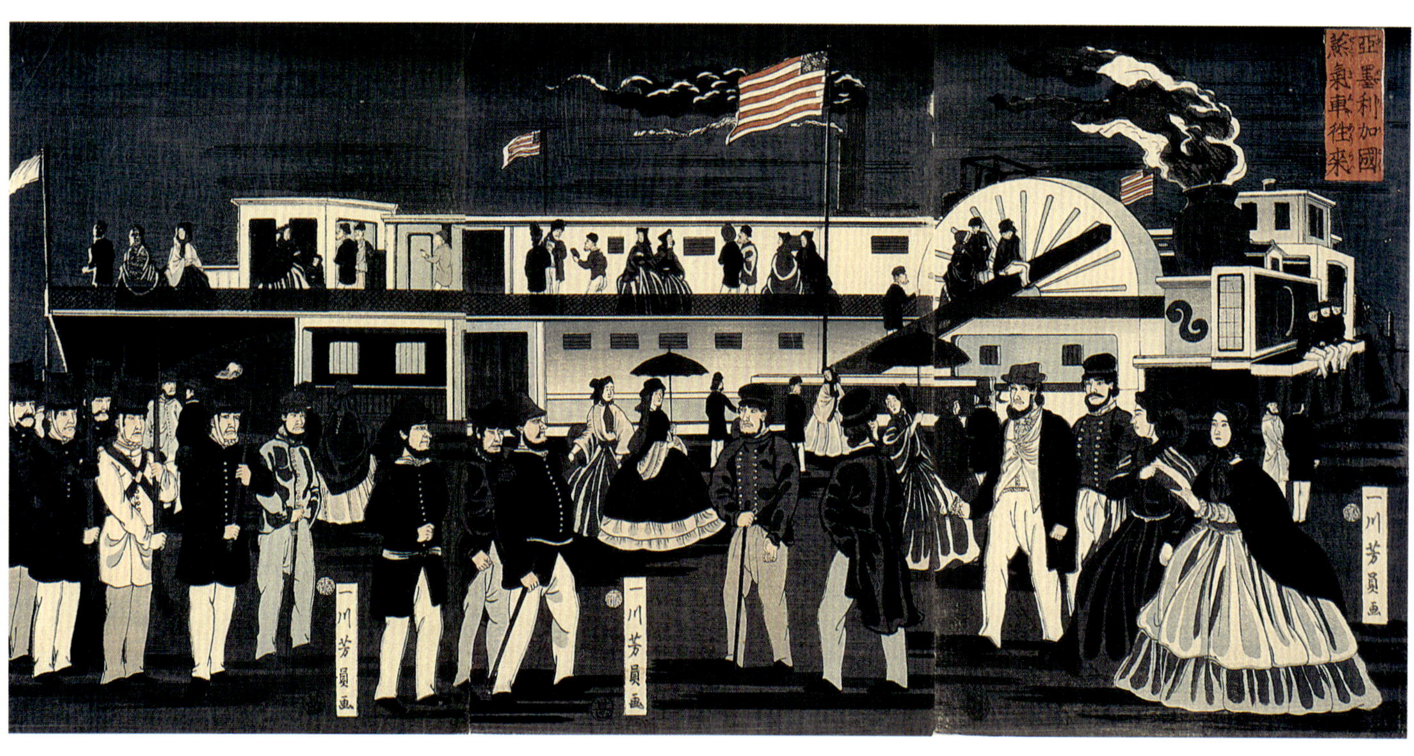

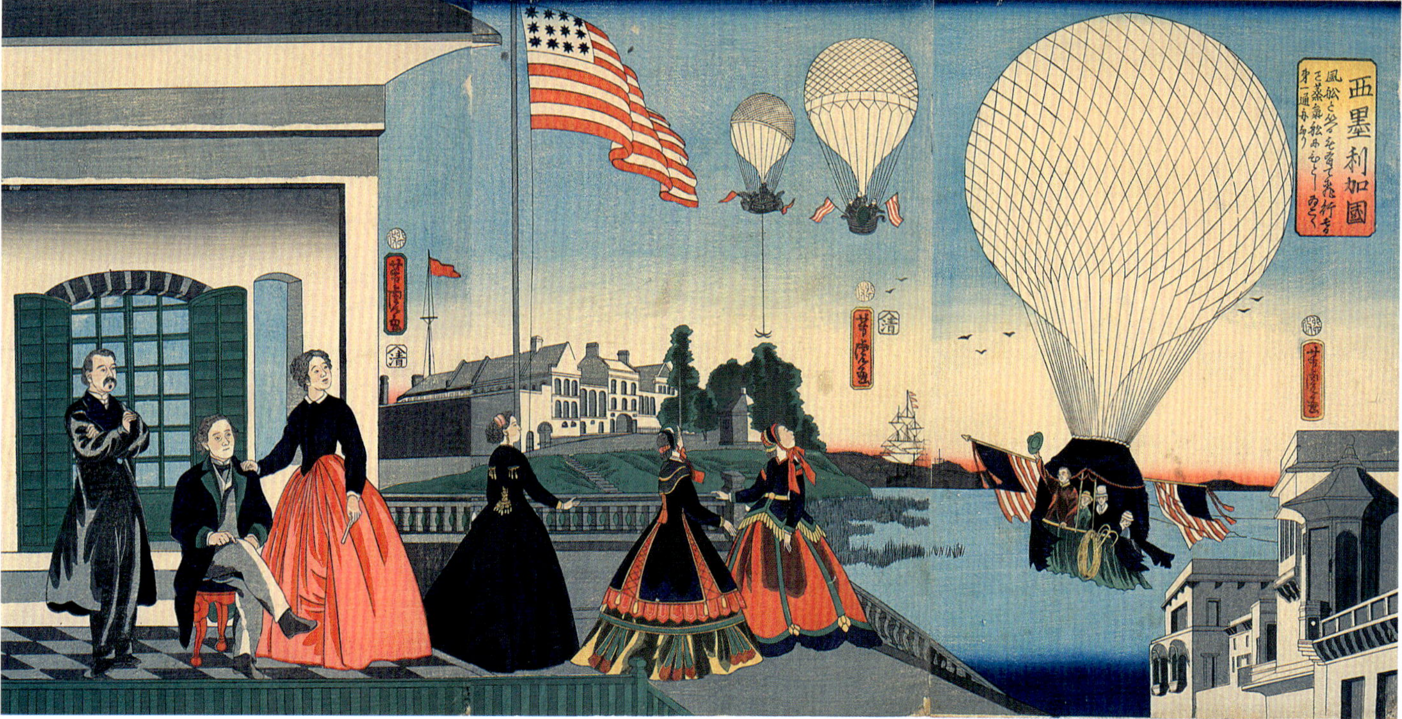

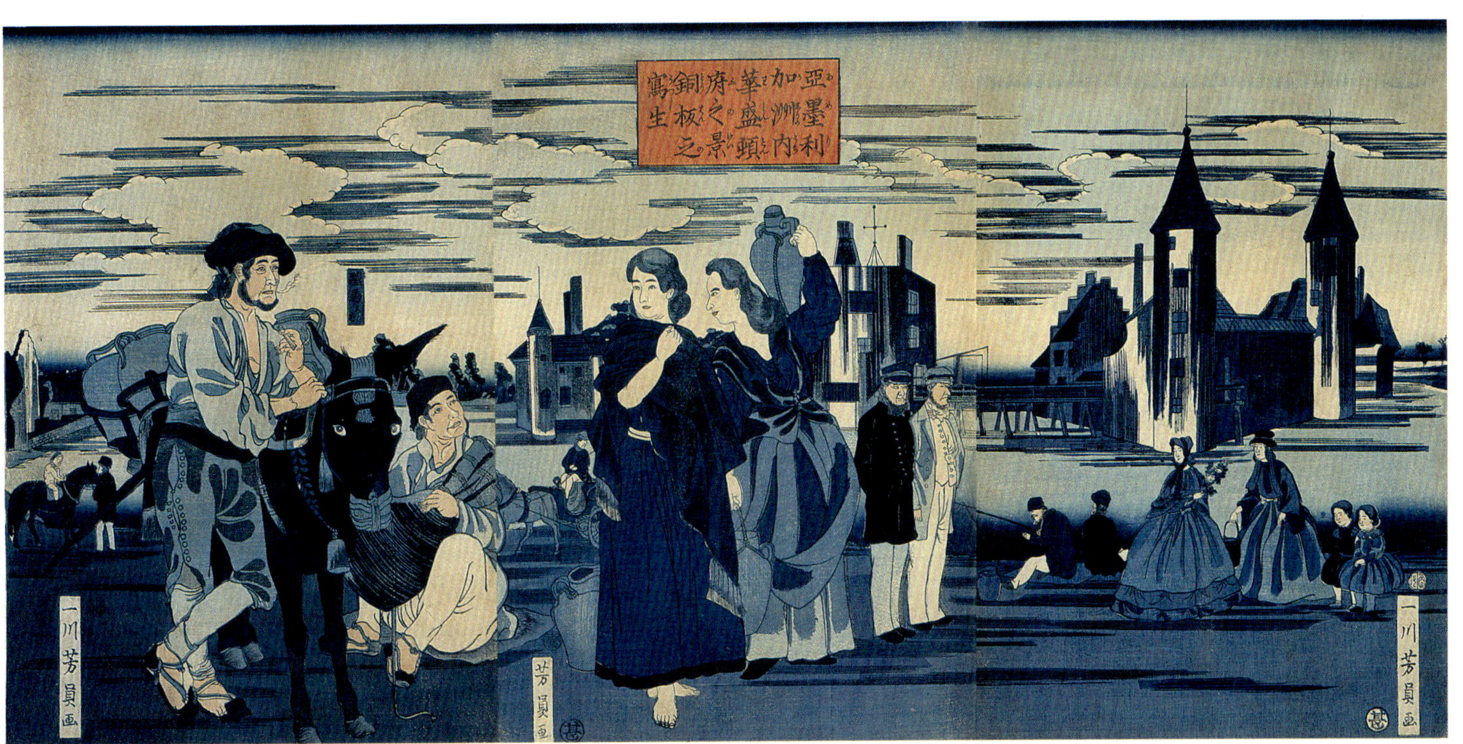

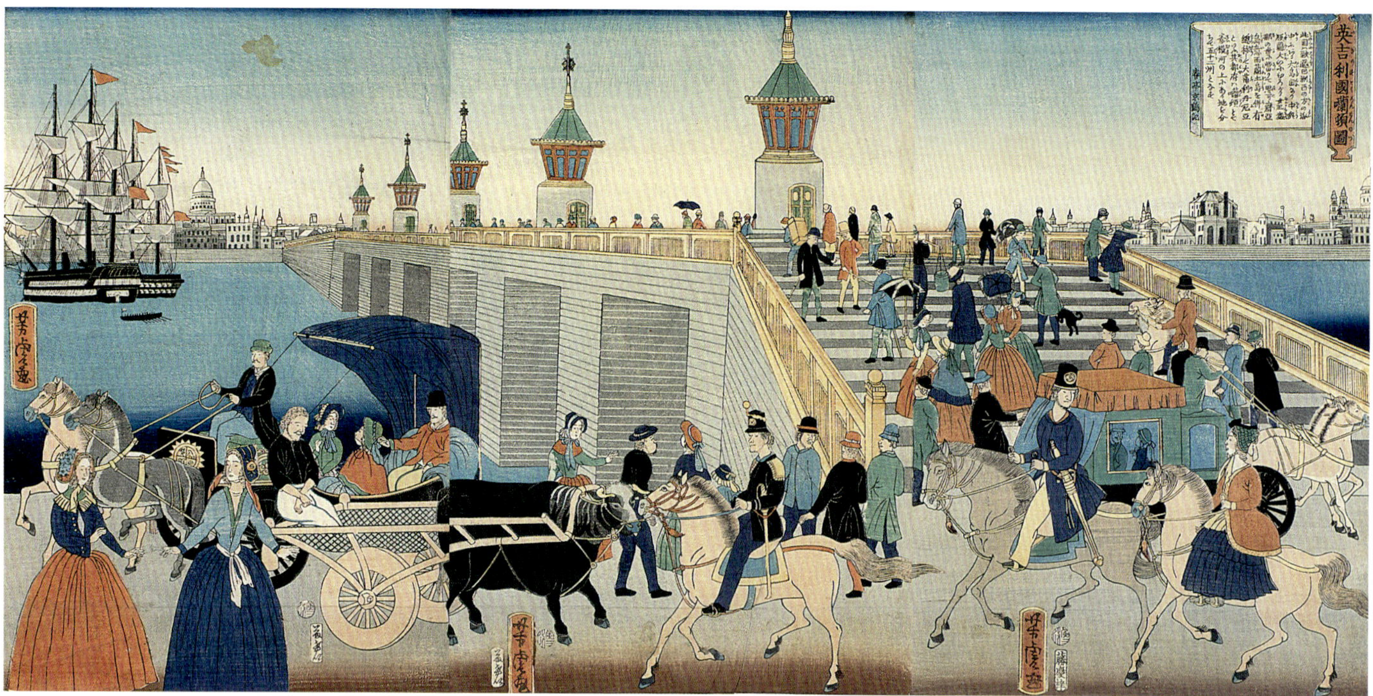

News to create a view of what he called Washington, D.C. (plate 173). While America had gained a place in the Japanese popular consciousness by the middle of the nineteenth century, much about it remained misunderstood and misinterpreted.

In Yokohama prints, such fantastical or misguided representations of foreign lands and peoples were not limited to images of the United States or the American people. In one image of Paris, the city was portrayed as a port. Views of England and London (plate 174), however, were executed with little exaggeration or error. This accuracy can perhaps be attributed to the greater familiarity the Japanese had with the British, who had a majority presence in the expatriate community in Yokohama at the time and enjoyed the largest trading volume with the Japanese.

The seaman William Cleveland had made some pointed observations and criticisms of the Dutch and their handling of information when he visited Nagasaki only a half-century earlier in 1800. Perhaps the British, the dominant players in trade and society in Yokohama, had a part in manipulating information in their era. In the Yokohama prints, it is clear that a degree of misrepresentation was at play, especially in how the British and the Americans were portrayed.

Japanese exposure to the outside world was not limited to what could be seen in the Yokohama prints. As the nineteenth century progressed, the Japanese people themselves were permitted to travel abroad, and, in doing so, they formed their own perceptions of the larger world. Their contacts and encounters contributed to a new perception of Japan's place in the global community and its relationship with other peoples and nations.

NOTES

1. Kontonkai/Kimura Kenkadō Kenshōkai, ed. *Kimura Kenkadō raikanshū senjin kyūkō shotoku* (Osaka: Nakaoshōsendō Shoten/Izumi Shoin, 2004), 105, 244.

2. Kanai Madoka, *A Diary of William Cleveland, Captain's Clerk on Board the Massachusetts,* Institute of Asian Studies monograph series no. 1 (Quezon City: University of the Philippines, 1965): 20 (July 22).

3. For general information about *Shintei bankoku zenzu* in English, see Ayusawa Shintarō, "The Types of World Map Made in Japan's Age of National Isolation," *Imago Mundi* 10 (1953): 123–27.

4. See Bob Tadashi Wakabayashi, "Opium, Expulsion, Sovereignty: China's Lessons for Bakumatsu Japan," *Monumenta Nipponica* 47, no. 1 (spring 1992): 1–25.

5. Matthew Perry, *Narrative of the Expedition of an American Squadron to China Seas and Japan, Performed in the Years 1852, 1853, and 1854,* ed. Francis L. Hawks (New York: Appleton, 1857), 286 (July 12, 1853).

6. S. Wells Williams, "A Journal of the Perry Expedition to Japan (1853–1854)," in *Transactions of the Asiatic Society of Japan* 37, part 2 (1910): 56–57.

7. Perry, *Narrative,* 286.

8. Williams, "Journal," 158–59 (April 6, 1854); 111–12 (February 24, 1854); and 137 (March 15, 1854).

9. The Bittinger incident was related in both American and Japanese documents; see for instance, Perry, *Narrative,* 359–61.

REFERENCES

Fune no Kagakukan, *Kurofune raikō, Fune no kagakukan shiryō guido* no. 4, 2nd ed. (Tokyo: Nihon kaiji kagaku Shinkōzaidan Fune no Kagakukan, 2005).

Hora Tomio, trans., *Perry Nihon ensei zuikōki,* Shin ikoku sōsho, vol. 8 (Tokyo: Yūshōdō Shuppan, 1970).

Ikokue no bōken—kinsei Nihon bijutsu ni miru jōhō to gensō, exh. cat. (Kobe: Kobe City Museum, 2001).

Iwashita Tetsunori, *Edo jōhō ron* (Tokyo: Hokuju Shuppan, 2000).

———, *Yokoku sareteita Perry raikō to bakumatsu jōhō sensō* (Tokyo: Yōsensha, 2006).

Kanai Madoka, "Kansei 9 nen Amerika yōsen Iraiza gō shodo no Nagasaki raikō," in *Annual Report of the Historiographical Institute,* Tokyo University, No. 12, 1977.

———, trans., "Kansei 12 nen (1800) beisen Massachūsettsu gō Nippon Nagasaki taizai nikki," *Yōgaku,* no. 1 (1993).

———, trans., *Perry Nihon ensei nikki,* Shin ikoku sōsho, vol. 2–1 (Tokyo: Yūshōdō Shuppan, 1985).

Kurofune—Perry raikō 150 shūnen kinen, exh. cat. (Yokohama: Kanagawa Prefectural Museum of Cultural History, 2003).

Nichibei kōryū no akebono, exh. cat. (Tokyo: Edo-Tokyo Museum, 1999).

Nichiran Gakkai and Hōsei Rangaku Kenkyūkai, *Oranda fūsetsugaki shūsei,* 2 vols. (Tokyo: Yoshikawa Kōbunkan, 1977–79).

Perry raikō to Yokohama, exh. cat. (Yokohama: Yokohama Kaikō Shiryōkan, 2004).

Qian Guohong, *Nihon to Chōgoku ni okeru "seiyō" no hakken: 19 seiki nicchū chishikijin no sekaizō no keisei* (Tokyo: Yamakawa Shuppansha, 2004).

Sayama Kazuo, *Waga na wa Kendorikku* (Tokyo: Kōdansha, 1991).

Tsukahara Akira, "Kansei 10 nen no Shiba Kōkan," in *Sasaki Gōzō sensei koki kinen ronshū—Nihon bijutsu zatsukō* (Tokyo: Meitoku Shuppan, 1998).

Yokohama Kaikō Shiryōkan and Yokohama Kyoryūchi Kenkyūkai, eds., *Yokohama kyoryūchi to ibunka kōryū* (Tokyo: Yamakawa Shuppansha, 1996).

Further Reading

Ayers, John, O. R. Impey, and J. V. G. Mallet. *Porcelain for Palace: The Fashion for Japan in Europe, 1650–1750*. London: Oriental Ceramic Society, 1990.

Beukers, Harmen. *The Mission of Hippocrates to Japan: The Contribution of Philipp Franz von Siebold*. Amsterdam: Foundation Four Centuries of Netherlands–Japan Relations, 1997.

Blussé, Leonard Williem Remmelink, and Ivo Smits, eds. *Bridging the Divide: 400 Years, The Netherlands–Japan*. Leiden: Hotei Publishing; Hilversum: Teleac/NOT, 2000.

Bruijn, Max de, ed. *Sawasa: Japanese Export Art in Black and Gold, 1650–1800*. Amsterdam: Rijksmuseum; Amsterdam/Zwolle: Waanders, 1998.

Campbell, Tony. *Japan: European Printed Maps to 1800*. London: Map Collectors' Circle, 1967.

Cortazzi, Hugh. *Isles of Gold: Antique Maps of Japan*. New York: Weatherhill, 1983.

Effert, F. R., ed. *The Court Journey to the Shogun of Japan: From a Private Account of Jan Cock Blumhoff*. Leiden: Hotei Publishing, 2000.

Elison, George. *Deus Destroyed: The Image of Christianity in Early Modern Japan*. Harvard, Mass.: Council on East Asian Studies, Harvard University, 1988.

Emerson, Julie, Jennifer Chen, and Mimi Gardner Gates. *Porcelain Stories: From China to Europe*. Seattle: Seattle Art Museum in association with University of Washington Press, 2000.

French, Cal. *Through Closed Doors: Western Influence on Japanese Art 1639–1853*. Rochester, Mich.: Meadow Brook Art Gallery, Oakland University, 1977.

Goodman, Grant K. *Japan and the Dutch, 1600–1853*. Richmond, Surrey: Curzon, 2000.

Houchins, Chang-su. *Artifacts of Diplomacy: Smithsonian Collections from Commodore Matthew Perry's Japan Expedition. 1853–1854*. Washington D.C.: Smithsonian Institution, 1995.

Impey, O. R. and Christiaan J. A. Jörg. *Japanese Export Lacquer: 1580–1850*. Amsterdam: Hotei Publishing, 2005.

Jackson, Anna, and Amin Jaffer, eds. *Encounters: The Meeting of Asia and Europe, 1500–1800*. London: V&A Publications, 2004.

Jansen, Marius B. *The Making of Modern Japan*. Cambridge, Mass.: Belknap Press of Harvard University Press, 2002.

Japanese Export Porcelain: Catalogue of the Collection of the Ashmolean Museum, Oxford. Amsterdam: Hotei Publishing, 2002.

Johnson, Hiroko. *Western Influence on Japanese Art: The Akita Ranga Art School and Foreign Books*. Amsterdam: Hotei Publishing, 2005.

Jörg, Christiaan J. A. *Fine and Curious: Japanese Export Porcelain in Dutch Collections*. Amsterdam: Hotel Publishing, 2003.

Massarella, Derek. *A World Elsewhere: Europe's Encounter with Japan in the Sixteenth and Seventeenth Centuries*. New Haven: Yale University Press, 1990.

Murase, Miyeko, ed. *Turning Point: Oribe and the Arts of Sixteenth-Century Japan*. New York: Metropolitan Museum of Art; New Haven: Yale University Press, 2003.

Nagatake, Takeshi. *Classic Japanese Porcelain: Imari and Kakiemon*. New York: Kodansha International, 2003.

Okamoto, Yoshitomo. *The Namban Art of Japan*. New York: Weatherhill/Heibonsha, 1972.

Parthesius, Robert, Kris Schiermeier, and Oka Yasumasa. *Japanese Amazement: Shiba Kōkan 1747–1818, Artist under the Spell of the West*. Amsterdam: Amsterdam Historisch Museum, 2001.

Plummer, Katherine. *The Shogun's Reluctant Ambassadors: Japanese Sea Drifters in the North Pacific*. Portland: Oregon Historical Society Press, 1991.

Screech, Timon. *The Lens within the Heart: The Western Scientific Gaze and Popular Imagery in Later Edo Japan*. Honolulu: University of Hawai'i Press, 2002.

The Spirit of Japanese Glass: From Magatama to Vidro/Diamant, exh. cat. Shigaraki, Japan: Miho Museum, 2006.

Sullivan, Michael. *The Meeting of Eastern and Western Art*. Berkeley: University of California Press, 1989.

Toby, Ronald P. *State and Diplomacy in Early Modern Japan: Asia in the Development of the Tokugawa Bakufu*. Princeton, N.J.: Princeton University Press, 1984.

Trubner, Henry, William J. Rathburn, and Michael Knight, et al. *A Thousand Cranes: Treasures of Japanese Art*. Seattle: Seattle Art Museum; San Francisco: Chronicle Books, 1987.

Walter, Lutz, ed. *Japan: A Cartographic Vision: European Printed Maps from the Early 16th to the 19th Century*. New York: Prestel-Verlag, 1994.

Wiley, Peter Booth, with Korogi Ichiro. *Yankees in the Land of the Gods: Commodore Perry and the Opening of Japan*. New York: Viking, 1990.

Worlds Revealed: The Dawn of Japanese and American Exchange. Salem, Mass.: Peabody Essex Museum, 1999.

Yonemura, Ann. *Yokohama Prints from Nineteenth-century Japan*. Washington, D.C.: Arthur M. Sackler Gallery and Smithsonian Institution Press, 1990.

The realization of *Japan Envisions the West: 16th–19th Century Japanese Art from Kobe City Museum* was possible only with the wholehearted support of the Kobe City Museum and its successive directors, Sugita Fumio, Nishikawa Kazuki, and Sasayama Kazutoshi. I first presented my idea for this exhibition and book in May 2003 to Oka Yasumasa, then Senior and now Chief Curator at the museum. I extend my sincere thanks and respect to him for generously sharing his curatorial expertise and a wealth of practical information on organizing the exhibition, which contributed greatly to the implementation of my ideas.

I express my deep appreciation to Nakamura Yoshinori, Director of the museum's curatorial division, and to the full curatorial team. Besides allowing me access to the collection, they guided my research in the fields of *namban* and *kōmō* art, areas outside my own expertise. My many discussions with curators Narusawa Katsushi, Katsumori Noriko, Onoda Kazuyuki, and Tsukahara Akira were truly enlightening, and their rich knowledge informed my selection process and the editorial direction of the book. I also thank the many other staff members of the Kobe City Museum and the Kobe City Board of Education for their kind support. Conservation treatment related to some of the scrolls in the exhibition was carefully carried out at Oka Bokkōdo, Kyoto.

The exhibition and book represent the collective efforts of many staff members at the Seattle Art Museum. My foremost appreciation goes to Mimi Gates, Illsley Ball Nordstrom Director; Chiyo Ishikawa, Deputy Director for Art; and her predecessor, Lisa Corrin, for their strong and thoughtful support from the start. Zora Hutlova Foy, Senior Manager of Exhibitions and Publications, kept me on track in many ways with her timely, experienced suggestions. For securing necessary funding, I thank Maryann Jordan, Senior Deputy Director; Michele Hasson, Acting Development Director; and the Development staff, particularly Laura Hopkins, Foundation Relations Officer; Carol Mabbott, Grants Manager; Kelly Hyde, Corporate Relations Manager; and Laurie Adams, Fundraising Liaison for Asian Art.

Initiated by Sarah Loudon, former Senior Museum Educator, the educational programming for the exhibition was created under the leadership of Sandra Jackson-Dumont, Deputy Director of Education. Michael McCafferty, Director of Exhibition Design and Museum Services, capably mastered a complicated installation to create beautifully designed galleries. Lauren Tucker, Associate Registrar, handled the complicated task of the safe handling and transporting of the objects. We owe Tsukahara Akira gratitude for orchestrating an extremely complex export/import process.

Members of the Seattle Asian Art Museum board committee and the Asian Art Council provided valuable feedback as I refined the project. Traci Timmons, Librarian, tracked down obscure volumes and fielded numerous research queries with persistence and grace. Zora Hutlova Foy was indefatigable as she tracked down an important map in the Czech Republic. Julie Emerson, Ruth J. Nutt Curator of Decorative Art, gave constructive suggestions regarding the descriptions of the many ceramic pieces. Josh Yiu, Foster Foundation Associate Curator of Chinese Art, was of great assistance in providing information about Chinese paintings. Pam McClusky, Curator of

African and Oceanic Arts, kindly facilitated the translation by Ralph and Miep Salmon of some Dutch documentation. Images of objects in the Seattle Art Museum were visualized by the keen eye of Paul Macapia, who recently retired as the museum's photographer. Others who were of great help include Sue Bartlett, Marketing Manager; Christina DePaolo, New Media Manager; and Nicholas Dorman, Chief Conservator, and the staff of the Conservation Division. Ellen Oppliger, Curatorial Coordinator, Asian Art Department, and Heather Pederson, Exhibitions/Curatorial Publications Coordinator, provided invaluable behind-the-scenes support.

I received tireless assistance from interns in the Asian Art Department. Melanie King, Blakemore Intern for Japanese and Korean Art, has been by my side since 2005, and I am thoroughly grateful for her extensive efforts on behalf of the project, particularly the publication, for which she compiled the list of further reading, among a host of other tasks. Mark Pitner, Blakemore Intern of Chinese Art, helped with his language skills in German and Chinese. I am grateful also to Fumi Suto, Sayaka Ito, and John Holt, previous Blakemore Interns for Japanese and Korean Art.

I found helpful allies in Karin Zaugg Black, Communications Director, City of Seattle, and Chair, Seattle-Kobe Sister City Association; Yamamoto Takeshi, former Director, and Uematsu Kenji, Director, Kobe Trade Information Office. I extend thanks for the support and friendship exhibited by countless other individuals at the Office of Intergovernmental Relations, City of Seattle; International Division of the City of Kobe; Sister City Association of Kobe; Port of Seattle; Port of Kobe; Trade Development Alliance of Greater Seattle; Japan–America Society of the State of Washington; Japan Business Association of Seattle (Shunjukai); and Hyōgo Business and Cultural Center of the City of Seattle. Tanaka Kazuo, Consul-General of Japan in Seattle, and his predecessor, Abe Tadahiro, offered crucial words of encouragement. Griffith Way, a trustee of the Seattle Art Museum, was a valued consultant from the early stages of the project.

Complementing the exhibition is this volume, a beautiful and significant compilation that includes essays by the respected scholars Christiaan J. A. Jörg, Katsumori Noriko, Narusawa Katsushi, Oka Yasumasa, Onoda Kazuyuki, and Tsukahara Akira. I thank them for their stimulating and insightful contributions. Joseph Loh led the Japanese translation team of Hirano Yuuki, Miyabe Kyoko, and Yoshida Kaori, and Mark Poysden translated the sole Dutch essay.

I am indebted to scholars, curators, and librarians around the world who offered invaluable assistance in clarifying important details in the stories of some of the exhibited objects: Ishihara Aeka, Associate Professor, Keio University; Matsuda Kiyoshi, Professor, Kyoto University; Günter Schilder, Professor Emeritus, University of Utrecht; Soňa Švábová, Castle Mnichovo Hradiště, Czech Republic; Miyoshi Tadayoshi, Senior Curator, Kobe City Museum; Hamish A. Todd, Head of Japanese Collections, Asia, Pacific and Africa Collections, The British Library; and Ken Vos, Curator, Japan and Korea, Rijksmuseum voor Volkenkunde, Amsterdam.

This handsome volume was realized through the skillful collaboration of editor Suzanne Kotz and designer John Hubbard, Marquand Books. I cannot count the many things I learned from them about the art of making a book. Because of them, my and the authors' thoughts and intentions are truly reflected in this publication.

The project benefited from the expert guidance of a number of scholars who graciously shared their time and counsel: Kawai Masatomo, Senior Academic Adviser, Idemitsu Museum of Arts, and Professor Emeritus, Keio University; Kobayashi Yoriko, Professor, Mejiro University; and Miyeko Murase, Takeo and Itsuko Atsumi Professor Emerita, Columbia University, and Former Special Consultant for Japanese Art, Metropolitan Museum of Art. Information about the Japanese drifter Otokichi was generously provided by Jim Mockford, Ken Nakano, Takeuchi Yasuo, Tanaka Keisuke, and the staff of the Makah Cultural and Research Center, Neah Bay, and the National Park Service, Fort Vancouver.

Finally, for their steadfast good wishes for my success in this project, I thank my family in Japan, especially my mother, Takako, who passed away two years ago.

Yukiko Shirahara
John A. McCone Foundation Curator of Asian Art

Illustrations and/or their captions are in **bold**. Japanese artworks are indexed by their English titles.

Notes to the Reader

Unless otherwise noted, the objects reproduced in this publication are from the collection of the Kobe City Museum. For a checklist of the objects included in the exhibition, please go to www.seattleartmuseum.org and follow the link to "Exhibitions."

For dimensions given, height precedes width precedes depth.

Japanese name order

Japanese names are presented in the traditional manner, with family name first, followed by given name. Exceptions are made for those individuals who reside primarily outside Japan.

Chronology

Japan

Muromachi period 1392–1573
Momoyama period 1573–1615
Edo period 1615–1868
Meiji period 1868–1912

China

Yuan Dynasty 1279–1368
Ming Dynasty 1368–1644
Qing Dynasty 1644–1912

© 2007 by the Seattle Art Museum
All rights reserved

Library of Congress Cataloging-in-Publication Data
    Japan envisions the West: 16th–19th century Japanese
   art from Kobe City Museum / edited by Yukiko Shirahara.
     p. cm.
     Issued in connection with an exhibition held Oct. 11,
    2007–Jan. 6, 2008, Seattle Art Museum Downtown.
    Includes bibliographical references and index.
    ISBN 978-0-295-98740-8 (hardcover: alk. paper)
    1. Art, Japanese—European influences—Exhibitions.
2. Japan—Relations—Europe—Exhibitions. 3. Europe
—Relations—Japan—Exhibitions. 4. Art—Japan—
Kobe-shi—Exhibitions. 5. Kobe Shiritsu Hakubutsukan—
Exhibitions. I. Shirahara, Yukiko. II. Seattle Art Museum.
  N7352.J362 2007
  709.52'074521874—dc22   2007023514

Edited by Suzanne Kotz
Proofread by Sharon Vonasch
Japanese translations by Joseph Loh with Hirano Yuuki,
  Miyabe Kyoko, and Yoshida Kaori
Dutch translation (Jörg) by Mark Poysden
Index by Robert Palmer

Designed by John Hubbard
Typeset by Maggie Lee
Produced by Marquand Books, Inc., Seattle
  www.marquand.com
Color separations by iocolor, Seattle
Printed and bound in China by C&C Offset
  Printing Co., Ltd.

Distributed by University of Washington Press
PO Box 50096
Seattle, WA 98145-5096
www.washington.edu/uwpress

Photo credits
Photographs of works of art from the Kobe City Museum were provided by the museum. Most of the photographs for the figure illustrations were provided by the owners as given in the captions. Additional credits include Leonid Fink/*Seattle Times*: p. 10 (right); Sandra Havermans: fig. 5; Christiaan J. A. Jörg: fig. 19; courtesy Kobe City Museum: p. 10 (left); Miroslav Kotěšovec: fig. 8; Paul Macapia: detail p. 164, plates 112a,b, 113, 127, 128, 130, 131, 133, 136–39, 142, 144; Nederlands Scheepvaartmuseum, Amsterdam: fig. 9; TNM Image Archives: figs. 1, 2.

Image credits
p. 8: Katsushika Hokusai (Japanese, 1760–1849). *Fūryū Nakute nanakuse* (Two Ladies Looking through a Telescope, from the series "Fanciful Presentation of Seven Useless Habits"), 1789–1804 (Kansei-Kyōwa era), published by Tsutaya Jūzaburō. *Ō-ban* woodblock print: ink on paper, 14½ × 9¾ in. (36.8 × 24.8 cm).

p. 12: Hasegawa Sadanobu II (Japanese, 1848–1941). Detail from *Sesshū Kobe kaigan han'ei no zu* (Bustling Port of Kobe, Settsu Province), 1871 (Meiji 4), published by Shibaya Kyūshirō and Yaoya Zensuke. *Ō-ban* woodblock triptych: ink and color on paper, 11¼ × 29⅛ in. (36.1 × 73.9 cm).

Details
p. 1: plate 59b; pp. 2–3: plate 34b; p. 16: plate 8; p. 32: plate 17; p. 56: plate 39a; p. 74: plate 57; p. 98: plate 69; p. 118: plate 89; p. 134: plate 97; p. 164: plate 144; p. 194: plate 168e

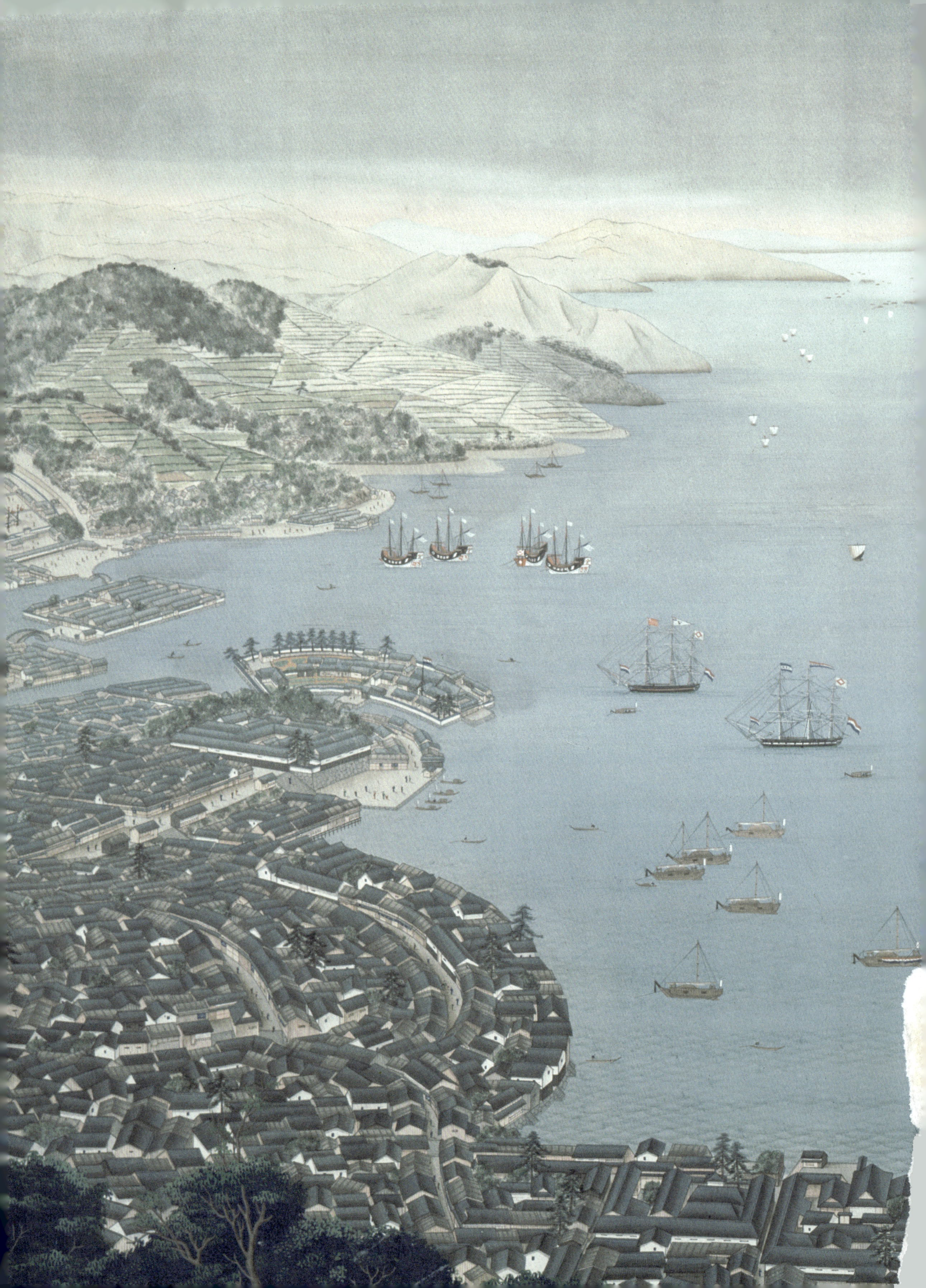